VENTURE CAPITAL

The *Robert W. Kolb Series in Finance* provides a comprehensive view of the field of finance in all of its variety and complexity. The series is projected to include approximately 65 volumes covering all major topics and specializations in finance, ranging from investments, to corporate finance, to financial institutions. Each volume in the *Kolb Series in Finance* consists of new articles especially written for the volume.

Each *Kolb Series* volume is edited by a specialist in a particular area of finance, who develops the volume outline and commissions articles by the world's experts in that particular field of finance. Each volume includes an editor's introduction and approximately 30 articles to fully describe the current state of financial research and practice in a particular area of finance.

The essays in each volume are intended for practicing finance professionals, graduate students, and advanced undergraduate students. The goal of each volume is to encapsulate the current state of knowledge in a particular area of finance so that the reader can quickly achieve a mastery of that special area of finance.

VENTURE CAPITAL

Investment Strategies, Structures, and Policies

Douglas J. Cumming

The Robert W. Kolb Series in Finance

WILEY

John Wiley & Sons, Inc.

Published by John Wiley & Sons, Inc., Hoboken, New Jersey.
Published simultaneously in Canada.

For general information on our other products and services or for technical support,
please contact our Customer Care Department within the United States at (800) 762-2974,
outside the United States at (317) 572-3993 or fax (317) 572-4002.

Wiley also publishes its books in a variety of electronic formats. Some content that
appears in print may not be available in electronic formats. For more information about
Wiley products, visit our Web site at www.wiley.com.

Library of Congress Cataloging-in-Publication Data:

Venture capital : investment strategies, structures, and policies /
Douglas J. Cumming, editor.
      p. cm. – (The Robert W. Kolb series in finance)
  Includes bibliographical references and index.
  ISBN 978-0-470-49914-6 (cloth)
 1. Venture capital.   I. Cumming, Douglas.
  HG4751.V472 2010
  332′.04154–dc22

                             2009050966

Printed in the United States of America

10 9 8 7 6 5 4 3 2 1

Contents

CHAPTER 1

Introduction to the Companion to Venture Capital

DOUGLAS CUMMING
Associate Professor and Ontario Research Chair,
York University—Schulich School of Business

INTRODUCTION

Venture capital is often referred to as the "money of invention" (see, e.g., Black and Gilson 1998; Gompers and Lerner 1999; Kortum and Lerner 2000), and venture capital fund managers as those that not only provide the money but also other value-added resources to entrepreneurial firms. Venture capital fund managers play a significant role in enhancing the value of their entrepreneurial investments as they provide financial, administrative, marketing, and strategic advice to entrepreneurial firms, as well as facilitating a network of support for an entrepreneurial firm with access to the best accountants, lawyers, investment bankers, and organizations specific to the industry in which the entrepreneurial firm operates (Sahlman 1990; Sapienza, Manigart, and Vermeir 1996; Gompers and Lerner 1999; Manigart et al. 2002, 2006; Leleux and Surlemont 2003; Wright and Lockett 2003). In terms of innovativeness (Kortum and Lerner 2000), profitability, and share price performance upon going public (Gompers and Lerner 1999), academic studies have shown that entrepreneurial firms backed by venture capital are on average significantly more successful than entrepreneurial firms that are not.

There are massive differences in the size and success of venture capital markets around the world. These differences have been attributable to differences in shareholder protection (Jeng and Wells 2000), government venture capital funds and other government policies (Jääskeläinen, Maula, and Murray 2007; Keuschnigg and Nielsen 2001, 2003a,b, 2004a,b), bankruptcy laws and capital gains taxes (Armour and Cumming 2006), and the strength of a country's stock market (Black and Gilson 1998). International differences in the size and success of venture capital and private equity markets are highlighted for select European and North American countries in Exhibit 1.1. As governments around the world recognize that entrepreneurship and innovation are important drivers of economic growth and that venture capital is an important source of capital for entrepreneurship and innovation, there has been a growing interest in rigorous theoretical and empirical analyses of venture capital markets worldwide.

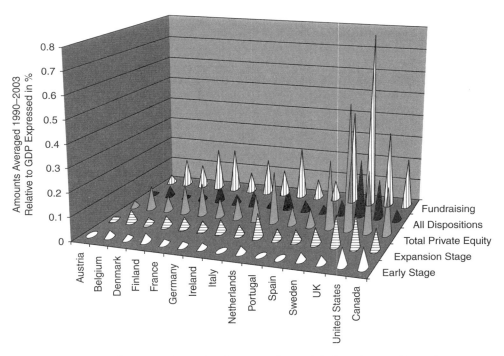

Exhibit 1.1   Size of Venture Capital and Private Equity Markets Across Countries
Source: Armour and Cumming (2006).

In the 1980s and 1990s, there was comparatively little academic work on venture capital finance. This gap in the literature was largely attributable to a dearth of systematic venture capital data. More recently, however, there have been a growing number of academics that have taken an interest in the topic and have collected systematic data for empirical studies both in the U.S. context and abroad. This empirical work has in turn inspired theoretical analyses of venture capital finance. As at 2009 there are a significant number of academics that have contributed greatly to our understanding of venture capital markets. These studies include, but are not limited to, work on fund-raising and fund structure, the nature of financing agreements with entrepreneurs, exit transactions and returns, impacts on regional development and employment, and international differences that are attributable to public policy, as well as legal and other factors. In view of these significant and rapid developments in the literature, a comprehensive review of the literature in a unified source is not only desirable but indeed essential.

The purpose of this book is to provide a comprehensive view of venture capital by describing the current state of research and practices on this topic. The chapters included here discuss sources of capital (angel investment, limited partnerships, corporate funds, government funds), due diligence, financial contracts and monitoring, the efficiency implications of VC investment, investment returns and performance, international differences in venture capital markets, and regulation and public policy. This book is organized into five parts, which collectively cover each of these areas, as explained below. This brief introduction serves as a roadmap to the range of topic areas.

Part One of this book begins with a review of alternative forms of venture capital. In Chapter 2, Andrew Zacharakis explains some of the unique features of venture capital markets, including how venture capitalists source deals, screen investments, and negotiate deals. The ways in which venture capital finance differs from bank finance is explained by Jean Etienne de Bettignies in Chapter 3. In Chapter 4, Vladimir Ivanov and Fei Zie explain differences between corporate venture capital funds and limited partnerships. Andrew Wong analyzes differences between venture capital and angel investment in Chapter 5 and focuses on unique features of financing from earlier-stage angel investors. In Chapter 6, Darek Klonowski analyzes the connection between business incubators and venture capital. Thereafter, Luisa Alemany and Mariarosa Scarlata describe in Chapter 7 the philanthropic model of venture capital, a model that has been significantly growing in importance in recent years as this market segment continues to expand.

Part Two of this book highlights the structure of venture capital investments. Venture capitalists write detailed contracts that separately allocate cash flow and control rights. These contracts have the potential to significantly affect the performance of venture capital–backed firms. Catherine Casamatta and Roberta Dessi in Chapters 8 and 9, respectively, explain how venture capital contracts influence the incentives for venture capital fund managers to monitor and advise their portfolio firms.[1] In Chapter 10, Dima Leschinskii explains how investment structures and portfolio design for a venture capitalist can influence venture capitalist investment activities and outcomes.[2] In Chapter 11, Dirk De Clercq and Dimo Dimov examine the role of syndication in venture capital, including the rationales for syndication and the implications of syndication for investment performance.

Part Three of this book examines various aspects of the role of venture capitalists in adding value to their investee firms. In Chapter 12, John Hand provides evidence on how venture capital–backed firms mature over time. Empirical evidence on the various things that venture capitalists do to add value to their investees is reviewed in Chapter 13 by Tom Chemmanur, Karthik Krishnan, and Debarshi Nandy. The role of venture capital in stimulating innovation is studied in Chapter 14 by Masako Ueda. There are significant differences in the reputations of different venture capital funds; the implications of these reputational effects are discussed in Chapter 15 by Rajarishi Nahata. Of course, not all venture capitalists are of sound repute, and sometimes venture capitalists take advantage of their investee firms. These governance issues in venture capital are discussed by Brian Broughman in Chapter 16. Conflicts of interest between venture capitalists and their investees are analyzed in Chapter 17 by Vladimir Atanasov.

Part Four of this book examines drivers of venture capitalists' returns. Because venture capital–backed firms typically do not have cash flows to pay interest on debt or dividends on equity, venture capitalists seek capital gains by exiting from their investments. The five main exit routes are initial public offerings, acquisitions, secondary sales, buy-backs and write-offs, as explained by Armin Schwienbacher in Chapter 18. Factors that influence the financial return to venture capital–backed firms are surveyed by Mike Wright and Riya Chopraa in Chapter 19. Whether or not venture capitalist control helps or hinders venture capital–backed firms is empirically studied in Chapter 20 by April Knill.

Finally, Part Five of this book examines international differences in venture capital and the role of public policy. It is worthwhile to provide a comparative perspective on international venture capital markets to understand how and why venture capital markets differ across countries in terms of size and success, and the role of government policy in stimulating venture capital investment and international venture capital investment. Markku Maula explores cross-border venture capital investment activities in Chapter 21. Unique features of venture capital in Canada are analyzed in Chapter 22 by Cécile Carpentier and Jean-Marc Suret, which is interesting to examine given the large amount of public subsidies in Canada, and the relatively low level of success of those government expenditures. To understand why government-created venture capital programs are difficult to implement in practice, it is useful to have a strong theoretical perspective. Christian Keuschnigg theoretically examines the role of public policy for stimulating venture capital finance in Chapter 23.[3] Finally, practical lessons on the role of government policy in stimulating venture capital and private equity are offered by Gordon Murray and David Lingelbach in Chapter 24.

Specific features of later-stage private equity deals are not covered in this volume, but are covered in *The Companion to Private Equity*, a related volume published by Wiley in the Companion to Finance Series. There are various other topics related to entrepreneurial finance, and other authors have made important contributions, many of which are highlighted in each of the chapters herein. Areas where further research is needed are likewise highlighted in each chapter. In view of the empirically documented importance of venture capital in stimulating entrepreneurship, innovation, and economic growth, we hope and expect that venture capital research will help guide the theoretical understanding and practical implementation among students, academics, practitioners, and policy makers alike.

NOTES

1. Note that in practice, venture capital contracts differ significantly across countries. Most notably, for entrepreneurs resident in the United States, venture capitalists typically use convertible preferred securities in their contracts, and the use of this security has been attributed to unique aspects of U.S. tax practice (Gilson and Schizer 2003), in addition to theoretical arguments that this security is uniquely optimal. However, in all other countries and regions around the world where venture capital contracting data have been collected—including Canada, Europe, and various developing countries—venture capitalists use a variety of securities, and convertible preferred equity has not been the most frequently used security (Cumming 2005, 2008; Lerner and Schoar 2005; Kaplan, Martel, and Strömberg 2007; Cumming and Johan 2009). One explanation for the use of these different securities is that agency problems differ across different transactions, and efficient security design varies depending on which agency problems are most pronounced in the particular transaction.

2. For related work, see Kanniainen and Keuschnigg (2003, 2004) and Keuschnigg (2004).

3. For related work, see, e.g., Keuschnigg (2004), Keuschnigg and Nielsen (2001, 2003a, b, 2004a, b), and Jääskeläinen, Maula, and Murray (2007).

REFERENCES

Armour, J., and D. J. Cumming. 2006. The legislative road to Silicon Valley. *Oxford Economic Papers* 58:596–635.

Black, B. S., and R. J. Gilson. 1998. Venture capital and the structure of capital markets: Banks versus stock markets. *Journal of Financial Economics* 47:243–277.

Cumming, D. J. 2005. Capital structure in venture finance, *Journal of Corporate Finance* 11:550–585.

———. 2008. Contracts and exits in venture capital finance. *Review of Financial Studies* 21:1947–1982.

———, and S. A. Johan. 2009. *Venture capital and private equity contracting: An international perspective.* San Diego: Elsevier Science Academic Press.

Gilson, R., and D. Schizer. 2003. Venture capital structure: A tax explanation for convertible preferred stock. *Harvard Law Review* 116:875–916.

Gompers, P. A., and J. Lerner. 1999. *The venture capital cycle.* Cambridge: MIT Press.

Jääskeläinen, M., M. Maula, and G. Murray. 2007. Performance of incentive structures in publicly and privately funded "hybrid" venture capital funds. *Research Policy* 36:7, 913–929.

Jeng, L., and P. Wells. 2000. The determinants of venture capital funding: Evidence across countries. *Journal of Corporate Finance* 6:241–89.

Kanniainen, V., and C. Keuschnigg. 2003. The optimal portfolio of start-up firms in venture capital finance. *Journal of Corporate Finance* 9:521–534.

———. 2004. Start-up investment with scarce venture capital support. *Journal of Banking and Finance* 28:1935–1959.

Kaplan, S. N., F. Martel, and P. Strömberg. 2007. How do legal differences and experience affect financial contracts? *Journal of Financial Intermediation* 16:273–311.

Keuschnigg, C. 2004. Taxation of a venture capitalist with a portfolio of firms. *Oxford Economic Papers* 56:285–306.

———, and S. B. Nielsen. 2001. Public policy for venture capital. *International Tax and Public Finance* 8:557–572.

———, and S. Bo Nielsen. 2003a. Tax policy, venture capital and entrepreneurship. *Journal of Public Economics* 87:175–203.

———, and S. Bo Nielsen. 2003b. Taxes and venture capital support. *Review of Finance* 7:515–538.

———, and S. Bo Nielsen. 2004a. Progressive taxation, moral hazard, and entrepreneurship. *Journal of Public Economic Theory* 6:471–490.

———, and S. Bo Nielsen. 2004b. Start-ups, venture capitalists and the capital gains tax. *Journal of Public Economics* 88:1011–1042.

Kortum, S., and J. Lerner. 2000. Assessing the contribution of venture capital to innovation. *RAND Journal of Economics* 31:674–692.

Leleux, B., and B. Surlemont. 2003. Public versus private venture capital: Seeding or crowding out? A pan-European analysis. *Journal of Business Venturing* 18:81–104.

Lerner, J., and A. Schoar. 2005. Does legal enforcement affect financial transactions? The contractual channel in private equity. *Quarterly Journal of Economics* 120:223–246.

Manigart, S., K. De Waele, M. Wright, K. Robbie, P. Desbrières, H. Sapienza, and A. Beekman. 2002. The determinants of the required returns in venture capital investments: A five-country study. *Journal of Business Venturing* 17:291–312.

Manigart, S., A. Lockett, M. Meuleman, M. Wright, H. Landstrom, H. Bruining, P. Desbrieres, and U. Hommel, 2006. Venture capitalists' decision to syndicate. *Entrepreneurship Theory and Practice* 30:131–153.

Sahlman, W. A. 1990. The structure and governance of venture capital organizations. *Journal of Financial Economics* 27:473–521.

Sapienza, H., S. Manigart, and W. Vermeir. 1996. Venture capital governance and value-added in four countries. *Journal of Business Venturing* 11:439–469.

Wright, M., and A. Lockett. 2003. The structure and management of alliances: Syndication in the venture capital industry. *Journal of Management Studies* 40:2073–2104.

ABOUT THE AUTHOR AND EDITOR

Douglas Cumming, B.Com. (Hons.) (McGill), M.A. (Queen's), J.D. (University of Toronto Faculty of Law), Ph.D. (Toronto), CFA, is an Associate Professor of Finance and Entrepreneurship and the Ontario Research Chair at the Schulich School of Business, York University. His research is primarily focused on law and finance, market surveillance, hedge funds, venture capital, private equity, and IPOs. His work has been presented at the American Finance Association, the Western Finance Association, the European Finance Association, the American Law and Economics Association, the European Law and Economics Association, and other leading international conferences. His recent publications have appeared in numerous journals including the *American Law and Economics Review, Cambridge Journal of Economics, Economic Journal, European Economic Review, Financial Management, Journal of Business, Journal of Business Venturing, Journal of Corporate Finance, Journal of International Business Studies, Oxford Economic Papers,* and *Review of Financial Studies.* He is the coauthor (along with his wife, Sofia Johan) of the new book *Venture Capital and Private Equity Contracting: An International Perspective* (San Diego: Elsevier Science Academic Press, 2009). His work has been reviewed in numerous media outlets, including *Canadian Business,* the *Financial Post,* and *The New Yorker.* He was the recipient of the 2004 *Ido Sarnat Award* for the best paper published in the *Journal of Banking and Finance* for a paper on full and partial venture capital exits in Canada and the United States. In addition, he received the *2008 AIMA Canada-Hillsdale Research Award* for his paper on hedge fund regulation and performance, and the 2009 Canadian Institute for Chartered Business Valuators Award for his paper on private equity returns and disclosure around the world. He is a research associate with the Paolo Baffi Center for Central Banking and Financial Regulation (Bocconi University), Groupe d'Economie Mondiale at Sciences Po (Paris), Capital Markets CRC (Sydney), Venture Capital Experts (New York), Cambridge University ESRC Center for Business Research, Center for Financial Studies (Frankfurt), Amsterdam Center for Research in International Finance, and the University of Calgary Van Horne Institute. He has also consulted for a variety of governmental and private organizations in Australasia, Europe, and North America, and most recently is working with Wilshire Associates.

## PART I

Alternative Forms of Venture Capital

CHAPTER 2

Venture Capitalists Decision Making

An Information Processing Perspective

ANDREW ZACHARAKIS
The John H. Muller, Jr. Chair in Entrepreneurship, The Arthur M. Blank
Center for Entrepreneurship, Babson College

INTRODUCTION

Venture capital is the fuel for high potential growth firms, especially in the United States. New venture survival is tenuous at best, but those backed by venture capitalists (VCs) tend to achieve a higher survival rate than those that are not (Kunkel and Hofer 1990; Sandberg 1986). Studies find that survival for VC-backed ventures range from around 65 percent (Sahlman 1990) to 85 percent of the VC's portfolio (Dorsey 1979). Venture capital predominantly focuses on high technology industries (84 percent of all investments in 2004 in the United States), and U.S. companies receive over 60 percent of all venture capital disbursed among the largest markets: the United States, Europe, and Japan (Minniti, Bygrave, and Autio 2006). VCs focus on knowledge-based businesses that have the potential to change the way people live. Some examples of businesses that VCs have backed include Genetech, Apple, Google, Amazon, and Federal Express (Bygrave and Hunt 2005). Although venture capital investments have fallen from a peak of $100 billion in 2000 to around $30 billion in 2007 in the United States, it is still higher than the level of investment in 1998 (Money Tree Report 2008). Reflecting the overall importance to entrepreneurship, venture capital has received considerable academic attention.

Wright, Sapienza, and Busenitz (2003) compiled a list of the most important research articles on venture capital. Perusing the chapters, several important research streams emerge, such as the VC investment decision process with a heavy emphasis on decision criteria, how VCs add value postinvestment, macromarket factors that influence the development of venture capital industries across the United States and around the world, how VCs value and structure deals, and harvesting those investments, among others. This chapter will focus on the investment decision process. The basic motivation behind this stream is to understand how VCs make their investment decisions (e.g., MacMillan, Zeman, and SubbaNarasimha 1987; Shepherd and Zacharakis 2001; Tybejee and Bruno 1984; Zacharakis and Meyer 1998; Zacharakis and Shepherd 2005). As such, much of the research has investigated what decision criteria VCs use and how they use them. The main decision criteria categories are entrepreneur/team, market, product, and financing issues (MacMillan, Zeman, and SubbaNarasimha 1987; Zacharakis and Meyer 1998). The primary focus of most of this research centers on the investment screening stage. As such, the full VC decision process is under-researched. To better capture the full richness, this chapter will review past research and suggest future areas to explore across a larger portion of the VC investment process. Specifically, we look at VC decisions during deal origination, screening, evaluation (due diligence), and negotiation (Tyebjee and Bruno 1984).

The chapter proceeds as follows. First, it sets up a theoretical lens, Information Processing Theory, and builds a model that highlights what information captures *attention*, how it is *interpreted*, and the *action* that comes from that process across preinvestment stages. The subsequent sections of this chapter more deeply explore the decision process at each stage, reviewing research and suggesting future avenues of study.

INFORMATION PROCESSING THEORY

Cognitive science, the study of how people make decisions, provides a fruitful source for theories that have been applied to the VC decision process. Barr, Stimpert, and Huff (1992) delineate a simple information processing model that describes decisions as a function of what information attracts the manager's *attention*, how that information is *interpreted*, and what *actions* follow from that interpretation. The expert decision making model (Lord and Maher 1990) best fits the VC environment (Shepherd, Zacharakis, and Baron 2003). Expert models can be characterized as fitting between a truly rational decision model where all information and alternatives are considered and evaluated, on the one hand, and a limited capacity model, which recognizes the cognitive limits of decision makers (Cyert and March 1963), on the other. Experts learn which factors best distinguish between successful and unsuccessful ventures (Shepherd et al. 2003), although this is often at an unconscious level (Zacharakis and Meyer 1998). These expert mental models are efficient and effective in helping VCs select the most promising ventures, yet are subject to biases that may hinder decision accuracy.

VCs possess a multitude of mental models that can be called into action depending upon the situation (i.e., based on past experience in the industry, or past experience with the lead entrepreneur, etc. [Zacharakis and Shepherd 2001]). Thus, when the VC perceives a somewhat familiar situation that requires action, an appropriate mental model is summoned from long-term memory (Moesel et al. 2001). In unfamiliar situations, the VC uses an evaluation strategy (a mental model of how to approach new situations) to formulate the information into a mental model, which is then manipulated to make a decision. The VC's mental model of the situation influences what information is *attended* to and how that information is *interpreted*; the mental model acts as a filter that preserves limited cognitive processing capacity (Moesel et al. 2001; Zacharakis and Shepherd 2001). An example may better illustrate the mental model concept. Imagine two VCs examining the same proposal. The first VC is very familiar with the industry and, in fact, also has extensive knowledge of the team. As such, the VC is likely to base her judgment on these two chunks of information. Other important information that doesn't fit

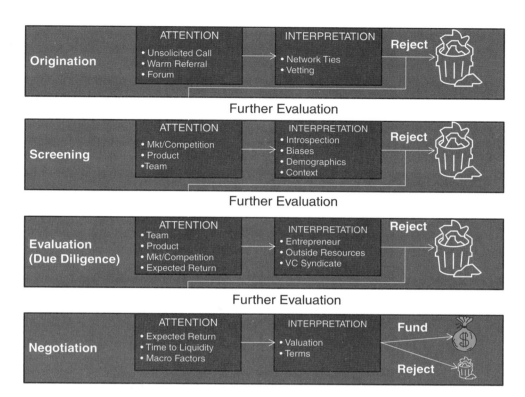

Exhibit 2.1 Information-Processing Perspective of VC Decision Making

neatly within this configuration receives limited consideration. The second VC, on the other hand, is not familiar with the industry or the entrepreneurial team. In this case, the VC doesn't possess a mental model based on the larger chunks of information. The VC assesses the entire array of information and uses various decision strategies to make his decision. For example, he may use a satisfying strategy (Simon 1955) and assess whether the proposal meets the minimum criteria on each decision factor.

While information processing theory has most often been applied to the screening stage of the investment process, it can provide a useful framework to examine questions across all stages. Exhibit 2.1 views the VC investment decision with information processing theory. The model suggests that at each stage, some stimuli captures the VC's *attention* and based upon the VC's *interpretation*, the VC takes *action* by either moving to the next stage or terminating consideration of the venture. The remainder of the paper looks at this process by VC decision making phases.

ORIGINATION (DEAL FLOW)

Origination is the number of potential ventures that VCs see as they look for the best investment opportunities (Manigart et al. 2006; Sorenson and Stuart 2001). Deal flow comes to the VC in a number of ways. Entrepreneurs can directly solicit VCs, often by sending them a business plan, executive summary, or a PowerPoint slide deck. Trusted friends may refer a business opportunity to the VC; this is what is called a "warm referral." Other VCs may refer a project to a different VC or approach each other to co-invest in a particular opportunity. Finally, VCs may actively seek deal flow by attending networking events, judging business plan competitions, or prospecting for exciting opportunities and then approaching the entrepreneur. Origination is critical for VC success. The more, higher-quality deals a VC sees, the more likely she is to fund high-return ventures. On the other hand, the greater the deal flow, the more pressure on the VC's most valuable resource, her time. From an information processing lens, the source of the deal flow directly impacts how much, if any, of the VC's *attention* the opportunity captures. Certain sources of deal flow are more apt to capture the VC's *attention* than other sources. Likewise, certain sources of deal flow are easier to *interpret* and thus more efficient and effective with which to make a decision. Specifically, VCs with direct ties to the entrepreneurs can quickly lower the information asymmetries between the VC and entrepreneur (Shane and Cable 2002). Indirect ties, meaning through a mutual direct tie to both the VC and entrepreneur respectively, are a bit less efficient, and a lack of ties is the least efficient in reducing information asymmetries. Whether an opportunity captures a VC's *attention* and how he *interprets* it will lead to the *action* taken.

Unsolicited Entrepreneurs Sending in Material

VCs receive hundreds, if not thousands, of unsolicited proposals every year. These proposals have a difficult time capturing the VC's *attention* as the VC protects his most rare asset, time. Often, junior associates screen unsolicited proposals and send more promising ones to the partner. Even if partners screen unsolicited proposals themselves, they do so quickly. Hall and Hofer (1993) find that VCs spend as little as six minutes screening a deal. For this reason, unsolicited proposals rarely capture the VC's *attention*, and even if they do so, the VC is unlikely to *interpret* them favorably because the proposal hasn't garnered any previous vetting or endorsements from trusted sources (Stuart, Hoang, and Hybels 1999). Thus, *action*, if taken at all, is likely to be a polite rejection.

Warm Referrals

Shane and Cable (2002) suggest that VC financing is a function of network ties, both direct and indirect. The stronger the ties between entrepreneurs and investors, the more likely VCs will fund entrepreneurs. Thus, network theory suggests that VCs generate deal flow by tapping their networks. Specifically, better quality entrepreneurs will get warm referrals to VCs by knowing someone in the VC's network that the VC respects and trusts (Fried and Hisrich 1994; Tyebjee and Bruno 1984). Tyebjee and Bruno (1984) observe that out of 90 deals, only 23 (26 percent) materialized pursuant to an unsolicited call from the entrepreneur. The majority of deals (65 percent) were recommended to the VC by other VCs (33 percent) or through sources such as previous investees and personal contacts (roughly 40 percent). Ten percent received endorsement from investment banks or investment brokers. Considering that the Tyebjee and Bruno (1984) research is relatively older and that the industry has matured and grown dramatically since that time, the number of funded unsolicited proposals is likely to be much lower. Anecdotally, in many panel discussions geared to would-be entrepreneurs that I've attended or participated in, VCs often warn that they never look at unsolicited proposals. Those firms that systematically review all unsolicited proposals likely have lower deal flow and need to supplement warm referrals with unsolicited proposals.

From an information processing perspective, warm referrals are more likely to lead to positive *action*; moving onto the screening stage. In essence, a warm referral is basically a first screen if the venture comes to the VC through a trusted gatekeeper. At the minimum, a deal originated through a trusted gatekeeper creates an endorsement effect (Stuart, Hoang, and Hybels 1999) that suggests the entrepreneur and concept has received some vetting.

VCs often co-invest with other VCs or refer deals that don't fit their investment charter to a more appropriate VC with the idea that in the future, the other VC will reciprocate. However, reciprocity is likely a function of the relative power and prestige of each VC. Lower-quality VCs may refer deals to more prestigious VCs in an attempt to garner the spillover reputation effect, even though the higher-status VC firms are less likely to offer to syndicate their deals in return. Yet being associated with a premier VC on a deal that becomes a blockbuster can build reputation and lead to higher prestige for the lower-status firm in the future. As such, lower-quality VCs act as feeders to larger more reputable firms, often funding seed and early-stage deals that larger firms avoid.

Active Prospecting

In today's venture capital industry, competition is fierce. The old adage that "there is too much money chasing too few [quality] deals" holds true. One way to minimize the amount of competition for a given deal is to actively pursue it, rather than passively wait for it to cross the transom. VCs seek deals in a number of ways including forums, university events, and even cold-calling interesting prospects. In active prospecting, the VC's *attention* is aroused; they are alert for interesting opportunities. Moreover, active prospecting implies prevetting. In venture capital forums and university events, such as business plan competitions, the event organizers have done some prescreening to eliminate less attractive ventures and identify more promising ones. When VCs cold-call on entrepreneurs, it often suggests that the VC has been looking at firms that have garnered outside attention (e.g., favorable media) or are searching for prospects that meet certain predefined criteria. As such, VCs are primed to positively *interpret* the venture and move it to the next stage.

Future Research

Deal flow is critical to a VC's success. Roure and Keeley (1990) contend that most of the variance in VC success stems from selecting the right investments. The more deal flow that a VC sees, the better their odds of finding attractive investments. Yet, for the most part, VC decision-making literature has ignored this phase of the VC decision process. So the key questions in this area are these: How do VCs increase their deal flow, especially how do they increase quality deal flow? Network theory (Shane and Cable 2002) and reputation play an important role in deal flow.

The more central a VC is within a network, the more deals that he will see. This chapter has identified three categories of deal flow (cold-calling, warm referrals, and active prospecting), and posits that the different sources are likely to receive differing levels of *attention* and be predisposed to either more positive or negative *interpretation*.

A number of interesting research questions present themselves. First, when and how often do unsolicited proposals get VC *attention*? We need to update the work of Tyebjee and Bruno (1984). What percentage of unsolicited proposals receive funding? Related to the above question is whether entrepreneurs can increase the odds that an unsolicited proposal will receive *attention* and be *interpreted* favorably? Another set of research questions centers around warm referrals. Where do VCs get warm referrals? Which sources of warm referrals provide more accurate vetting? How can VCs establish and maintain relationships with the best conduits of warm referrals? Research on warm referrals should also be looked at from the perspective of the entrepreneur. How can entrepreneurs network into the best warm referral conduits? Finally, there needs to be research on active prospecting. Is active prospecting equally productive for all VCs? It is likely that younger VC firms find active prospecting more productive because they don't have the reputation to get quality warm referrals. Another question is what types of active prospecting are most fruitful?

An interesting extension to the basic research questions proposed above is how the source of deal flow may bias the decision process. Warm referrals, for example, may lead VCs to limit their analysis or may focus the decision on certain salient factors such as the entrepreneur over other important factors, like market conditions. Likewise, active prospecting may lead to an escalation of commitment effect (Staw 1997) where the VC, having devoted so much time to find the best deals, continues on with a venture despite disconfirming evidence of its attractiveness. Active prospecting may also be susceptible to the bandwagon effect or herding towards those prospects in industries that are deemed hot (Gompers and Lerner 1998). There are numerous other factors that may impact the deal origination phase, but to date little research has explored this arena.

SCREENING

During the screening stage, VCs quickly decide whether a potential venture merits further evaluation. Many researchers have investigated how VCs make their decisions, focusing heavily on the decision criteria that distinguish those ventures that have a greater chance of providing strong returns (Wells 1974; Poindexter 1976; Tyebjee and Bruno 1984; MacMillan, Siegel, and SubbaNarasimha 1985; MacMillan, Zeman, and SubbaNarasimha 1987; Robinson 1987; Timmons et al. 1987; Sandberg, Schweiger, and Hofer 1988; Hall and Hofer 1993; Zacharakis and Meyer 1995). The underlying justification for these studies is that a better understanding of the VC process may lead to better decisions and more successful ventures. The criteria derived from these studies appear to fit four categories: (1) entrepreneur/team capabilities, (2) product/service attractiveness, (3) market/competitive conditions, and (4) potential returns if the venture is successful (Hall and Hofer 1993).

While early studies (e.g., MacMillan, Siegel, and SubbaNarasimha 1985; MacMillan, Zeman, and SubbaNarasimha 1987; Robinson 1987; Timmons et al.

1987; Tyebjee and Bruno 1984) identified those decision criteria that best discriminate between success and failure, it relied primarily on interviews and surveys that are prone to post hoc recall and rationalization biases (Zacharakis and Meyer 1998). Subsequent research called into question expert decision makers' ability to accurately introspect about their decision processes (e.g., Hall and Hofer 1993; Sandberg, Schweiger, and Hofer 1988; Zacharakis and Meyer 1995, 1998). While the criteria identified from earlier studies were correct, the relative importance of those criteria appears to be different from the VCs' introspection, at least at the screening stage. The gist of these studies is that VCs were not attending to or interpreting information in a manner consistent with early research. Specifically, VCs focus more on market conditions than on the entrepreneur in the screening stage, despite believing otherwise (Hall and Hofer 1993; Zacharakis and Meyer 1998). A lack of understanding has implications for VCs, especially when it comes to training new associates (Zacharakis and Shepherd 2005).

More recent research investigates other factors and situations that may impact *interpretation*, such as biases (Zacharakis and Shepherd 2001; Gompers and Lerner 1998), demographics [human capital] (Shepherd, Baron, and Zacharakis 2003; Dimov, Shepherd, and Sutcliffe 2007), and context (Zacharakis, McMullen, and Shepherd 2007; Bruton and Ahlstrom 2003).

Introspection

Although insightful, many early studies suffer from introspection biases since they use ex post collection methods (Hall and Hofer 1993; Sandberg et al. 1988; Shepherd 1999; Zacharakis and Meyer 1998). For instance, most VCs state that the entrepreneur is the most important factor in making their decisions, but studies using real-time data collection methods, such as verbal protocols (Hall and Hofer, 1993) and policy-capturing experiments (Zacharakis and Meyer, 1998), find that market-based factors are more important in the screening phase of the decision. There are several reasons why introspection is inaccurate. First, the screening stage is generally very quick (Hall and Hofer 1993), and VCs use decision heuristics that speed the decision process. While the entrepreneur is critical to successfully implementing an opportunity, certain markets are more promising than others. So VCs may screen using a satisficing heuristic (Simon 1955) in a hierarchical manner to quickly eliminate those proposals that don't have as much potential (Zacharakis and Meyer 2000). For example, many VCs specialize by industry or stage and will screen out proposals that fall outside of those parameters.

Real-time methods have also allowed researchers to gain a deeper picture of the complexity of the VC decision process. While VCs typically screen on market factors first, entrepreneur criteria impact how market factors are *interpreted* (Zacharakis and Shepherd 2005). While previous findings suggest that the entrepreneur isn't a central decision cue during the screening, VCs do consider it in conjunction with other factors. Specifically, leadership experience is more valued in markets with lots of competitors who are relatively weak (Zacharakis and Shepherd 2005). So while the market originally captures the VC's *attention*, the entrepreneur's leadership ability helps in *interpreting* how likely the venture is to succeed, considering the market conditions.

Biases

Biases may cause VCs to use information incorrectly thereby affecting which mental models are used for any particular decision (Zacharakis and Shepherd 2001). For example, VC experience within an industry may cause the VC to more rigorously evaluate available industry information because he knows the industry well (i.e., industry indicators and benchmarks), an availability bias. Hence, biases impact what information captures the VC's *attention* and how he *interprets* that information. Biases may cause the VC to evaluate the other aspects of the proposal less rigorously, such as product and entrepreneur attributes. The point is that such knowledge biases the VC; the VC evaluates or uses different mental models for this proposal from a VC who is unfamiliar with the industry.

Just because mental models bias decisions does not mean that they result in errors (Barr et al. 1992). However, these biases most likely prevent decision makers from reaching optimal solutions (in the rational model sense) because they may reduce the amount of information and alternatives considered. The number of potential biases to any decision is enormous. Few biases have received attention within the VC decision-making literature, but some that have include herding, overconfidence, and first-impression biases.

VCs may fall victim to a "herding" phenomenon where they invest in similar companies as do the leading VC firms, especially if the potential returns that other VCs are likely to receive appear to be great (Gompers and Lerner 1998). In a sense, herding influences what kinds of companies VCs pay *attention* to. It also impacts how information is *interpreted*; information is viewed more favorably as late-coming VCs see the returns of earlier VCs. Several examples of herding have occurred over time. Sahlman and Stevenson (1985) found that VCs herded into the hard disk drive industry, leading to overinvestment and unsustainable valuations. The dynamics play out as follows: early investments in the sector start to pay off and then other VCs seek to cash in on the sure bet, each player hoping that "a greater fool" will help them harvest the investment before the bubble bursts. Sahlman and Stevenson (1985) found that from 1977 to 1984, VCs invested $400 million into the hard disk drive industry with $270 million coming in the last two years. It seems that the VC industry goes through herding cycles on a regular basis. The most current example is the dot.com boom and bust. While herding can be efficient, in that VCs are following the lead and returns of other VCs as they seek attractive industries and investments, the subsequent bubble has negative effects. In many cases, herding leads to overcrowding in the market space with lots of me-too competitors that damage the overall sector dynamics and increase the failure rate within that space.

Zacharakis and Shepherd (2001) looked at VC overconfidence. Using a conjoint experiment, Zacharakis and Shepherd (2001) find that VCs are overconfident (96 percent of the 51 participating VCs exhibited significant overconfidence) and that overconfidence negatively affects VC decision accuracy (the correlation between overconfidence and accuracy was –0.70). The experiment controlled for the amount of information each VC reviewed and the type of information reviewed. The study finds that more information leads to increased overconfidence. What this means is that VCs believe more information leads to better decisions, yet they don't necessarily use all that information, and their overall decision accuracy is lower. Likewise, VC confidence increases when they view information criteria that they are more familiar and comfortable with. Finally VCs are more overconfident in their failure predictions than in their success predictions. As such, Zacharakis and Shepherd (2001) posit that overconfident VCs may limit their information search (although they believe that they are fully considering all relevant information) and focus on salient factors (e.g., how similar this deal is to a past successful deal) despite other information factors that would suggest this deal may fail. Unlike Busenitz and Barney (1997) who suggest that overconfidence can have positive ramifications for entrepreneurs—they will launch the venture in the first place and then work harder to make sure the venture succeeds—overconfidence in VCs is likely mostly a negative in that it is overconfidence in decision-making ability, and it may not lead to increased effort to help failing ventures succeed, especially when VCs often attribute failure to outside, uncontrollable events (Zacharakis, Meyer, and DeCastro 1999).

Traditionally, screening research has focused on the business plan, but more recently, researchers are looking at the oral presentation (Mason and Harrison 2003). These studies find that first impressions matter. VCs may be biased by the effectiveness of pitching the venture, appearance and so forth. Gregoire, de Koning, and Oviatt (2009) take this line of research to the next level by having investors react to specific statements within the entrepreneur's pitch. This type of experiment will allow researchers and, by extension, entrepreneurs to understand what aspects of their presentation capture the VC's *attention*.

Demographics

Research has looked into how different VC demographics impact investment success. The main idea behind this research is that different demographics influence the decision process. For example, Shepherd and colleagues (2003) find that VC experience has a curvilinear effect on decision performance. While more experience is generally better, they find that after 14 years of experience, VC decision effectiveness declines, possibly due to over-reliance on gut feelings rather than on a concrete examination of all the decision factors. In other words, VCs are limiting their information search and making decisions based upon past experiences (an availability bias).

More recent research looks at the expertise that a VC brings to a new fund and how that impacts the VC firm's success (Walske and Zacharakis 2009). From this research, we may infer that the decision processes these VCs bring to the table differ. For instance, Walske and Zacharakis (2009) found that VCs with past venture capital experience and VCs with past senior management experience were more likely to succeed, and VCs with past entrepreneurship experience were more likely to fail. Walske and Zacharakis (2009) speculate that VCs with past experience are better at managing portfolios of companies, those with senior management experience are better at guiding their portfolio companies to grow, while those with entrepreneurship experience fall in love with a particular company and may not fully evaluate the criteria that disconfirms the venture's potential. Thus, demographics influence what and how much information VCs *attend* to and *interpret*.

Context

Institutional differences across countries also influence how VCs attend and use information (Zacharakis, McMullen, and Shepherd 2007). While previous research finds that VCs from different countries such as Korea, New Zealand, and Canada use similar information cues as in the United States (Knight, 1994; Rah, Jung, and Lee 1994), they seem to use those cues differently. For instance, Zacharakis and colleagues (2007) find that U.S. VCs are more attuned to market-based factors whereas Chinese VCs are relatively more focused on human capital factors. Zacharakis and colleagues assert that the differences in which factors VCs *attend* to and how they *interpret* those factors are a function of differing country institutions. VCs in more mature economies such as the U.S. follow rules-based institutions where the rule of law protects parties to a relationship to a greater degree from opportunistic behavior, whereas VCs from countries where relationship-based institutions prevail rely on strong personal relationships to minimize opportunistic behavior (Zacharakis et al. 2007). Thus, country context, and possibly even differing contexts within regions of a country, will impact what information captures *attention* and how it is *interpreted.*

Future Research

The work on screening revolves around *attention* and *interpretation*. From the research, we know that not all criteria receive the same amount of *attention,* and we know that biases, demographics, and context greatly influence how the criteria are *interpreted*. Although study of this area is well developed, there is much more room to research these topics.

The topic of biases has received considerable attention, but the number of unexplored biases for VCs remains large. For example, Baron (1998) suggests that entrepreneurs are prone to counterfactual thinking: the tendency to think about what might have been. He proposes that entrepreneurs are more likely to regret actions not taken (e.g., a missed opportunity), rather than the mistakes they may have actually made. A counterfactual bias may also have a strong impact on VCs. Anecdotally, we read about VCs who bemoan passing up investments in big winners, such as Amazon or Google. This regret may increase the tendency to take bigger risks without fully evaluating all the information around a venture decision because the VC doesn't want to miss out again. It may also lead to chasing bubbles as VCs see others succeed in a particular space and feel that they need to get in there or lose out (e.g., the dot.com bubble). A slew of other biases may also prove insightful in this field of inquiry (see Hogarth and Makridakis 1981).

Decision context also impacts how information around screening is evaluated. While VCs from different countries seem to have different decision policies, it is also likely that VCs within a country *attend* to and *interpret* information differently. Florida and Kenney (1988) identify seven venture capital clusters within the United States and suggest that these clusters form around either technology-oriented companies and invest locally within that cluster or form around finance-oriented companies and export their capital to other clusters, or are some hybrid of the two. Florida and Kenney suggest that venture capital formation is path dependent and driven by the institutions in the regions in which the venture capital firms develop.

From an institutional perspective, we may expect financial complex VCs to use information differently from their brethren in technology clusters. More specifically, finance cluster VCs may tend to focus more on later-stage deals. As such, they may rely more heavily on technology cluster VCs to feed earlier-stage deals to them and as such do much of the evaluation of the quality of the venture.

In addition to geography, the industry and stage focus also likely influence how VCs view information (Elango et al. 1995). Elango and colleagues find that VCs focused on early-stage deals pay more *attention* to the nature of a product's proprietary protection and the market's size whereas later-stage VCs look at the venture's previous performance.

Testing a main hypothesis (derived from the finding that entrepreneurs have difficulty introspecting about their personal decision policies) and also understanding that VCs suffer from decision biases, several studies have set out to build actuarial decision aids that can improve the screening process (Astebro 2004; Riquelme and Rickards 1992; Zacharakis and Meyer 2000; Zacharakis and Shepherd 2005). These studies consistently find that actuarial decision aids are better in screening ventures than are actual VCs themselves due to consistency in applying decision policies and removing decision biases, yet few VCs have adopted these aids. Research exploring this reluctance could be insightful.

DUE DILIGENCE

In the due diligence phase, VCs are engaged in a continuous loop between *interpretation* and *action*. The VC collects information from the entrepreneur and a multitude of other sources. How this information is *interpreted* influences the *action* that the VC takes. For instance, some information may raise questions that need to be answered and lead to additional information search. Once this loop is complete to the VC's satisfaction, the process moves to either negotiation or a polite rejection.

There hasn't been a lot of research on the VC due diligence process, and what work there has been hasn't focused on the relative importance of criteria, which *has* been the case for screening. Nonetheless, anecdotally, the importance of criteria differs in due diligence from its importance in screening. While screening starts with market factors, due diligence is a drill down on the entrepreneurial team and product (Smart 1999). The VC believes there is potential, but due diligence looks hard at whether the team is capable of executing on that promise as well as whether the product is not only technically feasible but likely to be adopted by the customer. Kaplan and Stromberg (2004) categorize these issues in terms of risk. There is internal risk, which centers on the VC's difficulty in gauging the entrepreneur's human capital and monitoring the entrepreneur's activity, particularly in regard to how the investment is used. There is external risk, which looks at market acceptance, competitive reaction, and so forth. Finally, there is execution risk, which involves the complexity of developing a winning strategy and product. Due diligence helps to minimize these risks.

Due diligence takes a considerable amount of the VC's time. Smart (1999) estimates that VCs spend on average 120 hours just evaluating the entrepreneur's human capital, trying to reduce the internal risk. This doesn't include the time VCs spend on due diligence of the market, product, or the financial standing of the portfolio company (Smart 1999). This means that due diligence on the entrepreneurial team requires anywhere from 1 to 10 weeks of full-time effort; however, VCs rarely spend all that time sequentially, so in calendar terms due diligence can last anywhere from six weeks to six months (Fiet 1995). The level of due diligence is influenced by time constraints, cost of reducing information asymmetries, and any number of situational aspects that can make thorough due diligence more difficult (Harvey and Lusch 1995). As such, due diligence is a cost/benefit trade-off; how much effort and time should VCs commit to reduce the adverse selection (Sah and Stiglitz 1986), which is an internal risk. Investors will refrain from investing if they foresee an expensive due diligence process. The ebb and flow of the due diligence process on a particular venture, as well as the cost to acquire and evaluate relevant information influences what captures the VC's *attention* and how the VC *interprets* that information.

Due diligence involves evaluating both tangible assets (e.g., patents, accounts receivable, etc.) and intangible ones (quality of leadership, know how, culture, etc. [Harvey and Lusch 1995]). Entrepreneurial firms seeking venture capital likely have more intangible assets, which are much harder to assess and *interpret* (more costly), especially for earlier-stage deals (Norton and Tenenbaum 1993a). Smart (1999) conducted an exploratory study of VC due diligence on the entrepreneurial team's human capital potential (an intangible asset); basically, VCs must assess the likelihood that the team's behaviors will lead to a desired outcome. His study of 51 VCs finds three primary areas of due diligence effort: (1) work samples where the VC quizzes the entrepreneur on a number of what-if scenarios; (2) reference checks on people who can attest to the entrepreneur's capabilities; and (3) fact-based interviews to assess the entrepreneur's past performance. These are the areas that capture the VC's *attention*. From Kaplan and Stromberg's (2004) perspective, the focus is on internal and execution risks. While VCs can protect themselves from agency issues by contingent financing and entrepreneur compensation contracting, it is harder to protect themselves from execution risks. Thus, execution risk takes on more importance.

The entire due diligence process can be subject to VC biases. Franke and colleagues (2006) find that VCs evaluate entrepreneurs more favorably if they are similar to the VCs themselves. In a study of 51 VCs, Franke and colleagues find that VCs view entrepreneurs more favorably if the entrepreneur shares similar prior work experience and education background as the VC. Within due diligence, this similarity bias may led VCs to shorten their due diligence process, possibly overlooking key factors that may suggest the venture isn't as attractive as the VC believes. In other words, similarity biases may affect *attention* and *interpretation*.

The due diligence areas of emphasis change by stage of the investment. For earlier-stage deals, Smart (1999) finds that work samples take more of the VC's time whereas for later-stage deals, fact-based interviews become more important. These findings have face validity in that in later-stage deals, the VC can gauge the entrepreneur's efforts in the venture in question and assess how likely the entrepreneur is to continue on a successful course. On the other hand, for earlier-stage deals, VCs are looking at the entrepreneur's decision-making process to assess whether the entrepreneur will develop a strategy that can lead to success.

Venture capitalists focus on informants as a means of conducting due diligence. These experts can offer insight to market potential, and are often other VCs who may become co-investors (Fiet 1995). In essence, co-investing (or forming a syndicate) reduces the costs of due diligence as it brings more minds to the evaluation process. If we look at the above work from an information-processing perspective, VCs bring in outside help to filter and *interpret* relevant information.

Syndication is a common practice in financing transactions (Brander, Amit, and Antweiler 2002; Bygrave 1987; Lerner 1994; Sorenson and Stuart 2001). Syndication is highly relevant to VCs, for it allows VCs to pool information prior to investment decisions as well as throughout the investment process (Brander, Amit, and Antweiler 2002; Florida and Smith 1990). Information on investments is considered a valuable resource because information reduces risk without negatively affecting returns (Bygrave 1987). Thus, syndication reduces the cost of *attending* and *interpreting* information. Furthermore, two parties are likely to hold different information on the same subject, resulting from different backgrounds, experiences, and perspectives (Subrahmanyam and Titman 1999), so that pooling the knowledge of several parties increases the diversity of information considered. Venture capitalists *attend* and *interpret* more information. Sah and Stiglitz (1986) show that syndicated investments are superior to those that are based only on the knowledge base of one individual, suggesting that this minimizes biases in *interpretation*. Scholars thus argue that a selection process for VC investments becomes all the more effective the larger the number of VCs who actively participate (Lerner 1994; Sorenson and Stuart 2001). In essence, the pooling of experiences and knowledge eases information asymmetries between VCs and entrepreneurs, and reduces the syndicate's exposure to adverse selection risk and improves the *interpretation* of the information surrounding the decision.

Since VCs can never make due diligence costless, VCs add a discount to their valuation (Cornell and Shapiro 1988; Cumming and MacIntosh 2001). Therefore, better-quality entrepreneurs benefit if they can reduce information asymmetries. Busenitz, Fiet, and Moesel (2005) suggest that entrepreneurs can reduce the information gap and thereby cut the VC's cost of due diligence by signaling the entrepreneur's personal commitment to the venture. In essence, such signaling reduces the VC's concern over some agency risks, such as shirking, adverse selection, and holdups (Kaplan and Stromberg 2004). However, Busenitz, Fiet, and Moesel (2005) did not find that signaling was correlated to long-term venture success. The lack of findings may suggest that signaling biases VCs in their due diligence process, possibly by encouraging them to take shortcuts (less time devoted to due diligence) or pay more *attention* to certain factors (such as the team) and less to others (such as the market).

Future Research

While several aspects of due diligence have received attention, more work can be done. Smart (1999) finds better due diligence performance by smaller VC firms and speculates it's because they make fewer deals per partner, but he was unable to test that proposition. From an information-processing perspective, it implies that these VCs have more time and therefore more fully *attend* to and *interpret* the information around a decision. A good future study may look at difference in due diligence by VC firm size, stage focus, technology focus, and so forth. Smart (1999) also questions whether there is a curvilinear effect on time/effort expended and value of due diligence. In other words, does a fully rational evaluation of a decision become inefficient? Following Kaplan and Stromberg (2004), research may use investment memorandums written by VCs to assess the level of due diligence and then see if there is a correlation to ultimate venture performance.

As mentioned earlier in this chapter, the VC's most important asset is time. From an information-processing perspective, time constraints likely lead to short-cuts, meaning limits in information *attended* to and shortcuts in *interpreting* that information. Time can be further constrained in situations where the VC is prone to grandstanding (Gompers 1996). Newer venture capital firms feel pressure to find and harvest deals quickly in order to demonstrate returns and improve their position in raising subsequent funds. This may lead newer VCs to try and push potential deals into the pipeline as quickly as possible and thereby shortchange the amount of information they *attend* to and the time they spend *interpreting* it.

Syndication brings multiple perspectives on a deal and should lead to a more thorough consideration of the information. However, the partnership's ability to fully evaluate that information may hinge on how similar (homogeneous) or dissimilar (heterogeneous) the two VC firms are. For instance, the relative status of each firm may influence the exchange and consideration of information (Walske, Zacharakis, and Smith-Doerr 2008). There is an opportunity to evaluate how syndicate partners handle and manage due diligence in regard to *attention, interpretation,* and *action* and what if any interactions occur.

NEGOTIATION

If due diligence proves favorable, the VC and the entrepreneur enter negotiations on the investment's specific terms. During this phase, VCs take *action* on the information they have previously *interpreted*. Several issues are pertinent in this stage, including valuation, contract provisions that provide protection against agency risks, staging of future rounds, and board representation and oversight (Sahlman 1990).

Valuation

As Wright and Robbie (1998) point out, valuation for a new venture is quite different from formal corporate valuation. Wright and Robbie underscore the importance of proper valuation models to incorporate the two facets that make VC investments distinctive: relatively high uncertainty compared to investments in mature companies and rapid growth. Techniques anticipating steady future developments and constant earnings on the basis of the company's history cannot entirely capture the potential inherent in such investment. Seppä and Laamanen (2001) therefore summarize that in the VC context the absence of a performance history by which to judge the company and uncertainties about the young business particularly hamper the use of conventional valuation methods such as benchmark valuations on the basis of Price/Earnings (P/E) ratios of public companies or calculation of a company's Discounted Cash Flow (DCF).[1] A young company's earnings may, for instance, be subject to great jumps at the beginning, which are not predictable on the basis of its previous performance; this increases the error of forecasts. Cornell and Shapiro (1988), Kaplan and Ruback (1996), and Keeley and Punjabi (1996) observe that VCs revert to benchmarks more specifically related to the business to assess the potential value an investment can attain given its prospects. This may lead to an availability bias. How similar is this venture to other deals? What has been the valuation on those deals? Such benchmarking may lead VCs to limit their information search (*attention*) and analysis (*interpretation*).

An anchor and adjust bias is likely at this stage (Hogarth and Makridakis 1981). In the anchor and adjust bias, two parties base their negotiation on the "sticker price" (anchoring) and then adjust from that "price" based upon their perspective (Northcraft and Neale 1987). Considering that the final valuation will largely be determined by the initial anchor (Hogarth 1988), understanding the process is critical. Since VCs have more negotiating power and deeper knowledge of previous deals, it is likely that their valuation will act as the anchor. Thus, from an information-processing perspective, we would expect they will use benchmarks to anchor the valuation and *interpret* the adjustment in relation to how the current venture stacks up to previous deals. If the VC and entrepreneur are in agreement on the anchor, it is more likely that they will take *action* and fund the deal.

Contract Terms

Since valuation is highly susceptible to future performance of the venture, which is impacted by entrepreneur actions, unforeseen conditions, and so forth, VCs often contract to protect themselves from agreeing to an inflated valuation (Cornelli and Yosha 2003; Kaplan and Stromberg 2001; Kirilenko 2001; Wright and Robbie 1998). One way is to use hybrid financing, which allows VCs to alter the financing structure throughout the investment period in reaction to newly emerging information. Norton and Tenenbaum (1992, 1993b) researched the financing methods of 98 U.S. VC firms and found that preferred convertible equity dominates in general, since it allows VCs an effortless use of ratchets (Trester 1998). Cornelli and Yosha (2003) demonstrate that in the course of a staged investment, convertible securities afford VCs a strong position to work against window-dressing problems as they can increase their stake (diluting the entrepreneur's stake) in case predefined goals are not accomplished. Gilson and Schizer (2003) suggest that convertible securities predominate in the United States due to favorable tax treatment for the entrepreneur and because they have become the accepted form, but other means can achieve the same goals of protecting the VC. Depending on the business and the industry sector, the extent of these measures varies. Thus, outside the United States, convertible securities are used less often (Cumming 2005). For instance, high technology investments with a higher risk for failure generally entail more contract provisions related to milestones than low technology companies (Gompers and Lerner 2000). High tech investments are also more likely to use convertible securities (Cumming 2005). Structure and covenants also economize the VC's time as they provide postinvestment protection from faulty decisions. In essence, these provisions protect the VC against missed information (*attention*) and poor *interpretation*.

Besides looking into capital structure–related covenants, scholars have researched the application of other governance means, which are usually stipulated in advance to an investment. Barney and colleagues (1989) looked into 270 VC contracts during 1983 and 1985 and observed that VCs occupy a disproportionably high number of board seats either with representatives or affiliates in relation to their actual ownership position (Baker and Gompers 2003; Sorenson and Stuart 2001). It is argued that stronger board representation of VCs increases the entrepreneur's receptivity to financial, operational, and strategic advice (Fried, Bruton, and Hisrich 1998). Rosenstein (1988) finds that boards of VC-backed ventures have even greater power than the company's management (e.g., entrepreneurs). VCs use their board presence to supervise the management and initiate strategic changes if necessary (Barry et al. 1990). In the long run, however, Barney and colleagues (1994) find that VCs forego board seats the more the company's performance improves and the longer the management is in place. Barney and colleagues (1994) add that VCs grow keen to seek covenants protecting proprietary knowledge and impede entrepreneurs from engaging in rivaling activities the more competitive the venture's environment. Kaplan and Strömberg (2003) provide an overview on the extent of specific governance methods that are commonly applied in VC finance on the basis of 213 investments in the United States. They show that if companies lack significant turnover, VCs apply staging mechanisms, vesting, voting rights, and board influence in order to supervise the investment effectively. However, VCs tend to release these stringent conditions the more the venture matures and the more uncertainty is resolved. Again, governance structures are a means to economize on preinvestment decision making and protect against missed information and faulty interpretation.

Future Research

Although control and monitoring economize on decision making, they may also have negative effects. Shepherd and Zacharakis (2001) warn that undue reliance on negative covenants such as ratchets may so diminish entrepreneur motivation that it negatively impacts overall venture performance. For this reason, Shepherd and Zacharakis (2001) propose a model of trust building that recognizes that any VC-entrepreneur relationship is based not only on control (from an agency perspective) but also on trust. They assert that entrepreneurs (as well as VCs) can build trust in the other party by signaling commitment, taking fair and just actions, obtaining a good fit, and open and frequent communication. While many scholars have focused on control mechanisms (Barney et al. 1996; Fiet 1995; Sahlman 1990), less work has looked at the interaction of trust and control in the VC-entrepreneur relationship. One exception is that Sapienza and Korsgaard (1996) have investigated VCs' responses to the timeliness with which entrepreneurs shared information and the level of influence the VC had over the strategic direction of the venture. By comparing the relations of two panels of Master's-level business students on the one hand and experienced VCs on the other hand with management teams of their portfolio companies, Sapienza and Korsgaard (1996) unveil that prompt feedback positively impacts the relationship. This turns into greater trust between investors and investees, which eventually softens principal-agent concerns and relieves monitoring efforts. It is thus beneficial for VCs to seek timely cooperation with entrepreneurs. Future research could look at how trust building interacts with information processing. Does it reduce asymmetric information? Does it lead the VC to shorten the due diligence process?

While negotiation and contracting has drawn heavily on the shape of contracts and how the provisions tie to an agency perspective, most of the research seems to view the process from the VC's eyes. There is an opportunity to examine how entrepreneurs enter negotiations and how they improve the valuation through this process. How do entrepreneurs provide information to VCs to facilitate or possibly hinder VC decision making? We suspect that the ability of the entrepreneur to negotiate successfully will be contingent upon a number of contextual factors, such as the entrepreneur's previous experience, the perceived potential of the venture, current economic conditions (e.g., the dot.com boom and bust), and so forth. How does the negotiation process evolve? Does the way the process moves from initial meetings, to term sheets, to final valuation and terms influence the entrepreneur's incentives?

CONCLUSION

Over the last 30 years, we have gained a strong understanding of the VC decision process, but there is still ample room to gain deeper understanding. This chapter examines the VC investment decision process from an information-processing perspective. While certain aspects of the VC decision process have received considerable attention, namely screening and valuation, others are under-researched. In particular, deal origination and due diligence have received far less attention than is warranted by the importance of these steps in the VC process. Although the basic information-processing model of *attention, interpretation,* and *action* is simple, it is also robust. Using this platform, a whole slew of extensions to the basic process can be examined, including interactions between decision criteria, biases, and heuristics. In addition, learning can be applied to the model. As VCs go through the process multiple times, they inevitably learn. This learning can lead them to better understand what aspects deserve more *attention* and deeper *interpretation* than other aspects. The model laid out in Exhibit 2.1 highlights a few aspects that are pertinent in *attention* and *interpretation* across stages. The difficulty, as highlighted in the chapter, is that learning can also be suboptimal and lead to biases that may not improve the decision process. Future research can use this as a starting point to add depth to our understanding of the VC process.

NOTE

1. A DCF valuation computes the risk and time adjusted value of a company's future cash flows.

REFERENCES

Astebro, T. 2004. Key success factors for technological entrepreneurs' RandD projects. *IEEE Transactions on Engineering Management* 51(3):314–321.

Baker, M., and P. Gompers. 2003. The determinants of board structure at the initial public offering. *Journal of Law and Economics* 46(2):569–598.

Barney, J., L. Busenitz, J. Fiet, and D. Moesel. 1989. The structure of venture capital governance: An organizational economic analysis of the relations between venture capital firms and new ventures. *Academy of Management Proceedings:* 64–68.

———. 1994. The relationship between venture capitalists and managers in new firms: Determinants of contractual covenants. *Managerial Finance* 20(1):19–30.

_____. 1996. New venture teams' assessment of learning assistance from venture capital firms. *Journal of Business Venturing* 11(4):257–272.

Baron, R. 1998. Cognitive mechanisms in entrepreneurship: Why and when entrepreneurs think differently than other persons. *Journal of Business Venturing* 13, 275–294.

Barr, P., J. Stimpert, and A. Huff. 1992. Cognitive change, strategic action, and organizational renewal. *Strategic Management Journal*, 13:15–36.

Barry, C., C. Muscarella, J. Peavy, and M. Vetsuypens. 1990. The role of venture capital in the creation of public companies: Evidence from the going-public process. *Journal of Financial Economics* 27(2):447–471.

Brander, J., R. Amit, and W. Antweiler. 2002. Venture capital syndication: Improved venture selection versus the value-added hypothesis. *Journal of Economics and Management Strategy* 11(3):423–452.

Brush, C., N. Carter, P. Greene, M. Hart, and E. Gatewood. 2002. The role of social capital and gender in linking financial suppliers and entrepreneurial firms: A framework for future research. *Venture Capital: An International Journal of Entrepreneurial Finance* 4(4): 305–323.

Bruton, G., and D. Ahlstrom. 2003. An institutional view of China's venture capital industry: Explaining the differences between China and the West. *Journal of Business Venturing* 18(2):233–259.

Busenitz, L., and J. Barney. 1997. Differences between entrepreneurs and managers in large organizations: Biases and heuristics in strategic decision making. *Journal of Business Venturing* 12:9–30.

Busentitz, L., J. Fiet, and D. Moesel. 2005. Signaling in venture capitalists—new venture team funding decisions: Does it indicate long-term venture outcomes? *Entrepreneurship Theory and Practice* 29(1):1–12.

Bygrave, W. 1987. Syndicated investments by venture capital firms: A networking perspective. *Journal of Business Venturing* 2(2):139–154.

Bygrave, W., and S. Hunt. 2005. *Global Entrepreneurship Monitor: 2004 Financing Report.* Babson Park, MA; London, UK: Babson College-London Business School.

Cornell, B., and A. Shapiro. 1988. Financing corporate growth. *Journal of Applied Corporate Finance* 1 (Summer):6–22.

Cornelli, F., and O. Yosha. 2003. Stage financing and the role of convertible securities. *Review of Economic Studies*, 70(1):1-32.

Cumming, D. 2005. Agency costs, institutions, learning, and taxation in venture capital contracting. *Journal of Business Venturing* 20:573–622.

_____, and J. MacIntosh. 2001. Venture capital investment duration in Canada and the United States. *Journal of Multinational Financial Management* 11(4–5):445–463.

Cyert, R., and J. March. 1963. *A Behavioral Theory of the Firm.* Engelwood Cliffs, NJ: Prentice Hall.

Dimov, D., D. Shepherd, and K. Sutcliffe. 2007. Requisite expertise, firm reputation, and status in venture capital investment allocation decisions. *Journal of Business Venturing* 22(4):481–502.

Dorsey, T. 1979 *Operating Guidelines for Effective Venture Capital Funds Management.* Austin: University of Texas.

Elango, B., V. Fried, R. Hisrich, and A. Polonchek. 1995. How venture capital firms differ. *Journal of Business Venturing* 10(2):157–179.

Fiet, J. 1995. Reliance upon informants in the venture capital industry. *Journal of Business Venturing* 10(3):195–223.

Florida, R., and M. Kenney. 1988. Venture capital and high technology entrepreneurship. *Journal of Business Venturing* 3(4):301–319.

Florida, R., and D. Smith. 1990. Venture capital, innovation and economic development. *Economic Development Quarterly* 4(4):345–360.

Franke, N., M. Gruber, D. Harhoff, and J. Henkel. 2006. What you are is what you like—Similarity biases in venture capitalists' evaluations of start-up teams. *Journal of Business Venturing* 21: 802–826.

Fried, V., G. Bruton, and R. Hisrich. 1998. Strategy and the board of directors in venture capital–backed firms. *Journal of Business Venturing* 13(6):493–503.

Fried, V., and R. Hisrich. 1994. Toward a model of venture capital investment decision making. *Financial Management* 23(3):28–37.

Gilson, R., and D. Schizer. 2003. Understanding venture capital: A tax explanation for convertible preferred stock. *Harvard Law Review* 116: 874–916.

Gompers, P. 1996. Grandstanding in the venture capital industry. *Journal of Financial Economics* 42(1):133–156.

———, and J. Lerner. 1998. What drives venture capital fundraising. *Brookings Papers on Economic Activity*: 149–204.

———, and J. Lerner. 2000. *The venture capital cycle*. Cambridge, MA; London: MIT Press.

Greene, P., C. Brush, M. Hart, and P. Saparito. 2001. Patterns of venture capital funding: Is gender a factor? *Venture Capital: An International Journal of Entrepreneurial Finance* 3(1):63–83.

Gregoire, D., A. de Koning, and B. Oviatt. 2009. Do VC's evaluate "live" presentations like they do business plans? *Frontiers of Entrepreneurship Research* 65–77.

Hall, J., and C. Hofer. 1993. Venture capitalists' decision criteria and new venture evaluation. *Journal of Business Venturing* 8(1):25–42.

Harvey, M., and R. Lusch. 1995. Expanding the nature and scope of due diligence. *Journal of Business Venturing* 10(1):5–22.

Hogarth, R. M. 1988. *Judgment and choice*. Chichester, UK: John Wiley & Sons.

Hogarth, R., and S. Makridakis. 1981. Forecasting and planning: An evolution. *Management Science* 27(2):115–138.

Kaplan, S., and R. Ruback. 1996. The market pricing of cash flow forecasts: Discounted cash flow vs. the method of "comparables." *Journal of Applied Corporate Finance* 8(4): 45–60.

Kaplan, S., and P. Strömberg. 2001. Venture capitalists as principals: Contracting, screening and monitoring. *American Economic Review* 91(2):426–430.

———. 2003. Financial contracting theory meets the real world. *Review of Economic Studies* 70(2):281–315.

———. 2004. Characteristics, contracts, and actions: Evidence from venture capitalist analyses. *Journal of Finance* 59(5):2173–2206.

Keeley, R., and S. Punjabi. 1996. Valuation of early-stage ventures: Option valuation models vs. traditional approaches. *Journal of Entrepreneurial and Small Business Finance* 5(2):114–138.

Kirilenko, A. 2001. Valuation and control in venture finance. *Journal of Finance* 56(2): 565–587.

Knight, R. 1994. Criteria used by venture capitalists: A cross cultural analysis. *International Small Business Journal*, 13(1):26–37.

Kunkel, S., and C. Hofer. 1990. Why study the determinants of new venture performance: A literature review and rationale. *Presented at Academy of Management meetings*.

Lerner, J. 1994. The syndication of venture capital investments. *Financial Management* 23(3):16–27.

Lord, R., and K. Maher. 1990. Alternative information-processing models and their implications for theory, research, and practice. *Academy of Management Review*, 15(1): 9–28.

MacMillan, I., R. Siegel, and P. SubbaNarasimha. 1985. Criteria used by venture capitalists to evaluate new venture proposals. *Journal of Business Venturing* 1(1): 119–128.

MacMillan, I., L. Zeman, and P. SubbaNarasimha. 1987. Criteria distinguishing unsuccessful ventures in the venture screening process. *Journal of Business Venturing* 2(2):123–137.

Manigart, S., A. Locket, M. Meuleman, M. Wright, H. Landstrom, P. Desbrieres, and U. Hommel. 2006. Venture capitalists' decision to syndicate. *Entrepreneurship Theory and Practice* 30(2):131–153.

Mason, C., and R. Harrison. 2003. "Auditioning for money": What do technology investors look for at the initial screening stage? *Journal of Private Equity* 6(2):29–42.

Minniti, M., W. Bygrave, and E. Autio. 2006. *Global Entrepreneurship Monitor Executive Report 2005*. Babson Park, MA; London, UK: Babson College-London Business School.

Moesel, D., J. Fiet, and L. Busenitz. 2001. Embedded fitness landscapes—part 1: How a venture capitalist maps highly subjective risk. *Venture Capital: An International Journal of Entrepreneurial Finance* 3(2):91–106.

Money Tree Report. 2008. Historical trend data. Retrieved from https://www.pwc moneytree.com/MTPublic/ns/nav.jsp?page=historical.

Northcraft, G., and M. Neale. 1987. Experts, amateurs, and real estate: An anchoring-and-adjustment perspective on property pricing decisions. *Organizational Behavior and Human Decision Process* 39 (February):84–97.

Norton, E., and B. Tenenbaum. 1992. Factors affecting the structure of U.S. venture capital deals. *Journal of Small Business Management* 30(3):20–29.

———. 1993a. Specialization versus differentiation as a venture capital investment strategy. *Journal of Business Venturing* 8(5):431–442.

———. 1993b. The effects of venture capitalists' characteristics on the structure of the venture capital deal. *Journal of Small Business Management* 31(4):23–41.

Poindexter, E. 1976. The efficiency of financial markets: The venture capital case. PhD diss. New York University.

Rah, J., K. Jung, and J. Lee. 1994. Validation of the venture evaluation model in Korea. *Journal of Business Venturing* 9(6):509–524.

Riquelme, H., and T. Rickards. 1992. Hybrid conjoint analysis: An estimation probe in new venture decisions. *Journal of Business Venturing* 7(6):505–518.

Robinson, R. 1987. Emerging strategies in the venture capital industry. *Journal of Business Venturing* 2: 53–77.

Roure, J., and R. Keeley. 1990. Predictors of success in new technology based ventures. *Journal of Business Venturing* 5: 201–220.

Rosenstein, J. 1988. The board of strategy: Venture capital and high technology. *Journal of Business Venturing* 3(2):159–170.

Sah, R., and J. Stiglitz. 1986. The architecture of economic systems: Hierarchies and polyarchies. *American Economic Review* 76(4):716–727.

Sahlman, W. 1990. The structure and governance of venture capital organizations. *Journal of Financial Economics* 27:473–521.

Sahlman, W., and Stevenson, H. 1985. Capital market myopia. *Journal of Business Venturing*, 1(1):7–30.

Sandberg, W. 1986. *New Venture Performance*. Lexington, MA: Lexington.

Sandberg, W., D. Schweiger, and C. Hofer. 1988. The use of verbal protocols in determining venture capitalists' decision processes. *Entrepreneurship Theory and Practice* (Winter):8–20.

Sapienza, H., and M. Korsgaard. 1996. Procedural justice in entrepreneur-investor relations. *Academy of Management Journal* 39: 544–574.

Seppä, T., and T. Laamanen. 2001. Valuation of venture capital investments: Empirical evidence. *Rand Management* 31(2):215–230.

Shane, S., and D. Cable. 2002. Network ties, reputation, and the financing of new ventures. *Management Science* 48(3):364–381.

Shepherd, D. 1999. Venture capitalists' assessment of new venture survival. *Management Science* 45(5):621–632.

_____, and A. Zacharakis. 2001. The venture capitalist-entrepreneur relationship: Control, trust and confidence in co-operative behavior. *Venture Capital: An International Journal of Entrepreneurial Finance* 3(2):129–149.

Shepherd, D., R. Baron, and A. Zacharakis. 2003. Venture capitalists' decision processes: Evidence suggesting more experience may not always be better. *Journal of Business Venturing* 18(3):381–401.

Simon, H. 1955. A behavioral model of rational choice. *Quarterly Journal of Economics* 69: 99–118.

Smart, G. 1999. Management assessment methods in venture capital: An empirical analysis of human capital valuation. *Venture Capital: An International Journal of Entrepreneurial Finance* 1(1):59–82.

Sorensen, O., and T. Stuart. 2001. Syndication networks and spatial distribution of venture capital investments. *American Journal of Sociology* 106(6):1546–1588.

Staw, B. 1997. The escalation of commitment: An update and appraisal. In *Organizational Decision Making*, ed. Z. Shapira (191–215). Cambridge: Cambridge University Press.

Stuart, T., H. Hoang, and R. Hybels. 1999. Interoganizational endorsements and the performance of entrepreneurial ventures. *Administrative Science Quarterly* 44: 315–249.

Subrahmanyam, A., and S. Titman. 1999. The going-public decision and the development of financial markets. *Journal of Finance* 54(3):1045–1082.

Timmons, J., D. Muzyka, H. Stevenson, and W. Bygrave. 1987. Opportunity recognition: The core of entrepreneurship. *Frontiers of Entrepreneurship Research*: 109–123.

Trester, J. 1998. Venture capital contracting under asymmetric information. *Journal of Banking and Finance* 22(6–8):675–699.

Tyebjee, T., and A. Bruno. 1984. A model of venture capitalist investment activity. *Management Science* 30(9):1051–1066.

Walske, J., and A. Zacharakis. 2009. Genetically engineered: Why some venture capital firms are more successful than others. *Entrepreneurship Theory and Practice* 33(1): 297–318.

_____, and L. Smith-Doerr. 2008. Effects of venture capital syndication networks on entrepreneurial success. *Frontiers of Entrepreneurship Research*: 38–52.

Wells, W. 1974. Venture capital decision-making. PhD Diss. Carnegie-Mellon University.

Wright, M., and K. Robbie. 1998. Venture capital and private equity: A review and synthesis. *Journal of Business Finance and Accounting* 25(5 and 6):521–570.

Wright, M., H. Sapienza, and L. Busenitz. 2003. *Venture capital*, vols. 1, 2, 3. London: Edward Elgar.

Zacharakis, A. L., J. McMullen, and D. A. Shepherd. 2007. Venture capitalists' decision making across three countries: An institutional theory perspective. *Journal of International Business Studies* 38(5):691–708.

Zacharakis, A., and G. Meyer. 1998. A lack of insight: Do venture capitalists really understand their own decision process? *Journal of Business Venturing* 13(1):57–76.

Zacharakis, A., and G. Meyer. 1995. The venture capitalist decision: Understanding process versus outcome. *Frontiers of Entrepreneurship Research*: 465–478.

_____. 2000. The potential of actuarial decision models: Can they improve the venture capital investment decision? *Journal of Business Venturing* 15(4):323–346.

_____, and J. DeCastro. 1999. Differing perceptions of new venture failure: A matched exploratory study of venture capitalists and entrepreneurs. *Journal of Small Business Management* 37(3):1–14.

Zacharakis, A. L., and D. A. Shepherd. 2001. The nature of information and overconfidence on venture capitalists' decision making. *Journal of Business Venturing* 16(4):311–332.

Zacharakis, A. L., and D. Shepherd. 2005. A non-additive decision-aid for venture capitalists' investment decisions. *European Journal of Operational Research* 162(3):673–689.

ABOUT THE AUTHOR

Andrew Zacharakis is the John H. Muller, Jr. Chair in Entrepreneurship and the Director of the Babson College Entrepreneurship Research Conference, the leading academic conference on entrepreneurship worldwide. Zacharakis's primary research areas include the (1) venture capital process and (2) entrepreneurial growth strategies. Zacharakis received a BS (finance/marketing) from the University of Colorado; an MBA (finance/international business) from Indiana University; and a PhD (strategy and entrepreneurship/cognitive psychology) from the University of Colorado.

CHAPTER 3

Banks Versus Venture Capital in the Financing of New Ventures

JEAN ETIENNE DE BETTIGNIES
Associate Professor, Queen's School of Business, Queen's University

INTRODUCTION

How do entrepreneurs finance their ventures? This is one of the fundamental questions of entrepreneurship, which until recently had been addressed—theoretically—in two ways in particular. On the one hand, the security design literature, building on Grossman and Hart's (1986) and Hart and Moore's (1990) classic work on incomplete contracting, examined the conditions for the optimality of debt in the financing of new projects (Bolton and Scharfstein 1990, 1996; Hart and Moore 1994, 1998) as well as various trade-offs between debt and equity financing (Aghion and Bolton 1992; Dewatripont and Tirole 1994; Fluck 1998; Myers 2000; Dybvig and Wang 2002).

On the other hand, much of the entrepreneurial finance literature has focused on trying to explain the predominant use of convertible securities in venture capital contracts in the United States today.[1] Indeed, convertible securities have been shown to emerge as a response to single-sided (Bergmann and Hege 1998), double-sided (Casamatta 2003; Repullo and Suarez 2004, Hellmann 2006) or sequential (Schmidt 2002) moral hazard issues affecting the entrepreneur/investor relationship; to potential signal manipulation ("window-dressing") by the entrepreneur (Cornelli and Yosha 2003); as well as to conflicts of interest between the entrepreneur and the investor in exit situations such as trade sales and IPOs (Berglöf 1994; Bascha and Walz 2001) or liquidation events (Marx 1998).

While both literatures provide very valuable insights, neither one can fully address the question posed at the beginning of this introduction. The security design literature does not address the financing of entrepreneurial ventures specifically (e.g., the particularity of venture capital, etc.). And the convertible security literature ignores key features of entrepreneurial financing, namely that (1) 90 percent of all start-ups are *not* financed with venture capital, and more than 95 percent of small-firm financing comes from sources other than venture capital (Davis 2003); and (2) Within the set of start-ups backed by venture capital, the prevalence of convertible securities is not as universal as was once thought: in Canada and Europe for example, common equity, rather than convertible equity, tends to predominate (Bottazzi, Da Rin, and Hellmann 2004; Cumming 2005).[2]

A new theoretical literature has recently emerged that addresses these limitations. Indeed, this line of research does focus specifically on entrepreneurial ventures, but restricts itself neither to venture capital backed start-ups, nor to convertible preferred equity contracts. It examines the entrepreneur's choice between VC financing and bank financing.

Our purpose here is to review this small but rapidly growing literature. Clearly, the contribution here is not in the results themselves, which by the very nature of this exercise are not novel to the paper. Rather, we hope to contribute by presenting one or two key results from each paper, in a simplified model that allows the reader to grasp the intuitions easily and rapidly, without compromising too much the structural choices made by the initial authors. Thus, this review may be useful to researchers new to the field, who wish to get a quick yet deep enough overview of the literature before digging into each model specifically, and as an easy reference to researchers more familiar with the field.

Naturally, from an economics and finance point of view, the trade-offs between VC financing and bank financing can be viewed as comparisons of the various economic inefficiencies associated with one type of financing or the other. Accordingly, we organize the various papers reviewed here in terms of the key inefficiencies that they highlight.

We start in the second section with hidden action models. The simplest possible framework is a single-sided moral hazard model in the spirit of Elitzur and Gavious (2003), where only the entrepreneur exerts nonverifiable effort. In such a framework, the optimal contract is to "backload all incentive payments to the entrepreneur," very similar, in fact, to simple debt contracts such as the ones offered by banks. Next, we allow for moral hazard on the side of the investor as well, at least in the case where the investor is a venture capitalist. This allows us to transition to a framework closer to Bettignies and Brander (2007), and to show that in this richer type of environment, and in contrast to the single-sided moral hazard environment, bank debt need not be optimal. Indeed, the choice between bank financing and venture capital in that case depends on the relative efficiency at performing value-increasing activities, between the VC and the entrepreneur: there exists a threshold level of VC efficiency relative to entrepreneurial efficiency, such that above that threshold an equity contract with the VC dominates a debt contract with a bank.

The third section focuses on problems of hidden information, and particularly on Ueda's (2004) model of asymmetric information and expropriation. This is a model where the bank cannot evaluate entrepreneurial projects, and must elicit this information from the entrepreneur in a screening framework. The venture capitalist, on the other hand, can acurately evaluate the project, but may be tempted to expropriate the entrepreneur. Thus the trade-off between the two types of financing for the entrepreneur involves trading off the cost of asymmetric information versus the risk of expropriation.

The fourth section examines inefficiencies associated with problems of contractual incompleteness and reviews three main papers. Bettignies (2008) suggests that one of the key factors affecting the entrepreneur's optimal contractual choice, and the consequent optimal choice between banks and VCs, is the complementarity of efforts by the entrepreneur and the investor. In high-growth ventures (i.e., classic start-ups), for example, where entrepreneur/investor effort complementarity is crucial, equity-type contracts are shown to be optimal; while in lifestyle ventures (e.g., restaurants, hair salons, etc.) where effort complementarity is relatively low, debt-type contracts are optimal. The relationship between the type of venture and the type of financing can therefore be explained as follows: High-growth entrepreneurs tend to seek financing from VCs because (1) they can offer complementary skills, and (2) they typically offer equity contracts, which are optimal for these types of entrepreneurs. In contrast, lifestyle entrepreneurs tend to seek bank financing because (1) they don't need complementary skills from the investor, and (2) banks offer debt contracts that are optimal in these types of venture. Landier (2003) proposes a model where entrepreneurs and investors can hold each other up once the game is started. As a result, the choice between bank finance and venture capital depends on the quality of the entrepreneur's exit option, which itself depends on the legal environment and on the stigma of failure faced by the entrepreneur. And Winton and Yerramilli (2008) derive a model of choice between banks and venture capitalists where it is strategic uncertainty (uncertainty in continuation strategy choices) that is crucial in determining the optimal type of financing institution.

Finally, in concluding remarks in the fifth section, we underline the set of empirical predictions generated by the theory, in an attempt to stimulate new empirical research in a literature that currently seems overwhelmingly (exclusively?) theoretical.

MORAL HAZARD ISSUES

One of the key differences between bank financing and venture capital is that in the latter case the investor makes value-increasing contributions to the venture, in contrast to bank financing where value-increasing activities are more limited. The activities performed by the entrepreneur and the investor typically are difficult to verify, leading to what is known as a double-sided moral hazard problem. In this section we present a simplified version of Bettignies and Brander (2007), which can be used to examine the trade-off between VC financing and bank financing in the context of single-sided, that is, entrepreneur only, moral hazard as in Elitzur and Gavious (2003), as well as in the context of double-sided moral hazard.[3]

Consider a wealth-constrained entrepreneur who wants to start a new venture. The venture will yield profits Π with probability $1/2$, or zero otherwise, at date 2. To get started, the project requires a (very small) cash injection k at date 0, and to obtain k the entrepreneur can turn to one of two types of investors: She can turn to a venture capitalist, in which case she offers an equity stake equivalent to a share s of profits; or she can turn to a bank and offer a debt contract with a debt repayment d at date 2, which is paid out in the good state and not in the bad state. Finally, the entrepreneur and the investor can exert effort levels e and i, at personal costs $e^2/2$ and $i^2/2$, respectively, at date 1, which affect profits at date 2 in the following way: $\Pi = e + \theta i$. Parameter θ represents the efficiency of the investor relative to that of the entrepreneur. We examine venture capital (VC) financing and bank financing in turn, proceeding by backward induction.

VC Financing
Date 1: Effort Choices

Given that a share s of the equity has been given to the investor at date 0, the entrepreneur and the investor face the following maximization programs at date 1, respectively:

$$\max_e (1 - s) \frac{1}{2} (e + \theta i) \frac{1}{2} e^2 \tag{3.1}$$

$$\max_i s \frac{1}{2} (e + \theta i) - \frac{1}{2} i^2 - k$$

which yield $e = (1-s)/2$ and $i = s\theta/2$.
Date 0: Equity Choice

If the entrepreneur chooses to request funding from the venture capitalist, she offers an equity stake that maximizes the following program (having substituted the equilibrium levels of effort as functions of s):

$$\max_s (1 - s) \frac{1}{2} \left(\frac{1 - s}{2} + \frac{s\theta^2}{2} \right) - \frac{1}{2} \left(\frac{1 - s}{2} \right)^2, \text{ subject to} \tag{3.2}$$

$$s \frac{1}{2} \left(\frac{1 - s}{2} + \frac{s\theta^2}{2} \right) - \frac{1}{2} \left(\frac{s\theta}{2} \right)^2 - k \geq 0 \tag{3.3}$$

If a unique solution exists, let us denote it s^*. Then conditional on choosing VC financing, the entrepreneur offers an equity stake s^* in her venture in exchange for the initial investment k, and her expected payoff from a date 0 point of view is:

$$R_E^{VC} = (1 - s^*) \frac{1}{2} \left(\frac{1 - s^*}{2} + \frac{s^*\theta^2}{2} \right) - \frac{1}{2} \left(\frac{1 - s^*}{2} \right)^2 \tag{3.4}$$

Bank Financing
Date 1: Effort Choices

Given the date 2 debt repayment specified at date 0, we can describe the maximization programs for the entrepreneur and the investor, respectively, as follows:

$$\max_e \frac{1}{2} [(e + \theta i) - d] - \frac{1}{2} e^2 \tag{3.5}$$

$$\max_i \frac{1}{2} d - \frac{1}{2} i^2$$

which yields $e = 1/2$ and $i = 0$.
Date 0: Debt Choice

Since the debt repayment does not affect effort levels or expected profits, the entrepreneur simply chooses the smallest possible d, subject to the banker's participation constraint, $d/2 - k \geq 0$ that is, $d = 2k$, yielding the following expected payoff for the entrepreneur from a date 0 standpoint:

$$R_E^B = \frac{1}{2}\left(\frac{1}{2} - 2k\right) - \frac{1}{8} = \frac{1}{8} - k \tag{3.6}$$

Clearly, at date 0 the entrepreneur chooses VC financing over bank financing if and only if $R_E^{VC} \geq R_E^B$. As we shall now see, whether or not this condition holds depends on θ, the efficiency of the investor relative to the entrepreneur.

Single-Sided Moral Hazard: Elitzur and Gavious (2003)

We start with the simplest scenario where $\theta = 0$. In that case, the investor has zero marginal productivity and exerts zero effort at date 1, regardless of the type of financing. Indeed the problem reduces to a single-sided moral hazard model not dissimilar to Elitzur and Gavious (2003).

Under bank financing, the problem remains as we described above, and at date 0 the entrepreneur expects a return $R_E^B = \frac{1}{8} - k$. Under VC financing, an increase in the equity stake s allocated to the investor reduced the expected profits, via its negative effect on entrepreneurial incentives; and reduces the share of these profits that the entrepreneur takes home ex post. Thus, for the entrepreneur it is optimal to set s as low as possible, subject to the investor's participation constraint: that is, to set s such that (3.3) is binding. There are three possibilities here: there may be either zero, only one, or more than one value $s^* \in [0,1]$ of s such that the investor's participation constraint is binding.

It is easy to see that regardless of these three possibilities, they always yield an outcome for the entrepreneur that is strictly dominated by bank financing. In that case where $s^* = \emptyset$, VC financing is not feasible, and bank financing is optimal de facto. In the other two cases, the expected payoff for the investor is the same as under bank financing: he gets his reservation utility of zero. However total profits are higher under bank financing than under VC financing because in the former the entrepreneur has first-best incentives while in the latter she gets a share $1-s^* < 1$ of the profits and hence exerts less than first-best effort. Since the payoff to the entrepreneur is total profits minus the investor's payoff, it must be higher under bank financing than under VC financing.

Thus, when the investor brings nothing but cash to the venture, it is optimal for the entrepreneur to choose bank financing, because the associated debt contract "backloads all incentive payments to the entrepreneur" as suggested by Elitzur and Gavious (2003).

Double-Sided Moral Hazard: Bettignies and Brander (2007)

Let us now consider the scenario in which the investor's effort has a strictly positive impact on profits: $\theta > 0$. Under bank financing the equilibrium is as before: the equilibrium debt repayment $d = 2k$ is set such that the investor's participation constraint is binding, and the expected return to the entrepreneur as date 0 is $R_E^B = \frac{1}{8} - k$.

Under VC financing, the entrepreneur faces two concerns when deciding how large an equity stake s to offer the venture capitalist. First, increasing s has an ambiguous effect on expected profits: it increases the investor's incentives and equilibrium effort, which in turn has a positive impact on profits, but it decreases the entrepreneur's incentives and effort, which tends to reduce profits. Second, increasing unambiguously reduces the share of profits that the entrepreneur receives ex post.

In the case where $0 < \theta \leq 1$, the investor is less efficient than the entrepreneur in generating profits, and consequently, when increasing s the positive impact on investor incentives and profits is more than offset by the negative impact of that increase on entrepreneur incentives and on profits. Thus in that case increasing s has no benefits for the entrepreneur and only costs, and at date 0 it is optimal for the entrepreneur to offer as small an equity stake as possible, subject to the investor's participation constraint. This is the same outcome as in the case where $\theta = 0$, in which case we have shown that VC financing is strictly dominated by bank financing.

In contrast, in the case where $\theta > 1$, the investor is more efficient than the entrepreneur, who faces a real trade-off when deciding on the equity stake to be offered to the investor: On the one hand, an increase in s, though decreasing her own incentives, increases the investor's incentives sufficiently to generate a positive net effect on profits. On the other hand, an increase in s reduces the fraction of those profits that the entrepreneur can claim at date 2. Solving the program described in equations (3.2) and (3.3), it can be shown that for k "small enough," there exists an optimal equity stake $s^* = (1-\theta^2)/(1-2\theta^2)$ that maximizes the entrepreneur's expected payoff under VC financing and simultaneously satisfies the investor's participation constraint. Substituting this value of s^* into (4), the date 0 expected return for the entrepreneur simplifies to $R_E^{VC} = (\theta^4/8)/(2\theta^2-1)$. It is easy to show that $dR_E^{VC}/d\theta > 0$, and since $R_E^{VC} = 1/8$ at $\theta = 1$, we must have $R_E^{VC} > 1/8$ for all $\theta > 1$. This in turn implies $R_E^{VC} > R_E^B$: VC financing strictly dominates bank financing whenever the investor is more efficient than the entrepreneur. The intuition is simple: unlike a debt contract, which gives maximum incentives to the entrepreneur but none to the investor, an equity contract provides the investor with incentives to exert effort. When the investor's effort is sufficiently productive, equity capital provided by a venture capitalist is optimal.

The key empirical implication here is therefore clear: an increase in the efficiency of the investor relative to the entrepreneur should lead to a higher likelihood of VC financing over bank financing.

ASYMMETRIC INFORMATION ISSUES

Aside from moral hazard considerations, another issue that plagues the entrepreneur-investor relationship is that of asymmetric information: entrepreneurs are usually considered to be better informed about prospects of the venture than investors,[4] and even when both parties respond optimally to resolve this problem, economic inefficiencies usually remain. Ueda (2004) addresses this issue head-on in the context of VC versus bank financing. She proposes a model where the bank cannot evaluate entrepreneurial projects, and must elicit this information from the entrepreneur in a screening framework. The VC, on the other hand, can acurately evaluate the project, but may be tempted to expropriate the entrepreneur. Thus the entrepreneur must trade off the cost of asymmetric information against the risk of expropriation. In what follows we present the main insights of her analysis.

Project Evaluation and Expropriation: Ueda (2004)

Consider an entrepreneurial project that requires an initial capital outlay F, and returns profits RF with probability p ex post (and zero otherwise). The probability of success depends on the entrepreneur's "quality." If the entrepreneur is of type h (high quality), $p = p_h$, and if she is of type l (low quality), $p = p_l$, with $p_h > p_l$. The prior probability of being of either type is $1/2$. The type h project yields an expected payoff $p_h RF - F = \Phi > 0$ and hence is worth undertaking, while the type l project yields $p_h RF - F < 0$ and should not be undertaken. All players are risk neutral and the entrepreneur has zero initial wealth.

The entrepreneur sequentially negotiates with a bank and, if negotiations break down, with a venture capitalist. There are two key differences between the bank and the venture capitalist in this model: on the one hand, the bank does not know the entrepreneur's type while the venture capitalist does, once the project is disclosed to him. On the other hand, the venture capitalist can, once the project is disclosed to him, expropriate the project from the entrepreneur by undertaking it on his own, while the bank cannot do that. These two differences are the key drivers of the entrepreneur's choice between the two types of financing.

Negotiation with the Venture Capitalist

This scenario is very simple to describe, because there is no problem of information asymmetry here. In the case of a type l entrepreneur, the investor will simply refuse to finance the project. In the type h case, the entrepreneur offers that the venture capitalist pay the project initiation cost F, and keep the proceeds from the project Φ, minus a payment π_{VC} to the entrepreneur. Clearly, the entrepreneur wants to make π_{VC} as large as possible, subject to avoiding expropriation. Suppose that in case of expropriation the venture capitalist must pay compensation L to the entrepreneur. Clearly the investor will expropriate if and only $\pi_{VC} > L$, and hence in equilibrium the entrepreneur sets $\pi_{VC} = L$. The type h entrepreneur's expected payoff under VC financing is $U_{VC} = L$.

Negotiation with the Bank

Ueda points out—building on Rothschild and Stiglitz (1976) and Bester (1985) —that in this asymmetric information scenario, the optimal contract is one where the bank offers a menu of payments that (1) elicit truthful revelation of the entrepreneur's type and (2) maximize the type h entrepreneur's payoff while satisfying the type l's participation constraint. Let this menu of payments be $\{\pi_R, \pi_0, T\}$, where π_R and π_0 represent payments to the type h entrepreneur following success and failure of the venture, respectively, and T is the payment to a type l entrepreneur (in that case the venture is not undertaken).

In that case the maximization program can be expressed as follows:

$$\max_{\pi_R, \pi_0, T} \quad p_h \pi_R + (1 - p_h) \pi_0 \qquad (3.7)$$

$$\frac{1}{2}[\Phi - (p_h \pi_R + (1 - p_h) \pi_0)] - \frac{1}{2}T \geq 0 \qquad (3.8)$$

$$p_l \pi_R + (1 - p_l) \pi_0 \leq T \qquad (3.9)$$

$$\pi_0 \geq 0 \qquad (3.10)$$

$$T \geq 0 \qquad (3.11)$$

where (3.8) represents the bank's participation constraint, (3.9) represents the incentive compatibility constraint for the type l entrepreneur, (3.10) represents the limited liability constraint for the entrepreneur (her net wealth must be non-negative in all states of the world), and (3.11) represents the participation constraint for the type l entrepreneur. (The incentive compatibility and participation constraints for the type h entrepreneur always hold and can thus be ignored.)

One can easily show that there exists a unique solution to this program such that $\pi_0 = 0$, $\pi_R = \Phi/(p_h + p_l)$, and $T = p_l \Phi/(p_h + p_l)$. Substituting these values into the type h entrepreneur's expected payoff yields $U_B = p_h \Phi/(p_h + p_l)$.

Thus, at the beginning of the game the type h entrepreneur chooses VC financing over bank financing if and only if $U_{VC} \geq U_B$; that is, if and only if:

$$L \geq p_h \Phi/(p_h + p_l) \qquad (3.12)$$

Noting that absent informational asymmetry and project expropriation problems, the type h entrepreneur would obtain a payoff of Φ; it is intuitively helpful to rewrite condition (3.12) in terms of the inefficiencies associated with one type of financing or the other. Indeed, the entrepreneur will choose VC financing over bank financing if and only if:

$$\Phi - L \leq p_l \Phi/(p_h + p_l) \qquad (3.13)$$

that is if and only if the inefficiency associated with project expropriation under VC financing is smaller than the inefficiency associated with informational asymmetry under bank financing.

INCOMPLETE CONTRACTING ISSUES

The models of hidden action or hidden information described above can be described as models of "complete" contracting, to the extent that contracts therein . . . specify all parties' obligations in all future states of the world, to the fullest extent possible as a result of which there is never a "need for the parties to revise or renegotiate the contract as the future unfolds" (Hart 1995, 22). In what follows, we review the trade-off between bank financing and VC financing in the context of incomplete contracting; that is, when it is not possible to specify all possible future contingencies in a date 0 contract, and when as a result the potential for renegotiation must be taken into account.

Entrepreneur/Investor Input Complementarity: Bettignies (2008)

Bettignies (2008) proposes an incomplete contracting model of the entrepreneur's optimal financial contracting choice. One of the key insights of the paper is to highlight the importance of entrepreneur/investor effort complementarity for the entrepreneur's design of the optimal contract and for her choice of financing institution, namely a bank or a venture capitalist. Bettignies shows for example that in high-growth ventures, where the complementarity of effort between the entrepreneur and investor is crucial, equity-type contracts are optimal. In contrast, in lifestyle ventures where entrepreneur/investor complementarity is relatively low, debt-type contracts are shown to be optimal. The relationship between the type of venture and the type of financing can therefore be explained as follows: high-growth entrepreneurs tend to seek financing from VCs because (1) VCs can offer complementary skills and (2) they typically offer equity contracts, which are optimal for these types of entrepreneurs. In contrast, lifestyle entrepreneurs tend to seek bank financing because (1) they don't need complementary skills from the investor and (2) banks offer debt contracts, which are optimal in these types of venture. To provide an intuition for this insight, let us present the key elements and results of the model. Note that some parts of the model description presented below are drawn directly from Bettignies (2008).

Technology
Consider that wealth-constrained entrepreneur e who has in mind a one-period, positive NPV project, which requires an initial capital outlay $k = \$1$ from an investor i. Both e and i are risk-neutral. At date 0, the entrepreneur offers a contract to the investor, whose (dollar) net opportunity cost of capital over the course of the game is r. The project yields profit opportunities u and v each with probability p, at dates 1 and 2, respectively.

At date 1.5, the entrepreneur and the investor exert nonverifiable efforts q^e and q^i, respectively, which increase the expected profits: $v(q^e, q^i, \alpha) = (q^e + q^i) + \alpha q^e q^i$, where α is a measure of entrepreneur/investor effort complementarity. When $\alpha = 0$ entrepreneur effort and investor effort are perfect substitutes, the two efforts become more complementary as α increases. Cost of effort for both e and i is $c(q) = \frac{1}{2}(q)^2$ with $q = q^e, q^i$.

Contracts and Equilibrium Efforts
Profit opportunity u is assumed to be privately observable by the entrepreneur (and hence can be costlessly diverted by her), v is observable by both parties, but is not verifiable.[5] Contractual incompleteness in this model stems from these problems of observability and verifiability, and indeed the initial contract specifies only the allocation of control (or property) rights over the venture, which can be of three types.

With entrepreneur-control (E), the entrepreneur is the sole owner of the venture and has complete control over the assets and the decisions to be made. This brings two types of benefits to the entrepreneur. First, it brings a private (nonverifiable) benefit b^e. Second, it brings pecuniary benefits. If the profit opportunity v arises, e can unilaterally seize it and extract all rents for herself, and i gets nothing. At date 1.5, anticipating this, e maximizes $[b^e + pv(q^e, q^i \alpha) - ce(q^e)]$ w.r.t. q^i, taking q^e as given; and i exerts no effort (i.e., no involvement). The unique Nash equilibrium (NE) is $q_E^{e*} = p$ and $q_E^{i*} = 0$, with total expected surplus $V_E = b_e + pv(q_E^{e*}, q_E^{i*}) - c(q_E^{e*}) = b^e + \frac{1}{2}p^2$.

With investor-control (I) it is the investor who is the sole owner of the venture and has complete authority over assets and decisions. He enjoys private benefits b^i and access to 100 percent of the rents at date 2. The entrepreneur gets nothing.

In equilibrium, e exerts $q_I^{e*} = 0$ and i exerts $q_I^{i*} = p$, generating total expected surplus $V_I = b^i + pv(q_I^{e*}, q_I^{i*}) - c(q_I^{i*}) = b^i + \frac{1}{2}p^2$. The natural assumption that $b^e > b^i$ is made, which implies $V_E > V_I$.

Finally, with joint control (J), the entrepreneur and the investor jointly own the venture and share control rights. If v arises, bargaining takes place, yielding a payoff of $\frac{1}{2}v$ to both e and i. Anticipating this outcome, at date $1/2$ e and i exert efforts q^e and q^i to maximize $[p\frac{1}{2}v(q^e), q^i\alpha) - c(q^e)]$ and $[p\frac{1}{2}v(q^e), q^i\alpha - c(q^i)]$, respectively. This gives $q_J^{e*}(\alpha) = q_J^{i*}(\alpha) = \frac{p}{2-p\alpha}$, total expected surplus $V_J(\alpha) = pv(q_J^{e*}(\alpha), q_J^{i*}(\alpha), \alpha) - c(q_J^{e*}(\alpha)) - c(q_J^{i*}(\alpha)) = \frac{(3-p\alpha)}{(2-p\alpha)^2}p^2$ at date 2. Both e and i obtain the same expected payoff $V_J^e(\alpha) = V_J^i(\alpha) = \frac{1}{2}V_J(\alpha)$.

Profit u, which is not observable to i, is diverted by e regardless of the allocation of control.

Key Results

The model shows that under these assumptions, and given these three possible allocations of control, four distinct types of contracts emerge as optimal, depending on the entrepreneur/investor complementarity α, and on the investor's cost of capital r:

Standard debt (SD) assigns entrepreneur control if a (verifiable) debt repayment d_{SD} is paid out to i at date 1; and investor-control in the event of default.

Debt with reorganization (DR) assigns entrepreneur control if debt repayment d_{DR} is made and converts to joint control otherwise. With this contract, default is followed by reorganization with both agents sharing control, rather than liquidation as in the SD contract.

Voting equity (Q) assigns joint control regardless of the state of the world. The reason why this contract is interpreted as voting equity is simply that, in entrepreneurial ventures where cash flows are arguably difficult to verify and consequently contracts contingent on cash flows only are unlikely to be honored, it is the delegation of control rights to the investor, which is nearly always included in entrepreneurial contracts involving equity, rather than the cash flow rights themselves, which enables the investor to extract some rents ex post. And indeed, here joint control generates a stream of payoffs to the investor that is similar to the one typically obtained in an equity contract.

Preferred equity (P) assigns joint control conditional on debt payment d_P being made, and investor-control otherwise. This contract bears its name from two similar types of contracts observed in practice. Straight preferred contracts (SP)—and the similar participating preferred contracts—typically specify the redemption value of the investment (say d), the redemption date (say date 1.5), and the amount of common stock to be issued in combination with the preferred stock, which gives the investor some cash flow rights *in addition* to the prespecified redemption value ("double dipping"). If the company cannot make the redemption payment, the assets are liquidated, with the proceeds accruing to the investor first ("liquidation preference"). This is very similar to the P contract with strictly positive equilibrium d.

Similarly, convertible preferred contracts (CP) give the investor the choice between redeeming his stock at the prespecified redemption value d, and converting it into common stock. In the bad state—which in this model corresponds to the case where the profit opportunity u is not realized—the investor does not convert, thus forcing liquidation and making use of the liquidation preference attached to his security to extract as much out of the liquidation value as possible. In contrast, in the good state—when u is realized—he converts, provided that the rents he can get with the common stock after conversion are higher than the redemption value. This resembles the P contract when d tends to zero.

Exhibit 3.1 represents the optimality of each contract as a function of r and V_J, keeping V_E and V_I constant. Since $dV_J/d\alpha > 0$ but $dV_E/d\alpha = dV_I/d\alpha = 0$, changes in V_J in Exhibit 3.1 are equivalent to changes in α.

Several implications can be drawn from the results depicted in Exhibit 3.1. The first interesting result is that a number of contracts resembling financial instruments commonly used in practice—such as common equity, convertible and straight (or participating) preferred equity, as well as secured and unsecured debt—can emerge as optimal; a result consistent with recent evidence on the financing of new ventures. Indeed, even if we restrict our attention to the VC-financed ventures, the evidence suggests that entrepreneurs use a variety of financing contracts. As shown in Exhibit 3.2, for instance, in Canada and Europe they use both equity-type instruments and debt-type instruments.

Even in the United States where, as mentioned at the beginning of the introduction, the prevalent use of convertible preferred equity in VC-financed ventures is well documented, entrepreneurs have access to other forms of financing. As mentioned in Bettignies (2008), venture lending has recently emerged, providing debt-type instruments in the form of venture leasing, venture debt, or subordinated debt (Hardymon, Lerner, and Leamon 2005). Venture lenders have been very active recently,[7] offering an interesting alternative to equity financing for start-ups in the United States.

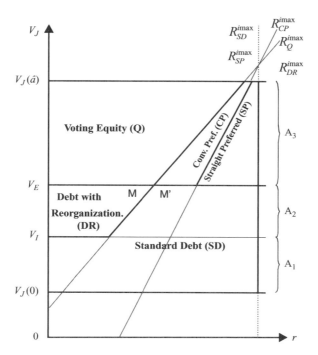

Exhibit 3.1 Optimal Contracts

Exhibit 3.2   Financial Instruments in Venture Capital Deals (as percentage of Total Deals)

	Equity	Debt	Conv. Debt	Pref. Equity	Other
Europe (Bottazzi et al. 2004)	55.5	6.5	7.5	25.5	5
Canada, Can. VCs (Cumming 2005)	36.3	15	12.4	18.1	18.2
Canada, U.S. VCs (Cumming 2007)	34.6	12	12	36.5	4.8
Germany (Bascha and Walz 2002)	26.6	38.7	0	10.6	25.1

Source: Bettignies, 2008

Second—and most directly relevant to the trade-off between bank financing and VC financing—is the result that while debt-type contracts such as standard debt and debt with reorganization are optimal when entrepreneur/investor effort complementarity is low, equity-type contracts such as voting equity and preferred equity are optimal when α is high enough. The intuition for this result is simple: equity-type contracts tend to place more emphasis on joint control, relative to debt-type contracts. Joint control is the only control allocation that encourages simultaneous efforts by both entrepreneur and investor. As effort complementarity rises, the relative value of these collaborations, and hence of equity-type contracts, also increases. The implication for the choice between bank financing and VC financing is then clear: ventures in which effort complementarity is high should turn to venture capitalists and offer equity-type contracts to elicit collaboration incentives; while ventures in which effort complementarity is less crucial should be financed with bank debt.

Note that while VC financing is often associated with equity financing, the evidence illustrated in Exhibit 3.2 suggests that debt contracts are not that uncommon in VC deals. A natural question to ask, then, is "what's the difference between getting debt from a bank and getting debt from a venture capitalist?" Exhibit 3.1 suggests that—to the extent that entrepreneur/investor collaboration (and hence joint control) is more important in VC-financed ventures than in bank-financed ventures—the two types of debt may be different: Bank-financed ventures may use standard debt (*SD*), where in case of default the bank takes complete control of the venture and usually liquidates, while VC-financed ventures may use something closer to debt with reorganization (*DR*), where in case of default the entrepreneur is more likely to remain involved in a reorganization of the venture. Whether this is indeed the case in practice remains an open empirical question.

The Stigma of Failure: Landier (2003)

Landier (2003) proposes a model where entrepreneurs and investors can hold each other up once the game is started. As a result, the choice between bank finance and venture capital depends on the "quality" of the entrepreneur's exit option, which itself depends on the legal environment and on the "stigma of failure." When the stigma of failure is large enough, the first-best outcome can be achieved with bank financing; otherwise VC financing is optimal even if only a second-best outcome can be reached. To help understand this result and the intuition behind it, in what follows we present a simplified version of the model.

Timing of the Game

At date 0, the entrepreneur contracts, with a competitive investor, a contract that specifies the amount of the initial date 0 investment I_0, the amount of debt repayment D at date 3, and the amount of investment in technological expertise H to be made, at cost γH, by the investor at date 0. An amount I_0 is invested in the project.

At date 1, the entrepreneur and the investor learn whether or not the entrepreneur is competent. If she is of low competence, which occurs with probability p, the project is terminated at neither cost (the initial investment can be recouped) nor benefit. If the entrepreneur is of high competence, the project is continued, and she exerts effort e at personal cost $e^2/2$. The purpose of this effort is to affect the distribution of the project cost C, which is revealed at date 2.

At date 2, the actual cost of the project is realized. C is uniformly distributed over $[0, 2C(e)]$, and the expected project cost, $C(e)$, is negatively affected by entrepreneurial effort: $C'(e) < 0$. C is observable but not verifiable. If $C > I_0$, then an additional investment $I_2 = C - I_0$ must be secured from the (same) investor.

At date 3, the project generates nonverifiable cash flow V. The entrepreneur can either make the debt repayment D and keep $V-D$ or default, in which case she receives nothing from the project, while the investor, who takes control of the assets receives $V(H) < V$. The difference $V-V(H)$ is some sort of transaction cost associated with default and the transfer of ownership, and Landier assumes that the larger the investor's investment in technological expertise, the smaller this cost: $V'(H) > 0$. Once the payoffs of the project have been allocated, the entrepreneur moves on to a competitive labor market, where she earns her expected productivity, which itself depends on her past success or failure: following success or failure, she can expect to earn w_s or w_f, respectively. The difference in wages $\Delta = w_s - w_f$ > 0 captures the notion of stigma of failure.

Contractual Incompleteness and Renegotiation

In this model, contractual incompleteness arises from the nonverifiability of project cost C and of project payoff V. If V were verifiable, the date 0 contract could specify a transfer $D = \alpha V$ from the entrepreneur to the investor whenever V is generated. Because this is not the case here, D will only be repaid at date 3 if it is in the interest of the entrepreneur to do so. If the entrepreneur defaults at date 3, renegotiation will take place, since the surplus from trading, $V + w_s$, is larger than the surplus in case of a breakdown, $V(H) + w_f$. Assuming Nash bargaining, this implies that the payment D from the entrepreneur to the investor is replaced by a payment $t = (1/2)(V + w_s + V(H) - w_f)$, yielding payoffs $U_E = w_f + (1/2)(V + w_s - V(H) - w_f)$ and $U_I = V(H) + (1/2)(V + w_s - V(H) - w - f)$ for the entrepreneur and the investor, respectively. If the entrepreneur repays the debt at date 3, she gets $w_s + V - D + (I_0 - C)$ if $I_0 > C$ and $w_s + V - D$ otherwise. Hence, a sufficient condition to ensure the entrepreneur's repayment of D at date is:

$$w_s + V - D > U_E \tag{3.14}$$

Similarly, the nonverifiability of C prevents the entrepreneur from contracting at date 0 on a potential date 2 cash injection $I_2 = C - I_0$. As a result, renegotiation will occur at date 2, if $I_2 > 0$ is needed, yielding the same Nash bargaining outcomes as the ones described above: a transfer t from the entrepreneur to the investor at date 3, yielding payoffs U_E and U_I for the entrepreneur and the investor, respectively. Note that although this renegotiation occurs at date 2, there is no incentive for the entrepreneur to renege at date 3, as default would trigger renegotiation with exactly the same payoffs.

First-Best
The first-best levels of investment in technological expertise and of entrepreneurial effort maximize total surplus:

$$\max_{e,H} \; (1 - p)\left[V - C\,(e) - e^2/2\right] - \gamma H \tag{3.15}$$

Clearly, $e^* = -C'(e^*)$ and $H^* = 0$.

Optimal Contract
Two key results emerge from this simple model. The first result is that when the stigma of failure Δ is sufficiently large, the optimal contract is one where there is no investor technological expertise and entrepreneurial effort e^* (i.e., first-best levels), no staging of investment (all financing requirements are channelled through I_0, and $I_2 = 0$), and no renegotiation, similar in many regards to a bank financing contract.

To see this, suppose that $\Delta \geq \Delta^*$, with $\Delta^* = 4C(e^*) - V$, which can easily be shown to imply that:

$$V - 2C\left(e^*\right) + w_s \geq w_f + (1/2)\left(V + w_s - w_f\right) \tag{3.16}$$

Now suppose that at date 0 the entrepreneur offers a contract that includes $I_0 = 2C(e^*)$, $D = I_0 = 2C(e^*)$, and $H = 0$. If it turns out at date 2 that $C < 2C(e^*)$, then there is no renegotiation: $C < I_0$ ensures no renegotiation at date 2, and condition (3.16) ensures no renegotiation at date 3 (debt is repaid). Thus in that case the entrepreneur gets $V + (I_0 - C) - D + w_s = V - C + w_s$. On the other hand, if it turns out that $C \geq 2C(e^e)$, then a cash injection of $C - 2C(e^*)$ is needed at date 2, and renegotiation occurs, yielding payoff U_E to the entrepreneur. Note also that given C's uniform distribution, the probability that $C < 2C(e^*)$ is $2C(e^*)/2C(e)$, and the probability that $C > 2C(e^*)$ is $1 - 2C(e^*)/2C(e)$.

Anticipating all this, at date 1 the entrepreneur chooses $e \in [0, e^*]$ to maximize the following program:

$$\max_e \; \frac{2C\left(e^*\right)}{2C\,(e)}\,(V - C\,(e) + w_s) + \left(1 - \frac{2C\left(e^*\right)}{2C\,(e)}\right) U_E - \frac{e^2}{2} \tag{3.17}$$

which can be rewritten as:

$$\max_e \; \left[(V - C\,(e) + w_s) - \frac{e^2}{2}\right] + \left(1 - \frac{C\left(e^*\right)}{C\,(e)}\right)\left[U_E - (V - C\,(e) + w_s)\right] \tag{3.18}$$

with $C(e) < 2C(e^*)$. Condition (3.16) thus ensures that $U_E - (V - C(e) + w_s) < 0$, and it then follows immediately that e^* is the program maximizing choice for the entrepreneur. Importantly, note that with effort e^* the realized value of C is bound from above by $2C(e^*) = I_0$, and hence we always have sufficient initial cash to cover the entire cost of the project. There is no staging of investment, and no renegotiation in equilibrium. Finally, there is no investor expertise, and the debt repayment $D = I_0$ such that the investors' net payoff is $D - I_0 = 0$, that is, such that his participation constraint is binding and he extracts no rents.

Now suppose instead that $\Delta < \Delta^*$. In that case condition (3.16) no longer holds, and the only way the entrepreneur can commit not to renegotiate for $C < 2C(e^*)$ is if $I_0 - D$ is positive and sufficiently large for

$$V + (I_0 - D) - 2C\left(e^*\right) + w_s \geq w_f + (1/2)\left(V + w_s - w_f\right) \qquad (3.19)$$

to hold. But if $I_0 - D > 0$, and if as in the first case discussed ($\Delta \geq \Delta^*$) there is no renegotiation on the equilibrium path, then the investor's participation constraint cannot hold, and he would refuse to finance the project in the first place. To alleviate this problem, the entrepreneur offers two complementary solutions. First, she specifies a smaller level of $I_0 < 2C(e^*)$. This has two impacts: (1) it has a direct impact in "easing" the participation constraint, and (2) it makes it more likely that $I_0 < C$, in which case a further cash injection I_2 will be needed, requiring renegotiation. Note that this occurs not only because a reduction of I_0 has a direct negative effect on $I_0 - C$, but also because a lower I_0 reduces equilibrium effort (since excess cash that the entrepreneur can expect to retain is smaller), and this in turn increases the expected value of C, from an ex ante point of view.

The second partial solution to the participation constraint problem is to specify a strictly positive investment in technological expertise by the investor: $H > 0$. From our discussion of U_E and U_I above we know that a higher H tends to shift bargaining power in renegotiation away from the entrepreneur and towards the investor. Since in this case renegotiation does occur with some non-zero probability, doing so tends to increase the expected payoff of the investor and to ease his participation constraint.

Thus—and this is the second key result of the paper—when the stigma of failure Δ is not large enough, the optimal contract is one where there is strictly positive investor technological expertise, second-best entrepreneurial effort $e^{**} < e^*$, lower initial cash injection, and some probability of a second cash injection and renegotiation at date 2 (i.e., staging of investment), similar in many regards to a venture capital contract.

Strategic Uncertainty: Winton and Yerramilli (2008)

Winton and Yerramilli (2008) also examine the entrepreneur's choice between banks and venture capitalists in an incomplete contracts framework, although as we shall see the source of contractual incompleteness is different here. In what follows, we summarize the intuition for the main insight of the paper, which is that VC financing may be a better way than bank financing for the entrepreneur to commit not to take risky strategies that, though they maximize her utility at the time of the action choice, may not be optimal from an ex ante point of view. To see the intuition for this result, consider a simplified version of the game described in Winton and Yerramilli.

Simplified Model Setup
A project requiring a cash investment I at date 0 can turn out to be either of high quality or of medium quality at date 1. At that moment an action must be taken: either a safe strategy is pursued, in which case the project yields profits X_S regardless of its quality; or a risky strategy is pursued, which yields X_R with probability p and zero otherwise. The probability of success is $p = p_h$ if the project is of high quality, and $p = p_m$ if the project is of medium quality, with $p_h > p_m$. The variance of profits under the risky strategy from a date 0 point of view can be expressed as $\sigma^2 = \Phi(1 - \Phi)(p_h - p_m^2 X - R^2)$, and is labeled "strategic uncertainty" in the model.

The parameters of the model are set such that profit maximization requires a risky strategy in good quality projects and a safe strategy in medium quality projects, but the manager enjoys private benefits such that, from a date 1 point of view, playing a risky strategy is optimal in both types of projects.

The state of world at date 1, that is, the quality of the project, is not verifiable, and hence cannot be contracted at date 0. Therein lies the contractual incompleteness of the model. Realized profits are contractible, but for the investor's participation constraint to hold, he must have some control over the strategic choice made at date 1. Thus, the question facing the entrepreneur at date 0 is whether the financing should be obtained from, and the control rights assigned to, a venture capitalist or a bank.

VC Financing versus Bank Financing
The results of the model rest on two key assumptions about the differences between banks and venture capitalists. On the one hand, for reasons described in the paper, banks are assumed to have the advantage of a lower cost of capital. On the other hand, venture capitalists are assumed to be better than banks at monitoring. In the model, this is captured by assuming that the venture capitalist can discover the quality of the project at date 1, while the bank cannot. This translates into an advantage for VC financing, as the informed investor can make better use of his control rights to affect strategic decisions at date 1, an advantage that benefits the entrepreneur at date 0.

Importantly, Winton and Yerramilli show that this advantage is increasing in the degree of strategic uncertainty. The intuition for this is clearly stated in the paper: "[T]he value of active monitoring is the value of the option to use better information to choose between the safe and risky strategies. As the conditional variance of risky cash flows increases, the value of this option increases, making active monitoring more attractive."

The key insight of the paper thus is two-fold: it is to point to this interesting trade-off between bank and VC financing, namely monitoring ability versus cost of capital; and to suggest that, ceteris paribus, higher strategic uncertainty is likely to favor VC financing over bank financing.

CONCLUDING REMARKS

This paper examines the small but growing theoretical literature on the entrepreneur's choice between her two main sources of financing: bank debt and venture capital. The purpose of this paper is not to propose new results or theoretical insights. Rather, it is to review the existing research in a way that is detailed enough to provide the reader with a glimpse of the methodology used, yet simple enough to allow her to understand the key results easily and intuitively.

A further contribution of this paper is to bring together and underline the various empirical implications of the theory. This is particularly important in this line of research, where empirical work has been disappointingly absent so far. Indeed a number of empirical predictions—and associated empirical research questions—emerge from the papers reviewed. They suggest for example that when the investor has no project-specific expertise, the project should be financed with bank debt (Elitzur and Gavious 2003). In contrast, factors that favor a choice of VC financing over bank financing include higher expertise of the investor relative to that of the entrepreneur (Bettignies and Brander 2007); lower "stigma of failure" plaguing the entrepreneur's experience (Landier 2008); and higher "strategic uncertainty" (Winton and Yerramilli, 2008). Tighter protection of intellectual property, and "high-techness" of the project, also favor VC financing, because they lower the expected expropriation costs and increase the informational advantage, respectively, associated with that type of financing (Ueda 2004). Finally, high-growth ventures (i.e., classic start-ups), where entrepreneur/investor input complementarity will likely be important ought to be financed with venture capital; in contrast with lifestyle ventures (e.g., restaurants, hair salons, etc.) where input complementarity will likely be low and where bank financing may be optimal (Bettignies 2008). There is still much to do to improve our understanding of the trade-offs between VC financing and bank financing, theoretically, and empirically in particular. We look forward to more research in that line of research.

NOTES

1. The prevalent use of convertible preferred equity in start-ups financed by venture capitalists in the United States today is well documented: see, for example, Sahlman (1990), Lerner (1994), Gompers (1995), Bergmann and Hege (1998), Gompers and Lerner (1999), and Kaplan and Strömberg (2002).

2. Even within the United States, convertible preferred equity was not always the security of choice in venture capital deals: until the mid-1980s, straight preferred equity was the dominant contract used (Hardymon and Lerner, 2001).

3. There are several other papers that address the question of single-sided and double-sided moral hazard in the entrepreneur-investor relationship—Innes (1990), Bergmann and Hege (1998), Cassamatta (2003), Inderst and Muller (2004), Repullo and Suarez (2004), Hellmann (2006)—but not specifically the trade-off between VC financing and bank financing.

4. Garmaise (2007) argues on the contrary that the investor may be better informed than the entrepreneur about the venture, and proposes an optimal contracting model based on this type of information asymmetry.

5. The difference in observability between u and v can be motivated by the fact that, although information asymmetry between the entrepreneur and the investor is a common problem early in the venture, it may be alleviated over time.

6. In Cumming (2005), the preferred equity category consists of 7.27% straight preferred equity and 10.87% convertible preferred equity. In Cumming (2007), the preferred equity category consists of 15.38% straight preferred equity and 21.15% convertible preferred

equity. Finally, Bascha and Walz (2002) explain that in Germany, the so-called silent parternship, a debt-type instrument, is commonly used (33.1%); it is categorized as debt in Exhibit 3.2. Moreover, private limited companies are not allowed to use convertible debt. They use other instruments instead, which are categorized as "other" in Exhibit 3.2.

7. Debt providers such as Western Technology Investments and Lighthouse Capital raised $720 million and $366 million, respectively, in May 2003 (Hardymon, Lerner, and Leamon et al. 2005). Perhaps better known is Silicon Valley Bank (Leamon and Hardymon 2001), and its spin-off Gold Hill Venture Lending, which raised $200 million in the Summer of 2004 (Hardymon, Lerner, and Leamon et al. 2005).

REFERENCES

Aghion, P., and Patrick Bolton. 1992. An incomplete contracts approach to financial contracting. *Review of Economic Studies* 59:473–494.

Bascha, A., and U. Walz. 2001. Convertible securities and optimal exit decisions in venture capital finance. *Journal of Corporate Finance* 7:285–306.

_____, 2002. Financing practices in the German venture capital industry: An empirical assessment. Working paper, University of Tubingen.

Berglöf, E. 1994. A control theory of venture capital finance. *Journal of Law, Economics, and Organization* 10:247–267.

Bergmann, D., and U. Hege. 1998. Venture capital financing, moral hazard, and learning. *Journal of Banking and Finance* 22:703–735.

Bester, H. 1985. Screening versus rationing in credit markets with imperfect information. *American Economic Review* 75:850–855.

Bettignies, J. de. 2008. Financing the entrepreneurial venture. *Management Science* 54: 151–166.

_____ and James Brander. 2007. Financing entrepreneurship: Bank finance versus venture capital. *Journal of Business Venturing* 22:808–832.

Bolton, P., and D. Scharfstein. 1990. A theory of predation based on agency problems in financial contracting. *American Economic Review* 80:94–106.

_____.1996. Optimal debt structure with multiple creditors. *Journal of Political Economy* 104:1–25.

Bottazzi, L., M. Da Rin, and T. Hellmann. 2004. The changing face of the European venture capital industry: Facts and analysis. *Journal of Private Equity* 7:26–53.

Cassamatta, C. 2003. Financing and advising: Optimal financial contracts with venture capitalists. *Journal of Finance* 58:2059–2085.

Cornelli, F., and O. Yosha. 2003. Stage financing and the role of convertible debt. *Review of Economic Studies* 70:1–32.

Cumming, D. J. 2005. Capital structure in venture finance. *Journal of Corporate Finance* 11:550–585.

_____. 2007. United States venture capital financial contracting: Foreign Securities. In *Advances in Financial Economics* 12, ed. M. Hirschey, K. John, and A. Makhija: 405–444.

Davis, C. 2003. Venture capital in Canada. In *The growth of venture capital: A cross-cultural comparison*, ed. D. Cetindamar: 175–206. Praeger, Westport, CT,

Dewatripont, M., and J. Tirole. 1994. A theory of debt and equity: Diversity of securities and manager-shareholder congruence. *Quarterly Journal of Economics* 39: 1027–1054.

Dybvig, P., and Y. Wang. 2002. Debt and equity. Working paper, Washington University in Saint Louis and Boston University.

Elitzur, R., and A. Gavious. 2003. A multi-period game theoretic model of venture capital investment. *European Journal of Operational Research* 144:440–453.

Fluck, Z. 1998. Optimal financial contracting: Debt versus outside equity. *Review of Financial Studies* 11:383–418.

Garmaise, M. 2007. Informed investors and the financing of entrepreneurial projects. Working paper, UCLA.

Gompers, P. A. 1995. Optimal investment, monitoring, and the staging of venture capital. *Journal of Finance* 50:1461–1489.

——— and J. Lerner. 1999. *The venture capital cycle.* Cambridge: MIT Press.

Grossman, S., and O. Hart. 1986. The costs and benefits of ownership: A theory of vertical and lateral integration. *Journal of Political Economy* 94:691–719.

Hardymon, F., and J. Lerner. 2001. A note on private equity securities. Harvard Business School Case.

Hardymon, F., J. Lerner, and A. Leamon. 2005. Gold Hill Venture Lending. Harvard Business School Case.

Hart, O. 1995. *Firms, contracts, and financial structure.* Oxford, UK: Oxford University Press.

——— and J. Moore. 1990. Incomplete contracts and the nature of the firm. *Journal of Political Economy* 98:1119–1158.

——— and J. Moore. 1994. A theory of debt based on the inalienability of human capital. *Quarterly Journal of Economics* 109:841–879.

——— and J. Moore. 1998. Default and renegotiation: A dynamic model of debt. *Quarterly Journal of Economics* 113:1–41.

Hellmann, T. 2006. IPOs, acquisitions and the use of convertible securities in venture capital. *Journal of Financial Economics* 81:649–679.

Inderst, R., and H. Muller. 2004. The effect of capital market characteristics on the value of start-up firms. *Journal of Financial Economics* 72:319–356.

Innes, R. D. 1990. Limited liability and incentive contracting with ex-ante action choices. *Journal of Economic Theory* 52:45–67.

Kaplan, S., and P. Strömberg. 2002. Financial contracting meets the real world: An empirical analysis of venture capital contracts. *Review of Economic Studies* 70: 281–316.

Landier, A. 2003. Start-up financing: From banks to venture capital. Working paper, New York University.

Leamon, A., and F. Hardymon. 2001. Silicon Valley Bank. Harvard Business School Case.

Lerner, J. 1994. The syndication of venture capital investments. *Financial Management* 23:16–27.

Marx, L. 1998. Efficient venture capital financing combining debt and equity. *Review of Economic Design* 4:371–387.

Myers, S. 2000. Outside equity. *Journal of Finance* 55:1005–1037.

Repullo, R., and J. Suarez. 2004. Venture capital finance: A security design approach. *Review of Finance* 8:75–108.

Rothschild, M., and J. Stiglitz. 1976. Equilibrium in competitive insurance markets: An essay on the economics of imperfect information. *Quarterly Journal of Economics* 82: 629–649.

Sahlman, W. A. 1990. The structure and governance of venture capital organizations. *Journal of Financial Economics* 27:473–521.

Schmidt, K. 2002. Convertible securities and venture capital finance. *Journal of Finance* 58:1139–1166.

Ueda, M. 2004. Banks versus venture capital: Project evaluation, screening, and expropriation. *Journal of Finance* 59:601–621.

Winton, A., and V. Yerramilli. 2008. Entrepreneurial finance: banks versus venture capital. *Journal of Financial Economics* 88:51–79.

ABOUT THE AUTHOR

Jean-Etienne de Bettignies is an Associate Professor of Managerial Economics at Queen's School of Business. He received his Ph.D. from the Graduate School of Business at the University of Chicago in 2001. Prior to joining Queen's in the summer of 2007, Jean was on the faculty at the Sauder School of Business at the University of British Columbia. His research examines applications of contract theory to entrepreneurial and corporate finance, industrial economics, and public policy. His work has been published in academic journals such as *Management Science*, *Journal of Business Venturing*, *Journal of Industrial Economics*, *International Journal of Industrial Organization*, and *Canadian Journal of Economics*, among others.

CHAPTER 4

Corporate Venture Capital

VLADIMIR I. IVANOV
Assistant Professor, School of Business, University of Kansas

FEI XIE
Assistant Professor, School of Management, George Mason University

INTRODUCTION

Corporate venture capital (CVC) is one of the relatively underexplored areas in venture capital. Although the origin of CVC can be traced back to the early 1960s, more systematic examination of CVC activity did not commence until the late 1990s. In this chapter we summarize the existing empirical evidence on CVC. We show that CVC contributes to the prosperity of parent corporations as well as the development of start-up firms. We also provide some directions for future CVC research.

THE NATURE OF CORPORATE VENTURE CAPITAL

Corporate venture capital stands for organized efforts of nonfinancial corporations to make private equity investments in young and risky firms. Since its inception in early 1960s, CVC investment has gone through boom and bust cycles that mirrored the peaks and troughs of the overall VC industry (Gompers and Lerner 2000). Over the period from 1980 to 2007, CVC investment represents about 6 percent of total VC investments, with the percentage higher in early 1980s when traditional venture capitalists (TVCs) were still underdeveloped.[1] After its meteoric rise in the 1990s and peaking in 2000, the dollar amount of annual CVC investment experienced significant declined in 2001 and 2002 and began to gradually pick up only more recently (see Exhibit 4.1).

CVCs differ from TVCs in several important aspects (Gompers and Lerner 2000). First, CVCs are usually organized as separate units within corporations with a certain degree of autonomy from corporate headquarters. Sometimes, they can also be structured as informal groups within units, for instance, as part of a corporation's research and development (R&D) department. TVCs, on the other hand, are mostly structured as limited partnerships (LPs). Second, CVCs usually lack the high-powered incentive schemes typical for TVCs. While substantial profit sharing ("carried interest") is common among TVCs, most corporate venture capitalists are compensated with salary and bonuses. For example, MacMillan and

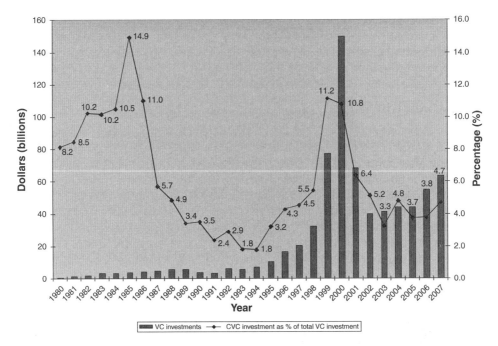

Exhibit 4.1 CVC Investments from 1980 to 2007
The figure plots the annual VC dollar investments in entrepreneurial firms (the shaded bars)
and the percentage of CVC investments in total VC investments (the line with diamond).

colleagues (2008) survey 48 CVC programs and report that only 21 percent of
senior personnel receive carried interest and 13 percent receive bonuses similar to
carried interest. Third, unlike TVCs, CVCs do not invest in entrepreneurial companies for financial returns only. Instead, they often pursue investments to provide
their corporate parents with strategic benefits such as access to new technology
and markets and opportunities to develop strategic alliances or joint ventures.[2] In
fact, most corporations establish CVCs programs with strategic motives in mind
(Yost and Devlin 1993 and Ernst&Young 2002).

DO CVCs BENEFIT THEIR
PARENT CORPORATIONS?

Given the purported strategic motives behind most CVC programs, CVCs' contributions to their parent corporations cannot be measured in financial returns alone,
especially since CVCs may be willing to accept lower financial returns on an investment if the strategic benefits are high enough. CVCs generate financial benefits to
their parent corporations by successfully exiting from entrepreneurial companies
in which they invest. Strategic benefits are more diverse in nature and can include
acquisitions of new technologies, nurturing new customers or suppliers, development of complementary products and services, penetrating new markets, and so
on. Even learning about new products, technologies or practices or observing the
failure of those could be considered a valuable strategic benefit from corporate

venture investing. While strategic benefits are generally harder to quantify than purely financial benefits, there have been some attempts in the CVC literature to measure the benefits that corporations receive from starting and operating a corporate venture unit.

Increased Firm Value

A direct test of whether CVCs are beneficial to their parent corporations is to measure the marginal effect of corporate venture investing on the value of the parent company after controlling for other factors that drive firm value. Such valuation effect may be absent for a couple of reasons. First, the purported benefits of CVCs either have been exaggerated or can be achieved by traditional research and development efforts. Second, CVC investing may indeed be value increasing but the ability to add value depends on the interaction of several factors—the establishment of coherent goals and objectives for the CVC arm, the use of effective compensation and organizational structure, and the ability to select and nurture high-quality start-ups. It is possible that any superior industry knowledge and expertise that CVCs possess are offset by their inferior organizational and compensation structure, or by a lack of clearly-defined mission and goals. Thus, a more relevant question is *when* CVCs can create value for their parent corporations.

Dushnitsky and Lenox (2005) investigate whether CVC activity is associated with an increase in firm value in a panel of U.S. public firms during the period from 1990 to 1999. In their analysis, they use Tobin's q as a measure of firm value and relate that to both the presence of a CVC program and the dollar value of CVC investments. They find evidence of value creation. Specifically, firms with CVC programs have higher Tobin's q. Moreover, the greater the amount of CVC investments, the more pronounced the increase in firm value. Another important finding of their study is that value creation is greater when CVC programs have a strategic focus, that is, when firms explicitly pursue CVCs to harness entrepreneurial inventions. The valuation effect of CVCs also appears to be industry specific, as Dushnitsky and Lenox (2005) find that firms with CVC programs have higher Tobin's q only in devices and information sectors.

Increased Innovation Output

One of the main reasons for establishing a CVC unit is to capture external innovations by making private equity investments in start-ups. There are various ways in which CVCs can gain knowledge of valuable technologies and products. Those include evaluating business plans for future funding, interacting with co-investors participating in the monitoring and governance of start-ups (e.g., by serving on the boards and committees), working closely with start-ups, and entering into strategic alliances with start-ups (Gompers and Lerner 2000, Maula, Keil, and Zahra 2003, and Ivanov and Masulis 2008). The successful acquisition and utilization of external knowledge obtained through CVC can result in significant improvements in parent corporations' innovation outputs over time. The development of potential customers through venture investing could have similar effects, since it can increase the demand for the parent corporations' products and services and hence accelerate the pace of corporate innovations (Brandenburger and Nalebuff 1996).

Dushnitsky and Lenox (2005) examine whether a firm's CVC investments are related to its innovation rate using panel data from 1975 to 1995. Their sample includes 247 firms with CVC investments and 2,042 firms without CVC investments during that period. Controlling for a number of factors that could affect changes in innovation rates, they find that increases in CVC investments are associated with an increase in a firm's future innovation rate as proxied by citation-weighted patenting rates. In addition, they find that the degree to which CVC investing affects innovation outcomes depends on the absorptive capacity of the CVC parent. The absorptive capacity is the ability of a firm to make productive use of external technologies. Previous studies (Mowery 1983, Pisano 1991, Kleinknecht and van Reijnen 1992, and Veugelers 1997) show that firms with better absorptive capacity acquire greater benefits when outsourcing research and are more likely to cooperate on research with other firms. Dushnitsky and Lenox (2005) document that higher absorptive capacity (usually associated with high levels of R&D spending) leads to a stronger effect of CVC on the parent firm's innovation output. Along the same lines, they find that the effect of CVC on innovation is stronger the weaker the intellectual property regime in which the parent firm operates. In a weak intellectual property protection environment, start-ups rely on secrecy to protect their innovations from competitors, and they usually do not have enough resources to receive and defend patents for their technology (Cohen, Nelson, and Walsh 2001). CVCs' investments in and interactions with start-ups provide a channel for them to gain access to the valuable information.

A few other studies also provide evidence that CVC investing can boost the innovation rates of parent companies. For example, Maula, Keil, and Zahra (2003) document that firms with CVC programs are more likely to recognize technological discontinuities. Shildt, Maula, and Keil (2003) show that firms with CVC arms are more likely to engage in explorative learning.[3]

Improved Acquisition Performance

Another potential benefit from CVC programs is that companies can utilize the information on emerging technologies and industries that they obtain through venture investing to make more informed acquisition decisions by selecting better targets and negotiating better deal terms. Acquisitions are among the largest corporate investments and are fraught with uncertainty about how much synergy they can generate and how much value they can create for acquiring shareholders. It is well documented in the finance literature that acquirers on average do not gain from acquisitions, as evidenced by the negative or insignificant average abnormal stock returns around acquisition announcements (Andrade, Mitchell, and Stafford 2001).

Benson and Ziedonis (2005, 2007) examine the effect of a firm's CVC investments on its acquisition performance. They find that when corporations with CVC arms acquire entrepreneurial firms, on average they experience an abnormal stock return of 0.76 percent around deal announcements. However, when the acquired entrepreneurial company is backed by the acquirer's CVC unit, the average acquirer announcement-period abnormal return is –1.01 percent. These findings suggest that on average acquisitions of own portfolio firms (private or public) tend to be value destroying. However, this does not necessarily reject the value-increasing argument because only in 20 percent of the cases do CVCs acquire their own portfolio firms. Benson and Ziedonis put forth three possible explanations as to why such acquisitions are value decreasing. First, it could be that acquirers systematically overpay for the targets in which they hold equity, possibly to induce higher competing offers, and thus generate higher returns on their investments. Second, the value-destroying transactions could be driven by managerial hubris or over-confidence (Roll 1986 and Malmendier and Tate 2005). Overconfident management of the acquirer may overvalue the synergies from the acquisition. Lastly, acquirers may be susceptible to agency problems where managers have incentives to make value-reducing acquisitions to extract private benefits for themselves (Jensen 1986).

Benson and Ziedonis (2005) find evidence consistent with managerial overcon-fidence and agency problems at the CVC parent. For example, the announcement returns tend to be negative mainly for CVCs with an inferior organizational structure—the ones that are organized not as a separate autonomous unit within a corporation but rather as a part of a product group or the R&D department. They argue that these CVCs are likely to have lower deal flow and their investments will be more difficult to monitor, thus leading to value-destroying deals. In addition, Benson and Ziedonis (2007) document that CVCs with better absorptive capacity tend to do better at acquisitions. However, the effect of the absorptive capacity is concave—the beneficial effects of CVC investing on acquisition performance decreases as the ratio CVC investments to total firm R&D increases.

DO CVCs ADD VALUE TO THEIR PORTFOLIO FIRMS?

Academics and practitioners alike have long suggested that CVCs add value to their portfolio companies, but the empirical evidence on this is rather limited. Previous studies such as Gompers and Lerner (2000) and Santhanakrishnan (2003) find that CVC backing increases entrepreneurial firms' likelihood of going public or being acquired. However, it remains unclear how CVC-backed start-ups fare once they arrive at these stages. It would be premature to conclude that CVCs add value if their portfolio companies consistently go public or get acquired at valuation levels below those attained by non–CVC-backed companies. Since CVCs almost always co-invest with TVCs, whether CVC backing adds value to start-up companies depends on whether CVCs can make contributions incremental to those from TVCs. Some of the institutional differences between the two types of venture organizations suggest that CVCs can, while other differences suggest otherwise. These differences will jointly determine how valuable CVC services and support are to entrepreneurial companies.

Potential Advantages of CVCs

The defining feature of CVCs is their close affiliation with large established indus-trial corporations: they are usually created as either separate corporate subsidiaries or informal units within corporations' research and development departments. As a direct result of this affiliation, they can leverage the assets and capabilities of their parents to facilitate the growth and development of portfolio companies (Block and MacMillan 1993). For example, they can provide start-ups with technological and R&D support, product development assistance, manufacturing capacities, and access to marketing and distribution channels (Chesbrough 2000). Sometimes, certain technologies require the development of complementary technologies in order to generate value, and corporations may be better positioned than TVCs to provide and coordinate such complementarities (Chesbrough 2000). CVCs can also connect entrepreneurial firms with various business units of their parent corporations and help establish cooperative relationships between them. The CVC parent may be a potential customer or supplier, which could significantly increase the start-up's odds of success.

Ivanov and Xie (forthcoming) examine the forms of collaboration that exist between a CVC parent and its portfolio firms. Their study of CVC-backed IPOs yields evidence consistent with a value-adding role of CVCs. They find that CVCs provide a variety of valuable services and support to their portfolio companies. Specifically, between start-up companies and their CVC investors, there often exist customer or supplier relations, marketing/sales/distribution agreements, and joint research or product development agreements. These relations exhibit interesting variations across different industries. For example, joint research agreements are more common for pharmaceutical and biotech firms, while firms from industries such as Internet/business services, electronics, and machinery and computer equipment have more product development and marketing/sales/distribution relations with their corporate venture investors (see Exhibit 4.2.).

Being part of large industrial corporations also gives CVCs access to the intrafirm information network. Their contacts with other divisions of the parent corporations can generate inside knowledge about the industries and product markets in which those divisions operate. CVCs can use this information to help entrepreneurial companies devise better business strategy and compete more effectively in the product market. Also, since CVCs are a part of large corporations, they can tap the financial resources of their parent corporations (deep pockets) and hence may be able to finance start-ups even during periods in which the VC industry is in recess (Chesbrough 2000).

Another way in which CVC backing benefits start-ups is by bringing credibility to these young, unproven enterprises (McNally 1997). Most CVC parent corporations are well-known leaders in their respective industries. Their presence as investors can send a positive signal about a start-up's prospects and mitigate the information asymmetry surrounding the start-up. The reduced uncertainty should facilitate the start-up's interactions with potential alliance partners, suppliers, and customers, and help the start-up obtain a higher valuation in the capital market. Consistent with this argument, Stuart, Hoang, and Hybels (1999) find that biotech start-ups with prominent strategic alliance partners arrive at the IPO stage faster and receive higher valuations than comparable firms without such connections. In addition, the credibility provided by CVC parent corporations can help with the rapid internalization of their portfolio firms (Maula and Murray 2002).

Potential Disadvantages of CVCs

The unique organizational structure of CVCs also puts them at certain disadvantages compared to TVCs. Most of the traditional venture funds are set up as limited partnerships in which the venture capitalists are the general partners and they

Exhibit 4.2 Types of Services and Support Provided by CVCs

The exhibit presents the type of development relations between CVCs and start-ups at 123 strategic CVC-backed IPOs during the period from 1981 to 2000. C, S, PD, RAD, and MSD stand for the five types of services and support provided by CVCs as listed in Panel A. In Panel A, the percentages (numbers) represent the proportions (numbers) of strategic CVC-backed IPOs where a given type of service or support exists. In Panel B, the percentages (numbers) represent the proportions (numbers) of strategic CVC-backed IPOs from a same industry where a given type of service or support exists. In each row, the percentages for C, S, PD, RAD, and MSD add up equal to 100%.

Panel A: Types of Relations between CVCs and IPOs

Type of Services and Support	Percentage (Number) of IPOs
The CVC parent is a customer of the IPO firm (C)	30.1% (38)
The CVC parent is a supplier of the IPO firm (S)	23.6% (29)
Product development agreement (PD)	26.8% (33)
Research agreement for joint development of drugs, chemicals, agricultural products, and so on (RAD)	17.9% (22)
Marketing/Sales/Distribution agreement (MSD)	35.0% (43)

Panel B: Relations between CVCs and IPOs—Distribution by Industry

Industry Description	SIC	Type of Services and Support					Total
		C	S	PD	RAD	MSD	
Chemicals and Allied Products (Pharmaceutical)	SIC 28	10% (2)	5% (1)		60% (12)	25% (5)	100% (20)
Industrial Machinery and Equipment	SIC 35	33.3% (3)		33.3% (3)		33.3% (3)	100% (9)
Electronic and Other Electrical Equipment	SIC 36	34.8% (8)	21.7% (5)	26.1% (6)		17.4% (4)	100% (23)
Instruments and Related Products	SIC 38	9.1% (1)	36.3% (4)	18.2% (2)	18.2% (2)	18.2% (2)	100% (11)
Communications	SIC 48	42.9% (3)	28.5% (2)	14.3% (1)		14.3% (1)	100% (7)
Business Services	SIC 73	22.7% (17)	18.6% (14)	24.0% (18)		34.7% (26)	100% (75)
Research (Biological and Laboratory)	SIC 87	16.7% (2)	8.3% (1)		66.7% (8)	8.3% (1)	100% (12)

invest the money contributed by limited partners. The prespecified finite life of the limited partnerships (usually 10 years) and the covenants in the contractual agreements between limited partners and general partners ensure that venture capitalists put their best efforts into selecting and managing portfolio companies (Gompers and Lerner 1996). However, both features are largely missing from corporate venture programs. Therefore, it is questionable whether corporate venture capitalists have enough incentives to exert best efforts in the selection and development of start-up companies.

The problem is exacerbated by the fact that CVCs do not have the high-powered compensation schemes that TVCs usually adopt, probably due to their less autonomous status as part of a larger industrial company.[4] Therefore, CVCs frequently experience difficulties in recruiting and retaining talented employees (Gompers and Lerner 2000), which further undermines their ability to provide value-added services to entrepreneurial companies. In addition, CVCs can become victims of intraorganizational politics as various business units compete over scarce resources (Sykes 1990).

CVCs' incentives may also be called into question when conflicts of interest arise between their corporate parents and their portfolio companies due to similar or competing products and technology. As active equity investors, CVCs have access to the business strategy and trade secrets of the entrepreneurial firms and should try to prevent any leakage of such sensitive information. However, in cases of a conflict, CVCs most likely will side with their parent corporations, which they are a part of, and engage in activities such as information sharing and technology transfer that may jeopardize the survival and growth of start-ups (Hamel 1991). Hellmann (2002) shows that when a CVC parent and a start-up are potential competitors, the start-up is better off receiving financing from a TVC. In addition, sometimes CVC investments in start-ups are preludes to acquisitions later on McNally (1997); Siegel, Siegel, and MacMillan (1998); Sykes (1990); and Winters (1988). Sykes reports that entrepreneurs are often wary of such intentions. Having a corporate venture investor can also constrain start-ups from developing interorganizational relationships. For example, CVCs may prevent their portfolio companies from forming alliances with their parent corporations' competitors, even though such alliances can bring significant strategic benefits to the start-ups.

Empirical Evidence

The unique attributes that distinguish corporate venture capitalists from their independent counterparts make the investigation of CVC value adding an interesting empirical question. Some of the differences suggest that corporate venture capitalists could benefit entrepreneurial firms in ways that traditional venture capitalists may not be able to emulate. Specifically, corporate venture capitalists are usually closely affiliated with large, established industrial companies, and this vantage point enables them to draw upon their corporate parents' resources to aid in the growth and maturation of their portfolio companies. At the same time, however, there are also reasons to suspect that CVCs may not be able to add much value to entrepreneurial firms. In addition, many general partners of TVCs have substantial prior business experiences, through which they have acquired significant industry expertise and developed a wide network of connections within their specialized industries. These two factors may enable TVCs to match CVCs in providing resource-based services and support to start-up companies. Therefore, it is an empirical question whether CVCs can add value to their portfolio companies in addition to the contributions by TVCs.[5]

So far the empirical work on the value added by CVCs has focused on primarily two questions. First, does CVC backing improve the start-up's likelihood of a successful exit? Second, does CVC backing lead to higher valuations and better performance? In answering both questions, one of the main issues has been to distinguish strategic from purely financial CVC investing. As mentioned above, investing for strategic reasons may have very different implications for the motivation and ability of CVCs to nurture their start-ups. Another key issue is to disentangle selection from value added. Specifically, do CVCs simply select better start-ups to finance, or do they add value beyond that added by other investors in the start-up? The answer to this question would undoubtedly provide us with a much clearer understanding of what role CVCs play in the financing of entrepreneurial ventures.

Gompers and Lerner (2000) were the first to show that CVC backing is associated with a higher probability of a successful exit. They examine the performance of start-ups backed by TVCs and CVCs during the period from 1983 to 1994. As a unit of analysis they use an investment in a start-up by CVCs or TVCs. They find that CVC-backed start-ups are more likely to go public or be acquired than TVC-backed start-ups. In addition, they find that it is not CVC backing per se that is associated with better exit outcomes, but the presence of a strategic fit between the start-up and the CVC parent. Gompers and Lerner define strategic fit on the basis of the degree of proximity between the lines of business of the CVC parent and the start-up. Their study, however, does not deal with the selection versus value added issue.

One potential explanation for the positive relationship between successful exits and strategic fit with the CVC parent is provided by Hellmann (2002). In his theoretical model, the CVC has an incentive to offer support to a start-up when the two have complementary products. Santhanakrishnan (2003) tests Hellmann's prediction using a unique measure of complementarity between start-ups and CVC parent corporations and finds that in the presence of complementarities CVCs are more likely to provide product market support to their portfolio firms, which in turn increases their probability of successful exit. Santhanakrishnan (2003) also controls for the endogeneity between product market support and start-up exit strategies and finds that his results remain unchanged.

Most of the current empirical evidence on CVC value added is based on CVC-backed start-ups that go public because a lot more information is available for those firms than for CVC-backed start-ups that are acquired or remain private. Maula and Murray (2002) examine the effect of CVC backing on the market value of IPO firms for a sample of 325 information technology firms going public during the period from 1998 to 1999. Market value is measured as shares outstanding multiplied by the price at the close of the offer day. Controlling for several factors that may affect the firm value at IPO, they find that CVC-backed IPOs tend to have higher market value than other IPOs. The valuations are higher when the start-up is backed by more than one CVC. However, their empirical analysis does not address whether the documented CVC effect reflects CVC value added or is simply due to superior project selection abilities of CVCs, as CVCs may be able to leverage their industry knowledge and expertise to choose better entrepreneurial companies to back without adding any value. Also, Maula and Murray (2002) do not distinguish between CVCs making strategic investments and those making purely financial investments.

Ivanov and Xie (forthcoming) provide further insights into whether CVCs add value to start-ups by analyzing a large sample of 1,510 VC-backed IPOs during the period from 1981 to 2000, of which 219 were backed by CVCs. They examine whether CVC backing affects the valuations that start-ups obtain when they go public and how persistent the effect is. Unlike other studies, they also study a sample of acquisitions of VC-backed targets to investigate whether CVC backing has any effect on the takeover premiums that CVC-backed start-ups receive when acquired.

Their analyses show that the valuable services and support from CVCs translate into higher IPO valuations for the start-up companies. Using a method of propensity score matching to control for the endogeneity of CVC backing, they find that IPOs with CVC backing are able to obtain significantly higher valuations than those with TVC backing only, suggesting that CVCs add value to their portfolio companies and that the value added is incremental to that from TVCs. Moreover, they find that the higher valuations mostly accrue to start-ups that have a strategic fit with the parent corporations of their CVCs, where strategic fit is defined as the existence of a strategic alliance or close business relation. This is consistent with the argument that the benefits of CVC backing primarily come from asset or operation complementarities between start-ups and corporate venture investors. The results hold for a number of widely used price multiples and are robust to controlling for a host of IPO pricing determinants. The valuations of CVC-backed IPOs with the presence of strategic fit remain higher than those of other IPOs for at least six months after the offering, and in the three years after the IPO the return performance of CVC-backed IPOs is similar to that of their TVC-backed peers. To investigate whether the higher valuation of CVC-backed IPOs is simply driven by the superior project selection ability of CVCs, they estimate a system of simultaneous equations in which both CVC backing and IPO valuation are endogenous. The results suggest that CVCs do exhibit some project selection ability, but they also add value to their portfolio firms (see Exhibit 4.3.).

To shed more light on the incremental value added by CVCs, Ivanov and Xie (forthcoming) also compare the offer-day valuations between strategic

Exhibit 4.3 Tests for Differences in Valuations of CVC-Backed and TVC-Backed IPOs (P/V Ratios Based on Offer Prices)

Panels A and B present the median P/V ratios for the three types of IPOs over the entire sample period and the period from 1981 to 1998. The P/V ratio is the ratio of the price multiple of the CVC-backed IPO to the price multiple of its matching firm, where a matching firm is a TVC-backed IPO with the closest propensity score. For example, P/V = (Price/Sales$_{CVC}$)/(Price/Sales$_{TVC}$). In parentheses in Panel A are two-sided p-values based on heteroskedasticity-consistent standard errors. In parentheses in Panels B and C are two-sided p-values from the Wilcoxon signed-rank tests.

Panel A: 1980 ~ 2000

Multiple	CVC IPOs Number of Issues	CVC IPOs Median P/V Ratio (p-value)	Strategic CVC IPOs Number of Issues	Strategic CVC IPOs Median P/V Ratio (p-value)	Nonstrategic CVC IPOs Number of Issues	Nonstrategic CVC IPOs Median P/V Ratio (p-value)
Price/Sales	219	1.29 (0.00)	123	1.51 (0.00)	96	1.01 (0.92)
Enterprise Value/Sales	219	1.30 (0.00)	123	1.57 (0.00)	96	0.96 (0.94)

Panel B: 1981 ~ 1998

Multiple	CVC IPOs Number of Issues	CVC IPOs Median P/V Ratio (p-value)	Strategic CVC IPOs Number of Issues	Strategic CVC IPOs Median P/V Ratio (p-value)	Nonstrategic CVC IPOs Number of Issues	Nonstrategic CVC IPOs Median P/V Ratio (p-value)
Price/Sales	117	1.34 (0.01)	59	1.73 (0.00)	58	1.05 (0.19)
Enterprise Value/Sales	117	1.35 (0.01)	59	1.63 (0.00)	58	1.06 (0.17)

CVC-backed IPOs and TVC-backed IPOs that have strategic alliances with other corporations. They find that strategic CVC-backed IPOs continue to have significantly higher valuations, suggesting that IPO companies benefit more from strategic CVC backing than from general corporate alliances. One possible reason for that is that strategic CVCs hold substantially larger ownership in portfolio companies than do other corporate alliance partners. As a result, CVCs have stronger incentives to develop and nurture entrepreneurial firms. The higher equity stakes may also help resolve potential hold-up problems between partners in strategic relationships (Klein, Crawford, and Alchian 1978, Grossman and Hart 1986, and Hart 1988, 2001).

Ivanov and Xie (forthcoming) also supplement their IPO analysis with an examination of acquisitions of VC-backed targets, since acquisitions and IPOs are the two most successful exit outcomes for start-ups. They find that targets with CVC backing tend to receive higher takeover premiums than their counterparts with only TVC backing, and the higher premiums again concentrate in targets with strategic overlap with their CVCs' corporate parents. This result echoes the evidence based on IPO valuation and lends further credence to the CVC value added claim (see Exhibit 4.4.).

Exhibit 4.4 CVC Backing and Takeover Premiums of VC-Backed Targets

The sample used in this panel consists of 187 TVC-backed targets, 22 CVC-backed targets with strategic CVC investments, and 30 CVC-backed targets with financial CVC investments from 1996 to 2000. The dependent variable is the logarithmic transformation of the Purchase Price/Book Value of Assets. *Stock acquisition* is a dummy variable equal to one if the deal is financed entirely with common stock, and zero otherwise. *Relative deal size* is the ratio of deal size to acquirer market value of equity at the end of the month prior to the announcement date. *Target industry MTB* is the median target industry market-to-book ratio during the year of the deal, where industry is defined using 2-digit SICs. *Intraindustry deal* is a dummy variable equal to one if the target and the acquirer share a 2-digit SIC code. In parentheses are two-sided p-values based on heteroskedasticity-consistent standard errors.

Independent Variables	Dependent Variable: Log (Purchase Price/Book Value of Assets)	
	(1)	(2)
Intercept	−1.06 (0.14)	−0.99 (0.16)
CVC	0.07 (0.24)	−0.26 (0.43)
Strategic CVC		0.88 (0.05)
Stock acquisition	0.70 (0.01)	0.68 (0.01)
Relative deal size	0.04 (0.01)	0.04 (0.01)
Target industry MTB	0.87 (0.03)	0.88 (0.02)
Intra-industry deal	0.15 (0.54)	0.15 (0.59)
Industry fixed effects	Included	Included
Year fixed effects	Included	Included
Adjusted R^2	0.40	0.42
Number of observations	239	239

CVCs AND THE GOVERNANCE
OF PORTFOLIO FIRMS

A distinctive feature of VC investors is that they hold large equity stakes and obtain significant control rights in the start-ups they finance. These enhanced control rights enable them to manage the significant moral hazard risk and uncertainties associated with venture investments. Previous studies by Lerner (1995) and Kaplan and Stromberg (2003, 2004) document that the strength of a VC's control rights is inversely related to a start-up's performance. VCs gradually relinquish their control rights as the start-up's performance improves and it nears an IPO. As major investors, CVCs have significant influence over a start-up firm's choice of governance systems. As Ivanov and Xie (forthcoming) show, CVCs investing for strategic reasons hold significant equity stakes and frequently sit on the board of their portfolio firms that eventually go public. Bottazzi, Da Rin, and Hellmann (2008) also document that CVCs sit on the board of their portfolio firms in roughly 60 percent of the cases. Thus, it will be interesting to see to what extent CVCs are involved in the corporate governance of their portfolio firms, and whether the motivation for investing—strategic versus purely financial—plays a role.

Current studies on the participation of CVCs in the governance of their portfolio firms focus on CVC-backed IPOs. The IPO event represents a shock to a start-up's corporate governance since a VC's powerful control rights disappear as their convertible preferred stock with its enhanced control rights is forced to convert into ordinary shares. Also, prior to going public, private firms usually restructure their corporate governance to meet exchange listing and disclosure standards, and also to become more attractive to outside investors.

To enhance both their expected returns and private equity reputations, VCs have incentives to set up effective corporate governance systems before start-ups go public. VCs raise new funds usually every three to four years. This means that very frequently they must find investors (limited partners) willing to commit capital to their new VC funds. However, investor interest is strongly related to the performance of the VC's previous funds. VCs typically realize their highest returns when they take portfolio firms public. However, VCs generally do not exit from their companies immediately at the IPO as documented in Brav and Gompers (2003). Instead, VCs usually must wait for a six-month lock-up period to expire, which underwriters typically require of all private equity investors. Interestingly, VCs frequently keep a portion of their equity stake even after the IPO lock-up period expires (Barry et al. 1990). Thus, VCs need to ensure that their portfolio firms have good governance systems in place when they go public in order to protect the value of their ongoing investments in these firms.

Likely TVCs, CVCs repeatedly access the IPO market by bringing their young portfolio companies public, and their reputations affect the willingness of investment bankers to underwrite their IPOs. If CVC-backed IPO firms are known to have poor performance, then future IPOs backed by these same CVCs are likely to experience weak investor and underwriter interest. To preserve their reputational capital, CVCs have incentives to implement good governance systems in the start-ups they finance.

CVCs have several additional incentives to establish effective governance mechanisms to curb managerial entrenchment and private benefits of control. Unlike TVCs, CVCs primarily invest for strategic reasons. As a result, their corporate parents often enter into formal or informal strategic or business relationships with their portfolio firms, which tend to last for a number of years after these firms go public, and these business relationships can offer important strategic as well as financial benefits to CVC parent corporations. Strategic alliances can be plagued by a host of contracting problems, especially in highly risky industries in which CVCs usually invest. This contracting environment with asymmetric information can lead to opportunistic behavior by one party that exploits the other by exerting insufficient effort, underinvesting, or appropriating a disproportionate share of the joint surplus created by the relation. The literature on incomplete contracting (see Klein, Crawford, and Alchian 1978, Grossman and Hart 1986, Hart 1988, 2001, and Aghion and Tirole 1994) conclude that equity ownership and its associated control rights can be used to mitigate potential hold-up problems between strategic alliance partners, which in our case are CVC parents and start-ups.

As strategic investors, CVCs have incentives to seek greater control rights than other investors because they have more to lose due to their strategic goals. CVCs are motivated by financial considerations just as TVCs are. However, they obtain financial gains from two sources: (1) the financial gains of the start-up investment, like TVCs, and (2) the financial benefits of the parent's strategic business relationship with the start-up. These parent business relationships can be hurt if (1) a start-up's management is unwilling to pursue operating and investment decisions that are complementary or at least not damaging to a CVC's parent or (2) the start-up is acquired by a third party, which could threaten its commercial relationships with the parent. CVCs generally have important strategic objectives that can be consistent with, independent of, or in conflict with the goal of maximizing a start-up's financial returns. Since manager incentives are generally aimed at maximizing a portfolio firm's financial returns, strategically oriented CVCs are taking greater risks when they allow start-up firm managers unchecked decision-making power. Thus, CVCs have incentives to seek greater decision-making power in start-ups than other VCs do and to limit start-up management influence by establishing effective corporate governance systems that can help protect their strategic goals after a start-up goes public, when they lose their special control rights.

TVCs have an incentive to support efficient start-up governance structures to maximize their exit payments. Stronger governance can limit managers' ability to behave opportunistically, which can also help protect a CVC's strategic investment. So in this regard, the interests of CVCs and TVCs can be aligned. Aghion and Tirole (1994), in their model of the organization of R&D activity, show that it is optimal for CVCs ("customer" in their model) to have TVCs as co-investors since it can help raise CVC profits. Thus, syndication with TVCs can benefit CVCs, both from a strategic and a financial viewpoint, while alleviating some entrepreneurial concerns about CVC expropriation.

Ivanov and Masulis (2008) investigate this important issue by assessing whether IPO issuers backed by strategic CVCs or TVCs with an outside strategic partner have distinctly different corporate governance systems from other IPO issuers backed by TVCs without an outside strategic partner or financially oriented CVCs. Using a sample of 542 venture-backed IPOs from the 1992 to 1999 sample period, they document significant differences in the corporate governance of IPO issuers backed by strategic CVCs compared to control samples of IPO issuers that are backed by either TVCs or financially oriented CVCs. They find that strategic CVCs hold large shareholding positions in IPO issuers relative to financial CVCs or other outside strategic alliance partners. This suggests that having a CVC-affiliated strategic alliance partner is likely to have an impact on corporate governance, given a CVC's much stronger voting power in these IPO issuers. Consistent with the above predictions, they find that IPO issuers backed by strategic CVCs have stronger internal corporate governance mechanisms. Specifically, they observe that IPO issuers backed by strategic CVCs have significantly more independent directors on their boards than control samples of firms that lack strategic alliances and are backed by either TVCs or financially motivated CVCs. Examining another important element of corporate governance, they find that strategic CVC-backed IPOs tend to sell fewer primary shares at the IPO, which is consistent with strategic CVCs having particularly strong incentives to preserve their voting rights after their portfolio firms go public, and also consistent with the arguments of Williamson (1979, 1985) concerning the governance of transactions characterized by a high degree of uncertainty and idiosyncratic risk (see Exhibit 4.5.).

Turning to external corporate governance mechanisms, they document that IPO firms backed by strategic CVCs have a higher frequency of strong antitakeover protections (ATPs) than IPO firms backed by financially oriented CVCs and TVCs. Furthermore, IPO issuers backed by strategic CVCs are more likely to adopt a staggered board, which is often considered the strongest form of takeover defense, compared to other VC-backed IPO issuers. They hypothesize that strategic CVCs have incentives to support strong ATPs to help ensure the continued viability of their parents' strategic alliances, which can be threatened by competitors acquiring control of the IPO firm and then terminating the alliances. The downside associated with such takeover defenses is potentially greater management entrenchment. However, this effect can be at least partially offset by weaker management influence over the board of directors. Consistent with weaker management power, we find IPO issuers backed by strategic CVCs exhibit higher forced CEO turnover compared to other VC-backed IPOs.

Lastly, Ivanov and Masulis (2008) compare IPO firms backed by TVCs with outside strategic relationships (and having no strategic CVC investor) to matched IPOs backed by TVCs without strategic partners and to IPOs backed by strategic CVC investors. Since a large majority of CVCs are strategically oriented where their parents have business relationships with these start-ups, it is important to be able to separate the effects of the strategic relationships from the effects of CVC backing per se. They then investigate whether CVC strategic relationships are more or less beneficial than other strategic relationships. On first glance, one might expect any VC-backed firm with a strategic alliance to exhibit a similar governance structure and economic benefits. For these newly public firms, we would expect the outside strategic partner to act similarly to strategic CVCs in many dimensions. Since these partners are concerned with expropriation by the management of the IPO issuer and with protecting their strategic relationship, they will have similar incentives with respect to desirable equity ownership and board structure. The authors document that the main difference between non-CVC strategic alliance

Exhibit 4.5 Board Composition for IPO Issuers Backed by Strategic CVC Investors and Other VC Investors

The exhibit presents the results of a pooled cross-sectional time series regression of the fraction of independent directors on the company's board on a number of explanatory variables for a sample of 542 CVC-backed and TVC-backed IPOs during the period from 1992 to 1999. Strategic CVC is an indicator that equals one if there is a strategic CVC investor. Financial CVC is an indicator that equals one if there is a financial CVC investor. Outside SA is an indicator that equals one if there is an outside strategic partner (but not a strategic CVC investor). SA Ownership is an indicator variable equal to one if the strategic partner has an equity stake in the TVC-backed IPO. Outside SA * SA Ownership is an interaction term indicating an outside strategic partner with an equity stake. CEO-chairman and CEO-founder are respectively indicators that equal one if the CEO is also a chairman of the board and if the CEO is a firm founder. Standard errors are robust to heteroskedasticity and firm clustering. The t-statistics are reported in brackets.

| | Percentage of Independent Directors on the Board | | | | |
| | Pooled Cross-Sectional Time Series Regressions | | | Random Effects GLS | General Linear Model |
Variables	(1)	(2)	(3)	(4)	(5)
Strategic CVC	0.022 [2.10]	0.031 [2.19]		0.030 [2.24]	0.119 [1.89]
Financial CVC		0.020 [2.04]	0.021 [1.60]		
Outside SA		0.004 [0.31]	−0.006 [−0.45]	0.001 [0.08]	−0.005 [−0.08]
Outside SA * SA Ownership		0.011 [1.58]	0.022 [1.21]	0.022 [0.95]	0.121 [1.33]
CEO characteristics:					
CEO ownership	0.001 [0.92]	0.001 [0.97]	0.001 [1.06]	0.001 [1.10]	0.004 [0.89]
Log (CEO tenure)	−0.004 [−0.50]	−0.003 [−0.33]	−0.004 [−0.50]	0.005 [1.04]	−0.018 [−0.45]
CEO-chairman	0.006 [0.59]	0.007 [0.64]	0.007 [0.67]	0.014 [2.13]	0.034 [0.68]
CEO-founder	0.044 [3.52]	0.042 [3.36]	0.045 [3.56]	0.028 [3.20]	0.203 [3.31]
Firm characteristics	Included	Included	Included	Included	Included
Year dummies	Included	Included	Included	Included	Included
Number of Observations	2318	2318	2318	2318	2318
Adjusted R^2 / Log-likelihood	0.16	0.16	0.15	0.15	−815.79

partners and CVCs investing for strategic reasons is that the CVCs generally have larger equity stakes in their alliance partners (an average of 20.7 percent versus 2.8 percent before the IPO). The greater control rights of strategic CVCs are likely to yield stronger effects. Consistent with these differences, they find that strategic CVCs are more likely to sit on the board of their strategic partners, that these IPO firms have more independent boards and are associated with higher likelihood of forced CEO turnover and have stronger takeover defenses.

Another study that investigates the participation of CVCs in the governance of start-up firms is Masulis and Nahata (2007). They study how strategic CVC investing affects the allocation of control rights among a start-up's founders and various investors. They find that CVCs have more board power when making strategic investments. On the other hand, insiders appear to have significantly bigger board representation in cases where the CVC is a potential competitor to the start-up. They argue that in such instances insiders may fear the formation of a controlling block of shareholders or directors dominated by an unfriendly CVC. In addition, they find that when CVCs are the lead VCs in a syndicate investing in a particular start-up, they have lower board representation than lead TVCs for the same level of shareholdings (they receive a board seat in less than 70 percent of the deals they syndicate, while lead TVCs almost always sit on the board). They interpret this as a sign that entrepreneurs may be wary of the presence of strategic investors since those may be able to influence the development of the start-up in unison with their own goals and needs.

CONCLUDING REMARKS AND DIRECTIONS FOR FUTURE RESEARCH

Prior research on corporate venture capital has documented some important benefits to both portfolio firms and parent companies from CVC investing. However, the field of corporate venturing is still relatively unexplored. We see several fruitful areas for future research:

Syndication. Keil, Maula, and Wilson (2007) study the participation of CVCs in VC centrality networks using data on U.S. venture capitalists during the period from 1996 to 2005. They find that CVCs tend to quickly ascend to central positions in VC networks and attribute this to the valuable services that CVCs can provide to start-ups. However, questions remain as to with whom CVCs syndicate their investments and whether strategic focus affects the ability of CVCs to syndicate and their position in VC networks?

CVC investing. Ivanov (2004) shows that VC investments are affected by the degree of openness of IPO and M&A markets. Gompers and colleagues (2007) document that improvements in business opportunities drive VC investments and show some important differences between reputable and less-reputable VCs. However, more research efforts are needed to understand what type of companies start CVC units, what determines the change in a firm's mixture of internal R&D and acquisition of external R&D through CVC over time, and what drives (strategic) CVC investing in general.

CVC contracting. Kaplan and Stromberg (2003) document some interesting features of VC contracts. It would be interesting to find out what the main characteristics of CVC contracts are and how closely they resemble those of TVCs. Using Canadian VC data, Cumming (2006) shows some important differences between types of claims used by CVCs and TVCs. Clearly, further analysis is needed on this topic.

CVC around the world. Most of the empirical studies are based on U.S. and U.K. data. It would be interesting to examine what drives CVC activity in other parts of the world and whether there are significant differences in CVC programs in other countries. Haemmig (2002) represents a first step in this direction.

NOTES

1. By "traditional venture capitalists," we refer to stand-alone venture capital firms that are independent of government agencies, industrial firms, and financial firms such as commercial banks, investment banks, and insurance companies.

2. Other strategic benefits include establishing a toehold for future acquisitions, developing potential customers or suppliers, supporting the growth of complementary products and services, utilizing excess capacity, and exposing middle management to entrepreneurship (Silver 1993).

3. Compared to exploitative learning, which is characterized by reliance on existing knowledge within a firm, explorative learning is associated with more risk taking, discovery, flexibility, and innovation, and it generates knowledge that is distant from a firm's existing knowledge base.

4. For example, jealousy from other divisions and bureaucracy in a large corporation can deter the use of high-powered compensation schemes.

5. There is evidence that VCs can help start-ups develop more strategic alliances (Hsu 2006 and Lindsey 2008), contribute to their professionalization (Hellmann and Puri 2002, and accelerate their speed to bring products to the market (Hellmann and Puri 2000). However, these studies are silent on whether there is any differential effect between CVCs and TVCs on the provision of these services. Bottazzi, Da Rin, and Hellmann (2008) touch upon this issue, and they find that CVCs in general are less involved in the recruiting of directors and managers at entrepreneurial companies than TVCs. However, they make no distinction between strategic CVCs and financial CVCs, which play quite different roles at entrepreneurial companies as indicated by the former's significantly greater board control and equity ownership (Ivanov and Xie Forthcoming).

REFERENCES

Aghion, P., and J. Tirole. 1994. On the management of innovation. *Quarterly Journal of Economics* 109:1185–1207.

Andrade, G., M. Mitchell, and E. Stafford. 2001. New evidence and perspectives on mergers. *Journal of Economic Perspectives* 15:103–120.

Barry, C., C. Muscarella, J. W. Peavy III, and M. Vetsuypens. 1990. The role of venture capital in the creation of public companies. *Journal of Financial Economics* 27:447–471.

Benson, D., and R. Ziedonis. 2005. Corporate venture capital and the return to acquiring entrepreneurial firms. Working paper. University of Michigan.

_____. 2007. Corporate venture capital as a window on new technologies: Implications for the performance of corporate investors when acquiring start-ups. Working paper. University of Michigan.

Block, Z., and I. MacMillan. 1993. *Corporate venturing: Creating new business within the firm.* Boston: Harvard Business School Press.

Bottazzi, L., M. Da Rin, and T. Hellmann. 2008. Who are the active investors? Evidence from venture capital. *Journal of Financial Economics* 89:488–512.

Brandenburger, A., and B. Nalebuff. 1996. *Co-opetition.* Boston: Harvard Business School Press.

Brav, A., and P. Gompers. 2003. The role of lockups in initial public offerings. *Review of Financial Studies* 16:1–29.

Chemmanur, T., and E. Loutskina. 2007. How do corporate venture capitalists create value for entrepreneurs? Working paper. Boston College.

Chesbrough, H. 2000. Designing corporate ventures in the shadow of private venture capital. *California Management Review* 42(3):31–49.

_____. 2002. Making sense of corporate venture capital. *Harvard Business Review* 80:90–99.

Cohen W., R. Nelson, and J. Walsh. 2001. Protecting their intellectual assets: Appropriability conditions and why U.S. manufacturing firms patent (or not). NBER working paper #7552. National Bureau of Economic Research.

Cumming, D. J. 2006. Corporate venture capital contracts. *Journal of Alternative Investments:* Winter 2006, 40–53.

Dushnitsky, G., and M. Lenox. 2005. Corporate venture capital and incumbent firm innovation rates. *Research Policy* 34:615–639.

———. 2006. When does corporate venture capital create firm value? *Journal of Business Venturing* 21:753–772.

Ernst&Young. 2002. Corporate venture capital report.

Gompers, P., and J. Lerner. 1996. The use of covenants: An empirical analysis of venture partnership agreements. *Journal of Law and Economics* 39:463–498.

———. 1999. *The venture capital cycle.* Cambridge: MIT Press.

———. 2000. The determinants of corporate venture capital success. In *Concentrated Corporate Ownership*, ed. R. Morck (17–50). Chicago: University of Chicago Press.

———. 2001a. The venture capital revolution. *Journal of Economic Perspectives* 15:145–168.

———. 2001b. *The money of invention: How venture capital creates new wealth.* Boston: Harvard Business School Press.

———, A. Kovner, and D. Scharfstein. 2007. Venture capital investment cycles: The impact of public markets. *Journal of Financial Economics* 87:1–23.

Grossman, S., and O. Hart. 1986. The costs and benefits of ownership: A theory of vertical and lateral integration. *Journal of Political Economy* 94:691–719.

Haemmig, M. 2002. The globalization of venture capital: A management study of international venture capital firms. PhD diss. California School of International School of Management, San Diego.

Hamel, G. 1991. Competition for competence and inter-partner learning with international strategic alliances. *Strategic Management Journal* 12:83–103.

Hart, O. 1988. Incomplete contracts and the theory of the firm. *Journal of Law, Economics, and Organization* 4:119–139.

———. 2001. Financial contracting. *Journal of Economic Literature* 39:1079–1100.

Hellmann, T. 2002. A theory of strategic venture investing. *Journal of Financial Economics* 64:285–314.

———, and M. Puri. 2000. The interaction between product market and financing strategy: The role of venture capital. *Review of Financial Studies* 13:959–984.

———, and M. Puri. 2002. Venture capital and the professionalization of start-up firms: Empirical evidence. *Journal of Finance* 57:169–197.

———, L. Lindsey, and M. Puri. 2008. Building relationships early: Banks in venture capital. *Review of Financial Studies* 21:513–541.

Hsu, D. 2006. Venture capitalists and cooperative start-up commercialization strategy. *Management Science* 52:204–219.

Ivanov, V. 2004. What determines the dynamics of venture capital investments? Working paper. University of Kansas.

———, and R. Masulis. 2008. Strategic alliances and corporate governance in newly public firms: Evidence from corporate venture capital. Working paper. University of Kansas.

———, and F. Xie. Forthcoming. Do corporate venture capitalists add value to start-up firms? Evidence from venture-backed IPOs and acquisitions. *Financial Management*.

Jensen, M. C. 1986. Agency costs of free cash flow, corporate finance, and takeovers. *American Economic Review* 76(2):323–330.

Kaplan, S., and P. Stromberg. 2003. Financial contracting meets the real world: An empirical analysis of venture capital contracts. *Review of Economic Studies* 70:281–316.

———. 2004. Characteristics, contracts and actions: Evidence from venture capitalist analyses. *Journal of Finance* 59:2173–2206.

Keil, T., M. Maula, and C. Wilson. 2007. Unique resources of corporate venture capitalists as a key to entry into rigid venture capital syndication networks. Working paper. Helsinki University of Technology.

Klein, B., R. Crawford, and A. Alchian. 1978. Vertical integration, appropriable rents, and the competitive contracting process. *Journal of Law and Economics* 21:297–326.

Kleinknecht, A., and J. van Reijnen. 1992. Why do firms cooperate in R&D? An empirical study. *Research Policy* 21:347–360.

Lerner, J. 1995. Venture capitalists and the oversight of private firms. *Journal of Finance* 50:301–318.

Lindsey, L. 2008. Blurring firm boundaries: The role of venture capital in strategic alliances. *Journal of Finance* 63:1137–1168.

Loizos, C. 2005. Dell, other corporations shut venture units. *Venture Capital Journal*, February 1.

MacMillan, I., E. Roberts, V. Livada, and A. Wang. 2008. Corporate venture capital (CVC): Seeking innovation and strategic growth. National Institute of Science and Technology report (NIST GCR 08-916).

Malmendier, U., and G. Tate. 2005. CEO overconfidence and corporate investment. *Journal of Finance* 60:2661–2700.

Masulis, R., and R. Nahata. 2007. Strategic investing and financial contracting in start-ups: Evidence from corporate venture capital. Working paper. Vanderbilt University.

Maula, M., and G. Murray. 2002. Corporate venture capital and the creation of U.S. public companies: The impact of sources of venture capital on the performance of portfolio companies. In *Creating value: Winners in the new business environment*, ed. M. A. Hitt, R. Amit, C. Lucier, R. D. Nixon. 164–187. Oxford: Blackwell.

Maula, M., T. Keil, and S. Zahra. 2003. Corporate venture capital and recognition of technological discontinuities. Working paper. Helsinki University of Technology.

McNally, K. 1997. *Corporate venture capital: Bridging the equity gap in the small business sector*. London: Routledge.

Mowery, D. C. 1983. The relationship between intrafirm and contractual forms of industrial research in American manufacturing, 1900–1940. *Explorations in Economic History* 20:351–374.

Pisano, G. 1991. The governance of innovation: Vertical integration and collaborative arrangements in the biotechnology industry. *Research Policy* 20:237–249.

Roll, R. 1986. The hubris hypothesis of corporate takeovers. *Journal of Business* 59:197–216.

Santhanakrishnan, M. 2003. The impact of complementarity on the performance of entrepreneurial companies. Working paper. Idaho State University.

Schildt, H., M. Maula, and T. Kiel. 2003. Explorative and exploitative learning from external corporate ventures. Working paper. Helsinki University of Technology.

Siegel, R., E. Siegel, and I. MacMillan. 1988. Corporate venture capitalists: Autonomy, obstacles and performance. *Journal of Business Venturing* 3:233–247.

Silver, D. A. 1993. *Strategic partnering*. New York: McGraw-Hill.

Stuart, T. E., H. Hoang, and R. Hybels. 1999. Interorganizational endorsements and the performance of entrepreneurial ventures. *Administrative Science Quarterly* 44:315–349.

Sykes, H. B. 1990. Corporate venture capital: Strategies for success. *Journal of Business Venturing* 5:37–47.

Veugelers R. 1997. Internal R&D expenditures and external technology sourcing. *Research Policy* 26-3:303–315.

Williamson, O. 1979. Transaction-cost economics: the governance of contractual relations. *Journal of Law and Economics* 20:233–261.

Williamson, O. 1985. *The economic institutions of capitalism: Firms, markets, relational contracting*. New York: Free Press.

Winters, T. B. 1988. Venture capital investing for corporate development objectives. *Journal of Business Venturing* 3:207–223.

Yost, M., and K. Devlin. 1993. The state of corporate venturing. *Venture Capital Journal* 37–40.

ABOUT THE AUTHORS

Vladimir I. Ivanov received his Ph.D. from Vanderbilt University. He specializes in venture capital and private equity, corporate governance, strategic alliances, securities issuance, and entrepreneurship. His research has been published in academic journals such as *Financial Management* and the *Journal of Corporate Finance*.

Fei Xie received his Ph.D. from Vanderbilt University. He specializes in corporate governance, mergers and acquisitions, venture capital, and executive compensation. His research has been published in top academic journals such as the *Journal of Finance*, *Review of Financial Studies*, and *Financial Management*.

CHAPTER 5

Angel Finance

The Other Venture Capital

ANDREW WONG
Analysis Group Inc.

INTRODUCTION

With the rise (and fall) in the returns and prominence of new entrepreneurial ventures, much attention has focused on the genesis of new firms. One of the most important considerations these new entities face in the transformation from entrepreneurial ideas to revenue-generating companies is the procurement of capital. Because traditional avenues of finance such as debt are often not available, entrepreneurs must seek risk capital by offering equity. While some companies may be able to generate capital by forming alliances, most new ventures must rely on two sources of outside equity: venture capital and angel financing.[1]

Institutional venture capital has been glamorized in the press and academic research as the primary source of outside equity finance. However, many studies estimate that institutional venture capital contributes less than half of the total equity financing for new firms. The less-scrutinized, yet equally important, source of start-up capital is the informal venture capital market, known as "angel financing." It is difficult to precisely quantify the size of the angel market due to its informal nature. Studies estimate the size of the angel market to be at least twice that of the institutional venture capital market.[2] In 2000, the National Venture Capital Association assessed the size of the angel market to be $100 billion in the United States while the institutional venture capital market was estimated to be less than half this size at $48.3 billion.[3] The Global Entrepreneurship Monitor (GEM) assessed the size of the angel market to be $107.8 billion in 2002 while the institutional venture capital market was estimated to be only $21.2 billion.[4] More recently, Shane (2008), compiling data from several different surveys conducted between 2001 through 2003, finds between 140,000 and 266,000 angels commit between $12.7 and $36 billion to between 50,000 and 57,000 companies annually. Using data from the 1993 National Survey of Small Business Finance, Berger and Udell (1998) find 3.59 percent of all small businesses are funded by angels, while only 1.85 percent are funded by venture capital. Freear, Sohl, and Wetzel (1992) suggest angels provide the largest amount of capital among early-stage financiers and fund more than 10 times the number of firms as venture capitalists. In the United Kingdom,

71

Mason and Harrison (1990) find angel investors finance at least five times as many small firms as venture capitalists.

Despite the importance of angel funding, much of what is known about angels is incomplete and not well understood. Very few academic studies have examined angels, in part because data on angel investment is difficult to obtain. The lack of research leaves many questions unanswered. Specifically, why do two types of equity-based start-up financing exist, and do these investors operate in the same manner with respect to control? Asymmetric information and uncertainty problems in new firms make corporate governance an important issue. If angel financiers are similar to institutional venture capital, they should maintain a comparable degree of control over their investments. Moreover, as angel financing usually occurs earlier in a firm's life than venture financing, the degree of uncertainty surrounding the firm is comparatively greater. This suggests angels may desire stronger controls. Previous research has found the implementation of control mechanisms with venture capital investments to be more important as expected agency costs or uncertainty increase. Alternatively, if angels do not behave similarly to venture capitalists with regard to the use of traditional control rights, what mechanisms (if any) do angels use to protect themselves from expropriation?

Using a unique dataset of angel-financed firms, I examine the role of angels in funding, monitoring, and providing assistance to their investments. While many of my results are different from conclusions that other researchers have found with institutional venture capital, some similarities exist. However, angel investors do not employ the same type of control mechanisms as venture capitalists. For example, I find that angels seldom receive board seats in the firm they invest in. When board seats are allocated, the founders usually retain board control, indicating board control is not the primary control mechanism utilized by angels. The allocation of board seats is not sensitive to measures of agency costs or greater uncertainty. Gompers (1995) finds venture capitalists use staged capital infusions as a mechanism to control agency costs. In contrast, I find little support for the use of staging in angel investments. While some investors follow-on their initial investments, the majority of angels do not stage their investments. The use of staging does not increase in response to higher degrees of uncertainty or expected agency costs in the firm. Kaplan and Strömberg (2003) report venture capitalists employ many contractual clauses as protection. Unlike venture capitalists, I find angels do not appear to use contractual design to safeguard their investment. Angels usually take common equity claims, which do not afford them a higher degree of protection in the event of bankruptcy or liquidation. The majority of contracts between firms and angels also do not contain clauses for anti-dilution or contingent equity claims.

Instead, I find angels use alternative mechanisms of control. On average, less than a quarter of the firm is sold to outsiders in each round. Potential moral hazard problems are mitigated because the entrepreneur retains a large share of the equity. While their funding levels are not sensitive to measures of investment uncertainty or expected agency costs, angels receive a higher level of equity ownership to compensate for investing in earlier rounds. The average contribution per angel decreases as the amount of uncertainty increases. Additionally, many investors syndicate risky investments to share the risk and minimize the losses for any single investor. However, venture capitalists also use syndication and incentive alignment in their investments, yet they maintain strong traditional control rights as well.

An important facet of angel investing appears when investigating the geographical proximity of the investors. Geographic proximity is a substitute for many of the formal control mechanisms and a complement to other mechanisms such as syndication. Taken together, these results suggest that the entrepreneur appeals to sociological networks and uses local ties to generate initial funding for the venture. The angels rely on trust in lieu of more formal control mechanisms. As the need for more capital arises, the entrepreneur exhausts local funding sources. The entrepreneur must appeal to more professional and remote funders, such as venture capitalists, for assistance. Because the new funders are not as familiar with the entrepreneur as the local investors, more formal control mechanisms need to be implemented to protect their investment. This finding provides some insight into the extensive control mechanisms used by institutional venture capital and the relative lack of formal control with angels.

While much empirical and theoretical research has been conducted on venture capital, there are few empirical studies of angel investing. Much of what is known is based on anecdotal evidence or small, regional surveys of angel investors (see Van Osnabrugge and Robinson (2000) for an overview of survey results). These papers tend to focus mainly on descriptive statistics of investment size, while my paper focuses on the control aspects of angel investment. Wetzel (1983) provides one of the earliest profiles of angel investment in his survey of New England–area angels. Lerner (1998) analyzes the plausibility of public efforts to fund new firms via angels. Prowse (1998) describes the characteristics of angel investors in the Dallas area. Ehrlich and colleagues (1994) publish survey results comparing the level of investor involvement of venture capitalists and angels. Freear and Wetzel (1990); Freear, Sohl, and Wetzel (1992); and Sohl, Van Osnabrugge, and Robinson (2000) provide survey evidence on the investment behavior of angels within certain industries. Fenn and Liang (1998) offer a preliminary investigation of angel control rights, but focus only on firms that are about to go public. Their sample may only reflect the habits of the most successful firms and not the typical characteristics of the market.

More recent empirical research on angel financing has corroborated the initial findings from my sample. Becker-Blease and Sohl (2007) find angels purchased a similar percentage of companies they invested in. In their sample, angels acquired an average of 21 percent of the firms. Goldfarb and colleagues (2008) find that preferred stock is most frequently used by angel investors in Series A transactions. Their finding may be a result of their sample. They study Series A transactions obtained from legal offices. Incorporating a lawyer into a deal may signal complexity, resulting in a more complex security. My results of geographic proximity are also reinforced by Goldfarb and colleagues' (2008) findings. They find that 60 percent of investors are no more than three hours drive from the firms they invested in, and 18 percent of investors are within the same zip code. With respect to control rights, Wiltbank and Boeker (2007) finds that a sample of accredited angel-group investors make follow-on investments only 29 percent of the time. In contrast, Goldfarb and colleagues (2008) find that angel-only and mixed groups follow-on more often than venture capital–only investors. Ibrahim (2008) also notes that a burdensome or complicated angel round contract is more costly to remove and can be an impediment to important venture capital financing at a later date.

The study that is most similar to this is Kaplan and Strömberg (2003), one of the first papers to formally study the details of venture capital contracting and the control rights accorded to venture investors. In their paper, Kaplan and Strömberg provide detailed empirical evidence on the degree of board control, cash flow, liquidation, and voting rights in venture capital financings. They find that control rights are held mostly by venture capitalists, particularly when the performance of the firm is poor.

In addition to Kaplan and Strömberg (2003), a related line of empirical work examines investor control in venture capital literature. Sahlman (1990) and Gompers and Lerner (1996) examine venture capital contracts and report some typical stipulations in these contracts. Gompers (1995) finds staged capital infusions to be more prevalent in situations of higher agency costs. Lerner (1995) and Baker and Gompers (2003) investigate the degree of board control of venture capitalists in their investments. Both papers find venture capitalists maintain active board participation.

The existing theoretical literature on outside investors and control rights can be divided into distinct groups. The first group makes predictions that coincide with the behavior of venture capitalists. Berglöf (1994), Cornelli and Yosha (2003), and Hellmann (2006) investigate the role of convertible debt in venture financings. Admati and Pfleiderer (1994) offer one of the first analyses on venture capital contracting in asymmetric information environments. Hellmann (1998) analyzes the effect of replacement help on the allocation of control rights. Kirilenko (2001) argues that venture capitalists should get more control rights to compensate for information problems. Other papers such as Hart and Moore (1994), Bergemann and Hege (1998), and Neher (1999) stress the role of staging in their theoretical models.

My results do not support some of these theoretical findings, in large part because much of this theoretical research does not explicitly distinguish between angel investors and venture capital. As is the case with much of the literature, it is possible the authors did not consider angel finance as a viable source of start-up capital since very little is known about angels. For example, Admati and Pfleiderer (1994) argue investors should hold a fixed fraction of equity through each investment stage. However, my results show angels do not follow-on, meaning that the fraction of equity held by angels decreases. Trester (1998) suggests investors should only use common equity in later stages; I find common equity is most frequently used in the earliest stages of investment. Gompers (1997) argues control rights should be assigned to investors in periods of highest asymmetric information, such as early in the life of the project. I find that control rights are actually retained by entrepreneurs even though investment occurs when the firms are young. My results also do not support the results of Neher (1999), Bergemann and Hege (1998), and Cornelli and Yosha (2003), who advocate the staging of capital and the optimality of convertible securities. The results of many of these models rely on assumptions based on the stylized facts of venture capital investing and do not consider angel investors as a financing alternative.

Other authors allow for the possibility of angel financing in their models. Repullo and Suarez (2004) allow for a pure financier and a venture capitalist in their moral hazard model. Casamatta (2003) develops a model that captures some of the differences between angel investment and venture capital. She finds the optimal choice of security is a function of the size of investment. She finds also that smaller investments (typically by angels) should use common equity and straight preferred, while larger investments (typically by venture capitalists) should use more complicated securities. The empirical results from this paper support her predictions. Finally, Bernhardt and Krasa (2005) allow for an angel financing equilibrium in their model. Angel financing is optimal if the financier has sufficient expertise to screen investments, and no information regarding the proper action choice.

This paper proceeds as follows. The following section is a brief background on angels and angel investments. Then comes a study of the details of the sample and the data collection process. The empirical tests and results are discussed after that, followed by the conclusion.

ANGEL BACKGROUND

The term "angel investor" originates from funders for theatrical shows. Today, an angel investor refers to a high-net worth individual who typically invests in small, private firms on her own account. Formally, angel investors are "accredited investors" according to the SEC. SEC Rule 501 of Regulation D states an accredited investor is an individual who has a net worth of more than $1 million or an expected individual (household) yearly income of more than $200,000 ($300,000). While the Federal Reserve's Survey of Consumer Finances estimates that over 6 million households qualify to be accredited investors, many studies estimate of the number of active angel investors in the United States to be between 250,000 to 400,000.[5]

Sohl (1999) reports that angels are usually cashed-out entrepreneurs who continue to yearn for the next high-growth venture. Because angels have to perform their own due diligence, they typically invest in ventures in their familiar industries. Prowse (1998) reports that angels are diverse in background, with some being financially sophisticated and others relatively inexperienced. In addition to making a financial investment, some angels actively participate in the firm's operations; however, such participation varies by angel. He reports that angels usually invest close to home. Using information collected from interviews with angels, Linde and Prasad (1999) find the average angel has a total of $335,000 invested in 4 different companies. As individual investors, angels exhibit great heterogeneity in personal characteristics such as age, experience, and investment preferences.

Studying several sources of data, Shane (2008) finds that accredited investors account for approximately 23 percent of the angel population between 2001 and 2003. He finds that accredited investors tend to make larger investments than unaccredited investors. In his sample, some angels are one-time investors; for 20.8 percent of people who made an angel investment it was their first and only investment.

Preston (2004) reports that angels also co-invest in angel investment groups. She finds that they are active investors that typically invest locally. She also finds that angels invest in groups to benefit from the greater power of combined investment dollars, for collective due diligence, and for greater quality in deal flow.

SAMPLE DESCRIPTION
Data Gathering

To investigate the hypotheses of the model, I needed a sample of angel-backed firms. The task is complicated by the fact that no commercial database exists that systematically records angel transactions. The angel market involves private transactions that are not subject to public disclosure with very little institutional infrastructure supporting the market. Additionally, much of the market is fragmented and unorganized. These factors make data difficult to obtain.

To conduct this study, I collected data through surveys and interviews with entrepreneurial firms. Over 800 angel-backed firms were identified via newswires, periodicals (such as Angel Investor), press releases, angel networks, and web sites (such as Red Herring's Herringtown and Localbusiness.com). Firms were asked if they had received any outside funding. Angel-backed firms were contacted for information regarding all financing received since firm initiation. In addition to financial information, the firms were asked to provide descriptive information on their firm such as the number of employees, revenues (if any), and background information on the founders. Due to issues of confidentiality and competition, some respondents only provided partial responses. Whenever possible, a founder or person responsible for investor relations was contacted for information. The final sample consists of 215 investment rounds made by angel investors in 143 companies from 1994 to 2001.

All funding rounds consisted of some financial participation by angels, whether it was angels only or co-investing with venture capitalists, strategic investors, or other investors such as friends and family. For my purposes, any funding conducted by "angel venture" funds or limited-liability organizations acting as "early-stage-angel" funds are considered venture capital funds because I only wanted investments by individuals. For example, entities such as Angel Investors LLP and the Band of Angels Fund are considered a venture fund. However, investments from individual Band of Angels members are classified as angel investments. Investments by friends and family are also not considered to be angel investments.

This sample of firms has many advantages. Since entrepreneurial firms were asked for information (instead of angels), the sample is free from the bias caused by investors reporting information from only successful ventures. Although surveys are imperfect for the usual reasons, the approach allowed for subjective answers from entrepreneurs on questions such as the quality of help from outside investors. While it is impossible to obtain information on every completed angel financing due to the very nature of the transactions, every effort has been made to make the sample as unbiased and representative as possible. The 215 financings are a large enough sample to draw representative conclusions.

Sample Selection Issues

In this section, I discuss potential selection issues concerning my sample. The financings are not a completely random sample in that the data is from firms that were willing to respond to inquiries and provide confidential information.

I contacted 801 companies for information and received information from 143 companies. Of the 143 companies in the sample, 56 companies are identified via newswires, 48 companies from Red Herring's Herringtown web site,[6] 33 from angels or angel networks, and 6 from other miscellaneous sources.[7] It is possible that the companies surveyed were more successful, having released some information publicly. However, many of the companies surveyed have since been acquired, ceased operations, or continued to operate successfully. As of November 2001, 102 of the companies are still operating, 9 have been acquired, 22 have ceased operations. No companies have gone public. I am not able to verify the status of 10 companies.

The average age of the companies when surveyed was 24.5 months (with a median of 19 months), relatively close to the age of the companies at funding in Exhibit 5.1. The proximity between the survey age and the funding age should reduce selection bias problems.

Despite the possibilities of modest selection bias existing in the sample, the biases should not be of great concern since I am not attempting to measure performance. Instead, I am trying to detail the specifics of angel investments and the role of angel investors. In this respect, the sample is likely to be similar to typical angel investments.

Summary Statistics

Exhibit 5.1 presents summary information for the sample.

Panel A of Exhibit 5.1 reports the geographical distribution of the dataset.[8] In comparison to venture capital investments, the dataset has fewer observations in California and New England, although the sample remains heavily weighted toward California. For the time period from 1995 to 2000, Venture Economics reports slightly more than 22 percent of venture-capital–backed companies are located in California. A major difference between Venture Economics, and my data is the high representation of firms in the Southeast and an under-representation of firms from New England. Venture Economics reports approximately 12 percent of venture-backed companies are located in New England whereas less than 6 percent of my sample comes from New England. If angel activity is concentrated in the highest areas of venture capital activity, then the sample has minor geographical differences. The data's geographic breakdown falls roughly in line with Angel Society's survey of angel group activity and the Angel Capital Associations survey of angel group industry preferences.[9]

Panel B shows the date of company formation. Most of the companies were founded between 1998 and 2000. While it is easy to state the founding date of the company as the date of legal incorporation, many firms had other significant events occur, such as hiring an employee or the beginning of business operations, before legal incorporation. I take the founding date as the earliest date that I have for any significant firm activity. Most of the angel rounds were completed between 1998 and 2000, with over half of my sample financing rounds from 2000. While the young age of the companies does not allow for long-term panel studies, the relative youth of our companies and the freshness of the funding are positive for many aspects. First, the findings in this paper will not suffer from survivorship bias caused by analyzing data from older companies. Second, the companies reflect the current state and trends in angel financing.

Exhibit 5.1   Sample Description

Summary information for 215 investments in 143 angel-financed companies. Investments were made between January 1994 and March 2001. Panel A specifies the location of the financed firm into their respective regions. The regions are specified by Venture Economics. Panel B provides founding dates for the companies in the sample. The column labeled First Fund denotes the year in which the firm first received angel financing. Panel C provides information on the number of angel-financed rounds in each year and the years that a company has first received angel financing. Panel D provides the industry decomposition of angel investments. Industry classifications are the same as reported by Venture Economics. Panel E reports the type of investor per funding round. Other investors include strategic alliances and corporate venture capital.

Panel A: Geographic Location

Region	Companies	Percent	Funding Rounds	Percent
Great Lakes	11	7.8	19	8.9
Great Plains	6	4.2	11	5.1
New York	11	7.8	15	7.0
MidAtlantic	10	7.0	16	7.5
California	31	21.8	46	21.5
New England	8	5.6	10	4.7
Northwest	13	9.2	24	11.2
Ohio Valley	7	4.9	9	4.2
Rocky Mountains	6	4.2	9	4.2
South	3	2.1	4	1.9
Southeast	20	14.1	25	11.7
Southwest	16	11.3	26	12.15
Total	142	100.0	214	100.0

Panel B: Date Founded and Rounds Financed

Year	Companies Founded	Percent	Rounds Completed	First Fund
1991	1	0.7	0	0
1992	0	0.0	0	0
1993	2	1.4	0	0
1994	2	1.4	1	1
1995	4	2.8	0	0
1996	6	4.2	1	1
1997	10	6.9	5	5
1998	18	12.5	18	13
1999	65	45.1	51	38
2000	35	25.0	130	80
2001	0	0.0	7	5
Total	143	100.0	213	143

Exhibit 5.1   (*Continued*)

Panel C: Industry Distribution of Companies and Rounds

Industry	Companies	Percent	Rounds	Percent
Communications	4	2.8	7	3.3
Computers	0	0.0	0	0.0
Computers-Related	78	54.6	117	54.4
Computer Software	33	23.1	49	22.8
Electronic Components	7	4.9	11	5.12
Other Electronics	5	3.5	7	3.3
Biotechnology	3	2.1	5	2.3
Medical/Health	3	2.1	5	2.3
Energy	0	0.0	0	0.0
Consumer Products	3	2.1	6	2.8
Industrial Products	1	0.7	1	0.5
Transportation	3	2.1	3	1.4
Other Industries	3	2.1	4	1.9
Total	143	100.0	215	100.0

Panel D: Prerevenue and Postrevenue Funding Rounds

	Number of Rounds
Prerevenue rounds	151
Postrevenue rounds	59
First funding round	137
Later rounds	78

Panel E: Age at First Funding

	Months
1st quartile	2
Median	7
3rd quartile	12
Mean	10.5

Panel F: Number of Employees

Employees	First Funding	All
1	12	13
2	20	20
3	14	17
4	21	24
5	24	30
6–10	26	34
11–20	17	37
21 and higher	7	27

Panel C divides the sample into different industries as defined by Venture Economics. Most of the sample are from the "Computer-Related" industry, reflecting the technology boom in the late 1990s. "Computer-Related" firms include Internet services, Internet content and design firms, and business-to-business/consumer companies. This may be oversampling of one industry, or it may represent the trend in the late 1990s to invest heavily in computer-related companies, an industry that experienced rapid growth during this time. Data from venture capital disbursements seem to support this idea. Gompers and Lerner (2001) find 60 percent of all venture capital disbursements went to information technology industries.

As panel D indicates, the majority of the rounds in my sample are pre-revenue. Sixty-nine percent (99 of 143 companies) of the firms were pre-revenue for all funding rounds. This is significantly different from the sample of firms in most venture capital research. For example, less than 40 percent of the firms in Kaplan and Strömberg's (2003) sample are pre-revenue firms. If a revenue stream is an indicator of development, my analysis focuses on firms that are earlier in their life cycle rather than analysis on venture capital–financed firms. Panel E indicates the age of the firms in the sample at first funding. The average age of first funding is 10.5 months. Most firms that receive funding are less than 12 months old. In comparison, the average age at first funding for venture-backed firms is greater than one year (Gompers 1995). If information quality is linked to age, then the uncertainty should be much greater in angel-financed than in venture capital–financed firms. Panel D and E of Exhibit 5.1 support the idea that angels typically finance earlier-stage companies.

Panel A of Exhibit 5.2 shows that most of my sample (157 rounds) is financed entirely by angels. Co-investment by angels and venture capitalists accounts for less than 20 percent of all funding rounds. This indicates that angels are a different type of venture investor, not merely co-investors with institutional venture capital.

Panel B of Exhibit 5.2 describes the funding amounts for the financing rounds. The median investment per investment round is $1 million. Not surprisingly, firms with positive revenue or those that are in later stages of financing receive greater amounts of financing, suggesting that as asymmetric information decreases in later rounds or with observable revenue streams, financing increases. In rounds having only angel participation, the mean investment is $1.28 million (median of $850,000). Compared to the results in Kaplan and Strömberg (2003), the average amount of financing provided by venture capitalists is twice the size of the amount of financing provided by angels only for companies at comparable stages.

Comparing the results from Exhibit 5.2 with data from institutional venture capital data from Venture Economics yields many differences between angels and venture capital. In rounds completed between 1998 and 2000, the average round of venture capital investment is $17.95 million per round. Considering only venture capital–funded seed and start-up rounds, the size of the average venture capital investment remains larger than angel contributions. From 1998 to 2000, an average of $4.77 million was received from venture capitalists by companies in these start-up/seed stages. The average angel funding was $2.16 million across all rounds. Panel C and D of Exhibit 5.2 report that angel financing is smaller than venture capital fundings in comparable industries.

The difference in funding size provides some evidence that angels play a complementary role to venture capital. Instead of competing with venture capitalists

Exhibit 5.2 Firm Funding Information

This exhibit reports funding information in funding rounds. Panel A reports the number of rounds funded by financier type. Panel B reports the total funding amount in each round. Panel C reports the funding amounts in selected industries for seed and start-up rounds. Panel D reports funding information for all rounds in the selected industries. Venture capital funding information is from venture economics. The total columns denote the entire funding or equity stake in the round. Total funding in co-invested rounds denotes the total funding in rounds where angels and venture capital, angels and other, or angels, venture capital, and others. Angel funding in co-invested rounds refers to the angel contributed amounts in rounds whose investors are angels and venture capital, angels and other, and angels, venture capital, and others. Angels only refers to rounds where only angel investment was made.[1] In Panel B, the number beneath the means is the t-statistic for differences in means assuming unequal variances. The number beneath the median column is the z-score for Mann-Whitney test for differences in percentages in ownership.

Panel A: Financiers

Financier	Number of Rounds
Angels only	157
Angels and venture capital	38
Angels and other	12
Angels, venture capital, and other	8

Panel B: Funding Amounts in Each Round (Amounts in Millions)

	Total			Total Funding in Co-Invested Rounds		
	Mean	Median	N	Mean	Median	N
All Firms	2.16	1.00	212	4.80	2.20	57
Prerevenue	1.49	1.00	149	2.79	2.00	41
Postrevenue	3.76	1.00	59	11.50	6.50	13
	(2.26)	(1.87)		(2.43)	(2.82)	
First round	1.29	0.87	135	2.37	1.50	29
Later rounds	3.69	1.50	77	7.33	3.15	28
	(3.02)	(3.03)		(2.51)	(3.18)	

	Angel Funding in Co-Invested Rounds			Angels Only		
	Mean	Median	N	Mean	Median	N
All Firms	0.88	0.70	42	1.28	0.85	155
Prerevenue	0.79	0.60	35	1.01	0.72	108
Postrevenue	1.41	1.04	6	1.85	1.00	46
	(1.51)	(1.98)		(1.67)	(1.50)	
First round	0.60	0.50	23	1.00	0.63	106
Later rounds	1.23	1.00	19	1.87	1.00	49
	(3.14)	(3.18)		(1.91)	(2.75)	

(Continued)

Exhibit 5.2   *(Continued)*

Panel C: Seed and Start-Up Rounds (Amount in Millions)

Industry	Angels & Co-Invested Rounds	Angel Only	VC
Computer-Related (Internet)	1.40	0.94	4.80
Computer Software	1.05	0.64	3.34
Semiconductors and Other	1.37	1.37	4.94

Panel D: All Rounds (Amount in Millions)

Industry	Angels & Co-Invested Rounds	Angel Only	VC
Computer-Related (Internet)	2.47	1.38	20.03
Computer Software	1.31	0.90	13.31
Semiconductors and Other	1.71	1.08	20.58

[1]N is different because I do not have funding for every round.

for firms at similar stages of development, angels provide a smaller amount of funding to younger firms.

Empirical Tests and Results

In this section, I use my sample to provide detailed evidence on the aspects of the angel investment process with a focus on control mechanisms. Inferences regarding the differences in the allocation of control rights between venture capital and angel investors are drawn by comparing existing results on venture capital to my findings. Subsequently, I investigate the variation of the distribution of control rights within angel investments. I test for other determinants that may influence distribution of control rights. These factors are culled from existing literature on venture capital.

In addition to control rights, I examine the reasons for angel financing. Research indicates venture capitalists often provide professionalization assistance. I examine whether angels can provide the same nonmonetary benefits to the new enterprise such as professionalization and assistance in locating additional funds.

Control Rights

Many investors seek to protect their investment from expropriation through the use of control rights. I consider three common control mechanisms used by institutional venture capital. The first measure is representation on the board of directors. Receiving board rights is an indication that investors maintain a degree of authority over the manager. Secondly, the control of investments through staging has been documented in the venture capital literature (Gompers 1995) as a control mechanism. Staging an investment can effectively halt the progress of a wayward venture as capital is no longer available for the new firm. Lastly, as Kaplan and Strömberg (2003) demonstrate in venture capital contracts, contracting mechanisms such as security choice and contractual provisions can be effective methods of control. If angels are similar to venture capitalists, they should maintain similar protections, particularly in ventures where the threat of expropriation is the highest.

Many theories emphasize the role that capital providers such as venture capital provide after the investment is made. Lerner (1995) finds venture capitalists exercise control through board representation and the active recruitment and dismissal of CEOs. Kaplan and Strömberg (2000) find many venture capitalists anticipate having an active role in management and the hiring of new management. If angel investors are similar to venture capital organizations, angels should actively participate in the lives of the firms.

Board Rights

Board seats give outside investors the ability to affect corporate decisions. Board rights are particularly important in environments with greater uncertainty since it is not feasible to specify all possible contingencies in the ex ante contract. Sahlman (1990) finds board seats are typically allocated to venture capitalists as part of a financing round.

Panel A of Exhibit 5.3 shows this is not the case with angel investments. Board seats are granted in 42.5 percent of all funding rounds. The likelihood of providing a board seat does not change much when considering pre- and postrevenue funding rounds. Initial rounds of angel financing tend to have a slightly higher (though not statistically significant) probability of board seat allocation, although fewer than half of all first rounds relinquish board seats to outside investors.

Lerner (1995) reports an average of 1.12 board seats are added in each venture capital round. As shown in panel B of Exhibit 5.3, an average of only 0.59 board seats are added to the board of directors in a typical angel-financed investment round. Board sizes in angel-financed ventures are much smaller than board sizes in public companies[10] or venture-backed firms.[11] Panel C shows that the average board size of the firms is 3.71 members with a median of 4 members. Panel D reports, on average, angels only represent 18 percent of the board of directors. Kaplan and Strömberg (2003) find venture capitalists control between 37 percent to 47 percent of the board seats in the firms they invest in. In my sample, insiders have the majority of board seats on 100 boards (out of 116 where I have information on board composition subsequent to funding), which is consistent with Kaplan and Strömberg's (2003) finding that outside board control is less common for early-stage companies. However, in venture capital–funded firms, insiders comprise the majority in only 13.9 percent of the boards. Exhibit 5.3 shows that angels take a much smaller degree of control through board representation than venture capitalists.

The results on boards of directors are consistent with other theories that suggest a passive role for angels. Fama and Jensen (1983) hypothesize that the composition of the board should be shaped by the need for monitoring. If the threat of managerial expropriation is high, then the board will bear a greater responsibility for oversight. Additionally, at the early age of the firm, much of the value of the venture is embodied in the human capital of the entrepreneurs, so the replacement of the founders would not seem to increase the value of the company.

Similarly, the need for a board seat may be determined by the need for oversight within each company. Larger investments (and equity stakes) by outsiders will increase the need for oversight. Ventures with larger potential agency costs should be monitored more often. Firms in industries with higher market-to-book

Exhibit 5.3 Board Rights

This exhibit details the security issued in exchange for investment and the composition of the board of directors. Panel A provides information on the board seats given to the group of investors in each round. The number in parentheses represents t-statistics for tests of equality of means under an unequal variance specification between consecutive rows. Panel B displays information on the number of board seats given in each round. Panel C provides postinvestment board size. Panel D shows the angel composition of the board subsequent to investment. Prerevenue refers to firms that do not have any revenue at the time of funding.

Panel A: Round with Granting of Board Seats

	Percentage	N	
All rounds	0.425	193	
Angels only	0.439	139	(0.63)
Angels with co-investment	0.389	54	
Prerevenue	0.439	132	(0.36)
Postrevenue	0.411	56	
First round	0.459	122	(1.26)
Later rounds	0.366	71	

Panel B: Number of Board Seats Granted on Investment

	Mean	Median	N	Min	Max
Board seats	0.59	0.00	193	0	6
Board seats if granted	1.39	1.00	82	1	6
Prerevenue	0.58	0.00	132	0	6
Postrevenue	0.64	0.00	56	0	3
First round	0.45	0.00	71	0	3
Later rounds	0.67	0.00	122	0	6

Panel C: Board Size

	Mean	Median	N	Min	Max
Board size	3.71	4.00	116	1	9
Board size if granted	4.29	5.00	63	1	9
Prerevenue	3.65	3.00	80	1	9
Postrevenue	3.97	4.00	33	2	7
First round	3.53	3.00	76	1	9
Later round	4.05	4.00	40	1	7

Panel D: Angel Representation on Board

	Mean	Median	N	Min	Max
Angel percentage	0.18	0.20	116	0.00	0.80
Angel percentage if granted	0.33	0.33	63	0.17	0.80
Prerevenue	0.18	0.20	80	0.00	0.80
Postrevenue	0.19	0.17	33	0.00	0.67
First round	0.22	0.23	76	0.00	0.80
Later round	0.11	0.00	40	0.00	0.67

ratios may need more monitoring as agency costs are often associated with growth options. Tangible assets lower the expected agency costs in inefficient continuation, decreasing the need for board seats. Industry volatility should increase the need for a board seat if the volatility is a measure of the uncertainty in the project. Firms with intensive R&D may need more oversight, since it is likely that these firms will have more specific assets that can be expropriated. Entrepreneurs with previous entrepreneurial history may not need as much oversight because their reputations have already been established. Finally, early rounds, when uncertainty is the highest, should have more board seats allocated.

Exhibit 5.4 reports results from the probit regressions on the factors determining the allocation of board seats.

Panel A examines the results for all funding rounds and panel B only considers funding rounds composed entirely of angel funders. The coefficient on industry volatility has the opposite sign, as predicted, and is different from Kaplan and Strömberg's (2003) finding that outsider board control is positively related to industry volatility. Though the coefficients on R&D are economically large, they are not always statistically significant. However, the coefficient on the ratio of fixed assets has the opposite sign from expectations. It appears that angels do not increase the use of board representation as a control mechanism in projects with higher agency costs or uncertainty.

Staging

Empirical and theoretical works have emphasized the importance of staging as a control mechanism for venture capitalists. Instead of providing the entirety of capital in a lump sum, the investment is provided in stages, preserving the investor's option to abandon. Models such as Hart and Moore (1994), Bergemann and Hege (1998), and Neher (1999) stress the importance of staging as a control mechanism. Gompers (1995) finds that venture capitalists use staging as an important method to control agency costs.

Panel A of Exhibit 5.5 provides mixed results for the use of staging. Consecutive rounds funded entirely by angels tend to have follow-on investors from earlier rounds. However, if the subsequent financing round involves venture capital–participation, angels do not follow-on. This finding supports the complementary nature of angel and venture capital investment. Once the firm has been nurtured to success, with success being venture capital investment, the angels step aside for more professional or deep-pocketed investors.[12] Panel B shows that even when angels follow-on, only an average of 40 percent of investors from previous rounds participate in the subsequent rounds.

I investigate the factors that affect the probability of staging investment in the probit regressions in panels C and D of Exhibit 5.5. Similar to the predictions on board seats, investors in ventures with high degrees of agency costs and uncertainty should have a higher probability of staging their investments. The predictions for the coefficients of the independent variables are similar to the predictions for board rights. However, the results indicate that many of the variables do not significantly affect whether angels stage investment. Most of the variables are not statistically significant. Investigating only angel-financed rounds, none of the independent variables are statistically significant although the coefficient on research

Exhibit 5.4   Determinants of Board Seats

This exhibit presents two-stage instrumented probit regressions using the approach of Newey (1987). Panel A uses all funding rounds and panel B only examines rounds entirely funded by angels. The dependent variable is equal to 1 if a board seat was assigned to an angel investor in the financing round. The logarithm of funds is instrumented with the number of angels and the number of employees at funding. The percentage ownership is instrumented with the number of employees and the financing round. First round is equal to one if this is the firm's first round of outside financing. Round is the number of outside financing rounds. Age of firm at financing refers to the number of months since founding. Geography equals 1 if the closest angel investor is less than 50 miles away. Previous entrepreneur equals 1 if the founders have been previous entrepreneurs. Industry Market/Book is the mean 3-digit SIC market to book ratio. Industry R&D/assets is the aggregate R&D expense to total assets for public firms in the company's 3-digit SIC industry according to COMPUSTAT. Industry fixed assets/total assets is the median fixed total assets for all (public as well as closely held) firms with sales less than $1 million in the company's 4-digit SIC industry according to OneSource. Industry Volatility is the volatility of the value weighted industry portfolio return from months t-61 to t-1 where t is the date of funding, where industries are defined according to the Fama and French (1997) industry classification. Previous entrepreneur equals one if the founders had previously started another venture. The absolute values of z-statistics are reported in parentheses beneath the coefficients. A star (*) denotes statistical significance at a 10 percent level; Two stars (**) denotes statistical significance at a 5 percent level; Three stars (***) denotes statistical significance at a 1 percent level.

Panel A: All Rounds

	(1)	(2)	(3)	(4)	(5)	(6)
Log of funds (instr.)	0.207		−0.092		0.195	
	(1.18)		(0.70)		(0.91)	
Percent owned (instr.)		3.037		5.446		3.105
		(0.82)		(1.64)		(0.87)
First round	0.514	0.183			0.707	0.459
	(1.63)	(0.51)			(1.86)*	(1.23)
Geography	−0.316	−0.505			−0.209	−0.342
	(1.17)	(1.65)*			(0.66)	(0.98)
Previous entrepreneur	−0.439	−0.504			−0.097	−0.224
	(1.58)	(1.63)			(0.30)	(0.62)
Industry market/book			0.025	0.032	0.005	0.023
			(1.22)	(1.37)	(0.16)	(0.65)
Industry volatility			−0.225	−0.120	−0.383	−0.304
			(2.55)**	(1.12)	(3.15)***	(2.10)**
Industry R&D/assets			5.804	0.861	12.444	8.493
			(1.01)	(0.12)	(1.63)	(0.79)
Industry fixed assets/ total assets			3.712	3.441	3.341	2.975
			(2.51)**	(2.14)**	(1.77)*	(1.39)
Constant	−2.852	−0.180	1.498	−1.276	−1.754	0.322
	(1.12)	(0.24)	(0.81)	(1.10)	(0.57)	(0.25)
Observations	108	98	156	142	94	84
Pseudo-R^2	0.05	0.06	0.07	0.09	0.17	0.18
χ^2	7.68	8.50	15.69	16.83	21.99	20.81

Exhibit 5.4 *(Continued)*

Panel B: Angel-Only Rounds

	(1)	(2)	(3)	(4)	(5)	(6)
Log of funds (instr.)	0.175		−0.126		0.150	
	(0.87)		(0.67)		(0.58)	
Percent owned (instr.)		6.058		4.755		5.392
		(1.11)		(1.50)		(0.98)
First round	0.583	−0.144			0.591	0.092
	(1.66)*	(0.22)			(1.38)	(0.14)
Geography	−0.295	−0.539			−0.259	−0.326
	(0.97)	(1.61)			(0.69)	(0.75)
Previous entrepreneur	−0.318	−0.321			0.100	0.019
	(1.03)	(0.93)			(0.26)	(0.04)
Industry market/book			0.036	0.043	0.017	0.028
			(1.57)	(1.69)*	(0.48)	(0.62)
Industry volatility			−0.282	−0.155	−0.381	−0.283
			(2.79)***	(1.26)	(2.79)***	(1.54)
Industry R&D/assets			4.575	2.386	14.722	8.583
			(0.63)	(0.29)	(1.44)	(0.58)
Industry fixed assets/ total assets			3.260	3.779	2.606	2.289
			(1.80)*	(1.96)**	(1.15)	(0.89)
Constant	−2.603	−0.630	2.479	−0.968	−1.160	0.002
	(0.92)	(0.83)	(0.92)	(0.74)	(0.30)	(0.00)
Observations	83	74	112	103	71	62
Pseudo-R^2	0.05	0.07	0.09	0.10	0.18	0.19
χ^2	5.86	7.13	14.05	13.86	17.43	15.86

and development is economically large. Angels may want to wait for the product to be closer to development before committing additional funds. In summary, staging is not a frequently used control mechanism by angels. Staging does not appear to be used to control agency costs or relieve uncertainty in investment decisions.

Contractual Provisions

Angel investors may use contractual provisions as protection from expropriation. More complex securities may provide investors stronger protections in the event of liquidation. Contractual clauses may give the investor additional protection from expropriation. Common protections in venture contracts include ratcheting and antidilution agreements.

Panel A of Exhibit 5.6 reports the types of security used in each round. Common equity is the most prevalent security, used in 34 percent of all rounds and 39.5 percent of angel-only rounds. In contrast, Sahlman (1990), Gompers (1998), and Kaplan and Strömberg (2003) report that convertible preferred is the dominant security in venture capital financing. The high usage of preferred and common equity is consistent with the theoretical predictions of Casamatta (2003). In her model, Casamatta finds common equity is better suited to smaller investments (such as those made by angels), while larger investments should use preferred

Exhibit 5.5 Follow-On Investment

This exhibit presents results on the follow-on investment behavior of angel investors. Panel A provides frequency data on the number of follow-on investments. Panel B provides information on the percentage of angels who have funded previous rounds. Panels C and D present probit regressions where the dependent variable is equal to 1 if a funding round contained investors from previous investment rounds. The independent variables are described in Exhibit 5.4. Industry dummies are included in Columns 1–7. All financing rounds are included in the regressions in panel C. Panel D examines rounds funded by only angels. The absolute values of White (1980) t-statistics are reported in parentheses beneath the coefficients in panel C. Robust z statistics are reported in parentheses beneath the coefficients in panel D. A star (*) denotes statistical significance at a 10% level; two stars (**) denotes statistical significance at a 5% level; three stars (***) denotes statistical significance at a 1% level.

Panel A: Number of Follow-On Investments

	All Rounds	Angel Only Rounds	VC investment
No follow-on	64	18	46
Follow-on	42	27	15

Panel B: Follow-On Percentage

	Mean	Median
Percentage of investors from previous rounds	40.25%	25%

Panel C: All Rounds

	(1)	(2)	(3)	(4)	(5)	(6)	(7)	(8)
Log of funds	−0.074 (0.80)							
Percent owned		0.424 (0.43)						
Board seat			−0.170 (0.66)					
Previous entrepreneur				0.460 (1.20)				
Number of angels					−0.007 (0.64)			
Geography						−0.269 (0.81)		
Postrevenue							0.353 (1.18)	
Industry market/book								0.018 (0.89)
Industry volatility								0.022 (0.17)
Industry R&D/assets								20.000 (2.61)***
Industry fixed assets/ total assets								0.558 (0.31)
Constant	0.800 (0.62)	−0.151 (0.60)	−0.119 (0.68)	−0.489 (1.48)	−0.054 (0.29)	0.000 (0.00)	−0.298 (2.10)**	−1.671 (1.54)

Exhibit 5.5 (*Continued*)

Panel D: Angel Rounds Only

	(1)	(2)	(3)	(4)	(5)	(6)	(7)	(8)
Observations	104	86	97	59	97	59	104	93
Pseudo-R^2	0.00	0.00	0.00	0.02	0.00	0.01	0.01	0.07
χ^2	0.64	0.19	0.43	1.45	0.41	0.65	1.40	7.96
Log of funds	0.071							
	(0.36)							
Percent owned		0.875						
		(0.51)						
Board seat			0.072					
			(0.18)					
Previous entrepreneur				−0.181				
				(0.31)				
Number of angels					−0.010			
					(0.68)			
Geography						−0.619		
						(1.11)		
Postrevenue							0.220	
							(0.45)	
Industry market/book								−0.012
								(0.40)
Industry volatility								0.295
								(1.47)
Industry R&D/assets								16.289
								(1.58)
Industry fixed assets/ total assets								2.657 (1.08)
Constant	−0.643	0.320	0.210	0.566	0.476	0.842	0.210	−3.033
	(0.25)	(0.86)	(0.81)	(1.11)	(1.80)*	(1.83)*	(0.99)	(1.86)*
Observations	44	38	42	27	42	27	45	39
Pseudo-R^2	0.00	0.01	0.00	0.00	0.01	0.04	0.00	0.10
χ^2	0.13	0.26	0.03	0.09	0.46	1.24	0.21	4.74

or convertible preferred securities. Equity may be used more often with angel investments because the higher costs of writing a complex security with a small investment outweigh the benefits.

Panels B and C of Exhibit 5.6 report regression results from probit regressions where the dependent variable is equal to one if the security used is equity and 0 otherwise. Smaller investments may not justify the use of complex securities because of the higher costs of implementing a more complex security. Complex securities should be used when the threat of expropriation is greater. Thus, a negative coefficient is expected for the market-to-book ratio, R&D, and industry volatility. Firms that have an identifiable revenue stream and entrepreneurs with prior entrepreneurial experience may not need as strong a security as other firms.

The results in Exhibit 5.6 support the relation between funding and security choice. Large investment rounds use more complex securities. The transactions costs from writing a more detailed contract may be more warranted with larger investments. However, if the size of the investment is measured by equity stake,

Exhibit 5.6   Security Issuance and Contractual Terms

This exhibit presents information on security issuance and other contractual terms. Panel A lists the type of security used in each round. Panel B reports regression results from probit regressions where the dependent variable equals 1 if equity is issued and 0 otherwise using all rounds of funding. Panel C reports results using only angel-financed rounds. Columns 1 to 7 of panels B and C include industry dummy variables. Panel D presents the types of dilution protection for angel investors. The "Other" category includes dilution protection such as verbal agreements in the event of a down round. Panel E provides data on the number of rounds where repurchase agreements are in the contract. A repurchase option gives the entrepreneur the right to repurchase an angel's stake in the firm. The absolute values of z-statistics are reported in parentheses beneath the coefficients in panels B and C. A star (*) denotes statistical significance at a 10% level; two stars (**) denotes statistical significance at a 5% level; three stars (***) denotes statistical significance at a 1% level.

Panel A: Security Issuance

Security	All Rounds	Angel Rounds Only
Common equity	72	60
Preferred equity	56	34
Convertible note	14	12
Convertible preferred	67	46

Panel B: Determinants of Security

	(1)	(2)	(3)	(4)	(5)	(6)	(7)	(8)
Log of funds	−0.347							
	(4.09)***							
Percent owned		−0.640						
		(0.70)						
Board seat			−0.129					
			(0.64)					
Previous entrepreneur				−0.076				
				(0.27)				
Number of angels					−0.007			
					(0.68)			
Geography						0.361		
						(1.36)		
Postrevenue							0.135	
							(0.65)	
Industry market/book								−0.002
								(0.48)
Industry volatility								0.044
								(0.60)
Industry R&D/assets								1.948
								(0.40)
Industry fixed assets/ total assets								−0.987
								(0.82)
Constant	5.116	6.076	6.045	6.052	6.052	5.691	0.617	−0.587
	(3.88)***	(9.68)***	(8.09)***	(7.52)***	(8.76)***	(7.57)***	(0.90)	(0.90)
Observations	208	166	187	112	189	112	206	191
Pseudo-R^2	0.14	0.07	0.07	0.08	0.07	0.10	0.06	0.01
χ^2	26.59	115.63	86.50	75.66	96.13	71.18	16.48	1.88

Exhibit 5.6 (*Continued*)

Panel C: Determinants of Security—Angels Only

	(1)	(2)	(3)	(4)	(5)	(6)	(7)	(8)
Log of funds	−0.400							
	(3.98)***							
Percent owned		−0.320						
		(0.31)						
Board seat			−0.087					
			(0.37)					
Previous entrepreneur				−0.040				
				(0.12)				
Number of angels					−0.015			
					(1.17)			
Geography						0.282		
						(0.95)		
Postrevenue							0.102	
							(0.43)	
Industry market/book								0.013
								(0.76)
Industry volatility								0.046
								(0.55)
Industry R&D/assets								9.475
								(1.54)
Industry fixed assets/ total assets								−1.505
								(1.01)
Constant	5.789	6.067	6.055	6.056	6.068	5.775	0.631	−0.780
	(3.87)***	(6.34)***	(6.88)***	(8.29)***	(6.38)***	(6.48)***	(0.91)	(0.97)
Observations	151	123	134	86	137	86	151	137
Pseudo-R^2	0.13	0.05	0.06	0.07	0.07	0.07	0.05	0.03
χ^2	22.50	52.69	56.82	96.18	50.56	48.73	8.63	5.78

Panel D: Contractual Provisions

Type of Protection	N	Percent
Right to participate in future funding	27	24%
Weighted ratchet	18	26%
Warrants at lower valuation	5	4%
Other ratcheting protection	3	11%
No reported ratcheting provision	66	55%
Right to force bankruptcy	3	4.6%
Contingent board or equity rights	2	1.7%
Veto management decision	6	5.1%

Panel E: Buyback Provision

	N
Repurchase provision	38
No repurchase provision	80

the coefficient is not statistically significant, lending support to the fixed costs of security choice. The other independent variables do not affect the choice of security, indicating that the cross-sectional variation in security choice is not influenced by concerns with reducing agency costs or expropriation.

In addition to security choice, many investment contracts have provisions that protect and empower the investor. Panel D contains information on many of these contractual clauses. Many contracts contain a follow-on right of first refusal provision that allows angels to participate in future rounds to capture the potential upside in successful ventures. However, as Exhibit 5.5 shows, many angels do not exercise this right; 26 percent of financing rounds contain weighted ratchet clauses for protection against future rounds at decreased valuations. Full ratcheting protection was not given in any investment round. In comparison, Kaplan and Strömberg (2003) find that 21.9 percent of their sample use full ratcheting and 78.1 percent of their sample use weighted ratcheting. Kaplan and Strömberg (2003) find contingent equity ownership prevalent in venture capital contracts. However, very few angel contracts contain provisions for contingent equity stakes.

Contractual protection from expropriation is not one-sided. Panel E indicates 38 financing rounds contain provisions that allow the firm to repurchase the stake of the angel, similar to the call provisions explained in Sahlman (1990). Many entrepreneurs cite this clause as a way to rid themselves of "bad apples" or investors whose vision does not coincide with that of the founders.

Alternative Mechanisms

In contrast to previous results on the control mechanisms adopted by venture capitalists, I find angels do not implement the same methods of managerial oversight. In particular, angels typically do not receive board seats, stage investments, or use particularly strong contractual claims to protect their claims. The use of the conventional control mechanisms is not very sensitive to commonly used measures of agency costs and uncertainty. Little support is found for the idea that increases in potential agency costs and uncertainty lead to increased use of protection. The puzzle remains: How do angel investors mitigate the increased risks of investing at early stages?

Funding

This section investigates the factors affecting the amount of funding. If investors are concerned with large degrees of uncertainty, then the average contribution per investor, total funding amounts, and number of investors will be sensitive to industry proxies for uncertainty, characteristics of the entrepreneur and management team, and the presence of a revenue stream. Intangible factors such as the entrepreneur's prior experience may provide signals to alleviate investor uncertainty. Funders may feel more secure investing with entrepreneurs who have a previous track record. More mature firms and larger firms also should have more existing information, decreasing the uncertainty with investment. Having a management team or a revenue stream signals to investors that the firm has completed the initial research and development phases. Hellmann and Puri (2000) find the hiring of a marketing and sales vice president to be an indicator for product development. Other methods to protect against large potential losses are investing

smaller amounts in firms with greater uncertainty and to syndicate riskier investments. Lerner (1994) finds venture capitalists syndicate early rounds as a method
to verify their decision making processes.

Exhibit 5.7 provides evidence on the factors that influence the amount of funding in a round. The results on the total funds raised in the round are displayed
in panel A, and the funds in angel-only investment rounds are shown in panel B.
Focusing on the angels-only results in panel B, during postrevenue phases firms

Exhibit 5.7 Determinants of Round Funding

This exhibit presents ordinary least-squares estimates of the size of funding in a round.
The dependent variable is the logarithm of the total amount of funding received in a
round of financing from all outside investors divided by the total number of employees
in the round. Panel B presents regression results from rounds entirely funded by angels.
Venture Capital is equal to 1 if the round includes investment from venture capitalists.
The other independent variables are described in Exhibit 5.4. Regressions 1 through 5 in
Panels A and B have industry dummies. The absolute values of White (1980) t-statistics
are reported in parentheses beneath the coefficients. A star (*) denotes statistical
significance at a 10% level; two stars (**) denotes statistical significance at a 5% level;
three stars (***) denotes statistical significance at a 1% level.

Panel A: Total Investment in Round

	(1)	(2)	(3)	(4)	(5)	(6)
Venture capital	0.937	0.906	0.970	1.042	1.114	0.860
	(5.91)***	(5.74)***	(4.85)***	(4.21)***	(4.35)***	(5.40)***
First round	0.243					
	(1.67)*					
Postrevenue		−0.334				
		(2.30)**				
Management team			0.084			
			(0.45)			
Geography				−0.305		
				(1.47)		
Previous entrepreneur					−0.207	
					(0.82)	
Industry market/book						−0.001
						(0.08)
Industry volatility						−0.054
						(0.94)
Industry R&D/assets						−1.457
						(0.39)
Industry fixed assets/ total assets						−0.369
						(0.38)
Constant	10.821	11.170	11.726	12.074	11.768	12.217
	(20.53)***	(18.81)***	(15.84)***	(16.30)***	(16.56)***	(24.46)***
Observations	209	207	122	119	119	185
R^2	0.17	0.18	0.21	0.20	0.19	0.12
F-statistic	5.46	6.14	4.24	15.60	6.24	6.06

(*Continued*)

Exhibit 5.7 (*Continued*)

Panel B: Angel Funding Only

	(1)	(2)	(3)	(4)	(5)	(6)
First round	0.208					
	(1.13)					
Postrevenue		−0.334				
		(1.95)*				
Management team			0.117			
			(0.52)			
Geography				−0.266		
				(1.11)		
Previous entrepreneur					−0.043	
					(0.17)	
Industry market/book						0.033
						(2.73)***
Industry volatility						−0.055
						(0.88)
Industry R&D/assets						−3.927
						(0.90)
Industry fixed assets/						−0.908
total assets						(0.80)
Constant	10.848	11.170	11.710	12.035	11.768	12.327
	(20.30)***	(18.65)***	(15.36)***	(15.88)***	(16.37)***	(21.98)***
Observations	154	153	92	93	93	134
R^2	0.12	0.13	0.19	0.17	0.16	0.07
F-statistic	3.11	4.41	7.19	18.80	9.69	3.55

actually receive less funding. High growth firms, as measured by the industry market-to-book ratio, receive more funding in each round. However, there is little support for the idea that any other measures of uncertainty strongly influence the amount of funding as most of the coefficients are not statistically significant.

As evidenced by the statistics on cash flow rights in Exhibit 5.8, the majority of residual claims belong to management. Outside investors typically own less than a quarter of the new firm.

Angels may not need a high degree of control because the threat of expropriation is minimized by the large residual claim held by the founders. The incentives of the founders are aligned with the prospects of the firm. In comparison, Kaplan and Strömberg (2003) find venture capitalists hold a larger proportion of cash flow rights (on average 40 percent) in the investments that they make. Because the incentives of the entrepreneur are not as aligned with the outside investors, the need for formal control mechanisms may be greater. However, it is questionable whether such a difference in ownership drastically increases the need for formal controls.

Exhibit 5.9 presents estimates from two-stage least squares regressions where the dependent variable is the equity ownership allocated to the outside investors in each round. Angels receive a higher equity stake to compensate for the extra risk of investing under greater uncertainty. The statistically significant and positive

Exhibit 5.8 Investor Ownership

This exhibit reports the total equity stake relinquished in each round. The total columns denote the entire funding or equity stake in the round. Total percentage ownership in co-invested rounds denotes the total percentage ownership in rounds where angels and venture capital, angels and other, or angels, venture capital, and others. Angel percentage ownership in co-invested rounds refers to the ownership stake in rounds whose investors are angels and venture capital, angels and other, and angels, venture capital, and others. Angels only refers to rounds where only angel investment was made. The number beneath the means is the t-statistic for differences in means assuming unequal variances. The number beneath the median column is the z-score for Mann-Whitney test for differences in percentages in ownership. For firms that used convertible notes, the percentage ownership amount is adjusted for conversion.

	Total			Total Percentage Ownership in Co-Invested Rounds		
	Mean	Median	N	Mean	Median	N
All firms	0.20	0.18	173	0.24	0.21	44
Prerevenue	0.20	0.19	119	0.24	0.22	32
Postrevenue	0.19	0.16	54	0.25	0.21	12
	(0.30)	(0.49)		(0.25)	(0.21)	
First round	0.21	0.20	107	0.24	0.21	24
Later rounds	0.18	0.15	66	0.24	0.28	20
	(1.53)	(1.89)		(0.96)	(0.30)	

	Angel Ownership in Co-Invested Rounds			Angels Only		
	Mean	Median	N	Mean	Median	N
All firms	0.10	0.08	35	0.18	0.15	129
Prerevenue	0.10	0.08	30	0.19	0.17	87
Postrevenue	0.09	0.10	5	0.13	0.18	42
	(0.59)	(0.40)		(0.36)	(0.38)	
First round	0.11	0.09	18	0.20	0.20	87
Later rounds	0.09	0.07	17	0.14	0.10	42
	(0.74)	(0.48)		(2.61)	(2.77)	

coefficient on the first round dummy indicates that angels receive a premium for investing early. Having a management team in place, an indication that the firm has progressed past the initial development stages, decreases the equity ownership purchased by outsiders. Investors in firms with more uncertainty, as measured by industry volatility, receive more cash flow rights. Greater research and development intensity leads to a decreased equity stake for angels. These results agree with the results from Kaplan and Strömberg (2003).

Syndication

Another method of reducing risk is to syndicate investment with other investors. By syndicating investments, the investors may be able to share the risks and share in the monitoring of the firm. Additionally, a larger syndicate may indicate that the firm has passed the evaluations of more screeners. Some angels may cooperate (or free-ride) on the due diligence of others. Syndication may also act as a verification mechanism; thus it is expected that earlier funding rounds will have more investors.

Exhibit 5.10 shows the average number of angels participating in each round. On average, twelve angels co-invest in a round. In comparison, Kaplan and Strömberg (2003) find venture rounds are normally syndicated with two to nine

Exhibit 5.9   Determinants of Cash Flow Rights

This exhibit presents two-stage least-squares estimates of the percentage of cash flow rights exchanged in a round. The dependent variable is the total percentage ownership given to investors in a round of financing from all outside investors. Log of Funds is instrumented by the number of employees and a venture capital dummy. Columns 1 through 4 have industry dummy variables as controls. Panel B uses only rounds entirely funded by angel investors. The other independent variables are described in Exhibit 5.4. The absolute values of White (1980) t-statistics are reported in parentheses beneath the coefficients. A star (*) denotes statistical significance at a 10% level; two stars (**) denotes statistical significance at a 5% level; three stars (***) denotes statistical significance at a 1% level.

Panel A: All Rounds

	(1)	(2)	(3)	(4)	(5)	(6)
Log of funds (instr.)	0.041	0.046	0.072	0.070	0.050	0.103
	(2.73)***	(2.32)**	(3.26)***	(3.52)***	(3.11)***	(2.89)***
First round	0.052	0.059	0.104	0.099	0.067	0.088
	(3.10)***	(2.79)***	(4.13)***	(4.43)***	(3.81)***	(2.57)**
Postrevenue	−0.027					−0.035
	(1.52)					(0.93)
Management team		−0.036				−0.060
		(1.51)				(1.81)*
Geography			0.026			0.046
			(0.71)			(0.92)
Previous entrepreneur				−0.031		−0.045
				(0.98)		(1.06)
Industry market/book					−0.001	0.000
					(2.73)***	(0.07)
Industry volatility					1.359	2.186
					(3.17)***	(2.56)**
Industry R&D/assets					−0.023	−0.016
					(3.30)***	(1.26)
Industry fixed assets/ total assets					−0.011	0.213
					(0.10)	(1.32)
Constant	−0.489	−0.569	−0.981	−0.922	−0.422	−1.247
	(2.44)**	(2.15)**	(3.06)***	(3.44)***	(1.98)*	(2.40)**
Observations	172	107	104	104	152	65
R^2	0.27	0.30	0.26	0.27	0.24	0.25
F-statistic	8.22	4.54	4.51	4.50	8.26	4.26

Exhibit 5.9 (*Continued*)

Panel B: Angel Rounds

	(1)	(2)	(3)	(4)	(5)	(6)
Log of funds (instr.)	0.069	0.094	0.085	0.079	0.075	0.288
	(2.01)**	(2.80)***	(1.97)*	(2.01)**	(2.03)**	(2.84)***
First Round	0.078	0.097	0.129	0.114	0.073	0.156
	(4.06)***	(3.41)***	(4.05)***	(4.17)***	(3.26)***	(1.87)*
Postrevenue	−0.031					−0.214
	(1.48)					(1.43)
Management team		−0.057				−0.102
		(2.11)**				(1.27)
Geography			0.067			0.187
			(1.44)			(1.41)
Previous entrepreneur				−0.045		−0.212
				(1.10)		(1.76)*
Industry market/book					−0.001	−0.002
					(0.67)	(0.30)
Industry volatility					1.594	3.354
					(2.90)***	(1.52)
Industry R&D/assets					−0.023	0.035
					(2.73)***	(0.93)
Industry fixed assets/ total assets					−0.133	−0.008
					(0.91)	(0.02)
Constant	−0.871	−1.207	−1.208	−1.045	−0.741	−4.008
	(1.94)*	(2.68)***	(1.99)*	(2.01)**	(1.51)	(2.55)**
Observations	128	80	80	80	112	50
R^2	0.21	0.20	0.19	0.20	0.10	
F-statistic	3.97	2.74	2.26	7.73	5.41	2.37

venture funds co-investing. While the increase in syndication may increase the monitoring capacities of the angel investment group,[13] venture capitalists also syndicate their investments while maintaining more formal control mechanisms.

Panel A of Exhibit 5.10 shows that the number of angels in each round is higher in earlier rounds. As firms develop, later rounds and postrevenue firms receive larger average contributions per angel. On average, each angel owns between 3 to 5 percent of the firm.

I run regressions to further examine the factors that influence the variation of contribution amounts.

Panels A and B of Exhibit 5.11 show that the average contribution per angel is only affected by early rounds, although the coefficient is not statistically significant in panel B. In panel B, angels have a higher average contribution when a management team is in place at the firm.

Panel C and D of Exhibit 5.11 provide results on the factors that determine the number of angels investing in a round. The model is an instrumental variables estimate of a poisson model, following the 2SQML method detailed in Mullahy (1997). Using this procedure, the estimates are consistent, but the standard errors

Exhibit 5.10   Angel Funding Information

This exhibit reports information on angel participation in financing rounds. Panel A reports the number of angels in each round. The columns titled Angels Only refer to deals in which only angel investors participated in the round. The columns titled Angels with Co-Investment refer to rounds funded jointly by angels and a combination of venture capitalist or other miscellaneous investors. Panel B reports the average contribution per angel in each round. Panel C reports the equity ownership percentage for the average angel investor and the maximum angel ownership position.

Panel A: Number of Angels per Deal

	Total			Angel Funding with Co-Investment			Angels Only				
	Mean	Median	N	Mean	Median	N	Mean	Median	N	t-test	MW
All fundings	11.8	8.0	193	10.9	8.0	52	12.2	8.0	141	(0.61)	(0.46)
Prerevenue	10.8	6.0	133	9.7	4.0	38	11.2	7.0	95	(0.66)	(1.22)
Postrevenue	14.5	11.5	58	14.9	15.0	13	14.4	11.0	45	(0.14)	(1.34)
	(1.23)	(2.00)		(1.77)	(2.70)		(1.04)	(0.79)			
First round	12.4	8.0	125	12.5	9.0	26	12.4	8.0	99	(0.05)	(0.08)
Later rounds	10.7	7.5	68	9.2	7.5	26	11.6	7.5	42	(1.05)	(0.58)
	(0.85)	(0.05)		(1.05)	(0.17)		(0.24)	(0.32)			

Panel B: Average Contribution per Angel (numbers in thousands)

	Total			Angel Funding with Co-Investment			Angels Only				
	Mean	Median	N	Mean	Median	N	Mean	Median	N	t-test	MW
All fundings	222.0	91.1	178	225.0	100.0	39	221.1	87.5	139	(0.06)	(0.58)
Prerevenue	179.3	92.0	127	252.2	116.7	33	153.7	86.6	94	(1.42)	(1.14)
Postrevenue	328.3	88.0	51	75.9	77.0	6	362.0	88.0	45	(2.44)	(0.75)
	(1.40)	(0.30)		(2.65)	(1.25)		(2.35)	(0.19)			
First round	145.2	75.0	119	113.2	50.0	21	152.1	78.5	98	(0.92)	(1.13)
Later rounds	376.8	120.0	59	355.5	144.2	18	386.2	100.0	41	(0.19)	(1.38)
	(2.43)	(3.09)		(2.17)	(2.75)		(2.59)	(1.74)			

Panel C: Ownership Percentage per Angel

	Total			Angel Funding with Co-Investment			Angels Only		
	Mean	Median	N	Mean	Median	N	Mean	Median	N
All fundings	4.2	1.6	158	3.0	1.2	34	4.5	1.7	124
Prerevenue	4.6	1.7	111	5.1	1.7	29	5.1	1.7	82
Postrevenue	3.2	1.3	47	3.5	1.6	5	3.5	1.4	42
First round	4.8	1.7	102	2.6	0.8	17	5.3	1.8	85
Later rounds	3.1	1.4	56	3.5	1.6	17	2.6	1.3	39

Exhibit 5.11 Syndication and Average Contribution

Panels A and B present estimates from OLS regressions on average angel contribution. In panel A, the dependent variable is the logarithm of the average contribution per angel in all financing rounds. Panel B reports results for only angel-financed rounds. Panels C and D report the results from a poisson regression with instrumental variables as specified in Mullahy (1997). The dependent variable is the number of angel investors. Panel D only uses rounds entirely financed by angels. The natural logarithm of funds is instrumented by the number of employees and the presence of venture capital. The other independent variables are defined in Exhibit 5.4. The regressions in Columns 1–6 of panels A and B and Columns 1–6 of panels C and D have industry dummy variables. The absolute values of White (1980) t-statistics are reported in parentheses below the coefficients in panels A and B. The absolute values of z statistics are reported in parentheses below the coefficients in panels C and D. A star (*) denotes statistical significance at a 10% level; two stars (**) denotes statistical significance at a 5% level; three stars (***) denotes statistical significance at a 1% level.

Panel A: Average Contribution per Angel

	(1)	(2)	(3)	(4)	(5)	(6)	(7)	(8)
Venture capital	0.237							0.336
	(1.04)							(0.78)
Postrevenue		0.077						0.353
		(0.37)						(1.05)
First round			−0.559					−0.745
			(2.89)***					(2.33)**
Management team				0.391				0.445
				(1.58)				(1.53)
Geography					−0.811			−0.528
					(3.13)***			(1.55)
Previous entrepreneur						0.442		0.352
						(1.52)		(0.96)
Industry market/book							−0.007	0.028
							(2.91)***	(0.87)
Industry volatility							0.021	−0.123
							(0.29)	(0.98)
Industry R&D/assets							−5.148	−4.091
							(1.07)	(0.49)
Industry fixed assets/ total assets							3.630	2.723
							(2.76)***	(1.42)
Constant	13.214	13.136	13.493	13.018	14.024	13.214	10.834	12.210
	(29.98)***	(26.85)***	(20.68)***	(21.56)***	(26.98)***	(29.32)***	(15.31)***	(10.68)***

(Continued)

Exhibit 5.11 (*Continued*)

Observations	178	178	178	111	111	111	158	70
R^2	0.09	0.08	0.14	0.11	0.21	0.15	0.09	0.30
F-statistic	3.39	6.81	9.55	9.14	7.13	4.48	3.77	2.97

Panel B: Average Contribution per Angel—Angels Only

	(1)	(2)	(3)	(4)	(5)	(6)	(7)
Postrevenue	0.221						0.286
	(0.92)						(0.83)
First round		−0.395					−0.387
		(1.65)					(1.01)
Management team			0.679				0.630
			(2.42)**				(1.97)*
Geography				−0.568			−0.179
				(1.86)*			(0.48)
Previous entrepreneur					0.358		0.131
					(1.08)		(0.31)
Industry market/book						0.002	0.011
						(0.11)	(0.32)
Industry volatility						−9.750	−14.026
						(1.76)*	(1.46)
Industry R&D/assets						3.679	1.300
						(2.40)**	(0.49)
Industry fixed assets/ total assets						−0.018	−0.182
						(0.21)	(1.22)
Constant	12.992	13.411	12.874	13.782	13.214	11.235	13.027
	(25.67)***	(22.22)***	(17.84)***	(25.06)***	(28.87)***	(13.03)***	(8.18)***
Observations	139	139	87	89	89	122	54
R^2	0.09	0.10	0.18	0.18	0.15	0.12	0.31
F-Statistic	8.39	9.07	3.36	5.62	7.62	2.85	2.34

Panel C: Number of Angel Investors per Round

	(1)	(2)	(3)	(4)	(5)	(6)	(7)	(8)
Log of funds (instr.)	0.139	0.011	−0.071	0.057	0.073	0.008	0.035	0.178
	(4.68)***	(0.46)	(2.12)**	(2.21)**	(1.67)*	(0.19)	(1.45)	(2.13)**
Venture capital	−0.335							0.071
	(4.48)***							(0.47)
Postrevenue		0.177						0.221
		(3.71)***						(2.03)**
Management team			0.255					0.230
			(4.15)***					(2.54)**
First round				0.056				0.639
				(1.09)				(5.91)***
Geography					0.488			0.111
					(6.88)***			(1.12)
Previous entrepreneur						−0.115		−0.078
						(1.61)		(0.79)
Industry market/book							0.001	0.010
							(1.13)	(1.16)
Industry volatility							−0.044	0.021
							(2.50)**	(0.62)
Industry R&D/assets							−1.698	−3.024
							(1.52)	(1.39)
Industry fixed assets/ total assets							−0.635	−1.003
							(2.15)**	(1.82)*
Constant	−1.838	−0.328	0.803	−0.782	−1.456	−0.107	2.556	−0.738
	(2.27)**	(0.42)	(0.97)	(0.99)	(1.57)	(0.12)	(7.26)***	(0.62)
Observations	191	190	118	191	114	114	170	70
χ^2	581.03	573.82	127.94	561.95	152.36	105.56	17.49	56.81

(Continued)

Exhibit 5.11 *(Continued)*

Panel D: Number of Angel Investors per Round—Angels Only

	(1)	(2)	(3)	(4)	(5)	(6)	(7)
Log of funds (instr.)	0.197	0.138	0.217	0.093	0.066	0.274	0.029
	(5.87)***	(3.34)***	(6.52)***	(1.99)**	(1.42)	(8.57)***	(0.38)
Postrevenue	0.041						0.275
	(0.71)						(2.42)**
Management team		0.131					0.089
		(1.72)*					(0.88)
First round			0.025				0.202
			(0.41)				(1.58)
Geography				0.273			−0.187
				(3.56)***			(1.69)*
Previous entrepreneur					−0.022		0.241
					(0.27)		(2.09)**
Industry market/book						0.013	0.025
						(2.80)***	(2.80)***
Industry volatility						−0.038	−0.007
						(1.87)*	(0.17)
Industry R&D/assets						0.036	2.653
						(0.03)	(1.04)
Industry fixed assets/ total assets						−1.130	0.399
						(3.15)***	(0.61)
Constant	−2.643	−1.889	−2.874	−1.496	−0.868	−0.668	1.235
	(3.21)***	(2.13)**	(3.42)***	(1.57)	(0.93)	(1.44)	(1.07)
Observations	139	89	140	89	89	123	54
χ^2	592.30	163.50	594.54	109.07	96.15	75.74	29.00

may be positively biased using this procedure. The results in panel D for angels-only rounds indicate more investors in firms in higher market-to-book industries, suggesting that more investors want to invest in ventures with higher growth. Entrepreneurial experience seems to attract more investors.

Geographic Proximity

The results on geographical proximity deserve further elaboration and may provide insight into the investing behavior of angels. Entrepreneurs may begin their search for capital by exploring local resources. A localized bond of trust may exist between the entrepreneur and investor, making formal control mechanisms unnecessary. Because of the strong trust and familiarity many local investors may have with each other, syndication is greater among local investors. Subsequent larger fundings may exhaust the resources of the local investors and need to be funded by more professional investors. Additionally, as a firm progresses, the need for professionalization is greater, leading the entrepreneur to turn to more professional investors who require more formal control because of their lack of familiarity with the founders.

If investment size is related to the degree of uncertainty and the cost of information dissemination is related to geography, the amount of investment should increase as the angels are closer. Alternatively, investments made by investors at a distance can be most costly (either to monitor, to negotiate, etc.). The results in Exhibit 5.7 show that the total funding and the angels' contribution to the round decrease when the nearest angel is less than 50 miles away, supporting the second idea.

Panel B of Exhibit 5.11 shows that the average contribution per angel also decreases as the angels are closer, suggesting that local investors may not be as wealthy as more professional investors. However, this is offset by the increase in the number of angels who invest if they are located closer to the entrepreneur. Lastly, from Exhibit 5.12 local investors provide more help, given their local proximity. However, geographical proximity may delay venture capital investment. A possible explanation is that local angels do not have as large a contact network as more professional investors.

Some additional validation for this idea is provided by examining the results on the formal control mechanisms: board seats, staging, and security choice. In contrast to Lerner's (1995) finding that close geographical proximity increases the likelihood of board representation, I find geographical proximity has a negative effect on the probability of board representation in angel-funded rounds (Exhibit 5.4), albeit the results are not highly significant. The need for contractual monitoring (via a board seat) may be reduced because of the geographic proximity of investors. Although not statistically significant, geographic proximity also decreases the use of staging and increases the use of equity, consistent with the localized investor hypothesis.

Taken together, these results suggest that many entrepreneurs begin their search for capital with local resources, relying on local ties to encourage investment. Local angel investors may not be as sophisticated as more professional investors, but may be more trusting.

Exhibit 5.12   Postinvestment Assistance

This exhibit presents evidence on the amount of assistance angel financiers provide. Panel A gives the number of rounds where the angel investors helped form the management team. Panel B presents results on the determinants of funding duration leading up to venture capital financing. The dependent variable is the number of months from completion of one funding round until the completion of the next funding round from venture capital. The distribution of the hazard duration is assumed to be Weibull. Panel C presents results from ordered logit regressions where the dependent variable is the amount of help that angel investors provide. Responses are 1 (for very little or no help) to 5 (the angel provided a great deal of help). The other independent variables are defined in Exhibit 5.4. Robust z statistics are reported in parentheses below the coefficients in panel C. A star (*) denotes statistical significance at a 10% level; two stars (**) denotes statistical significance at a 5% level; three stars (***) denotes statistical significance at a 1% level.

Panel A: Management Team Assistance

Do the angels help form the management team (N = 119)?	23.5%

Panel B: Time until Venture Capital Financing

	(1)	(2)	(3)	(4)
Postrevenue	0.224	0.207	0.024	0.183
	(0.79)	(0.79)	(0.17)	(1.58)
Log of funds	0.035		0.029	
	(0.40)		(0.56)	
Number of angels	−0.018	−0.012		
	(1.70)*	(1.46)		
First round	−0.007	−0.211		
	(0.02)	(0.78)		
Geography	0.254	0.535		
	(1.06)	(2.59)***		
Percent owned		1.489		0.390
		(1.32)		(0.82)
Industry market/book			−0.006	−0.008
			(0.69)	(0.78)
Industry volatility			−0.158	−0.087
			(2.94)***	(1.51)
Industry R&D/assets			6.559	6.699
			(3.39)***	(3.46)***
Industry fixed assets/total assets			2.010 (3.12)***	1.208 (1.23)
Constant	1.856	1.855	2.071	2.024
	(1.41)	(4.99)***	(3.52)***	(5.09)***
Observations	28	26	47	38
χ^2	4.23	14.28	40.39	37.54

OTHER POSTINVESTMENT ACTIVITIES

In this section, I consider the role angels have in the success of the firm. Gorman and Sahlman (1989), Sahlman (1990), and Ehrlich and colleagues (1994) find that venture capitalists actively participate in their investments after funding.

Exhibit 5.12 (*Continued*)

Panel C: Amount of Help

	(1)	(2)	(3)
Number of angels	−0.003	−0.001	−0.001
	(0.12)	(0.03)	(0.05)
Geography	1.149	1.105	1.105
	(3.00)***	(2.85)***	(2.88)***
Log of funds		−0.021	−0.013
		(0.18)	(0.11)
Previous entrepreneur			−0.231
			(0.49)
Observations	97	96	96
Pseudo-R^2	0.03	0.03	0.03
χ^2	9.16	8.68	8.95

In addition to funding, angel investors may play an active role in professionalizing the firm or bringing a product to market, similar to some of the activities that venture capitalists provide (Hellmann and Puri 2002). Since many angels are former entrepreneurs or industry executives, many angels may derive some private benefits from assisting in the development of a new firm.

Building the management team is an important responsibility of the founders. In Exhibit 5.7, a complete management team leads to larger funding amounts. Hellmann and Puri (2002) find that venture capitalists help form the management team. In panel A of Exhibit 5.12, 23.5 percent of respondents said that angel investors assisted in identifying and recruiting members of the management team. Kaplan and Strömberg (2000) find that 50 percent of venture capitalists expect to replace the CEO or help recruit the management team. I find that angels tend to provide less assistance than venture capitalists in recruiting top management.

Angels can provide assistance in another important area, helping to locate and secure subsequent financing from venture capital. Gorman and Sahlman (1989) report that venture capitalists consider raising additional funds the most important activity. If angels are helpful in securing additional funding from venture capital, the time until venture funding should decrease as the number of angels increases because of a larger network of contacts. Panel B of Exhibit 5.12 presents hazard rate duration regressions on the time until venture capital financing, assuming that the hazard rate follows the Weibull distribution. There are 57 financing rounds where the subsequent round is financed by venture capital. I find that having more angel investors leads to a faster time to venture financing. This is evidence that angels can play a networking role; a larger number of angels leads to a larger network of contacts and faster venture capital financing. Ibrahim (2008) stresses the importance of angel finance as a precursor to venture capital, suggesting that angels agree to less complex contract terms to expedite future venture capital financing.

Panel C of Exhibit 5.12 presents results from ordered logit regressions where the dependent variable is the amount of help that angel investors provided the firm. The amount of help is a subjective response from the founders, so it is tainted by the usual problems with subjective responses. The variable is separated into five categories with the lowest category representing "little or no help" and the highest category corresponding to "a lot of beneficial help from angel investors." In all the regressions, geography is statistically significant at the 5 percent level. Angels who are in closer proximity tend to provide better assistance. Familiarity with issues confronting new ventures may require more interaction; therefore geographical proximity may encourage more assistance. Other variables do not appear to affect the degree of assistance.

CONCLUSION

This paper presents an examination of angel investing. Using a hand-collected dataset, I detail the characteristics of angel finance, from the implemented control mechanisms to the determinants of funding levels. I find that angels are not given the traditional control rights that venture capitalists typically use. Rather, one of the primary mechanisms to control agency costs is the alignment of the entrepreneur's interests with those of the firm through the large ownership positions. Additionally, angels make smaller investments and increase syndication when investing in the riskier ventures.

The results suggest a difference between venture capital investors and angel investors. The summary statistics show angels fund smaller amounts than venture capital. Firms that require larger amounts will seek venture capital investment, while angels may be preferred for small capital. Closer examination reveals that venture capitalists may not like to co-invest with angels. Angel investors appear to nurture younger firms until the company is established enough for venture capital consideration.

A puzzle still remains as to why angels provide capital in highly uncertain operations without much formal protection from expropriation. I suggest a geography-based explanation. Geographical proximity plays a large role in determining the funding amount, control, and degree of postinvestment assistance from angels. These results are similar to the networking effects for venture capital found by Sorenson and Stuart (2001), who find close geographic proximity increases the likelihood of funding and the ease of monitoring. Additionally, some support is found for the idea that investors may receive private benefits from investing. Other theories cannot be excluded. It is entirely possible that the returns from investing at early stages may be commensurate to the risk involved. Exhibit 5.9 shows first round investments receive a significantly higher equity claim, enhancing the possible return for early investors. To address this hypothesis, reliable estimates on private equity returns need to be obtained. As Cochrane (2005) shows, private equity returns are problematic to measure.

Another explanation may be that angels have specialized information and have a high ability to screen for higher quality projects. Many investors have made their fortunes in the same industries that they subsequently invest in. Industry knowledge is difficult to measure and examine since the identities of the investors need to be known. In such a confidential environment, the screening ability of angels would be difficult to examine.

In a larger scope, this paper provides an examination into direct versus intermediated financing. The results suggest traditional control rights and mechanisms may not be as important with direct financing.

NOTES

1. See Robinson (2008) for a detailed examination on strategic alliances.
2. Many people refer to angels as informal venture capital. Unless otherwise specified, I use the term *venture capital* to refer to institutional venture capital partnerships.
3. Venture Economics press release, January 2000, www.ventureeconomics.com.
4. Global Entrepreneurship Monitor, http://gemconsortium.org/files.aspx?Ca_ID=112.
5. *Forbes,* November 2, 1998, "200 Best Small Companies: Celestial cast of characters" and see Markova and Petkovska-Mircevska (2009).
6. Herringtown was a database of young start-up companies maintained by the publishers of Red Herring.
7. These include companies personally referred by angels.
8. A superconductor firm refused to give its geographical location for confidentiality purposes.
9. Angel Society, January 2001, and Preston (2003).
10. See Denis and Sarin (1999), Yermack (1996). or Gertner and Kaplan (1996) for evidence on public companies.
11. See Barry, Muscarella, Peavy, and Vetsuypens (1990); Lerner (1995); Baker and Gompers (2003); and Kaplan and Strömberg (2003) for evidence on board seats and board size in venture-backed firms.
12. Alternatively, venture capitalists may not want to co-invest with angels, thereby forcing angels aside. Evidence for this idea is provided in panel C of Exhibit 5.11. The number of angels is significantly lower in rounds with venture capital co-investment.
13. The increased syndication may lead to free-rider problems as well.

REFERENCES

Admati, A. R., and P. Pfleiderer. 1994. Robust financial contracting and the role of venture capitalists. *Journal of Finance* 49(2):371–402.

Baker, M., and P. Gompers. 2003. The determinants of board structure and function at the initial public offering. *Journal of Law and Economics* 46(2):569–598.

Barry, C. B., C. J. Muscarella, John W. Peavy III, and Michael R. Vetsuypens. 1990. The role of venture capital in the creation of public companies: Evidence from the going-public process. *Journal of Financial Economics* 27(2):447–472.

Becker-Blease, J. R., and J. Sohl. 2007. Do women-owned businesses have equal access to angel capital? *Journal of Business Venturing* 22(4):503–521.

Bergemann, D., and U. Hege. 1998. Venture capital financing, moral hazard, and learning. *Journal of Banking and Finance* 22(6–8):703–735.

Berger, A. N., and G. F. Udell. 1998. "The economics of small business finance: The roles of private equity and debt markets in the financial growth cycle." *Journal of Banking and Finance* 22(6–8):613–673.

Berglöf, E. 1994. A control theory of venture capital finance. *Journal of Law, Economics, and Organization* 10(2):247–267.

Bernhardt, D., and S. Krasa. 2005. "Informed Finance?" Department of Economics, University of Illinois, Champaign.

Casamatta, C. 2003. Financing and advising: Optimal financial contracts with venture capitalists. *Journal of Finance* 58(5):2059–2085.

Cochrane, J. H. 2005. The risk and return of venture capital. *Journal of Financial Economics* 75(1):3–52.

Cornelli, F., and O. Yosha. 2003. Stage financing and the role of convertible securities. *Review of Economic Studies* 70(1):1–32.

Cumming, D. J., and S. A. Johan. 2008. Preplanned exit strategies in venture capital. *European Economic Review* 52:1209–1241.

Denis, D. J., and A. Sarin. 1999. Ownership and board structures in publicly traded corporations. *Journal of Financial Economics* 52(2):187–223.

Ehrlich, S. B., A. F. De Noble, Tracy Moore, and Richard R. Weaver. 1994. After the cash arrives (A comparative study of venture capital and private investor involvement in entrepreneurial firms). *Journal of Business Venturing* 9(1):67–82.

Fama, E. F., and K. R. French. 1997. Industry costs of equity. *Journal of Financial Economics* 43(2):153–193.

Fama, E., and M. Jensen. 1983. Separation of ownership and control. *Journal of Law and Economics* 26(2):301–325.

Fenn, G. W., and N. Liang. 1998. "New resources and new ideas: Private equity for small businesses." *Journal of Banking and Finance* 22(6–8):1077–1084.

Freear, J., J. E., Sohl, and W. E., Wetzel, Jr. 1992. The Investment Attitudes, Behavior and Characteristics of High Net Worth Individuals. In N. C. Churchill, S. Birley, W. D. Bygrave, D. F. Muzyka, C. Wahlbin and W. E. Wetzel Jr. (eds.), *Frontiers of Entrepreneurship Research* (Wellesley, MA: Babson College), 374–383.

Freear, J., and W. E. Wetzel Jr. 1990. Who bankrolls high-tech entrepreneurs? *Journal of Business Venturing* 5:77–89.

Garmaise, M. 2000. Informed investors and the financing of entrepreneurial projects. University of Chicago Working Paper.

Gertner, R., and S. Kaplan. 1996. The value-maximizing board. University of Chicago Working Paper.

Goldfarb, B., G. Hoberg, D. Kirsch, and A. Triantis. 2008. Does angel participation matter? An analysis of early venture financing. Robert H. Smith School Research Paper No. RHS-06-072.

Gompers, P. A. 1995. Optimal investment, monitoring, and the staging of venture capital. *Journal of Finance* 50:1461–1489.

_____. 1997. An examination of convertible securities in venture capital. Harvard University Working Paper.

_____. 1998. Venture capital growing pains: Should the market diet? *Journal of Banking and Finance* 22(6–8):1089–1104.

_____, and J. Lerner. 1996. The use of covenants: An empirical analysis of venture partnership agreements. *Journal of Law and Economics* 39(2):463–498.

_____, and J. Lerner. 2001. The venture capital revolution. *Journal of Economic Perspectives* 15(2):145–168.

Gorman, M., and W. A. Sahlman. 1989. What do venture capitalists do? *Journal of Business Venturing* 4(4):231–248.

Hart, O., and J. Moore. 1994. A theory of debt based on the inalienability of human capital. *Quarterly Journal of Economics* 109(4):841–879.

Hellmann, T. 1998. The allocation of control rights in venture capital contracts. *RAND Journal of Economics* 29:1, 57–76.

Hellmann, T. 2006. IPOs, acquisitions and the use of convertible securities in venture capital. *Journal of Financial Economics* 81(3):649–679.

_____, and M. Puri, 2000. The interaction between product market and financing strategy: The role of venture capital. *Review of Financial Studies* 13(4):959–984.

_____, and M. Puri. 2002. Venture capitalists and the professionalization of start-up firms: Empirical evidence. *Journal of Finance* 57(1):169–197.

Ibrahim, D. M. 2008. The (not so) puzzling behavior of angel investors. *Vanderbilt Law Review* 61:405–1452.

Kaplan, S. N., and P. Strömberg. 2000. How do venture capitalists choose investments? *University of Chicago Working Paper.*

_____. 2003. Financial contracting theory meets the real world: An empirical analysis of venture capital contracts. *Review of Economic Studies* 70(2):281–315.

Kirilenko, A. A. 2001. Valuation and control in venture finance. *Journal of Finance* 56(2):567–587.

Lerner, J. 1994. The importance of patent scope: An empirical analysis. *RAND Journal of Economics* 25(2):319–333.

_____. 1995. Venture capitalists and the oversight of private firms. *Journal of Finance* 50(1):301–318.

_____. 1998. "Angel" financing and public policy: An overview. *Journal of Banking and Finance* 22(6–8):773–783.

Linde, L., and A. Prasad. 1999. Venture Support Systems Project: Angel Investors. MIT Entrepreneurship Center.

Markova, S., and T. Petkovska-Mircevska. 2009. "Financing Options for Entrepreneurial Ventures." *Amfiteatru Economic* 11(26):597–604.

Mason, C., and R. T. Harrison. 1990. Informal risk capital: a review and research agenda. *Venture Finance Research Project Working Paper No. 1* (University of Southampton and University of Ulster).

Mullahy, J. 1997. Instrumental-variable estimation of count data models: Applications to models of cigarette smoking behavior. *Review of Economics and Statistics* 79(4): 586–593.

Neher, D. V. 1999. Staged financing: An agency perspective. *Review of Economic Studies* 66(2):255–274.

Newey, W. K. 1987. Efficient estimation of limited dependent variable models with endogenous explanatory variables. *Journal of Econometrics* 36(3):231–250.

Preston, S. 2004. Angel investment groups: An introduction and analysis. Wisconsin Angel Investment Groups Presentation.

Prowse, S. 1998. Angel investors and the market for angel investments. *Journal of Banking & Finance* 22(6–8):785–792.

Repullo, R., and J. Suarez. 2004. Venture capital finance: a security design approach. *Review of Finance* 8(1):75–108.

Robinson, D. T. 2008. Strategic alliances and the boundary of the firm. *Review of Financial Studies* 21(2):649–681.

Sahlman, W. A. 1990. The structure and governance of venture-capital organizations. *Journal of Financial Economics* 27(2):473–521.

Shane, S. 2008. The importance of angel investing in financing the growth of entrepreneurial ventures. Small Business Administration Office of Advocacy Working Paper.

Sohl, J. E. 1999. The early stage equity market in the USA. *Venture Capital* 1(2):101–120.

_____, M. Van Osnabrugge, and R. Robinson. 2000. Models of angel investing: Portals to the early stage market. In P.D. Reynolds, E. Autio, C.G. Brush, W.D. Bygrave, S. Manigart, H.J. Sapienza and K.G. Shaver (eds.), *Frontiers of Entrepreneurship Research* (Wellesley, MA: Babson College), 289.

Sorenson, O., and T. Stuart. 2001. Syndication networks and the spatial distribution of venture capital investments. *American Journal of Sociology* 106(6):1546–1588.

Trester, J. J. 1998. Venture capital contracting under asymmetric information. *Journal of Banking & Finance* 22(6):675–699.

Van Osnabrugge, M., and R. J. Robinson. 2000. *Angel investing: Matching start-up funds with start-up companies.* San Francisco: Jossey-Bass.

Wetzel, W. E. 1983. Angels and informal risk capital. *Sloan Management Review* 24(4):23–34.

White, H. 1980. A heteroskedasticity-consistent covariance matrix estimator and a direct test for heteroskedasticity. *Econometrica* 48(4):817–838.

Wiltbank, R., and W. Boeker. 2007. Returns to angel investors in groups. Ewing Marion Kauffman Foundation research paper series.

Yermack, D. 1996. Higher market valuations of companies with a small board of directors. *Journal of Financial Economics* 40(2):185–211.

ABOUT THE AUTHOR

Andy Wong received his MBA and Ph.D. in Finance from the Booth School of Business at the University of Chicago. He is currently a managing principal at Analysis Group. A specialist in corporate finance, venture capital, securities, and company valuation, Dr. Wong has managed case teams supporting multiple experts in areas involving securities fraud, accounting, and financial statement analyses.

This work is largely based on a chapter from Dr. Wong's doctoral dissertation at the University of Chicago. Since his original work in 2002, other authors have expanded the frontiers of angel investing research. Dr. Wong has supplemented his results with their findings where appropriate. This document has benefitted from comments and conversations with Qi Chen, Mark Garmaise, Steve Kaplan, Raghu Rajan, Christopher Malloy, Arek Ohanissian, David T. Robinson, Jeff Sohl, Per Strömberg, Bill Wetzel, and Brian Wong. Dr. Wong also thanks seminar participants at the University of Chicago Corporate Finance Brown Bag Workshop, Columbia University, Indiana University, the University of Oklahoma, the University of Oregon, the Federal Reserve Board of Governors, and Ohio State University. Input, comments, and guidance from Julian Chan, Jeff Cohn, Ron Conway, James Geshwiler, Bijoy Goswami, Mark Harrington, Andrew Hoyne, Ray Hurcombe, Cary Nourie, Phil Polishook, Roliff Purrington, John Van Dyke, Pete Viti, the Texas Angel Investors, and countless other angels and entrepreneurs have contributed tremendously. This version would not have been possible without the exceptional research assistance and diligence of Mihir Bhatia and Zachary Freeman.

CHAPTER 6

Business Incubation and Its Connection to Venture Capital

DAREK KLONOWSKI
Professor, Brandon University

INTRODUCTION

Small and medium-sized (SME) enterprises play a key role in shaping any local economy. They are a source of growth and innovation in the industry for owners and provide jobs for the local population. SMEs are believed to offset economic declines and help restructure existing industry. A healthy SME sector is critical to any local economy and imperative to economic growth for several reasons. Firstly, it is estimated that 6 out of every 10 jobs are created by the SME sector. Secondly, SMEs are spearheading the industrial transformation from traditional industries into the high technology sector. Thirdly, SMEs are at the forefront of developing innovations with a clear competitive advantage. Lastly, these firms are making significant inroads in developing global markets.

For firms from the SME sector in many countries, pursuing technological innovation is a viable alternative. Not only is technological innovation important for the prosperity of individual private firms, it is also one of the fundamental contributors to a nation's economic growth. Many countries' economic growth and prosperity depend on how effective local firms are in commercializing new technologies and innovations, and converting firms from the SME sector into viable business ventures with a sustainable competitive advantage. The role of science and technology in fostering economic growth has received increased attention from economists and policy makers in recent years—technological change and innovation is widely recognized as a key driver of economic development.

The development of a successful and flourishing SME sector faces two major problems. The first concerns access to finance. Access to finance is one of the major problems firms from the SME sector face and poses a particular constraint on these firms' ability to increase the level of technology in their enterprises. The constraint comes from both equity and debt markets. In terms of equity markets, the existing venture capital firms are growing in size and, consequently, aim to employ capital in larger increments in order to improve deal economics. As a result, they are increasingly uninterested in pursuing smaller transactions. This phenomenon has been termed "the liquidity gap." The capital constraint is most pronounced for small firms, which require small investments, are at early stages of development, are technology-oriented, and have suboptimal geographic locations. Evidence from Western countries suggests that the liquidity gap is most pronounced in the range of $100,000 to $2,000,000. In terms of debt provision (i.e., commercial banking), private entrepreneurial firms are not attractive candidates for financing from the banking sector. Banks are generally unwilling to finance smaller, private firms if they lack a track record, appropriate collateral, or have an insufficient credit rating. These constraints result in a sizeable pool of entrepreneurial projects being precluded from possible debt financing.

The second problem concerns access to know-how. Newly created enterprises with entrepreneurs inexperienced in a commercial environment may suffer from shortcomings in their managerial skills and abilities. Young entrepreneurial firms struggle in running their businesses. Many firms, even with sizeable levels of sales and operations, do not employ functional specialists (especially in the areas of finance and accounting) and, consequently, rarely prepare business plans or formal budgets. Another functional department often neglected by entrepreneurs is marketing and promotion. Additionally, there are two fundamental areas where know-how assistance is required. First, in the early stages, beginner enterprises are often "virtual" in their development; there is only an idea, concept, or invention driving the ultimate development of a full business. The key problem to address is business survival. Second, enterprises in the small-sized stages of development require different assistance. The key issue for these enterprises is management of growth. The aim is to ensure sustainability in the long term and the successful transition to another stage of development.

The problems of access to finance and the provision of know-how are closely related, since access to finance may be necessary for addressing some of the operational challenges, and effective managerial skills assure proper utilization of capital. Providing capital without managerial assistance is likely to translate into developmental stagnation for firms (a lack of know-how often leads to limited investment, which, in turn, leads to limited employment growth), as well as a greater sensitivity to external factors and business potential that is unlikely to be captured. Providing know-how without finance is likely to lead to an immediate downfall of a young entrepreneurial firm, a freeze of private initiative, and a lack of propensity for taking business risk. In both circumstances, the unintended consequences of these two challenges are the possible chain reaction for business failure in other firms.

These problems may be addressed with the introduction of business incubators, which can resolve the dual problem of inadequate know-how and access to finance. Business incubators offer funding, technical support, and networking capabilities and have become central to the development of early-stage firms around the world.

The objective of this paper is to provide an overview of recent developments in business incubation. The paper is organized in the following manner. The first section describes the concept of business incubation and different types of business incubators. This section also summarizes some of the existing research on the effectiveness of business incubators. The second section outlines the mechanics of a business incubator, while the third section outlines the international setting for business incubators by discussing national associations in the most active geographic regions, namely North America (i.e., the United States) and Europe.

The last section describes the evolving relationship between business incubators and venture capital. The paper is based on desk research of secondary data and the author's direct professional experience in venture capital financing and business incubation activities.

BUSINESS INCUBATION

Concept Overview

The definition of business incubation has evolved in recent years to reflect the specific institutional, regional, and technological economic conditions of a specific country, but it generally denotes targeted programs developed to accelerate the development of entrepreneurial firms through a wide range of businesses support services. Business incubators are places where low-cost, real estate–based facilities are provided to nurture the development of new firms. Business incubators provide the temporary use of shared premises, capital equipment, business and technical services, and access to finance (through networking with venture capital firms, business angels, and other financiers) through an active and dynamic development process that occurs between the start-up firm and the business incubator (Phan, Siegel, and Wright 2005; Aernoudt 2004; Lalkaka and Abetti 1999). These facilities are provided at below-market rates and on flexible terms with the aim of reducing business start-up costs. The main objective of business incubation is to provide incentives for business start-ups and to support already existing businesses in the development of new and innovative products and services, helping them to survive their most vulnerable stage of development and dramatically lower early-stage failure rates (Callegati, Grandi, and Napier 2005; Hansen et al. 2000). It is important to note here that business incubators differ from research and technology parks in their approach to young entrepreneurial firms. Research and technology parks tend to be large-scale projects that house a variety of firms ranging from corporate, government, and university laboratories to small firms. Most research and technology parks do not offer business assistance services, which are the cornerstone of business incubation programs.

The concept of modern business incubation was initially developed in Europe and rooted deeply in medical science. In ancient times, the practice of sacrificing animals for the purpose of obtaining a vision, enlightenment, and sometimes overcoming disease was termed *incubatio*. Later, the term was used to provide temporary assistance to prematurely born infants requiring controlled conditions and technical assistance. The development of the incubation concept in our more recent era has revolved around revitalizing declining manufacturing regions in the United States during the 1950s by providing entrepreneurs with the necessary resources to develop new ventures (thus enabling them to become instruments for promoting a more diversified industrial base for a regional economy and stimulating local job creation). During the late 1970s, business incubators became methods of improving regional and national competitiveness by promoting the development of innovative and technology-oriented firms. In the 1980s, business incubators shifted to linking the incubator concept with academic institutions and publically funded research institutes. In the 1990s, there was a trend to develop business incubators around specific industrial and technological clusters such as biotechnology, information technologies, and environmental technologies.

Business incubation has become a permanent component of national small enterprise strategies in many countries around the world. Centers of entrepreneurial development see business incubators as a vehicle for economic growth and meeting social-economic needs. Some of these developmental goals may include creating jobs, fostering a community's entrepreneurial climate, inspiring the commercialization of technology, diversifying local economies, encouraging women or minority entrepreneurship, identifying potential spin-in or spin-out business opportunities, and so on. Economic development planners are known to help revitalize economic development at military bases that are closing and in rural communities in distress.

There is no precise international data on the development of business incubators around the world, as academic studies focus on regional or national developments in this area. It is estimated that there are about 5,000 business incubators worldwide, of which 1,000 are located in North America (100 in Canada; 900 in the United States) and 850 are located in Western Europe. About 800 business incubators are estimated to exist in developing countries.

Typology of Business Incubators

Academic researchers in the area of business incubation have not been able to agree on one consistent method of classifying business incubators. The classification of business incubators has evolved over time to reflect the existing financial and human resources, business culture and environment, and social agenda (O'Neal 2005; Clarysse et al. 2005). In the last two decades, academic researchers have proposed classifications ranging from basic to more complex. In the early 1980s, initial studies limited classification of business incubators with respect to the source of financing into private and public. The late 1980s saw the emergence of numerous academic studies of business incubation, and, consequently, the definitions and classifications have expanded. New typologies of business incubation emerged, defined in basic terms as business incubation clusters with respect to location (rural versus urban), social agenda and objectives (not-for-profit versus for-profit), lead sponsors (corporate versus public), the type of firm accepted into the incubator (i.e., all firms accepted, industrial or manufacturing focus only, technology orientation only), and the type of tenants (i.e., resident versus virtual). The 1990s saw an emergence of new research into the incubation process centering on the type of service provided to the tenant firm. Consequently, researchers defined business incubators not as different clusters of focus, but along the spectrum of the value-added service provided by the business incubator (i.e., from low value-added to high value-added). The 1990s also saw a rapid expansion of the incubation phenomenon beyond the United States and Europe into emerging markets. These newly developed markets have modified the business incubation concept to fit into their social and economic realities. Emerging markets have arguably seen the most advanced and sophisticated types of business incubators when compared to some of the more traditional brick-and-mortar (i.e., real estate–based) incubators established in the United States and Europe. As a result, new concepts such as "scholar parks," "knowledge management centers," and "entrepreneurial networks" emerged. The new millennium saw the emergence of technology parks and dot.com incubators. Two other types of business incubators also emerged. The first were "international enterprise centers," often referred to as "third generation" business incubation systems, which provide a full range of services for the development of knowledge-based businesses with established links to academic centers, research facilities and institutions, venture capital, corporate businesses, and international partners. Secondly, "networked incubators" were developed on the basis that the most important part of any newly created firm is its business contacts. These incubators primarily focus on establishing relationships with existing large businesses (Bollingtoft and Ulhoi 2005; Hansen et al. 2000).

With high growth and increasing diversity in the nature of incubators in developed and developing markets, the objective of this paper is to describe the most common types of business incubators and their characteristics. Exhibit 6.1 presents the simplified landscape of the main types of business incubators. The key criteria selected for mapping the business incubation spectrum were profit orientation (for-profit, not-for-profit) and the operational model (virtual, brick-and-mortar, full service—these operational models will be described in detail below in the operational overview). The oval around each type of business incubator represents the breadth of the business services provided and the source of financing.

Exhibit 6.2 provides a brief summary of key characteristics of different types of business incubators. The following section provides a brief description.

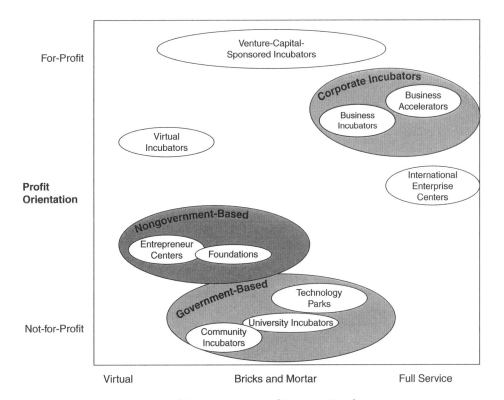

Exhibit 6.1   The Landscape of the Major Types of Business Incubators

Exhibit 6.2   Typology of Business Incubators

Type	Objective	Sectoral Focus	Services Provided	Financial Orientation	Lead Sponsor
University incubators	Research	Sciences	Brick-and-mortar	Nonprofit	Public
Corporate incubators	New product development	All	Full-service	For-profit	Private
Community incubators	Job creation	All	Limited	Nonprofit	Public
Technology parks	Product development	Sciences	Various	Nonprofit	Public
Entrepreneur centers	"Know-how" assistance	All	Various	Nonprofit	Public
Foundations	"Know-how" assistance	All	Limited	Nonprofit	Public/private
Virtual incubators	"Know-how" assistance	All	Limited	Nonprofit	Public
International enterprise centers	Business development	All	Full	For-profit/non-profit	Public/private
Venture capital-sponsored	Business development	Sciences	Full	For profit	Private
Business accelerators	Business development	All	Limited	For-profit/nonprofit	Public/private

University Incubators: Academic entrepreneurship is a growing phenomenon. University-based incubators, housed in university campuses and generally connected with science faculties (i.e., medicine, engineering, biotechnology, computer science), are focused on promoting the development of new research and enhancing universities' research agendas. These are operated as faculty divisions or as separate entities under the faculty's jurisdiction. These incubators provide tenant firms with well-equipped and staffed laboratories, extensive research libraries, powerful computer systems, and the support of faculty members. The incubators provide standard business support services, including business plan preparation and planning and managerial assistance. The key role of this type of incubator relates to linking research, technology, know-how, and capital. Tenant firms are typically founded by one or more scientists who participate in academic research. It is estimated that out of the total number of 5,000 business incubators around the world, approximately 1,500 are university-related. Researchers argue that their socioeconomic impact on the community is very significant due to their symbiotic networking of entrepreneurs, students, university faculty members, and the business community.

Corporate Incubators: The growth of corporate incubation has been a relatively recent phenomenon, as corporations have realized that their intellectual assets may become a source of increasing profits and growing shareholder value. Corporate incubation is based on a cooperative relationship between the parent corporation, corporate incubator, and the technology venture where physical, knowledge-based, and intangible resources can be bridged. These incubators are generally established by larger corporations and aimed at leveraging and disseminating intellectual capital within the corporation (consequently reducing the acquisitions of entrepreneurial firms at premium-priced valuations). These incubators either establish new ventures on the basis of their own teams of professionals or admit independent tenants under their corporate umbrella. In the second case, the corporations make gains through service fees or an equity stake in the new venture.

International Enterprise Centers: These structures, often called "third generation incubators," offer the most sophisticated range of services, including links between universities, research institutes, and international joint ventures. These intense support programs are effectively paid for by sharing in the success of tenant firms by taking equity stakes, royalty payments, or brokerage, or by underwriting fees on arranged capital. The majority of them provide in-house debt or equity capital and have strong channels with external providers of finance. Many of these structures focus on export activities and are related to other industrial incubators. They are very popular in emerging markets.

OPERATIONAL OVERVIEW OF BUSINESS INCUBATORS

In many countries, business incubation programs are sponsored by regional or national government institutions as a part of their overall economic development strategy. In other countries, incubation programs are independent, community-based, and resourced projects where national or local economic development offices finance the initial start-up phase.

Defining the operational model establishes the structure and parameters of the business incubator. The operational and structural model of the business incubator defines the structure of the incubator, the scope of the service offered, and the available financing options. Current academic research suggests three basic models of operations for the business incubator. First, there is a virtual operational model where the incubator does not provide premises for the incubated firms. Instead, support and services are offered from a central office via telephone, television, and the Internet, allowing newly created firms in different geographic locations to access the business support service. While some virtual incubators offer an address and mailbox, others offer a wide array of services, including hands-on management assistance, access to financing, and orchestrated exposure to other businesses. Most offer shared office services such as reception, answering service, and web page maintenance. Financing is sometimes available through this type of business support structure. Secondly, there is the common operational approach of providing brick-and-mortar (BAM) physical facilities to tenant firms. The entire process of developing a business is concentrated in a building. An advantage of this model is the interaction, the formation of partnerships between tenant businesses, and the resolution of common problems by resident entrepreneurs. Support services are generally few, and financial assistance is limited. Third, there are business incubators that offer a wide range of services, including know-how assistance and financing availability.

The Process

The business incubator and the entrepreneurial firm enter into a business arrangement for a period ranging from one to three years. The business incubation process can be divided into five distinct phases of cooperation: initial consultation, tenancy application submission, screening and decision, business development, and exit (see Exhibit 6.3).

Initial Consultation: The process of cooperation between the business incubators and the entrepreneurial firms begins with the initial consultation. For the business incubator, the objective of the initial meeting is to ascertain whether the potential tenant is able to meet the entry criteria of the incubator and its own potential to assist the firm. The incubator's management also aims to provide an overview of its application process and the range of services offered. For the entrepreneurial firm, the objective is to test the potential fit between the firm's requirements and the offered services, to meet other tenant firms, and to understand whether the incubator can provide suitable facilities, production, and otherwise. An initial decision to cooperate is made at this juncture.

Tenancy Application Submission: Unlike many business assistance programs developed by local and national government institutions, business incubators do not serve all entrepreneurial firms. Entrepreneurs who wish to enter a business incubator must apply for admission. Acceptance criteria vary from program to

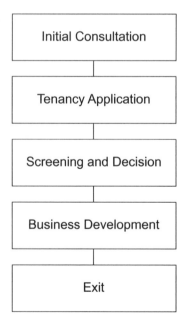

Exhibit 6.3 The Steps in Business Incubation

program, but in general only those with feasible business ideas are admitted to the incubator. The most important business arrangement for the two parties is to define ultimate goals of cooperation and the exit parameters and criteria (some business incubators define exit goals strictly in terms of tenancy, a period of one to three years).

Screening and Decision: The prepared application is screened by the incubator's selection committee. Some business incubators have low entry requirements. Consequently, tenant firms provide the business incubator with basic information on the business concept and some supportive information on the founding entrepreneurs. The application forms range from one to five pages in length. These incubators assume that young entrepreneurial firms are unlikely to prepare a comprehensive business plan on their own and see the business plan as an evolutionary process. Only after being admitted to the incubator can the tenant firm begin to develop a preliminary concept description and a budget, to be later converted into a more professional business plan. Once the business plan is created, the decision is made whether to pursue the project further.

Other business incubators operate in a different manner. Their entry requirements are high. They have an application form, which ranges from 15 to 25 pages in length. Some of the expectations may be that the entrepreneurial firms have a product suitable for production; a professionally prepared and comprehensive business plan, including a full set of financial projections for a period of at least two years (the incubator may agree to pay for the plan or co-share the development costs of the business plan); adequate financial resources for working capital to produce and distribute products, as well as to pay rent, wages, supplies and overhead; and a comprehensive plan to hire professional management and develop the business skills of employees.

It takes between one to three months for the business incubator to make a final decision on admitting a new candidate firm.

Business Development: Once entrepreneurial firms are accepted into the incubators, they obtain the advantages of developmental programs structured to the needs of each individual firm. It is the general expectation of the business incubator that the entrepreneurial firm validate production parameters and establish production facilities, establish a sustainable market presence, develop distribution channels, and secure financial resources for future growth and development. It is also expected that the firm establish a strong advisory board. A mentor (project manager) is generally assigned to work with the business. Professional staff working at the incubator work with the firm to help complete its defined activities and tracks progress.

Exit: The objective of the business incubator is to mentor and assist entrepreneurial firms in the development and commercialization of new products and technologies, leading to the successful establishment of a viable business. Many business incubators expect to graduate one to five tenants every year upon the successful completion of the program.

If the financial resources are made available to the tenant firm (these, on average, range from $15,000 to $500,000) to cover the preparation of the business plan and operational costs, the tenant firm agrees to reimburse these costs at the point of exit. If repayment is not possible, the provided capital is converted into a loan (generally at below-market rates and preferential repayment terms) or equity (generally at the valuation accepted in the first round of subsequent financing of the tenant firm).

The Determinants of Successful Business Incubation

While numerous academic studies (see O'Neal 2005; Hansen et al. 2000; Mian 1994; Lichtenstein 1992; Smilor 1987; Allen and Bazan 1990) have attempted to focus on the determinants of a successful business incubator, no final consensus has been reached by academics with respect to identifying the successful factors of business incubation. Academic research has focused on two main aspects of the incubation process: the tenant firm and the incubator (Phan et al. 2005). Studies (Hansen et al. 2000; Lichtenstein 1992; Weinberg 1987) have focused on the characteristics of tenant firms and the incubation programs and services they provided (i.e., range of services, quality of managerial assistance). These studies highlighted the importance of networked relationships. Other studies (O'Neal 2005; Allen and Bazan, 1990) have focused on the operational aspects of incubators. These studies focused on entry criteria, tenancy timing, and the types of businesses admitted into the incubation program. Studies by Lalkaka and Schafer (1998), Bearse (1998), Sherman and Chapel (1998) and Tornatsky and colleagues (1996) have discussed the evaluation matrix applied to measuring the success of business incubators. These related to job creation, the number of clients served, and the number of successful exits from the program.

In essence, however, three basic aspects of business incubator performance seem to ultimately translate into success for tenant firms: services, a network of contacts, and availability of financing. For the incubator to be successful, the services offered must be adequate to the geographic area of its activity and to the development stage of the entrepreneurial firms it aims to support. A key aspect of this success is the quality of the network of firms and people connected with the incubator. For example, traditional brick-and-mortar incubators limit their network of contacts to tenant firms in the incubator, while networked incubators rely on their network for the firm's survival and ultimate success. In addition to the services and this network of relationships, availability of financing at appropriate stages of the tenant firm's development may reduce business risk and shorten the incubation period.

INTERNATIONAL PERSPECTIVES ON BUSINESS INCUBATION

There are no representative global studies pertaining to business incubation. The most advanced empirical studies have been initiated by Lalkaka (2003) and Lalkaka (2002). Other empirical studies (Clarysse et al. 2005; Aernoudt 2004; Allen and Bazan 1990; Smilor 1987) have predominantly taken national or regional approaches, while case studies have attempted to discuss the operational aspects of business incubation in a specific type of business incubator or setting. The lack of depth may be due to at least two factors. First, government policies in different countries with respect to entrepreneurship and the SME sector are not homogenous. This makes it virtually impossible to capture the essence of these programs on a comparative basis. Second, researchers (for example, see Lalkaka 2002 and Weinberg 1987) have outlined the different sensitivities of business incubators to different socioeconomic conditions.

The geographic allocation of business incubation activity is presented in Exhibit 6.4. Academic studies, international and local associations, and government institutions estimate that there are about 5,000 business incubators in the world, of which about 1,000 are located in North America (approximately 900 in the United States; 100 in Canada), 1,000 in Asia, 850 in Europe, and 400 in Latin America (Aernoudt 2004; Lalkaka 2003; Lalkaka 2002). Of these, approximately 500 could be classified as technology parks, and 300 could be classified as for-profit incubators. There are about 60 national or regional business incubation associations. The most experienced geographic regions in terms of assistance to entrepreneurial firms are located in North America and Asia. The European region is regarded by academics as a laggard in the areas of business incubation and SME support systems. The European Union has recently begun to focus on research, development, and innovation due to its perceived lack of competitiveness when compared to other regions (Aernoudt 2004).

Numerous academic studies have assessed country-specific initiatives and provided exhaustive descriptions of them. The objective, therefore, would be to provide an overview of the leading business incubation associations in Europe and in North American (i.e., the United States) and their most innovative programs rather than to discuss country-specific approaches to incubators, which have been described in numerous academic studies. An understanding of these national organizations is critical to setting the tone of development and coordinating the activities of business incubators in each country. Strong national organizations result in effective local business incubators.

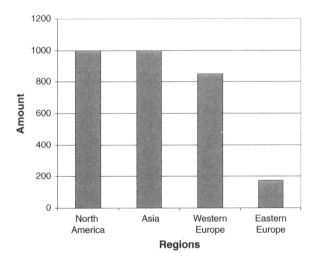

Exhibit 6.4   Business Incubation around the World

North America (the United States)

One of the leading and perhaps best known business incubation organizations in the world is the U.S.-based National Business Incubation Association (NBIA). NBIA aims to provide individuals, business owners, and academic centers with information, education, advocacy, and networking resources. Its mission is also to provide specialized training to help business assistance professionals create and administer effective business incubation programs. Its staff is comprised of business incubator developers and managers, technology commercialization specialists, educators, and business assistance professionals. The organization prides itself on being a research center on business incubation in the United States and as such has one of the most comprehensive databases on the subject.

NBIA estimates that there are 900 business incubators in the United States, 40 percent of which have in-house financing programs or investment funds. On average, 25 percent of business incubators take an equity stake in their tenant firms; this number is larger (i.e., 75 percent) for incubators focusing on technology. According to NBIA, its associated incubation programs have assisted more than 27,000 entrepreneurial firms employing more than 100,000 people. The combined generated revenues for these businesses were around $17 billion. NBIA also claims that the tenant firms have a 90 percent survival rate.

The most successful business incubators in the United States are sector-specific, corporately sponsored, or university affiliated (Lalkaka 2002). Business incubators are developed in geographic clusters where collective efforts in capital raising and sustainable competitiveness are possible (the most well known cluster being Silicon Valley).

Europe

The goals of most business incubators in Europe differ from country to country, reflecting the level of development of the SME sector, the level of political support to the SME sector, and the aspirations of the business community. In Germany, for example, the main objective was to focus on economic development; in Belgium, Spain, and Italy, the existing programs aimed to provide incentives for larger multinational firms to enter their markets. In the United Kingdom, the Netherlands and France, the academic, university-based model of business incubation prevailed. Due to such a diverse nature of business incubation, it is difficult to construct a standardized model of business incubation across Europe. In spite of this diversity, Aernoudt (2004) attempted to provide a simplistic typology of European business incubators based on an Anglo-Saxon incubation model (based on profit orientation, strong networking to the industry, and prompt, commercial innovation) and a Germanic model (based on a wide network of nonprofit innovation centers aimed at stimulating regional economic development, job creation, and the transfer of technology).

The leading business incubation organization in Europe is the European Business Network (EBN), which, along with other, similar centers, was established following a series of reports prepared by the European Union outlining Europe's stagnation within the areas of research, development, and innovation. EBN, founded in 1984 by the European Commission, is a nonprofit organization based in Brussels that offers a wide range of services to member incubators (or Business Incubator Centers, also known as BICs). EBN has approximately 150 full members and 70 associate members in 21 countries across Europe. BICs are nonprofit and for-profit organizations mandated to provide consultancy and managerial services, initiate and navigate technology transfers, and educate firms from the SME sector. EBN also networks other similar organizations such as centers for innovation and entrepreneurship. EBN offers a formalized way to organize and coordinate business incubation activities across different regions in Europe. The organization continually stimulates the development of its incubation network through developing new initiatives and programs and involving the member incubators to participate in these initiatives.

In terms of innovative programming, EBN has been able to develop a number of programs recognizing the migratory nature of firms in the SME sector in Europe. For example, the DELOC program has been developed to address the problem of delocalization within the SME firms. The ECON IT program was developed to better coordinate available business advisors and mentors for the development of the SME sector. VIPIA is a preincubation program aimed at assisting entrepreneurs in refining their business concepts for further development through venture capital or angel financing.

While it has not been an objective of this paper to provide a detailed description of specific business incubators around the world, Exhibit 6.5 presents a sample of business incubators in specific countries. These incubators are described in terms of key characteristics. Additionally, web pages are provided.

BUSINESS INCUBATION AND VENTURE CAPITAL

Business incubation activity and venture capital investing have many common characteristics. First, business incubators and venture capitalists share a common interest in successfully growing young entrepreneurial firms. Business incubators are regarded as valuable tools for assisting firms from the SME sector, while venture capital is often regarded as a "business of building businesses." Both instruments are characterized by providing entrepreneurial firms with hands-on assistance. Second, incubators and venture capitalists want to see measurable business success at the end of their relationship with an entrepreneurial firm. In the case of business incubators, success is described as a graduation of a tenant firm from the business incubator to a viable, long-term business. For venture capitalists, success is financial in nature and measured in cash-on-cash or an internal rate of return. Third, the process for entrepreneurial firms to enter the business incubator or receive financing from venture capital is, broadly speaking, the same. Both processes are multistage, even though the one used by venture capitalists may be regarded as more comprehensive and exhaustive. Tyebjee and Bruno (1985) proposed a five-stage model of venture capital investing (i.e., deal generation, screening, evaluation, deal structuring, postinvestment activities), while Fried and Hisrich (1994) proposed a six-stage model (i.e., origination, venture capitalist firm's specific screen, generic screen, first-phase evaluation, second-phase evaluation, closing). The business incubation model may be described as a shorter, five-stage model (described earlier). Fourth, venture capitalists can be a source of assistance to business development, which

Exhibit 6.5 A Sample of Business Incubators around the World

City (Country)	Name (Abbreviated Name) (Sponsor, Profit Orientation)	Number of Firms Incubated at Present*	Networking Potential (L/M/H)	Financing Availability (L/M/H)	Value-Added Services	Web Page Address
London (UK)	Harrow in Business (HIB) (public, not-for-profit)	5	M	N/A	• Property • Advice	harrowinbusiness.com
London (UK)	London Bio-Science Innovation Centre (LBIC) (public, not-for-profit)	23	M	L	• Laboratories • Property • Advice	londonlifesciences.com
Scranton (USA)	Scranton Business Incubator (public, not-for-profit)	15	M	L	• Property • Advice	scrantonenterprisecenter.com
Seattle (USA)	Accelerator Corporation (private, for-profit)	4	H	H	• Property • Advice	acceleratorcorp.com/
Leduc (Canada)	Agrivalue Processing Business Incubator (APBI) (public, not-for-profit)	4	L	N/A	• Laboratories • Property • Advice	agric.gov.ab.ca
Toronto (Canada)	Medical and Related Sciences Incubator (MaRS) (public/private, not-for-profit)	17	M	L	• Property • Advice	marsdd.com
Markham (Canada)	Innovation Synergy Center in Markham (ISCM) (public, not-for-profit)	0	L	N/A	• Virtual • Advice	iscm.ca

Please note that for assessing the networking potential and finance provision capabilities of the selected business incubators, qualitative measures are applied:
L—Low, M—Medium, and H—High.
*This information was gathered in December 2008.

can be perceived as complementary to the services offered by business incubators. This relationship appears to be symbiotic, as venture capitalists seek access to attractive deal flow, and the tenants of business incubators need capital for business survival and growth.

In spite of these similarities and potential synergies between business incubation and venture capital, limited academic research exists that explores this topic; hence, this section of the paper draws heavily from nonacademic literature. Academic studies aimed at understanding venture capital activities in the context of business incubation by Callegati, Grandi, and Napier (2005), Gullander and Napier (2003), and Bearse (1998) reported the problems of venture capitalists when working with business incubators. In fact, access to venture capital is regarded as one of the major challenges faced by business incubators (Callegati, Grandi, and Napier 2005). Venture capitalists appear less interested in nurturing this potentially beneficial relationship. This may be due to lower general interest in early-stage firms (and the perceived risk associated with them), limited knowledge of the business incubation process, and a perception of low value.

Over the years, the relationship between business incubators and venture capital has evolved quite profoundly. In the early years (prior to 1998), venture capitalists' exposure to business incubation was virtually nonexistent. Venture capitalists sought exposure to the start-up and early-stage sector through direct investment in early-stage firms rather than through some indirect means (i.e., business incubation, advisory service). Venture capitalists' exposure to early-stage investing was relatively stable prior to 1998; the investment in early-stage entrepreneurial firms as a percentage of total investment was at around 22 percent in the United States and 12 percent Europe. The venture capital firms committed around $9 billion to early-stage entrepreneurial firms on an annual basis.

The period from 1998 to 2001 (the so-called Internet bubble) has permanently redefined the relationship between venture capitalists, early-stage firms, and business incubators (Valliere and Peterson 2004). In the United States, for example, the number of venture capital firms increased from 288 in 1998 (with $31.1 billion under management) to 635 firms in 2000 (with $107.7 billion under management). During this time period, the proportion of capital dedicated to early-stage firms increased from 41 percent in 1998 to 62 percent in 2000. The total investment in the sector increased from $29 billion to $118 billion over the same time period. While no official data exists on the subject, it is estimated that approximately 25 percent of such a commitment came in the form of indirect venture capitalist investment in business incubators. Fueled by some of the early commercial success stories of firms such as Amazon, Yahoo, and VeriSign, early-stage firms (especially from the dot.com sector) saw substantial increases to their business valuation, and there was an unprecedented number of IPOs from the early-stage sector. To increase their exposure to the early-stage entrepreneurial firms' sector, venture capitalists placed their capital in untested entrepreneurial firms either directly or through business incubators (Henricks 2006).

The rationale for venture capitalists to be involved in business incubation was threefold. First, most venture capitalists perceived business incubation as a way to locate new technologies in early stages of development in order to improve overall deal flow. Venture capitalists instinctively realized that access to a strong and more focused deal flow of early-stage firms was likely to translate to more potential success stories (Sheahan 2005a). Second, venture capitalists believed that their involvement in the early stages of an entrepreneurial firm's development would validate the underlying business model or concept for the entrepreneurial firm (Christopher 2001). By working with a larger cluster of early-stage firms (perhaps from the same industry), venture capitalists were better able to monitor their financial and operational performance. Venture capitalists expected that such collaboration was likely to translate to a reduction of problem cases and write-offs. Third and most importantly, business incubation offered large venture capital firms their only chance of exposure to an important asset class (i.e., early-stage firms). Venture capital firms were growing in size and had less appetite to complete smaller transactions due to deal economics. In 2001, the Internet bubble burst. As a consequence, the venture capital community (as well as other investors) has seen a significant increase in the rate of business failure among their investee firms, a sharp decrease in the value of their portfolios, and a decrease in their chances of raising additional capital from limited partners.

In the aftermath of the burst of the Internet bubble, venture capitalists changed their approach to involvement in early-stage firms. This was manifested in reducing the amount of capital invested in early-stage firms and in limiting capital exposure to traditional business incubation. While the bursting of the Internet bubble continues to play a major, negative role in venture capitalists' perception of business incubation, they began to revisit the concept of business incubation in the mid 2000s, spurred by sporadic acquisitions of early-stage firms by large, multi-national conglomerates at premium valuations (for example, NewsCorp acquired Myspace.com; eBay acquired Skype). The venture capitalists' interests primarily centered on information technologies, telecommunications (3G, wireless), and medical sciences (new drug development, treatments). Venture capitalist interest in the area of information technology, for example, is spurred by a new generation of software applications based on open standards and application programming interfaces, new web service opportunities, and identity management. Nonacademic literature reports a number of initiatives pertaining to venture capitalist involvement in business incubation (Hibbard and Green 2006; Goldfisher 2006; Sheahan 2005b). Some venture capitalists are currently interested in pursuing two basic models of participation in business incubation: the multiple-venture capital partnership model and the university model. While there is no data or academic studies to confirm the extent of these activities, the scale appears small. It is also still too early to confirm whether these efforts will be successful. It is clear, however, that venture capital firms are likely to benefit from a larger pool of entrepreneurial firms in attractive market sectors. The following section will touch briefly on these two approaches.

One model of collaboration emerging between business incubators and venture capitalists is an incubator financed by multiple venture capital firms. Some incubators do not have a fund of their own, but rely on an exclusive relationship with venture capital firms to cover some of the operational expenses and take equity stakes in the tenant firms. The most popular approach involves the cooperation of three venture capital firms in funding one incubator (Sheahan 2005a). This allows for a diversity of opinions while not complicating the investment decision-making process. A slight variation of this model sees the involvement of an industry partner in this arrangement that assumes some of the market-oriented activities of the tenant firms. The most significant risk lies with venture capital firms that selectively take equity stakes in the tenant firms.

Venture capitalists have also structured deals with business incubators operated by universities. The attractiveness of university-based incubators relates to universities being on the cutting edge of technology, a lower burn rate (some of the costs are covered by universities from other pools of funds), and access to a well-educated employee base. The drawbacks of such arrangements are that some universities may be less committed to the commercialization of their inventions and that some of the exit arrangements with universities may be unfavorable (i.e., they may expect high royalty rates).

CONCLUSION

Business incubators have established themselves as a tool for supporting the development of entrepreneurial firms from the SME sector. Business incubators serve as a source of know-how to managers of young entrepreneurial firms. They are in the business of providing a wide range of services aimed at decreasing a firm's failure rate and at increasing their chance of becoming a viable business in the long term.

The relationship between business incubators and venture capitalists has evolved in recent years. In the aftermath of the Internet bubble, venture capitalists seemed to lose interest in pursuing firms in early stages of development and indirectly participating in business incubation activities. This has inevitably left a gap in the market place where entrepreneurial firms from the SME sector have a more challenging time securing financial partners. In this respect, business incubators have filled an important role, though their ability to assist the SME sector is limited without proper access to capital.

Unanswered Questions and Future Research

The section above describing the symbiotic relationship between venture capitalists and business incubators has numerous implications for academics. The overview confirms that there are multiple areas where venture capitalists and business incubators can effectively collaborate, since strong similarities and goals between the two sides exist. While the topic of business incubation has been widely covered in academic literature, the relationship between business incubators and venture capitalists is not well understood. There are at least three possible areas of investigation for researchers to understand the dynamics between the two groups. First, it is important to understand the key lessons from venture capitalist participation in business incubators during the Internet bubble period of 1998 to 2001. Such lessons are valuable for business practitioners who have been negatively influenced by events. While some research exists in the area of financial anomalies, no research exists on this specific topic. Second, a long-term study is needed to investigate the benefits of such cooperation to both sides. For venture capitalists, the actual venture capital returns received from participating in business incubators or investing in the firms residing in them would need to be understood—academic researchers have not been able to obtain factual data on the actual performance of venture capital-based incubators. For business incubators, the rate of successful graduation from business incubators based on venture capital financing warrants further investigation. Third, researchers need to understand the economics of venture capitalist participation in business incubation activities. In principle, it should be answered whether this method of developing entrepreneurial firms is a viable business model for venture capitalists. There must be an understanding as to how the two sides can combine their business models and effectively improve cooperation. It is particularly important to the operators of business incubators to establish operations in such a manner as to increase the attractiveness of the incubation model to venture capitalists. While some business incubators have already forged successful relationships with financiers, the factors that contribute to such positive relationships are not well understood. Ideally, a study is needed to confirm the key factors of success.

REFERENCES

Aernoudt, R. 2004. Incubators: Tool for entrepreneurship? *Small Business Economics* 23(2):127–135.

Allen, D., and E. Bazan. 1990. Value-added contributions of Pennsylvania's business incubators to tenant firms and local economies. Appalachian Regional Commission and the Pennsylvania Department of Commerce.

Bearse, P. 1998. A question of evaluation: NBIA's impact assessment of business incubators. *Economic Development Quarterly* 12:322–333.

Bollingtoft, A., and J. Ulhoi. 2005. The networked business incubator—Leveraging entrepreneurial agency. *Journal of Business Venturing* 20(2):265–290.

Callegati, E., S. Grandi, and G. Napier. 2005. Business incubation and venture capital: An international survey of synergies and challenges. Joint IPI/KED working paper, Malmo, Sweden.

Christopher, A. 2001. Incubators lose favor, some still see potential. *Venture Capital Journal* 41(5):1–2.

Clarysse, B., et al. 2005. Spinning out new ventures: A typology of incubation strategies from European research institutions. *Journal of Business Venturing* 20(2):183–216.

Fried, V., and R. Hisrich. 1994. Towards a model of venture capital investment decision making. *Financial Management* 23(3):28–37.

Goldfisher, A. 2006. Garage parks new fund. *Venture Capital Journal* 46(5):14.

Gullander, S., and G. Napier. 2003. Business angel network handbook. Nordic Innovation Centre, Stockholm School of Entrepreneurship.

Hansen, M., et al. 2000. Networked incubators: Hothouses of the new economy. *Harvard Business Review* 78(5):24–28.

Henricks, M. 2006. Bubble 2.0? *Entrepreneur* 34(8):17–18.

Hibbard, J., and H. Green. 2006. It feels like 1998 all over again. *Business Week* 3985:30–32.

Lalkaka, R. 2002. Technology business incubators to help build innovation-based economy. *Journal of Change Management* 3(2):167–176.

———. 2003. Business incubators in developing countries: Characteristics and performance. *International Journal of Entrepreneurship and Innovation Management* 3(1):31–55.

———, and P. A. Abetti. 1999. Business incubation and enterprise support systems in restructuring countries. *Creativity and Innovation Management* 8(3):197–209.

———, and D. Schafer. 1998. Nurturing entrepreneurs, creating enterprises: Technology business incubation in Brazil. International Labor Organization.

Lichtensten, G. 1992. The significance of relationship in entrepreneurship: A case study of the ecology of enterprise in two business incubators. PhD diss., Wharton School, University of Pennsylvania.

Mian, S. 1994. US university-sponsored technology incubators: An overview of management, policies, and performance. *Technovation* 14(8):515–528.

O'Neal, T. 2005. Evolving a successful university-based incubator: Lessons learned from the UCF technology incubator. *Engineering Management Journal* 17(3):11–24.

Phan, P., D. S. Siegel, and M. Wright. 2005. Science parks and incubators: Observations, synthesis and future research. *Journal of Business Venturing* 20(2):165–182.

Sheahan, M. 2005a. Revisiting incubators: Back to school. *Venture Capital Journal* 45(5):8–12.

———. 2005b. VCs try partnering for successful incubation. *Venture Capital Journal* 45(2):7–10.

Sherman, H., and D. S. Chapel. 1998. Methodological challenges in evaluating business incubator outcomes. *Economic Development Quarterly* 12(4):313–321.

Smilor, R. 1987. Commercializing technology through new business incubators. *Research Management* 30(5):36–41.

Tornatsky, L., et al. 1996. The art and craft of technology business incubation—Best practices, strategies and tools from more than 50 programs. National Business Incubation Association.

Tyebjee, T. T., and A. T. Bruno. 1985. The entrepreneurs search for capital. *Journal of Business Venturing* 1(1):61–64.

Valliere, D., and R. Peterson. 2004. Inflating the bubble: Investing dot.com investor behavior. *Venture Capital: An International Review* 6(1):1–22.

Weinberg, M. 1987. Business incubators give new firms in rural areas a head start. *Economic Research Service* 3(2):6–10.

ABOUT THE AUTHOR

Darek Klonowski received a Ph.D. in Economics from the Warsaw School of Economics. He has worked in the venture capital industry for nearly 15 years, making investments throughout Central and Eastern Europe (CEE). As Managing Director of Copernicus Capital Management (currently Abris Capital), a venture capital fund affiliated with Boston-based Advent International, he has focused on investments in the CEE region. He previously worked for Enterprise Investors, the largest and most successful venture capital fund in the CEE region. Dr. Klonowski has also advised multiple clients on asset allocation strategies regarding CEE, including the European Bank for Reconstruction and Development (EBRD) and the International Finance Corporation (IFC).

## CHAPTER 7

Philanthropic Venture Capital

A New Model of Financing for Social Entrepreneurs

LUISA ALEMANY
Associate Professor, ESADE Business School

MARIAROSA SCARLATA
PhD candidate, ESADE Business School

INTRODUCTION

In recent years, philanthropic venture capital has attracted great interest due to its novelty and to the combination of two terms that are seldom heard in the same breath: *philanthropy* and *venture capital*. On the one hand, philanthropy implies donating; on the other hand, venture capital implies investing in companies with the explicit purpose of realizing capital gains.

So what exactly is philanthropic venture capital also called venture philanthropy? It attempts to apply the strategies and techniques developed within the venture capital industry to the financing needs of social enterprises. Venture capital is characterized by the temporary financing of new ventures or growing businesses, usually through equity and by the provision of knowledge and expertise by investors. Venture capitalists are active investors since they often sit on the board of directors, participating in the definition of the company's strategy and its key decisions, that closely monitor and control the company's financial results.

Similarly, philanthropic venture capital consists of treating social funding, traditionally provided by foundations, as an actively managed investment rather than as a grant. As such, the involvement and the knowledge of these investors, combined with the need to provide funds to social groups, not only facilitates the development of new ventures to social issues but also helps support and sustain these approaches in the long-term.

Philanthropic venture capital is indeed different from socially responsible investments, also known as SRI and the recently named venture capital for sustainability. The exact definition of both is still not clear, but some general ideas and guidelines allow to classify the respective investment models.

Socially responsible investment (SRI) refers to asset allocation based on "negative screens," strategies based on which certain securities (such as tobacco, alcohol or weapons) are excluded from investment consideration based on social and/or environmental criteria; also, "positive screens," strategies make investments in activities and companies believed to have a positive social impact (such as clean tech or education); and, last "best in class," strategies which evaluate investments in terms of the impact of firms' socially responsible or environmental policies (USSIF 2007).

Venture capital for sustainability (VC4S), by contrast, is a specific area within venture capital where profit objectives are supplemented with a mission to have a direct impact on sustainability. However, the main difference with philanthropic venture capital is that in VC4S profit objectives are a top priority and the expected returns, or the internal rate of return (IRR), are in the range of 20 to 25 percent annually (Eurosif 2007). A typical example of investments in this category is the clean tech industry.

Despite the great interest in philanthropic venture capital among both the philanthropic and the venture capital communities, academics have as yet paid little attention to this area. As a result, no common definition of philanthropic venture capital and philanthropic venture capitals exists, and no clear boundaries between the "fathering" venture capital model and its "offspring" (i.e., philanthropic venture capital financing model) have been set. Therefore, the aim of this chapter is twofold: (a) to help the reader to understand what philanthropic venture capital is and how it differs from similar concepts such SRI and VC4S; and b) to analyse how the typical for-profit VC cycle (e.g., Gompers and Lerner 2001) works in philanthropic venture capital.

CURRENT CHALLENGES FACED IN FOUNDATION GRANTMAKING

The State of the World

In the last decade, an unprecedented set of changes have raised fundamental issues concerning the future of the world and of humankind.

The Human Development Report (2007) explains that on a variety of levels climate alterations as well as changing demographics and social tensions have been threatening to jeopardize social order. As a result, a variety of social, ecological, and economical programs have been institutionalized and many attempts have been taken in order to increase the effectiveness of institutions. Yet the latter have been shaped by these continuous changes themselves.

The United Nations is having mixed success as a global problem solver. The collapse of the European Union constitutional process as well as the waning influence of institutions such as NATO may be seen as a weakening of faith in global integration. Similarly, the contributions made by international treaties, conventions, and gatherings—such as the G8—have been limited as regards the wider field of global problem solving. For example, the financial crisis started in the summer of 2007 with subprime mortgages in the United States, but it soon became a problem around the world after the collapse of the top investment bank, Lehman Brothers. The crisis thus expanded across the globe, putting greater pressure on governments and global organizations.

As a result, economic and social divisions widen. UNICEF (2007), among others, reports that nearly 4 million infants die within a month of birth every year.

One child in six is severely undernourished, and one in seven receives no health care. Over a billion people do not have access to safe drinking water, and some 115 million children of primary school age do not attend school.

Social Enterprises and Social Problems

Given the state of the world, social enterprises are playing an increasingly important social role. In fact, they appear to be able to create innovative solutions to pressing social problems (e.g., Alvord et al. 2004; Dart 2004). Their mission is to solve a given social issue, have a social impact, and create social value. This is in clear contrast with the concept of shareholder value maximization, which is at the heart of any commercial enterprise. Even so, social enterprises need to acquire greater expertise if they are to successfully respond to the ongoing challenges and maximize their social impact. However, an increase in expertise is not achievable without greater funds. At the same time, those organizations that traditionally supply both expertise and capital for the development of new projects with a social impact (i.e., foundations) are finding it hard to provide enough support for social enterprises (e.g., Van Slyke and Newman 2006).

There are several factors that hinder foundations as key supporters of social entrepreneurs:

Foundations are not inclined to invest in an entire organization.

They tend to be project-driven and prefer to support a program or project that addresses a specific social problem. They are thus less interested in the overall capabilities of a social enterprise and its long-term needs. This approach does not seem to properly support social enterprises since directed gifts do not give the organization the flexibility to use funds where the need is greatest (Larson 2002). In turn, this hampers the enterprise from developing long-term programs and achieving sustained growth.

Donations represent the main source of financing for the social enterprise, and therefore these may face a problem of undercapitalization.

Some studies find that debt coverage and operating cost ratios on social sponsored projects are rather low. Additionally, U.S. foundations donate only 5.5 percent of their assets to charities, which is slightly above the legal minimum requirement of 5 percent; the rest is invested in activities that create financial rather than social returns (Porter and Kramer 1999). The same studies claim that for each $100 donated to a charity, $250 of social benefit is forgone through lost tax revenue. On the other hand, such donations only yield a social benefit to foundations equivalent to 14 percent of the tax revenue lost. As a result, undercapitalization may force social entrepreneurs to continuously focus on scrambling for funds, preventing them from achieving their social goals. The likelihood of their obtaining new resources and developing new social programs is thereby reduced.

Foundations mainly look for social projects with a high potential for replication by organizations other than the original one.

Although many organizations have succeeded in developing solutions to a given social problem, their efforts have not been broadly disseminated, adopted or scaled up (e.g., Morino 2000). It is a fact that governments' net social expenditures with respect to GDP ratios have fallen over the last 10 years. This, together with increasing disillusionment with governments' unwillingness and inability to come up with solutions to social problems has led foundations to re-evaluate their grant-making strategy in order to support the long-term needs of social enterprises.

Foundations often allocate funds based on need rather than on performance.

As a consequence, foundations pay little attention to strategic thinking and to measuring the results achieved by fund recipients. However, without considering the results obtained, foundations and their donors will never be sure whether the money was well spent. Furthermore, this might imply that good results may not be rewarded, resulting in a lack of stimuli: *"rarely excellent performance is rewarded with an increased flow of philanthropic capital"* (Grossman 1999, 3).

Foundations do not provide resources to help grantees improve their management practices.

Foundations are not involved in recruiting and training qualified staff members for the social enterprise or in improving their computer and accounting systems, or in developing sophisticated tools to track the results of social-service programs. In fact, in most cases this is completely beyond the scope of their mission. Many social organizations often ignore the value added by better management, usually preferring to be managed by organizational founders rather than by experienced managers. Additionally, pay is seldom performance-related.

The system by which foundations operate is similar to a fragmented merchant banking system.

The relationship between demand and supply of funds is institutionally mediated (Wood and Marti 2007). This implies little connection between social and economic needs and the supply of money. Rather, social enterprises have to apply to grant-making foundations for support, submitting to different concepts of social impact and theories of change.

Nonetheless, it would be wrong to portray traditional grantmaking as completely divorced from the organizations that foundations back. Over decades, many foundations have pursued close working relationships with their grantees, playing a role that goes far beyond more than a mere cash channel. There are many excellent examples of traditional grantmakers developing long-term, engaged relationships with a small number of organizations, delivering value far beyond check writing. Most grantmakers, however, have neither the inclination nor the skills to manage a relatively small number of highly engaged relationships.

The Change Needed: Value Creation

In this context, recognizing the importance and role of foundations as the "research and development arm of society," some authors propose they should focus on creating new value (e.g., Bernholz 1999; Porter and Kramer 1999). Actually, foundations "create value when achieving an equivalent social benefit with fewer dollars or when creating greater social benefits for a comparable cost" (Porter and Kramer 1999, 126).

Foundations can take four key steps to boost value creation:

1. Selection of the best grantee so that resources are channelled to the most productive recipient
2. Building on point 1, signal other funders of the social value, which attracts other donors who will support the organization

3. Building on points 1 and 2, improve the performance of the recipient organization
4. Building on points 1, 2, and 3, advance knowledge

Porter and Kramer have argued, "The value created in this way extends beyond the impact of one grant: it raises the social impact of the grantee in all that it does and, to the extent that grantees are willing to learn from one another, it can increase the effectiveness of other organizations as well" (1999, 124).

SOCIAL ENTREPRENEURS AND THE FINANCING OF SOCIAL ENTERPRISES

Social entrepreneurship concerns enterprises that mainly pursue social ends, and it involves building commercially viable and socially constructive organizations. Considering that the central driver for social entrepreneurship is the social problem being addressed, the legal organizational form a social enterprise takes should be the one that most effectively mobilizes the resources needed to address social problems. Thus, the legal form a social enterprise takes may range from nonprofit to purely for profit.

How is it possible to distinguish between social and commercial entrepreneurship then? The debate is still open, but the following four elements, identified by Austin and colleagues (2006), could be of help in distinguishing between the two:

1. Social entrepreneurship emerges when there is a social-market failure, i.e., commercial market forces do not meet a social need.
2. Social entrepreneurship involves the creation and maximization of social value for public good. The primary goal of commercial entrepreneurship is the creation and maximization of shareholder value, resulting in private gains. This does not imply that social enterprises are banned from making profits. Indeed they can, but this is not their central goal.
3. The nondistributive-profits restriction, which holds for nonprofits, as well as the social purpose of social enterprises, limits the access for social entrepreneurs to the same capital markets as commercial entrepreneurs.
4. The social purpose of social enterprises creates greater challenges for measuring performance than for commercial entrepreneurs, who can rely on relatively tangible and quantifiable measures of performance such as financial indicators, market share, customer satisfaction, and quality. In this respect, no common indicator of social performance and social impact has been developed by either practitioners or scholars. Each social entrepreneur identifies the tool that he feels best measures social impact.

PHILANTHROPIC VENTURE CAPITAL: DEFINITIONS, KEY DATA, AND MAIN PLAYERS

Authors such as Letts and colleagues (1997) and John (2006) suggest that philanthropic venture capital can be a way of improving the traditional financing methods available for social enterprises.[1] This subject has been raised particularly after the dot.com boom of the late 1990s and the successful New Economy entrepreneurs' belief that they can transfer the wealth created during the boom to future generations. The application of the for-profit entrepreneurial and finance models to social organizations gave birth to many philanthropic venture capital funds first in the United States, and in Europe thereafter.

What exactly is philanthropic venture capital, then? In order to provide a definition, we take the venture capital definition and then transpose it to philanthropic venture capital. Additionally, we discuss the meaning and reach of the other two terms which are sometimes confused with this concept: socially responsible investment (SRI) and venture capital for sustainability (VC4S). The three terms are quite new and for that reason it is important to differentiate them.

Definitions

Philanthropic venture capital is the application of the venture capital investment model to the financing of social enterprises. By financing the founding or growth of social enterprises, philanthropic venture capital is an intermediated investment aiming at maximizing the social return on investment.[2]

Following the professional language used by practitioners, philanthropic venture capital can also be called "venture philanthropy," a term first coined by John D. Rockefeller III. In a 1969 speech before the Committee on Ways and Means, leading to the Tax Reform Act, Rockefeller claimed: "Private foundations often are established to engage in what has been described as 'venture philanthropy' or the imaginative pursuit of less conventional charitable purposes than those normally undertaken by established public charitable organizations."

It is worthy to note that, as with the term *social entrepreneurship*, there is still no consensus on how "venture philanthropy" should be defined. However, the key elements that characterize *philanthropic venture capital investments* in social enterprises are

- Provision of capital as well as expertise
- Implementation of risk management practices in the invested company
- Prevalence of an accountability-for-results process
- Managing partner relationship between the investor and the company invested in
- Long-term investment perspective (three to six years business plans)
- Definition of a clear exit strategy

As such, social enterprises, thanks to the financial and nonfinancial support provided by philanthropic venture capitalists, are in principle able to create a higher social impact, which is transferred to society. Besides, the financial return that may be obtained from the investment can be reinvested in the philanthropic venture capital fund itself and used to support new social ventures. The philanthropic venture capital model is depicted in Exhibit 7.1.

Following the same logic used while defining *philanthropic venture capital*, this chapter provides a definition of the investors, that is, the philanthropic venture capitalists:

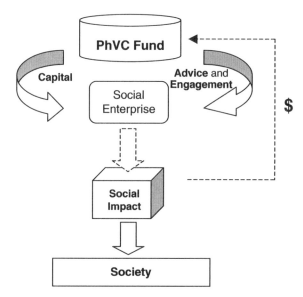

Exhibit 7.1 The Philanthropic Venture Capital Model (PhVC)
Source: Drawn up by the authors, based on the model presented by the European Venture Philanthropy
Assocation (EVPA 2007).

Philanthropic venture capitalists are professionals whose aim consists of investing
those funds raised from different donors—who may be wealthy individuals, enterprises, and/or foundations—in organizations with high social impact. In order
to maximize the social return from the investment, they engage in a value-added
partnership with the target organization and compromise funds depending on the
milestones reached. They monitor the progress of the social organizations they
back, not only providing capital but also expertise and strategic guidance. Furthermore, the philanthropic venture capitalist may take a seat on the board of directors
of the venture-backed organization, giving the right to intervene in the company's
operations when necessary.

The two concepts that are often related to philanthropic venture capital and
can lead to some level of confusion are *socially responsible investment* and *venture
capital for sustainability*.

Socially responsible investment (SRI) refers to the way assets are allocated in
order to maximize the positive impact of these on society. However, they always
expect reasonable if not top-end returns to compensate for the risk involved in
the investment. Asset selection is based on some negative screens (exclusion),
positive screens (inclusion), and "best in class." The negative screens specify
any assets to which the fund or the investor will not allocate money. The assets that are typically excluded belong to sectors or industries such as tobacco,
alcohol, casinos, or weapons. By contrast, positive screens identify those sectors
that should be favoured such as clean tech, education, or health care. Finally,
the best in class category includes policies such as the firms' socially responsible or environmental practices and their impact on their region or stakeholders
(USSIF 2007).

Venture capital for sustainability (VC4S), also known as socially responsible investment private equity, is a specific area within traditional venture capital. Here profit objectives are supplemented by a mission to have a direct impact on sustainability. However, profit objectives are still a top priority and the expected returns, IRR, are in the range of 20 to 25 percent annually (Eurosif 2007; USSIF 2007). In the United States, VC4S started to flourish after some of the larger pension funds, such as the California state funds, CalPERS and CalSTRS, decided in 2004 to allocate assets to this area, especially in clean tech. Silicon Valley venture capitalists also saw VC4S as an opportunity, and they have made significant inroads in the last few years. Some of the top investors, such as Kleiner Perkins, who were famous for their investments in companies like Amazon and Google, are boosting their involvement in green investments. In February 2006, the Prize for Green Innovation fund for $100 million was created specifically for green investing. In addition, the Nobel Prize winner Al Gore joined the firm in 2007. They have also sponsored legislation to benefit investing in renewable energy sources.

In Europe VC4S is also taking off, and it is estimated that around €1.25 billion of committed capital was raised by European venture capitalists in 2006. A recent study by Cummig and Johan (2007) based on Dutch investors identifies two of the characteristics that encourage institutional funds to allocate funds to this type of investment: (1) the existence of a centralized Chief Investment Officer and (2) the fund's degree of international focus.

To conclude, philanthropic venture capital is a way of giving resources to social entrepreneurs. It is called "venture capital" because it uses some of the techniques and processes of for-profit investors; however, the investors do not expect to receive any return to compensate for the risk. In the case of profits the money would be invested back in the fund to keep on supporting social enterprises.

Philanthropic Venture Capital: Key Data from the United States and Europe

At the end of 2008, 74 philanthropic venture capitalists were identified, 36 in the United States and 38 in Europe.[3]

The geographical location of the philanthropic venture capital funds is summarized in Exhibit 7.2.

Looking at the characteristics of the philanthropic venture capitalists, it is clear that most are quite new (see Exhibit 7.3, Panel A). In fact, this is quite a recent

Exhibit 7.2 Location of Philanthropic Venture Capitalists

	Number of Investors	%
Continental Europe	20	27.0%
Eastern Europe	3	4.1%
UK	15	20.3%
Total Europe	*38*	*51.4%*
United States	36	48.6%
TOTAL	**74**	**100.0%**

Exhibit 7.3   Foundation of Philanthropic Venture Capital Funds

Panel A: Number of Philanthropic Venture Capital Funds by Year of Foundation

	United States		Europe		Total	
	#	%	#	%	#	%
1980–1990	2	5.6%	-	-	2	2.7%
1991–1999	15	41.7%	11	28.9%	26	35.1%
Total 1980–1999	*17*	*47.3%*	*11*	*28.9%*	*28*	*37.8%*
2000–2004	13	36.1%	18	47.4%	31	41.9%
2005–2008	4	11.1%	7	18.4%	11	14.9%
Total 2000–2008	*17*	*47.2%*	*25*	*65.8%*	*42*	*56.8%*
N/A	2	5.6%	2	5.3%	4	5.4%
Total	36	100%	38	100%	74	100%

Panel B: Number of Philanthropic Venture Capital Funds Created around the Dot.com Boom

	United States		Europe		Total	
	#	%	#	%	#	%
Before 1995 (excluded)	7	19.4%	1	2.6%	8	10.8%
1995–2001 (included)	20	55.6%	13	34.2%	33	44.6%
After 2001 (excluded)	7	19.4%	22	57.9%	29	39.2%
N/A	2	5.6%	2	5.3%	4	5.4%
Total	36	100%	38	100%	74	100%

phenomenon. In the United States, 17 of the 36 funds have less than 10 years. This represents 47 percent of the total number of U.S. philanthropic venture capital funds. In Europe they are even younger: two-thirds were created during this same time period. In fact, the first philanthropic venture capital fund in the United States was incorporated in 1980, while the first one in Europe was established almost 15 years later, in 1993.

Comparing these figures with Panel B of Exhibit 7.3, we realize that philanthropic venture funds were primarily funded in the early years of the dot.com boom, with 56 percent of the total number of funds being created from 1995 to 2001. In Europe the majority of philanthropic venture capital funds were created in the later years of the dot.com boom, when the bubble had already burst: 58 percent of European philanthropic venture capitalists were created after 2001.

From this data it can be inferred that American and European capitalism tends to create wealth through entrepreneurship and reconstitute wealth through philanthropy. On the one hand, for-profit capital market principles have been applied to the philanthropic environment, that is, transparent objective criteria to make early- and later-stage investment decisions, balance risk with return, and reward improvements in top and bottom lines. In other words, from the financial (top) and social (bottom) perspectives, social enterprises might have better access to capital. On the other hand, philanthropic venture capital allows venture capital players

Exhibit 7.4　Classification of U.S. and EU Philanthropic Venture Capitalists by Legal Structure

Panel A: US vs. Europe

	US		Europe		Total	
	#	%	#	%	#	%
Public charity	15	41.7%	13	34.2%	28	37.8%
Foundation	12	33.3%	17	44.7%	29	39.2%
For profit	2	5.6%	7	18.4%	9	12.2%
Other	6	16.7%	1	2.6%	7	9.5%
N/A	1	2.8%	0	0.0%	1	1.4%
Total	36	100%	38	100%	74	100%

Panel B: Details of the European Philanthropic Venture Funds by Country

	Number of Investors	Foundation	Public Charity	For Profit	Other
UK	15	3	8	3	1
Netherlands	5	3		2	
Italy	4	3		1	
France	3	3			
Germany	3		2	1	
Ireland	2	1	1		
Spain	1	1			
Switzerland	1	1			
Czech Republic	1		1		
Estonia	1	1			
Hungary	1		1		
Liechtenstein	1	1			
Total	38	17	13	7	1

to reinvest the proceeds of their traditional for-profit businesses in social purpose enterprises whose aim is to create social wealth, thus allowing them to redistribute the wealth they create. This can be seen as a marketing tool for those venture capital funds sponsoring the philanthropic fund. However, the reality is that the philanthropic funds have different denominations, thus making it difficult for the general public to relate the for-profit investment business with the philanthropic activity.

Exhibit 7.4 lists the number of philanthropic venture capitalists by the legal structure they have adopted. In the United States, 41.4 percent use a foundation organizational structure, while in Europe it is by 58.6 percent of philanthropic venture capitalists. Also, 53.6 percent of American funds are public charities, compared with 46.4 percent in Europe. Panel B in Exhibit 7.4 provides more details by country in Europe.

The Philanthropic Venture Capital Approach

Considering the financing model proposed by foundations and the peculiar needs of social enterprises described, in 1997 Letts, Ryan, and Grossman suggested that foundations could benefit from the use of the for-profit venture capital model, bringing up the concept of philanthropic venture capital. In their view, foundations may benefit from the distinctive ability of venture capitalists in screening potential grantees, in developing a sound strategy, and in sustaining social enterprises in their long-term needs. The reasons for this are manifold:

Philanthropic venture capitalists, like their for-profit counterparts, offer indispensable expertise, advice, and consultation on organizational growth.

Since philanthropic venture capitalists do not provide a large number of recipients with project-oriented grants that cover only a small proportion of the costs of a typical social enterprise, they are able to cover the majority of the costs of the enterprise by increasing the size of the funds.

Thanks to multiyear investments in a relatively small number of organizations, philanthropic venture capitalists encourage organizational development and capacity building.

Responding to an array of challenges associated with more traditional forms of philanthropy, philanthropic venture capital models vary along many dimensions: some philanthropic venture capitalists focus their support on an issue area (e.g., education) or a region (e.g., United States or India); others are issue neutral with a national scope; some focus more on investor engagement, while others emphasize the relationship with their portfolio of organizations; still others focus on seed-stage organizations and their leaders, while others focus on replicating scalable models. Most of the time, the ultimate goal is to create an environment in which visionary social entrepreneurs have the necessary strategic and financial resources to grow their organizations to scale and to achieve a sustainable, transformative social impact.

Grant making is thus assumed to be like any other financial transaction, and it requires a multidimensional decision-making effort. Acting as investors instead of donors ensures that grants will not merely be spent on any kind of project but rather valuably expended on intelligent programs with a lasting social impact.

At this point, it is worth noting that philanthropic venture capital does not constitute a critique of traditional philanthropy, or a substitute to replace it in the world of finance. It represents a viable and complementary alternative to more traditional philanthropic endeavours:

> *[T]he three main elements of venture philanthropy—building operating capacity, close engagement between donors and recipients, and clear performance expectations—are not new at all. Many would argue that those have been the trademarks of effective philanthropists for decades, and that they were well on the rise long before venture philanthropy gained public attention.... Perhaps venture philanthropy is more of an evolution than the revolution it first seemed to be. Already, it is beginning to blend in, taking its place as one style of grantmaking among many.... In short, venture philanthropy's greatest lasting effect may be to reinforce a few basic principles of effective philanthropy that were already emerging. And, like many of the dot.coms that made venture capitalists so successful for a while, what seemed so new about venture philanthropy may have been the sizzle, not the content (Kramer 2002).*

It is thereby clear that both types of funders are necessary in providing the array of capital necessary for success in gaining social returns.

Some Examples of Successful Philanthropic Venture Capitalists in the United States

Silicon Valley Community Foundation (SVCF)

This is one of the philanthropic venture capitalists with the highest assets under management, with almost $2 billion invested. In 1999 SVCF launched its first philanthropic venture capital fund, focusing mainly in the support of the education of poor children. In addition, SVCF is active in coordinating teachers, schools, agencies, and local nonprofits to provide a six-year environmental curriculum centred on local ecosystems and their interconnections (Silicon Valley Community Foundation 2008). SVCF was started by Silicon Valley venture capitalists in the middle of the dot.com boom. It takes the form of a "community foundation" classified under the category "Others" in Exhibit 7.4.

Roberts Enterprise Development Fund (REDF)

Another example of U.S. philanthropic venture capitalists is the Roberts Enterprise Development Fund (REDF), a foundation previously known as Robin Hood Trust. REDF was one of the first philanthropic venture capital funds to be established, founded by George Roberts, a founding partner of the well known leveraged buy-out (LBO) firm Kolberg, Kravis & Roberts (KKR) in 1990. The fund focuses on investing in social enterprises that aim to train or employ people with barriers to work. They offer to the social enterprises they back financial support, business assistance, and human and intellectual capital. "REDF is an excellent model of high-engagement philanthropy in the way they have actively learned from their experience with their investees, have improved on their model over the years, and have been willing to share their experience broadly within the field" (Letts and Hauser 2007).

Some Examples of Successful Philanthropic Venture Capitalists in Europe

In Europe, unlike the United States, where no philanthropic venture capital association existed, the European Venture Philanthropy Association (EVPA) was founded by Stephen Dawson in 2003. EVPA aims at raising standards across the charity sector by providing governance models as well as investment disciplines and accountability for social enterprises. By the end of 2008, 25 funds had already joined the European association.

Impetus Trust

In the same year Dawson, thanks to the experience gained at a venture capital fund specialized in midmarket buy-outs, founded the philanthropic venture capital fund Impetus Trust. Impetus takes the legal form of a public charity and has significant funding commitments from the major European venture capital and private equity firms. So far, it has approximately raised $6 million to invest in charities—such as Speaking Up! and St. Giles Trust—making a demonstrable, significant, and sustainable difference to the lives of a substantial number of disadvantaged people.

Phi Trust Foundation
This was established as a foundation in 2004 by Gilles Cahen-Salvador, the co-founder of the Paris based buy-out company LBO France. Phi Trust focuses on financing social entrepreneurs who are involved in the education, health care, culture, and housing social sectors.

THE PHILANTHROPIC VENTURE CAPITAL MODEL COMPARED TO THE VENTURE CAPITAL MODEL

The typical venture capital model includes three main stages: fund-raising, investing, and exiting (Gompers and Lerner 2001). Exhibit 7.5 presents the venture capital cycle with details of the key issues taking place in each stage.

The fund-raising stage starts well before any investment has been analyzed and is the process of getting the venture capital entity funded. The investment stage is the longest one as it starts with the selection of the deal, goes through the entire process of analysis, due diligence, and negotiation to the closing of the deal, and then focuses on adding value and controlling the investee company in order to maximize value creation. Finally, the exit stage focuses on finding the most appropriate way to sell the portfolio company's stake in order to maximize the investor's return.

This chapter analyzes the investing and exiting stages of the venture capital model and how these are applied to philanthropic venture capital. Fund-raising is not reviewed as it does not involve the creation of a relationship between the social enterprise and the philanthropic venture capitalists. Indeed, it involves a

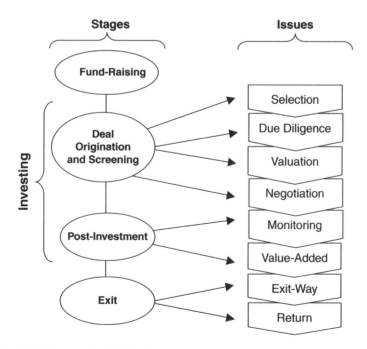

Exhibit 7.5   The Venture Capital Cycle

relationship between the philanthropic venture capitalists and other types of actors, i.e., its donors.

Selection Process

As shown in Exhibit 7.5, once the stage of fund-raising is closed and the money is available the venture capital model moves to the screening of new potential investments. Given that venture capitalists operate in environments with higher levels of information asymmetries than faced by other investors, this type of investors have developed specialized abilities in selecting entrepreneurial projects (Amit et al. 1998). By considering variables such as the attractiveness of the investment opportunity in terms of management team, market size, strategy, customer adoption, competition, deal terms, and technology (cf. Kaplan and Stromberg 2000; Elango et al. 1995; MacMillan et al. 1989), venture capitalists select those deals that offer the highest return with the lowest level of risk. Is this also the case for philanthropic venture capitalists?

Indeed the philanthropic venture capital deal origination stage analyzes the characteristics of the target company, its business arena, and the investments of the enterprise, with a particular focus on social impact. In particular, New Profit and other philanthropic venture capital funds, such as Acumen Fund and REDF, employ four main criteria for selecting the target company:

1. Social enterprises are required to have the ability to meet an urgent, widespread social need with a high quality service or product through a model with the potential to grow to scale and to have a potential high social impact.
2. Social entrepreneurs are required to have the ability to build and execute on a compelling vision for transformational social change by recruiting and inspiring a talented, committed management team and board of directors.
3. Evidence must be shown of the ability of the organization to deliver high quality results, navigate growth challenges, manage finances effectively, and build a brand identity.
4. A clearly defined and broadly understood organizational mission and strategy must be evident along with a vibrant culture in support of that mission, strong prospects for growth, and willingness to invest in critical systems and infrastructure as the foundation for growth.

Due Diligence Process

The philanthropic venture capital due diligence process involves the selection of a small number of investments from a pool of several hundred candidates. This includes extensive interviews with management teams and board members of the social enterprise, competitive landscape analysis, review of financial performance and interviews with other key stakeholders, as in venture capital practices. Given that philanthropic venture capitalists, as venture capitalists, aim at investing in the best promising enterprise, they focus on developing an internal as well as external strategy through the analysis of the market in which the social target company operates. This process represents a critical preparation for undertaking long-term partnerships with potential portfolio organizations: philanthropic venture capitalists, on average, spend 80 hours with finalists to determine the organization's fit (New Profit 2008).

Valuation and Negotiation Process

It is still not clear which are the valuation methods adopted by philanthropic venture capitalists nor how the negotiation process is structured, that is, how control rights are assigned and which financial instruments are used to support social enterprises. Typically, in venture capital, contracts are drawn up in such a way that adverse selection problems due to hidden information are minimized. The process of investment followed by philanthropic venture capitalists is currently being researched by the authors of this chapter, and the results will shed more light on the process.

Monitoring and Value Added Process

Concerning postinvestment activities, venture capitalists focus on

- Finding key management personnel.
- Participating in strategic and operational planning, both by serving the venture-backed company by being part of the board of directors and by frequent informal visits to the company and meetings with its customers and suppliers.
- Helping with additional financing either by staging the total amount of funds to be given to the backed company or by searching for other investors that could enter in the capital of the portfolio company. Stage financing allows venture capitalists to gather information and to monitor the progress of firms, maintaining the option to periodically abandon projects (cfr. Tyebjee and Bruno 1984; MacMillan et al. 1989; and Sahlman 1990).

The amount and the quality of the value added by venture capitalists seems to be related to

- The amount of face-to-face interaction between the venture capitalist and the CEO of the venture-backed company.
- The number of hours that venture capitalists put in each individual venture.
- The venture capitalists' network of contacts as well as their advice on strategic and financial issues (cfr. Sapienza et al. 1996; Hochberg et al. (2007); Manigart et al. 2002).

In the philanthropic venture capital model, once the target organization is selected, it is monitored by the provision of expertise alongside financial support. As such, the philanthropic venture capital approach entails a close relationship between the investor and the social enterprise, which can last for a number of years. The relationship is characterized by a partnership rather than oversight, with a mutual interest in organizational capacity building. Accordingly, philanthropic venture capitalists tend to undertake an active role in the portfolio company by the involvement in management, governance, and organizational problem solving (e.g., REDF or Venture Philanthropy Partners in the case of the United States and Bridges Community Ventures or Oltre Venture in the case of Europe). As board members, philanthropic venture capitalists regularly engage in strategic guidance, oversighting the venture operations and outcomes, as well as providing project-specific support.

Like traditional venture investors, philanthropic venture capitalists inject capital in the target social enterprise by staging the total amount of funding. Stage-specific focus requires philanthropic venture capitalists to think differently about their role as funders and about how they can work with other funders. Philanthropic venture capitalists are starting to borrow the venture capitalists' habits of syndicating deals by trying to bring enough funding from a variety of sources to guarantee success for each stage in an organization's growth.

Exit Way

The last phase of the venture capital model consists in exiting from the investment. Generally speaking, five exit ways are commonly used to exit investment:

1. The venture is brought public via an IPO.
2. The venture is bought by a strategic investor.
3. The venture goes back to the incumbent management (management buy-outs, i.e., MBOs) or to external managers (management buy-in, i.e., MBIs).
4. The venture is acquired by another venture capital investor (secondary buy-outs) or by a financial investor.
5. The venture fails and goes out of business.

In the philanthropic venture capital setting, not all the opportunities available to venture capitalists can be adopted: clearly the stock market is not the place to look for funds for a social enterprise developing a new social program. Besides, due to the intrinsic definition of nonprofit organization, these cannot distribute net earnings/profit to individuals who can exercise control over it: as a result, in this case, exits are bounded to the nondistribution of profits.

As a consequence, a philanthropic venture capital exit can be defined as a shared commitment between philanthropic venture capitalists and the funded social enterprise to

- Determine a strategy for accessing different types of funding over the organization's life cycle to ensure its long-term viability
- Provide assistance in building the organization's capacity to access these different types of funding
- Specify capacity, placing milestones, time periods, and roles for the philanthropic venture capitalists, given the overall funding strategy

As in venture capital investments, the exit strategy is a vital part of the philanthropic venture capital model, and philanthropic venture capitalists plan to exit from the initial investment after a holding period of two to six years, exactly like venture capitalists. Similarly, for venture capital, an exit strategy means that the investor starts explicitly discussing it with the investee early in the relationship. The awareness that philanthropic venture capitalists will exit may encourage social entrepreneurs to be more disciplined about their organizational capacity-building efforts. Furthermore, exiting may be an honest representation of both parties' intentions, and it can represent a continuation of the working relationship between the philanthropic venture capitalists and the investee. As a result, wider and more consistent application of exits may help to segment the nonprofit capital markets and to diversify financial products, aligning donor funding with organizational development and financial need. The expectation is that philanthropic venture capital may facilitate the availability of next-stage funding for those social enterprises that have achieved capacity-building targets.

While in the case of venture capitalists the exit-way represents a crucial phase, given that it is when the investor realizes financial returns, philanthropic venture capital exits constitute a signal of the attainment of social goals. Some of the preconditions for a "successful exit strategy" are:

- A good leadership and management
- A solid organizational infrastructure
- A track record of meeting short-term objectives on a consistent basis
- Positive social outcomes and evidence of progress toward meeting the organization's social mission
- A clear social mission for the future

These may be indicators of the fact that organizational capacity building has been attained and that the social enterprise is in a good position to access new funding sources and has good chances of long-term success.

Returns

The issue of measuring results has been faced by philanthropic venture capital practitioners with the development and implementation of a performance measurement tool capable of grasping both the financial and the social component of the return on the investments, that is, the social return on investment (SROI). This was first proposed by the fund REDF, and it enables philanthropic venture capital funds to understand the link between the financial funds provided to the investee organizations on the one hand and the social results those organizations achieve on the other hand, as opposed to the internal rate of return (IRR) criterion employed by venture capitalists, which grasps merely financial returns. To the best of our knowledge, no performance data is currently available.

CONCLUSION

This chapter focuses on a new way of giving based on the venture capital model. It could be a solution to the challenges faced by foundations while financially supporting social enterprises. Social enterprises are being considered important actors in solving some of the problems of today's society. The traditional project-based allocation of funds by foundations as well as a lack of focus on performance measurement poorly supports the growth and the sustainability of social enterprises.

After defining the concept of philanthropic venture capital, the market is presented with an analysis of the actors in both the United States and Europe. Furthermore, some key players from both regions are identified. It can be seen that most philanthropic venture capitalists (a) are less than 10 years old and were mainly created in the dot.com period and (b) tend to adopt the public-charity legal structure. Subsequently, the philanthropic venture capital approach is presented comparing the philanthropic venture capital model with the traditional for-profit venture capital model. In both regions philanthropic venture capitalists do implement venture capitalists' practices in the screening and monitoring stages, but it still is not clear how do they do it when investing and exiting.

More research, currently under way, is needed in this area to answer this and other related questions: Do philanthropic venture capitalists valuate social enterprises in the same way that venture capital investors do? How do they include the social component of the enterprise in their valuation? Do philanthropic venture capitalists retain equity rights? How are these equity rights being assigned? Which are the exit-ways used by philanthropic venture capitalists?

These questions have become particularly urgent in the light of the development of the field in the last years. Academic research is addressing them and will hopefully provide answers to these and many other open questions.

NOTES

1. On an academic level, see Letts et al. (1997), John (2006), Edelson (2004), as well as Kramer and Porter (1999). On the more professional perspective, see Morino and Shore (2004), Walker (2004), Gose (2003), Morino Institute (2001), Ryan (2001), Tuan and Emerson (2000), and Emerson, Wachowicz, and Chun (2000).

2. The authors' definition combines the definitions by Letts and colleagues (1997) and Edelson (2004), as well as the National Venture Capital Association (NVCA 2007) and the European Venture Philanthropy Association (EVPA 2007).

3. In order to identify philanthropic venture capitalists two main databases were consulted, the National Venture Capital Association (NVCA) database for the United States and the European Venture Philanthropy Association (EVPA) for Europe. The data was then integrated with the list of organizations reported by Morino (2002). In addition, other philanthropic venture capitalists active in the field, but not reported in these sources, have been identified by analyzing the board of directors of the previously identified funds.

REFERENCES

Alter, K., P. Shoemaker, M. Tuan, and J. Emerson. 2001. When is it time to say good-bye? *Exit Strategies and Venture Philanthropy Funds.* REDF Publications. Retrieved from http://www.redf.org

Alvord, S. H., L. D. Brown, and C. W. Letts. 2004. Social entrepreneurship and societal transformation—An explanatory study. *Journal of Applied Behavioural Science* 40(3): 260–282.

Amit, R., J. Brander, and C. Zott. 1998. Why do venture capital firms exist? Theory and Canadian evidence. *Journal of Business Venturing* 13(6):441.

Austin, J., H. Stevenson, and J. Wei-Skillern. 2006. Social and Commercial entrepreneurship: same, different, or both? *Entrepreneurship: Theory & Practice* 30:1, 1–22.

Bernholz, L. 1999. *Foundations for the future: Emerging trends in foundation philosophy.* San Francisco: Blue Print R&D.

Cochrane, J. 2005. The risk and return of venture capital. *Journal of Financial Economics* 75(1):3–52.

Cumming, D. and S. Johan. 2007. Socially responsible institutional investment in private equity. *Journal of Business Ethics* 75, 395–416.

Cumming, D., and J. G. MacIntosh. 2003. A cross-country comparison of full and partial venture capital exits. *Journal of Banking & Finance* 27(3):511–548.

Dart, R. 2004. The legitimacy of social enterprise. *Nonprofit Management & Leadership* 14(4):411–424.

Edelson, H. 2004. Philanthropic venture capital: Its time has come. *Venture Capital Journal* 44(1):36–37.

Elango, B., V. H. Fried, R. D. Hisrich, and A. Polonchek. 1995. How venture capital firms differ? *Journal of Business Venturing* 10(2):157–179.

Emerson, J., J. Wachowicz, and S. Chun. 2000. Social return on investment: Exploring aspects of value creation in the non-profit sector. Chapter 8, REDF Publications. Retrieved from http://www.redf.org

European Venture Philanthropy Association (EVPA). 2007. Brussels. Retrieved from http://www.evpa.eu.com

Eurosif. 2007. *Venture capital for sustainability 2007*. Paris: Author.

Gompers, P., and J. Lerner. 2001. The venture capital revolution. *Journal of Economic Perspectives* 15(2):145–168.

Gose, B. 2003. A revolution was ventured, but what did it gain? *Chronicle of Philanthropy*. Retrieved from http://philanthropy.com

Grossman, A. 1999. Philanthropic social capital markets: Performance-driven philanthropy. *Harvard Business School Working Paper*. Social Enterprise Series, no. 12.

Hochberg, Y. V., A. Ljungqvist, and Y. Lu. 2007. Whom you know matters: Venture capital networks and investment performance. *Journal of Finance* 62(1): 251–301.

Human Development Report 2007. 2007. Report: Human development and climate change. Retrieved from http://hdr.undp.org/

John, R. 2006. Venture philanthropy: The evolution of high engagement philanthropy in Europe. Skoll Centre for Social Entrepreneurship, Saïd Business School Publications. Oxford, UK. Retrieved from http://www.redf.org

Kaplan, S., and P. Stromberg. 2000. How do venture capitalists choose and manage their investments? Working paper, University of Chicago.

Kramer, M. 2002. Will venture philanthropy leave a lasting mark on charitable giving?. *Chronicle of Philanthropy*. Retrieved from http://philanthropy.com

Larson, B. 2002. The new entrepreneurs: new philanthropy or not? *New Directions for Philanthropic Fundraising* 37:79–84.

Letts, C., and R. Hauser. 2007. Hauser Center for Nonprofit Organizations, Harvard University, REDF. Retrieved from http://www.redf.org/support-intro.htm

Letts, C. W., W. Ryan, and A. Grossman. 1997. Virtuous capital: What foundations can learn from venture capitalists. *Harvard Business Review* 75(2):36–44.

MacMillan, I. C., D. M. Kulow, and R. Khoylian. 1989. Venture capitalists' involvement in their investments: Extent and performance. *Journal of Business Venturing* 4(1): 27–47.

Manigart, S., H. Bruining, A. Lockett, and M. Meuleman. 2002. Why do European venture capital companies syndicate? Vlerick Leuven Gent Management School Working Paper, Series 2002–20.

Morino, M., and B. Shore. 2004. High-engagement philanthropy: A bridge to a more effective social sector. VPP Publications. Retrieved from http://www.venturephilanthropy partners.org

Morino Institute. 2000. Venture philanthropy 2000: Landscape and expectations. VPP Publications. Retrieved from http://www.venturephilanthropy partners.org

Morino Institute. 2001. Venture philanthropy: The changing landscape. VPP Publications. Retrieved from http://www.venturephilanthropy partners.org

Morino Institute. 2002. Venture philanthropy 2002: Advancing nonprofit performance through high-engagement grantmaking. VPP Publications. Retrieved from http://www. venturephilanthropy partners.org

National Venture Capital Association (NVCA). 2007. Retrieved from www.nvca.org

New Profit. 2008. Retrieved from www.newprofit.com

Porter, M. E., and M. R. Kramer. 1999. Philanthropy's new agenda: Creating value. *Harvard Business Review* 77(6):121–130.

Ryan, W. P. 2001. Nonprofit capital: A review of problems and strategies. Rockefeller Foundation and the Fannie Mae Foundation. Retrieved from http://www.knowledgeplex.org/showdoc.html?id=73673

Roberts Enterprise Development Fund (REDF). 2008. Retrieved from www.redf.org

Sahlman, W. 1990. The structure and governance of venture capital organizations. *Journal of Financial Economics* 27(2):473–521.

Sapienza, H. J., S. Manigart, and W. Vermeir. 1996. Venture capitalist governance and value added in four countries. *Journal of Business Venturing* 11(6):459–82.

Silicon Valley Community Foundation (SVCF). 2008. Retrieved from http://www. siliconvalleycf.org/

Tuan, M. and J. Emerson. 2000. The Roberts enterprise development fund: A case study on venture philanthropy. REDF Box Set—Social Purpose Enterprises and Venture Philanthropy in the New Millennium 2. Retrieved from http://www.redf.org

Tyebjee, T. T. and A. V. Bruno. 1984. A model of venture capitalist investment activity. *Management Science* 30(9):1051–1056.

UNICEF. 2007. Annual Report 2006. Retrieved from http://www.unicef.org

USSIF. 2007. 2007 Report on socially responsible investing trends in the United States. Author.

Van Slyke, D. M. and H. K. Newman. 2006. Venture philanthropy and social entrepreneurship in community redevelopment. *Nonprofit Management & Leadership* 16(3):345–368.

Walker, L. J. 2004. The growth of venture philanthropy. *On Wall Street* 14(1):107–107.

Wood, A. and M. Marti. 2007. Market–based solutions for financing philanthropy. Retrieved from http://ssrn.com/abstract=980097

Wright, M., K. Robbie, Y. Romanet, S. Thompson, R. Joachimsson, J. Bruining, and A. Herst. 1993. Harvesting and the longevity of management buy-outs and buy-ins: A four-country study. *Entrepreneurship: Theory & Practice* 18(2):90–109.

ABOUT THE AUTHORS

Luisa Alemany is an associate professor of finance at ESADE Business School in Barcelona (Spain). She received an MBA from Stanford (USA), and a Ph.D. in Finance from U. Complutense (Spain). She has gained professional experience in consulting with McKinsey & Co, in finance with Goldman Sachs, and in venture capital with The Carlyle Group. Her main research interests are venture capital, valuation of start-ups, entrepreneurial finance, and corporate finance.

Mariarosa Scarlata holds an undergraduate degree in Financial Market and Institution Economics (University Luigi Bocconi, Milan) and is preparing her Ph.D. in Business Administration (ESADE). She works as a teaching assistant for ESADE undergraduate and MBA courses in finance. She is also a researcher for the ESADE Entrepreneurship Institute and the Institute for Social Innovation. Her research focuses on the application of capital risk models in the philanthropic area.

## PART II

The Structure of Venture Capital Investments

## CHAPTER 8

Financial Contracts and Venture Capitalists' Value-Added

CATHERINE CASAMATTA
Professor of Finance, Toulouse School of Economics (CRG, IDEI) and Europlace Institute of Finance

INTRODUCTION

Innovative projects are plagued by a high level of uncertainty that varies over time. Because new pieces of information arrive frequently, crucial decisions have to be taken during the early years of start-ups: strategic orientation of the project, allocation of resources, etc. Investors have a major role to play to obtain precise information on the prospects of the firms and to take appropriate measures. For that reason, it is often said that *who* finances the firm is as important as *how much* is financed to determine the future success of early ventures. The objective of this chapter is to review the sources of value-added of venture capitalists, and to understand what contractual tools can help them to take relevant decisions and enhance firm value. The chapter is organized as follows. The next section rapidly surveys the literature on the forms and means of value-added of venture capitalists. The following section develops a model of start-up financing to investigate the advising role of venture capitalists. The analysis of the model first provides a comparison of the efficiency of venture capital advice compared to pure consultant advice. It then studies the shape of the optimal financial contract between entrepreneurs and venture capitalists. The last section discusses to what extent the results presented in the model can explain observed patterns of venture capital.

FORMS OF VALUE-ADDED OF VENTURE CAPITALISTS

The idea that venture capital is a source of value-added for start-up firms is not new. Several empirical studies have tried to measure how much value is created when venture capitalists are on board. For instance, Kortum and Lerner (2000) measure ex post the contribution of venture capitalists by comparing the patent output of venture capital-backed and non-venture-capital-backed firms. They report that venture capital investments amount to 3 percent of R&D expenses in the United States but to more than 8 percent of the number of industrial patents. Other ex post measures of the value created by venture capital include the financial performance of venture-capital-backed firms. The early studies of Brav and Gompers (1997) and Gompers and Lerner (1999) document that venture capital-backed firms achieve a higher performance five years after their IPO, compared to non-venture-capital-backed firms.

How do those investors enhance the value of the firms in their portfolio? Several explanations have been identified in the literature. The first one is the *screening* role of venture capitalists. Venture capitalists carefully analyze and select their investment projects (the so-called due-diligence process). By retaining only the best projects, venture capital investments can achieve higher performance. Fenn, Liang, and Prowse (1995) illustrate dramatically the importance of the screening process by computing the selection rate of United States venture capital funds. They estimate that only 1 percent of the investment projects received by venture capitalists obtain financing. How do VCs select projects? What are the key elements to assess the value of a new venture? Kaplan and Strömberg (2004) provide a detailed study of 67 investment analyses performed by 11 venture capital firms. The novelty of their analysis is that they had access to the detailed memoranda prepared by the partners in charge of a given investment project. Those memoranda constitute the basis for discussion among VC partners to decide whether to invest into a project or not. A first lesson from this study is that investors try to measure accurately all sources of risk. Second, Kaplan and Strömberg (2004) identify three sources of risk. The first one refers to internal risk factors: management quality, past performance, downside risk, valuation, and monitoring costs. These factors are related to management actions and/or to the quality of the management team. The second source of risk contains external factors, mainly market size, exit conditions, and competitors. The third source of risk relates to the complexity of the project: it may reflect the difficult execution or implementation of the technology, or the business strategy. One reason why Kaplan and Strömberg (2004) adopt such a classification is that some of those risks can be better controlled for, or insured against, than others. For instance, internal risk factors can to some extent be controlled by a careful monitoring by VCs. External factors are by essence beyond control. Complexity reflects the possible reliance on the entrepreneur's human capital, and the difficulty to find a successor if needed. All sources of risk are important determinants of the VCs' decision to invest. For instance, the quality of the management team is mentioned in 60 percent of the cases as a reason to invest, while the market development is mentioned in 69 percent of the investments. The technology and business model were a reason to invest in 40 percent of the cases. This selection role has also been studied theoretically. Ueda (2004) explains the use of venture capital by arguing that those investors can obtain more precise information than banks on the future prospects of firms. Building on this role, Casamatta and Haritchabalet (2007) explore how the syndication of deals can help venture capitalists gather additional useful information before supporting projects.[1]

The second source of value-added is the *monitoring and advising* role of venture capitalists. Monitoring and advising encompass all interventions of venture capitalists into portfolio firms once investment is realized. While monitoring relates to the venture capitalists' control over entrepreneurs' actions, advising is seen as more supportive. Advising has been documented in various ways since the earlier studies of Sahlman (1988, 1990) or Gorman and Sahlman (1989). For example, Hellmann and Puri (2000) analyze a sample of high tech Silicon Valley start-ups and find that the presence of venture capital fosters innovative strategies by reducing the time to bring a product to market. Hellmann and Puri (2002) document that venture capitalists alternate between a monitoring and an advising role according to the situation of the firm. Using a sample of 173 start-ups, they report that venture capitalists provide more support to the founder when things go well (for instance by helping to recruit key employees), but favor his replacement in harder times. This active intervention is not homogenous across venture capitalists. Bottazzi, Da Rin, and Hellmann (2008) explore this issue with a sample of European venture capital investments. They find that the organization structure of venture capital funds (in particular whether they are independent or affiliated to a bank or industrial group) as well as their human capital are important determinants of their supporting activity. Independent venture capital firms, as well as venture capital firms with experienced partners are more likely to be actively involved in the start-up firms after the investment phase.

VENTURE CAPITALISTS' CONTRACTS

Many of those interventions that enhance firm value are not easy to describe or to contract on. While it is conceivable to sign a contract that fixes a number of working hours, the efficiency of venture capital advice is less easy to verify. Also, the nature of the venture capitalists' intervention depends on the type of project. For instance, VCs may not have the same involvement with a young and inexperienced entrepreneur as with a more seasoned founder. Depending on their own experience or business specialization, they will not provide the same type of advice. For that reason, the value-added process and the active role of venture capitalists are generally considered sources of moral hazard in the literature. This raises the question of how to incentivize venture capitalists, that is, how to design optimal financial contracts to cope with the specific agency problems between entrepreneurs and VCs.

The empirical literature on venture capital contracts has highlighted the numerous specificities of the field. Kaplan and Strömberg (2003) are certainly the first to offer an in-depth analysis of venture capital contracts, based on 200 venture capital investment rounds in 118 portfolio firms, performed by 14 venture capital funds. Their first finding is that venture capital contracts allocate separately cash flow rights and control rights, measured as voting rights, board rights, and liquidation rights. This stands in sharp contrast with most standard financial contracts where cash-flow and control rights are usually bundled. An illustration of this separate allocation of cash-flow and control rights is that venture capitalists typically hold half of the cash flow rights of a given venture, but are unlikely to have the majority of the board seats (this happens only in 25 percent of the cases in the study sample). Their second finding is that the most widely used financial instruments are convertible preferred stocks, which appear in 189 financing rounds out of 200. However, the superiority of convertible preferred stocks has to be taken with caution. First, Kaplan and Strömberg (2003) study a sample of U.S. investments, where tax advantages favor the use of convertible preferred. Cumming (2005) studies a sample of over 3000 Canadian venture capital investments and finds that common equity is used in 36.33 percent of the investments, followed by straight debt (14.99 percent), and convertible debt (12.36 percent). In the Canadian sample, convertible preferred equity is used in hardly more than 10 percent of the investments. Second, Kaplan and Strömberg (2003) note that other securities are used in addition to the convertible preferred stocks, recognizing that what matters is the way cash flows are allocated, not the way financial securities are gathered to achieve a given allocation of cash flows. The last and more important result in view of the theoretical literature on agency conflicts is that both cash flow and control rights allocations are contingent on the achievement of some performance milestones, or on the occurrence of some observable variable. For instance, a typical financing round has the following features: venture capitalists hold an average stake of 50 percent of the cash flows, while the entrepreneur holds an average 30 percent and previous investors and employees hold 20 percent. However, the average stake of a venture capitalist can decrease by 8 percent between the less favorable and the most favorable performance states. This gap is even larger for early-stage rounds, and reaches an average 12 percent. Thus it is typical to find that when performance increases, the founder's stake increases due to the presence of vesting provisions, and the venture capitalist's stake decreases.

The overwhelming use of convertible preferred in the United States has certainly biased the theoretical literature to explore the optimality of such claims. Indeed, many papers advocate the use of convertible securities to alleviate moral hazard problems. It is important to notice, though, that in most theoretical models, convertible securities are just one, but not the unique way, to implement an optimal contingent allocation of cash flows. An illustration of this is the fact that in most models it is impossible to distinguish between convertible debt, convertible preferred, and preferred stocks. With this caveat in mind, we now turn to the theoretical results on optimal venture capital contracts. According to Dessì (2005), the use of convertible bonds guarantees an effective monitoring role of venture capitalists, and induces them to take appropriate continuation decisions. On the advising role of venture capitalists, Casamatta (2003) mentions that a key determinant of the use of convertible bonds is the amount of money invested into the venture. The next sections will develop a simple model to deal with this issue. Repullo and Suarez (2004) consider the problem faced by entrepreneurs in a sequential investment model. When venture capitalists intervene only at a later stage, it is optimal to finance the initial stage with convertible claims to compensate the initial investor while preserving the incentives of the venture capitalist.[2] Considering explicitly the dual role of venture capitalists (monitoring and advising), Schindele (2006) also concludes that convertible bonds, with a contingent allocation of control rights, are an optimal way to incentivize venture capitalists. Last, some papers have considered that the efficiency of venture capital intervention depends on the nature of the project. Maybe the support of venture capitalists is valuable for the most promising projects only. When it is difficult to forecast what should be the degree of support of venture capitalists, Schmidt (2003) shows that convertible bonds induce the venture capitalist to intervene precisely in those states where his action is desirable. A related idea is developed in Cestone (2000), who points out that giving too many incentives to the venture capitalist to exert effort increases his willingness to intervene in the strategic decisions: this can discourage the initiative efforts of the entrepreneur. A careful allocation of contingent cash flow and control rights is then needed to balance the two effects. The next section studies more deeply a situation of moral hazard on venture capitalist advice. In particular, it analyzes how to design optimally the financial structure of a venture to cope with the double task to incentivize an entrepreneur and a venture capitalist.

A MODEL OF START-UP FINANCING

Let us consider the following model of entrepreneurial financing based on Casamatta (2003). For simplicity, assume that all agents are risk-neutral and the riskless interest rate is normalized to zero. An entrepreneur has an investment project that requires a fixed initial outlay I. The project lasts one period, and delivers a risky cash flow that can be high (R^h) or low ($R^l < R^h$). For the moment, fix $R^l = 0$.[3] The probability of success of the project is denoted p. This probability of success depends on two inputs, the level of effort provided by the entrepreneur, and the level of advice provided by an advisor. This assumption captures the idea that the success of an innovative project depends on the combination of different competences and that no individual agent possesses all these competences. To fix ideas, think about the entrepreneur as a technical expert, and think about the advisor as a management expert. The level of effort provided by the entrepreneur (resping the advisor) can be high, in which case it is denoted e (resp. a), or low, in which case it is denoted ℓ (resp. $\measuredangle$). Efforts affect the probability of success of the project in the following way:

$$p(e, a) = p_h$$
$$p(\ell, a) = p(e, \measuredangle) = p_m$$
$$p(\ell, \measuredangle) = p_l$$

with $p_h > p_m > p_l$. The cost of exerting effort e (resp. a) is c (resp. k). The cost of exerting ℓ or $\measuredangle$ is simply zero. To highlight the fact that the entrepreneur's effort is really key to the success of the venture, assume that his effort is more efficient than the advisor's effort. Given that both efforts affect the probability of success in a symmetric way, this implies: $c < k$.

Last, the value of the project depends on the effort provided as follows:

$$p_h R^h - I - c - k > p_m R^h - I - c > 0 > p_m R^h - I - k > p_l R^h - I \qquad (8.1)$$

Condition 8.1 states that the project cannot have a positive NPV, unless the entrepreneur exerts high effort. In other words, managerial talent is not enough to make a venture profitable. Suppose first that effort is verifiable. The first best investment decision is simply to implement the project and exert a high level of effort and advice. Since effort can be contracted upon, any investor can provide financing I, and the type of financial contract signed between the investor, the entrepreneur, and the advisor is irrelevant. Any financial contract that guarantees the investor an expected payoff of I when e and a are exerted is acceptable.[4] The next section considers the case where efforts are not observable.

MORAL HAZARD AND VENTURE CAPITALIST INTERVENTION

Let us turn to the case where efforts are not observable. Denote

$$R_E^\theta$$

the entrepreneur's revenue if the final cash flow is R^θ with $\theta \in \{h, l\}$. Equivalently denote R_A^θ, the advisor's revenue in state R^θ if an advisor participates to the venture. Let us introduce some further terminology. If the advisor does not provide financing to the venture, he is called a *consultant*. If the advisor also provides financing, he is called a *venture capitalist*. This terminology accounts for the fact that venture capitalists do not act as mere investors but provide managerial advice to the start-up firms in their portfolio.[5]

To understand the role of a venture capitalist, let us first explore the entrepreneur's decision to hire a pure consultant, that is, an advisor who does not provide financing. To do this, assume that the entrepreneur is wealthy enough to finance the initial investment I. We will then compare this to the case where the entrepreneur contracts with a venture capitalist.

If the entrepreneur hires an advisor, he proposes a contract such that both he and the advisor are induced to exert effort. The contract thus solves the following program:

$$\max_{R_A^\theta} \quad p_h\left(R^h - R_A^h\right) - (1 - p_h)R_A^l - I - c$$
$$\text{s.t.} \quad p_h\left(R^h - R_A^h\right) - (1 - p_h)R_A^l - c \geq p_m\left(R^h - R_A^h\right) - (1 - p_m)R_A^l \quad (IC_E)$$
$$p_h R_A^h + (1 - p_h)R_A^l - k \geq p_m R_A^h + (1 - p_m)R_A^l \quad (IC_C)$$
$$R_A^\theta \geq 0 \quad (LL)$$

The condition (LL) expresses the fact that the consultant is protected by limited liability. For consistency, since the entrepreneur is assumed to invest I, this constraint is not imposed on him. It is easy to see that a necessary condition for constraints (IC_E) and (IC_C) to be consistent is:

$$R^h \geq \frac{c + k}{(p_h - p_m)} \tag{8.2}$$

which is assumed to hold for the rest of the analysis. The following proposition presents the result of the entrepreneur's program when he chooses to hire a consultant.

Proposition 1. *If condition (2) holds, the entrepreneur can hire a consultant and induce him to exert effort. The optimal compensation of the consultant is*

$$R_A^h = \frac{k}{p_h - p_m}$$
$$R_A^l = 0$$

As is standard in moral hazard settings, a higher cash flow is a better signal of effort, and the compensation of the agent has to increase with the final cash flow. Here, it is optimal to reward the consultant only in the state R^h. Note that since the final cash flow is 0 in case of failure, the entrepreneur is also rewarded in state R^h only.

Even if hiring a consultant is feasible, it may not be the best choice of the entrepreneur. Remember that the project is valuable with the entrepreneur's effort only (see condition (1)). The next proposition explores the choice of the entrepreneur whether or not to hire a consultant.

Proposition 2. *There exists a threshold* R^* *such that the entrepreneur chooses not to hire a consultant when* $R^h \leq R^*$ *, and to hire a consultant when* $R^h > R^*$*. The threshold* R^* *is equal to* $\frac{p_h k}{(p_h - p_m)^2}$*. When the cost of the entrepreneur's effort* c *is sufficiently low compared to the cost of the consultant's effort* k *in the sense that*

$$c < \frac{p_m}{p_h - p_m} k \tag{8.3}$$

the threshold R^* *is strictly larger than* $\frac{c+k}{(p_h - p_m)}$ *.*

Proposition 2 illustrates the cost for the entrepreneur to hire a pure consultant. To induce the consultant to exert effort for the project to be successful, the entrepreneur has to abandon to him an incentive rent that depends on the consultant's cost of effort k. When this rent is sufficiently large compared to what the entrepreneur earns by staying on his own, the latter prefers not to hire a consultant *even if hiring a consultant is feasible*. Because of the cost to provide incentives, the entrepreneur is better off launching his venture alone when the future proceeds of the project are not very high ($R^h \leq R^*$). To understand to what extent this result is due to the entrepreneur's effort being more efficient than the advisor's effort, one can look at the polar case, that is, the case where the advisor has to decide whether to hire the entrepreneur as an employee. In that case, the program to be solved is the following:

$$\max_{R_E^\theta} \quad p_h \left(R^h - R_E^h \right) - (1 - p_h) R_E^l - I - k$$
$$\text{s.t.} \quad p_h R_E^h + (1 - p_h) R_E^l - c \geq p_m R_E^h + (1 - p_m) R_E^l \tag{IC_E}$$
$$p_h \left(R^h - R_E^h \right) - (1 - p_h) R_E^l - k \geq p_m \left(R^h - R_E^h \right) - (1 - p_m) R_E^l \tag{IC_C}$$
$$R_E^\theta \geq 0 \tag{LL}$$

This program means that the advisor-investor finances the project, and proposes to the entrepreneur a contract that induces the latter to exert effort.

Proposition 3. *There exists a threshold* R^{**} *such that the advisor chooses not to hire an entrepreneur when* $R^h \leq R^{**}$*, and to hire an entrepreneur when* $R^h > R^{**}$*. The threshold* R^{**} *is strictly smaller than* R^**.*

As before, the advisor who finances the project may renounce hiring the entrepreneur because the incentive rent to pay is too high compared to the project's value. However, because the entrepreneur's effort is more efficient, the advisor is more likely to hire the entrepreneur as an employee than the reverse. In other words, there are parameter values for which the entrepreneur prefers to stay on his own, while the advisor prefers to hire an entrepreneur as an employee. There are *no* parameter values for which the reverse holds. Proposition 3 reflects the fact that the difficulty to implement the joint provision of efforts depends on the relative efficiency of the two efforts: when the entrepreneur's effort is more efficient, he finds it less valuable to hire a consultant.

To complete this section, let us now explore the role of venture capitalists. The question raised here is whether the intervention of venture capitalists can improve the situation faced by entrepreneurs. To answer that question, let us consider the case where the entrepreneur asks for financing from a venture capitalist. In this situation, the venture capitalist provides effort a and financing I_{VC}. For sake of comparison, and to make the problem interesting, we maintain the assumption of limited liability for the venture capitalist. The program of the entrepreneur is now written:

$$
\begin{aligned}
\max\nolimits_{R_A^\theta, I_{VC}} \quad & p_h\left(R^h - R_A^h\right) - (1 - p_h)R_A^l - (I - I_{VC}) - c \\
\text{s.t.} \quad & p_h\left(R^h - R_A^h\right) - (1 - p_h)R_A^l - c \geq p_m\left(R^h - R_A^h\right) - (1 - p_m)R_A^l \quad (IC_E) \\
& p_h R_A^h + (1 - p_h)R_A^l - k \geq p_m R_A^h + (1 - p_m)R_A^l \quad (IC_{VC}) \\
& p_h R_A^h + (1 - p_h)R_A^l - k - I_{VC} \geq 0 \quad (PC_{VC}) \\
& R_A^\theta \geq 0 \quad (LL)
\end{aligned}
$$

The program is different from the pure consultant case in several respects. First, the entrepreneur can set the optimal amount of outside financing I_{VC} to maximize his expected utility. Second, one needs to introduce a participation constraint for the venture capitalist to accept the deal offered by the entrepreneur. This constraint was not needed before, because it was redundant with the advisor's incentive compatibility condition. This is no longer the case when the venture capitalist has to invest I_{VC}.

Proposition 4. *The optimal amount of venture capital financing is strictly positive.*

Proposition 4 states that the expected utility of the entrepreneur is strictly larger when he contracts with a venture capitalist than when he contracts with a pure consultant. Indeed, the case where he hires a consultant is deducted from the program above by setting $I_{VC} = 0$. The result that the optimal amount of venture capital financing is strictly positive implies that the entrepreneur's utility increases with the amount of outside financing.[6] Venture capitalists are always depicted as hands-on investors, who provide more than money to cash-poor entrepreneurs. The commonly accepted idea is that they monitor and advise entrepreneurs *because they invest money* into their venture. This result complements this idea by showing that venture capitalists invest *because they provide advice*. The corporate finance literature has often emphasized the view that firms or entrepreneurs are financially constrained because of agency problems and that the cost of external financing increases with those agency costs. In the specific setting of venture capital, where venture capitalists themselves have to provide advice, this is not necessarily true. Because entrepreneurs also face a moral hazard problem related to the effort provided by venture capitalists, outside financing can help reduce incentive costs, and it increases the value of the firm. To complete this study of venture capital financing, the next section explores the design of the optimal financial contracts between entrepreneurs and venture capitalists.

OPTIMAL FINANCIAL CONTRACTS BETWEEN ENTREPRENEURS AND VENTURE CAPITALISTS

We now turn to the question of the type of contract signed between entrepreneurs and venture capitalists. The empirical literature on venture capital reports that convertible claims (bonds or preferred stocks) are widely used in venture capital financing. To understand the use of those claims, let us consider the case where $R^l > 0$. To be more realistic, let us assume that both the venture capitalist and the entrepreneur are protected by limited liability.[7] As before, the financial participation of the venture capitalist is denoted I_{VC}. The program to be solved is now:

$$
\begin{aligned}
\max_{R_A^\theta, I_{VC}} \quad & p_h\left(R^h - R_A^h\right) + (1 - p_h)\left(R^l - R_A^l\right) - (I - I_{VC}) - c \\
\text{s.t.} \quad & p_h\left(R^h - R_A^h\right) + (1 - p_h)\left(R^l - R_A^l\right) - c \geq p_m\left(R^h - R_A^h\right) \\
& \quad + (1 - p_m)\left(R^l - R_A^l\right) && (IC_E) \\
& p_h R_A^h + (1 - p_h)R_A^l - k \geq p_m R_A^h + (1 - p_m)R_A^l && (IC_{VC}) \\
& p_h R_A^h + (1 - p_h)R_A^l - k - I_{VC} \geq 0 && (PC_{VC}) \\
& R_A^\theta \in \left[0, R^\theta\right] && (LL)
\end{aligned}
$$

Note that the main difference from the previous case is the fact that the repayment to the venture capitalist is bounded above by the value of the final cash flow R^θ. The type of financial contract according to the amount invested by the venture capitalist is defined in the next proposition.

Proposition 5. *The optimal amount of venture capital* (I_{VC}) *lies in the interval* $[\underline{I}_{VC}, \bar{I}_{VC}]$. *The optimal financial contract offered to the venture capitalist has the following properties:*

- *When I_{VC} is equal to $\underline{I}_{VC}$, the venture capitalist's contract can be implemented with common stocks. The entrepreneur then holds preferred stocks.*
- *When I_{VC} is equal to $\bar{I}_{VC}$, the venture capitalist's contract can be implemented with convertible bonds or preferred stocks. The entrepreneur then holds common stocks.*

Proposition 5 provides several insights on venture capital financial contracts. First, there is a maximum and a minimum amount of venture capital that can be provided in order to preserve the two agents' incentives to exert effort. We already know from Proposition 4 that it is optimal to let the venture capitalist invest a strictly positive minimum amount of money into the venture. This minimum investment compensates the entrepreneur for the incentive cost of inducing effort a. For the same reason, there is a maximum feasible level of venture capital investment: this maximum level is determined by the incentive compatibility condition of the entrepreneur himself. In other words, to maintain the entrepreneur's incentive to exert effort, the venture capitalist cannot be pledged too large a fraction of the final cash flow. This in turn limits the amount that the venture capitalist is willing to invest. Second, the type of financial claim issued by the entrepreneur depends on the level of investment of the venture capitalist. When his financial investment is low, what matters is his incentive to exert effort: the venture capitalist is then given some common stocks, while the entrepreneur obtains preferred stocks. This capital structure ensures that the venture capitalist is only rewarded in case of success. When the venture capitalist invests a lot, he has to be given a large fraction of the final cash flow. What matters then is to preserve the entrepreneur's incentive to exert effort and the latter is given common stocks while the venture capitalist holds convertible bonds. In that case, the allocation of cash flows is reversed, and the entrepreneur is only rewarded in case of success.

DISCUSSION AND EMPIRICAL PREDICTIONS

The stylized model developed here explains several features of venture capital financing and allows us to derive some empirical implications. Before developing these predictions, it should be noted that the situation explored here is one in which the involvement of the entrepreneur as well that of a business advisor are needed. For this reason, it is better suited to fit the situation of a young company, at an early stage of development. When the product and the business strategy still need to be more accurately defined, and when the management team is still incomplete, both the presence of a technical expert (the entrepreneur) and that of a business advisor are crucial for the success of the venture. Therefore, the conclusions of the model apply more specifically to early-stage financing rather than to private equity investments at later stages of a firm's life as, for instance, at the buy-out or expansion stages. The extent to which the model can fit later stages of financing depends on the particular situation of each firm. For instance, if the presence of a technical expert is less needed, the entrepreneur and the venture capitalist's efforts can substitute for one another, a situation not depicted here. In the remainder of the text, we will focus on empirical implications for early-stage firms.

First, we have shown that venture capital intervention is particularly desirable when entrepreneurs need some form of management advice. One important result of the model is that it is preferable (and sometimes only possible) to entrust a venture capitalist with the provision of business advice, rather than to hire a consultant. This theory implies the following testable predictions:

1. The first prediction of the model is related to the presence of consultants in start-up firms: the model implies that those firms asking for consultant services should be managed by entrepreneurs with not very specific skills or knowledge. One way to test this prediction would be to gather a cross-section of start-up firms, and to estimate the probability that they will ask for consulting services. This probability should depend on the entrepreneur's educational background. For instance it should be negatively correlated with entrepreneur's education unrelated to business administration. This prediction is supported by the result of proposition 2: when the cost of the entrepreneur's effort is low compared to that of the consultant, the former

prefers not to hire a consultant. The cost of the entrepreneur's effort is likely to be different from that of the consultant if the entrepreneur has specific skills, for instance, if he has a degree unrelated to business management. A related prediction is that venture capital financing is more likely when entrepreneurs have no business experience, and strong technical human capital.

2. A second prediction is that one should expect less venture capital in the capital structure of start-up firms when management teams are complete, and more when key personnel are missing. Again, this result calls for a more precise investigation of the organization of firms, and in particular of their human resources. This prediction is supported by an important idea of the model, which is that venture capital financing is sought when entrepreneurs need more than money, for instance when they need business advice. This is more likely when entrepreneurs miss such competencies inside the firm, that is, at the beginning of the firm's life, when such valuable employees have not yet been hired. When firms grow and get more mature, the need for business advice decreases, and venture capital should be less frequent.

A second important insight of the model is that the type of financial claim held by venture capitalists should vary with the amount of money they invest into the firms. For instance, one should observe that the probability of buying convertible claims increases with the financial investment of the venture capitalist. One should also observe that venture capitalists who do not invest much have much riskier claims than venture capitalists who invest a lot. At the opposite the entrepreneur should have more cash flow rights in low states of nature, the larger his financial investment. The reason behind this prediction is that when the investment of one agent is low, he needs to be given high-powered incentives in order to exert effort. This prediction is supported by the empirical observation that business angels, who typically invest much less than venture capitalists, more frequently hold common stocks, while venture capitalists hold convertible claims.

CONCLUSION

This chapter surveys the forms of value-added provided by venture capitalists. It explores the types of interventions that can increase the value of start-up firms, as well as the tools used by venture capitalists to add value. A simple model is presented that explains both why venture capitalists have a relative advantage compared to consultants in providing business advice to entrepreneurs, and why venture capitalists do not always buy the same type of financial claims. A key insight of the model is that the desirability of venture capital intervention, as well as the financial contract between entrepreneurs and investors depends on the relative efficiency of the efforts of the two agents. A natural extension of the above analysis would be to consider how this relative efficiency varies with the characteristics of projects, experience and educational background of agents, as well as with the legal and economic environment of start-up firms. One could then obtain comparative statics regarding the frequency of venture capital intervention, and regarding the type of financial contracts used.

This could be useful to better understand cross-country differences in the working of the venture capital industry. As already mentioned in the introduction, there is a striking difference between the financial contracts used in the United States and those used in other countries.[8] Some of the reasons for such differences lie beyond the scope of this chapter: as argued by Cummings (2005), favorable tax treatments can explain the widespread use of convertible preferred stocks in the United States. The legal system in which the company operates may also affect the design of financial contracts by rendering some contractual provisions more costly to enforce. The model developed in this chapter emphasizes that the structure of financial contracts depends on the relative efficiency of the venture capitalist's and the entrepreneur's effort. In countries where venture capitalists are less experienced, it is harder to induce them to exert effort, and higher-powered incentive schemes have to be provided to venture capitalists: venture capitalists have to be given more common stocks, and less liquidation rights when their cost of effort is higher. Venture capitalists may not always intervene in the management of the portfolio firm. Another consequence of the model is that when VCs do not play an active role, they should hold debt-like claims, to foster the entrepreneur's incentives to effort. Debt-like instruments can also arise in the context of venture capital financing. A natural consequence of this is that the lead syndicate partner should hold different claims from the other members of the syndicate, because his involvement in the venture is likely to be greater.

APPENDIX

Proof of Proposition 1. See first that at the optimum, (IC_C) is binding, otherwise the entrepreneur could reduce R_A^h and increase his expected utility. For the same reason, $R_A^l = 0$.

We then obtain

$$R_A^h = \frac{k}{p_h - p_m}$$

Replacing R_A^h into (IC_E), one sees that this contract is feasible if and only if condition (2) holds.

Proof of Proposition 2. Note that by staying alone, the entrepreneur can secure an expected profit of $p_m R^h - I - c$. Using the result of Proposition 1, the optimal contract signed with a consultant gives the entrepreneur an expected payoff of $p_h R^h - I - c - \frac{p_h k}{p_h - p_m}$. See that:

$$p_h R^h - I - c - \frac{p_h k}{p_h - p_m} > p_m R^h - I - c \Leftrightarrow R^h > \frac{p_h k}{(p_h - p_m)^2}$$

Last see that:

$$\frac{p_h k}{(p_h - p_m)^2} > \frac{c + k}{(p_h - p_m)} \Leftrightarrow c < \frac{p_m}{p_h - p_m} k$$

Proof of Proposition 3. Proceed as before to state that $R^h{}_E = \frac{c}{p_h - p_m}$ and that the expected payoff of the advisor, if he hires an entrepreneur, is: $p_h R^h - I - k - \frac{p_h c}{p_h - p_m}$. Because $c < k$, we have:

$$p_h R^h - I - k - \frac{p_h c}{p_h - p_m} > p_h R^h - I - c - \frac{p_h k}{p_h - p_m} \tag{8.4}$$

Denote $R^h = R^0$ the point at which the RHS of equation (4) is equal to zero. Because $p_m R^h - I - c$ is strictly positive, we have : $R^0 < R^*$. Denoting $R^h = R^{**}$ the point at which the LHS is equal to zero, it follows from equation (4) that $R^{**} < R^0 < R^*$.

Proof of Proposition 4. It is easy to see that at the optimum (PC_{VC}) is binding; otherwise one could increase I_{VC} to increase the objective function. We then have :

$$I_{VC} = p_h R^h_A + (1 - p_h) R^l_A - k. \tag{8.5}$$

From the constraint (IC_{VC}), one sees easily that the RHS of equation (5) is strictly positive, thus I_{VC} is strictly positive. Last, see that this increases the expected utility of the entrepreneur by replacing I_{VC} (using equation (5)) into the objective function. The entrepreneur's payoff is then : $p_h R^h - I - k - c$ which is strictly larger than $p_h R^h - I - c - \frac{p_h k}{p_h - p_m}$.

Proof of Proposition 5. Remember from the proof of Proposition 4 that (PC_{VC}) is binding. Therefore, at the optimum, the expected utility of the entrepreneur is fixed (and equal to the project NPV) and does not depend on the parameters of the contract as long as the constraints of the program are satisfied. The minimum and maximum amount of venture capital investment are simply determined by different contract parameter values. See from (PC_{VC}) that I_{VC} increases with R^θ_A. See also that R^h_A is bounded below by (IC_{VC}) and bounded above by (IC_E). To compute the minimum amount of venture capital financing, set $R^l_A = 0$ and use (IC_{VC}) to see that the minimum value of R^h_A is $\frac{k}{p_h - p_m}$. Replacing these parameters into (PC_{VC}) gives:

$$\underline{I}_{VC} = \frac{p_m k}{p_h - p_m}.$$

To find the maximum amount of venture capital financing, fix $R^l_A = R^l$, and use (IC_E) to see that the maximal value of R^h_A is $R^h - \frac{c}{p_h - p_m}$. Replace those into (PC_{VC}) to obtain:

$$\overline{I}_{VC} = p_h R^h + (1 - p_h) R^l - \frac{p_h c}{p_h - p_m} - k.$$

To complete the proof, note that when the venture capitalist invests $\underline{I}_{VC}$, he is only rewarded in case of success, while the entrepreneur obtains R^l in case of failure. Therefore, the venture capitalist's contract can be implemented by giving him common stocks and giving the entrepreneur preferred stocks. The opposite holds when the venture capitalist invests $\overline{I}_{VC}$. In that case, he obtains R^l in case of failure, and the entrepreneur is only rewarded in case of success, which can be implemented by giving the venture capitalist convertible bonds with a face value at least equal to R^l.

NOTES

1. On this issue, see also Cestone, Lerner, and White (2006).
2. The reader can refer to Cumming and Johan (2007) for an empirical analysis on European investments of the link between advice intensity and financial contracts.
3. This assumption will be relaxed when discussing the optimal financial contract between the entrepreneur and a venture capitalist.
4. Note that when efforts are contractible, the entrepreneur or the advisor can themselves act as investors.
5. See among others Gorman and Sahlman (1989); Sapienza, Manigart, and Vermeir (1996); or Hellmann and Puri (2002) on the venture capitalists' value-added process.
6. If the entrepreneur is also protected by limited liability, the optimal amount of outside financing is bounded above.
7. This helps reduce the range of optimal contracts.
8. For instance, see Cumming (2005) for the case of Canada, and Kaplan, Martel, and Strömberg (2007) for an international comparison.

REFERENCES

Bottazzi, L., M. Da Rin, and T. Hellmann. 2008. Who are the active investors? Evidence from venture capital. *Journal of Financial Economics* 89(3):488–512.

Brav, A., and P. Gompers. 1997. Myth or reality? The long-run underperformance of initial public offerings: Evidence from venture and nonventure-capital-backed companies. *Journal of Finance* 52(5):1791–1821.

Casamatta, C. 2003. Financing and advising: Optimal financial contracts with venture capitalists. *Journal of Finance* 58(5):2059–2086.

———, and C. Haritchabalet. 2007. Experience, screening and syndication in venture capital investments. *Journal of Financial Intermediation* 16(3):368–398.

Cestone, G. 2000. Venture capital meets contract theory: Risky claims or formal control? Working paper. UT1 and UAB.

———, J. Lerner, and L. White. 2006. The design of syndicates in venture capital. Working paper. CSEF, University of Salerno.

Cumming, D. 2005. Capital structure in venture finance. *Journal of Corporate Finance* 11(3):550–585.

———, and S. Johan. 2007. Advice and monitoring in venture capital finance. *Financial Markets and Portfolio Management* 21(1):3–43.

Dessí, R. 2005. Start-up finance, monitoring and collusion. *Rand Journal of Economics* 36(2):255–274.

Fenn, G., N. Liang, and S. Prowse. 1995. The economics of the private equity market. Board of Governors of the Federal Reserve System.

Gompers, P., and J. Lerner. 1999. Conflicts of interest in the issuance of public securities: Evidence from venture capital. *Journal of Law and Economics* 42(1):1–28.

Gorman, M., and W. Sahlman. 1989. What do venture capitalists do? *Journal of Business Venturing* 4(4):231–248.

Hellmann, T., and M. Puri. 2000. The interaction between product market and financing strategy: The role of venture capital. *Review of Financial Studies* 13(4):959–984.

_____. 2002. Venture capital and the professionalization of start-up firms: Empirical evidence. *Journal of Finance* 57(1):169–197.

Kaplan, S., F. Martel, and P. Strömberg. 2007. How do legal differences and experience affect financial contracts? *Journal of Financial Intermediation* 16(3):273–311.

Kaplan, S., and P. Strömberg. 2003. Financial contracting theory meets the real world: An empirical analysis of venture capital contracts. *Review of Economic Studies* 70(2):281–316.

_____. 2004. Characteristics, contracts, and actions: Evidence from venture capitalist analyses. *Journal of Finance* 59(5):2177–2210.

Kortum, S., and J. Lerner. 2000. Assessing the contribution of venture capital to innovation. *RAND Journal of Economics* 31(4):674–692.

Repullo, R., and J. Suarez. 2004. Venture capital finance: A security design approach. *Review of Finance* 8(1):75–108.

Sahlman, W. 1988. Aspects of financial contracting in venture capital. *Journal of Applied Corporate Finance* 1(2):23–36.

_____. 1990. The structure and governance of venture-capital organizations. *Journal of Financial Economics* 27(2):473–522.

Sapienza, H., S. Manigart, and W. Vermeir. 1996. Venture capitalist governance and value-added in four countries. *Journal of Business Venturing* 11(6):439–469.

Schindele, I. 2006. Advice and monitoring: Venture financing with multiple tasks. EFA 2004 Maastricht Meetings Paper No. 4637.

Schmidt, K. 2003. Convertible securities and venture capital finance. *Journal of Finance* 58(3):1139–1166.

Ueda, M. 2004. Banks versus venture capital: Project evaluation, screening, and expropriation. *Journal of Finance* 59(2):601–621.

ABOUT THE AUTHOR

Catherine Casamatta is Professor of Finance and head of the Ph.D. program in management at Toulouse University. She is a board member of the French Finance Association and academic fellow of the Europlace Institute of Finance. Her research interests cover many areas of corporate finance theory (capital structure, managerial compensation, venture capital), financial intermediation, and the organization of the fund management industry. Her research has been published in international academic journals such as the *Journal of Finance* and the *Journal of Financial Intermediation*. She holds a Ph.D. from Toulouse University and graduated from ESSEC business school.

## CHAPTER 9

Venture Capitalists, Monitoring and Advising

ROBERTA DESSÍ
Associate Professor of Economics, Toulouse School of Economics (IDEI and GREMAQ)

INTRODUCTION

Venture capitalists are widely regarded as financial intermediaries who provide not just financing but also advice and monitoring. This view rests on solid empirical foundations: according to Gorman and Sahlman (1989), for example, lead venture investors visit each portfolio company an average of 19 times per year, and spend 100 hours in direct contact (on site or by phone) with the company. Venture capitalists play a very active role in negotiating with suppliers, helping to recruit and compensate key individuals, replacing founders with outside CEOs, providing strategic advice and access to consultants, investment bankers, and lawyers (Gompers and Lerner 1999; Hellmann and Puri 2002; Lerner 1995; Kaplan and Strömberg 2003, 2004; and Sahlman 1990).

This chapter develops a unified theoretical framework to analyze the implications of venture capitalists' multiple roles as financiers, monitors, and advisers. The model is used to address three main questions:

1. What is the optimal allocation of cash flow rights and control rights between entrepreneurs and venture capitalists? Does this correspond to what is commonly observed in venture capital contracts?
2. What are the different implications of venture capitalists' roles as financiers, monitors, and advisors?
3. In what way does the desirability of deterring potential collusion between entrepreneurs and venture capitalists, at the expense of other investors, shape the structure of venture capital deals?

Each of these questions can obviously be investigated with a variety of approaches. The use of a single model to address all three questions has the advantage, beyond parsimony and simplicity, of exploring the connections between these different issues. For example, how does the allocation of control rights and cash flow rights affect incentives to monitor or advise relative to incentives to collude? This is one of the issues addressed below. On the other hand, the three questions set out above are very broad, and the answers generated here will be necessarily (very) incomplete; other chapters in this volume will provide plenty of additional insights.

The analysis developed below focuses on how financial contracts can be designed to achieve several objectives that are particularly important in the venture capital context. First, entrepreneurs need to be motivated to take efficient decisions for the venture; this may entail the provision of significant effort and the willingness to sacrifice some personal benefits in order to increase the chances of commercial success of the company. For example, an entrepreneur may be tempted to pursue an investment project that he finds particularly interesting (e.g., it was "his idea"), or one that could give him considerable personal prestige, even though their expected profitability is much lower than for an alternative project. It may be possible to solve this potential moral hazard problem and provide appropriate incentives to the entrepreneur by giving him a sufficient monetary stake in the venture; however, this reduces the returns available for investors and hence their willingness to contribute capital. When entrepreneurs are sufficiently capital-constrained, as is often the case for innovative start-ups, they may therefore turn to venture capitalists, who can alleviate the problem of entrepreneurial moral hazard through monitoring and intervention. This in turn leads to a second objective for venture capital contracts: they also need to induce venture capitalists to monitor efficiently.

As noted earlier, venture capitalists may play another valuable role, by providing advice on matters on which they have considerable knowledge and expertise. For example, venture capitalists will typically know the industry very well and be able to advise on strategic decisions, as well as helping to recruit key personnel. Thus a third objective of venture capital contracts may be to induce venture capitalists to provide advice efficiently. Finally, a crucial objective is to ensure that the venture is liquidated if its future prospects become sufficiently poor, or, on the contrary, that it is able to obtain the additional funding it needs to grow and invest when future prospects are sufficiently favorable.[1]

While this is by no means an exhaustive list of the objectives that need to be taken into account in the design of venture capital contracts, it does capture several of the key issues. Indeed, the need to elicit both entrepreneurial effort and VC advice has been the focus of numerous recent contributions to the theoretical literature on venture capital, while the importance of inducing the efficient decision to continue or liquidate is central to the work of, for example, Admati and Pfleiderer (1994). The approach developed in this chapter extends this literature in two key respects; first, by studying all the issues outlined above within a single theoretical framework and exploring the connections between them; second, by identifying and exploring a crucial new factor in the design of venture capital contracts: the need to ensure that entrepreneurs and venture capitalists have no incentive to collude at the expense of other investors, whether these investors be the limited partners in the venture capital fund, non-venture investors involved at an early stage, or later-stage investors such as those acquiring shares in the company at an IPO.

The need for contracts to be collusion-proof rules out a number of otherwise feasible contracts. This makes it possible to obtain a number of implications, for example concerning the optimal allocation of cash flow rights and control rights, without imposing exogenous restrictions on the set of contracts that can be used.

In this respect, the approach developed here differs from the one adopted in a number of contributions to the literature, which simply assume that contracts will be incomplete and that general control (ownership) rights will have to be allocated to the entrepreneur, the venture capitalist, or both (e.g., de Bettignies [2008]). In this chapter, on the other hand, the efficient allocation of control rights emerges endogenously through the analysis of optimal collusion-proof contracts. This makes it possible to obtain implications about the optimal allocation of specific control rights, which is consistent with observed practice in venture capital contracts.

The approach developed below sheds light on three features of venture capital financings, including:

1. The widespread use of convertible securities, such as convertible debt or preferred stock, especially in the United States
2. The allocation of control rights over the decision to continue or liquidate the project to venture capitalists, through the use of redemption rights, combined with negative covenants and staged financings
3. The certification role played by venture capitalists, whereby their decision to continue the project and exercise their securities' conversion option acts as a credible "good" signal to other investors (e.g., in an IPO)

The chapter is organized as follows. I first introduce the model, based on Dessí (2005). The theoretical analysis developed in Dessí (2005) focused on the monitoring role of venture capitalists: this is studied in the section after the model is discussed. Advice (support) is examined, which establishes how the results are modified if venture capitalists act purely as financiers and advisers—a case that has received considerable attention in the theoretical literature, but in different settings. The main innovation here is the analysis of how the possibility of collusion shapes optimal financial contracts between entrepreneurs and financiers/advisers.

THE MODEL

The model, based on Dessí (2005), has three types of agent: entrepreneurs, venture capitalists (intermediaries), and investors. For simplicity, they are all assumed to be risk neutral and protected by limited liability. There are two periods. At the beginning of the first period, $t = 0$, each entrepreneur has the opportunity to invest in a project, provided he can finance the required initial expenditure of value C_0. The interesting case, which will be the focus of our analysis, occurs when the entrepreneur does not have enough capital to undertake the project on his own. He can then seek finance from venture capitalists and/or other investors. In the presence of such external financing, there is a potential moral hazard problem at this stage, associated with the entrepreneur's choice of project. At the end of the first period, $t = 1$, a "good" or a "bad" state is realized; the state determines the expected payoffs from continuing or liquidating the project. If the project is continued, it requires further financing of value C_1. It will then yield return $R > 0$ at $t = 2$ if it succeeds, and zero otherwise. If the project is liquidated at $t = 1$, it generates a liquidation value L. There may then be a second moral hazard problem, associated with the decision to continue or liquidate the project. The model is described in greater detail below.

Entrepreneurs

At the beginning of the first period, each entrepreneur possesses some capital, $A_f < C_0$. He therefore needs to raise some external funds. At this point, there is substantial uncertainty about the returns that the project will generate. Some of the uncertainty is resolved at $t = 1$, when the state, γ, is realized. The state may be "good" (γ_G) or "bad" (γ_B), where $\gamma_G > \gamma_B > 0$. If the project is continued, it will either succeed, with probability γ, yielding verifiable returns R at $t = 2$, or fail, yielding returns equal to zero. The state γ therefore represents the probability of success in the second period.

The entrepreneur's choice of project determines the probability of the good ($\gamma = \gamma_G$) or bad ($\gamma = \gamma_B$) state occurring. Specifically, the entrepreneur chooses between a "good" project, in which the good state occurs with probability p_H, and a "bad" project, in which the good state occurs with a lower probability p_L, but the entrepreneur obtains a private benefit of value $B > 0$ during the first period. In what follows I denote by $\Delta p = p_H - p_L > 0$ the increase in the probability of the good state occurring associated with choosing the good project, and by $\Delta \gamma = \gamma_G - \gamma_B > 0$ the difference in the probability of success between the good state and the bad state.

Venture Capitalists (Intermediaries)

Beyond providing capital, venture capitalists can perform one of two functions, advising and monitoring, or both. Advising (or "support") entails a variety of value-adding activities, such as helping to recruit and compensate key individuals, working with suppliers and customers, and helping to establish tactics and strategy. I shall formalize these by assuming that a venture capitalist can, by incurring a private cost $c_a > 0$, increase the probability of the "good" state occurring by q, where $1 - p_H > q > 0$. Monitoring, on the other hand, enables the venture capitalist to limit the scope for opportunistic behavior by the entrepreneur. I model this formally by assuming that, through monitoring, the venture capitalist can reduce the entrepreneur's private benefit from undertaking the bad project to b, where $B > b > 0$. This alleviates the moral hazard problem associated with project choice. It can be interpreted as a restriction on the scope for opportunistic behavior by the entrepreneur as follows: suppose there is a third project that the entrepreneur could choose, identical to the bad project described above except for a lower private benefit, of value b. Then by becoming informed, the venture capitalist can identify the bad project yielding the large private benefit B, and intervene to prevent the entrepreneur from undertaking this project. On the other hand, monitoring is not perfect and cannot eliminate moral hazard altogether: the entrepreneur can still choose the project with low success probability and private benefits b.

Monitoring (intervention) entails a private cost $c_m > 0$ for the venture capitalist. Both costs, the cost of monitoring and the cost of advising, cannot be contracted on. Appropriate financial incentives must therefore be provided to the venture capitalist to induce him to engage in either activity. These will need to take into account not only the need to compensate for the costs c_a and c_m, but also any rents that venture capitalists may be able to earn because of the relative scarcity of financial intermediaries possessing both the skills and expertise of venture capitalists and substantial capital. In particular, I shall denote by α the gross expected rate of return on capital (per period), net of monitoring and advising costs, demanded by venture capitalists at $t = 0$. The equilibrium value of α will be determined by the interaction between supply and demand for venture capital (see Dessí 2005 for details). Typically, this will exceed the rate of return demanded by other investors, for the reason just given. Entrepreneurs will therefore raise from venture capitalists only the minimum amount of capital consistent with obtaining their monitoring and/or advice. Any remaining need for external finance will be met by turning to other investors.

Investors

In contrast to venture capitalists, other investors are assumed to be small and/or to lack the necessary skills to become informed and intervene (monitor) or advise. For this reason, I will often refer to them as "uninformed investors" or "outside investors" in what follows. There are many of these uninformed investors in each period, so that it is always possible to raise finance from them by offering them their required gross expected rate of return, which is normalized to one. In the venture capital context, there are several possible interpretations of "uninformed investors." First, these investors could be the limited partners in a venture capital fund. Typically, these investors provide most of the fund's capital, but they are not closely involved with the portfolio companies and remain "uninformed" relative to the venture capitalist. A second possible interpretation of the outside investors is that they represent non-venture investors, who are sometimes brought on board by venture capitalists to participate in financing but without becoming closely involved with the companies that receive the funds.[2] A third possible interpretation is that of new investors who acquire shares in the company when it is taken public, and who will be less informed at this stage than the venture capitalist who has been involved with the company from the start.

The Projects

To make the analysis interesting, I shall make the following five assumptions, where the model timeline is indicated in Exhibit 9.1:

1. $\gamma_G R - C_1 > L$
   Continuation is efficient at $t = 1$ in the good state.
2. $\gamma_B R - C_1 < L$
   Liquidation is efficient at $t = 1$ in the bad state.
3. $q[\gamma_G(R - C_1) - L] > c_a$
   Advice is efficient.
4. $p_H(\gamma_G R - C_1) + (1 - p_H)L \geq C_0 + c_m$
   It is efficient to invest in the good project ex ante, even if it requires monitoring and there is no advice.
5. $B + (p_L + q)(\gamma_G R - C_1) + (1 - p_L - q)L < C_0 + c_a$
   It is never efficient to invest in the bad project.

Exhibit 9.1   Timeline

$t = 0$	$t = 1$	$t = 2$
Financial contracts signed. Monitoring? Entrepreneur chooses good or bad project. Advice?	Realization of γ. Decision to continue or liquidate.	Project returns realized.

Information

I shall assume that the entrepreneur and the venture capitalist observe the realization of γ at $t = 1$, but outside investors do not. This kind of informational advantage for "insiders" relative to "outsiders" as in, for example, Admati and Pfleiderer (1994), Dessí (2005, 2009), Rajan (1992), and Schmidt (2003). It seems very plausible in the case of entrepreneurial start-up companies. It captures the idea that the venture capitalist has easier access to information about the firm's progress and prospects than outside investors, as well as the knowledge and expertise required to interpret the information correctly. Indeed, venture capitalists typically concentrate their investments in industries or sectors that they know and understand particularly well, often having worked in them (e.g., as entrepreneurs) prior to becoming venture capitalists. This is likely to be especially important for high technology industries, where considerable technical expertise may be needed to evaluate progress in the early stages of a venture.

MONITORING

This section studies the case where venture capitalists engage in monitoring but do not advise. Monitoring may entail a variety of interventions on the part of the board of directors (e.g., to recruit and change management,[3] which in turn affects the firm's strategy and the entrepreneur's (founder's) ability to pursue his preferred project). I begin by assuming that collusion is never feasible. This assumption is then relaxed to study how venture capital contracts can be optimally designed when the possibility of collusion is allowed for. As we shall see, the resulting contracts ensure that collusion does not occur in equilibrium; moreover, the allocation of cash flow rights and control rights in these contracts is consistent with common practice in the venture capital industry.

Collusion Ruled Out A Priori

If entrepreneurs possess enough of own capital, they can obtain the external finance they require to undertake their project directly from uninformed investors, with no need for (costly) monitoring: see Dessí (2005) for details. Since this entails no role for venture capitalists, I shall focus instead on the case where entrepreneurs do not have enough of their own capital and cannot finance their project without monitoring by a venture capitalist.

The venture capitalist's informational advantage relative to other investors means that there are two informed parties at $t = 1$, the entrepreneur and the venture capitalist. Ex ante, contracts can be designed to ensure that information about the realized state γ will be obtained from these informed parties at $t = 1$, and that the information will be used to make the efficient choice between continuing and liquidating the project. In fact, when collusion is ruled out exogenously, this can be achieved at no additional cost relative to a situation in which the state γ is publicly observable and contractable; in other words, the informational asymmetry between entrepreneur and venture capitalist on the one hand, and outside investors on the other hand, need not impose any restriction on financing possibilities relative to the case of symmetric information about the state. The intuition for this is the following: if the two informed parties cannot collude with each other, it is possible to induce them to reveal their information truthfully, by providing incentives for one party to call the other's bluff if the other lies. More formally, we can rely on subgame perfect implementation to elicit information about γ from the two informed parties without needing to increase their share of project income in equilibrium.

This effectively removes any potential moral hazard problem ex post, associated with the decision to continue or liquidate the project. Ex ante, on the other hand, the venture capitalist has to be given incentives to monitor, and the entrepreneur incentives to choose the "good" project. This entails pledging to them a sufficiently large share of the project's returns in the event of success, R. Intuitively, efficient provision of incentives also implies that their returns should be as low as possible when the project is liquidated (i.e., when the state γ is "bad"); specifically, they should be equal to zero, because of limited liability.

We therefore obtain the following result.

Proposition 1. *Assume that γ is observed by the entrepreneur and the venture capitalist at $t = 1$ but not by outside investors, and that collusion is not feasible. Then:*

    (i) *The entrepreneur can undertake the good project if, and only if, $A_f \geq A^*(\alpha)$, where $A^*(\alpha)$ is the critical threshold under symmetric information, and is given by $A^*(\alpha) \equiv C_0 - L - p_H[\gamma_G R - C_1 - L - ((b + c_m)/\Delta p)] - c_m\, p_L/\alpha^2 \Delta p$.*

    (ii) *Optimal contracts, which allow the project to be financed whenever $A_f \geq A^*(\alpha)$, have the following properties: (a) the equilibrium payoffs of the entrepreneur and the venture capitalist in the event of liquidation are equal to zero; and (b) information about γ is obtained from the venture capitalist and the entrepreneur at $t = 1$ through a sequential mechanism that requires their agreement for the project to be continued.*

The critical threshold for entrepreneurial capital, $A^*(\alpha)$, reflects the need to pledge part of the project's returns in case of success to the entrepreneur, for incentive reasons. This reduces the returns that can credibly be promised to outside investors, and hence the capital that they are willing to contribute towards funding the project. Of course, the venture capitalist can provide capital, but he will require the expected rate of return α on the capital he provides. As noted earlier, this will exceed the outside investors' required rate of return as long as venture capitalists' skills and capital are relatively scarce in the economy, implying some rents for venture capitalists. The need to provide these rents, as well as compensation for the monitoring cost c_m, further reduces the amount of project income that can be pledged to investors. Thus higher values of α and/or c_m increase the critical threshold $A^*(\alpha)$.

The second part of the Proposition shows that, in general, optimal contracts with asymmetric information between the informed insiders and the uninformed outside investors and no possibility of collusion are *not* consistent with the fact that venture capitalists typically hold convertible securities. These represent a claim on at least some of the proceeds in the event of liquidation, which is not consistent with Proposition 1(ii)(a). Moreover, the sequential mechanism required to elicit information about γ cannot be interpreted as a convertible security.

The allocation of control rights over the liquidation decision that emerges in these optimal contracts does embody an important feature of observed venture capital contracts, namely the fact that the intermediary has the power to force liquidation. This is consistent with the widespread use of redemption rights, discussed in detail below. On the other hand, the optimal contracts described by Proposition 1 also require the entrepreneur to have the power to force liquidation. The empirical evidence on this is less clear-cut. The reason is that the entrepreneur would typically need to have control of the board to initiate a liquidation; moreover, he may need a voting majority to ensure that the decision is approved (see Smith 2001 and Kaplan and Strömberg 2003).[4] In their study of 213 venture capital investments, Kaplan and Strömberg (2003) found that entrepreneurs (founders) had the majority of the board seats in 14 percent of cases, and venture capitalists in 25 percent of cases. In the remainder of cases neither had control, implying an important role for other board members; however, these were individuals mutually agreed upon by the venture capitalists and the entrepreneurs (founders), suggesting that they could not be counted upon to side systematically with the latter. As for voting rights,[5] the same study revealed that entrepreneurs had a voting majority in at most 24 percent of all financings, the corresponding figure for venture capitalists being 53 percent.[6] This suggests that in many cases entrepreneurs do not have the power to force liquidation.

Some intuition for the results described by Proposition 1(ii) can be obtained by comparing them with those that would apply under symmetric information about the state γ. In this case too, ex ante incentives could be provided by pledging to the entrepreneur and to the intermediary a sufficiently large share of the project's success returns, and a zero share of any proceeds in the event of liquidation. Ex post efficiency, on the other hand, could be guaranteed simply by specifying in the contract the efficient continuation decision contingent on γ, since γ would be contractable. However, when γ is only observed by the entrepreneur and the venture capitalist, it is not directly contractable; the information has to be elicited from the two informed parties.

There is some tension between the need to elicit information about γ and the allocation of cash flow rights that would be optimal under symmetric information. In particular, when the entrepreneur and the venture capitalist receive nothing in the event of liquidation (all the proceeds go to uninformed investors), they both always prefer continuation to liquidation, which might lead them to claim that the state is good even when in fact it is bad. This potential problem can be solved using a simple sequential mechanism, with the property that the entrepreneur and the venture capitalist share (sequentially) the control rights over the continuation decision; in particular, each party can force liquidation, so that continuation requires agreement. Notice though that this type of mechanism is not collusion-proof: in the bad state, the venture capitalist and the entrepreneur will have an incentive to collude to secure higher payoffs. This suggests that we need to investigate the implications of allowing for the possibility of collusion.

Collusion Deterred Through Contract Design

It might be argued that we should just assume away the possibility of collusion a priori, as was done above. Why? One argument in favor of such an assumption might be that the entrepreneur is capital-constrained: Where would he find the resources necessary to induce the venture capitalist to collude? This objection does not seem convincing, since the entrepreneur will typically be able to generate some private benefits for the venture capitalist, if he wishes, by using corporate resources (including ideas, knowledge, and information). He may, for example, allow the venture capitalist to influence decisions concerning supplier contracts or the recruitment of key employees, in a way that benefits the venture capitalist. Indeed, there is plenty of empirical evidence showing that venture capitalists play a very active role in negotiating with suppliers, recruiting senior management, and providing entrepreneurs with access to consultants, investment bankers, and lawyers (Gompers and Lerner 1999, Hellmann and Puri 2002, Kaplan and Strömberg 2003, and Sahlman 1990). This kind of involvement by venture capitalists could, in principle, facilitate collusion with entrepreneurs.

A more persuasive argument might be that venture capitalists will not be willing to collude because they will be concerned about the possible damage to their reputation. There are two aspects to this argument. First, there is the possibility that investors might discover ex post that collusion has taken place. However, this is unlikely if sufficient care is taken in choosing the form of the "favo." A good example here, particularly in the case of high technology start-ups, would be the sharing of valuable knowledge and information that the entrepreneur possesses and/or acquires in the early stages of the venture. Second, an intermediary who systematically colludes with entrepreneurs instead of monitoring the projects will build up, over time, a poorer track record for project success than an intermediary who never shirks on monitoring. This will obviously affect his reputation in the market and hence his ability to stay in business. While concern over such long-term reputational effects will undoubtedly play a role, it seems unlikely that it will provide, on its own, a sufficiently powerful deterrent to collusion at all times. Thus simply ruling out the possibility of collusion by assumption does not seem justified.

We now study instead how collusion can be deterred endogenously, through an appropriate design of financial contracts. Note first that collusion may occur at two different stages. The entrepreneur and the venture capitalist may collude ex ante, at $t = 0$, so that the venture capitalist does not monitor, and the entrepreneur chooses the bad project yielding private benefits B. They may also collude ex post, at $t = 1$, so as to induce continuation even in the bad state, which gives them strictly positive expected payoffs (unlike liquidation).

Ex ante collusion would require some form of transfer (favor) from the entrepreneur to the venture capitalist, to induce the latter not to monitor. The simplest way to capture the different possible ways in which collusive transfers might occur is through a linear collusion technology: that is, by assuming that a transfer that costs S to the giver benefits the receiver by an amount kS. We assume that $1 \geq k > 0$: the case where $k < 1$ implies the existence of transactions costs of collusion, including, for example, the effect of reputational concerns as discussed above, which would tend to reduce the benefit to the receiver. In principle, the case where $k > 1$ cannot be ruled out: for example, the entrepreneur might possess some private information that is potentially more valuable to the venture capitalist than to himself. For simplicity, we focus attention on what we consider to be the most plausible case, $1 \geq k > 0$. As for ex post collusion, this could occur even in the absence of any collusive transfers. The reason is that when the entrepreneur and the venture capitalist do not receive any of the proceeds in the event of liquidation, both parties stand to gain from continuing the project in the bad state, and can agree to coordinate on this outcome without any need for favors.

The following result summarizes the main implications of the need to deter collusion through the design of venture capital contracts.

Proposition 2. *Assume γ is observed by the entrepreneur and the venture capitalist at $t = 1$, but not by outside investors. Then:*

    (i) *Allowing for the possibility of collusion raises the minimum amount of entrepreneurial capital required to undertake the good project to:*
$$A_C^*(\alpha) \equiv A^*(\alpha) + p_H \, k(B-b)[1-(1/\alpha^2)]/\Delta \ p + \gamma_B(c+kB)[1-(1/\alpha^2)]/\Delta p \Delta \gamma,$$
where $A^*(\alpha)$ is the critical threshold when collusion is not feasible, given in Proposition 1.

    (ii) *Optimal collusion-proof contracts, which allow the good project to be financed whenever $A_f \geq A_C^*(\alpha)$, have the following properties: (a) the venture capitalist is given control rights over the decision to continue or liquidate the project at $t = 1$; and (b) the allocation of cash flow rights provides the venture capitalist with incentives to take the efficient continuation/liquidation decision; this entails giving him a share of the proceeds in the event of liquidation.*

Financing constraints are clearly exacerbated by the need to deter collusion. This is because there are essentially two ways of deterring collusion: making it less attractive to the entrepreneur, which requires increasing his share of the project's expected income, or making it less attractive to the venture capitalist, which requires giving him a greater share of the project's expected income instead. When the entrepreneur is sufficiently capital-constrained, the first option is not feasible, as the entrepreneur cannot increase his capital contribution to make up for the shortfall. The venture capitalist, on the other hand, can provide additional capital to "pay" for his higher expected income from the project, but he will also extract some rents ($\alpha > 1$): this makes the financing constraint tighter (i.e., it increases $A_C^*(\alpha)$).

Proposition 2(ii) shows that optimal collusion-proof contracts are consistent with commonly observed characteristics of venture capital contracts. First, the venture capitalist is given control rights over the continuation decision. In particular, he is given both *the right and the incentives to liquidate the project* in the bad state. The intuition for this is as follows. The possibility of collusion means that we can no longer implement the optimal continuation/liquidation decision while reducing the two informed parties' equilibrium payoffs in the bad state to zero by giving one party the incentive to call the other's bluff as the parties would collude to secure higher payoffs. The optimal continuation decision can only be implemented (and collusion deterred) by increasing the entrepreneur's and/or the venture capitalist's equilibrium payoffs in the event of liquidation. To minimize the need for entrepreneurial capital, we rely on the second option. This implies giving the venture capitalist the power and the incentives to liquidate the project in the bad state. This is consistent with the use of redemption rights[7] in venture capital contracts: as Gompers (1997) notes, these rights imply that "essentially, the venture capitalists can force the firm to repay the face value of the investment at any time. This mechanism can often be used to force liquidation."[8]

Second, the allocation of cash flow rights is also consistent with common practice in venture capital finance, where convertible securities (convertible preferred equity and convertible debt) are the most commonly used financial instruments.[9]

In particular, under plausible assumptions, *the venture capitalist's payoffs can be interpreted as the payoffs to a convertible security:* a debt claim with face value equal to his share of liquidation proceeds and an option to convert this to an equity share that will have the appropriate value at $t = 2$ if the project succeeds. The values of the debt claim and the equity share are chosen so that the venture capitalist has an incentive to continue the project and exercise the conversion option in the good state, while in the bad state he will prefer to liquidate without exercising the conversion option.

One implication of this interpretation is that *the intermediary's decision to continue and exercise the conversion option can act as a credible signal* to uninformed investors that the firm's prospects are good: this too seems consistent with the empirical evidence on venture capital financing. Continuation finance is often raised through IPOs, and venture capitalists are required to exercise their conversion option at this point. Megginson and Weiss (1991), in their study of 320 venture-backed and 320 nonventure IPOs over the period from 1983 to 1987, find that venture capitalists retain a majority of their equity after the IPO, and that the underpricing of venture-backed IPOs is significantly less than the underpricing of nonventure IPOs. They interpret this as evidence that venture capitalists certify to investors the quality of the firms they bring to market. Their argument for this *certification hypothesis* is based on reputational considerations: the idea is that venture capitalists have an incentive to build a reputation for bringing high-quality firms to market, which in turn will reduce the costs of taking firms public in the future. The results described above suggest that venture capitalists' certification role does not rely only on reputation, but also on the design of financial contracts, which provides the appropriate incentives for certification.

Finally, note that while the optimal collusion-proof contract can be implemented with convertible securities or a combination of debt and equity, *it cannot, in general, be implemented with straight debt or straight equity* : this may provide an explanation for the difference between the financial claims typically held by venture capitalists (convertible securities), and those held by business angels for whom the possibility of collusion is not an issue (straight equity).[10]

ADVISING

This section examines the case where venture capitalists provide advice (e.g., strategic advice, customer introductions) but do not monitor (intervene). This case has been studied, in different settings, in a number of contributions, including Bottazzi and Hellmann (2005), Casamatta (2003), Cestone (2000), Hellmann (1998), Kaplan, Martel, and Strömberg (2003), Lerner and Schoar (2005), Repullo and Suarez (2000, 2004), and Schmidt (2003). The main novelty here is is the analysis of how the possibility of collusion shapes optimal financial contracts between entrepreneurs and financiers/advisers. As in the previous section, I begin by assuming that collusion is never feasible. I will then relax this assumption and investigate the optimal design of contracts that deter collusion. I focus throughout on the more interesting case where α is not too large, so that it is indeed in the entrepreneur's interest to obtain the venture capitalist's advice.

Collusion Ruled Out A Priori

If collusion is not feasible, we can once again design contracts that will elicit information about the realized state γ from the entrepreneur and the venture capitalist at $t = 1$, at no additional cost relative to the case where the state is publicly observable and contractable. As in the monitoring case studied in the previous section, this removes any potential moral hazard problem associated with the decision to continue or liquidate the project. The venture capital contract then needs to provide appropriate incentives ex ante: it needs to motivate the venture capitalist to advise, and the entrepreneur to choose the good project. This yields a very similar result to the one described by Proposition 1:

Proposition 3. *Assume that γ is observed by the entrepreneur and the venture capitalist at $t = 1$ but not by outside investors, and that collusion is not feasible. Then:*

(i) *The entrepreneur can undertake the good project if, and only if, $A_f \geq A^{**}(\alpha)$, where $A^{**}(\alpha)$ is the critical threshold under symmetric information, and is given by $A^{**}(\alpha) = C_0 - L - (p_H + q)[\gamma_G R - C_1 - L - B/\Delta p - c_a/q] - c_a p_H/\alpha^2 q$.*

(ii) *Optimal contracts, which allow the project to be financed whenever $A_f \geq A^{**}(\alpha)$, have the following properties: (a) the equilibrium payoffs of the entrepreneur and the venture capitalist in the event of liquidation are equal to zero; and (b) information about γ is obtained from the venture capitalist and the entrepreneur at $t = 1$ through a sequential mechanism that requires their agreement for the project to be continued.*

Intuitively, when collusion is ruled out exogenously, the main difference between advice and monitoring is simply that advice increases the project's net present value (NPV), while monitoring decreases NPV but is nevertheless valuable because it relaxes financing constraints by reducing the share of expected income that needs to be pledged to the entrepreneur for incentive reasons, hence increasing pledgeable income.

Collusion Deterred Through Contract Design

Once we allow for the possibility of collusion, a further difference emerges between advising and monitoring. If the venture capitalist's role is to provide financing and advice, but no monitoring, there is no scope for ex ante collusion between the entrepreneur and the venture capitalist. There remains, on the other hand, scope for collusion ex post. The reason is that the optimal contracts described by Proposition 3 entail a payoff of value zero in the event of liquidation for both the entrepreneur and the venture capitalist, while continuation would give them positive expected payoffs. It is therefore in their interest to collude to ensure that the project is continued even when the realized state γ is bad.

Taking this into account, we obtain the following result.

Proposition 4. *Assume γ is observed by the entrepreneur and the venture capitalist at $t = 1$, but not by outside investors. Then:*

(i) *The minimum amount of entrepreneurial capital required to undertake the good project once we allow for the possibility of collusion is given by: $A_C^{**}(\alpha) = C_0 - L - (p_H + q)(\gamma_G R - L - B/\Delta p) + c_a/\alpha^2 + (1 - 1/\alpha^2)k\gamma_B B/\Delta p \Delta \gamma + (1 - 1/\alpha^2)\pi c_a/ q\Delta\gamma$.*

(ii) *Optimal collusion-proof contracts, which allow the good project to be financed whenever $A_f \geq A_C^{**}(\alpha)$, have the following properties: (a) the venture capitalist is given control rights over the decision to continue or liquidate the project at $t = 1$; and (b) the allocation of cash flow rights provides the venture capitalist with incentives to take the efficient continuation/liquidation decision; this entails giving him a share of the proceeds in the event of liquidation.*

Clearly, the key result concerning the allocation of control rights and cash flow rights that was obtained for the monitoring case also applies when the venture capitalist provides advice rather than monitoring. In particular, the venture capitalist is given control rights over the decision to continue or liquidate the project, and cash flow rights that provide the right incentives for him to exercise those control rights efficiently. Once again, these cash flow rights can be interpreted as payoffs to a convertible security. As discussed earlier in detail, these characteristics are consistent with observed practice in the venture capital industry. The results of this section show that they emerge as part of optimal collusion-proof contracts not only when venture capitalists act as monitors, as in Dessí (2005), but also when they act as advisers, as in a number of other recent contributions to the literature.

CONCLUSIONS

In this chapter, I have explored some of the implications of venture capitalists' roles as financiers, monitors, and advisors. I have done this using a simple, unified theoretical framework, which brings out the connections and differences between monitoring and advising. The results show that some of the key findings on the optimal allocation of control rights and cash flow rights in Dessí (2005), which focused exclusively on venture capitalists' role as monitors, also apply when we consider instead their role as providers of advice and support. Of course, there are many aspects of venture capitalists' roles that are not captured here. For example, their role in replacing founders with outside CEOs is not studied here; Hellmann (1998) provides an excellent analysis. The provision of advice and support has also been studied in a variety of settings, as already noted earlier: the contributions cited then provide many additional insights. One issue that has received relatively less attention in the theoretical literature is the joint allocation of control rights and cash flow rights. Some important exceptions include Cestone (2000) and Hellmann (2000). Cestone focuses on the potential trade-off between the need to encourage entrepreneurial initiative in the early stages of a venture and the need to elicit the venture capitalist's support (help and advice) in later stages. Hellmann examines the optimal allocation of cash flow rights and control rights between entrepreneurs and venture capitalists when there is ex ante uncertainty as to whether exit should eventually occur through an acquisition or an IPO. In view of the diversity, richness, and complexity of venture capital financings (see, among others, Bottazzi and Da Rin 2002, Gompers and Lerner 1999, Kaplan and Strömberg 2003, 2004), there remains nevertheless plenty of scope for further research on these issues.

APPENDIX

Proofs of Propositions 1 and 2
See Dessí (2005).

Proof of Proposition 3
Denote by $C3 = \{A_f, A_u, A_m, \Psi, L_f, L_u, L_m, R_f, R_u, R_m\}$ the contract proposed by the entrepreneur to the venture capitalist and the uninformed investors at $t = 0$. The subscript f refers to the entrepreneur, u to the uninformed investors, and m to the venture capitalist. The first three terms represent each party's initial capital contribution to the project; the next term denotes the mechanism that will be played by the entrepreneur and the venture capitalist at $t = 1$ to elicit information about the state γ and implement the efficient continuation/liquidation decision; the following three terms represent each party's payoff in the event of liquidation; the last three terms denote the payoffs if the project is continued and succeeds.

The proof proceeds as follows: I first characterize the contract that would make it possible to finance the good project with the lowest possible level of entrepreneurial capital in the presence of symmetric information; that is, if the contract could simply specify that at $t=1$ the project will be continued when $\gamma = \gamma_G$ and liquidated otherwise. I will then give an example of a mechanism that makes it possible to implement the same decision rule for project continuation/liquidation without imposing any additional restriction, thereby completing the proof.

In the presence of symmetric information as just described, we can specify the entrepreneur's problem (P3) as follows:

$$Max \quad (p_H + q)\gamma_G R_f + (1 - p_H - q)L_f - A_f \tag{9.1}$$

$$s.t. \quad (p_H + q)\gamma_G R_f + (1 - p_H - q)L_f \geq B + (p_L + q)\gamma_G R_f + (1 - p_L - q)L_f \tag{9.2}$$

$$R_f + R_u + R_m = R \tag{9.3}$$

$$L_f + L_u + L_m = L \tag{9.4}$$

$$A_f + A_u + A_m = C_0 \tag{9.5}$$

$$(p_H + q)(\gamma_G R_u - C_1) + (1 - p_H - q)L_u \geq A_u \tag{9.6}$$

$$(p_H + q)\gamma_G R_m + (1 - p_H - q)L_m \geq c_a + p_H \gamma_G R_m + (1 - p_H)L_m \tag{9.7}$$

$$(p_H + q)\gamma_G R_m + (1 - p_H - q)L_m - c_a \geq \alpha^2 A_m \tag{9.8}$$

Expression (9.1) represents the entrepreneur's expected payoff, while his incentive compatibility constraint is given by (9.2). Expressions (9.3) to (9.5) are feasibility constraints, and (9.6) is the investors' participation constraint. The venture capitalist's incentive compatibility and participation constraints are given by (9.7) and (9.8), respectively.

The method of proof is the following: first, obtain lower bounds for R_f, R_m, L_f, and L_m, using the entrepreneur's and the venture capitalist's ICCs, together with limited liability. Second, using these lower bounds together with the participation constraints, derive the minimum amount of entrepreneurial capital required for the project to be undertaken. Notice that, since $\alpha^2 \geq 1$, we can focus without loss of generality on the case where the intermediary's capital investment, A_m, is just equal to the minimum amount necessary to satisfy his participation and incentive compatibility constraints; any additional external finance is raised directly from investors.

From the entrepreneur's ICC, together with limited liability, we have:

$$R_f \geq B/\Delta p \gamma_G + L_f/\gamma_G \tag{9.9}$$

$$L_f \geq 0 \tag{9.10}$$

and from the venture capitalist's ICC, together with limited liability, we have:

$$R_m \geq c_a/q\gamma_G + L_m/\gamma_G \tag{9.11}$$

$$L_m \geq 0 \tag{9.12}$$

Using the lower bounds implied by (9.11) and (9.12), and the venture capitalist's participation constraint, we obtain:

$$A_m = c_a p_H/\alpha^2 q \tag{9.13}$$

Using conditions (9.9) to (9.12), together with the feasibility constraints (9.3) and (9.4), gives the following upper bounds for R_u and L_u:

$$R_u^{\max} = R - B/\Delta p \gamma_G - c_a/q\gamma_G \tag{9.14}$$

$$L_u^{\max} = L \tag{9.15}$$

Hence the maximum amount of capital that can be raised from investors is obtained from their participation constraint:

$$A_u^{max} = L + (p_H + q)[\gamma_G R - C_1 - L - B/\Delta p - c_a/q] \tag{9.16}$$

Expressions (9.5), (9.13), and (9.16) together imply that the project can only be financed if the entrepreneur's capital satisfies the following condition:

$$A_f \geq A^{**}(\alpha) = C_0 - L - (p_H + q)[\gamma_G R - C_1 - L - B/\Delta p - c_a/q] - c_a p_H/\alpha^2 q \tag{9.17}$$

When the above condition is satisfied, it can be easily checked that the following is a solution to P3: let $A_f = A^{**}$, $A_m = c_a p_H/\alpha^2 q$, $A_u = C_0 - A_f - A_m$, $L_f = 0$, $L_m = 0$, $L_u = L$, $R_f = B/\Delta p\gamma_G$, $R_m = c_a/q\gamma_G$, $R_u = R - R_f - R_m$.

Now consider the following mechanism Ψ:

- *Stage 1*: the venture capitalist chooses between continuation and liquidation. If he chooses liquidation, the project is liquidated; payoffs are L_f, L_u, and L_m. If the venture capitalist chooses continuation, go on to stage 2.
- *Stage 2*: the entrepreneur decides whether to agree with the venture capitalist or disagree. If he agrees, the project is continued, investors provide the required finance C_1, and payoffs are R_f, R_u, and R_m if the project succeeds; zero otherwise. If the entrepreneur disagrees, the project is liquidated; the entrepreneur receives $\gamma_B R_f + \epsilon$, the investors any remaining liquidation proceeds, and the venture capitalist zero.

For Ψ to work, it has to satisfy the following conditions:

$$\gamma_G R_f \geq \gamma_B R_f + \epsilon \tag{9.18}$$

$$\gamma_B R_f + \epsilon \geq \gamma_B R_f \tag{9.19}$$

$$L_m \geq 0 \tag{9.20}$$

$$\gamma_G R_m \geq L_m \tag{9.21}$$

The first two conditions ensure that in stage 2 the entrepreneur agrees if $\gamma = \gamma_G$, and disagrees if $\gamma = \gamma_B$. The last two conditions ensure that in stage 1 the intermediary prefers to liquidate if $\gamma = \gamma_B$ and to continue if $\gamma = \gamma_G$. Clearly ϵ can always be chosen to satisfy the first two conditions. Comparing the last two conditions with those for problem P3, given above, shows that they impose no additional restriction: it is therefore possible to implement the lower bounds for R_f, R_m, L_f, and L_m obtained earlier. Thus the minimum level of entrepreneurial capital required for the project to be feasible satisfies the condition:

$$A_f \geq A^{**}(\alpha) \tag{9.22}$$

as in the case of symmetric information.

Proof of Proposition 4

The entrepreneur at $t = 0$ proposes a contract $C4 = \{A_f, A_u, A_m, \Psi, L_f, L_u, L_m, R_f, R_u, R_m\}$ to the venture capitalist and the uninformed investors. The difference with contract $C3$ in Proposition 3 is that the contract needs to be collusion-proof. Once we allow for the possibility of collusion, the entrepreneur and the venture capitalist can always agree to make the same announcements when $\gamma = \gamma_B$ as when $\gamma = \gamma_G$, giving the outcome {continuation, success payoffs R_f, R_m} with expected payoffs equal to $\gamma_B R_f$, $\gamma_B R_m$. Thus it is no longer possible to implement the equilibrium payoffs that were optimal when collusion was ruled out a priori. To implement the optimal continuation/liquidation decision while minimizing the returns pledged to the entrepreneur (hence minimizing the need for entrepreneurial capital), we must have:

$$L_f = 0 \tag{9.23}$$

and set L_m so that the venture capitalist prefers liquidation to continuation when $\gamma = \gamma_B$ (in particular, so that he cannot be induced to collude with the entrepreneur to choose continuation):

$$L_m \geq \gamma_B R_m + k\gamma_B R_f \tag{9.24}$$

The venture capitalist's ex ante ICC (see below) requires that he prefer continuation when $\gamma = \gamma_G$ (otherwise he has no incentives to advise). Without loss of generality we can therefore specify the mechanism Ψ as follows:

- at $t = 1$ the venture capitalist decides whether to continue the project or liquidate it. If the project is liquidated, the entrepreneur receives $L_f = 0$, the venture capitalist $L_m = \gamma_B R_m + k\gamma_B R_f$, and the investors any remaining liquidation proceeds. If the project is continued, investors provide the required finance C_1, and payoffs are given by R_f, R_u, R_m (0) in the event of success (failure).

The venture capitalist's ex ante ICC is given by

$$(p_H + q)\gamma_G R_m + (1 - p_H - q)L_m \geq c_a + p_H\gamma_G R_m + (1 - p_H)L_m \tag{9.25}$$

The lower bounds for R_f and L_f are the same as in Proposition 3, and are given by (9.9) and (9.10), implying that the lower bound for R_m is given by (9.11); substituting for L_m using (9.24) gives the following condition:

$$R_m \geq c_a/q\,\Delta\gamma + \gamma_B k B/\gamma_G \Delta p\Delta\gamma \tag{9.26}$$

Let $R_m^{\min} = c_a/q\Delta\,\gamma + \gamma_B k B/\gamma_G\Delta p\Delta\gamma$. Then the amount of capital provided by the venture capitalist is equal to:

$$A_m = [(p_H + q)\gamma_G + (1 - p_H - q)\gamma_B]R_m^{\min}/\alpha^2 + (1 - p_H - q)k\gamma_B B/\alpha^2\Delta p\gamma_G - c_a/\alpha^2 \tag{9.27}$$

Further manipulation shows that the project can be financed if and only if $A_f \geq A_C^{**}(\alpha)$, where

$$A_C^{**}(\alpha) = C_0 - L - (p_H + q)(\gamma_G R - L - B/\Delta p) + c_a/\alpha^2 + (1 - 1/\alpha^2)k\gamma_B B/\Delta p \Delta \gamma$$
$$+ (1 - 1/\alpha^2)\pi c_a/q \Delta \gamma \qquad (9.28)$$

and $\pi \equiv (p_H + q)\gamma_G + (1 - p_H - q)\gamma_B$.

NOTES

1. As will be clear from this list, the analysis developed here is particularly relevant to companies at the start-up and expansion stages, where monitoring by venture capitalists is most valuable.

2. The involvement of nonventure investors in the financing of venture-backed companies is documented for example by Gompers and Lerner (1999).

3. On this see Kaplan and Strömberg (2004).

4. Board rights and voting rights can differ in venture capital contracts through the use of explicit agreements on the election of directors [see Kaplan and Strömberg 2003].

5. The calculation of voting rights is complicated by the fact that some of these are contingent on subsequent management performance and stock vesting milestones or contingencies. Kaplan and Strömberg deal with this difficulty by calculating both a minimum and a maximum number of votes for the venture capitalists, depending on future contingencies, and the corresponding votes for the entrepreneurs.

6. These figures refer to the minimum contingency case, which tends to overestimate the control rights of the entrepreneurs. In the maximum contingency case, venture capitalists have a voting majority in 69% of all financings, and entrepreneurs have a voting majority in only 12% of financings.

7. Venture capitalists' redemption rights can take one of two forms: mandatory redemption rights and optional investor redemption ("put") rights. Mandatory redemption requires the company to begin repurchasing shares at a specified date, usually subject to waiver by the venture capitalists. Optional investor redemption rights, which are much more common, allow venture capitalists to force the repurchase of their shares at their discretion. They can typically be exercised after a given date.

8. With both types of redemption right, the venture capitalist essentially acquires liquidation rights from a given date onwards. Earlier in the venture capital relationship, the venture capitalist effectively controls the continuation liquidation decision through the use of staged financing and negative covenants. For a more detailed discussion, see Smith (2001) and Kaplan and Strömberg (2003).

9. Convertible securities are the most commonly held securities by venture capitalists in the United States [see Gompers and Lerner 1999, Kaplan and Strömberg 2003]. Outside the United States, a variety of securities are used, notably in Canada (where common equity dominates), Europe, and in developing countries. On this see Cumming (2005a, 2005b, 2006), Cumming, Schmidt, and Walz (2010), Hege, Palomino, and Schwienbacher (2003), Kaplan, Martel, and Strömberg (2003), Lerner and Schoar (2005), and Schwienbacher (2002). Interestingly, Cumming (2005a), using Canadian data, finds that high tech firms are more likely to be financed with convertible preferred equity than other firms. High tech firms, as discussed earlier, may be particularly vulnerable to potential collusion

problems; moreover, in view of the high risks involved, the need to induce the efficient decision between continuation and liquidation would seem to be especially important.

10. See Fenn, Liang, and Prowse (1998) on business angels and Gompers and Lerner (1999), and Kaplan and Strömberg (2003) on venture capitalists.

REFERENCES

Admati, A. R., and P. Pfleiderer. 1994. Robust financial contracting and the role of venture capitalists. *Journal of Finance* 49:371–402.

Barclay, M. J., and C. G. Holderness. 1989. Private benefits from control of public corporations. *Journal of Financial Economics* 25:371–395.

Bergemann, D., and U. Hege. 1998. Venture capital financing, moral hazard, and learning. *Journal of Banking and Finance* 22:703–735.

Berglof, E. 1994. A control theory of venture capital finance. *Journal of Law, Economics and Organisation* 10:247–267.

Bergstrom, C., and K. Rydqvist. 1990. Ownership of equity in dual-class firms. *Journal of Banking and Finance* 14:255–269.

Bottazzi, L., and M. Da Rin. 2002. Venture capital in Europe and the financing of innovative companies. *Economic Policy* 17 (34):231–269.

———, and T. Hellmann. 2005. What role of legal systems in financial intermediation? Theory and evidence. Mimeo, Università Bocconi.

Brickley, J. A., R. C. Lease, and C. W. Smith Jr. 1988. Ownership structure and voting on antitakeover amendments. *Journal of Financial Economics* 20:267–291.

Casamatta, C. 2003. Financing and advising: Optimal financial contracts with venture capitalists. *Journal of Finance* 58:2059–2085.

Cestone, G. 2000. Venture capital meets contract theory: Risky claims or formal control? Mimeo, Institut d'Analisi Economica, Barcelona.

Cornelli, F., and O. Yosha. 2003. Stage financing and the role of convertible debt. *Review of Economic Studies* 70:1–32.

Cumming, D. J. 2005a. Agency costs, institutions, learning and taxation in venture capital contracting. *Journal of Business Venturing* 20:573–622.

———. 2005b. Capital structure in venture finance. *Journal of Corporate Finance* 11:550–585.

———. 2006. Adverse selection and capital structure: Evidence from venture capital. *Entrepreneurship Theory and Practice* 30:155–184.

———, D. Schmidt, and U. Walz. 2010. Legality and venture capital governance around the world. *Journal of Business Venturing*. 25 (1):54–72.

de Bettignies, J.-E. 2008. Financing the entrepreneurial venture. *Management Science* 54 (1):151–166.

Dessí, R. 2005. Start-up finance, monitoring, and collusion. *Rand Journal of Economics* 36 (2):255–274.

———. 2009. Contractual execution, strategic incompleteness, and venture capital. IDEI Working Paper, Toulouse School of Economics.

Diamond, D. 1984. Financial intermediation and delegated monitoring. *Review of Economic Studies* 51:393–414.

Felli, L. 1990. Collusion in incentive contracts: Does delegation help? Mimeo, MIT.

Fenn, G., Liang, N., and Prowse, S. 1998. The role of angel investors in financing high-tech start-ups. Mimeo, CEPR.

Freixas, X., and J. C. Rochet. 1997. *Microeconomics of banking*. Cambridge: MIT Press.

Gompers, P. 1997. Ownership and control in entrepreneurial firms: An examination of convertible securities in venture capital investments. Mimeo, Harvard and NBER,

———, and J. Lerner. 1999. *The venture capital cycle*. Cambridge: MIT Press.

Gorman, P., and W. Sahlman. What do venture capitalists do? *Journal of Business Venturing* 4 (1989):231–248.

Hege, U., F. Palomino, and A. Schwienbacher. 2003. Determinants of venture capital performance: Europe and the United States. Working Paper. RICAFE Working Paper No.1

Hellmann, T. 1998. The allocation of control rights in venture capital contracts. *Rand Journal of Economics* 29:57–76.

———. 2000. IPOs, acquisitions and the use of convertible securities in venture capital. Research Paper No. 1702, Stanford Graduate School of Business.

———, and Puri, M. 2002. Venture capital and the professionalization of start-up firms: Empirical evidence. *Journal of Finance* 57:169–197.

Holmstrom, B., and J. Tirole. 1997. Financial intermediation, loanable funds, and the real sector. *Quarterly Journal of Economics* 112:663–691.

Kaplan, S. N., F. Martel, and P. Strömberg. 2003. How do legal differences and learning affect financial contracts? Mimeo, University of Chicago.

Kaplan, S. N., and P. Strömberg. 2003. Financial contracting theory meets the real world: An empirical analysis of venture capital contracts. *Review of Economic Studies* 70:281–315.

———. 2004. Characteristics, contracts, and actions: evidence from venture capitalist analyses. *Journal of Finance* 59, 2177–2210.

Laffont, J. J., and J. C. Rochet. 1997. Collusion in organizations. *Scandinavian Journal of Economics* 99:485–495.

Lerner, J. 1995. Venture capitalists and the oversight of private firms. *Journal of Finance* 50:301–318.

———, and A. Schoar. 2005. Does legal enforcement affect financial transactions? The contractual channel in private equity. *Quarterly Journal of Economics* 120:223–246.

Maug, E. 2002. Insider trading legislation and corporate governance. *European Economic Review* 46:1569–1597.

Megginson, W. L., and K. A. Weiss 1991. Venture capitalist certification in initial public offerings. *Journal of Finance* 46:879–903.

Moore, J. 1992. Implementation in environments with complete information. In *Advances in economic theory*, ed. J. J. Laffont. Mass.: Cambridge University Press.

———, and Repullo, R., 1998. Subgame perfect implementation. *Econometrica* 56:1191–1220.

Pagano, M., and A. Roell. 1998. The choice of stock ownership structure: Agency costs, monitoring, and the decision to go public. *Quarterly Journal of Economics* 113:1985–2225.

Pound, J. 1988. Proxy contests and the efficiency of shareholder oversight. *Journal of Financial Economics* 20:237–265.

Rajan, R. 1992. Insiders and outsiders: The choice between informed and arm's length debt. *Journal of Finance* 47:1367–1400.

Repullo, R., and J. Suarez. 2000. Entrepreneurial moral hazard and bank monitoring: A model of the credit channel. *European Economic Review* 44:1931–1950.

———. 2004. Venture capital finance: A security design approach. *Review of Finance* 8:75–108.

Sahlman, W. 1990. The structure and governance of venture-capital organizations. *Journal of Financial Economics* 27:473–521.

Schmidt, K. 2003. Convertible securities and venture capital finance. *Journal of Finance* 58:1139–1166.

Schwienbacher, A. 2002. Venture capital exits in Europe and the United States. Working Paper. University of Amsterdam.

Shleifer, A., and R. W. Vishny. 1986. Large shareholders and corporate control. *Journal of Political Economy* 94:461–488.

Smith, D. G. 2001. Control over exit in venture capital relationships. Paper presented at the EFMA Meeting in Lugano, Switzerland.

Tirole, J. 1986. Hierarchies and bureaucracies: On the role of collusion in organizations. *Journal of Law, Economics, and Organization* 2:181–214.

_____. 1992. Collusion and the theory of organizations. In *Advances in economic theory*, vol. 2, ed. J. J. Laffont. Mass.: Cambridge University Press.

Zingales, L. 1994. The value of the voting right: A study of the Milan stock exchange experience. *Review of Financial Studies* 7:125–148.

ABOUT THE AUTHOR

Roberta Dessí obtained her Ph.D. in Economics from the University of Cambridge. She has taught at the University of Cambridge and the Toulouse School of Economics. Dr. Dessí has published in academic journals such the *American Economic Review*, the *RAND Journal of Economics*, the *Economic Journal*, and the *Journal of Economics and Management Strategy*. Her research contributes to a number of fields, notably corporate finance and capital structure, the role of financial intermediaries, managerial and employee incentives, incomplete contracts, financing and innovation, and the links between financial and product market competition.

## CHAPTER 10

Project Externalities and Moral Hazard

DIMA LESHCHINSKII
Adjunct Professor, University of Maryland University College

INTRODUCTION

When financing entrepreneurial projects, investors typically provide capital and other support to a portfolio of projects. For example, according to the Venture Expert database, on average a venture capital fund would invest over its lifetime into 24 companies, with some funds investing into more than a hundred companies over their lifetime. Most of these portfolio companies belong to the same industry sector, which creates a potential for strategic interaction between them, for example, R&D spillover or complementarity/substitutability of their products. In this paper we develop a theoretical framework to study how externalities between portfolio companies affect the investment contracts offered by investors. Using this framework, we analyze entrepreneurs' choice of investors for their innovative projects.

Due to the self-interests of investors and entrepreneurs, externalities between the projects' outcomes can potentially lead to suboptimal solutions, even if contracts are publicly observable (see, e.g., Segal 1999). Suboptimality can be exemplified as underinvestment or no investment at all into a worthy project.

The situation is only aggravated by the moral hazard problem caused by the noncontractibility of an investment's nonmonetary element. Our objective is to study the mechanisms that would alleviate the moral hazard problem and to identify which group of investors is more likely to finance a particular project. We consider two possible solutions to the problem. First, by internalizing externalities and coordinating investments in order to maximize the overall value of their investment portfolio, portfolio investors are in a better position to commit to providing higher effort that will benefit all their portfolio firms. Another mechanism uses the fact that the financial component of an investment is contractible. Investors then ask for higher stakes in return for giving more money, a significant part of which becomes personal compensation to entrepreneurs. Such high-compensation contracts can relieve the moral hazard problem and tend to shift entrepreneurs' preferences to these contracts, whenever they are offered.

"Portfolio" contracts often lose out to "high-compensation" contracts, which come out as surprise winners. Under such contracts investors are earning zero profit not as a fair return on necessary investment, but by receiving a higher stake in return for overinvestment in projects. When portfolio contracts are chosen, the investors earn strictly positive profit despite the competition with other investors.

Our paper builds upon a growing body of literature studying investors in risky innovative projects and their contracts with entrepreneurs. As stated earlier, these studies have identified two major groups emerging as the main suppliers of capital to this type of projects—business angels and VCs. Angels are rich individuals who invest their own money. VCs are professionals, who raise money for VC funds from individuals and institutional investors and act as the general partners of VC funds managing the capital raised.

From the literature we know that both angels and VCs not only provide financial capital, but are also actively involved in monitoring, advising, and formulating business strategy, (see, e.g., Gorman and Sahlman 1989; Ehrlich et al. 1994; Prowse 1998; Kaplan and Stromberg 2001; Wong forthcoming; Lange, Leleux, and Surlemont 2003; Stanco and Akah 2005). Ehrlich and others (1994) find that in comparison with business angels, VCs are more involved in the management of portfolio companies. This is probably due to the fact that angels' resources, such as personal time, are more limited than VCs'. As a result, the size of the angels' investment portfolio is smaller than VCs'. For example, Lange, Leleux, and Surlemont (2003, 19) observe that "angels tend to devote very significant amounts of time postinvestment supporting the ventures; as a consequence, their average investment portfolio size is often constrained by the amount of time they are prepared to commit to their investment activities." Van Osnabrugge (1998) reports that VCs have average portfolios of 10.3 investments compared with 2 by business angels. Based on Canadian data, Cumming (2006) reports that the average number of portfolio firms per VC limited partnership is 8.2. If other forms of VCs are included, this number goes up to 19.7. While Mason and Harrison (2002) do not provide the portfolio size, they provide overall investment experience by angel investors; 53.5 percent of respondents to their survey made 1 to 3 investments throughout their entire angel experience.

Our paper is not the first one to study the effect of a portfolio approach in VC investment. For example, Kanniainen and Keuschnigg (2003, 2004) have studied model portfolio investment and optimal portfolio size. In their models, the VC faces a trade-off between rents from a bigger number of companies and the correspondingly diminishing quality of advice. Bernile, Cumming, and Lyandres (2007) also study the optimal size of VC portfolio. In addition, they also endogenize the shares retained by entrepreneurs, which makes their model similar in spirit to this paper.

In our model, portfolio investment does not diminish the quality of the advising effort, if this effort is exerted. The problem arises from the fact that unlike the amount of financial investment, the effort exerted by an investor is not contractible. This leads to the moral hazard problem, which can be resolved by a specific contract design. For example, Repullo and Suarez (2004) find that in a double-sided moral hazard problem the optimal contract between VCs and an entrepreneur has the characteristics of convertible preferred stock. Hellmann, in a series of papers (1994, 1998a, 2002), studies why and under what circumstances entrepreneurs would voluntarily relinquish control to VCs. This happens, for example, when VCs have better expertise in decisions affecting the value of the firm. Casamatta (2000) shows that when a VC's investment (in terms of both cash and effort) is high, it is optimal to give him convertible bonds, and when it is low, he should receive common stock.

Our model is close to those of Bhattacharya and Chiesa (1995) and Cabral (2000). In Cabral (2000) different parties commit together to a potentially rewarding joint venture. However, the free-rider problem hinders innovation—if the project is successful, the discovery (technological innovation) becomes a public good, and so the parties have incentive to deviate from jointly-optimal behavior (to under-invest) at the outset, in order to free-ride. Bhattacharya and Chiesa (1995) have a similar model with implications closer to those of this paper, although they do not consider a moral hazard problem—in their model all investment is contractible. They study the interaction between financial decisions and the disclosure of interim research results to competing firms. Technological knowledge revealed to a firm's financier(s) need not also flow to its R&D and product market competitors. The authors show that the choice of financing source can serve as a precommitment device for pursuing ex ante efficient strategies in knowledge-intensive environments.

Hellmann (1998b) and Ueda (2004) have models where the entrepreneur's choice of investors takes into account the possibility that investors can steal the entrepreneur's idea. Unlike Ueda's paper, where stealing by a VC is seen necessarily as a bad thing, in our model information spillover is two-directional and can bring more value to the entrepreneur, because he could be the one who benefits from using others' ideas.

Our model features two entrepreneurs, each with a risky two-stage project that requires investment from outside investors. The first stage develops a new technology and requires a small, but contractible financial investment, plus an expert human capital investment, which is not contractible. The second stage commercializes this technology. The externalities in the model are due to the fact that the results of the R&D stage of one project affect the success/failure of the second stage of both projects.

Only angels and VCs possess the necessary financial and human capital. In return for their investment, investors receive a share in a project.

We understand that in real life the angel investors form a heterogeneous group. They have varying levels of wealth, and some of them are rich enough to provide financing and expertise for both projects. However, for the purposes of this paper we assume that angels can invest human capital into only one company, even if they are wealthy enough to provide financing for several companies. This is in line with empirical findings by Mason and Harrison (2002) and Van Osnabrugge (1998) cited before. Since angel investors invest their own money, they can be more lenient than VCs over what entrepreneurs do with their money. VCs invest other people's money and accordingly seek to limit their investment to what is necessary and no more. On the other hand, each VC has enough human capital resources to support two projects at the same time. This simplifying assumption helps us to make a clear distinction between angel investors and VCs.

In our paper we show that coordinated investment by VCs guarantees profitable investment in some projects for which angel investment would be suboptimal in terms of exerted effort. In this case the VCs' profits are strictly positive, although they do not depend on the value of the projects' payoff.

Surprisingly, the effect of information spillover between two projects does not give VCs as much of an advantage as one would expect. VCs do not usually provide better terms for entrepreneurs than the angel investors do, and underinvestment remains in a disappointingly large area. What is even more surprising is that in the regions where indulgent angels achieve the first best outcome, a VC can never match them.

Our results imply that in innovation-driven industries, we should observe single project investment into relatively safe projects with high compensation to entrepreneurs, whereas portfolio investors (VCs) play a more dominant role in financing more risky projects characterized by lower probability of success and higher payoff to the successful projects.

MODEL

The model has three dates $t = 0$, 1, and 2. Two entrepreneurs, E_1 and E_2, are endowed with their own innovative projects. E_1 has project 1 and E_2 has project 2. Each project comprises two stages. The first stage, which we call the R&D stage, investigates the feasibility of a potentially promising technology for a given project. Each project can test only one technology at this stage. Technology is very broadly defined here. It includes, but is not limited to, new business models, distribution channels, markets, products, and services. Amazon's "one-click" shopping, Dell's direct sales, and FedEx' hub system are just few examples of such new technologies.

The R&D stage requires investment into a project of financial capital, K, and expert effort (human capital), e, in addition to the entrepreneur's own effort, which is here normalized to zero.[1] Unlike K, which is observable and verifiable, e can be interpreted as the advising and monitoring process of investors, which is observable, but not verifiable, and therefore cannot be contracted upon. Since the object of our attention is the effort provided by investors, to simplify our analysis we assume that K is very small, but still positive.

For a project that receives both K and e, the R&D stage has a probability of success, β. If the effort is zero, $e = 0$, then the R&D stage is unsuccessful. We interpret the result of the first stage as a costly answer to the question "Will this technology work?" Investing K and e gives an entrepreneur and investor the right to put the question and obtain the answer, while investing only K simply entitles them to observe the other project's research result. If the project does not even receive K, then it goes out of business and cannot proceed to the next stage.

The success and failure of the R&D stage of individual projects are independent of the other project's outcome. However, as in Bhattacharya and Chiesa (1995), the final payoff of each project is affected by the other project. If at least one project is successful at the R&D stage, this technology can then be freely adopted by both projects provided that they have funding for the second stage. In other words, only failure of the R&D stage for both projects renders it impossible to go to the second stage, which we call the market stage.

At the market stage, the technology is actually implemented and production takes place. Projects 1 and 2 have payoffs V and RV, net of the second stage capital investment. R characterizes the degree of asymmetry between the projects. For clarity, we assume that $R \geq 1$.

Investors and Contracts

Entrepreneurs need both financial and human external capital. As discussed in the introduction, only two categories of investors can provide both money and expertise. In comparison with VCs, the angels' human capital resources are more limited; therefore we assume that one angel investor can invest e into only one project, while a VC investor has enough resources to invest K and e into both projects. This is consistent with empirical evidence, such as Prowse (1998) and Ehrlich et al. (1994). Since K is small, in general we assume that rich angel investors can provide financing for both projects. Since angel investors invest their own money, we also allow them to invest more than K, if they deem it necessary. We denote financial investment in project i as I_i.

Entrepreneurs choose their investors from a pool of angel investors and VCs. We assume that there are more than two angel investors and more than two VCs. All investors in the pool have financial wealth of no less than K. Expressed formally, investors offer financial investment I_i in project i in return for α_i share of the future cash flow.[2] An investor can also make a conditional offer to both entrepreneurs proposing I_1 in return for α_1 to E_1 and I_2 in return for α_2 to E_2 conditional on this offer's acceptance by both entrepreneurs.

As mentioned, we also allow wealthy individual investors to offer I_i that is greater than K. If $I_i > K$, then $(I_i - K)$ is appropriated by E_i for his personal use. Each entrepreneur's objective is to maximize his final cash flow, that is, the sum of his share in the project plus the diverted cash flow $(I_i - K)$.

Entrepreneurs observe investors' offers and choose one investor for one project (investor i invests in project i). In other words, E_i observes all α_i's offered and chooses the investor offering the most attractive one. A joint offer is considered accepted only if both entrepreneurs accept their respective parts of the offer. We assume that entrepreneurs cannot make transfer payments to each other. No investment is made until all the parties are satisfied with the share allocations and capital offered.

Only financial investment I_i is verifiable, but although the effort levels are not verifiable, entrepreneurs correctly anticipate them in equilibrium. To simplify our analysis we also assume that the effort levels are observed by entrepreneurs and investors, and that investor 2 observes the degree of effort made by investor 1 before exerting his own effort.[3]

Since investors act competitively, the competition drives their profits down, although not necessarily to zero. Investors have zero reservation utility, so they prefer to participate in projects even if they have zero expected return.

We assume that everybody is risk-neutral.

As several authors have pointed out, such as Hellmann (1994), the VC-entrepreneur relationship should be analyzed as a two-sided incentive problem. Our model is simpler than the double-sided moral hazard problem in Repullo and Suarez (2004), because K is very small, and this means that, when entrepreneurs act as agents, they will never divert the total capital investment I_i to their own benefit.

We focus on a single-aspect moral hazard problem, in which entrepreneurs act as principals and investors act as agents.

Information Structure

There is no information asymmetry at $t = 0$. The project characteristics, such as β, R, V and required investments K and e are common knowledge: α_1, I_1, α_2, and I_2 are publicly observable. Investor 2 observes investor 1's effort before exerting his own effort, although the effort is not verifiable. At $t = 1$ the R&D results become known, and if at least one project is successful, all projects still in business (meaning those that received financing $I \geq K$ at $t = 0$) can freely use its result, provided that they have financing for the second stage.

The Timeline

The timeline can be summarized as follows.

At $t = 0$, the entrepreneurs announce their projects. Investors decide whether to participate in projects and offer financial investment I_i in return for share α_i in project i. E_1 and E_2 choose their investors. If investors in projects 1 and 2 are different, we call them investor 1 and investor 2, respectively. Once the choice of investors becomes final, that is, when both E_1 and E_2 are satisfied with α_1 and α_2, investment of financial and human capital takes place. Investor 1 makes his investment first; investor 2 observes his exerted effort and makes his own investment.

Projects that receive financial investment of less than K do not get off the ground.

At $t = 1$ the success or failure of the R&D stage is observed by all parties that are still in business. The failed projects can potentially use the technology of the successful project, if there is one.

At $t = 2$, the net payoffs are realized.

Externality

The R&D externality is created by the transferability of R&D results of one project to the other project. It is characterized by the probability of success of an individual project, which depends on the level of effort put into the project. If no effort is put in any project, then the payoff to each project is zero. Investing e only in project 2 creates the externality for project 1, because its payoff becomes βV, which is the measure of externality in this case, and it reaches its maximum at $\beta = 1$. The payoff to project 2 is βRV. If e is put in both projects, the expected payoff to project 2 becomes $\beta(2 - \beta)RV$. The difference between the two payoffs, $\beta(1 - \beta)RV$, is the externality that project 1 investment creates for project 2. This externality reaches its maximum at $\beta = \frac{1}{2}$.

Results

First we consider the first best outcome, defined as the result that maximizes the joint surplus (NPV) of both projects. Since $R \geq 1$ and K is very small,[4] it is never optimal to have only one project running at the second stage; therefore, there are three possible candidates for the first best outcome:

None of the projects receives financing. The NPV is zero.

One project receives both K and e, while the other project has only K. In the case of success, both projects continue at the second stage. The expected NPV is $\beta(1 + R)V - (K + e) - K$.

Both projects receive both K and e. In the case of success, both projects continue at the second stage. The expected NPV is $\beta(2 - \beta)(1 + R)V - 2(K + e)$.

We can easily see that investing e into both projects is the first best outcome whenever

$$\begin{cases} \beta(2 - \beta)(1 + R)V - 2(K + e) > 0 \\ \beta(2 - \beta)(1 + R)V - 2(K + e) > \beta(1 + R)V - (K + e) - K \end{cases}$$

Since K is small, $K < \dfrac{\beta^2}{2}(1 + R)V$, this is equivalent to

$$e < \beta(1 - \beta)(1 + R)V \tag{10.1}$$

Similarly, we see that investing e into only one project is optimal for

$$\begin{cases} e > \beta(1 - \beta)(1 + R)V \\ e \leq \beta(1 + R)V - 2K \end{cases}$$

Finally, the projects are not worth investing in, if

$$\begin{cases} e > \beta\left(1 - \dfrac{\beta}{2}\right)(1 + R)V - K \\ e > \beta(1 + R)V - 2K \end{cases}$$

Again, for small K, $K < \dfrac{\beta^2}{2}(1 + R)V$, this is equivalent to

$$e > \beta(1 + R)V - 2K \tag{10.2}$$

All other things being equal, the zone of investment into both projects grows with R. It is also more advantageous for β to be close to $\frac{1}{2}$. If β gets any bigger, then it becomes more advantageous to invest only into one project, because of the externality effect.

Interestingly, due to the externality effect, investment into project 1 can be optimal, even if the expected net payoff to this project is negative, that is, if $\beta(2 - \beta)V < K + e$ and $\beta(1 - \beta)(1 + R)V > e$.

Two sources of inefficiency might preclude from achieving the first best result: (1) the selfish interests of participants, both entrepreneurs and investors, and (2) the coordination problem for the investors. In the remaining part of this section we describe these inefficiencies and show how investors can restore the first best result.

ANGEL INVESTMENT

We will first examine the possible outcomes with angel investment, if VC investment is not available and angel investors are only competing with each other. This competition drives their profits down to the level determined by the incentive compatibility (IC) and participation constraints (PC) of investors and entrepreneurs.

In order to understand what kind of contracts between entrepreneurs and angel investors can be observed in equilibrium, we start our analysis from the effort choice by two angel investors, who become involved in projects 1 and 2. The angel investing in project i selects his level of effort (zero or e) so as to maximize his expected profit given his share α_i in project i and the share α_j in project j attributable to investor j.

The outcome should be the Nash equilibrium of the game described by the tree in Exhibit 10.1 and by the following payoff matrix

effort	0	e
0	$(0;0)$	$(\alpha_1\beta V; \alpha_2\beta RV - e)$
e	$(\alpha_1\beta V - e; \alpha_2\beta RV)$	$(\alpha_1\beta(2-\beta)V - e; \alpha_2\beta(2-\beta)RV - e)$

where the elements of the matrix are the investors' expected payoffs net of the effort exerted. Rows correspond to the level of effort exerted by investor 1, and columns correspond to the level of effort exerted by investor 2.

Possible equilibria are described at the end of this chapter. There are three subgame perfect equilibria: $(e;e)$, $(0;e)$, and $(0;0)$.

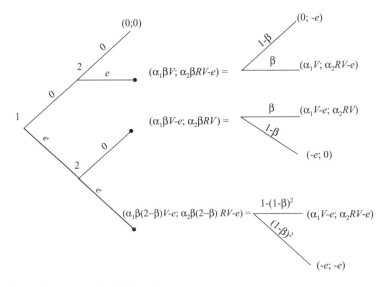

Exhibit 10.1   The Tree of the Effort Choice by Investors

The minimum values of $\alpha^e_{A,1}$ and $\alpha^e_{A,2}$ that can provide the $(e;e)$ outcome are:

$$\alpha^e_{A,1} = \frac{e}{\beta(1-\beta)V}, \qquad \alpha^e_{A,2} = \frac{e}{\beta(1-\beta)RV} \qquad (10.3)$$

Despite the competition, the net profits of the investors involved in each can remain strictly positive even at the minimum values $\alpha^e_{A,1}$ and $\alpha^e_{A,2}$ and are equal to

$$\Pi^e_{A,i} = \frac{1}{1-\beta}e - I_i \qquad (10.4)$$

where I_i is the financial investment into project i provided by the angel investor. For example, if $I_1 = I_2 = K$, then both investors make positive profits.

The profits of entrepreneurs are

$$\begin{cases} \Pi^e_{E_1,A} = \left(1 - \dfrac{e}{\beta(1-\beta)V}\right)\beta(2-\beta)V + (I_1 - K) = \beta(2-\beta)V - \dfrac{2-\beta}{1-\beta}e + (I_1 - K) \\[2ex] \Pi^e_{E_2,A} = \left(1 - \dfrac{e}{\beta(1-\beta)RV}\right)\beta(2-\beta)RV + (I_2 - K) = \beta(2-\beta)RV - \dfrac{2-\beta}{1-\beta}e + (I_2 - K) \end{cases}$$

The minimum values of $\alpha^{ne}_{A,1}$ and $\alpha^{ne}_{A,2}$ that can provide the $(0;e)$ outcome are:

$$\alpha^{ne}_{A,1} = \frac{K}{\beta V}, \qquad \alpha^{ne}_{A,2} = \frac{K+e}{\beta RV} \qquad (10.5)$$

where the superscript "ne" refers to "no effort" by investor 1. Investor 2 still exerts e. The necessary condition for this equilibrium to exist is

$$K + e \leq \beta RV \qquad (10.6)$$

If investors receive $\alpha^{ne}_{A,1}$ and $\alpha^{ne}_{A,2}$, their profits are zero. The entrepreneurs' profits are equal to the NPVs of their projects:

$$\Pi^{ne}_{E_1,A} = \beta V - K, \qquad \Pi^e_{E_2,A} = \beta RV - K - e$$

At the end of this chapter we show that for fixed α_1 and α_2 these two equilibria do not coexist, and from observing α_1 and α_2 we can accurately infer the effort level exerted by investor 1.

If $(0;0)$ is the equilibrium both projects have zero gross payoff; hence, none of the investors is interested in investing in them. We can infer that if

$$e > \beta RV \qquad (10.7)$$

then no investment is possible, although for $e < \beta(1-\beta)(1+R)V$ the first best outcome might be to invest money and effort into *both* projects!

Possible Outcomes When Angel Investment Is Financially Constrained

Investors' efforts are not observable. However, as we have mentioned, in equilibrium entrepreneurs correctly anticipate them by observing α_1 and α_2. If $\beta(1-\beta)V < e < \beta RV$, then $(e;e)$ equilibrium in the effort choice is impossible and $(\alpha_{A,1}^{ne}, \alpha_{A,2}^{ne})$ is the equilibrium allocation of shares received by investors. On the other hand, for $e < \beta(1-\beta)V$, both equilibria are possible depending on the choice of $\alpha_{A,i}$ by entrepreneurs.

For small e, $e \leq \beta(1-\beta)V$, angel investors offer E_1 and E_2 financing K in return for investors' shares $\alpha_{A,1}$ and $\alpha_{A,2}$, respectively, such that $\alpha_{A,1} \geq \alpha_{A,1}^e$ and $\alpha_{A,2} \geq \alpha_{A,2}^e$. If their offers are accepted, both investors provide money and effort e.

If e satisfies the inequality $e \leq \beta RV$, E_1 can be offered financing in return for investor's share $\alpha_{A,1}'$, in project 1, $\alpha_{A,1}^{ne} \leq \alpha_{A,1}' < \alpha_{A,1}^e$, and E_2 can be offered financing in return for $\alpha_{A,2}'$ share in project 2, $\alpha_{A,2}^{ne} \leq \alpha_{A,2}' < \alpha_{A,2}^e$. Only the project 2 investor provides money and effort e, while the project 1 investor provides money and zero effort.

For $e > \beta RV$ no angel financing is possible.

We will now turn to the contracts that can be offered in the equilibrium. Suppose that angel investors are financially constrained and cannot invest more than K—an assumption that we will relax later. Since they cannot invest more than K, they compete with each other by asking entrepreneurs for a smaller α_i share that would still elicit investors' choice of effort most preferred by entrepreneurs. Since in both equilibria investor 2 provides e, the situation is not symmetrical. It is the preference by E_1 that plays the crucial role in determining the outcome.

For example, if both entrepreneurs prefer an outcome in which investors both provide e, then the smallest α_i share asked for by investor i will be $\alpha_{A,i}^e$. In this case an investor cannot win a contract by asking for a slightly smaller share, $\alpha_{A,1} = \alpha_{A,i}^e - \varepsilon$, because he cannot commit to provide e at the later stage. However, if $(e;e)$ is not an outcome preferred by E_1, then investor 1 cannot enforce it by asking for $\alpha_{A,1}^e$. Any investor who concedes ε of this share, thus signaling that he will not exert e, will leave investors asking for $\alpha_{A,1}^e$ without a chance of winning the contract. As in Bertrand competition, the decision to ask for the share $(\alpha_{A,i}^e - \varepsilon)$ is not sustainable in this case, and $\alpha_{A,1}$ will go down to $\alpha_{A,i}^{ne}$, generating zero profit for investor 1.

When $e \leq \beta(1-\beta)V$, angel investors are prepared to provide effort for both projects, which would lead to the first best outcome. In this case, the profits of participating investors are strictly positive. However, due to the incentive compatibility constraints of entrepreneurs, the condition $e \leq \beta(1-\beta)V$ is not sufficient to achieve the first best outcome. We have to check whether the IC constraints for entrepreneurs are satisfied when $e \leq \beta(1-\beta)V$ and investors are receiving $\alpha_{A,1}^e$ and $\alpha_{A,2}^e$. Suppose that alternatively E_1 could choose an investor who would provide investment K and zero effort in return for $\alpha_{A,1}^{ne}$. He would still prefer to choose an investor offering investment for $\alpha_{A,1}^e$, that is, to give the investor a bigger share of project 1 if and only if the value of his share $(1 - \alpha_{A,1}^e)$ in the project were higher in this case than the value of his share $(1 - \alpha_{A,1}^{ne})$ in the project with zero effort:

$$\left(1 - \frac{e}{\beta(1-\beta)V}\right)\beta(2-\beta)V \geq \left(1 - \frac{K}{\beta V}\right)\beta V$$

which gives us

$$e \leq \frac{\beta(1-\beta)^2 V + K(1-\beta)}{2-\beta} \tag{10.8}$$

As we have mentioned, because investor 2 always provides effort, the preferences of E_2 do not really matter. In fact it turns out that E_2 prefers to receive $\left(1 - \alpha^e_{A,2}\right)$ if

$$e \leq \beta(1-\beta)^2 RV + K(1-\beta)$$

which holds, if inequality (10.8) holds.

It is easy to see that if inequality (10.8) does not hold, E_1 will prefer an investor who asks for $\alpha^{ne}_{A,1}$ in return for his investment. We have already seen why such investors exist despite the fact that the profit will be zero, while with $\alpha^e_{A,1}$ the investor's profit would be strictly positive.

We summarize the results in the following proposition:

Proposition 1. *If no angel investor can invest more than K, then angel investment leads to the following outcomes:*

For small e satisfying inequality (inequality for e, (e, e) positive externality), angel investors offer E_1 and E_2 financing K in return for investors' shares $\alpha^e_{A,1} = \frac{e}{\beta(1-\beta)V}$ and $\alpha^e_{A,2} = \frac{e}{\beta(1-\beta)RV}$, respectively. Both investors provide money K and effort e. Each investor makes strictly positive profit $\frac{1}{1-\beta}e - K$. E_1 has positive return $\beta(2-\beta)V - \frac{2-\beta}{1-\beta}e - K$, and E_2 has positive return $\beta(2-\beta)RV - \frac{2-\beta}{1-\beta}e - K$.

For e satisfying the double inequality

$$\frac{\beta(1-\beta)^2 V + K(1-\beta)}{2-\beta} < e \leq \beta RV - K \tag{10.9}$$

investors 1 and 2 receive, respectively, shares $\alpha^{ne}_{A,2}$ and $\alpha^{ne}_{A,2}$ from $(0,e)$ alphas) in return for financial investment K. Investor 2 exerts e, while investor 1 does not exert any effort.

For $e + K > \beta RV$ no angel financing is possible.

As we see from Proposition 1, quite often angel investment leads to a suboptimal outcome. For example, if $e < \beta(1-\beta)(1+R)V$, then exerting e for both projects is the first best action, while the angel investment achieves this result only under a much more restrictive condition of inequality (10.8). Similarly, no projects should receive funding only if $e + 2K > \beta(1+R)V$, while angel investors refuse financing whenever $e + K > \beta RV$.

The inefficiency of angel investment stems mainly from the angels' self-interest, because they make their investment decisions without regard for the impact on the other project's outcome. However, it is also partly attributable to entrepreneurs' selfish interests—even when angels are ready to provide investment and effort to achieve the first best outcome, entrepreneurs may choose a solution that is in fact suboptimal in terms of the total value created.

Also, although investors act competitively and do not intentionally coordinate their investments, they do still take the existence of other projects into account.

If we ignored the externality effect of other existing projects, assumed the expected value of project 1 to be βV, and tried to analyze the returns to angel investors on an isolated basis, then for e satisfying inequality (10.8) we would encounter the following "paradox": angel investors receive a smaller than "fair" share in the projects but nevertheless obtain strictly positive returns in the competitive world.

Of course, in reality there is no paradox once the externality effect is properly factored in.

So far in our analysis we have not allowed investors to invest money in more than one project, or to invest more than strictly necessary for the project's success. Therefore, even despite keeping this seemingly "smaller than fair" share $\alpha_{A,i}$, investors cannot be called indulgent—they do not give entrepreneurs more than the necessary investment K.

In the coming part of our paper, we will relax these two constraints by allowing angel investors to make financial, but not the human capital, investment, into two projects and by allowing them to invest more than K into one project. Of course, all players still remain rational and are not prepared to accept negative profits.

Possible Outcomes with Financially Unconstrained Angel Investment

If angel investors do not have monetary constraints, then two separate factors can now affect the outcome: (1) the same angel investor can finance both projects, while exerting e for only one of them, and (2) the amount of money invested into one project can exceed K. We have to emphasize that the same angel investor cannot exert effort e for both projects, because his human capital resources are limited.

Let us consider first that our angel investors are rich and the same investor can invest K into both projects. Investing into two projects makes sense either if it leads to a different outcome or if it gives the investor a higher profit without lowering that of the entrepreneurs.

If inequality (10.8) holds, then a rich angel investor cannot provide a viable alternative, for an obvious reason—he cannot exert e for both projects. If $(0; e)$ is an outcome in Proposition 1, then the rich investor cannot change the outcome, as he cannot increase his profit (making it positive) without asking for a higher share in at least one project, and the entrepreneur who owns the project concerned will not agree to that.

The only situation in which the two-project investment by the same angel investor may make a difference is where $e + K > \beta RV$ and $(0; 0)$ is the outcome in Proposition 1. This gives the following result:

Proposition 2. *If the system of inequalities*

$$\begin{cases} K + e > \beta RV \\ 2K + e \leq \beta(1 + R)V \end{cases} \tag{10.10}$$

holds, then one rich angel investor finances both projects in return for shares $\alpha_{RA,1}$ and $\alpha_{RA,2}$ in projects 1 and 2 respectively, such that

$$(\alpha_{RA,1} + \alpha_{RA,2}R)\beta V = 2K + e \tag{10.11}$$

Proof. The angel investor will demand α_1 and α_2 such that

$$(\alpha_1 + \alpha_2 R)\beta V \geq 2K + e$$

with competition driving it down to equality. Such an allocation with $\alpha_{RA,i} < 1$ always exists. For example, $\alpha_{RA,1} = \alpha_{RA,2} = \frac{2K+e}{\beta V(1+R)} < 1$. QED

The exact values of $\alpha_{RA,1}$ and $\alpha_{RA,2}$ are the result of bargaining between entrepreneurs and the investor and are outside the scope of this paper.

The second and, we believe, more interesting situation is the one in which individual investment can exceed K. This would appear to be an unusual situation, because everybody knows that the required financial investment is K. So for institutional investors, like VCs, investing more than necessary is highly unlikely. Since angel investors do not have such restrictions, they can invest more than K if they deem it necessary. Obviously, this can happen only if investors make non-negative profit as a result. Since in the $(0, e)$ equilibrium investors have zero profits, they will have an incentive to give entrepreneurs more than K only if this leads to an (e, e) equilibrium outcome.

In Proposition 1, for any e satisfying the double inequality

$$\frac{\beta(1-\beta)^2 V + K(1-\beta)}{2-\beta} < e \leq \beta(1-\beta)V$$

both investors were prepared to exert e, but the IC constraints for entrepreneurs, especially for E_1, precluded this outcome. By offering entrepreneurs a choice between $\alpha_{A,i}^{ne}$ in return for investment K and $\alpha_{A,i}^{e}$ in return for investment I_i, with $I_i > K$, investors can shift entrepreneurs' preferences to the second option if the following system of inequalities holds:[5]

$$\begin{cases} \left(1 - \frac{e}{\beta(1-\beta)V}\right)\beta(2-\beta)V + (I_1 - K) \geq \left(1 - \frac{K}{\beta V}\right)\beta V - K \\ \left(1 - \frac{e}{\beta(1-\beta)RV}\right)\beta(2-\beta)RV + (I_2 - K) \geq \left(1 - \frac{K+e}{\beta RV}\right)\beta RV - K \end{cases}$$

or

$$\begin{cases} I_1 \geq \frac{(2-\beta)}{1-\beta}e - K - (1-\beta)\beta V \\ I_2 \geq \frac{1}{1-\beta}e - K - (1-\beta)\beta RV \end{cases} \tag{10.12}$$

From (10.4) we derive that the investors' participation constraints (non-negative profit condition) are

$$I_i \leq \frac{e}{1-\beta}$$

Combined with (10.12) this gives us an inequality

$$e \leq \beta(1-\beta)V + K \qquad (10.13)$$

which always holds whenever angels' IC constraints for the $(e;e)$ outcome hold. Of course, in equilibrium, competition between angel investors will increase I_i until $I_i = \frac{e}{1-\beta}$ unless *all* investors' disposable financial resources investment are strictly smaller than $\frac{e}{1-\beta}$, in which case the outcome depends on whether or not there are at least two investors who can invest I_1 and I_2 that satisfy (10.12). We thus come to the following proposition:

Proposition 3. *If inequality (10.13) holds and there are at least two investors capable of and willing to provide financial investment that satisfies the system of inequalities (10.12), then in return for shares $\alpha^e_{A,1}$ and $\alpha^e_{A,2}$ satisfying condition (10.3), both projects will receive human capital investment e and financial investment I_1 and I_2, each in excess of K, such that $I_1 = I_2 = \frac{(2-\beta)}{1-\beta}e - K - (1-\beta)\beta V$, if there are only two such investors. Both investors earn positive profits*

$$(1-\beta)\beta V - e + K$$

$I_1 = I_2 = I_{third}$*, if all but two investors can invest only strictly less than $\frac{e}{1-\beta}$. I_{third} is the third biggest amount that can be invested. The two richest investors earn positive profits*

$$\frac{e}{1-\beta} - I_{third}$$

$I_1 = I_2 = \frac{e}{1-\beta}$ *if at least three investors can invest $\frac{e}{1-\beta}$. Investors' profits are equal to zero.*

We call these angel investors indulgent, because they know that the entrepreneurs will appropriate for personal use part $(I_i - K)$ of their financial investment, and nevertheless allow it to happen.

The good news is that e is now put into both projects. The bad news for investors is that if there are enough rich investors, they lose all their profits, even in the area satisfying inequality (10.8) where angel investors would have positive profit, if they were not rich and indulgent. Of course, this is good news for entrepreneurs, who make higher profit. Since the combined net value of investors and entrepreneurs coincides with the first best outcome, we may call this result the "quasi" first best outcome.

VC INVESTMENT

Let us now suppose that VC investment is possible as well. If VC investors enter the market, then the only time they create higher value for the projects than angel investors would be in a situation where putting e into both projects is the first best outcome, while angel investors would put e only into one project. On the other hand, we assume that as institutional investors, VCs cannot make a financial investment in excess of the strictly required level, that is, they cannot invest more than K in each project. Without this assumption, VCs could always at least match the angels' investments. We also assume that if VCs and angels create identical value for entrepreneurs, the entrepreneurs will prefer angel investors, due to the less formal nature of angel investment and the higher search costs involved in obtaining VC investment.

If K is small, then angel financing is always possible outside the no investment area determined by (10.2).[6] In order to win a contract, VCs must offer better deals to both entrepreneurs. The VC who wins the contract must credibly commit to put e into both projects and continue both projects at $t = 1$, while both entrepreneurs obtain higher value for their stakes thanks to the VC's investment. The next proposition establishes when these conditions hold.

Proposition 4. *If the system of inequalities*

$$\begin{cases} e < \beta(1-\beta)(1+R)V \\ e > \beta(1-\beta)V \\ e \le \beta RV - K \\ e \le (1-\beta)^2\beta(1+R)V + 2K(1-\beta) \end{cases} \tag{10.14}$$

holds, then VC investment provides a more attractive alternative to angel investment. The VC investor provides financial capital K and human capital e for each project in return for shares $\alpha^*_{VC,1}$ and $\alpha^*_{VC,2}$, such that

$$\alpha^*_{VC,1} + \alpha^*_{VC,2}R = \frac{e}{\beta(1-\beta)V}$$

and

$$\begin{cases} \alpha^*_{VC,1} \le \dfrac{1-\beta}{2-\beta} + \dfrac{K}{\beta(2-\beta)V} \\ \alpha^*_{VC,2} \le \dfrac{1-\beta}{2-\beta} - \dfrac{e-K}{\beta(2-\beta)RV} \end{cases}$$

The VC makes a strictly positive profit

$$\Pi_{VC} = \frac{\beta}{1-\beta}e - 2K$$

The proof is at the end of this chapter. It follows from the IC constraints for the VC and for the entrepreneurs.

The VC receives a strictly positive profit, because only then is his commitment to exert e for both projects credible. By assumption, VCs cannot "waste" money by overinvesting, therefore the profit remains strictly positive. If we relaxed this assumption, then the situation would resemble that described in Proposition 3, and instead of K, the VC investor would provide I_1 and I_2 such that $I_1 + I_2 = \frac{\beta}{1-\beta}e$, $I_i \geq K$.

The ability of VC investors to provide the first best result is not sufficient, because it can be obstructed by entrepreneurs' lack of interest in such a result. To summarize our results, we can write that the first best outcome that maximizes the combined value of the two projects is attainable in the following regions:

If either system of inequalities (10.14) or (10.1) holds, then entrepreneurs will choose a VC who exerts e for both projects.

If inequality (10.13) holds, then indulgent angel investors are the entrepreneurs' best choice. Both projects receive e.

If inequality (10.10) holds, then the same rich angel investor provides financing for both projects and exerts e for one of them.

For $\beta(1-\beta)(1+R)V \leq e \leq \beta RV - K$ two angel investors finance both projects, with only one project getting e.

Corollary   If the system of inequalities

$$\begin{cases} e < \beta(1-\beta)(1+R)V \\ e > \beta(1-\beta)V \\ e \leq \beta RV - K \\ e > (1-\beta)^2 \beta(1+R)V + 2K(1-\beta) \end{cases}$$

holds, then the first best outcome is never achieved by investors.

Proof. The proof follows from Proposition 4.

The corollary shows that despite strictly positive expected profit of a participating VC investor, when competing for contracts the VCs cannot lure entrepreneurs by conceding part of it (without investing more than K) due to the moral hazard problem. On the other hand, E_1 is adherent to the suboptimal outcome, because of his higher profits from it. If transfer payment from E_2 to E_1 were possible, it would make interests of E_1 and E_2 congruent, but it would not eliminate the VC's moral hazard problem.

The fact that in order to guarantee an input of e into both projects, VCs must earn strictly positive profit, means that when compared with indulgent investment from Proposition 3, VC investment will always be less attractive. In this case VCs cannot offer entrepreneurs terms that are comparable to the angels' contracts. We express this formally in the following proposition.

Proposition 5. *If $e \leq \beta(1-\beta)V$, then VCs' offers are always strictly dominated by indulgent investors' offers.*
   The proof is at the end of this chapter.

DISCUSSION AND EMPIRICAL IMPLICATIONS

Exhibits 10.2 to 10.6 provide an illustration of our results. Areas numbered 1, 2, and 3 in these exhibits correspond to the areas of "poor," "rich," and "indulgent" angel investment, respectively, area with number 4 corresponds to the region of VC investment, and in area 5 "no investment" is the first best outcome. Tildes denote underinvestment in the corresponding area. For computational simplicity we assume that $K = 0$.

Exhibit 10.2 shows how areas of angel and VC investment depend on e/V and β if there is no asymmetry between projects, i.e., $R = 1$. We see that the region of VC investment (area 4) is quite small in comparison with angels' investment. VCs invest in relatively risky but profitable projects.

As the asymmetry between projects grows (on Exhibit 10.3 $R = 2$), the area of the "two-projects effort" first best outcome also increases, and VCs start investing in a bigger number of projects, now including projects that are less risky and less profitable conditional on success, that is, project 1 has a lower profitability index, $\frac{V}{e}$ of the realized payoff. The growth of VC investment area 4 is outpaced by the overall growth of the area where "two-projects effort" is optimal, thus creating inefficiency due to the angel underinvestment (areas 1ı and 2ı).

The way the area of VC investment grows as the asymmetry between the projects increases is illustrated more clearly in Exhibits 10.4 and 10.5. For projects with a high $\frac{V}{e}$ ratio (on Exhibit 10.4 $\frac{V}{e} = 4.1$) VC investment into less risky projects is the contributor to this growth, while for projects with a more moderate $\frac{V}{e}$ ratio (in Exhibit 10.5 $\frac{V}{e} = 2$) VC investment expands both into higher and lower risk projects as the asymmetry grows.

In one of the subsections we were considering equilibrium outcomes in an economy where angel investors are cash constrained. Exhibit 10.6 illustrates what happens in an economy that does not have rich individual investors. We see that VC investment takes over entire areas of the former portfolio investments of rich angels, creating additional efficiency in area 4* and encroaching on the former area

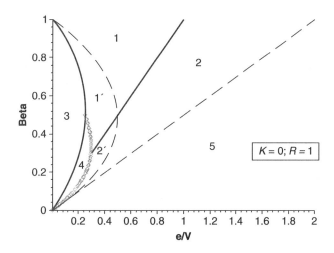

Exhibit 10.2   High Compensation and Portfolio Investment Contracts

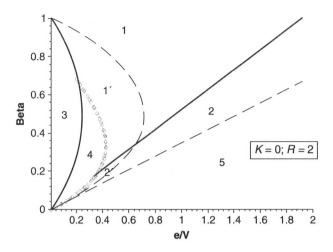

Exhibit 10.3 Regions of High Compensation and Portfolio Investment Contracts

of indulgent angel investment, but not completely—low risk projects are taken over by separate angel investors whose investment is suboptimal (area 1″). In area 4* the VC investor still makes a positive profit, while in the remaining areas, formerly the reserve of rich angel investment, his expected profit is zero.

Therefore, from Exhibit 10.6 we can infer that in comparison with rich economies, in poor economies one should observe more VC investment than angel investment, with angels holding the ground in investment into relatively safe and moderately profitable projects and VCs overtaking them in less profitable projects and highly profitable, but risky projects. In addition, unlike rich economies, where VC investment always makes positive profit despite competition, in poor economies VCs also make investments that generate zero profit.

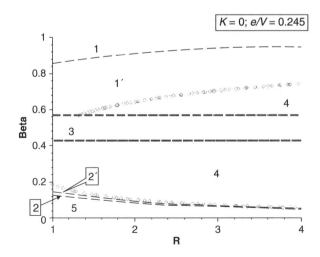

Exhibit 10.4 Contract Domination

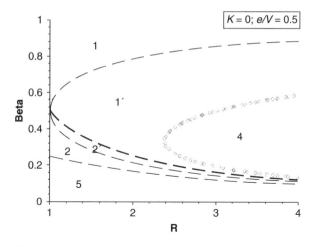

Exhibit 10.5   Different Contracts Domination

The existence of areas of underinvestment, the strictly positive profit obtained the participating VC, and the cash overspending by indulgent angels all raise legitimate questions as to whether or not the outcome can be further improved. One possible way of achieving the first best outcome could be to create a coalition of indulgent angels, with each investor holding stakes in both projects, while investing effort and (over)investing cash in only one project. Such a coalition would make the "two-project effort" first best outcome always attainable; both investors would make zero profit, essentially driving VCs out of business. A quick analysis shows that capital investment I_1 and I_2 and allocations of investors' stakes in both projects is a situation that is possible, although the exact solution involves bargaining between four parties and is beyond the scope of this paper.

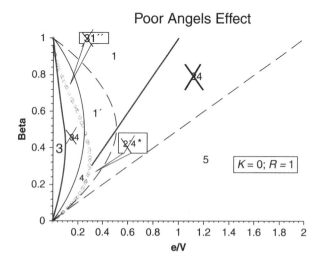

Exhibit 10.6   Regions of Different Contract Domination

In fact, such coalitions of angel investors are, in all but name, VC funds without limited partners. Therefore, another alternative to avoid underinvestment would be to allow VCs to invest excess cash in the project they support. Probably, this is what some VCs did in the late 1990s. The difficulty is that this solution leads to another agency conflict between VCs, who act as agents for the true owners of this money—the limited partners in venture capital funds.

EMPIRICAL IMPLICATIONS

Our results suggest the empirical implications of several types. First, there are implications concerning the VCs' returns in their portfolio companies. Second, we make inferences about investment patterns of angels' investment and VCs' investment. Third, we expect to observe some differences in start-up financing in countries with different per capita wealth of the richest angel investors.

To be more specific, when comparing VCs' investment portfolios to angels' portfolios, we should observe that VC-backed companies are relatively more heterogeneous in terms of their profitability or market share, but they nevertheless use compatible technology, that is, belong to the same industry or related industries, while companies in the angel investment portfolio are more closely related. This difference can be tested by constructing a heterogeneity index for VCs' and angels' investment portfolios. For both portfolios, we should observe more information spillover (e.g., adoption of the same technology, use of similar business models) between portfolio companies than between companies financed independently. It is interesting that Mason and Harrison (2002) report findings consistent with these predictions. They find that returns to business angels are less skewed than those of early-stage VC deals. Business angels have fewer investments in which they lose money (39.8 percent versus 64.2 percent by VCs), but a significantly higher proportion of their investments (23.8 percent versus 7.1 percent by VCs) either break even or generate only modest returns.

Second, regarding the ex ante probability of success for each company on an individual basis, we predict that VCs invest in more risky companies than angel investors. Ex ante valuation of some of these companies may not even justify the investment made, showing the negative NPV. This prediction can be tested by comparing the business plans of entrepreneurial companies.

Third, the ex post profitability of VC-backed companies is *higher* than for those financed by rich angels who also invest into a portfolio of companies, but *lower* than for companies backed by angels who are single-company investors.

Despite these differences in the profitability of portfolio companies, VC returns remain positive and are higher than angel returns. This is consistent with the previous prediction, because VC investors apparently consistently receive a higher project share than angel investors in return for investment of the same size. This is also consistent with some empirical evidence. For example, Stanco and Akah (2005) provide anecdotal evidence that angels tend to give start-ups overly high, unrealistic ex ante valuations, resulting in lower angels' share. Wong (forthcoming) reports that angels get on average 15 percent share in portfolio companies (8 percent if they co-invest), while the average investor's share in all types of investments is 18 percent (21 percent if more than one investor invests).

Finally, in the economies with lower per capita wealth of rich angel investors, we should observe a higher proportion of VC-backed start-ups. At the same time, VCs would receive on average lower profits from these start-ups than from their investments in fewer start-up in rich economies. The reason is the following: in rich economies VCs lose out to angel investors the projects in which investors earn zero expected profits and are able to finance only the projects that generate positive profits to VCs. As we have indicated before, these positive profits serve as a commitment mechanism in the investor's moral hazard problem.

ANSWERS TO PROOFS

In order to understand what kind of contracts between entrepreneurs and angel investors can be observed in equilibrium, we start our analysis from the effort choice by two angel investors, who become involved in projects 1 and 2. The angel investing in project i selects his level of effort (zero or e) so as to maximize his expected profit given his share α_i in project i and the share α_j in project j attributable to investor j.

The outcome should be the Nash equilibrium of the game described by the following matrix

effort	0	e
0	$(0; 0)$	$(\alpha_1 \beta V; \alpha_2 \beta RV - e)$
e	$(\alpha_1 \beta V - e; \alpha_2 \beta RV)$	$(\alpha_1 \beta (2 - \beta) V - e; \alpha_2 \beta (2 - \beta) RV - e)$

where the elements of the matrix are the investors' expected payoffs net of the effort exerted. Rows correspond to the level of effort exerted by investor 1 and columns correspond to the level of effort exerted by investor 2. Exhibit 10.1 shows the extensive form of the game.

For $R > 1$ four equilibria are possible. They include three pure strategy equilibria $(e; e)$, $(0; e)$, and $(0; 0)$ and a mixed strategy equilibrium.

Equilibrium $(e; e)$

$(e; e)$ is the equilibrium if and only if

$$\begin{cases} e \leq \alpha_1 \beta (1 - \beta) V \\ e \leq \alpha_2 \beta (1 - \beta) RV \end{cases}$$

Assuming that when indifferent between making effort e or zero effort, the investors will exert effort e, we obtain the minimum values of $\alpha_{A,1}^e$ and $\alpha_{A,2}^e$ that can provide the $(e; e)$ outcome:

$$\begin{cases} \alpha_{A,1}^e = \dfrac{e}{\beta(1 - \beta)V} \\ \alpha_{A,2}^e = \dfrac{e}{\beta(1 - \beta)RV} \end{cases}$$

Despite the competition, the net profits of both investors can remain *strictly positive* even at the minimum values $\alpha^e_{A,1}$ and $\alpha^e_{A,2}$ and are equal to

$$\Pi^e_{A,i} = \frac{1}{1-\beta}e - I_i$$

where I_i is the financial investment into project i provided by the angel investor. For example, if $I_1 = I_2 = K$, then both investors make positive profits.

We are not saying that $\alpha^e_{A,1}$ and $\alpha^e_{A,2}$ will necessarily be the allocations of shares received by investors in equilibrium. This outcome is possible if both E_1 and E_2 agree to receive $(1 - \alpha_1)$ and $(1 - \alpha_2)$ shares, respectively. The values obtained by entrepreneurs in this case are

$$\begin{cases} \Pi^e_{E_1,A} = \left(1 - \dfrac{e}{\beta(1-\beta)V}\right)\beta\,(2-\beta)\,V + (I_1 - K) = \beta\,(2-\beta)\,V - \dfrac{2-\beta}{1-\beta}e + (I_1 - K) \\[3mm] \Pi^e_{E_2,A} = \left(1 - \dfrac{e}{\beta(1-\beta)RV}\right)\beta\,(2-\beta)\,RV + (I_2 - K) = \beta\,(2-\beta)\,RV - \dfrac{2-\beta}{1-\beta}e + (I_2 - K) \end{cases}$$

From $\alpha_1 < 1$ and $\alpha_2 < 1$ it follows that the necessary condition for this equilibrium to exist is $e < \beta\,(1-\beta)\,V$. Due to the moral hazard problem, angel investor 1 will not provide a positive effort, e, if e lies in the area $\beta\,(1-\beta)\,V < e < \beta\,(1-\beta)\,(1+R)\,V$ despite the strictly positive profit that this investor would make, if he could commit to e.

Equilibrium $(0; e)$

The outcome in which effort e is invested in project 2 only, is the Nash equilibrium if and only if

$$\begin{cases} e > \alpha_1\beta(1-\beta)V \\ e \le \alpha_2\beta RV \end{cases}$$

Given the investors' participation constraints, that is, that investors' profits cannot be negative, we obtain the minimum values of $\alpha^{ne}_{A,1}$ and $\alpha^{ne}_{A,2}$ that can provide the $(0; e)$ outcome:

$$\begin{cases} \alpha^{ne}_{A,1} = \dfrac{K}{\beta V} \\[3mm] \alpha^{ne}_{A,2} = \dfrac{K + e}{\beta RV} \end{cases}$$

where the superscript "*ne*" refers to "no effort" by investor 1 and only by investor 1, because investor 2 still exerts e. From $\alpha_1 < 1$ and $\alpha_2 < 1$ it follows that the necessary condition for this equilibrium to exist is

$$K + e \le \beta RV$$

If investors receive $\alpha_{A,1}^{ne}$ and $\alpha_{A,2}^{ne}$, their profits are zero. The entrepreneurs' profits are equal to the NPVs of the projects:

$$\begin{cases} \Pi_{E_1,A}^{ne} = \beta V - K \\ \Pi_{E_2,A}^{e} = \beta RV - K - e \end{cases}$$

Notice that for fixed α_1 and α_2 this equilibrium is not compatible with the $(e;e)$ equilibrium, because $\alpha_1 < \alpha_{A,1}^{e}$.

Equilibrium $(0;0)$

$(0;0)$ is the equilibrium if and only if

$$\begin{cases} e > \alpha_1 \beta V \\ e > \alpha_2 \beta RV \end{cases}$$

In this case both projects have zero gross payoff; hence, none of the investors is interested in investing in them. We can infer that if

$$e > \beta RV$$

then no investment is possible, although for $e < \beta(1-\beta)(1+R)V$ the first best outcome might be to invest money and effort into *both* projects!

Mixed strategy equilibrium:

If the following system of inequalities holds

$$\begin{cases} e < \alpha_1 \beta V \\ e \geq \alpha_2 \beta(1-\beta)RV \end{cases}$$

then two Nash equilibria exist at the same time: $(0;e)$ and $(e;0)$. Each angel investor would prefer to provide zero effort if he knew that the other was investing e at the R&D stage.

A mixed equilibrium exists in which investor i decides to provide zero effort at the R&D stage with probability p_i and decides to provide e with probability $(1-p_i)$, where p_i is the solution to

$$\begin{cases} p_1 0 + (1-p_1)\alpha_2 \beta RV = p_1 \alpha_2 \beta RV + (1-p_1)\alpha_2 \beta (2-\beta) RV - e \\ p_2 0 + (1-p_2)\alpha_1 \beta V = p_2 \alpha_1 \beta V + (1-p_2)\alpha_1 \beta (2-\beta) V - e \end{cases}$$

The solution is: $\left\{ p_1 = \frac{-\alpha_2 \beta RV + \alpha_2 \beta^2 RV + e}{\alpha_2 \beta^2 RV}, p_2 = \frac{-\alpha_1 \beta V + \alpha_1 \beta^2 V + e}{\alpha_1 \beta^2 V} \right\}$. We thus have

$$p_1 = \frac{e - \alpha_2 \beta(1-\beta)RV}{\alpha_2 \beta^2 RV} \quad \text{and} \quad p_2 = \frac{e - \alpha_1 \beta(1-\beta)V}{\alpha_1 \beta^2 V}$$

The expected payoffs to investors 1 and 2 are

$$\Pi_{A,1} = \alpha_1 V - \frac{e}{\beta} - K \quad \text{and} \quad \Pi_{A,2} = \alpha_2 RV - \frac{e}{\beta} - K$$

$\alpha_{A,i}$ for this equilibrium cannot be less than

$$\alpha_{A,1}^m = \frac{e + \beta K}{\beta V} \quad \text{and} \quad \alpha_{A,2}^m = \frac{e + \beta K}{\beta RV}$$

for which the investors' profits are zero. Since

$$\begin{cases} e < \alpha_1 \beta V \\ e \geq \alpha_2 \beta (1 - \beta) RV \end{cases}$$

must hold as well as $\alpha_{A,i}^m < 1$, we have

$$\begin{cases} e < e + \beta K \\ e \geq (e + \beta K)(1 - \beta) \\ e + \beta K < \beta V \end{cases}$$

So, the necessary condition for the mixed equilibrium to exist is $e + \beta K < \beta V$. For $\alpha_{A,i} = \alpha_{A,i}^m$ entrepreneurs' profits are

$$\Pi_{E_1,A}^m = (\beta V - (e + \beta K)) \left(\frac{1}{\beta} - \frac{1}{\left(1 + \frac{\beta K}{e}\right)^2} \right)$$

$$\Pi_{E_2,A}^m = (\beta RV - (e + \beta K)) \left(\frac{1}{\beta} - \frac{1}{\left(1 + \frac{\beta K}{e}\right)^2} \right)$$

which are always positive.

Since investor 2 observes the other investor's effort before he makes his own effort, the mixed strategy equilibrium is not subgame perfect and it is never realized in our model.

Proof of Proposition 4. The incentive compatibility constraint for the VC is

$$(\alpha_{VC,1} + \alpha_{VC,2} R) \beta V - (2K + e) \leq (\alpha_{VC,1} + \alpha_{VC,2} R) \beta (2 - \beta) V - 2(K + e)$$

or

$$e \leq (\alpha_{VC,1} + \alpha_{VC,2} R) \beta (1 - \beta) V$$

with competition driving it down to equality

$$e = (\alpha_{VC,1} + \alpha_{VC,2} R) \beta (1 - \beta) V$$

Entrepreneurs are interested in VC investor, only if their profit will be higher than with angel investment. Participation constraints for entrepreneurs E_i and E_2 are, respectively

$$\begin{cases} (1 - \alpha_{VC,1})\,\beta(2 - \beta)V > \beta V - K \\ (1 - \alpha_{VC,2})\,\beta(2 - \beta)RV > \beta RV - (K + e) \end{cases}$$

or

$$\begin{cases} \alpha_{VC,1} \leq \dfrac{1 - \beta}{2 - \beta} + \dfrac{K}{\beta(2 - \beta)V} \\ \alpha_{VC,2} \leq \dfrac{1 - \beta}{2 - \beta} + \dfrac{(K + e)}{\beta(2 - \beta)RV} \end{cases}$$

Both incentive compatibility and participation constraints hold only if the following inequality is satisfied:

$$e \leq \left[\frac{1 - \beta}{2 - \beta}(1 + R) + \frac{(K + e) + K}{\beta\,(2 - \beta)\,V}\right]\beta(1 - \beta)V$$

which gives
$$e \leq (1 - \beta)^2\,\beta(1 + R)V + 2(1 - \beta)K \text{ QED.}$$

Proof of Proposition 5. IC constraints for VC and competition lead to

$$\alpha_{VC,1} + \alpha_{VC,2}R = \frac{e}{\beta(1 - \beta)V}$$

Indulgent angels hold $\alpha_{A,1}^e = \frac{e}{\beta(1-\beta)V}$ and $\alpha_{A,2}^e = \frac{e}{\beta(1-\beta)RV}$ in return for $\frac{e}{1-\beta}$.

In order for VC to win entrepreneurs contracts, the following IC constraints for entrepreneurs must hold:

$$\begin{cases} (1 - \alpha_{VC,1})\beta(2 - \beta)V \geq \left(1 - \dfrac{e}{\beta\,(1 - \beta)\,V}\right)\beta(2 - \beta)V + \dfrac{e}{1 - \beta} - K \\ (1 - \alpha_{VC,2})\beta(2 - \beta)RV \geq \left(1 - \dfrac{e}{\beta\,(1 - \beta)\,RV}\right)\beta(2 - \beta)RV + \dfrac{e}{1 - \beta} - K \end{cases}$$

which gives

$$\begin{cases} \alpha_{VC,1}\beta(2 - \beta)V \leq e + K \\ \alpha_{VC,2}\beta(2 - \beta)RV \leq e + K \end{cases}$$

or

$$\beta\,(2 - \beta)\,V\,(\alpha_{VC,1} + \alpha_{VC,2}) - 2\,(e + K) \leq 0$$

where the left-hand side expression is the VC's total profit. Since the VC's profit cannot be negative, we arrive at an equality

$$(\alpha_{VC,1} + \alpha_{VC,2}R) = 2\frac{e + K}{\beta(2 - \beta)V}$$

which contradicts VC's IC constraint (IC constraints VC).   QED.

CONCLUSION

In this article we study entrepreneurs' choice of investors, who must provide financial capital and effort for projects with externalities.

Each angel investor can exert effort for only one project, while VCs can invest in a portfolio of projects. When coordinated investment is necessary because of a strong externality effect, the VCs' portfolio approach can potentially lead to the first best outcome, whereas angels investing in separate projects may generate a suboptimal outcome, because they tend to undersupply effort for their projects and free-ride on competitors' results.

We have shown that angels can demonstrate their commitment to provide effort by supplying entrepreneurs with more cash than necessary for the projects' success. Because of the overinvestment, angels are then obliged to exert a high degree of effort in order to earn zero profit. This result offers an explanation for the lavish supply of cash attracted by certain entrepreneurial projects.

Due to the lack of coordination between angel investors, regions still remain where they either underinvest or fail to finance a group of projects, because they have negative NPV, if considered as stand-alone projects. Although portfolio investors, like angels and VCs, always manage to finance these projects, they are less successful in winning contracts from entrepreneurs running the underinvested projects.

The underinvestment problem can potentially be resolved by coalitions of angel investors who hold stakes in the portfolio of projects ("synthetic VCs"), or by allowing VCs to overinvest cash in their projects, which could be dangerous due to the principal-agency problem regarding relations between VCs (agents) and limited partners in venture capital funds (principals).

The results of this paper allow us to make the following conjectures.

First, a VC investment portfolio should include companies that are relatively heterogeneous in terms of their profitability or market share, but which nevertheless use compatible technology, that is, belong to the same industry or related industries with high interindustry externalities. Companies in the angel investment portfolio should be more closely related. For both portfolios, we should observe more information spillover (e.g., adoption of the same technology, use of similar business models) between portfolio companies than between companies financed independently.

Second, looking at the ex ante probability of success for each company on an individual basis, we will find that VCs invest in more risky companies than angel investors. Ex ante valuation of some of these companies might not even justify the investment made, showing the negative NPV.

Third, the ex post profitability of VC-backed companies is higher than for those financed by rich angels who also invest into a portfolio of companies but lower than for companies backed by angels who are single-company investors.

Finally, despite these differences in the profitability of portfolio companies, VC returns remain positive and are higher than angel returns. VC investors apparently consistently receive a higher project share than angel investors in return for investment of the same size. This result follows directly from our model, which made *no assumptions* about VCs' bargaining power or the scarceness of angel investment. On the contrary, if angel investors are poor and cannot invest cash into a portfolio of projects, VCs will invest in some zero profit projects. As individual investors become richer, VCs finance a smaller number of projects, but make higher profits on their investment!

Empirical evidence supports some of these predictions. Mason and Harrison (2002) find that returns to business angels are less skewed than those of early-stage VC deals. Business angels have fewer investments in which they lose money (39.8 percent versus 64.2 percent by VCs), but a significantly higher proportion of their investments (23.8 percent versus 7.1 percent by VCs) either break even or generate only modest returns. Stanco and Akah (2005) find that angels tend to give start-ups overly high, unrealistic ex ante valuations, resulting in lower angels' share. Wong (forthcoming) reports that angels get on average 15 percent share in portfolio companies (8 percent if they co-invest), while the average investor's share in all types of investments is 18 percent (21 percent if more than one investor invests).

NOTES

1. Casamatta (2003) looks for contracts soliciting effort from both entrepreneur and investor, because she studies relations between the entrepreneur and investors, modeling them as a double-sided moral hazard problem. Here we focus on the entrepreneur's choice of investor, thus only the investor's effort is important.

2. In Casamatta (2003) convertible debt should be used to elicit effort from the investor for a single-project model. Using convertible bonds does not change the results of this paper. Probably, this is due to the fact that we focus on a portfolio coordination problem.

3. The model works without this assumption, but analysis of the observed equilibrium becomes unnecessarily overcomplicated.

4. Although the value of K is negligible, we keep K in the formulas in order to make a distinction from the situation in which the project gets no investment at all.

5. Entrepreneurs are never interested in diverted K, because of the assumption that K is very small. Therefore, entrepreneurs always prefer to invest K rather than divert K and make the project fail.

6. For bigger K, there exists a region where angel financing is impossible, while investing into both projects is the first best result

$$\begin{cases} e < \beta(1-\beta)(1+R)V \\ e > \beta(1+R)V - 2K \end{cases}$$

In this case the VC investment is the entrepreneurs' only choice. The VC investor provides financial capital K and human capital e for each project in return for shares $\alpha_{VC,1}$ and

$\alpha_{VC,2}$, such that

$$\alpha_{VC,1} + \alpha_{VC,2}R = \frac{e}{\beta(1-\beta)V}$$

The VC makes a strictly positive profit

$$\Pi_{VC} = \frac{\beta}{1-\beta}e - 2K$$

REFERENCES

Bernile, G., D. Cumming, and E. Lyandres. 2007. The size of venture capital and private equity fund portfolios. *Journal of Corporate Finance* 13 (4):564–590.

Bhattacharya, S., and G. Chiesa. 1995. Proprietary information, financial intermediation and research incentives. *Journal of Financial Intermediation* 4:328–357.

Cabral, L. M.B. 2000. R&D cooperation and product market competition. *International Journal of Industrial Organization* 18:1033–1047.

Casamatta, C. 2003. Financing and advising: Optimal financial contracts with venture capitalists. *Journal of Finance* 58 (5):2059–2085.

Cumming, D. J. 2006. The Determinants of venture capital portfolio size: Empirical evidence. *Journal of Business* 79 (3):1083–1126.

Ehrlich, S. B., et al. 1994. After the cash arrives: A comparative study of venture capital and private investor involvement in entrepreneurial firms. *Journal of Business Venturing* 9:67–82.

Gorman, M., and W. Sahlman. 1989. What do venture capitalists do? *Journal of Business Venturing* 4:231–248.

Hellmann, T. 1994. Financial structure and control in venture capital. Stanford Working Paper.

_____. 1998a. The allocation of control rights in venture capital contracts. *Rand Journal of Economics* 29 (1):57–76.

_____. 1998b. A theory of corporate venture investing. Stanford Working Paper.

_____. 2002. A theory of strategic venture investing. *Journal of Financial Economics* 64 (2):285–314.

Kanniainen, V. and C. Keuschnigg. 2003. The Optimal Portfolio of Start-Up Firms in Venture Capital Finance. *Journal of Corporate Finance* 9:5, 521–34.

_____. 2004. Start-up investment with scarce venture capital support. *Journal of Banking and Finance* 28 (8):1935–59.

Kaplan, S., and P. Stromberg. 2001. Venture capitalists as principals: Contracting, screening, and monitoring. *American Economic Review* 91 (2):426–431.

Lange, J., B. Leleux, and B. Surlemont. 2003. Angel networks for the 21st century: An examination of practices of leading networks in Europe and the US (digest summary). *Journal of Private Equity* 6 (2):18–28.

Mason, C. M., and R. T. Harrison. 2002. Is it worth it? The rates of return from informal venture capital investments. *Journal of Business Venturing* 17 (3):211–236.

Prowse, S. 1998. Angel Investors and the market for angel investment. *Journal of Banking and Finance* 22:785–792.

Repullo, R., and J. Suarez. 2004. Venture capital finance: A security design approach. *Review of Finance* 8 (1):75–108.

Segal, I. 1999. Contracting with externalities. *Quarterly Journal of Economics* 114(2):337–388.

Stanco, T., and U. Akah. 2005. Survey: The relationship between angels and venture capitalists in the venture industry. George Washington University Working Paper. Ueda, Masako. 2004. Banks versus venture capital: Project evaluation, screening, and expropriation. *Journal of Finance* 59 (2):601–21.

Van Osnabrugge, M. 1998. The financing of entrepreneurial firms in the UK: A comparison of business angel and venture capitalist investment procedures. Doctoral diss., University of Oxford.

Wing, A. 2010. Angel finance: The other venture capital. In *Companion to venture capital*, Douglas J. Cumming. Hackensack, NJ: John Wiley & Sons, 71–110.

ABOUT THE AUTHOR

Dima Leshchinskii obtained his Ph.D. in Finance from INSEAD. He has had both industrial and academic experience. Dr. Leshchinskii worked as a Senior Economist at Cornerstone Research and he has held faculty positions in France and in the United States. His main research is on venture capital.

CHAPTER 11

Doing It Not Alone

Antecedents, Dynamics, and Outcomes of Venture Capital Syndication

DIRK DE CLERCQ
Associate Professor, Brock University

DIMO DIMOV
Assistant Professor, University of Connecticut

INTRODUCTION

An important and enduring feature of venture capital (VC) investing is syndication, specifically, the simultaneous investment by at least two venture capital firms (VCFs) in the same portfolio company (PFC). Formally, syndication represents a voluntary, long-term commitment by a VCF to a cooperative relationship with other VCFs, in which the firms exchange knowledge and resources (Wright and Lockett 2003). Although its prevalence varies by geographical regions and deal characteristics (Wright and Lockett 2003; Manigart et al. 2006), syndication is a widespread practice among venture capitalists. For example, a recent study of first-round investments by 2,498 U.S. VCFs between 1980 and 2004 reveals that 73 percent of these investments are syndicated (Dimov and Milanov in press).

Syndication also represents a rich and diverse research setting that enables researchers to focus on various aspects and topics. Broadly, its study can be classified in three general areas. First, the *antecedents of the decision to syndicate* pertain to both the motivation of VCFs to seek investment partners and their opportunity to attract such partners. Syndication motivations appear in a wide variety of recent studies (e.g., De Clercq and Dimov 2004; Manigart et al. 2006; Casamatta and Haritchabalet 2007; Kaiser and Lauterbach 2007; Dimov and Milanov in press), and a few studies of syndication opportunities have recently emerged (Abell and Nisar 2007; Dimov and Milanov in press). Second, the *internal dynamics of investment syndicates* covers both the level of involvement of individual VCFs in syndicates (De Clercq, Sapienza, and Zaheer 2008) and the contractual arrangements that characterize and affect syndication relationships (Wright and Lockett 2003; Cumming 2005). Third, research also addresses the *performance outcomes of syndication* (Dimov and De Clercq 2006; De Clercq and Dimov 2008). Together, these three research streams provide a comprehensive perspective of the phenomenon of syndication.

Research on VC syndication further embraces several conceptual perspectives, each focusing on and illuminating a distinct set of issues, theoretical constructs, and relationships. For example, the *financial* perspective typically focuses on the role of contractual arrangements in the governance of syndicate relationships (Cumming 2005, 2006), whereas the *economic sociology* perspective addresses how information about investments and partnering opportunities flows through social networks (Kogut, Urso, and Walker 2007), and the *management* perspective considers "managerial" aspects of syndication, with a specific focus on the combination and management of knowledge and other resources (e.g., De Clercq and Dimov 2008; Dimov and Milanov in press). Moreover, three general levels of analysis mark syndication research. At the *population* level, researchers attempt to describe the overall prevalence and characteristics of syndicated investments and relationships (Kogut, Urso, and Walker 2007). At the *portfolio* level, they investigate the role of syndication in the development and outcomes of investment portfolios (De Clercq and Dimov 2004; Dimov and De Clercq 2006). Finally, at the individual *investment* level, researchers examine why VCFs syndicate their investments and with whom they syndicate (Dimov and Milanov in press), how they manage those investments (De Clercq, Sapienza, and Zaheer 2008), and what benefits they derive from such investments (De Clercq and Dimov 2008).

Rather than offering a complete review of existing literature on VC syndication, however, this chapter draws from five recent empirical studies to illustrate and discuss a research program that uses the *management perspective* to study syndication at the portfolio or investment level. These studies cut across different research themes and thus illuminate various issues pertinent to VC syndication. We trace the predictions offered by each study to provide an overview of the theoretical streams and relationships that may help us understand syndication. We also offer a summary of the empirical findings for each prediction. In the final section, we provide concluding comments and directions for further research.

ANTECEDENTS OF VENTURE CAPITAL SYNDICATION

Venture capital investment practices include the decisions by VCFs to syndicate their investments, in which case *different* investors (syndicate partners) allocate capital to the same PFC, whether within a single investment or across subsequent investment rounds (Bygrave 1987; Lerner 1994; Sorenson and Stuart 2001).[1] Because of the high prevalence of syndication among VCFs, researchers seek to understand their motivations by applying a diverse set of theoretical perspectives and empirical methodologies (e.g., Bygrave 1987, 1988; Lerner 1994; Lockett and Wright 2001; Sorenson and Stuart 2001; Brander, Amit, and Antweiler 2002; Wright and Lockett 2003). Compared with relatively short-lived syndicates in investment banking (Chung, Singh, and Lee 2000; Podolny 1994), VC syndicates last longer and involve stronger partner commitments that are more difficult to terminate.

Exhibit 11.1 Overview of Motives for Syndication

Motive	Overview
Financial risk reduction	• The large size of the deal in proportion to the size of funds available • The requirement for additional rounds of financing • The large size of the deal in proportion to the firm's average deal size
Access to deal flow	• The possibility of the future reciprocation of deals (deal flow) • The reciprocation of past deal flow
Improved selection motive	• The need to seek the advice of other VCFs before investing
Knowledge sharing (value adding)	• The need to access specific skills to manage the investments • Difficulty in bringing in industry experts from outside • The deal is outside the investment stage(s) in which the VC usually invests • The deal is outside the industries in which the VC usually invests • The deal is located outside of the geographic region(s) in which the VC usually invests

Adapted from Manigart et al. (2006).

Therefore, the decision of whether and with whom to syndicate becomes very important.

Exhibit 11.1 summarizes four generic motives for syndicating VC investments, as reported by Manigart and colleagues (2006). These categories include financial concerns, access to deal flow, improved selection, and value-adding capabilities. Each motive relates to and can be examined within the context of specific factors associated with portfolio composition or investment selection.

Two recent studies examine various antecedents of VCF syndication, that is, the investment strategy of the VCF and the characteristics of the PFC (De Clercq and Dimov 2004) and the VCF's need for external knowledge and resources and its ability to attract syndicate partners (Dimov and Milanov in press). The first study focuses on antecedents of syndication at the portfolio level, whereas the second study addresses drivers for syndication for particular investments.

The Role of VCF Investment Strategy and PFC Characteristics

A VCF's investment strategy—in terms of its portfolio specialization and PFC characteristics—influences the extent to which it engages in syndication.[2] The VCF's investment strategy may relate to two competing rationales for syndication:

on the one hand, syndication can provide a VCF with a wide set of complementary information that facilitates better investment targets and increases value-adding capability (Lerner 1994; Lockett and Wright 2001; Brander, Amit, and Antweiler 2002), while on the other hand, syndication can spread financial risk among multiple investors (Bygrave 1987, 1988; Smith and Smith 2000), which allows the VCF to access a wider range of deals and reduce its overall portfolio risk.

Researchers note that a VCF may leverage its knowledge and experience across multiple portfolio companies (PFCs) by *specializing* in ventures in particular industries or at particular development stages (Gupta and Sapienza 1992; Norton and Tenenbaum 1993; De Clercq et al. 2001; De Clercq and Sapienza 2001). A portfolio with limited industry or development-stage scope can allow the VCF to exercise more effective control over its management of the financed companies (Gupta and Sapienza 1992). Furthermore, VCFs can develop more specialized understanding of the complexities of these industries or development stages, which encourages quick, incremental knowledge acquisition that applies horizontally across PFCs (Sahlman 1990; Gupta and Sapienza 1992; Hall and Hofer 1993; Norton and Tenenbaum 1993; De Clercq et al. 2001; Dimov and Shepherd 2005). From a knowledge-sharing perspective, specialized VCFs also may have a particular desire to access complementary skills, because their skill sets, even if abundant in particular industries or development stages, may be lacking in terms of the management and financial expertise that supports successful strategy execution and exit. In other words, VCFs with more specialized portfolios may have a greater need to engage in syndication to obtain the complementary knowledge necessary to oversee and manage the future affairs of their PFCs.

But from a risk-sharing perspective, VCFs have compelling reasons to *diversify* their investments across a wide range of industries or development stages (Gupta and Sapienza 1992; De Clercq et al. 2001). Involvement in a greater variety of industries could offer the VCF more investment opportunities and the ability to identify higher-return investments. Furthermore, by spreading investments across different industries, VCFs can reduce the industry-specific, diversifiable risk of their portfolio (Norton and Tenenbaum 1993; De Clercq et al. 2001). To the extent that this rationale is valid, VCFs with more diversified portfolios should employ more syndication.

Beyond industry and stage specialization, the point at which the VCF invests in a PFC, the PFC's development stage, and the PFC's age may entail various degrees of uncertainty for the VCF and thus affect its syndication behavior. From a knowledge-sharing perspective, combining diverse knowledge and opinions through syndication can lead to better judgments of the investment merit of a PFC. Such a knowledge advantage should be particularly salient in earlier investment rounds (Lerner 1994) and when the investment rounds are marked by PFC-specific uncertainty (Bygrave 1987). When viewed from the perspective of the focal VCF, this uncertainty is greater in earlier investment rounds, for less developed PFCs, and for younger PFCs, which suggests that VCFs that focus on such investments likely experience higher degrees of syndication. Alternatively, the desire to share financial risk through syndication can reflect VCFs' concern about or inability to undertake large deals by themselves. Because such deals are associated with later rounds and more developed and older PFCs, the investments should be associated with a higher degree of syndication

De Clercq and Dimov (2004) empirically test these alternative rationales for syndication by considering both within-firm and between-firm effects over more than a decade (from 1990 to 2001). The within-firm effects capture the change in syndication that each VCF experiences over time, whereas the between-firm effects capture overall differences in syndication across VCFs for the study period. The results are shown in Exhibit 11.2.

For portfolio specialization, the within-firm analysis shows that syndication increases when the VCF's industry specialization decreases, in support of a financial risk-reduction rationale for syndication. The absence of the knowledge-sharing rationale may occur because individual VCF expertise could be slow to build, which would make it slow to change. Thus, the extent to which a VCF undertakes investments outside its current domain of developed expertise and relies on the help of syndicate partners may be difficult to detect from year-to-year strategic investment decisions.

In the between-firm analysis, none of the portfolio specialization effects is significant, yet some interesting empirical trends emerge. Specifically, the signs of industry and stage specialization effects run opposite to those in the within-firm analysis, perhaps because syndication serves to offset any year-to-year variation in specialization. Such year-to-year changes in syndication behavior then may differ from the aggregate change over a longer time period. In addition, the effects for industry and stage specialization exhibit opposite signs in the within-firm versus the between-firm analyses. This result may indicate that industry specialization and stage specialization represent two distinct components of VCFs' investment strategies, each with a different influence on VCFs' syndication behavior, both on a year-to-year basis and over a longer period over time.

The within-firm analysis reveals a higher degree of syndication for later investment rounds, again attesting to the financial risk-reduction rationale. Similarly, in the between-firm analysis, VCFs investing in later rounds tend to have more syndicate partners, consistent with the financial rationale, because in later rounds, PFCs typically require more capital—likely more than one VCF can provide. Yet the between-firm results also support the knowledge-sharing rationale for syndication, in that VCFs that invest in companies in their early stages tend to have more syndicate partners. Because less-developed PFCs require less capital than

Exhibit 11.2 Predictors for Degree of Syndication

Predictor	Within-Firm Effect	Between-Firm Effect
Portfolio Investment Strategy		
Industry specialization	Negative effect	No effect (positive sign)
Stage specialization	No effect (positive sign)	No effect (negative sign)
Investment Characteristics		
Round number of first-time investment	Positive effect	Positive effect
PFC development stage	No effect	Negative effect
PFC age	No effect	No effect

Adapted from De Clercq and Dimov (2004).

their later-stage counterparts, the motivation for more extensive syndication cannot relate to VCFs' need to reduce their financial exposure. Rather, VCFs may attempt to bridge the greater uncertainty related to early-stage PFCs, in terms of their prospects for success, by accessing the knowledge base of a larger group of investors.

However, the increased syndication by VCFs that focus on earlier-stage deals also may stem from their need to maintain stable deal flow. Specifically, deal origination is more difficult at earlier stages (because of the uncertainty surrounding such companies), and deal sharing through syndication may be an effective way to maintain deal flow (Manigart et al. 2006). In this regard, a danger is that investments in early-stage companies could include more sharing of potentially "bad" deals, whereby VCFs try to keep really high-potential deals to themselves. Yet the repeated nature of deal sharing and interaction among VCFs (Wright and Lockett 2003) may make such behavior nonoptimal in the long run. That is, VCFs that continuously offer bad deals eventually may be excluded from the deal flow of their syndicate counterparts.

Overall, De Clercq and Dimov's (2004) study suggests that both the knowledge-sharing and financial rationales are evident in VCF syndication behavior. In addition, these rationales seem to have differential effects for the year-to-year variations in syndication behavior versus the stable, "baseline" behavior across a longer period of time. From a methodological point of view, this nuanced consideration of the motivation underlying VC syndication complements typical approaches that focus on between-firm syndication effects (e.g., Sorenson and Stuart 2001; Manigart et al. 2006) with an alternative method that acknowledges the distinct nature of within-VCF effects by also attributing variation in syndication behavior to VCFs' changing investment strategy decisions across time.

Interplay Between the Need and Opportunity for Syndication

Although VCFs exhibit general tendencies to syndicate, based on the structure and focus of their investment portfolios, these tendencies may not be sufficient to explain the syndication of particular investments.[3] As a type of alliance, syndication occurs when a firm *needs* additional resources or when it has the *opportunity* to know and attract potential partners (Eisenhardt and Schoonhoven 1996). The aforementioned knowledge-sharing rationale for syndication suggests that VCFs seek investment partners when they do not possess sufficient knowledge of the investment, because the partners enable them to evaluate and add value to it. This concept underlies their need to syndicate the investment, but it does not necessarily explain whether they have the opportunity to do so. Thus, VCFs in need of partners for particular investments may find it hard to attract such partners. Alternatively, VCFs with plentiful opportunities to syndicate—often because of their visibility or desirability as partners (Stuart 1998; Gulati 1999)—may not want to syndicate some of their investments.

Dimov and Milanov (in press) seek to understand how these strategic and social underpinnings of syndication may unfold in the context of specific investments. Each investment represents a certain degree of novelty to the VCF undertaking it. To this end, Podolny's (2001) framework helps distinguish between two types of investment uncertainty: *egocentric*, which pertains to the focal VCF's uncertainty about the necessary decisions for the investment to succeed, and *altercentric*, or uncertainty that the external parties face in judging the quality of the focal VCF as a potential investment partner. Whereas egocentric uncertainty increases the VCF's need to syndicate an investment, altercentric uncertainty reduces the VCF's opportunity to do so. Both types of uncertainty come to the fore when VCFs consider novel investments, such as those in industries in which they have not invested before. On the one hand, the VCF cannot rely fully on its past investment experience, so it faces uncertainty about how to appraise and manage these investments. On the other hand, information opacity and the relatively low odds of success make it hard for an external observer to appraise a VCF's ability to supervise such investment projects successfully.

Thus, VCFs are subject to altercentric uncertainty to the extent that information about their behavior is private, costly to acquire, and causally ambiguous (Podolny 1994, 2001). The attractiveness of the focal VCF in turn depends on whether others can directly evaluate its ability to contribute to a specific investment, as well as whether their more general perceptions of the focal VCF can help them make positive attributions about its potential contribution. This issue becomes particularly potent when the focal VCF has limited or no experience in the industry associated with the investment. In the absence of mechanisms to alleviate such altercentric uncertainty, prospective syndicate partners may be discouraged from joining the investment by their perceptions of high effort costs (Tykvova 2007), the possibility of free riding (Das and Teng 2001), or the suspicion that the ultimate success of the alliance depends too much on their own investment (Larsson et al. 1998). In such cases, the focal VCF's opportunity to syndicate the investment depends on the degree to which it can signal its quality to prospective investment partners. Two signals of quality are relevant to this process: the VCF's status and its reputation (Jensen and Roy 2008).

Formally defined, status represents how centrally positioned an organization is relative to other organizations in the industry network (Podolny 1993; Jensen 2003). An organization's status depends less on an actor's behaviors than on its relations and affiliations, which involve exchange or deference (Podolny 1994). In this regard, status serves as an important signal of quality when uncertainty exists about the quality of the organizations involved in a particular market and when the costs of carrying out an evaluative search are prohibitive. In the context of VC syndication, higher status provides the VCF with a greater chance of attracting syndication partners for novel investments (Podolny 2001). Higher-status VCFs also can access external expertise and recruit managerial talent to the companies in their portfolio. In addition, they have important affiliations with investment banks (Gulati and Higgins 2003), which facilitates investment exits through initial public offerings or acquisitions and thus enhances performance (Hochberg, Ljungqvist, and Lu 2007). These considerations suggest that when undertaking novel investments, higher-status VCFs can more easily soothe prospective partners' uncertainties and overcome the reduced opportunity for syndication.

In contrast, reputation is the "perceptual representation of a company's past actions and future prospects that describe the firm's overall appeal to all its key constituents when compared to other leading rivals" (Fombrun 1996, 72). As such, it serves as a signal of the firm's future performance, based on its past performance (Diamond 1989; Fombrun and Shanley 1990), and shapes the external audience's perceptions and expectations of the firm (Rao 1994). Similar to status, reputation can facilitate access to and the acquisition of resources (Gompers 1996), which ultimately should shape prospective partners' beliefs about future returns (Gompers, Blair, and Hellman 1998). The VCF's reputation, by providing a more direct reflection of its past performance, is instrumental for evaluating and selecting syndicate partners (Lerner 1994; Lockett and Wright 2001). It also enhances the VCF's ability to raise and invest new funds (Ippolito 1992; Gompers 1996; Siri and Tufano 1998) and attract PFCs (Hsu 2004). Therefore, when undertaking novel investments that demand external investor participation, reputable VCFs can signal trust and reliability, which helps them overcome the altercentric uncertainty inherent to such projects.

Dimov and Milanov (in press) test these ideas empirically by examining the likelihood that VCFs syndicate their first-round investments, as summarized in Exhibit 11.3. Overall, syndication is more likely for investments in industries that are less familiar to the VCF, consistent with the notion that the focal firm can access necessary knowledge externally when it does not possess that information itself (De Clercq and Dimov 2008). In line with the aforementioned importance of status as a signal of quality, they also find that investment syndication is more likely when investment novelty is combined with high status; yet the interaction effect between investment novelty and reputation is surprisingly negative. These results highlight the importance of dealing with altercentric uncertainty when seeking syndicate partners for unfamiliar investments. Status proves to be a more robust quality signal in the context of novel investments. Unlike reputation, status is dissociated from behavior and relates more to existing relations and affiliations (Podolny 2005). Therefore, it allows VCFs more resilience in situations in which uncertainties about their reputation arise (Podolny 2005). In contrast, reputation appears to be a counterproductive signal for attracting syndicate partners to unfamiliar investments, perhaps because a positive signal may not carry over to novel domains, especially if the signal content seems too closely aligned with the focal VCF's specific prior actions. Put differently, reputation appears to help VCFs find syndicate partners only to the extent that they stick to activities for which they are well known.

Exhibit 11.3   Predictors of Likelihood to Syndicate

Predictors	Nature of Effect
Investment novelty	Positive effect
VCF status	Positive effect
VCF reputation	Positive effect
Interaction between investment novelty × VCF status	Positive interaction
Interaction between investment novelty × VC reputation	Negative interaction

Adapted from Dimov and Milanov (in press).

DYNAMICS WITHIN VCF SYNDICATES

Internal dynamics govern interactions among syndicate partners, particularly with regard to the extent of *involvement* that VCFs extend to PFCs when the VCFs are part of the syndicate.[4] To this end, De Clercq, Sapienza, and Zaheer (2008) examine how VCFs' level of involvement in syndicates may depend on both their individual self-focused interests and the factors of their membership in a syndicate. Studying VCF involvement in syndicates is important, because it has the potential to increase the size of the investment payoff (Sapienza 1992), yet it also comes at a high cost with respect to time resources (Gorman and Sahlman 1989; Gifford 1997).

As members of a syndicate group, VCFs exchange information about their assessments of the opportunities, share the burden of capital contributions and monitoring efforts after investments have been made (Lerner 1994), and contribute to the success of the PFC through their value-adding activities (Sapienza 1992). As mentioned previously, syndication thus might not only enhance the quality of the preinvestment selection but also provide a vehicle for effective postinvestment involvement (Brander, Amit, and Antweiler 2002). Despite heterogeneity in the resources and efforts that the VCFs expend (Lockett and Wright 2001), each member of the syndicate receives rewards in proportion to its ownership shares, *regardless* of the specific value it may have created during the investment period through its involvement or reputational benefits (Sahlman 1990). The return on investment of a particular deal may provide a direct measure of the outcome of a syndicate relationship (Wright and Lockett 2003), but the question of how much each syndicate partner actually contributes to a given investment deal (through involvement and/or reputation) is less straightforward.

Significant debate also exists about whether investor involvement benefits the PFC, beyond the certification value associated with being selected by a highly reputable VCF (Sapienza 1992; Stuart, Hoang, and Hybels 1999). For example, VCFs face significant time pressures (Gorman and Sahlman 1989; MacMillan, Kulow, and Khoylian 1989; Gifford 1997), so the lack of a clear, demonstrable connection between their effort and their rewards creates a significant dilemma for them. Gorman and Sahlman (1989) show that individual VCFs participate in eight portfolio companies and four boards, on average, at any given point in time; furthermore, they estimate that such duties represent 60 percent of venture capitalists' working time. Because a VCF must carefully allocate its time, its involvement across PFCs likely varies depending on not only its own position and circumstances but also its consideration of the characteristics of the syndicate group (Wright and Lockett 2003). Although involvement is costly for the focal VCF, all members of the syndicate benefit from the involvement of any one VCF (Sahlman 1990), so each VCF must consider its own and the syndicate-related factors when it decides how much effort to expend to aid its PFCs.

Some VCFs determine their involvement on the basis of the formal positions they occupy. If a VCF obtains a seat on the PFC's board, it undertakes a certain, expected level of involvement (Fried and Hisrich 1995), yet studies find evidence of variation in involvement across board members (e.g., MacMillan et al. 1989; Sapienza 1992). Even if it is not formally designated, the role of the "lead" investor may be important in this regard, whether that lead investor is the VCF that originates the deal (Gorman and Sahlman 1989), the "most important"

Exhibit 11.4   Predictors of VCF Involvement

Predictor	Focal VCF Involvement
Focal VCF investment relative to all its investments	No effect
Focal VCF reputation	Negative effect
Focal VCF investment relative to average syndicate investment	Positive effect
Total reputation of other syndicate members	Negative effect
Dispersion of reputation among other syndicate members	No effect
Board membership	Positive effect
Lead investor	No effect

Adapted from De Clercq, Sapienza, and Zaheer (2008).

investor (Sapienza 1992), or the investor with the greatest financial stake (Wright and Lockett 2003).

De Clercq, Sapienza, and Zaheer (2008) extend research focused on VCFs' formal positions as board members or lead investors by noting that a VCF calibrates its efforts on the basis of its assessments of the importance of the investment for itself, the anticipated instrumentality of its own and others' involvement, and the behavior of the other members of the group, as well as how those other members expect the focal firm to behave. They consider two VCF-specific characteristics (i.e., the *focal* VCF's investment stake in the PFC relative to its total investments and its individual reputation) and three syndicate-related characteristics (i.e., its investment stake in the PFC relative to the investment stake of the syndicate partners, the total reputation of the syndicate partners, and the dispersion of this reputation among the syndicate partners). Understanding how these factors influence VCF involvement requires a combination of expectancy, equity, and collective action theories. A summary of De Clercq and colleagues' (2008) findings appears in Exhibit 11.4.

With respect to the two VCF-specific characteristics, De Clercq, Sapienza, and Zaheer (2008) find no support for the claim that VCF involvement varies with the size of the investment relative to its total investments, perhaps because VCFs tend to treat each investment as equally important, *regardless* of its weight in the portfolio, if their fiduciary responsibilities do not vary according to the level of their stake in a particular PFC. Furthermore, VCF involvement relates inversely to the VCF's individual reputation, which means VCFs may view their own reputation as a substitute for effort, irrespective of the total reputation of the other syndicate partners. Conversely, VCFs with *less* reputation may exert extraordinary effort to build standing within the VCF syndicate or increase their odds of raising funds in future (Wright and Lockett 2003), which accords with Emerson's (1962) explication of a power-balancing tactic, whereby the more dependent member of a syndicate (i.e., less reputable VCF) balances its dependence by increasing the dependence of the other group members on its input. If high-reputation VCFs economize on their efforts, entrepreneurs and syndicate partners may have cause to question their expectation of high value additions from those top VCFs.

De Clercq, Sapienza, and Zaheer (2008) find support for the effect of two syndicate-related factors: the VCF's investment stake relative to the average syndicate investment relates positively to VCF involvement in the syndicate, and the reputation of the other syndicate partners relates negatively to VCF involvement. These findings are consistent with an equity theory perspective (Walster, Walster, and Berscheid 1978; Barley 1990) that suggests individual VCF behavior derives from a comparative process through which VCFs adopt more or less active roles, as is appropriate for their relative contribution to the group. The negative effect of the total reputation of the syndicate members also supports Gifford's (1997) suggestion that VCFs may be tempted to economize on their efforts to assist PFCs. In this respect, the syndicate context may mimic a typical social loafing context—characterized by multiple players, joint outcomes, uncertain cause-and-effect relationships, and monitoring difficulties—though shirking behavior may not be loafing per se but rather reflect more equitable trade-offs with other syndicate partners. The fine line between an appropriate and equitable conservation of resources versus self-serving withholding of effort does not allow De Clercq, Sapienza, and Zaheer (2008) to determine whether such judgments are appropriate and functional or mistakenly self-serving.

In addition, they find no effect for the dispersion of syndicate reputation on VCF involvement, in contrast with the claim that when reputation is highly concentrated in a few marquee syndicate members, the individual VCF perceives less need for its own involvement to achieve its investment goals. This nonresult could indicate that individual VCFs pay attention to the total reputation of the other syndicate members and ignore the concentration of reputation.

Finally, De Clercq, Sapienza, and Zaheer (2008) note that the VCF's board membership significantly predicts VCF involvement. This relationship gives credence to Wright and Lockett's (2003) premise that VCFs assume and enact roles within syndicates and behave in manners that reflect their membership in syndicate groups. However, the results also extend their insights by showing that these roles depend not on the size of the investment or board position (or lack thereof) but on the relative contribution of the VCF in terms of its reputational capital.

Taken together, these results belie the popular notion of VCFs as excessively atomistic and self-focused in their behavior and emphasize instead the importance of the broader multiparty (i.e., syndicate) context for predicting individual VCF behavior. An individual VCF's involvement in a syndicate tends to be somewhat dominated by syndicate effects; specifically, its financial stake relative to that of the syndicate and the reputation of the other syndicate partners significantly influence a given VCF's involvement. Furthermore, the VCF's involvement relates negatively to its own reputation. If reputation is negatively associated with VCF involvement, entrepreneurs and potential syndicate entrants should be wary about their ability to leverage VCF reputation fully to achieve their goals.

OUTCOMES OF VENTURE CAPITAL SYNDICATION

The following sections discuss the performance outcomes of syndication, in terms of both the upside potential and failure of venture capital investments.

Interplay Between Internal and External Knowledge Strategies

Extant research acknowledges the importance of knowledge sharing and development as a motivation for VCF syndication (as we reviewed in the first section of this chapter); yet limited attention centers on whether knowledge-based factors pay off in terms of the performance associated with VC investing.[5] In a recent study that addresses this issue, De Clercq and Dimov (2008) examine the performance effects of two knowledge-driven VCF strategies: internal knowledge development through portfolio development and external knowledge access through syndication.

First, VCFs' internal knowledge development, especially through their prior investments, should have positive performance outcomes on their absorptive capacity to evaluate, select, and manage investment opportunities. As mentioned earlier in this chapter, the knowledge-based perspective of portfolio strategies emphasizes that VCFs differ in the extent to which they focus their investments in specific industries or stages of development (Ruhnka and Young 1991; Norton and Tenenbaum 1993). De Clercq and Dimov (2008) clarify that this knowledge-based perspective complements, rather than contrasting with, the alternative perspective that focuses on financial risk management. That is, spreading financial risk provides an important rationale for constructing an investment portfolio, but knowledge considerations may be particularly important for explaining investment outcomes. Arguably, whereas financial risk management may help reduce a portfolio's downside, knowledge management helps increase its upside potential (Dimov and Shepherd 2005).

De Clercq and Dimov (2008) focus in particular on the role of a VCF's *industry* expertise as a reflection of its internally accumulated knowledge and a driver for investment performance. A VCF should be more successful when it invests in industries in which it is more knowledgeable, such as those in which it has invested previously. In managing its current investments, the insights and lessons a VCF derives in that industry—including those related to monitoring company behavior and performance (Sapienza and Korsgaard 1996), providing strategic advice and network contacts (Busenitz, Moesel, and Fiet 2004), and recruiting management (Hellman and Puri 2002)—can increase its value contribution and hence investment performance (De Clercq et al. 2006). Empirical tests undertaken by De Clercq and Dimov (2008), based on longitudinal data about the investments, syndication, and performance of 200 U.S.-based venture capital firms, reveal that investing in industries in which a VCF has more knowledge enhances the resulting investment performance (Exhibit 11.5).

Second, with respect to VCFs' access to external knowledge through syndication, De Clercq and Dimov (2008) argue that the *number* of syndicate partners with which a VCF co-invests has positive performance outcomes. The selection of potential investment opportunities becomes more effective when multiple investors can help increase the quality of deal flow (Sorenson and Stuart 2001) and make the selection procedure more rigorous (Lerner 1994). Moreover, syndication increases the value-added potential of the focal VCF because syndicate partners bring additional operational and strategic knowledge to the table (Brander, Amit, and Antweiler 2002). Similarly, a positive relationship should exist between the number of *prior interactions* between the focal VCF and its syndicate partners and the VCF's investment performance. Because VCFs often interact repeatedly over

Exhibit 11.5   Predictors of VCF Investment Performance

Predictors	Nature of Effect
Industry knowledge (of focal VCF)	Positive effect
Number of syndicate partners	Positive effect
Number of prior interactions between focal VCF and syndicate partners	Positive effect
Interaction between industry knowledge and number of syndicate partners	Negative interaction
Interaction between industry knowledge and number of prior interactions	Negative interaction

Adapted from De Clercq and Dimov (2008).

long periods of time and across investments in different PFCs (Wright and Lockett 2003), taking alternating lead and nonlead investor roles (Gorman and Sahlman 1989), syndication with familiar parties should promote current knowledge flows and joint problem solving, assuming that the focal VCF learns from its prior (successful or unsuccessful) relationships (Argote 1996; Uzzi 1997). De Clercq and Dimov's (2008) empirical findings indeed show that when VCFs invest with more syndicate partners that are more familiar, they enjoy enhanced investment performance (Exhibit 11.5).

The most interesting aspect of their study, however, may be the argument that the role of syndication is more instrumental to the extent that greater *incongruity* exists between the VCF's knowledge and product domains (Grant and Baden-Fuller 2004). The *product domain* refers to the VCF's ability to guide a particular PFC from initial investment to successful exit, whereas the *knowledge domain* indicates its understanding of the decisions and processes involved in these activities. Incongruity exists when the VCF possesses knowledge that differs from that needed to make a particular company successful, in which case the VCF may benefit most from collaborating with syndicate partners. For a particular investment, the VCF's knowledge of the industry determines whether the investment fits the firm's expertise; high industry knowledge implies congruity, whereas low industry knowledge implies incongruity. Limited industry knowledge cannot enable the focal VCF to bring the portfolio company to a successful exit (Sahlman 1990; De Clercq et al. 2006), but the scope (i.e., number of syndicate partners) and embeddedness (i.e., prior relationships with syndicate partners) of its external relationships should help alleviate this incongruity between what the VCF knows and what it intends to do. Thus, when the VCF lacks sufficient knowledge of a specific industry, it has more to gain from syndicate partners. Similarly, accessing and converting partners' knowledge into successful performance outcomes should be more likely when the focal VCF collaborates with its familiar syndicate partners.

Empirical findings (i.e., the negative interaction effects in Exhibit 11.5) confirm this argument, in that access to external knowledge (with more or more familiar partners) is particularly beneficial when an investment exposes gaps in the VCF's own expertise (De Clercq and Dimov 2008). Thus, access to external knowledge through syndication is more effective to the VCF when an incongruity exists between what the VCF knows and what it intends to do. A VCF's internal knowledge matters substantially more when there are no syndicate partners involved or the partners are unfamiliar, but its importance *declines* as the VCF gains access to necessary knowledge from its external partners. Overall, the results suggest that VCFs can benefit if they devote sufficient attention to internal learning processes and to understanding the knowledge contributions of their potential syndicate partners. Investments in less familiar industry sectors can succeed if they are undertaken in collaboration with (more) familiar partners. In turn, those on the receiving end of investments, namely, the entrepreneurs, may extract higher benefits from VC investors if they conduct their own elaborate due diligence regarding the specific strategic and operational competences that investors offer, particularly in terms of the VCFs' prior investment record with various industries and syndication partners.

VCF Syndication and PFC Failure

Finally, VCF investment strategies may relate to the *failure* of their PFCs (Dimov and De Clercq 2006).[6] Starting a new venture entails a high level of risk, and the failure rates for new businesses hover around 40 percent in the first year and up to 90 percent over 10 years (Timmons 1990). In many cases, the venture's "liability of newness" prompts this failure (Stinchcombe 1965), because new ventures lack sufficient time to develop internal performance routines and working relationships. In addition, new ventures lack external legitimacy with potential investors, buyers, suppliers, employees, and other stakeholders (Stuart et al. 1999). Somewhat paradoxically, to overcome the liability of newness, new firms might form cooperative relationships with other firms, including VCFs, to gain access to critical resources and knowledge (Baum and Oliver 1991) and signal their legitimacy (Stuart, Hoang, and Hubels 1999).

Because new venture failure represents a key aspect of entrepreneurial reality, Dimov and De Clercq (2006) consider how two facets of VCFs' investment strategies—their level of investment specialization and their syndication—relate to portfolio failure rates. If VCFs differ in the amount and nature of expertise they possess, some VCFs should be better able to prevent PFC failure (Dimov and Shepherd 2005); such expertise differences also may relate to the differences in the investment strategies pursued by VCFs, with respect to (1) specialization and (2) syndication.

First, a VCF's ability to prevent failure relates inherently to its *learning* from past failures (Argote 1996). In the VC context, evidence indicates that the VCF's prior deal-related experience contributes to higher survival among its PFCs (Dimov and Shepherd 2005). In addition, learning outcomes increase when a firm assimilates new knowledge that pertains to its existing knowledge structure (Bower and Hilgard 1981; Cohen and Levinthal 1990). Failure-related learning may be more effective for VCFs that develop specialized expertise through their portfolio investments. Dimov and De Clercq (2006) then suggest specific ways in which a VCF's specialized expertise could reduce the failure rate of its portfolio investments. For example, specialized expertise facilitates control over the new venture's management (Gupta and Sapienza 1992), so the VCF can detect deteriorating performance and undertake corrective measures. Furthermore, specialized expertise offers a better understanding of the complexities associated with particular development stages or industries, which help them manage badly performing investments more effectively (De Clercq et al. 2001). New venture failure should be less likely, for example, when VCFs understand the critical challenges inherent in particular development stages or particular industries.

Second, the extent to which a VCF relies on *syndication* may influence its portfolio failure rates. Dimov and De Clercq (2006) develop parallel arguments for both negative and positive effects of syndication. On the one hand, several (rather than one) VCFs potentially provide more effective knowledge input to their PFCs, which enhances the companies' survival chances. That is, the greater the number of partners in the syndicate, the greater is the diversity of available expertise and thus the higher is the likelihood of access to a particular critical piece of information or advice (Lerner 1994; Brander, Amit, and Antweiler 2002). A venture managed by a syndicate may also be subject to quicker detection of, say, deteriorating performance. On the other hand, syndication could enhance failures (e.g., more PFCs get pushed into bankruptcy) by specific group dynamics that are at work within the investment syndicate, such as commitment and social loafing. In particular, individual VCFs who invest alone may be prone to keep investing in a PFC, even when it exhibits deteriorating performance (Birmingham, Busenitz, and Arthurs 2003). In contrast, when a VCF becomes part of an investment syndicate, it may not escalate its commitment, such that ventures facing failure get pushed into bankruptcy proceedings as the VCF and its co-investors attempt to salvage at least some value. These actors who function as part of a group, rather than alone, also may decrease their efforts and engage in social loafing (Harkins and Petty 1982). That is, the focal VCF may trade off its own effort against the potential effort undertaken by its syndicate partners. Considering the serious time allocation dilemmas that VCFs face, as we discussed previously (Gifford 1997), VCFs that are part of an investment syndicate may thus be less likely to become highly involved with PFCs that are in trouble, which in turn should increase their portfolio failure rate.

Dimov and De Clercq's (2006) empirical tests—summarized in Exhibit 11.6 and based on longitudinal data pertaining to the realized strategies of 200 U.S.-based VCFs over a 12-year period—confirm that VCFs' specialized expertise with respect to their PFCs' development stage has a negative effect on the proportion of defaults in a portfolio. When the compatibility between the VCF's investment expertise and the specific context of a portfolio company is limited, the VCF appears unable to detect the venture's needs or potential challenges; instead, it simply applies its own expertise, often to the company's detriment. Moreover, the VCF's level of

Exhibit 11.6   Predictors of Portfolio Failure Rate

Predictors	Nature of Effect
Industry specialization	No effect
Stage specialization	Negative effect
Syndication	Positive effect

Adapted from Dimov and De Clercq (2006).

syndication positively—rather than negatively—affects its portfolio failure rate. When multiple VCFs finance a PFC, the continued commitment by any single VCF in the syndicate may decline (Birmingham et al. 2003), which precludes additional involvement through value-added inputs or subsequent investments. This lower commitment may result from the VCFs' feeling of less responsibility toward a prior investment decision when it shares this responsibility with other investors (Staw 1976) and the increased likelihood to free-ride on syndicate partners' activities, trading off its own effort against the potential effort undertaken by others (Wagner 1995), ultimately resulting in an increased removal of PFCs from its portfolio.

Thus, though syndication may lead to positive investment outcomes, by granting the venture access to a broader range of relevant knowledge, it also and somewhat paradoxically can accelerate the risk of investment default. A VCF may be motivated to build its ventures to become spectacular successes, but it also may be more reluctant to prevent looming failure, especially when co-investors are involved. Specifically, each VCF may reason that, given the excessive demands on its time, it should rely on the efforts of its co-investors to address poor performance, which enables it to attend to more successful deals or other demanding tasks, such as raising new funds and screening additional deals (Gifford 1997). From an individual VCF perspective, this behavior may appear logical in the short term, but it also may have long-term consequences for the VCF by harming its reputation in the investor community and discouraging invitations to join other interesting syndicate partnerships.

CONCLUSION

This chapter provides an overview of five recent studies that examine VC syndication, focusing on the antecedents of syndication, the internal dynamics within syndicates, and the performance outcomes of syndication. As we discussed in the introduction, these studies represent but a small selection of the ecology of syndication research with respect to the theoretical perspectives and level of analysis employed. Therefore, although these studies shed light on various aspects of syndication, when viewed within the big picture of this research, they leave open several avenues for research.

Antecedents of Syndication

De Clercq and Dimov (2004) show that both knowledge-based and financial motives explain VCF syndication. Yet by using yearly aggregate data, they may have overlooked important variations in the data. Research should examine how a VCF expands its portfolio on a company-by-company basis. For example, it might be interesting to examine the types of syndicate partners that are attracted by the focal VCF, depending on the characteristics of the existing portfolio. Furthermore, De Clercq and Dimov (2004) consider the VCF as a black box. Research should investigate the links among the varied capabilities of a VCF's management, the VCF's investment strategy, and its syndication behavior. A possible explanation for variation in VCFs' syndication behavior could be the fit (or misfit) between investment strategies and the experiential background of the individual investment managers.

Although syndication is widespread (Lerner 1994; Hochberg, Ljungqvist, and Lu 2007) and offers buffers against various uncertainties (Bygrave 1987), Dimov and Milanov (in press) implicitly assume that syndication is always a desirable strategy to cope with uncertainty. In other words, they regard nonsyndicated investments as examples of the focal VCF seeking investment partners but failing. Unpacking this assumption suggests several research paths. In certain situations, VCFs may prefer to keep a deal to themselves (e.g., Snellman and Piskorski 2003), and thus their decisions may require more elaborate, motivational models. In addition, to the extent that an existing investment is part of a more extensive syndication agreement that covers a series of investments, unobserved interactions may occur among the syndicate partners, which in turn warrant additional considerations. Another issue involves whether VCFs are aware of each other's status and reputation and whether some firm signals actually emanate from individual investors who work within the VCF. In this regard, it would be interesting to study whether potential investments that are novel for the VC firm as a whole can leverage the knowledge or social capital of individual investors. Finally, the qualitatively different roles played by status and reputation, as Dimov and Milanov (in press) suggest, could create a spurious relationship between syndication and performance. That is, they can be helpful for attracting investment partners, but at the same time they can also facilitate easier access to resources and reflect some superior capabilities, both of which contribute to current performance.

Dynamics within Venture Capital Syndicates

De Clercq, Sapienza, and Zaheer (2008) show that focal VCF involvement in syndicates depends on a combination of both focal VCF and syndicate characteristics, beyond the formal roles that investors play (e.g., being a board member or lead investor). That is, VCF involvement is negatively affected by its own reputation and the reputation of the other syndicate members but positively influenced by its financial stake, relative to that of the syndicate group. To assess whether equitable, shared involvement actually exists across past and present relationships among VCFs and their syndicate partners, or whether individual VCFs are shirking, further research should attempt to gather data about the relative ownership stakes of the syndicate members across all joint undertakings.

From the point of view of new ventures, additional research might consider how VCFs' substitution of syndicate reputation for their own involvement could influence *performance* after an initial public offering. The substitution of others' (or own) reputation for involvement may explain the inconsistency in past findings regarding whether and when VCFs add value to new ventures (Steier and Greenwood 1995). Thus, research should consider the entire spectrum of value that might be added by the VCF and its syndicate partners, including both involvement with the PFCs and the certification value associated with their reputation.

Outcomes of Venture Capital Syndication

With respect to the *positive* outcomes of syndication, De Clercq and Dimov (2008) find that investing in industries in which a VCF has more knowledge and with more or familiar external partners enhances investment performance; furthermore, they identify important interactions, such that access to external knowledge is particularly beneficial when the investment exposes gaps in the VCF's own expertise. In contrast, Dimov and De Clercq (2006) find that the level of syndication increases, rather than decreases, portfolio failure rates. Research might benefit from combining examinations of both positive and negative outcomes in the same study to disentangle the trade-offs associated with the effect of syndication on portfolio performance. Finally, researchers could examine the performance effects of the varied timing at which syndicate partners join an investment syndicate (e.g., early versus later investment rounds; see Cumming 2005) and the internal coordination mechanisms that can most effectively manage dynamic changes in VC syndicate membership.

NOTES

1. Syndication differs from "co-investment," in which the same VCF makes investments sourced from the different funds it manages (Gompers and Lerner 1999). Empirical evidence shows that though syndication can facilitate investment returns, co-investment does not (Cumming and Walz 2008). The focus of the chapter is syndication.

2. This section is based on De Clercq and Dimov (2004).

3. This section is based on Dimov and Milanov (in press).

4. This section is based on De Clercq, Sapienza, and Zaheer (2008).

5. This section is based on De Clercq and Dimov (2008).

6. This section is based on Dimov and De Clercq (2006).

REFERENCES

Abell, P., and T. M. Nisar. 2007. Performance effects of venture capital firm networks. *Management Decision* 45 (5):923–936.

Argote, L. 1996. Organizational learning curves: Persistence, transfer and Turnover. *International Journal of Technology Management* 11:759–769.

Barley, S. R. 1990. The alignment of technology and structure through roles and networks. *Administrative Science Quarterly* 35:61–103.

Baum, J. A. C., and C. Oliver. 1991. Institutional linkages and organizational mortality. *Administrative Science Quarterly* 36:187–218.

Birmingham, C., L. W. Busenitz, and J. D. Arthurs. 2003. The escalation of commitment by venture capitalists in reinvestment decisions. *Venture Capital* 5 (3):218–230.

Bower, G. H., and E. R. Hilgard. 1981. *Theories of learning.* Englewood Cliffs, NJ: Prentice-Hall.

Brander, J. A., R. Amit, and W. Antweiler. 2002. Venture capital syndication: Improved venture selection versus the value-added hypothesis. *Journal of Economics and Management Strategy* 11 (3):423–452.

Busenitz, L. W., D. D. Moesel, and J. O. Fiet. 2004. Reconsidering the venture capitalists' "value added" proposition: An interorganizational learning perspective. *Journal of Business Venturing* 19:787–807.

Bygrave, W. D. 1987. Syndicated investments by venture capital firms: A networking perspective. *Journal of Business Venturing* 2:139–154.

———. 1988. The structure of the investment networks of venture capital firms. *Journal of Business Venturing* 3:137–158.

Cable, D. M., and S. Shane. 1997. A prisoner's dilemma approach to entrepreneur-venture capitalist relationships. *Academy of Management Review* 22(1):142–176.

Casamatta, C., and C. Haritchabalet. 2007. Experience, screening and syndication in venture capital investments. *Journal of Financial Intermediation* 16:368–398.

Chung, S. A., H. Singh, and K. Lee. 2000. Complementarity, status similarity and social capital as drivers of alliance formation. *Strategic Management Journal* 21:1–22.

Cohen, W. M., and D. A. Levinthal. 1990. Absorptive capacity: A new perspective on learning and innovation. *Administrative Science Quarterly* 35:128–152.

Cumming, D. J. 2005. Agency costs, institutions, learning and taxation in venture capital contracting. *Journal of Business Venturing* 20(5):573–622.

———. 2006. Adverse selection and capital structure: Evidence from venture capital. *Entrepreneurship Theory and Practice* 30(2):155–184.

———, and U. Walz. 2008. Private equity returns and disclosure around the world. *Journal of International Business Studies*, forthcoming.

Das, T. K., and B. S. Teng. 2001. Trust, control, and risk in strategic alliances: An integrated framework. *Organization Studies* 22(2):251–283.

De Clercq, D., and D. Dimov. 2004. Explaining venture capital firms' syndication behavior: A longitudinal study. *Venture Capital: An International Journal of Entrepreneurial Finance* 6(4):243–256.

De Clercq, D., H.J. Sapienza, and A. Zaheer. 2008. Internal knowledge development and external knowledge access in venture capital investment performance. *Journal of Management Studies* 45(3):585–612.

De Clercq, D., V. H. Fried, O. Lehtonen, and H. J. Sapienza. 2006. An entrepreneur's guide to the venture capital galaxy. *Academy of Management Perspectives* 20:90–112.

De Clercq, D., P. K. Goulet, M. Kumpulainen, and M. Mäkelä. 2001. Portfolio investment strategies in the Finnish venture capital industry: A longitudinal study. *Venture Capital* 3(1):41–62.

De Clercq, D., and H. J. Sapienza. 2001. The creation of relational rents in venture capitalist-entrepreneur dyads. *Venture Capital* 3(2):107–128.

De Clercq, D., H.J. Sapienza, and A. Zaheer. 2008. Firm and group influences on venture capital firms' involvement in new ventures. *Journal of Management Studies* 45(7):1169–1194.

Diamond, D. W. 1989. Reputation acquisition in debt markets. *Journal of Political Economy* 97:828–862.

Dimov, D., and D. De Clercq. 2006. Venture capital investment strategy and portfolio failure rate: A longitudinal study. *Entrepreneurship Theory and Practice* 30(2):207–223.

Dimov, D., and H. Milanov. in press. The interplay of need and opportunity in venture capital investment syndication. *Journal of Business Venturing*.

Dimov, D., and D. Shepherd. 2005. Human capital theory and venture capital firms: Exploring "home runs" and "strike outs." *Journal of Business Venturing* 20(1):1–21.

Eisenhardt, Kathleen M. 1989. Agency theory: An assessment and review. *Academy of Management Review* 14:57–74.

———, and C. B. Schoonhoven. 1996. Resource-based view of strategic alliance formation: Strategic and social effects in entrepreneurial firms. *Organization Science* 7(2): 136–150.

Emerson, R. M. 1962. Power-dependence relations. *American Sociological Review* 27:31–41.

Fombrun, C. 1996. *Reputation: Realizing value from the corporate image.* Boston: Harvard Business School Press.

———, and M. Shanley. 1990. What's in a name? Reputation building and corporate strategy. *Academy of Management Journal* 33:233–258.

Fried, V. H., and R. Hisrich. 1995. The venture capitalist: A relationship investor. *California Management Review* 37(2):101–113.

Gifford, S. 1997. Limited attention and the role of the venture capitalist. *Journal of Business Venturing* 12:459–482.

Gompers, P. 1996. Grandstanding in the venture capital industry. *Journal of Financial Economics* 43:133–156.

———, and J. Lerner. 1999. *The venture capital cycle*. Cambridge: MIT Press.

———, M. Blair, and T. Hellman. 1998. What drives venture capital fundraising? *Brookings Papers on Economic Activity: Microeconomics*:14–204.

Gorman, M., and W. Sahlman. 1989. What do venture capitalists do? *Journal of Business Venturing* 4:231–248.

Grant, R. M., and C. Baden-Fuller. 2004. A knowledge accessing theory of strategic alliances. *Journal of Management Studies* 41:61–84.

Gulati, R. 1999. Network location and learning : The influence of network resources and firm capabilities on alliance formation. *Strategic Management Journal* 20(4):397–420.

———, and C. M. Higgins. 2003. Which ties matter when? The contingent effects of interorganizational partnerships on IPO success. *Strategic Management Journal* 24(2):127–144.

Gupta, A., and H. Sapienza. 1992. Determinants of venture capital firms: Preferences regarding the industry diversity and geographic scope of their investments. *Journal of Business Venturing* 7:347–362.

Hall, J., and C. W. Hofer. 1993. Venture capitalists' decision criteria in new venture evaluation. *Journal of Business Venturing* 8:25–42.

Harkins, S. G., and R. E. Petty. 1982. The effects of task difficulty and task uniqueness on social loafing. *Journal of Personality and Social Psychology* 43:1214–1229.

Hellmann, T., and M. Puri. 2002. Venture capital and the professionalization of start-up firms: Empirical evidence. *Journal of Finance* 57:169–197.

Hochberg, Y., A. Ljungqvist, and Y. Lu. 2007. Whom you know matters: Venture capital networks and investment performance. *Journal of Finance* 62(1):251–301.

Hsu, D. J. 2004. What do entrepreneurs pay for venture capital affiliation? *Journal of Finance* 59:1805–1844.

Ippolito, R. A. 1992. Consumer reaction to measures of poor quality: Evidence from the mutual fund industry. *Journal of Law Economics* 35:45–70.

Jensen, M. C. 2003. The role of network resources in market entry: Commercial banks' entry into investment banking, 1991–1997. *Administrative Science Quarterly* 48(3):466–497.

———, and A. Roy. 2008. Staging exchange partner choices: When do status and reputation matter? *Academy of Management Journal* 51, 495–516.

Kaiser, D. G., and R. Lauterbach 2007. The need for diversification and its impact on the syndication probability of venture capital investments. *Journal of Alternative Investments* 10:62–79.

Kogut, B., P. Urso, and G. Walker. 2007. Emergent properties of a new financial market: American venture capital syndication, 1960–2005. *Management Science* 53:1181–1198.

Larsson, R., L. Bengtsson, K. Henriksson, and J. Sparks. 1998. The interorganizational learning dilemma: Collective knowledge development in strategic alliances. *Organization Science* 9(3):285–305.

Lerner, J. 1994. The syndication of venture capital investments. *Financial Management* 23(3):16–27.

Lockett, A., and M. Wright. 2001. The syndication of venture capital investments. *Omega* 29:375–390.

MacMillan, I. C., D. M. Kulow, and R. Khoylian. 1989. Venture capitalists' involvement in their investments. *Journal of Business Venturing* 4(1):27–47.

Manigart, S., A. Lockett, M. Meuleman, M. Wright, H. Bruining, H. Landström, P. Desbrières, and U. Hommel. 2006. The syndication decision of venture capital investments. *Entrepreneurship: Theory and Practice* 30(2):131–153.

Mynatt, C., and S. J. Sherman. 1975. Responsibility attribution in groups and individuals: A direct test of the diffusion of responsibility hypothesis. *Journal of Personality and Social Psychology* 32:1111–1118.

Norton, E., and B. H. Tenenbaum. 1993. Specialization versus diversification as a venture capital investment strategy. *Journal of Business Venturing* 8:431–442.

Podolny, J. M. 1993. A status-based model of market competition. *American Journal of Sociology* 98(4):829–872.

———. 1994. Market uncertainty and the social character of economic exchange. *Administrative Science Quarterly* 39(3):458–483.

———. 2001. Networks as the pipes and prisms of the market. *American Journal of Sociology* 107(1):33–60.

———. 2005. *Status signals: A sociological study of market competition.* Princeton, NJ: Princeton University Press.

Rao, H. 1994. The social construction of reputation: Certification contests, legitimation, and the survival of organizations in the American automobile industry: 1895–1912. *Strategic Management Journal* 15:29–44.

Ruhnka, J., and J. Young. 1991. Some hypotheses about risk in venture capital investing. *Journal of Business Venturing* 6:115–133.

Sahlman, W. A. 1990. The structure and governance of venture capital organizations. *Journal of Financial Economics* 27:473–521.

Sapienza, H. J. 1992. When do venture capitalists add value? *Journal of Business Venturing* 7:9–27.

———, and M. A. Korsgaard. 1996. The role of procedural justice in entrepreneur–venture capital relations. *Academy of Management Journal* 39:544–574.

Siri, E. R., and P. Tufano. 1998. Costly search and mutual fund flows. *Journal of Finance* 53:1589–1622.

Smith, J. K., and L. S. Smith. 2000. *Entrepreneurial finance.* New York: John Wiley & Sons.

Snellman, K. and M. Piskorski. 2003. Network structure of exploitation: Venture capital syndicate structure and time to IPO. Paper presented at Annual Meeting of the American Sociological Association Reference, Atlanta, GA, August 2003.

Sorenson, O., and T. E. Stuart. 2001. Syndication networks and the spatial distribution of venture capital investments. *American Journal of Sociology* 106(6):1546–1588.

Staw, B. M. 1976. Knee-deep in the Big Muddy: A study of escalating commitment to a chosen course of action. *Organizational Behavior and Human Performance* 16:27–44.

Steier, L., and R. Greenwood. 1995. Venture capitalist relationships in the deal structuring and post-investment stages of new firm creation. *Journal of Management Studies* 32:337–359.

Stinchcombe, A. 1965. Social structure and organizations. In *Handbook of Organizations*, ed. J. G. March (142–193). Chicago: Rand McNally.

Stuart, T. 1998. Network positions and propensities to collaborate: An investigation of strategic alliance formation in a high-technology industry. *Administrative Science Quarterly* 43:668–698.

Stuart, T. E., H. Hoang, and R. C. Hybels. 1999. Interorganizational endorsements and the performance of entrepreneurial ventures. *Administrative Science Quarterly* 44:315–349.

Timmons, J. A. 1990. *New venture creation: Entrepreneurship in the 1990s.* Homewood, IL: Irwin.

Tykvova, T. 2007. Who chooses whom? Syndication, skills and reputation. *Review of Financial Economics* 16(1):5–28.

Uzzi, B. 1997. Social structure and competition in interfirm networks: The paradox of embeddedness. *Administrative Science Quarterly* 42(3):69.

Wagner, J. A. 1995. Studies on individualism-collectivism: Effects on cooperation in groups. *Academy of Management Journal* 38(1):152–172.

Walster, E., G. W. Walster, and E. Berscheid. 1978. *Equity: Theory and research.* Boston: Allyn and Bacon.

Wright, M., and A. Lockett. 2003. The structure and management of alliances: Syndication in the venture capital industry. *Journal of Management Studies* 40:2073–2102.

ABOUT THE AUTHORS

Dirk De Clercq received a Ph.D. in Business Administration from the University of Minnesota. He is Associate Professor of Management and Chancellor's Chair for Research Excellence at Brock University. His research interests are in entrepreneurship, venture capital, social exchange relationships, firm internationalization, and cross-country studies. Dr. De Clercq's work is published in *Journal of Business Venturing, Entrepreneurship Theory and Practice, Journal of Management Studies, Journal of International Business Studies, Journal of the Academy of Marketing Science, Journal of Business Research, Journal of Small Business Management, International Small Business Journal, Small Business Economics,* and *Academy of Management Perspectives,* among others.

Dimo Dimov received a Ph.D. in Entrepreneurship (Management) from the University of London (London Business School). He is currently Assistant Professor of Management at the University of Connecticut. His research interests focus on entrepreneurial opportunities: how potential entrepreneurs create them and how potential (venture capital) investors select them. Dr. Dimov's work is published or forthcoming in *Journal of Business Venturing, Entrepreneurship Theory and Practice, Journal of Management Studies, Journal of the Academy of Marketing Science,* and *Small Business Economics,* among others.

## PART III

Venture Capital Value-Added and Conflicts

CHAPTER 12

Time to Grow Up

Large Sample Evidence on the Maturation Dynamics of Private Venture-Backed Firms

JOHN R. M. HAND
H. Allen Andrew Distinguished Professor, Kenan-Flagler Business School

INTRODUCTION

In this chapter, I describe and analyze how a wide range of venture-backed firms' economic characteristics develop as the firms mature through their private, pre-exit stages of life. Although venture-backed companies make significant employment, financial, scientific, and technological contributions to the U.S. economy (NVCA 2004), relatively little large sample research to date has focused on their business evolution. I seek to address this gap by providing scholars, venture investors, and entrepreneurial firms with a current, broad-ranging, and large-sample view of the early life-stage dynamics of venture-backed firms.

The economic characteristics whose maturation dynamics I study include realized annual revenues and one-year-ahead forecasted revenues; employees (in total and by functional area); organizational hierarchy; industry sectors; boards of directors; corporate policies; equity holdings; employee cash compensation and benefits; equity values; financings; and attributes of founders. The data that I employ are quasi-time-series observations derived from cross-sectional survey information collected primarily by VentureOne in 2004 and 2005. The cross-sectional data are converted into "as-if" or quasi-time-series data by grouping firms according to whether their last round of venture financing prior to the survey date was a seed, first round, second round, and so on. This method crucially assumes that round number (an observable variable) is a good proxy for firm maturity (an unobservable variable).

The statistical tests that I conduct on the quasi-time-series data are designed to detect the presence of linear maturation trends in firm's economic characteristics and identify significant deviations from such trends. The overall goal of the tests is to evaluate the degree to which the evolution of venture-backed firms conforms to a firm-level interpretation of Gort and Klepper's (1982) theory of the prototypical new industry's life cycle. Three main empirical maturity patterns emerge that collectively I interpret as being consistent with a Gort and Klepper–type view of firm-level evolution:

Most characteristics of venture-backed firms change linearly as a function of the number of venture funding rounds received. This suggests that in much the same way that Gort and Klepper propose that industry evolution has distinct stages produced by underlying economic primitives, so the maturation of venture-backed firms during the private, pre-exit portion of their lives consists of stages that are technologically or economically homogeneous when grouped by financing round. I conjecture that the staged nature of venture financing reflects this homogeneity because venture funds typically invest only after a firm has accomplished a given set of technological and/or business milestones.

Revenue per employee and the number of patents granted rise as venture-backed firms mature, and the fraction of firm employees in sales (technical) functions increases (falls). This is consistent with venture-backed firms experiencing stage 1 of Gort and Klepper's industry-level theory, the Introductory Stage. In this stage, maturing firms adjust their corporate focus away from proving the technological or scientific validity of their innovations toward demonstrating the business demand for those innovations.

Departures from linear maturation typically occur at the seed round, that is, the round that precedes the Series A round. At the seed round managers hold unusually large amounts of equity and firms are less likely to have adopted formal corporate policies or provide full benefits to employees. This suggests that venture investors exert their greatest influence on a firm at the Series A round, and that their influence is permanent rather than transitory. Although Gort and Klepper's life cycle theory is silent regarding venture investors, when viewed in the light of research that documents the beneficial roles that venture investors play in solving agency and information asymmetry problems in intangible-intensive, technology-based young companies (Gompers and Lerner 1999; Hellman 2000; Hellman and Puri 2000, 2002), I interpret my finding as indicating that by means of the financial and organizational capital they bring to bear, venture investors raise the probability that innovative firms will in aggregate be sufficiently successful so as to be able to mature sequentially through Gort and Klepper's more general and long-lived industry-level life stages.

In addition to these aggregate maturation patterns, I report descriptive statistics on a variety of venture-backed firms' business characteristics. By providing a contemporary and detailed depiction of the early life-stages of an increasingly important sector of the U.S. economy, my research adds to the contributions made by prior work that has looked into the evolution of young technology-centric firms (Houlihan Valuation Advisors 1998; Barron and Burton 1999, 2001; Kaplan, Sensoy, and Strömberg forthcoming).

The remainder of the chapter proceeds as follows. I first summarize the existing literature on industry-level and firm-level life cycles, both in general and specifically with regard to venture-backed companies. I then highlight my contributions relative to those of prior work, and develop the chapter's three main propositions. Next, I describe the proprietary databases used, explain how cross-sectional data are converted into quasi-time-series data, and outline the statistical framework used to test my propositions. The maturation dynamics of venture-backed firms' economic characteristics are then detailed together with the results of formal statistical tests. Finally, I note some of the limitations of my work, and provide a concluding perspective.

LITERATURE REVIEW

In this section I review the relevant prior literature pertaining to the economics of firms' life cycles.

Industry Life-Cycle Economics

Two main features characterize prior research into firms' life cycles. First, the lion's share of life-cycle research has been at the industry level. Relatively little work has examined the expansion or contraction paths of individual firms over their lives, or as a function of firm maturity. And second, both theoretical and empirical understanding at the industry level have been contributed by a wide range of social science disciplines, including accounting, economics, finance, management, and strategy (Dickinson 2007).

A key study of the economic determinants of industry life cycles is Gort and Klepper's (1982) evolutionary theory of the diffusion of product innovations. In contrast to the approaches taken by organizational ecologists (e.g., Baum and Pownell 1995) and technology theorists (e.g., Suarez and Utterback 1995), Gort and Klepper hypothesize that the prototypical industry based on the introduction of a new product proceeds through five periods or stages, each of which reflects a major transition in the forces that determine the number of producers of the product.[1] In the introductory stage, stage 1, a product innovation (which is exogenously assumed by Gort and Klepper to be technically fully developed) is introduced into the market by a single producer with the aim of building product awareness and market share (Jovanovic 1982). Stage 2, the growth stage, is characterized by large investments in tangible and intangible assets and a sharp increase in the number of producers (Jovanovic 1982; Spence 1977, 1979, 1981).

In stage 3, the maturity stage of the new industry's life cycle, obsolescence of initial investments relative to new investments such that the number of entrants is roughly balanced by the number of exiting firms, while in stage 4, the shakeout stage, there is substantial negative net entry. In the final stage, the number of firms in equilibrium is defined by market size and economies of scale until the product becomes obsolete and the industry either dies or is reborn through new technology launching a new product.[2]

Life-Cycle Analysis of Venture-Backed Firms

To the extent that Gort and Klepper's theory can be interpreted or hypothesized as applying at the level of an individual firm, my study focuses on the economic causes and consequences of the introductory and growth stages, together with the period of technical development that precedes the introductory stage. Research that examines these entrepreneurial life stages generally either has been focused on one aspect of the firm, or has been somewhat disadvantaged by having available relatively sparse data about firms' business characteristics.[3] A key source of data limitations is that firms in the youngest stages of their life cycles are almost always privately held. As a result, and unlike their more mature publicly traded cousins, they are not required by SEC rules or other regulatory bodies to disclose any financial information about their economic performance, nor are their equity values or returns publicly observable. This makes it difficult to systematically obtain broad-ranging business-related information on a large set of firms as they progress from birth to maturity.

Venture-backed private firms represent a significant exception to these general data constraints. The reason is that the longevity, size, and growth of the U.S. venture capital market mean that not only do venture funds themselves have rich data on their portfolio companies as they mature from birth to exit, but specialized companies have been formed whose key goal has been to actively collect broad and deep business-relevant information on large numbers of venture-backed entities, particularly during the private, pre-exit phases of their lives.[4]

Several studies have used small samples of richly detailed data on venture-backed firms, obtained either from venture funds or from direct contact with companies. In a sample of 213 VC investments in 119 portfolio companies by 14 VC firms, Kaplan and Strömberg (2003) find that founders' cash flow, voting, and board rights decline over financing rounds, while VC rights increase. Also, terms in contracts between VCs and investee companies are not always enforced but are not infrequently renegotiated, supporting the incomplete contracting theories that rely heavily on the presence of bargaining and renegotiation (e.g., Hart 1995).

More recently, Kaplan, Sensoy, and Strömberg (forthcoming) trace the real-time evolution of 49 venture-backed companies founded between 1975 and 1998, starting with their early business plan and progressing to their IPO and three years post-IPO.[5] Their focus is on empirically identifying either the "glue" that property rights theories of the firm argue holds firms together (Hart 1995; Holmström 1999) and/or the key resources on which critical resource theories hypothesize firms base their growth (Wernerfelt 1984; Rajan and Zingales 2001). They find support for both sets of theories, although they note that there exists significant ambiguity as to whether human capital is the modern young firm's most critical resource, as conjectured by Zingales (2000). Overall, Kaplan, Sensoy, and Strömberg (forthcoming) report:

- Venture-backed firms' business models remain very stable over time, despite the dramatic growth they experience.
- Venture-backed firms consistently sell to similar customers and compete against similar competitors.
- Venture-backed firms consistently claim to be differentiated by a unique product, service, or technology.
- Although venture-backed firms stress the importance of proprietary IP, their alienable assets (i.e., patents and physical assets) become ever more important as they mature.
- The human capital in venture-backed firms changes considerably over time—more so than their nonhuman capital—and is generally not tied to specific individuals.

Other studies have used large sample datasets obtained from either Venture-One or Venture Economics but typically in a way that targets one or two specific economic characteristics for in-depth analysis, conditional on firm maturity. For example, Houlihan Valuation Advisors (1998) describe changes in the value of venture-backed high tech and life-sciences companies between their initial equity financing round, their interim financing rounds, and their IPO. More rigorously, Gompers and Lerner (1999) examine the roles that a variety of proxies for firm maturity (firm age, stage of development, business status) play inter alia in explaining cross-sectional variation in firms' premoney valuations, the amount of money they raise, the time between financing rounds, and exits.

A last dataset that has recently been exploited is the U.S. Census Bureau's Longitudinal Research Database (LRD). Chemmanur, Krishnan, and Nandy (2008) use the LRD to show that venture capital backing improves the total factor productivity efficiency of private firms, particularly with regard to sales revenues, and that this improvement monotonically increases over the four years subsequent to the year of initial VC financing. Using the LRD, Puri and Zarutskie (2008) find that venture capital disproportionately finances firms born with no commercial revenues, is "patient" capital relative to non-VC financing in the early stages of firms' life cycles, and focuses on the potential for rapid business scalability rather than profitability.

CONTRIBUTIONS OF THIS STUDY

In this study, I also describe and analyze venture-backed firms' economic characteristics as they mature, but with several differences in data, methodology, and focus versus prior work.

Novel and Large Sample Quasi-Time-Series Dataset

I employ quasi-time-series data that are derived from cross-sectional survey information collected primarily by VentureOne but also by Advanced-HR, Inc. That is, my data are not a true time-series as in Kaplan, Sensoy, and Strömberg (forthcoming). Rather, I convert cross-sectional survey information into an "as-if" time-series by grouping firms according to whether their most recent financing round relative to the survey date was a seed, first round, second round, and so on, and then tracking firms' economic characteristics as a function of the most recent financing round. This approach assumes that firms' economic characteristics depend on where firms are in their life cycle, rather than on calendar time per se. In exchange for bearing the inferential risk that this method potentially creates, I am able to bring to bear a large and recent sample, namely 889 firm-year observations (one observation per firm).

Second, although I analyze many of the same features of venture-backed firms as does prior work by Houlihan Valuation Advisors (1998), Gompers and Lerner (1999), and Kaplan, Sensoy, and Strömberg (forthcoming), I also describe and investigate a number of previously unexplored but plausibly important firm characteristics. These include organizational structure (e.g., the number of VPs, directors and managers by functional area, and VP span of control by functional area), corporate policies (e.g., whether the firm has a formal pay policy in place), cash compensation by position and functional area, and employee benefits.

Firm-Level Characterization of Gort and Klepper's Industry-Level Theory of Product Innovation, Diffusion and Maturation

The statistical tests that I conduct on the large sample quasi-time-series dataset outlined above are designed to detect the presence of linear maturation trends in firm characteristics and to identify significant deviations from such trends. The motivation behind the tests is to shed light on three broad propositions pertaining to venture-backed firms, each of which emerges from or can be connected to a firm-specific interpretation of Gort and Klepper's (1982) industry-level theory of product innovation diffusion highlighted earlier.

Proposition 1. *That the maturation dynamics of venture-backed firms consist of economically and/or technologically homogeneous stages for which firms' financing rounds are good proxies. That is, in much the same way that Gort and Klepper propose that the entire life cycle of the typical industry consists of multiple, distinct stages, I conjecture that the staged nature of venture financing reflects a fundamental aspect of firm maturity because venture funds typically invest only when the firm has reached certain technological and/or business milestones.*

Proposition 2. *That the early stages of firm life focus on transitioning away from establishing technological or scientific milestones toward demonstrating the business viability of the firm's innovations. In effect, Proposition 2 conjectures that stage 1 of Gort and Klepper's view of how a prototypical new industry evolves—the introductory stage—also occurs at the firm level.*

Proposition 3. *That venture investors exert the most influence on a firm at the Series A financing round, and in a way that is permanent, not transitory. Although Gort and Klepper's theory is silent as to venture capital investors, I conjecture that the business expertise, networks, and financing that venture investors provide to young, innovative companies enhance the probability that those firms, and the industries they represent, will be sufficiently successful as to be able to sequentially mature through the life stages theorized by Gort and Klepper.*

By examining the degree to which the propositions above are empirically supported or rejected, I hope through this study to contribute to the entrepreneurial literature with regard to identifying and understanding the economic causes and consequences of the evolution of venture-backed firms' business characteristics as the firms mature through their private, pre-exit stages of life.

DATABASES

This study benefits from being granted confidential access to the databases of two companies that collect data on venture-backed firms—VentureOne and

Advanced-HR. VentureOne is the world's leading venture capital research firm, offers investors, service providers, and entrepreneurs the most comprehensive, accurate, and timely information on the venture capital industry. Its products and services help venture capital firms, corporate investors, investment banks, and accounting and law firms to identify private investment opportunities, perform due diligence, and evaluate market trends, including company valuations and industry preferences. Advanced-HR is a smaller company that specializes in employee benefits.

VentureOne Surveys

The data in this study come predominantly from proprietary surveys undertaken by VentureOne in spring 2004 and spring 2005.[6] VentureOne emailed a Web-based compensation questionnaire to each of the roughly 5,000 venture-backed firms in its financing database that it classified as being pre-IPO and independent. The questionnaire asked firms to provide data on a broad set of compensation- and business-related items. For example, companies were asked to report the dollar values of the base salary, bonus, and other cash compensation of every employee (up to a maximum of 50 people from the most senior person down); the number of employees that receive stock options; the total number of shares of founder's stock and exercised and unexercised options that each held; and the total number of both fully diluted and common shares that the firm had outstanding. VentureOne also asked each firm to report revenues for its most recently completed fiscal year; its forecast of revenues for the fiscal year in progress (which I refer to as "one-year-ahead" forecasts); the number of employees at the end of its most recent fiscal year, both in total and by job function (administrative, business development, finance, marketing, sales, technical, and other); and the total number of employees it expected to have at the end of the current fiscal year.[7]

The data from VentureOne's surveys were then merged with VentureOne's financing and general support databases. VentureOne's financing database contains a record of each firm's equity financing history, where available. For each round of funding, the financing database reports the amount of money raised, when the round closed, the pre- and postmoney valuations of the firm, the type of round (e.g., seed, first round, second round, and so on), the firm's business status (e.g., startup, product development, shipping), and the ID code and type of each investor that participated in the round. The general support database contains general information about each firm, such as its industry, state, and telephone area code, as well as details on current and former senior management and board members, such as their title, type (e.g., outside Board member, venture investor board member) and whether they are or were one of the firm's founders. Finally, the number of patents granted to each firm at June 30 of the most recently completed fiscal year as well as June 30 of the forecasted year ahead was obtained from www.uspto.gov.

Exhibit 12.1 lists the restrictions that I placed on VentureOne's databases to arrive at a robust set of observations. Of the roughly 5,000 venture-backed firms to which VentureOne emailed its compensation survey, a total of 1,296 responded.[8] Of these, 42 firms were eliminated because they had been acquired or merged, were

Exhibit 12.1   Maturation Profiles of Pre-IPO Venture-backed Firms (VentureOne Data)

Firms in VentureOne's financing database that were invited by VentureOne to participate in its spring 2004 or spring 2005 compensation survey	≈ 7,000
Firms that responded to the 2004 survey	796
Firms that responded to the 2005 survey	500
	1,296
Less firms that:	
Had been acquired or merged	20
Were in IPO registration	10
Were out of business	8
Were publicly traded	4
	42
= Pre-IPO venture-backed firms that responded to VentureOne's spring 2004 or 2005 surveys	1,254
Less firms where:	
Firm was in both 2004 and 2005 surveys, so to restrict the sample to one observation per firm, the 2005 survey was not used	193
Last financing round was not explicitly classified as being a seed, 1st, 2nd, . . . , 9th type of round	164
Type of the last financing round was missing	8
	365
= Pre-IPO venture-backed firms with sufficient VentureOne data for analysis of maturation profiles	**889**
Of which:	
Firms with only 2004 data	637
Firms with only 2005 data	252
	889

already public or in IPO registration, or had gone out of business. This yielded 1,254 firms that were truly private and independent venture-backed pre-IPO companies. Untabulated analysis indicated that respondents were not significantly different from nonrespondents.[9] To avoid oversampling, from this set I retained the 2004 survey data but excluded the 2005 survey data for the 193 firms that responded to both the 2004 and 2005 surveys. Firms were also excluded if their most recent presurvey financing round was not classified as being a seed, first round, second round, and so on.[10] These selection criteria resulted in 889 pre-IPO observations from by 889 different firms, 75 percent of which were from VentureOne's 2004 survey.

Advanced-HR's OptionImpact database

Distinct from VentureOne's company-specific dataset, my study also draws on aggregate information regarding the employee benefits and performance reviews of venture-backed firms from Advanced-HR, Inc.'s online OptionImpact database.[11] Advanced-HR's data are aggregate because OptionImpact does not provide information on a firm-by-firm basis. Rather, it reports the average of a given firm characteristic such as the number of paid days off per employee by the number of the most recent venture funding round (Pre-A = seed, Post-A = 1st, etc.). This study uses the set of 192 firms in the OptionImpact database.[12]

QUASI-TIME SERIES DATA, STATISTICAL ANALYSIS FRAMEWORK AND ECONOMIC HYPOTHESES

The VentureOne and Advanced-HR databases are cross-sectional in nature, consisting of one observation per firm. A natural question to ask is how then can such databases provide insights into how and why the economic characteristics of venture-backed firms evolve through their pre-IPO stages of life, given that evolution is a time-series phenomenon?

The answer is that under certain assumptions, cross-sectional data can be converted into quasi-time-series data. In this study the temporal dimension that I create to convert cross-sectional data into quasi-time-series data is *RoundNumber*, the number of the firm's most recent venture funding round, defined as *RoundNumber* = 0 (seed round), *RoundNumber* = 1 (1st round), *RoundNumber* = 2 (2nd round), *RoundNumber* = 3 (3rd round), *RoundNumber* = 4 (4th round) and *RoundNumber* = 5 (≥5th round). The key assumptions behind such a conversion are that the characteristics of pre-IPO venture-backed firms depend on maturity, and that the number of the most recent funding round is a good observable proxy for unobservable firm maturity.

The statistical framework that I employ to analyze the quasi-time-series data is illustrated in Exhibit 12.2. First, I report either the frequency or the mean of each firm characteristic according to *RoundNumber*. Second, I estimate the regression:

$$Y_i = \alpha + \beta \cdot DSeed_i + \theta \cdot RoundNumber_i + \varepsilon_i \qquad (12.1)$$

Exhibit 12.2 General Firm Characteristics

Last Round	Number of Observations	Firm Age (Years)	HQ in California	HQ in Massachussets	No. of Granted Patents	Growth in Granted Patents	% Firms in Same Telephone Area Code
Seed	29	3.1	34%	10%	0.1	0.1	3.3%
1st	279	4.4	33	10	0.6	0.2	2.8
2nd	273	5.7	37	15	0.8	0.5	3.3
3rd	183	6.4	42	15	1.5	0.9	3.1
4th	89	6.9	38	18	3.1	1.3	3.3
≥5th	36	8.5	36	11	4.9	1.1	2.4
DSeed		−0.6	1.7%	0.8%	0.7	0.2	0.3%
(t-stat)		(−1.0)	(0.2)	(0.1)	(0.9)	(0.5)	(0.5)
Slope		0.9	1.8%	1.8%	0.9	0.3	0.04%
(t-stat)		(9.7)**	(1.3)	(1.7)	(7.0)**	(5.4)**	(0.4)

Note: Single and double asterisks denote a coefficient estimate that is reliably different from zero at the 5% and 1% significance levels, respectively, under a two-tailed test.

Y_i = the characteristic being analyzed for firm i, and $DSeed_i = 1$ if the firm's most recent funding round prior to the survey date was a seed round, zero otherwise. The coefficient on *RoundNumber* measures the mean change in Y associated with a firm's moving through (in the quasi-time-series sense) one more round of venture funding. The coefficient on *DSeed* measures the degree to which a firm whose most recent funding was a seed round has an abnormally high or low average value of the firm characteristic being analyzed, after controlling for the linear effect, if any, of *RoundNumber*.

I use equation (12.1) to evaluate the validity of the assumptions delineated above concerning the conversion of cross-sectional data to quasi-time-series data. If these assumptions are valid, it should be the case that $\theta \neq 0$ — that is, firm characteristics depend in a reliably linear manner on *RoundNumber*. I also use equation (12.1) to test the proposition that venture investors exert their greatest influence on a young firm at the first round of funding. Although both seed and first rounds are technically venture capital financings, they differ in that seed rounds typically involve much smaller dollar investments and manifest a higher level of participation by individual angel investors.[13] As a result, I hypothesize that venture investors in seed rounds will only find it cost-effective to passively provide the investee firm with money, while in first rounds they will find it cost-effective to actively provide money, business expertise, and connections.[14] If so, and if firm characteristic Y_i is one that is supplied through venture investor business expertise or connections, then I expect to observe $\beta \neq 0$.

MATURATION DYNAMICS

Exhibit 12.1 presents the sample selection criteria used to derive the firms used to develop and analyze firms' maturation profiles.

This part of the chapter describes the results of estimating equation (12.1) for a wide variety of firms' economic characteristics. In the remainder of the chapter I highlight key findings in each exhibit, noting where the evolution of venture-backed firms conforms to the firm-level interpretation of Gort and Klepper's (1982) theory of the prototypical new industry's life cycle delineated in the three propositions developed earlier.

Exhibit 12.2 and the exhibits that follow share a common structure. The sample is predominantly the set of firms in VentureOne's spring 2004 and spring 2005 compensation survey databases that satisfied the requirements outlined in Exhibit 12.1.

Between the rows marked "Seed" and "$\geq$5th" are the means of firm characteristics by the round number of firms' most recent funding round prior to VentureOne's survey date (spring 2004 or spring 2005). After those six rows are reported, I report the estimated coefficients and associated t-statistics on the indicator *DSeed* and the variable *RoundNumber* in the following regression:

$$Y_i = \alpha + \beta \cdot DSeed_i + \theta \cdot RoundNumber_i + \varepsilon_i,$$

where:

Y_i = the variable being analyzed for firm i;
$DSeed_i$ = 1 if the firm's most recent funding round prior to the survey date was a seed round, zero otherwise; and
$RoundNumber_i$ = the number of the firm's most recent funding round prior to the survey date, with a seed round carrying a value of zero, a first round carrying a value of one, and so on.

The coefficient on *RoundNumber* measures the mean change in the dependent variable associated with a firm's going through (in the cross-sectional sense) one more or one less funding round. The coefficient on *DSeed* measures the degree to which a firm whose last funding was a seed round has an abnormally high or low average value of the firm characteristic being analyzed, after controlling for the linear effect of *RoundNumber*.

Single and double asterisks denote a coefficient estimate that is reliably different from zero at the 5 percent and 1 percent significance levels, respectively, under a two-tailed test. The number of observations in this exhibit ranges between 876 and 889.

As the number of financing rounds received from venture investors increases, so also do firm age, the number of patents granted, and the year-to-year growth in the number of patents granted. On average, financing rounds are 0.9 years apart, and one more financing round is associated with an additional 0.9 granted patents and an increase of 0.3 in the year-to-year growth in granted patents. In contrast, the across-state and within-state geographic densities of venture-backed firms (as proxied by the fraction of firms headquartered in California or Massachusetts and the percentage of firms that share the same telephone area code) do not change as firms mature.

Exhibit 12.3 presents mean and median revenues by last financing round for sample firms. "Prior year" denotes the most recent fiscal year completed prior to the date of the VentureOne survey. "Current year" denotes the fiscal year in which the date of the survey resides, such as 2005 for a firm surveyed in spring 2005. Prior year data are therefore actual numbers, while current year data are forecasts made by firms' managers. Revenue categories are defined by VentureOne as follows: 0 ($0 to $0.5 mil.), 1 ($0.5 to $1.0 mil.), 2 ($1.0 to $2.0 mil.), 3 ($2.0 to $3.0 mil.), 4 ($3.0 to $5.0 mil.), 5 ($5.0 to $10 mil.), 6 ($10 to $20 mil.), and 7 (>$20 mil.). Revenue category 7 is converted into dollars using the mean of the most recent fiscal year's revenues for a subset of firms for which annual dollar revenues are available (namely, $60 million). The number of observations in this exhibit ranges between 836 and 843.

Venture-backed firms' actual revenues for their most recent fiscal year increase by an average of $2.8 million per financing round (panel A, column 3). In contrast, and perhaps indicating the presence of managerial overoptimism, revenues for the current fiscal year are predicted by management to increase by an average of $4.5 million per financing round (panel A, column 4). Actual annual revenue growth rates on average exceed 200 percent.

Consistent with Proposition 2, revenue per employee increases rapidly as firms mature and establish the business viability of their technology and ideas,

Exhibit 12.3 Revenues

Panel A Mean Revenues

Last Round	Revenue Category		Revenue (in $ million)		Annual Growth in Revenues		Revenue per Employee ($000s)	
	Prior Year	Current Year	Prior Year	Current Year	$ Million	Rate (%)	Prior Year	Current Year
Seed	0.6	1.4	$ 0.8	$ 1.8	$ 1.0	189%	$ 66	$ 70
1st	1.7	3.0	5.2	8.7	3.6	376	92	151
2nd	2.1	3.3	4.5	8.7	4.3	277	92	157
3rd	3.1	4.2	9.6	15.3	5.7	218	130	178
4th	3.8	4.7	12.6	21.9	9.3	192	138	191
≥5th	4.5	5.3	18.1	28.6	10.5	363	156	226
DSeed	−0.3	−0.9	−0.2	−0.5	−0.4	−2.0	−2.9	−62
(t-stat)	(−0.6)	(−2.0)*	(0.1)	(−0.1)	(−0.2)	(−1.5)	(−0.1)	(−1.2)
Slope	0.7	0.6	2.8	4.5	1.7	−0.4	17	16
(t-stat)	(10.0)**	(8.3)**	(6.3)**	(7.9)**	(5.0)**	(−2.2)*	(3.5)**	(2.0)*

Panel B Median Revenues

Last Round	Revenue Category		Revenue (in $ million)		Annual Growth in Revenues		Revenue per Employee ($000s)	
	Prior Year	Current Year	Prior Year	Current Year	$ Million	Rate (%)	Prior Year	Current Year
Seed	0.0	0.5	$0.3	$ 0.5	$0.0	0%	$ 42	$ 50
1st	0.0	3.0	0.3	2.5	1.3	100	36	100
2nd	1.0	4.0	0.8	4.0	1.3	100	45	94
3rd	3.0	5.0	2.5	7.5	1.5	88	75	136
4th	5.0	5.0	7.5	7.5	1.5	100	90	163
≥5th	5.0	6.0	7.5	15.0	3.5	88	108	167

converting them into salable business products and services. Realized revenue per employee in the most recent fiscal year rises from $66 for firms whose most recent financing round was a seed round to $156 at the ≥5th round an average of 5.4 years later, with current year revenue per employee being forecasted by management to rise from $70 to $226 (panel A, columns 7 and 8).[15]

Exhibit 12.4 presents statistics on employees by last financing round for sample firms. "Prior year" denotes the most recent fiscal year completed prior to the date of the VentureOne survey. "Current year" denotes the fiscal year in which the date of the survey resides, such as 2005 for a firm surveyed in spring 2005. Prior year data are therefore actual numbers, while current year data are forecasts made by firms' managers. Headcount categories are defined by VentureOne as follows: 0 (0 to 10 employees), 1 (10 to 20), 2 (20 to 30), 3 (30 to 40), 4 (40 to 50), 5 (50 to 60), 6 (60 to 100), and 7 (>100). For the current year, employee category 7 is converted into a number using the mean number of employees for category 7 firms in the prior year (= 360). The number of observations in this exhibit ranges between 733 and 867.

Venture-backed firms' headcounts increase in a robustly linear manner by an average of between 18 and 26 employees per financing round, depending on whether one is considering actual employees in place at the end of the most recent

Exhibit 12.4 Number and Composition of Employees in Total and by Functional Areas

Panel A Means Regarding Total Employees

Last Round	Headcount Category		Number of Employees		Annual Growth in Employees		Employee Turnover (%)
	Prior Year	Current Year	Prior Year	Current Year	Number	Rate (%)	
Seed	0.6	1.4	10	29	8	100%	8%
1st	1.8	2.8	36	57	20	61	11
2nd	2.6	3.4	51	68	16	49	13
3rd	3.8	4.3	72	98	25	47	12
4th	4.5	4.8	84	132	52	60	13
≥5th	5.1	5.5	118	170	51	65	18
DSeed	−0.3	−0.7	−6.3	4.8	1.5	44	−3.1
(t-stat)	(−0.8)	(−1.6)	(−0.2)	(0.2)	(0.1)	(2.2)*	(−1.1)
Slope	0.9	0.7	18	26	8.2	−0.9	0.9
(t-stat)	(14.6)**	(11.1)**	(4.3)**	(8.0)**	(2.0)*	(−0.3)	(2.4)*

Panel B Mean Number of Employees in Functional Areas

Last Round	Administration	Business Development	Finance	Marketing	Sales	Technical	Other
Seed	1.2	0.6	0.7	1.1	1.1	4.9	0.4
1st	2.9	0.8	1.6	1.7	6.2	12	11
2nd	3.9	0.9	1.9	1.6	5.8	18	19
3rd	4.7	1.2	2.6	2.8	8.1	24	13
4th	4.8	1.3	3.3	3.8	13	29	20
≥5th	7.0	1.4	5.5	3.8	14	26	44
DSeed	−0.9	−0.04	0.02	0.3	−2.1	−3.0	−6.3
(t-stat)	(−0.8)	(−0.1)	(0.0)	(0.4)	(−0.5)	(−0.7)	(−0.4)
Slope	0.8	0.2	0.7	0.6	1.9	4.9	4.3
(t-stat)	(4.3)**	(3.5)**	(7.0)**	(5.1)**	(3.1)**	(7.1)**	(1.6)

Panel C Percentage of Employees in Functional Areas

Last Round	Administration	Business Development	Finance	Marketing	Sales	Technical	Other
Seed	17%	6.2%	6.4%	8.5%	6.9%	51%	4.4%
1st	12	3.4	5.8	5.4	12	47	14
2nd	11	2.9	4.9	4.3	12	50	15
3rd	10	2.4	5.4	5.0	15	42	19
4th	8.6	1.9	4.9	5.4	17	43	19
≥5th	7.9	2.0	6.0	4.8	15	32	33
DSeed	4.0	2.4	0.8	3.4	−3.1	−1.7	−6.0
(t-stat)	(2.2)*	(2.7)**	(0.8)	(2.8)**	(−1.2)	(−0.3)	(−1.3)
Slope	−1.1	−0.5	−0.1	−0.0	1.5	−2.8	2.9
(t-stat)	(−3.9)**	(−3.3)**	(−0.7)	(−0.3)	(3.8)**	(−3.8)**	(4.1)**

Note: Percentages are computed by round, not by functional area. Rows therefore sum to 100%, but columns do not.

fiscal year or forecasted employees at the end of the current fiscal year (panel A, columns 3 and 4). Annual growth rates in the number of employees average about 60 percent (panel A, column 6). Perhaps due to the desire by employees to remain with the firm more the less vested are stock options they may have been granted, employee turnover rates are lowest at the seed round and increase by a statistically significant average of 0.9 percent per financing round thereafter.

Panel B reveals that the mean number of employees increases with *Round-Number* across all seven functional areas: Administration, Business Development, Finance, Marketing, Sales, Technical, and Other. As they mature through one additional round of funding, firms add between 0.2 business development employees and 4.9 technical employees. After scaling by the total number of employees, however, panel C shows that the composition of the firms' workforce changes as they mature. In particular, and consistent with Proposition 2, there is a relative substitution away from technical personnel toward sales and nontechnical Other employees (columns 4 to 6). As firms mature and scale up their activities, they hire more of all types of employees. However, because firms shift from establishing the technical feasibility of their technology- or scientific-based innovations to proving business demand, they hire relatively more sales people (column 5) and Other employees (column 7) and relatively fewer technical personnel (column 6).

Exhibit 12.5 presents statistics on sample firms' organizational hierarchy by last financing round for sample firms. This is based on all available data provided on an employee-by-employee basis. In VentureOne's survey, firms are permitted, but not required, to provide employee-specific data on up to, but not more than, 50 employees. Employee seniority declines as one moves from senior executives (panel A) to Vice-Presidents (panel B) to Directors (panel C) to Managers (panel D). VentureOne's survey contains some information about employees below the manager level, but statistics for such employees are not reported in this exhibit. The number of observations in this exhibit is 889.

Exhibit 12.5 explores how the organizational hierarchy matures by exploiting the fact that each employee in VentureOne's survey not only has a specific job title but is also assigned a seniority level. In descending order of seniority, the five uppermost seniority levels are [1] CEO and President (panel A); [2] CFO, COO, CTO, and CSO (panel A); [3] Vice-Presidents (panel B); [4] Directors (panel C); and [5] Managers (panel D).

Three main findings emerge from Exhibit 12.5. First, firms set most of their organizational hierarchy in place at the seed round of venture funding. This is evidenced by the observation that in four of the five seniority levels (the two highest, [1] and [2], and the two lowest, [4] and [5]) the slope coefficient on *RoundNumber* is reliably nonzero at most 33 percent of the time. Taken as a group, none of the seed round dummies and only 18 percent of *RoundNumber* slope coefficients are reliably nonzero at these same seniority levels.

Second, the sole exception to the surprisingly strong pattern of firms seeming to organize their employee hierarchy very early in their lives occurs at the VP seniority level. In five of the seven functional areas where VPs exist, the percentage of firms with one or more VPs in those functions reliably increases as firms mature (finance, IT/technology, marketing, sales, and operations). Thus, the VP seniority level appears to be the one that plays a key maturity-based role in firms' organizational hierarchies.

Exhibit 12.5 Firm Organizational Hierarchy, and Hierarchy Within and Across Functional Areas

Panel A Percentage of Firms with Senior Executive Positions Filled

Last Round	CEO	President	CFO	COO	CTO	CSO
Seed	97%	0%	31%	10%	38%	14%
1st	92	10	36	14	44	11
2nd	95	10	42	14	44	13
3rd	93	13	55	17	37	16
4th	96	11	61	16	40	15
≥5th	92	6	72	11	31	14
DSeed	4.3	−10	4.9	−3.8	−9.7	3.2
(t-stat)	(0.9)	(−1.7)	(0.5)	(−0.5)	(−1.0)	(0.5)
Slope	0.5	0.0	8.9	0.3	−2.7	1.2
(t-stat)	(0.7)	(0.0)	(6.1)**	(0.3)	(−1.8)	(1.2)

Panel B Percentage of Firms with One or More VPs in Functional Areas

Last Round	Business Development	Finance	IT/Technical Services	Marketing	Sales	Operations	R&D
Seed	17%	0.0%	0.0%	6.9%	0%	17%	3.4%
1st	20	5.4	1.8	18	33	11	9.7
2nd	30	8.8	2.2	28	39	14	12
3rd	25	9.8	7.7	34	58	23	13
4th	27	15	9.0	35	64	20	16
≥5th	25	8.3	5.6	42	58	28	8.3
DSeed	−5.1	−4.1	0.6	−7.1	−23	10	−5.8
(t-stat)	(−0.6)	(−0.7)	(0.2)	(−0.8)	(−2.4)*	(1.4)	(−0.9)
Slope	1.3	2.0	2.1	6.0	9.8	4.1	1.1
(t-stat)	(1.0)	(2.4)*	(3.6)**	(4.6)**	(6.8)**	(3.7)**	(1.1)

Panel C Percentage of Firms with One or More Directors in Functional Areas

Last Round	Business Development	Finance	IT/Technical Services	Marketing	Sales	Operations	R&D
Seed	6.9%	0.0%	0.0%	0.0%	3.4%	0.0%	10%
1st	7.5	5.4	7.9	11	11	5.0	5.8
2nd	6.6	7.7	7.0	10	10	7.7	7.0
3rd	9.3	6.0	14	19	14	7.7	10
4th	9.0	10	12	17	12	11.2	13
≥5th	2.8	5.6	5.6	5.6	2.8	2.8	11
DSeed	−0.5	−5.3	−6.5	−9.8	−7.7	−5.0	7.0
(t-stat)	(−0.1)	(−1.1)	(−1.1)	(−1.5)	(−1.2)	(−1.0)	(1.3)
Slope	0.0	0.7	1.2	1.4	−0.0	0.8	2.1
(t-stat)	(0.1)	(0.9)	(1.4)	(1.4)	(−0.1)	(1.2)	(2.6)**

Panel D Percentage of Firms with One or More Managers in Functional Areas

Last Round	Administration	Controller	IT/Technical Services	Marketing	Sales	Operations	R&D
Seed	3.4%	6.9%	0.0%	0.0%	3.4%	−	3.4%
1st	6.8	15	7.5	3.9	2.9		2.5
2nd	5.9	16	7.7	6.6	4.8		6.6
3rd	5.5	26	9.8	6.0	9.3		4.9

(Continued)

Exhibit 12.5   (*Continued*)

4th	6.7	26	11	7.9	5.6		10
≥5th	0.0	14	2.8	2.8	2.8		5.6
DSeed	−4.2	−5.5	−7.4	−4.3	0.8	–	1.5
(t-stat)	(−0.9)	(−0.7)	(−1.4)	(−1.0)	(0.2)		(0.3)
Slope	−0.7	2.9	0.4	0.6	1.1	–	1.5
(t-stat)	(−1.1)	(2.5)*	(0.5)	(0.9)	(1.7)		(2.2)*

Third, organizational hierarchies are most homogeneous and standardized at the most senior levels of management, and least homogeneous and standardized at the least senior levels of management. Of firms, 96 percent have a CEO; 29 percent have CFOs, COOs, CTOs, and CSOs; 19 percent have VPs; 8 percent have Directors; and 7 percent have Managers.[16]

As seen in the clustering of observations on and around the diagonal of Exhibit 12.6, firm maturity is highly positively correlated with firm life stage. Other highlights of Exhibit 12.6 are that there appear to be noticeable jumps in the fraction of firms moving into the shipping product life stage going from seed to first round funding, and that very few venture-backed firms are profitable at any point in pre-IPO life cycle (even at the ≥5th financing round, a mere 22 percent report positive net income).

Two features stand out in Exhibit 12.7. These are that the percentage of firms classified by VentureOne as Internet in nature reliably increases with *RoundNumber*, but the alternative classifications of firms into four key industry sectors show no association with *RoundNumber*. An explanation for the former result is suggested by the negative relation between firms' average dates of founding and the percentage of firms classified as Internet. This almost certainly reflects the pre-2001 boom in the number of Internet firms that were started and the post-2001 bust in the number of Internet firms that failed.

In exchange for the capital and expertise they supply, venture investors commonly demand influence and/or control of investee firms' boards of directors. Indications of this can be seen in Exhibit 12.8 in two ways. First, consistent with Proposition 3 (that venture investors exert their greatest influence at the first funding round), the coefficient on the seed round dummy is reliably positive in the

Exhibit 12.6   Percentage of firms at different life stages (n = 889)

Exhibit 12.6 presents the percentage of firms at different life stages by last financing round.

Last Round	Start-up	Product Development	Product in Beta Test	Clinical Trials	Shipping Product	Profitable
Seed	31%	59%	0%	0%	10%	0%
1st	6	41	2	2	43	6
2nd	0	25	7	4	55	8
3rd	0	7	2	9	74	8
4th	0	6	2	11	73	8
≥5th	0	6	0	8	64	22

Exhibit 12.7 Mean founding date and percent of firms in key industries and sectors (n = 889)

Exhibit 12.7 presents sample firms' mean founding date and industry by last financing round.

Last Round	Date Firm Was Founded	Internet	Health Care	IT	Retail/ Services	Other
Seed	July 2001	38%	31%	52%	14%	3%
1st	Mar 2000	46	23	53	19	5
2nd	Nov 1998	50	30	52	16	2
3rd	Feb 1998	56	30	52	17	1
4th	Sept 1997	60	30	48	20	2
≥5th	Dec 1995	67	31	47	19	3
DSeed		−2.6	8.1	−2.4	−4.1	−1.7
(t-stat)		(−0.3)	(0.9)	(−0.2)	(−0.5)	(−0.5)
Slope		5.0	2.2	−1.2	0.0	1.1
(t-stat)		(3.3)**	(1.6)	(−0.8)	(0.1)	(2.3)*

regression of the dummy signifying a chairman who is also the CEO on the seed round dummy and *RoundNumber* (column 2). Of seed round firms, 11 percent have a CEO who is also Chairman of the Board, but this drops significantly to 4.1 percent at the first funding round. This suggests that at the first funding round, venture investors deliberately separate the responsibilities of CEO and Chairman, most likely for purposes of optimal governance from their point of view as shareholders who at the first funding round typically own a minority equity stake but who expect as the firm matures to become as a group majority stakeholders. Although not shown directly in Exhibit 12.8, the Chairman position is then almost exclusively held by one of the first round venture investors. Second, the number of founders on the board also declines significantly between the seed and first funding rounds.

The other clear pattern is the inexorable increase in the number of board members as firms mature. On average, with the passing of one more financing round a firm adds 0.6 new board members. The greatest portion of this increase derives from new venture investors being added to the board as they participate in the new financing round. The number of outsiders and insiders on the board does increase with maturity, but at a much slower rate. Not surprisingly, individual investors are only occasionally members of a venture-backed firm's board.

Exhibit 12.8 showed that venture investors influence firms' boards of directors. Exhibit 12.9 demonstrates that they also have a significant influence on firms' policies.

The results in panel A are derived from VentureOne's database and span two types of corporate policies—formal and discretionary. Formal policies consist of formal pay policies, established stock grant guidelines, formal sales commission plans, and defined bonus plans. Discretionary policies comprise discretionary bonus plans and the awarding of hire-on bonuses. Several findings stand out from panel A.

First, firms at the seed round have relatively few formal policies in place. This is not that surprising, since at the seed round the economic payback to allocating

Exhibit 12.8   Boards of Directors (n = 889)

Exhibit 12.8 presents data on sample firms' boards of directors by last financing round.

Last Round	Chairman Is a Founder	Chairman Is the CEO	Number of Board Members	Number of Founders on Board	Types of Board Members			
					Outsider	Individual Investor	Venture Investor	Insider
Seed	3.6%	11%	3.4	0.8	0.8	0.3	1.1	1.2
1st	2.2	4.1	4.1	0.5	0.8	0.2	1.7	1.3
2nd	0.4	0.8	4.9	0.5	1.0	0.2	2.2	1.5
3rd	1.1	2.2	5.6	0.6	1.2	0.2	2.7	1.5
4th	2.3	2.3	5.9	0.6	1.1	0.3	3.0	1.5
≥5th	0.0	0.0	6.1	0.5	1.4	0.3	2.9	1.6
DSeed	1.7%	7.0%	−0.2	0.3	0.07	0.07	−0.3	−0.05
(t-stat)	(0.7)	(2.2)*	(−0.5)	(2.4)*	(0.3)	(0.7)	(−1.1)	(−0.4)
Slope	−0.2	−0.7	0.6	0.02	0.1	0.02	0.4	0.07
(t-stat)	(−0.6)	(−1.4)	(12.1)**	(1.3)	(3.9)**	(1.0)	(10.8)**	(3.5)**

Exhibit 12.9   Corporate Policies

Exhibit 12.9 presents sample firms' corporate policies by last financing round. The data in panel A are from VentureOne. The data in panel B are from Advanced-HR, Inc.'s OptionImpact database. The number of observations in panel A ranges between 873 and 880. The number of firms in the OptionImpact database is 192, and they provided data items to Advanced-HR between 8/20/04 and 8/20/05.

Panel A Percent of Firms with Formal and Discretionary Corporate Policies in Place[1]

	Formal Policies				Discretionary Policies	
Last Round	Has a Formal Pay Policy	Has Established Stock Grant Guidelines	Has a Formal Sales Commission Plan	Has a Defined Bonus Plan	Has a Discretionary Bonus Plan	Provides Hire-On Bonuses
Seed	21%	45%	21%	58%	67%	14%
1st	55	73	56	69	49	15
2nd	54	71	64	77	63	17
3rd	52	80	73	82	53	14
4th	55	72	75	85	70	14
$\geq$5th	56	72	81	89	62	22
DSeed	−34	−27	−30	−6.2	19	−1.6
(t-stat)	(−3.4)**	(−3.1)**	(−3.2)**	(−0.7)	(1.2)	(−0.2)
Slope	−0.2	0.8	6.7	5.4	4.2	0.1
(t-stat)	(−0.1)	(0.6)	(4.7)**	(4.2)**	(1.9)	(0.1)

Panel B Percent of Firms That Conduct Performance Reviews and Have Established Pay Ranges for Staff Positions

	Conduct Performance Reviews			Has Established Pay Ranges for Staff Positions
Last Round	As Needed	At Employee Anniversary	Focal	
Seed	38%	38%	25%	22%
1st	12	31	58	57
2nd	17	17	66	53
3rd	7	32	61	64
4th	5	15	80	54
$\geq$5th	7	14	79	66
Number of Observations	18	37	103	Yes = 110/192

[1]The categorization of policies as formal or informal is by the author, not VentureOne.

scarce resources to the determination and then implementation of a set of formal corporate policies would seem small, there being only 10 employees on average in place at that time (see panel A in Exhibit 12.4).

Second, by the time they have matured to the $\geq$5th funding round, having formal policies in place is the rule rather than the exception. The increase in the intensity of formal policies from seed to the $\geq$5th funding round comes about in two ways. Consistent with Proposition 3, for three of the four formal policies described in panel A of Exhibit 12.9 there is a significant increase between the seed and first funding rounds. The percentage of firms with formal pay policies, established stock grant guidelines, and formal sales commission plans roughly doubles between the

Exhibit 12.10 Equity holdings

Exhibit 12.10 presents mean employee option holdings by last financing round for sample firms. Equity is defined by VentureOne as the sum of all outstanding preferred stock, common stock, stock options granted (whether vested or not), and stock options available for future grants. Means are calculated over all available observations for a firm, subject to data availability. In VentureOne's survey, firms are permitted, but not required, to provide equity holding data on up to, but not more than, 50 employees. The number of observations in panel A ranges between 748 and 877.

Panel A Mean Options Granted and Equity Concentrations

Last Round	Percent of Employees Granted Options	Percent of Options Granted to CEO	Executive Equity as Percent of all Equity	Average Vesting Period (years)	Percentage of Equity Held by: CEO or President	VCs
Seed	80%	48%	31%	3.4%	15%	43%
1st	86	48	22	3.8	11	54
2nd	89	47	17	3.8	8	64
3rd	94	49	14	3.9	7	69
4th	94	49	14	3.8	7	71
$\geq$5th	89	57	12	3.9	7	76
DSeed	−4.8	2.0	6.9	−0.3	4.1	−7.4
(t-stat)	(−1.0)	(0.4)	(2.2)*	(−2.1)*	(2.0)*	(−1.5)
Slope	2.3	1.0	−2.9	0.03	−1.1	5.9
(t-stat)	(3.2)**	(1.3)	(−6.1)**	(1.3)	(−3.9)**	(7.8)**

Panel B Mean Fractions of Firm Equity Held by Employees at Different Ranks

Last Round	CEO	President	CFO	CTO	VP	Director	Manager
Seed	15%	−[1]	1.8%	7.9%	3.4%	1.3%	0.1%
1st	10	8.2%	1.8	5.1	2.0	0.5	0.3
2nd	7.4	4.4	1.5	4.0	1.5	0.4	0.2
3rd	6.6	3.3	1.2	3.0	0.9	0.2	0.1
4th	6.9	4.4	1.3	2.6	0.9	0.2	0.2
$\geq$5th	7.5	2.0	1.6	2.0	0.8	0.3	0.2
DSeed	4.7	−	0.0	2.0	1.1	0.7	−0.2
(t-stat)	(2.4)*		(0.0)	(1.2)	(2.9)**	(4.4)**	(−1.2)
Slope	−1.0	−1.5	−0.1	−0.9	−0.4	−0.1	−0.04
(t-stat)	(−3.6)**	(−2.9)**	(−1.9)	(−4.0)**	(−9.6)**	(−5.8)**	(−2.9)**
Number of Observations	720	85	355	326	1,773	1,192	460

[1]Denotes where there were too few observations to create reliable statistics (typically two observations or less).

seed and first funding rounds. Alongside these one-time shifts, it is also the case that there is a maturation trend over time. Thus, the percentage of firms with formal sales commission plans and the percentage of firms with a defined bonus plan increase linearly with *RoundNumber*.

Finally, discretionary policies appear to be independent of both firm maturity and the move from seed to first funding rounds. This may be because the costs of determining and implementing discretionary corporate policies are smaller than is the case for formal policies.

The results reported in panel B, which are derived from Advanced-HR's OptionImpact database, also support Proposition 3, and in a way that moves investee firms from informal to formal corporate policies. Relative to VentureOne's database, the OptionImpact database reports two additional types of corporate policies: the percentage of firms that conduct performance reviews of their employees at different points in time and the percentage of firms that have established pay ranges for staff positions. From the figures reported in panel B, it appears that firms at the seed funding round are markedly more likely to conduct performance reviews on a discretionary as-needed basis, less likely to conduct focal performance reviews, and less likely to have established pay ranges for staff position.[17]

Equity incentives are widely used by firms to incentivize, motivate, and retain employees. This is especially so in venture-backed firms, where intensely technological or science-based assets and investment opportunities are fraught with information asymmetry and agency problems that can fruitfully be ameliorated by strong equity incentives. Exhibit 12.10 describes the equity holdings of employees and venture investors for firms in the VentureOne database. Overall, I interpret the results of Exhibit 12.10 to be consistent with Proposition 3, namely that venture investors exert their biggest influence at the Series A round, and that such influence is permanent, not transitory.

Panels A and B suggest four findings of note. First, venture-backed firms typically grant stock options very deeply into their organizations (see also Hand 2008). Second, the fraction of employees who are granted stock options reliably increases by 2.3 percent per financing round. While this result could be indicative of a genuine firm maturation trend, it may instead reflect a decline over calendar time. The latter explanation is possible because over the past several years the Financial Accounting Standards Board (FASB) has successfully sought to require firms to expense the costs of stock-based compensation. One of the responses that some have suggested firms will make to this requirement to show stock option expenses in their income statements is to cut back on how deeply in their organizations they grant options. The data in panel A are consistent with such a response occurring on a proactive, but limited, basis.

The second finding of note across panels A and B is that both as a group and by seniority level, employees hold a steadily declining fraction of total equity as firms mature. In contrast, the fraction of equity held by venture investors steadily increases. Third, CEOs hold a disproportionate share of the equity held by employees as a whole—roughly 50 percent at all stages of firm maturity (compare panel A, column 5 to column 3).

Fourth, consistent with Proposition 3, several equity attributes decline significantly between the seed and first rounds of venture funding. The attributes are executive equity as a percentage of all equity, and the percentage of equity held by the CEO, VPs, and Directors.

Using the OptionImpact database, Exhibit 12.11 reports the relations between firm maturity by *RoundNumber* and employee benefits. On the one hand, the results shown in panel A indicate that the mean number of vacation days, the total paid days off per employee, and the components of that total (company paid holiday and sick leave) are insensitive to the firm's maturity. On the other hand, firms

Exhibit 12.11   Employee Benefits

Exhibit 12.11 presents descriptive statistics on employee benefits in sample firms by last financing round. The data in this Exhibit are from Advanced-HR, Inc.'s OptionImpact database. The maximum number of firms over which statistics are calculated is 192. All data items were provided to Advanced-HR by firms between 8/20/04 and 8/20/05.

Panel A Mean Number of Paid Days Off per Employee

Last Round	Company Paid Holiday	Vacation	Sick Leave	Paid Time Off
Seed	9	11	7	14
1st	9	10	6	16
2nd	10	12	6	16
3rd	10	12	6	16
4th	10	14	6	16
$\geq$5th	10	13	7	17
Number of Observations	192	86	53	106

Panel B Percent of Firms that Provide Specialized Types of Benefits to Their Employees

Last Round	Medical	Dental	Vision	401k	Long-term Disability	Short-term Disability	Life Insurance	Pre-tax Spending
Seed	100%	78%	56%	56%	44%	33%	56%	33%
1st	100	95	59	70	68	49	73	59
2nd	100	100	91	91	71	42	89	71
3rd	100	100	84	91	87	67	80	87
4th	100	96	79	100	88	63	88	71
$\geq$5th	100	100	88	94	88	63	88	91
Number of Observations	192	187	153	167	149	105	157	142

appear to grant markedly more of the specialized types of employee benefits at the first funding round than at the seed round. This too is consistent with Proposition 3. It also echoes the findings reported in Exhibit 12.9 that indicated that a key area in which venture investors exert influence is corporate policies.

Exhibit 12.12 reports a variety of general information about the cash compensation earned by employees of venture-backed firms, as a function not only of firm maturity but also functional area, type of cash compensation (base vs. bonus), and employee rank.[18] The database analyzed is that of VentureOne. Several results warrant particular attention.

First, computed over all employees for whom firms provided compensation data to VentureOne, base, bonus, and cash compensation rise linearly and significantly as firms mature by *RoundNumber* (panel A). On average, annual total cash compensation per employee increases $7,200 as firms mature through one more financing round. Of this increase, $4,400 is in base compensation, $2,500 is in bonus compensation, and only $300 is in other compensation.

Second, total cash compensation increases with firm maturity across all ranks of employees—but at a rate that is increasing in employee rank (panel B). Thus, while CEOs earn $14,000 more per financing round, CFOs and CTOs earn $8,000 and $5,900 more, VPs earn $4,000 more, Directors earn $3,200 more, and Managers earn

Exhibit 12.12   Cash Compensation

Exhibit 12.12 presents mean employee cash compensation by last financing round. All cash compensation amounts are in $000s. Means are calculated over all available employee observations for a firm, subject to an employee receiving an annual base salary of at least $10,000 and being at or more senior than the manager level (i.e., senior management, vice-presidents, directors, and managers). Employees below the level of manager are not included. In VentureOne's survey, firms are permitted, but not required, to provide compensation data on up to, but not more than, 50 employees. Total cash compensation is base salary + bonus + other cash compensation.

Panel A Means of Each Component of Total Cash Compensation, and Total Cash Compensation Itself, Computed over All Employees for Whom Firms Provided Compensation Data to VentureOne (Number of Employees = 6,157)

Last Round	Base	Bonus	Other	Total
Seed	$ 129	$ 6	$ 2	$ 136
1st	138	12	2	152
2nd	142	15	3	160
3rd	146	18	2	166
4th	149	18	4	172
≥5th	158	24	3	185
DSeed	−4.9	−4.3	−0.3	−6.0
(t-stat)	(−1.0)	(−1.5)	(−0.2)	(−0.9)
Slope	4.4	2.5	0.3	7.2
(t-stat)	(7.5)**	(7.4)**	(1.6)	(9.1)**

Panel B Mean Total Cash Compensation by Employee Rank

Last Round	CEO	President	CFO	CTO	VP	Director	Manager
Seed	$ 167	—	$ 133	$ 123	$ 134	$ 118	$ 74
1st	214	195	162	161	160	113	87
2nd	237	197	167	164	170	117	87
3rd	267	227	183	185	181	122	91
4th	277	252	202	176	188	124	89
≥5th	288	290	200	197	183	126	119
DSeed	−20	—	−9.0	−18	−9.3	5.1	−6.1
(t-stat)	(−1.7)		(−0.7)	(−1.4)	(−1.3)	(0.8)	(−0.5)
Slope	14	15	8.0	5.9	4.0	3.2	2.8
(t-stat)	(7.9)**	(2.8)**	(5.2)**	(3.3)**	(6.0)**	(4.9)**	(2.9)**
Number of Observations	827	93	402	365	1,978	1,423	576

Panel C Mean Base Cash Compensation, by Employee Rank

Last Round	CEO	President	CFO	CTO	VP	Director	Manager
Seed	$ 155	—	$ 130	$ 123	$ 131	$ 107	$ 82
1st	189	164	150	148	143	105	83
2nd	202	162	152	150	149	109	83
3rd	224	203	162	165	154	113	86
4th	232	197	177	159	160	113	83
≥5th	236	213	175	173	150	119	119[1]
DSeed	−20	—	−9.0	−18	−9.3	5.1	3.5
(t-stat)	(−1.7)		(−0.7)	(−1.4)	(−1.3)	(0.8)	(0.2)

(Continued)

Exhibit 12.12   Cash Compensation (*Continued*)

Last Round	CEO	President	CFO	CTO	VP	Director	Manager
Slope	$ 14	$ 15	$ 8.0	$ 5.9	$ 4.0	$ 3.2	$ 2.8
(t-stat)	(7.9)**	(2.8)**	(5.2)**	(3.3)**	(6.0)**	(4.9)**	(2.9)**
Number of Observations	827	93	402	365	1,978	1,423	576

Panel D Probability of Receiving a Bonus by Employee Rank

Last Round	CEO	President	CFO	CTO	VP	Director	Manager
Seed	0.29	–	0.13	0.00	0.17	0.05	0.20
1st	0.41	0.31	0.42	0.39	0.40	0.31	0.20
2nd	0.51	0.50	0.48	0.47	0.42	0.36	0.32
3rd	0.53	0.50	0.61	0.48	0.53	0.42	0.26
4th	0.57	0.70	0.57	0.47	0.54	0.44	0.45
$\geq$5th	0.58	1.00	0.69	0.73	0.59	0.24	0.00
DSeed	−0.10	–	−0.24	−0.35	−0.18	−0.26	−0.01
(t-stat)	(−0.9)		(−1.3)	(−2.0)*	(−1.7)	(−2.4)*	(−0.1)
Slope	0.05	0.12	0.07	0.05	0.05	0.03	0.03
(t-stat)	(3.2)**	(2.6)*	(3.1)**	(1.9)*	(5.5)**	(2.3)*	(1.7)

Panel E Mean Bonus Conditional on Receiving a Bonus by Employee Rank

Last Round	CEO	President	CFO	CTO	VP	Director	Manager
Seed	$ 39	–	$ 25	–	$ 16	$ 15	$ 10
1st	56	$ 42	29	$ 33	34	19	11
2nd	64	53	31	29	38	18	10
3rd	79	49	34	40	41	18	14
4th	72	71	38	33	39	20	8
$\geq$5th	89	78	36	29	43	30	–
DSeed	−10	–	−1.3	–	−17	−1.6	−1.4
(t-stat)	(−0.6)		(−0.1)		(−1.0)	(−0.1)	(−0.1)
Slope	7.6	7.8	2.4	0.8	1.9	0.8	−0.3
(t-stat)	(3.7)**	(1.2)	(1.9)*	(0.5)	(2.0)*	(0.9)	(−0.3)
Number of Observations	400	44	208	161	926	520	164

[1]Of the 19 observations underlying this mean, 11 come from a single firm (their average is $124).

only $2,800 more. This likely reflects the decreasing decision rights and marginal product with respect to value creation of employees in lower ranks relative to those in higher ranks. This pattern is also observed in the base (panel C) and bonus (panels D and E) components of total cash compensation.

Third, the probability of receiving a cash bonus is increasing in firm maturity at all employee ranks except that of Manager (panel D). The amount of the increased probability per financing round varies between 3 percent for Directors and 12 percent for Presidents. It is also the case that for three of the seven employee ranks, the mean bonus conditional on receiving a bonus is reliably increasing in *RoundNumber* (CEOs, CFOs, and VPs, panel E).

Exhibit 12.13   Firm Equity Values and Financings

Exhibit 12.13 presents mean firm equity values and funding raised by last financing round.

Panel A Mean Firm Equity Values at the Last (i.e., the Most Recent) Funding Round for Which a Premoney Equity Value for the Firm was Available ($n = 445$ to 450)

Last Round	Premoney Value at Last Round ($ million)	Postmoney Value at Last Round ($ million)	Premoney Value per Employee ($000s)	Postmoney Value per Employee ($000s)
Seed	$ 2.7	$ 4.4	$ 388	$ 605
1st	11.2	17.8	523	852
2nd	22.3	34.6	774	1,266
3rd	44.9	60.5	1,184	1,623
4th	59.5	75.0	945	1,217
≥5th	64.6	74.3	2,301	2,543
DSeed	8.3	4.1	181	−15
(t-stat)	(0.6)	(0.3)	(0.4)	(−0.0)
Slope	16	18	296	288
(t-stat)	(7.9)**	(8.0)**	(4.5)**	(3.8)**

Panel B Mean Financing Characteristics at the Last (i.e., the Most Recent) Funding Round

Last Round	Equity Raised in Last Round ($ million)	Total Equity Firm's Life ($ million)	Time Since Last Round (years)	No. of VCs in Last Round	Dilution in Last Round (%)
Seed	$ 1.4	$ 1.4	$ 2.2	$ 2.0	$ 36%
1st	7.5	8.5	1.9	2.3	42
2nd	11.8	18.9	1.7	3.2	39
3rd	12.9	26.9	1.6	4.1	31
4th	14.3	34.8	1.4	4.6	29
≥5th	11.7	33.4	1.3	4.1	15
DSeed	−5.5	−0.6	0.07	0.2	−13
(t-stat)	(−2.7)**	(−0.2)	(0.3)	(0.4)	(−2.5)*
Slope	1.8	7.9	−0.2	0.7	−5.6
(t-stat)	(6.0)**	(14.4)**	(−4.1)**	(9.8)**	(−7.4)**
#obs.	889	889	889	889	448

Fourth, neither base nor bonus nor total cash compensation is unusually low at the seed round as compared to the linear maturity trends fitted by means of *RoundNumber*. Specifically, of the 21 different estimated coefficients on the seed dummy in panels A, B, C, and E combined, none is reliably different from zero. This implies that venture investors do not exert any particularly large influence on investee firms' cash compensation at the first funding round.

Exhibit 12.13 demonstrates that firm pre- and postmoney equity values increase with firm maturity in a purely linear manner (panel A). On average, premoney equity values rise by $16 million per financing round, and postmoney values rise by $18 million per round. Such patterns stem almost certainly from more than the pure value creation suggested by the strongly increasing equity value per employee (and revenue per employee, per Exhibit 12.3). In particular, reported equity values very likely also reflect the effects of selection bias and new equity investments. For example, while VentureOne's database is not restricted to only those firms that have successfully gone public, it *is* limited to firms that have been sufficiently successful so as to be alive and able to respond to VentureOne's survey. Also, firms' premoney values at a given funding round will heavily reflect investments made by venture investors at all prior rounds (hence pre- and postmoney values increase as firms scale up).

Panel B of Exhibit 12.13 describes how firms' financing-related characteristics change as firms mature. First of all, firms raise an average of $1.8 million more per round (t-statistic = 6.0), and the elapsed time between rounds falls by 0.2 years per round (t-statistic = −4.1). Second, supporting the notion that seed rounds are smaller and less rigorous than other rounds, the amount raised at seed rounds is a statistically significant $5.5 million less than that expected from the underlying linear relation between equity raised and *RoundNumber*. Third, indicative of the known tendency for venture investors to syndicate and spread the larger amounts of equity funding required by more mature firms across more venture funds, the number of venture investors participating in a round increases by 0.7 per *RoundNumber*. Finally, the amount of equity dilution created by the financing injected in any given round decreases as firms mature, with the notable exception that dilution is largest at the first round. This is once again consistent with venture investors exerting a particularly large influence on firms at the first funding round.

Exhibit 12.14 describes certain characteristics of company founders. The results reported in panel A indicate that in venture-backed firms, the influence of founders diminishes steadily as firms mature. This echoes one of the conclusions in Kaplan, Sensoy, and Strömberg (forthcoming), namely that the value of the human capital in venture-backed firms is generally not permanently tied to specific individuals. The typical founder sees his or her percentage of firm equity steadily diminish over time; is less likely to be on the board or Chairman of the Board at and after the first funding round; and is steadily less likely to remain as the firm's CEO.

Panel B indicates that, with the exception of Operations and Technical, founders tend to stay in their functional areas. There is some evidence that founders are less (more) likely to be in Operations (Technical) as firms mature, perhaps because founders tend to be more idea people than practical, get-it-done people. Finally, panel C suggests that founders tend to remain at the same managerial rank as firms mature.

LIMITATIONS OF THE STUDY

There are two key limitations to this study. First, and most important, the data used are quasi-time-series in nature, rather than a true time-series as in Kaplan, Sensoy, and Strömberg (forthcoming). The benefits obtained by using quasi-time-series data (namely, large sample size and the ability to conduct regression tests of maturity effects in firm characteristics) come at a cost. For example, the sample contains only those venture-backed firms that had not exited when VentureOne conducted its surveys. Since it is well documented that exits—particularly IPOs—do not occur randomly over time but in waves (so-called hot issue/cold issue markets), this

Exhibit 12.14 Founders

Panel A Means of Key Founder Characteristics

Last Round	For the Typical Founder			Number of Founders on Board	Probability Chairman is a Founder	Probability CEO is a Founder
	Percent of Equity Held	Percent of Options Granted	Base Salary ($000s)			
Seed	9.3%	28%	$ 134	0.8	0.05	0.75
1st	7.3	28	156	0.5	0.01	0.66
2nd	6.0	28	150	0.5	<0.01	0.44
3rd	4.6	27	171	0.6	0.01	0.44
4th	5.4	34	190	0.6	<0.01	0.34
≥5th	6.1	30	180	0.5	<0.01	0.35
DSeed	1.5	0.8	−9.6	0.3	0.03	0.06
(t-stat)	(1.3)	(0.2)	(−1.2)	(2.4)*	(3.3)**	(0.6)
Slope	−0.8	0.4	8.2	0.02	−0.00	−0.09
(t-stat)	(−3.8)**	(0.6)	(5.4)**	(1.3)	(−1.3)	(−6.0)
Number of Observations	1,146	1,132	1,282	889	866	866

Panel B Probability of a Founder Being in a Given Functional Area, by Round

Last Round	Leadership[1] (CEO, Pres.)	Bus. Dev. (VP)	Finance (CFO)	Marketing (VP)	Operations (VP, Dir)	Technical (CSO/CTO/VP/Dir)
Seed	0.44	0.04	0.06	0.02	0.10	0.35
1st	0.45	0.05	0.04	0.03	0.07	0.36
2nd	0.38	0.04	0.05	0.03	0.09	0.41
3rd	0.38	0.04	0.03	0.06	0.08	0.41
4th	0.45	0.01	0.02	0.01	0.06	0.44
≥5th	0.41	0.05	0.03	0.03	0.03	0.46

Panel C Probability of a Founder Being in a Given Management Rank, by Round

Last Round	CEO or President	CFO, CIO, CMO, COO, CSO, CTO	VP	Director	Manager
Seed	0.34	0.40	0.15	0.09	0.03
1st	0.38	0.40	0.19	0.03	0.01
2nd	0.34	0.43	0.19	0.03	<0.01
3rd	0.32	0.44	0.20	0.03	<0.01
4th	0.39	0.40	0.16	0.01	0.04
≥5th	0.38	0.33	0.20	0.00	0.00

[1]Denotes the management rank represented by the founders in each functional area.
Note: Operations consists of operations and product development. Technical is engineering, R&D, science, and technology.

may mean that the inferences arrived at in the study are biased because in terms of older firms the database only contains firms that were not successful enough to have exited in the last hot issue market.

Second, there are many important firm attributes that are not covered by this study. These include alliances (Nicholson, Danzon, and McCullough 2005), patent scope (Lerner 1994), international activities, management and employee gender and diversity, profitability and financial health, and entrepreneur experience, to name but a few. It would be worthwhile and enriching to examine such characteristics if and when data become available or could be created by researchers.

CONCLUSION

In this chapter, I have used a large quasi-time-series database to describe and analyze how and why a variety of venture-backed firms' economic characteristics develop as such firms mature through their private, pre-exit stages of life. In doing so, my study makes two contributions to research in entrepreneurship. First, by describing a wide variety of venture-backed firms' business characteristics, I provide a contemporary and detailed depiction of the early life stages of an increasingly important sector of the U.S. economy and add to the contributions of prior work that has looked into the evolution of young technology-centric firms (Houlihan Valuation Advisors 1998; Barron and Burton 1999, 2001; Kaplan, Sensoy, and Strömberg forthcoming). Second, by appealing to Gort and Klepper's theory of the life cycle evolution of a new industry, I have sought to provide a perspective on the maturation of young companies that complements that of other perspectives such as Kaplan, Sensoy, and Strömberg (forthcoming). It seems likely that the diversity, fluidity, and creativity of young companies are too rich to be neatly contained within one and only one theory. This suggests that there remains much to be learned about the maturation dynamics of private firms in general and venture-backed entities in particular.

NOTES

1. The most important force modeled by Gort and Klepper is the probability of entry by a new firm, which is proposed to be a positive function of the number of innovations coming from sources outside the industry, a negative function of the accumulated stock of experience held by incumbent producers, and a positive function of incumbent producers' profit (and thus the potential rewards to a new entrant).
2. Gort and Klepper's theory has been extended by Klepper and Graddy (1990) and Agarwal and Gort (2002), among others.
3. Robinson summarizes the results of a number of studies in entrepreneurship that have examined various measures of the economic performance of new ventures, including some studies that examine one or more performance measures as a function of firm life cycle (1999, 170).
4. Examples include VentureOne, Venture Economics, Sand Hill Econometrics, and Advanced-HR.
5. Other notable examples include Bhide (2000), who conducted interviews with the founders of 100 firms in *Inc. Magazine*'s 1989 list of the 500 fastest-growing companies, and Barron and Hannan (2002) and Barron and Burton (1999, 2001), who examine human resource management, employee turnover, gender mix, and the founder's employment model in approximately 100 Silicon Valley start-ups from 1991 to 1994.
6. The author was granted access to VentureOne's data after signing a nondisclosure agreement. He is most grateful to B. Hughes of VentureOne for his help in this regard.
7. A full listing of the items requested from survey participants is available from the author upon request.

8. The annual response rate of approximately 20 percent compares favorably with other compensation surveys.

9. I developed and estimated a logistic regression model to discriminate between respondents and nonrespondents. Using data available in VentureOne's aggregate financing and valuation database (which did not include compensation data), less than 1 percent of the variance could be explained. The independent variables used were the age of the firm, the date of its most recent round of equity financing, the number of its most recent round of equity financing (e.g., first, second, etc.), the amount raised in that round, the state in which it is headquartered, its life stage (e.g., start-up, product development, beta testing, shipping, profitable, clinical trials, and restart), and the industry sector of the firm. This analysis notwithstanding, in private correspondence VentureOne indicated that it is their belief that it is firms that anticipate seeking further funding from venture capital funds that are most likely to respond to the survey.

10. Funding rounds are sometimes labeled according to Series, where Series A is the first round, Series B is the 2nd round, etc. For simplicity I use the terms *first round*, *second round*, etc.

11. The author is most grateful to D. DiPietro, founder of Advanced-HR, for granting him access to her OptionImpact database.

12. Between October 20, 2004, and October 20, 2005, some 192 firms provided data items to Advanced-HR. These were the firms used by Advanced-HR on October 20, 2005 (the date that the relevant information in the OptionImpact database was viewed by the author), in calculating the means of the firm characteristics used in this study.

13. For example, in the VentureOne dataset the mean equity raised in a seed round was $1.4 million as compared to $7.5 million in a first round.

14. For example, Hellman (2000) and Hellman and Puri (2002) show that in first rounds and beyond, venture fund partners often serve on the firm's board of directors; provide financial sophistication, operating services, and business contacts; help recruit key personnel; and impart financial and strategic discipline.

15. From table 2, the figure of 5.4 years is the difference between the average age of firms whose last financing round was at the ≥5th round (8.5 years) and the average age of firms whose last round was a seed round (3.1 years).

16. These figures are computed crudely as the averages of the percentages shown in Exhibit 12.5 panels A to D across the seed through ≥5th financing rounds.

17. The nature of OptionImpact's figures precludes statistical tests of significance because OptionImpact reports the mean figure by financing round rather than firm-specific information.

18. Bengtsson and Hand (2008) analyze CEO compensation in the early life stages of venture-backed firms by seeking to understand how and why pay is used to align investor/manager incentives.

19. The categorization of policies as formal or informal is by the author, not VentureOne.

20. Denotes where there were too few observations to create reliable statistics (typically two observations or fewer).

21. Of the 19 observations underlying this mean, 11 come from a single firm (their average is $124).

22. Of the 19 observations underlying this mean, 11 come from a single firm (their average is $124).

23. Denotes the management rank represented by the founders in each functional area.

REFERENCES

Agarwal, R., and M. Gort. 2002. Firm and product life cycles and firm survival. *American Economic Association Papers and Proceedings 92*(2):184–190.

Armstrong, C., A. Dávila, and G. Foster. 2006. Venture-backed private equity valuation and financial statement information. *Review of Accounting Studies 11* (1):119–154.

Barron, J. N., and M. T. Hannan. 2002. Organizational blueprints for success in high-tech startups: Lessons from the Stanford Project on Emerging Companies. *California Management Review 44* (3):8–36.

_____, and M. D. Burton. 1999. Building the iron cage: Determinants of managerial intensity in the early years of organizations. *American Sociological Review 64*:4527–547.

_____. 2001. Labor pains: Change in organizational models and employee turnover in young, high-tech firms. *American Journal of Sociology 106* (4):960–1012.

Baum, J., and W. Powell. 1995. Cultivating an institutional ecology of organizations: Comment on Hannan, Carroll, Dundon, and Torres. *American Sociological Review 60* (4):529–538.

Bengtsson, O., and J. R. M. Hand. 2008. CEO compensation in private venture-backed firms. Working paper. Retrieved from http://ssrn.com/abstract=1079993

Bhide, A. 2000. *The origin and evolution of new businesses.* New York: Oxford University Press.

Chemmanur, T., K. Krishnan, and D. Nandy. 2008. How does venture capital financing improve efficiency in private firms? A look beneath the surface. Working paper. Retrieved from http://ssrn.com/abstract=1025322

Dickinson, V. 2007. Cash flow patterns as a proxy for firm life cycle. Working paper. Retrieved from http://ssrn.com/abstract=755804

Gompers, P. A., and J. Lerner. 1999. *The venture capital cycle.* Cambridge: MIT Press.

Gort, M., and S. Klepper. 1982. Time paths in the diffusion of product innovations. *The Economic Journal 92* (367):630–653.

Hand, J. R. M. 2008. Give everyone a prize? Employee stock options in venture-backed companies. *Journal of Business Venturing 23* (4):385–404.

Hart, O. 1995. *Firms, Contracts, and Financial Structure.* Clarendon Press, Oxford.

Hellman, T. F. 2000. Venture capitalists: The coaches of Silicon Valley. In *The Silicon Valley edge: A habitat for innovation and entrepreneurship*, ed. William F. Miller, Marguerite G. Hancock, and Henry S. Rowen. Pages 276–293. Stanford, CA: Stanford University Press.

_____, and M. Puri. 2000. The interaction between product market and financing strategy: The role of venture capital. *Review of Financial Studies 13* (4):959–984.

_____, and M. Puri 2002. Venture capital and the professionalization of start-up firms: Empirical evidence. *Journal of Finance 57* (1):169–198.

Holmström, B. 1999. The firm as a subeconomy. *Journal of Law, Economics and Organization 15* (1):74–102.

Houlihan Valuation Advisors. 1998. The pricing of successful venture capital-backed high-tech and life-science companies. *Journal of Business Venturing 13* (5):333–351.

Jovanovic, B. 1982. Selection and the evolution of industry. *Econometrica 50* (3):649–670.

Kaplan, S., and P. Strömberg. 2003. Financial contracting theory meets the real world: An empirical analysis of venture capital contracts. *Review of Economic Studies 70* (2):81–315.

Kaplan, S., B. Sensoy, and P. Strömberg. Forthcoming. Should investors bet on the jockey or the horse? Evidence from the evolution of firms from early business plans to public companies. *Journal of Finance.*

Klepper, S., and E. Graddy. 1990. The evolution of new industries and the determinants of market structure. *RAND Journal of Economics 21* (1):27–44.

Lerner, J. 1994. The importance of patent scope: An empirical analysis. *Rand Journal of Economics 25* (2):319–333.

National Venture Capital Association (NVCA). 2004. Venture impact 2004: Venture capital benefits to the U.S. economy.

Nicholson, S., P. M. Danzon, and J. McCullough. 2005. Biotech-pharmaceutical alliances as a signal of asset and firm quality. *Journal of Business 78* (4):1433–1464.

Puri, M., and R. Zarutskie. 2008. On the lifecycle dynamics of venture-capital- and non-venture-capital-financed firms. Working paper. Retrieved from http://ssrn.com/abstract=1231698

Rajan, R., and L. Zingales. 2001. The firm as a dedicated hierarchy: A theory of the origins and growth of firms. *Quarterly Journal of Economics 116* (3):805–851.

Robinson, K. C. 1999. An examination of the influence of industry structure on eight alternative measures of new venture performance for high potential independent new ventures. *Journal of Business Venturing 14* (2):165–187.

Spence, M. 1977. Entry, capacity, investment, and oligopolistic pricing. *Bell Journal of Economics 8* (2):534–544.

———. 1979. Investment strategy and growth in a new market. *Bell Journal of Economics 10* (1):1–19.

———. 1981. The learning curve and competition. *Bell Journal of Economics 12* (1):49–70.

Suarez, F., and J. Utterback. 1995. Dominant designs and the survival of firms. *Strategic Management Journal 16* (6):415–430.

Wernerfelt, B. 1984. A resource based view of the firm. *Strategic Management Journal 5* (2):171–180.

Zingales, L. 2000. In search of new foundations. *Journal of Finance 55* (4):1623–1653.

ABOUT THE AUTHOR

John R. M. Hand's research, teaching and consulting interests are in the intersection of finance, accounting and entrepreneurship. His current research focuses on understanding and optimizing accounting-based trading strategies in hedge fund contexts. He was a pioneer in documenting the inefficiency of the stock market with respect to accounting information, winning the 1988 American Accounting Association manuscript competition for his paper "A Test of the Extended Functional Fixation Hypothesis." His research has been published in many of the premier journals, and he twice won the American Accounting Association's competitive manuscript competition for his scholarship. Dr. Hand is co-author with Baruch Lev of New York University of *Intangible Assets: Values, Measures and Risks* (Oxford University Press, 2003). He received the 2008 UNC Kenan-Flagler Weatherspoon Distinguished Award for MBA Teaching. Before he joined UNC Kenan-Flagler, he served on the faculty at Yale University and the University of Chicago. He received his PhD and his MBA (with honors) from the University of Chicago. He earned his B.Sc. at the Bristol University, England, where he graduated first in his class and with highest honors.

CHAPTER 13

How Do Venture Capitalists Create Value for Entrepreneurial Firms? A Review of the Literature

THOMAS J. CHEMMANUR
Professor, Carroll School of Management, Boston College

KARTHIK KRISHNAN
Assistant Professor, Finance and Insurance Department,
College of Business, Northeastern University

DEBARSHI NANDY
Assistant Professor, Finance Area, Schulich School of Business, York University

INTRODUCTION

Venture capital (VC) financing is the predominant source of financing for riskier start-ups. VC financing is a strong driver of economic growth. Some of today's most prominent firms such as Microsoft, Google, Starbucks, Intel, Staples, and FedEx used venture capital financing to grow from fledgling entities to large corporations. A significant amount of practitioner discussion and academic research has focused on the value of venture capital financing. In this paper, we review the role of venture capital financing in adding value to entrepreneurial firms. We focus on value creation by VCs in three areas: First, how do venture capitalists create value in the early stages of a firm's life? We place particular emphasis on the

A portion of the research presented in this chapter was conducted while the authors were Special Sworn Status Researchers at the Boston Research Data Center of the U.S. Census Bureau and the National Bureau of Economic Research. Financial support for this research from the Social Sciences and Humanities Research Council of Canada and the Kauffman Foundation is gratefully acknowledged. The research results and conclusions expressed are those of the authors and do not necessarily indicate concurrence of the U.S. Bureau of Census. This chapter has been screened to ensure that no confidential data is revealed. Any errors and omissions are the responsibility of the authors.

nonpecuniary advantages that venture capitalists provide to entrepreneurial firms (e.g., professionalization of management). Second, how do contracting mechanisms between venture capitalists and entrepreneurs, and other features of venture capital financing, such as staging and syndication, create value? Third, how do venture capitalists create value at the time of exit?

Modern venture capital financing started in 1956, when the first VC firm, called American Research and Development (ARD), was formed.[1] Early VCs were closed end funds due to institutional investor reluctance to invest, but later VCs were structured as limited partnerships. Over time, the growth of venture capital investments has been extremely significant. Exhibit 13.1 reports the yearly distribution of VC investments, both in terms of number of new firms funded and amount of dollars invested in the first round of VC financing. The number of new firms getting VC funding has grown from 105 in 1970 to 2328 in 2007, which corresponds to an annual average compounded growth rate of 9 percent. Further the amount of investments raised has gone from $62.91 million in 1970 to $23,540.06 million in 2007, in nominal terms. In terms of real 1987 dollars, the investment value has gone up from $184 to $12,897 million, an average compounded yearly increase of 12 percent per year.[2] The patterns in Exhibit 13.1 also reflect how macroeconomic conditions are associated with VC investments over this time period. We see a spike of VC investments from 1998 to 2000, which corresponds to the Internet bubble period. After that, VC investments dropped significantly and started to increase at a more tempered pace.

Exhibit 13.2 reports the industry group distribution of VC investments. Consistent with expectations, a majority of VC investments go to the high tech, telecom, computer, biotechnology, and life science industries. At the same time however, VCs do not completely ignore non high-tech firms. In fact, VC investments in non high-tech firms have produced such prominent corporations as Federal Express, Starbucks, and Staples. Exhibit 13.3 shows the geographic locations of venture capital investments. Not surprisingly, a significant number of investments are made in California (21 percent) and Massachusetts (6.3 percent). About 29 percent of venture capital investments are made outside of North America, although North American VC investments account for the bulk of dollar investments (about 65 percent).

The remainder of this chapter is organized as follows. The next section reviews the literature and shows some new results on how venture capitalists add value in the early stages of the firms that they invest in. After that comes a discussion of how contracting between VCs and entrepreneurial firms, staging, and syndication add value. The following section discusses how venture capitalists add value to entrepreneurial firms at the time of exit. The Conclusion wraps up the whole discussion.

THE EXTRA-FINANCIAL FUNCTIONS OF VENTURE CAPITALISTS: SCREENING AND MONITORING

We start with the question of what exactly venture capitalists do other than providing financing that makes them different from other financial intermediaries. Anecdotal evidence suggests that venture capitalists provide significant

Exhibit 13.1   Time Trends in VC Financing (First Rounds Only)

Year	Number of Companies	Percent of Companies	Dollar Investment	Percent of Investment
1970	105	0.25	62.91	0.02
1971	101	0.24	89.89	0.03
1972	107	0.26	87.53	0.03
1973	151	0.36	138.61	0.05
1974	67	0.16	50.96	0.02
1975	68	0.16	47.31	0.02
1976	82	0.2	61.99	0.02
1977	112	0.27	105.83	0.04
1978	211	0.5	218.9	0.08
1979	235	0.56	330.2	0.12
1980	321	0.77	427.17	0.16
1981	544	1.3	828.74	0.31
1982	638	1.52	775.48	0.29
1983	742	1.77	1313.63	0.49
1984	656	1.57	1239.76	0.46
1985	548	1.31	1276.9	0.47
1986	648	1.55	1674.25	0.62
1987	719	1.72	1828.07	0.68
1988	750	1.79	2658.01	0.99
1989	628	1.5	2798.08	1.04
1990	454	1.09	1344.83	0.5
1991	349	0.83	970.56	0.36
1992	511	1.22	2827.95	1.05
1993	449	1.07	2786.78	1.03
1994	573	1.37	3266.77	1.21
1995	1123	2.68	5704.86	2.12
1996	1735	4.15	7423.78	2.75
1997	1850	4.42	8176.42	3.03
1998	2161	5.16	13392.73	4.97
1999	3651	8.73	29967.12	11.12
2000	6505	15.55	53200.31	19.74
2001	2909	6.95	20376.56	7.56
2002	1690	4.04	13464.97	5
2003	1666	3.98	15358.64	5.7
2004	1749	4.18	16078.65	5.97
2005	2172	5.19	15876.03	5.89
2006	2534	6.06	19698.09	7.31
2007	2328	5.56	23540.06	8.74

Source: Thomson Venture-Xpert.

support systems for the firms that they back. Practitioners argue that in addition to providing funding to private firms, venture capitalists contribute greatly to their success in many other ways. For example, VCs can add value by helping firms hire competent management, provide better incentives to management and employees, as well as allow them access to their network of contacts among suppliers and potential customers.[3] Such "monitoring" activities allow VCs to improve the

Exhibit 13.2   Industry Distribution in VC Financing

Industry Major Group	Number of Companies	Percent of Companies	Dollar Investment	Percent of Investment
Non–High-Technology	12674	30.29	108752.6	40.36
Computer Related	14427	34.48	69182.87	25.67
Communications and Media	5842	13.96	43310.35	16.07
Medical/Health/Life Science	3823	9.14	19930.82	7.4
Semiconductors/Other Electricals	2950	7.05	18710.64	6.94
Biotechnology	2126	5.08	9582.12	3.56

Source: Thomson Venture-Xpert.

value of the firms they back. Additionally, VCs also screen and pick out the better quality firms to invest in.

Various papers attempt to distinguish between these two effects (monitoring and screening). Sorensen (2007) uses an econometric approach with a structural matching model to account for the self-selection of firms into VCs with a certain level of experience. Sorenson finds evidence to support sorting (i.e., matching by firms into VCs of a certain level of experience) and influence (i.e., the ability of VCs to monitor the firms that they finance). Other studies use private (pre-IPO) data on venture-backed firms from various sources to test the role that VCs play in the firms that they back. Hellman and Puri (2000) analyze a sample of venture-backed firms and find that venture capitalists help firms bring products to the market faster. Hellman and Puri (2002) find that VCs help professionalize management, and provide incentive-based contracts to the firms they finance. Puri and Zarutskie (2008) use the Longitudinal Business Database (LBD) from the U.S. Census Bureau to analyze the life cycle dynamics and the eventual outcomes (successes and failures) of both VC and non–VC-financed firms. They find that VC backing is a function of market conditions and individual firm characteristics. More VC financing is observed in sectors that have higher IPO activity and Tobin's Q. Further, VC backing is more likely for firms that have no commercial revenue. They also find the VC-backed firms tend to be larger than non–VC-backed firms, based on employment and sales.

An interesting finding of Puri and Zarutskie (2008) is that VCs are "patient" at least in the first five years after investing in a firm. They find that the probability of a VC-financed firm failing is much lower than a non–VC-financed firm, but the probability of a VC-financed firm failing is actually higher than for non–VC-financed firms, conditional on their having survived for more than five years. They interpret their results as the VCs allowing some time for their portfolio companies to grow.

Chemmanur, Krishnan, and Nandy (2008) use the Longitudinal Research Database (LRD) from the U.S. Census Bureau data to analyze and compare the operating efficiency and productivity of VC-backed as well as non–VC-backed firms.[4] In addition, they also study the productivity or operating efficiency increases in VC-backed firms both before and after VC financing, thus providing direct evidence of the impact of screening and monitoring on the operating

Exhibit 13.3   Geographic Locations of Companies That Get VC Financing

Company Location	Number of Companies	Percent of Companies	Dollar Investment	Percent of Investment
Non-U.S.	12080	28.87	91923.54	34.11
California	8778	20.98	47374.28	17.58
Massachusetts	2637	6.3	11930.05	4.43
Texas	1770	4.23	12300.9	4.56
New York	1680	4.02	12284.15	4.56
Pennsylvania	988	2.36	5780.02	2.14
New Jersey	798	1.91	5970.45	2.22
Colorado	787	1.88	4156.13	1.54
Washington	748	1.79	4114.51	1.53
Illinois	742	1.77	5063.13	1.88
Georgia	730	1.74	4422.99	1.64
Virginia	687	1.64	4408.34	1.64
Florida	678	1.62	5115.5	1.9
Maryland	625	1.49	4072.01	1.51
Minnesota	557	1.33	2020.25	0.75
Connecticut	512	1.22	3113.07	1.16
North Carolina	502	1.2	3659.85	1.36
Ohio	455	1.09	2832.37	1.05
Ontario (Canada)	369	0.88	2154.28	0.8
Oregon	281	0.67	1160.27	0.43
Michigan	274	0.65	1615.49	0.6
Tennessee	274	0.65	2459.64	0.91
Quebec (Canada)	210	0.5	1055.65	0.39
Arizona	236	0.56	1540.04	0.57
Utah	230	0.55	1248.52	0.46
Missouri	190	0.45	1410.87	0.52
New Hampshire	166	0.4	960.49	0.36
Wisconsin	169	0.4	597.32	0.22
Indiana	164	0.39	790.45	0.29
Alabama	124	0.3	513.46	0.19
British Columbia (Canada)	115	0.27	1126.19	0.42
Washington, D.C.	107	0.26	860.67	0.32
Louisiana	100	0.24	685.01	0.25
Kentucky	98	0.23	559.2	0.21
Kansas	94	0.22	923.37	0.34
Iowa	80	0.19	365.67	0.14
Oklahoma	76	0.18	613.46	0.23
Rhode Island	76	0.18	293.44	0.11
South Carolina	75	0.18	505.85	0.19
New Mexico	69	0.16	202.11	0.08
Maine	61	0.15	209.02	0.08
Alberta (Canada)	55	0.13	504.47	0.19
Nevada	55	0.13	2911.32	1.08
Mississippi	45	0.11	166.46	0.06

(Continued)

Exhibit 13.3　*(Continued)*

Company Location	Number of Companies	Percent of Companies	Dollar Investment	Percent of Investment
Nebraska	40	0.1	464.11	0.17
Puerto Rico	38	0.09	118.49	0.04
Vermont	36	0.09	176.88	0.07
Hawaii	29	0.07	146.67	0.05
Arkansas	26	0.06	73.33	0.03
Idaho	26	0.06	561.59	0.21
Delaware	24	0.06	106.92	0.04
West Virginia	24	0.06	71.25	0.03
Montana	18	0.04	68.95	0.03
New Brunswick (Canada)	12	0.03	65.96	0.02
South Dakota	12	0.03	157.12	0.06
Saskatchewan (Canada)	10	0.02	34.74	0.01
North Dakota	9	0.02	29.77	0.01
Nova Scotia (Canada)	9	0.02	26.44	0.01
Manitoba (Canada)	6	0.01	25.4	0.01
Wyoming	6	0.01	14.82	0.01
Alaska	5	0.01	22.96	0.01
Newfoundland (Canada)	3	0.01	2.88	0
Prince Edward Island (Canada)	1	0	0.51	0

Source: Thomson Venture-Xpert.

efficiency of VC-backed firms.[5,6] This data allows them to analyze features of VC-backed firms at the time that they get VC financing. Unlike Puri and Zarutskie (2008), their paper analyzes the productivity of VC-backed firms before they are selected to obtain VC financing as well as changes in productivity subsequent to obtaining VC financing. The fundamental research questions analyzed in Chemmanur, Krishnan, and Nandy are (1) do VCs screen the firms that they back, or (2) do they improve their productivity by "monitoring" (or both?), and (3) if VCs do improve the productivity of the firms that they back, what are the channels by which they achieve such improvements (i.e., increase in sales or reductions in costs)?

Using data from LRD, we provide summary statistics on venture capital–backed firms and non–venture-backed firms in the U.S. manufacturing sector in Exhibit 13.4. Exhibit 13.4 reports means and quasi-medians for venture-backed firm-years and non–venture-backed firm-years.[7] Chemmanur, Krishnan, and Nandy (2008) find that venture–backed firms are larger (based on total sales) than non–venture-backed firms. Venture-backed firms have higher capital intensity, that is, capital per worker. Salaries and wages are higher at venture-backed firms than at non–venture-backed firms. The exhibit also reports that venture-backed firms have

Exhibit 13.4 Summary Data on Characteristics of Venture- and Non-Venture-Backed Firms

	Venture Backed Firms	Non–Venture-Backed Firms	Difference	p-value
Total revenues				
Mean	1035037.90	23662.78	1011375.10	0.00
Quasi-Median	65306.19	3554.35	61751.84	0.00
Observations	16824	771830		
Capital intensity (capital per worker)				
Mean	49.27	27.78	21.49	0.00
Quasi-Median	30.51	12.91	17.60	0.00
Observations	16676	756230		
Average salary and wages				
Mean	31.68	24.86	6.83	0.00
Quasi-Median	30.83	23.46	7.36	0.00
Observations	16676	756230		
Average skill level				
Mean	0.40	0.05	0.34	0.08
Quasi-Median	0.35	0.23	0.12	0.00
Observations	16676	756230		
Herfindahl Index				
Mean	0.12	0.08	0.03	0.00
Quasi-Median	0.08	0.06	0.03	0.00
Observations	16823	771798		

Source: Longitudinal Research Database (LRD).

higher skill levels. Skill levels are defined as the ratio of white collar worker wages to blue collar wages. This finding is consistent with the notion that venture financing typically goes to skilled entrepreneurs and in industries where human skill is important (e.g., high-tech, biotechnology, electronics, etc.). Consistent with this interpretation, Chemmanur, Krishnan, and Nandy (2008) find that venture-backed firms are more likely to be in the high-tech industry sector (firm's three-digit Standard Industrial Classification, SIC, code is 357, 366, 367, 372, 381, 382, or 384) than non–venture-backed firms. Finally, Exhibit 13.4 also reports that venture-backed firms have a higher Herfindahl index (three digit SIC). That is, venture-backed firms operate in more concentrated industries. This could be because many of the industries that VCs provide funding to are relatively new and not many players exist in these fields.

Chemmanur, Krishnan, and Nandy (2008) find evidence to suggest the existence of both a screening and a monitoring effect. In particular, VC-backed firms have higher productivity before VC financing, and this productivity increases after the VC financing. They also analyze the heterogeneity in VC-backed firms and find that while high reputation VC-backed firms have somewhat lower productivity prior to receiving financing, their productivity improvements are much higher than for low reputation VC-backed firms.

Exhibit 13.5 reports the mean productivity (calculated as TFP or total factor productivity) for non–VC-backed firms and high and low reputation VC-backed firms both before and after receiving financing (Chemmanur, Krishnan, and Nandy 2008). VC reputation is measured by the ratio of money raised by the funds of a VC firm in the past five years over the total amount of venture capital raised during the same time period. VC firms having a ratio greater than the sample median are classified as high reputation VCs. The pre–VC financing TFP is the average TFP over the years prior to VC financing and the post-VC financing TFP is the average TFP of a firm over the years after the firm receives VC financing. Chemmanur, Krishnan, and Nandy (2008) find that average TFP of non–VC-backed firms is lower than that for VC-backed firms. Further, the TFP increases after VC financing for VC-backed firms, and this increase in TFP is higher for higher reputation VC-backed firms than for lower reputation VC-backed firms. The pre–VC financing TFP is higher for VC-backed firms than for non–VC-backed firms, and is somewhat higher for higher reputation VC-backed firms than for lower reputation VC-backed firms. Thus, the overall univariate analysis does suggest that venture capitalists actively screen for better quality firms and improve the quality of the firms that they back. In addition, Chemmanur, Krishnan, and Nandy (2008) find that these productivity increases occur within the first two rounds of financing after which the productivity levels are stable.

The latter results hold in Chemmanur, Krishnan, and Nandy (2008) even after controlling for a matching group of firms. Specifically, they select a matching group of non–VC-backed firms to test whether VC-backed firms indeed have higher pre–VC financing TFP than the matched set of non–VC-backed firms having similar future TFP growth and size and belonging to the same industry. Similarly, they also select a group of matching firms that are in the same industry and have similar size and pre–VC financing TFP and test whether VC-backed firms indeed have higher TFP growth relative to the matched non–VC-backed firms.

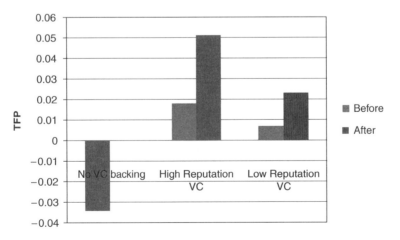

Exhibit 13.5   Mean TFP Levels for VC and Non–VC-Backed Firms

Exhibit 13.6 shows the mean and median TFP prior to VC financing after adjusting for the TFP of the matched sample. As can be seen, VC-backed firms have higher overall pre–VC financing TFP than the control sample. Further, the matched sample adjusted pre–VC financing TFP is similar at the mean for high and low reputation VCs but higher at the median for low reputation VCs than for high reputation VCs. Thus, the evidence suggests that low reputation VCs depend significantly on screening or selecting better firms. In addition, the evidence obtained for screening ability of low reputation VCs relative to high reputation VCs in the uncontrolled univariate analysis flips when we control for TFP growth, size, and industry. Overall, the evidence suggests that VCs may indeed engage in active screening of better firms.

Exhibit 13.7 shows the mean and median TFP growth after VC financing for sample firms in Chemmanur, Krishnan, and Nandy (2008) adjusted by the TFP growth of the matched control group of non–VC-backed firms. Consistent with monitoring, VC-backed firms have a higher overall growth in TFP after VC financing relative to the matched control sample. In addition, Chemmanur, Krishnan, and Nandy (2008) find that higher reputation VC-backed firms experience significantly higher growth in their TFP after VC financing than lower reputation VC-backed firms. Thus, the results suggest that VCs engage in monitoring activities of the firms they back, and higher reputation VCs are better at such monitoring activities. These results are consistent with the evidence of Hsu (2004) that a financing offer from a higher reputation VC is approximately three times more likely to be accepted by an entrepreneur and also that higher reputation VCs get better deal terms (i.e., lower valuations) when negotiating with start-ups. Thus, the empirical evidence in Chemmanur, Krishnan, and Nandy (2008) suggests the existence of monitoring by VCs as well.

Chemmanur, Krishnan, and Nandy (2008) also analyze the channels through which VCs obtain improvements in productivity. They find that VC-backed firms have increases in sales and costs after VC financing. Thus, the net effect of higher

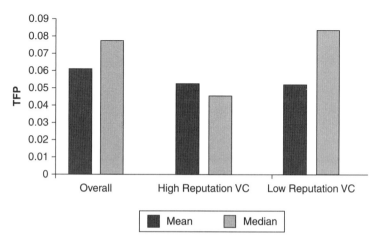

Exhibit 13.6 Productivity (TFP) of VC-Backed Firms prior to VC Financing (Match Sample Adjusted)

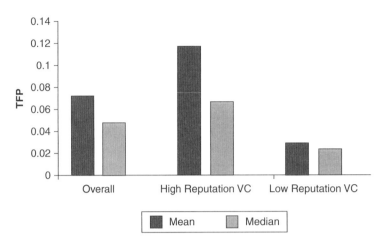

Exhibit 13.7 Productivity (TFP) Growth of VC-Backed Firms after VC Financing (Match Sample Adjusted)

productivity in VC-backed firms is due to VCs helping the firms to increase their sales at a higher rate than their costs. Interestingly, high reputation VC-backed firms have higher sales and lower growth in costs than low reputation VC-backed firms. They also find that both screening and monitoring have significant impact on the probability of exits through IPOs and mergers and acquisitions (M&A), particularly for high reputation VC-backed firms.

The evidence discussed above is also consistent with the literature analyzing how venture capital affects innovation. Kortum and Lerner (2000) find that the presence of venture capital has a significant impact on patenting activity. In particular, they find that a dollar of venture capital is three times more effective at stimulating patents than a dollar of traditional R&D by corporations. Further, patents backed by VCs are cited more frequently and more aggressively litigated, suggesting that these are higher quality patents.

VENTURE CAPITAL CONTRACTING, STAGE FINANCING, AND SYNDICATION

Contracts between venture capitalists (VCs) and portfolio companies contain explicit and implicit allocation of cash flow and control rights.[8] Such contracts are necessary since companies that get VC financing typically face significant information asymmetry and moral hazard problems. This section is divided into three parts. First, we discuss the literature on contracting between venture capitalists and portfolio companies. Further, VCs themselves are agents of their providers of capital (limited partners). Moral hazard and information asymmetry issues also may exist between limited partners (LPs) and the venture capitalists. The second section therefore discusses the literature on contracting between LPs and VCs. Finally, we discuss how VCs can obtain additional information and monitoring of their portfolio companies by syndicating with other VCs.

Value Addition through Contracting Between VCs and Portfolio Companies

Below we first discuss the literature on contracting and on setting of the contractual terms related to control and cash flow rights between venture capitalists and their portfolio companies.

Contractual Terms Related to Control and Cash Flow Rights

Kaplan and Stromberg (2003, 2004) provide evidence from private data on VC investments. Their empirical evidence is consistent with theoretical works on principal-agent models by Holmstrom (1979), Aghion and Bolton (1992), Dewatripont and Tirole (1994), etc., as well as hold-up problems related to such contracts, by (Hart and Moore 1994 and Neher 1999).[9]

Kaplan and Stromberg (2003) find that VC contracts are designed such that control, liquidation, and cash flow rights can be distributed independently. This can be achieved through various mechanisms such as nonvesting stock options (with no voting rights), unvested stocks, explicit contracting on voting rights, securities with different voting and director election rights, and explicit agreements on director election. Typical VC contracts make cash flow and control rights contingent on milestones. The milestones defining contingencies can vary and may be pecuniary (such as obtaining a certain level of ROA or earnings) or nonpecuniary (such as hiring a new CEO, providing certain level of dividends, obtaining patents, or obtaining FDA approval). This is consistent with the "informativeness" principal of Holmstrom (1979) that the principal should make payments contingent on as many contractible signals as possible as long as those signals are correlated with the agent's actual (and hidden) effort level.

Kaplan and Stromberg (2003) also find that control and voting rights are tied to the level of uncertainty about the entrepreneur and firm prospects. They use repeat entrepreneurship, firms without prior revenue, and the length of interaction between the entrepreneur and the VC as proxies for uncertainty and potential conflict of interest. They argue that this result supports the implications of Aghion and Bolton (1992). The latter propose a theoretical model where the investor only obtains financial benefits from the project and the (wealth constrained) entrepreneur gets both financial and nonpecuniary (private) benefits from the project (such as the ability to run a firm or the ability to hire a relative even if not qualified). Thus, the entrepreneur has to trade off giving control rights to the investor (and potentially lose his private benefits) with giving the investor his minimum required return if the former keeps control rights. When there is a higher likelihood of such a conflict of interest, entrepreneurs can make suboptimal decisions. Thus, it is better to give the investor control in such situations. On the other hand, when conflicts of interest are smaller, it is more efficient to give control rights to the entrepreneur. Lower conflict of interest reflected by lower uncertainty about the firm reduces the potential for opportunistic behavior on the part of the entrepreneur, making it more efficient to give control rights to the entrepreneur. Hart (2001) also provides a nice intuition for this result. He argues that firms where the risk is low should allocate more control and residual cash flow rights to the entrepreneur. In low risk firms, the entrepreneur can pay a fixed compensation to the investor (that gives the investor his minimum required return) and then maximize the social optimum since he gets residual cash flow rights and private benefits. The theoretical model by Hellman (1998) is also consistent with the latter result. Repeat entrepreneurship and the time of interaction between the VC and the entrepreneur can also reflect the VCs perception of the entrepreneur's quality. Hellman (1998) shows theoretically that the investor should get more control rights when the entrepreneur is less productive, since it may be more efficient to replace the entrepreneur with a more productive outside manager.

The empirical work of Kaplan and Stromberg (2003) also finds that the entrepreneur's incentive compensation (i.e., cash flow rights) becomes more high-powered with entrepreneur inexperience, moral hazard, and information asymmetry. Traditional principal agent theory trades off giving incentives based on uncertain output to the agent with the cost of the incentives arising from the risk aversion of the agent. This suggests that uncertainty may increase costs of providing such incentives, thus lowering the power of incentives compensation in more uncertain environments. Prendergast (1999) suggests that higher quality agents may prefer higher powered incentives in more uncertain environments (Lazear 1986). The empirical evidence on cash flow rights allocation in Kaplan and Stromberg (2003) is consistent with this latter argument.

Empirical evidence from Kaplan and Stromberg (2003) suggests that cash flow and control rights move towards the VC and away from the entrepreneur as firm performance gets poorer. This is also consistent with the model of Aghion and Bolton (1992), since poorer performance makes it harder to satisfy the investor's participation constraint, thus allocating more control rights to the VC in such cases. Hart (2001) suggests that while this result is consistent with Aghion and Bolton (1992), it need not necessarily follow from it. He suggests that VCs may also be better monitors when the firm performs well, and therefore control may also move to investors in such good states. For instance, while an entrepreneur can be creative and can add significant value to a start-up firm, he may not be well suited to managing a more mature firm (e.g., the replacement of Larry Page and Sergey Brin by Eric Schmidt as CEO of Google). Hart suggests that one reason why this argument may not hold is that the entrepreneur's incentives to exert effort may be diluted if he knows that he will be replaced even if the firm performs well.[10]

In addition, VC contracts typically include explicit redemption rights as well as vesting and noncompete clauses. The vesting and noncompete clauses can be reflective of the human capital that is crucial for the success of the firm. Models such as Hart and Moore (1994) and Neher (1999) suggest that human capital of the entrepreneur is inalienable, that is, inseparable from the entrepreneur. This can lead to future opportunistic rent seeking behavior on the part of the entrepreneur. Vesting and noncompete clauses protect VCs against such rent seeking behavior. Moreover, stocks not vested prior to the entrepreneur leaving the firm are often forfeited, further increasing the cost of opportunistic behavior by the entrepreneur.

Kaplan and Stromberg (2004) analyze how various risks faced by the VC shape the contract between him and the entrepreneur. Importantly, they connect the stated concerns of venture capitalists (which they classify into various categories of risk) to the contractual provisions they demand. They find that internal risks—such as moral hazard, information asymmetry, and the likelihood of future conflicts—are likely to lead to VCs demanding more control rights, higher levels of contingent compensation to the entrepreneur based on milestones, and more contingent financing in a given round (intraround staging).

External risks—risks that are equally uncertain to the VC and the entrepreneur—are associated with more contingent compensation for the entrepreneur, more VC control, stronger liquidation rights for the VC, and tighter staging (i.e., shorter duration between rounds). Examples of such risks include macroeconomic environment, new regulations, and so on. This is in contrast to the trade-off between risk and incentive compensation from the traditional principal-agent model (e.g., Holmstrom 1979). However, the latter results are consistent with the idea of Prendergast (1999) that higher uncertainty makes monitoring more difficult and higher pay-performance sensitivity is required.

Mixed risks—risks that are equally uncertain to the VC and the entrepreneur, but are partly under the entrepreneur's control, such as execution risk—are associated with more contingent compensation to the entrepreneur, higher VC control rights, and longer time vesting provisions. The prevalence of vesting provisions is consistent with hold-up theories (e.g., Hart and Moore 1994). Since the entrepreneur's skills are important in reducing such risks, it is important to reduce opportunistic rent-seeking behavior by the entrepreneur.

In addition, Kaplan and Stromberg (2004) are also able to analyze VCs' analysis of their investments and the actions they expect to take after investment. They find that VCs expect to intervene when they have control rights in the firm. An example of such intervention is the replacement of the management, possibly in conflict with the entrepreneur. VCs expect to provide support services, such as strategic advice or customer introductions when they have higher equity stakes (cash flow rights), but not necessarily more control rights. This result is reflective of a two-sided moral hazard problem (e.g., Casamatta 2003), where VCs also have to exert effort to improve firm value.

Chemmanur and Chen (2008) propose a theoretical model that analyzes the dynamics of the contracting between venture capitalists and entrepreneurial firms. In their model, an entrepreneur has more information than a potential financier about his firm. However, this information advantage diminishes as the financier interacts with the firm over time. Venture capitalists can add value by exerting effort, which together with the entrepreneur's effort, increases the chance of project success. The equilibrium VC contract maximizes value addition by ensuring that both the entrepreneur and the VC exert optimal effort. They show that, first, the optimal VC financing contract will resemble convertible debt. Second, for firms that use venture financing in earlier as well as later rounds, earlier-round financing contracts will have more of a fixed income component and more of a warrant ("upside") component compared to later-round financing contracts. Third, later-round financing contracts between an entrepreneur and a VC who financed it in an earlier round will have a greater warrant component compared to such a contract between a VC and a firm that was previously financed from non-VC private financing sources such as angels. The dynamic features of the contracting between venture capitalists and entrepreneurs, is consistent with the evidence in Kaplan and Stromberg (2003).

Use of Convertible Securities

Kaplan and Stromberg (2003), document that convertible securities are the predominant form of financing in venture capital financing. They find that 79.8 percent of VC financing rounds in their sample used convertible stocks (see also Sahlman

1997). In addition, they find that 38.5 percent of the rounds in their sample had participating convertible preferreds. A participating convertible preferred can be thought of as a combination of straight preferred stock and common stock. On liquidation or exit, holders of this security get back both the principal of the preferred as well as common stock as per the terms of conversion. Kaplan and Stromberg (2003) also document that VCs also use equity, straight preferreds, and a combination of securities.

There are multiple theories that explain the prevalence on convertible preferred stocks in VC financing.[11] Schmidt (2003) argues that convertibles can solve a two-sided moral hazard problem where the VC will only exert effort if he can exercise his conversion rights, and he will convert only if the entrepreneur exerts sufficient effort. He shows that convertibles are important where the investor's relationship-specific effort has sufficient value. Schmidt suggests that this can explain why convertibles are so popular in VC investments and not in more passive investments like bank loans. Cornelli and Yosha (1997) propose a theory where convertibles can mitigate the incentives of the entrepreneur to engage in window dressing to prevent the VC from liquidating the firm in the short run (by not funding in the next round or redeeming the current investment), since benefits from higher profits are more likely to go to the investor if the latter exercises his conversion option.

Hellman (2006) proposes another model of why convertibles may be optimal in VC financing. In his model, both the VC and the entrepreneur have to exert effort to make the firm successful. The trade-off then lies in keeping the entrepreneur's incentives while giving enough return to the investor. Importantly, the allocation of cash flow rights depends on the decision to exit through an IPO or an acquisition. The optimal contract in this model, implemented by a convertible security, allocates higher cash flows to the entrepreneur in case of an IPO and to the VC investor in the case of an acquisition. When VC investments are large, the venture capitalist requires higher compensation to participate, but such higher compensation can undermine the entrepreneur's incentives. Contingent cash flow rights, as described above turn, out to be optimal. The theory also squares well with the observation that convertible securities of VCs typically automatically convert to equity at the time of IPO.

An interesting outcome of the above model is that using convertible securities to allocate cash flow rights creates a new problem in terms of allocation of control rights: the VC will prefer to have an acquisition even when an IPO is more efficient (i.e., high states), and the entrepreneur will prefer to have an IPO even when an acquisition is more efficient.[12] Hellman (2006) suggests contingent control rights of the type described in Kaplan and Stromberg (2003) as a remedy. Importantly, he argues that contingent control rights emerge as a means to fix the inefficient exit problem caused by convertible securities, not because convertibles allocate contingent control rights. Typical convertibles in VC financing have voting rights on an "as-if-converted" basis.

Value Addition through Stage Financing

Typically, VC investments are provided in multiple rounds of investments. This allows VCs to monitor their investments at regular intervals and reduce moral hazard problems. VCs can also disburse funds already committed to a firm within a round over time, thus providing additional staged monitoring.

Gompers (1995) empirically analyzes staging in venture capital–backed firms. He motivates staging as a way of periodic monitoring of venture capital investments. VCs gather additional information about the portfolio company at each stage of investment. Consistent with this hypothesis, he finds that venture-backed firms that go public obtain venture capital finance over more rounds. He also argues that staging is affected by the uncertainty and the potential for opportunistic behavior on part of the entrepreneur. Consistently, his results indicate that early stage portfolio companies receive less funding per round. Further, as asset tangibility of the firm increases, the duration between rounds increase. Firms with more tangible assets require less monitoring since VCs can recover a larger fraction of their investment from liquidating the company's assets, thus lowering potential agency costs and the need for VC financing. Neher (1999) argues that this result is also consistent with the argument that asset tangibility reduces the importance of the inalienable human capital of the entrepreneur (e.g., Hart and Moore 1994), thus reducing potential hold-up problems that may require staging.

Gompers (1995) finds that VC funding duration decreases with R&D expenses of the firm. Higher R&D expenses can increase asset specificity and the potential for personal benefit–maximizing behavior by the entrepreneur. For instance, an academic entrepreneur may have the incentive to continue research that may not have any commercial potential, but has strong publication prospects and may bring him academic accolades. Gompers (1995) also finds that higher growth options (proxied by market to book ratio) lead to more frequent financing. Entrepreneurs have a higher ability to engage in personal benefit–maximizing behavior in industries where firm value depends largely on future growth opportunities. Since entrepreneurs are junior claimants (making them levered equity owners), they have the incentive to indulge in behavior such as underinvestment that can reduce firm value (Myers 1977). In addition, Kaplan and Stromberg (2003) find that entrepreneurs with previously successful ventures are likely to receive fewer rounds. A successful track record can reduce information asymmetry about the entrepreneur and thus requires less monitoring.

Thus, staging is an effective monitoring tool for venture capitalists. Staging can allow VCs to monitor the progress of a venture and stop investment if the firm has not progressed satisfactorily. It also provides a tool for VCs to protect themselves from opportunistic behavior on the part of the entrepreneur and as an incentive to work harder. Cornelli and Yosha (1997) suggest that staging might lead to window-dressing incentives for entrepreneurs. Yet, staging is a very commonly observed financing mode in venture capital, suggesting that any such negative effects may be outweighed by the benefits of staging.

Value Addition through VC Syndication

Similar to bank loans and securities underwriting, typical venture capital financings are syndicated between various VCs. The venture capital literature has examined multiple hypotheses regarding the reasons behind such syndications. Lerner (1994) examines a sample of biotechnology firms to explore why venture capitalists form syndicates. He finds support for three main hypotheses related to syndication.

First, the syndication of investments provides venture capitalists additional signals to verify their assessment of the portfolio company's prospects. Consistent with this hypothesis, Lerner (1994) finds that more experienced VCs syndicate with other experienced VCs for the first round. Since the signal of more experienced VCs are more reliable, such VCs can provide more valuable information in first round syndications. Casamatta and Haritchabalet (2007) propose a theoretical model consistent with this hypothesis. In their model, when a VC consults with another VC about a potential investment, it reveals proprietary information that can lead to competition for the investment opportunity. VCs thus form syndicates and share their returns to avoid such competition. Cestone, White, and Lerner (2006) also create a theory consistent with the "combination of signals" hypothesis. In their model, cash flow rights from the investment are appropriately allocated to VCs to induce them to expend effort to gather their signal and to get truthful reporting of the signal. Consistent with the empirical findings of Lerner (1994), their model predicts that more experienced VCs should syndicate with more experienced VCs.

Second, Lerner (1994) argues that VCs may use their private information about the quality of the portfolio company to sell overpriced securities in later rounds to other VCs. Since the original VC has to bear the cost of incentive problem (markets rationally price such incentives), he has to keep his ownership level in the firm constant. Consistent with this hypothesis, Lerner (1994) finds that VC investment in later rounds is such that the ownership level of the earlier VC stays constant. In addition, both more and less experienced VCs invest in later rounds. Since the signal of additional VCs is less important in later rounds, less experienced VCs are more likely to invest in later rounds.

Finally, VCs would like to show to prospective LPs that they invest in well-performing portfolio companies. VCs may therefore prefer to invest in companies that have performed well. Further, more experienced VCs can more easily get access to such investments if they can return the favor to early VCs in well performing companies by giving them access to their own good performers. Consistent with this hypothesis, Lerner (1994) finds that more experienced VCs typically invest in well performing companies in later rounds.

A different aspect of syndication, namely improvement in monitoring when multiple venture capitalists invest in a firm, is suggested by Brander, Amit, and Antweiler (2002). They argue that VCs form syndicates to complement management skills. For instance, some VCs may have experience in managing customer relationships, while others may have expertise in manufacturing processes, and yet others may be good at monitoring the management of the portfolio company. They use data from Canadian firms and find that syndicated VC investments have higher returns, which they interpret as supporting their "improved-monitoring" hypothesis.

VALUE ADDITION AT THE TIME OF EXIT

VCs typically expect to exit their investments after a fixed time period. Thus, the exit outcome is an important part of their investment decision. Bayar and Chemmanur (2008) provide a theoretical model of the exit choice of venture capitalist. The fundamental trade-off for a firm in their model is between going public and taking its chances against competitors in their product market and getting acquired and benefiting from the synergies obtained from a stronger market player in their segment. The downside of getting acquired is that the acquirer may have higher bargaining power in terms of the price she will pay the entrepreneur relative to the market. Their model also has additional factors affecting the equilibrium, including the entrepreneur's preference for maintaining control for the private benefits, and the VCs' preference for exiting quickly after their investments mature as compared to the entrepreneur who may be more concerned about long-term value.

Bayar and Chemmanur's (2008) model has many predictions regarding the exit decision of venture-backed firms. They predict that later-stage firms with mature business lines are more likely to go public rather than get acquired. Second, industries having more private benefits of control are more likely to see IPO exits of entrepreneurial firms than acquisitions. Third, industries that have a dominant market player are more likely to have acquisition of entrepreneurial firms, since the synergies from acquisitions in such industries are likely to be high. In addition, going up against a larger and well established competitor may be a much less successful strategy, thus increasing the probability of getting bought out. Fourth, higher IPO market valuation of the firm is likely to increase the probability that the firm would go public. Fifth, average IPO valuations are likely to be higher than acquisition valuations because both high and low quality can go public in their model, while only low quality firms get acquired. In addition, their model predicts that firms will get bought out at lower valuations than they could have obtained in the IPO markets because they realize that they may not survive product market competition.

Brau, Francis, and Kohers (2003) empirically investigate macroeconomic factors that drive the decision of a firm to go public or to get acquired. Consistent with the theory of Bayar and Chemmanur (2008), they find that larger firms are more likely to choose IPOs. In addition, the level of postdeal insider ownership tends to be higher for IPOs than for acquisitions. This suggests that insiders wanting to maintain a larger level of control will choose IPOs over acquisitions. They find that the degree of concentration of a private firm's industry, high tech industry affiliation, and the "hotness" of the IPO market increase the probability of an IPO. On the other hand, firms in high market to book industries, financial services sector, and high debt industries tend to prefer getting acquired. Brau, Francis, and Kohers (2003) also find an IPO premium, that is, insiders receive higher payoffs in IPOs than in acquisitions.

Poulsen and Stegemoller (2008) analyze firm-specific factors that may affect the choice of firms to conduct IPOs or to get acquired. They find that the exit decision depends on growth prospects, capital requirements, and information asymmetry of the private firm. Specifically, they find that IPO firms are more likely to face capital constraints, have fewer intangible assets, are less likely to be in the developmental stage, and are more likely to be backed by VC investors. The authors interpret this as evidence that IPO firms have lower information asymmetry. Further, firms that conduct IPOs tend to be higher growth firms, have higher valuation ratios, and need access to nondebt sources of funding. They also find that their results are the strongest for VC-backed firms.

Nahata (2003) analyzes exits by VC-backed firms. In particular, he compares three exit possibilities: IPOs, acquisitions, and write-offs. He finds evidence that factors related to venture capitalists as well as the entrepreneurial firms affect exit probability. Specifically, he finds that better performing firms are more likely to lead to successful exits through IPOs or acquisitions. In addition, early-stage companies are more likely to be acquired than to go public. Nahata (2003) argues that this result is consistent with early-stage firms having a promising product being able to benefit from the support of more well established firms. This argument is consistent with the trade-offs considered in Bayar and Chemmanur's (2008) model. He finds that VCs can time the market and take firms public when industry returns are higher. Firms backed by low reputation VCs are more likely to be liquidated, and firms backed by high reputation VCs are more likely to go public. VC backing by investment banks is less likely to lead to successful exit suggesting that these financial firms might lack the value-addition ability from extra-financial services provided by venture capitalists (e.g., Hellman and Puri 2000, 2002, Sorensen 2008, Chemmanur, Krishnan, and Nandy 2008). CVCs making strategic investments in firms correspond to a higher probability of exit through IPOs. Further, CVCs making strategic investments are also more likely to invest in firms that are written off relative to firms that are acquired. Nahata (2003) interprets this as evidence that strategic investments by CVCs are high risk/high return investments (more so than traditional VCs). He also finds that CVC-initiated deals of seed or early-stage firms are associated with a lower likelihood of successful exit. He argues that this could be because CVCs are not good at selecting better firms or because early-stage deals are inherently riskier and therefore should have higher failure probability.

The type of exit is also determined by the type of contracting between VCs and entrepreneurs. (We discuss a related model by Hellman [2006] below.) Cumming (2008) uses a novel dataset of European VC investments and exits and finds that the prediction of control rights theories hold in the venture capital setting. In particular, control rights models (e.g., Aghion and Bolton 1992) argue that since entrepreneurs derive nontransferable private benefits of control, they may not necessarily engage in monetary value maximizing actions. In such cases, the investor may have to retain more control if she has limited wealth. In particular, the investor is more likely to get higher control rights in firms with worse prospects and higher probability of conflicts of interest. The theory also predicts that higher VC control rights should be positively correlated with the probability of exit through acquisitions. Cumming (2008) tests the latter prediction about the association between control rights and exit outcome of the investment. He finds that higher control rights to the VC are linked to a higher probability of exit through acquisitions and lower probabilities of exit through IPOs and write-offs. This result holds even after controlling for the endogeneity between exits and contracting.

CONCLUSION

Venture capital is an important financing option for firms, particularly riskier firms with relatively short track records. We review recent academic literature and highlight some new results in this area on the value added by venture capitalists to the firms that they back, in particular the nonpecuniary aspects of value addition by venture capitalists. In this chapter, we have focused on three aspects of value addition by venture capitalists.

First, we review the literature on how VCs add value in early stages of a firm's life. The literature suggests that VCs add value by both screening start-up firms and monitoring them to improve their value (Chemmanur, Krishnan, and Nandy 2008). In addition, not all firms are suited for venture capital financing. VC financing is an equilibrium outcome where VCs may pick firms whose value they can improve the most. In addition, VCs increase sales and better reputation VCs can limit the increase in costs for the firms that they support. Thus, the literature also provides some guidance on the channels of these value increases. Both monitoring and screening activities by venture capitalists help improve the probability of a successful exit through IPOs and acquisitions.

Second, we review studies on how VCs may add value to firms through contracting, staging, and syndication. Venture capital contracts are designed to optimally incentivize the entrepreneur and provide enough returns for venture capitalists. Staging is considered to be a tool for monitoring of entrepreneurial firms by venture capitalists. Further, syndication may allow VCs in the process of screening by combining multiple information signals.

Third, we review studies on how VCs may create value at the time of exit. Theoretical models supported by empirical evidence seem to suggest that VC-backed firms may consider product market competition and synergies with potential acquirers when considering whether to get acquired or go public. The literature also suggests that a variety of factors can affect the propensity of a firm to exit through IPOs, acquisitions, and write-offs. These factors include macroeconomic and industry effects such as hotness of the IPO market, industry leverage, industry market to book, degree of concentration of a private firm's industry, and affiliation with the high tech industry or the financial industry. In addition, exit outcomes also depend on firm and VC characteristics such as asset tangibility, capital constraints, developments stage, VC reputation, and whether the VC is an investment bank or a CVC.

NOTES

1. See Gompers and Lerner (1996) for a more detailed account of the history of venture capital firms.
2. Average consumer price index (CPI) from the Bureau of Labor Statistics is used to calculate inflation adjustments.
3. Sahlman (1997) has argued that it is often more important from whom the entrepreneur raises capital than the terms that he gets for it.
4. In contrast to measures of innovation such as patent citations, TFP directly measures the operating efficiency of firms. It is not necessary that higher patent citations lead to greater operating efficiency or productivity. In particular, it is possible for more innovative firms to be inefficient (i.e., have a lower TFP). Thus, in this study, TFP measures the operating efficiency of innovative firms.
5. The LBD contains data on all firms, but has limited data on sales, costs, and other variables. On the other hand, the LRD contains data on manufacturing firms (SIC 2000-3999), but has detailed data on sales and costs required to calculate productivity.
6. The LRD dataset has also been used by Litchenberg and Siegel (1990) to analyze management buyouts in the United States. Harris, Siegel, and Wright (2005) use data similar to the LRD from the UK to analyze management buyouts in the UK.

7. The quasi-median is the average of the 43rd and the 57th percentile. This number is reported instead of medians because of disclosure restrictions on the Census (LRD) data.

8. Throughout this chapter, *portfolio company* or *company* will refer to the recipient of venture capital financing, while *VC firm* or *firm* will refer to the venture capitalist.

9. See Hart (2001) for an excellent review of some of these theories.

10. Hellman (1998) proposes a model where the entrepreneur may even voluntarily relinquish the control rights to fire management to the VC.

11. The pre-eminence of convertible securities in VC financing is explained mostly in terms of incentive and control issues in the finance literature. Gilson and Schizer (2003) argue that, in addition to such explanations, the prevalence of convertible securities in VC financing in the United States can also be explained by tax rules that reduce tax burden on incentive compensation when convertibles are used.

12. The VC's preference for an acquisition in the high state arises from the fact that she only gets part of the equity value from the IPO, while she always gets the full face value of the debt from the acquisition.

REFERENCES

Aghion, P., and P. Bolton. 1992. An incomplete contracts approach to financial contracting. *Review of Economic Studies* 59:473.

Bayar, O., and T. J. Chemmanur. 2008. IPOs or acquisitions? A theory of the choice of exit strategy by entrepreneurs and venture capitalists. Working paper. Boston College.

Brander, J. A., R. Amit, and W. Antweiler. 2002. Venture capital syndication: Improved venture selection vs. value-added hypothesis. *Journal of Economics and Managements Strategy* 11:422–452.

Brau, J. C., B. B. Francis, and Ninon Kohers. 2003. The choice of IPO versus takeover: Empirical evidence. *Journal of Business* 76:583–612.

Casamatta, C. 2003. Financing and advising: Optimal financial contracts with venture capitalists. *Journal of Finance* 58:2059–2086.

———, and C. Haritchabalet. 2007. Experience, screening and syndication in venture capital investments. *Journal of Financial Intermediation* 16:368–398.

Cestone, G., J. Lerner, and L. White. 2006. The design of syndicates in venture capital. Working paper. Harvard Business School.

Chemmanur, T. J., K. Krishnan, and D. Nandy. 2008. How does venture capital financing improve efficiency in private firms? A look beneath the surface. U.S. Bureau of Census, CES Working paper, CES-WP-08-16, 2008.

Chemmanur, T. J., and Z. Chen. 2008. Venture capitalists and angels: The dynamics of private firm financing contracts. Working paper. Boston College.

Cornelli, F., and O. Yosha. 1997. Stage financing and the role of convertible debt. *C.E.P.R. Discussion Papers*: 1735.

Cumming, D. J. 2008. Contracts and exits in venture capital finance. *Review of Financial Studies* 21:1947–1982.

Dewatripont, M., and J. Tirole. 1994. A theory of debt and equity: Diversity of securities and manager-shareholder congruence. *Quarterly Journal of Economics* 109: 1027–1054.

Gilson, R. J., and D. M. Schizer. 2003. Understanding venture capital structure: a tax explanation for convertible preferred stock. *Harvard Law Review* 116:874–916.

Gompers, P. A. 1995. Optimal investment, monitoring, and the staging of venture capital. *Journal of Finance* 50:1461–1489.

_____, and J. Lerner. 1996. The use of covenants: An empirical analysis of venture partnership agreements. *Journal of Law and Economics* 39:463–498.

_____, and J. Lerner. 1998. What drives venture capital fundraising? Brookings Paper on Economic Activity. *Microeconomics* 1998:149–204.

Harris, R., D. S. Siegel, and M. Wright. 2005. Assessing the impact of management buyouts on economic efficiency: Plant-level evidence from the United Kingdom. *Review of Economics and Statistics* 87:148–153.

Hart, O. 2001. Financial contracting. *Journal of Economic Literature* 39:1079.

_____, and J. Moore. 1994. A theory of debt based on the inalienability of human capital. *Quarterly Journal of Economics* 109:841–879.

Hellmann, T. 1998. The allocation of control rights in venture capital contracts. *Rand Journal of Economics* 29:57–76.

_____. 2006. IPOs, acquisitions, and the use of convertible securities in venture capital. *Journal of Financial Economics* 81:649–679.

_____, and M. Puri. 2000. The interaction between product market and financing strategy: The role of venture capital. *Review of Financial Studies* 13:959–984.

_____, and M. Puri. 2002. Venture capital and the professionalization of start-up firms: Empirical evidence. *Journal of Finance* 57:169–197.

Holmstrom, B. 1979. Moral hazard and observability. *Bell Journal of Economics* 10: 74–91.

Hsu, D. H. 2004. What do entrepreneurs pay for venture capital affiliation? *Journal of Finance* 59:1805–1844.

Kaplan, S. N., and P. Stromberg. 2003. Financial contracting theory meets the real world: An empirical analysis of venture capital contracts. *Review of Economic Studies* 70:281–315.

_____. 2004. Characteristics, contracts, and actions: Evidence from venture capitalist analyses. *Journal of Finance* 59:2177–2210.

Kortum, S., and J. Lerner. 2000. Assessing the contribution of venture capital to innovation. *RAND Journal of Economics* 31:674–692.

Lazear, E. P. 1986. Salaries and piece rates. *Journal of Business* 59:405–431.

Lerner, J. 1994. The syndication of venture capital investments. *Financial Management* 23:16–27.

Litchenberg, F. R., and D. Siegel. 1990. The effects of leveraged buyouts on productivity and related aspects of firm behavior. *Journal of Financial Economics* 27:165–194.

Myers, S. C. 1977. Determinants of corporate borrowing. *Journal of Financial Economics* 5:147–175.

Nahata, R. 2003. The determinants of venture capital exits: an empirical analysis of venture backed companies. Working paper. Baruch College, CUNY.

Neher, D. V. 1999. Staged financing: An agency perspective. *Review of Economic Studies* 66:255–274.

Poulsen, A. B., and M. Stegemoller. 2008. Moving from private to public ownership: Selling out to public firms versus initial public offerings. *Financial Management* 37:81–101.

Prendergast, C. 1999. The provision of incentives in firms. *Journal of Economic Literature* 37:7–63.

Puri, M., and R. Zarutskie. 2008. On the lifecycle dynamics of venture-capital- and non-venture-capital-financed firms. Working paper. Duke University.

Sahlman, W. A. 1997. How to write a great business plan. *Harvard Business Review* 75:98–108.

Schmidt, K. M. 2003. Convertible securities and venture capital finance. *Journal of Finance* 58:1139–1166.

Sorensen, M. 2007. How smart is smart money? A two-sided matching model of venture capital. *Journal of Finance* 62:2725–2762.

ABOUT THE AUTHORS

Thomas J. Chemmanur is Professor of Finance at the Carroll School of Management at Boston College. He received his Ph.D. in Finance from the Stern School of Business, New York University. Prior to joining Boston College, Dr. Chemmanur was Associate Professor of Finance at the Graduate School of Business, Columbia University. He has also taught at the Fuqua School of Business, Duke University, and the Stern School of Business, New York University. His main research interests are in theoretical and empirical corporate finance, with secondary research interests in applied game theory, contract theory, and industrial organization. One strand of his recent research focuses on various aspects of venture capital and angel financing contracts, value added by venture capitalists, and the role of venture capitalists in initial public offerings. Dr. Chemmanur's research has been presented at a number of national and international conferences, and several of his articles have been published in a number of top scholarly journals in finance, including the *Journal of Finance*, the *Journal of Financial Economics*, the *Review of Financial Studies*, the *Journal of Financial and Quantitative Analysis*, and the *Journal of Financial Intermediation*. He is currently serving as an associate editor of the *Review of Financial Studies*, and is editing a special issue of the *Journal of Economics and Business* on Venture Capital, Private Equity, and IPOs.

Karthik Krishnan obtained his Ph.D. in finance from Boston College and his bachelor's degree in Electrical Engineering from Delhi University. Dr. Krishnan is currently an Assistant Professor of Finance at Northeastern University in Boston. His research focus has been in empirical corporate finance, intermediation, corporate governance, and entrepreneurship. Dr. Krishnan is also affiliated as a Special Sworn Researcher with the Center for Economic Studies (CES), of the U.S. Census Bureau since 2006. His research has been cited in popular media outlets such as Reuters and Bloomberg and presented at various national and international conferences.

Debarshi K. Nandy obtained his Ph.D. in finance from Boston College, specializing in corporate finance and financial intermediation. Dr. Nandy is currently an Assistant Professor of Finance at the Schulich School of Business, York University and a Visiting Research Scholar at the National Bureau of Economic Research (NBER) at Boston. Dr. Nandy is also affiliated as a Special Sworn Researcher with the Center for Economic Studies (CES) of the U.S. Census Bureau since 2002. His research is in the areas of initial public offerings (IPOs), venture capital financing and entrepreneurship, security issuance, and financial intermediation. Dr. Nandy's research has been presented at a number of national and international conferences and has been published in academic journals such as the *Review of Financial Studies* and the *Journal of Financial and Quantitative Analysis*. Dr. Nandy has received several external research grants from the Social Sciences and Humanities Research Council of Canada (SSHRC) to fund his ongoing research.

CHAPTER 14

Venture Capital and Innovation

MASAKO UEDA
Assistant Professor, Wisconsin School of Business

INTRODUCTION

Having gone through a few boom and bust cycles, venture capital has rapidly grown over the last few decades and has fueled young innovative firms with strong financial appetites. The presence of VC backing for famous high-growth innovative companies such as Amazon.com, Apple, Cisco, Genentech, and Google has generated the hypothesis that venture capital stimulates innovation. Further, given that innovations in general may also benefit other firms through spillover effects, some policymakers attempt to stimulate their local VC markets hoping that such a policy will accelerate innovations and economic growth (e.g., see Lerner 2002; Cumming and McIntosh 2006). Nevertheless, the role of venture capital and its impact on innovations still largely remain open to discussion. This essay surveys literature in this issue and suggests future direction of research.

DEFINITION OF "VENTURE CAPITAL" AND "INNOVATION"

I would like to start with clarifying the two key words "venture capital" and "innovation." In particular, definitions of "innovations" vastly differ depending on contexts.

Definition of "Venture Capital"

Definitions of "venture capital" are slightly different across theoretical and empirical academic work, both of which will be discussed in this chapter. Theoretical academic work on venture capital portrays a venture capitalist as not only a financier but also either an intelligent evaluator who performs due diligence on ventures, a venture's partner who can add value to the venture, or both.[1] In short, theoretical academic work assumes that venture capital is smart money—the money accompanied by investor's expertise in evaluating and assisting the ventures. The scope of most empirical academic work on venture capital is on financial intermediaries that provide young firms with equity capital.

Since smart money may not be intermediated and financial intermediaries may not be "smart," the scope of theoretical work is not the same as the scope of

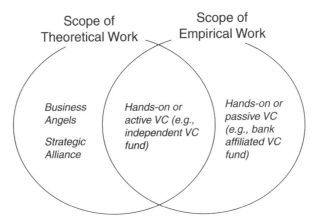

Exhibit 14.1 Definitions of Venture Capital

empirical work. For instance, smart money includes business angels and strategic alliance as venture financing. Business angels are high net worth individuals that provide funds to new firms at their very early stage (Freear, Sohl, and Wetzel 1995). They are often retired executives or former entrepreneurs who are willing to provide not only money but also their business expertise to the new firms they finance (Melloan 2005). Alternatively, a young firm may have an easier time obtaining funds from an established firm in the same industry, as the established firm has superior knowledge about the industry's business environment and therefore can evaluate the young firm's potential better than other type of investors, as illustrated by Sahlman (1990a).[2] For an example of financial intermediaries that may not be "smart," Hellmann, Lindsay, and Puri (2008) document that bank-affiliated venture capital in the United States tends to invest in later-stage ventures and to join a larger syndicate, suggesting that they rely on other investors' skill to evaluate the venture. Hellmann, Lindsay, and Puri argue that bank-affiliated venture capital in the United States provides equity finance to ventures, in order to obtain banking businesses from these ventures in the future.

Exhibit 14.1 summarizes the difference of the definitions between the theoretical work and the empirical work.

Definition of "Innovations"

Merriam-Webster online dictionary defines the word "innovation" as "the introduction of something new."[3] Some scholars directly follow this definition and study innovations by young and small firms. For instance, Acs and Audretsch (1988) study the number of new products that appeared in technology, engineering, and trade journals in 1982 and find that innovation per employee is higher for small firms than for large firms. Katila and Shane (2005) study the conditions under which licensed MIT patents are more likely to be commercialized and to generate sales than the license was to be terminated. The advantage of using the number of new products as a measure of innovation is its simplicity and intuitiveness. Nevertheless, this measure suffers from two issues. First, this type of data is infrequently collected or limited in the sample universe. Because of this limited focus, it is difficult to draw a conclusion that also applies to other contexts. Second, new products are vastly different in their qualities and their economic impacts. A mere count of new products is therefore a very noisy measure of innovation. For instance, it is natural to think that the new product that was sold widely and at a large quantity should receive a higher weight than the one that did not sell well and was withdrawn from the market quickly. However, this type of weighting is almost always impossible due to the limited nature of new product data.

Patent and productivity growth are two measures of innovation that are more comprehensively available than the aforementioned data sets of new products. Because both patent and productivity growth are available for extended periods, for a variety of industries, and for many countries, they are heavily used by scholars of technological innovation and economic growth. Research and development (R&D) expenditures at industry levels are also often used as an indicator of innovative activity, though they are not as widely available as patent and productivity growth. I am now going to discuss the limitation for each of these three measures.[4]

Patents as a measure of innovation are subject to two issues. First, like the problem of new products as a measure of innovation, patented inventions are heterogeneous in quality. In fact, this heterogeneity problem for patent is more acute than that for new products. New products emerge only if somebody is willing to incur costs of introducing them into markets. And this willingness indicates that the product has a potential economic value. Most patents are not even introduced to markets at all, however. For instance, Dechenaux and colleagues (2008) study 966 patents owned by MIT and document that only 192 patents led to a new product sale. Jaffe and Lerner (2004) list questionable patents without economic value and critically discuss the current U.S. patent system.[5] Second, not all innovations are patented. As patented innovations are publicly disclosed and this disclosure may allow the innovator's competitors to use the innovations illegally, the innovator may choose to hide her innovation instead of patenting it. Levin and colleagues (1987) indeed document that a patent is not the most important means of appropriating returns to innovation, and firms use a variety of other means such as secrecy and lead time in order to deter competitors from imitating the firms' innovations.

Different from simply counting the number of new products or patents, productivity growth quantifies the degree of each innovation. Roughly speaking, productivity is the ratio of output and input. One can compare the degree of two innovations by comparing their productivities. Productivity growth is the percentage increase of productivity. If it is higher, underlying innovation is bigger. There are two types of commonly studied productivity growth. The one is labor productivity growth; the other is total factor productivity (TFP) growth.[6] Labor productivity measures the amount of output produced per work hour. Though the simplicity of labor productivity is appealing, the biggest limitation of this measure is that it is a partial measure of productivity. Production requires not only labor but also other inputs such as material and equipment. Labor productivity is literally productivity of labor and does not measure productivity of other inputs. When labor productivity is growing, productivity of other inputs may be going down. As a consequence, it is not clear if the production process as a whole is becoming more efficient when labor productivity is growing. For instance, if a plant cuts the number of production workers, labor productivity may go up. Nevertheless, productivity of machines in the same plant may go down because fewer workers are now available for operating and maintaining the machines. TFP circumvents this problem of labor productivity and theoretically accounts for productivity of all inputs. Nevertheless, measurement of TFP requires measuring not only labor input but also other inputs. This is a difficult task, especially when quality of inputs is changing rapidly as in the case of computers and automated machinery in recent decades.

Different from patents and productivity growth, R&D expenditures are expressed by dollar amount and allow us to translate innovations into economic values easily. Nevertheless, to be precise, R&D expenditures are input for innovation and not innovation itself. The scale of innovation depends not only on how much R&D expenditures are spent but also on how efficiently they are spent. As a result, R&D expenditures are indirect measures of innovations, whereas patents and productivity growth are direct measures of innovations.

Given the limitations associated with each of the innovation measures, it is important to interpret any results on venture capital and innovation cautiously and also to validate the results using multiple measures of innovations.

Quick Facts on Venture Capital and Innovation

The statistical facts about VC investment and the three measures of innovation—patent, labor productivity growth, and TFP growth in the U.S. manufacturing industry—are summarized below.

Exhibit 14.2 summarizes the time series of VC investment and patent count. VC investment took off around 1980, due to a sequence of regulatory changes. These changes involve the clarification of the ERISA prudent man rule,[7] the reduction of capital gains tax rate,[8] and the introduction of Bayh-Dole Act that facilitated technology transfer from universities to private sectors.[9] In the early 1990s, the whole VC industry experienced downturns due to asset quality problems of pension funds. Those funds were pulled out from private equity investments to reduce riskiness of their portfolios. Pension funds are main financing sources for U.S. venture capitalists, and this assets reallocation by pension funds severely hit venture capitalists. In the later 1990s, VC investment explosively grew and then dropped in 2001 along with the bust of the NASDAQ bubble.

As shown in Exhibit 14.2, the patent count declined from 1970 to 1983 and created the concerns that technological opportunities may have been exhausted. Nevertheless, this declining trend was later reversed. Economists propose multiple causes for this reversal, including U.S. pro-patent policies as well as the resurgence of technological opportunities brought by innovations in information technology. (See Kortum and Lerner 1998; Hall 2004.) Since 1993, the trends of both VC investment and patent count have been upwards. Nevertheless, before 1993, two series appear to be negatively correlated.

Exhibit 14.3 summarizes the time series of VC investment and the two productivity growth measures. The two productivity growth measures are obviously and positively correlated. They, however, appear to be unrelated with VC investment. Together with the observations about the time series relation between VC investment and patents (Exhibit 14.2), there is no clear correlation between VC investment and innovation in the time-series data of the aggregated manufacturing industry.

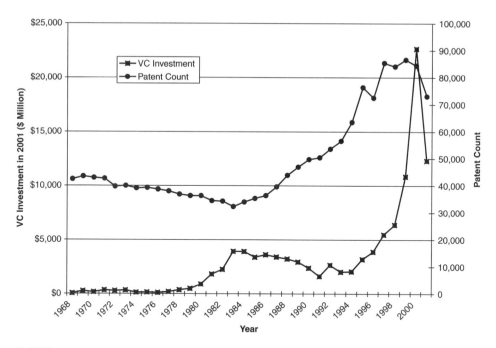

Exhibit 14.2 Investment and Patenting in U.S. Manufacturing Industries
Data sources are VentureXpert and USPTO. VC Investment is an estimated amount of VC
investment in U.S. manufacturing firms. Patent Count is the estimated number of utility
patents, applied to U.S. Patent and Trademark Office in each year, which are ultimately
granted. This patent count includes only ones that are potentially used in (not made by)
manufacturing firms. The method of estimating these two data series is detailed in Ueda
and Hirukawa (2008).

Unlike the time-series in Exhibit 14.2 and Exhibit 14.3, a positive relationship between VC investment and innovation is observed in cross-sectional data.
Exhibit 14.4 summarizes several innovation measures and VC investment in 19
U.S. manufacturing industries, together with the correlation coefficients of each
innovation measure and VC investment in dollars. These correlations are always
positive and, in particular, high if the two productivity growth measures are used
as proxies of innovation. Most notably, the "Office and Computing Machines" and
"Communication and Electronics" industries are both characterized by high innovations (labor productivity and TFP growth) and high venture capital investments
(in terms of dollars and the number of companies receiving VC funding). Note
that these two industries also have the highest R&D intensity next to the "Aircraft
and Missiles" industry. The "Drug" industry also has a relatively very high R&D
intensity and VC investment, but does not have high productivity growth.

In summary, a positive association between venture capital and innovation is
almost absent in the U.S. time-series data. This simple observation should alert
policy makers to be careful in using venture capital as a tool to stimulate local
innovation. The positive association between venture capital and innovation is
strong in the cross-sectional data. Nevertheless, we also have to be careful in
interpreting causality. (See Goldsmith 1969 about a general difficulty of establishing

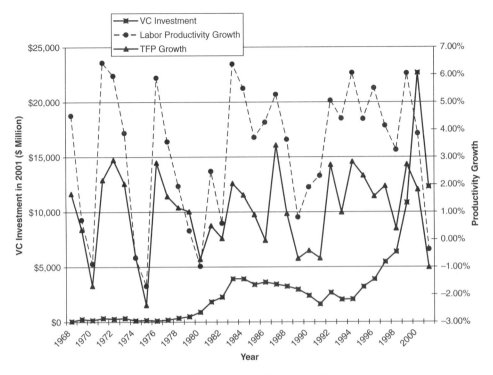

Exhibit 14.3 VC Investment and Productivity Growth in U.S. Manufacturing Industries
VC investment is an estimated amount of VC investment in U.S. manufacturing firms
and its data source is VentureXpert. Both labor and total factor productivity growths are
equal weight averages of U.S. manufacturing industries. The methods of estimating VC
investment and the two productivity growth figures are detailed in Ueda and Hirukawa
(2008).

the causality between finance and economic performance.) We will examine these
issues in detail at a later section of this chapter.

VENTURE CAPITAL AND INNOVATION: THEORETICAL LINKAGES

This section will survey the theories on financing innovations and to describe why
venture capitalists are particularly suitable for financing innovations. It is useful
to start with describing what makes financing of innovation different from other
types of financing. For this purpose, let us go back to the dictionary definition
of innovation—"introducing something new." By definition, something new has
been neither tried nor proven yet. Further, something new is often supported by
the most advanced technology only understood by experts in the field. These two
features of innovations create unique issues of financing and demand for special
financing arrangements. To be concrete, patient capital, value-adding investors,
investors with technical expertise, and less regulated institutions are particularly
important for financing innovations, as detailed in what follows.

Exhibit 14.4 Innovation Measures and VC Investment by Industry (Time Average)

Industry	SIC Codes	TFP Growth	Labor Productivity Growth	Number of Patent Applications	R&D Intensity (Industrial R&D/Sales)	Industrial R&D (MM$)	VC Investment (MM$)	# of Firms Receiving VC Funding
1 Food and kindred	20	0.56%	2.32%	433	0.92%	1,492	32	10
2 Textile and apparel	22,23	0.72%	3.00%	530	0.28%	319	27	6
3 Lumber and furniture	24,25	0.11%	1.51%	799	0.20%	299	13	3
4 Paper	26	0.48%	2.26%	575	1.08%	1,250	10	2
5 Industrial chemicals	281,282,286	0.72%	2.69%	2,803	3.25%	5,483	33	8
6 Drugs	283	−0.23%	2.58%	1,650	10.27%	6,648	393	43
7 Other chemicals	284–285,287–289	0.23%	2.28%	2,048	1.87%	2,098	15	4
8 Petroleum refining and extraction	13,29	0.52%	2.21%	295	1.38%	2,631	68	8
9 Rubber products	30	1.05%	2.30%	3,186	1.34%	1,491	27	5
10 Stone, clay and glass products	32	0.69%	1.75%	739	1.13%	864	18	5
11 Primary metals	33	0.55%	2.00%	586	0.57%	1,187	21	3
12 Fabricated metal products	34	0.24%	1.41%	3,580	0.55%	1,286	17	5
13 Office and computing machines	357	11.29%	18.75%	3,681	14.40%	9,090	706	115
14 Other non-electrical machinery	351–356,358–359	−0.09%	1.56%	11,278	1.28%	4,170	79	23
15 Communication and electronics	366,367	5.50%	9.65%	4,558	13.01%	15,553	976	121
16 Other electrical equipment	361–365,369	0.88%	3.27%	4,083	7.75%	6,592	145	28
17 Transportation equipment	371,373–375,379	0.50%	2.89%	1,484	3.74%	13,399	28	4
18 Aircraft and missiles	372,376	0.22%	2.86%	226	17.90%	22,908	8	1
19 Professional and scientific instruments	38	0.72%	3.81%	7,151	6.00%	8,738	558	115
Correlation with VC Investment (MM$)		*0.72*	*0.76*	*0.37*	*0.63*	*0.45*		

Note: Data sources are Bureau of Census, Bureau of Economic Analysis, National Science Foundation, VentureXpert, among others. All figures are average over respective annual U.S. data. The sample period is from 1968 to 2001. $ figures are 2001 constant values. See Ueda and Hirukawa (2008) for details.

Patient Capital

Since innovations have to be tested for viability before being brought to the marketplace, innovators often go through a long period of trials and errors without any financial returns. As a result, innovations need to be financed by patient capital that does not demand payback for a long period of time and therefore allows the innovative venture not to be liquidated prematurely. Patient capital is available when investors do not need liquidity for a long time or when initial investors can obtain liquidity by selling their financial claims easily. The latter condition often justifies NASDAQ-like stock markets where initial investors of innovative ventures can sell their shares even though the ventures have not generated any revenue yet. (See Black and Gilson 1998.)

Typical venture capital funds have a 10-year life with the option to extend 2 more years. Therefore, in principle, if a venture capitalist invests in a company at the beginning of the fund life, the venture capitalist and, in turn, the invested company do not have to pay back to the original investors of the fund for 10 to 12 years. This structure is superior in financing innovations compared to funds subject to redemption such as mutual funds and hedge funds. Nevertheless, in reality, venture capitalists would like to see returns much earlier than 10 to 12 years, because showing positive results allows them to raise the next fund more easily. Puri and Zarutskie (2008) highlight this limitation of VC in playing a role of patient capital. They find that VC-backed firms are less likely to exit than non-VC-backed firms for four to five years since the initial VC investment is received, whereas this relation is reversed after five years. This finding suggests that the VC's patience is limited to four to five years and after that VC becomes less patient than other financing sources.

Value-Adding Investors

Value-adding investors are those who provide not only financial resources to their portfolio firms but also other types of services to enhance the value of the firms. Value-adding investors are particularly important for financing innovations for a variety of reasons. When technical minds conceive business ideas, their goals are often to transform their ideas into products, not necessarily to make money. These technical minds often lack a sense of cost and of the viewpoints of prospective customers of the product. For this reason, to commercialize the ideas successfully and earn positive financial returns, business expertise needs to be brought into these new firms. Here, it becomes handy if the investors of these firms possess business expertise. These investors are naturally motivated to help their portfolio firms to commercialize the firms' ideas profitably, because their money is at stake (Casamatta 2003).[10]

Evidence supports the notion that venture capitalists provide valuable advice to their portfolio firms. Venture capitalists can assist new firms' innovation in several ways. Venture capitalists follow the progress of their portfolio firms through frequent phone calls and sitting on boards of directors. Knowing the needs of the portfolio firms, the venture capitalist can timely help the firms to obtain additional financing, to recruit a management team, to identify customers and suppliers, and to improve strategic and operational planning (Gorman and Sahlman 1989; Sapienza and Gupta 1994). Hellmann and Puri (2002) also examine the additional role played by venture capitalists compared to traditional financial intermediaries. The authors focus on the development of 170 young high technology firms in Silicon Valley. They find that venture capitalists intervene in a huge range of activities that are important for the professionalization and development of a start-up company, such as managerial advices, strategy formulation, communication skills, the formulation of human resource policies, the adoption of stock option plans and so on. Similarly, Stuck and Weingarten (2005) report that more than 64 percent of the general partners in a typical venture capital fund have advanced business degrees.

Because their ideas are unproven, new innovative ventures often have to change their operational directions. Hellmann and Puri also find that VC-backed companies are also more likely and faster to replace the founder with an outside CEO, both in situations that appear adversarial and those mutually agreed to. This evidence suggests that a VC's involvement makes new venture firms more sensitive to their profitability and less prone to managerial entrenchment.

Investors with Technical Expertise

In addition to business expertise, investors with technical expertise are also important for financing innovations for the following two reasons.

First, information problems such as moral hazard and asymmetric information are acute for new innovative ventures. These ventures are usually not prepared for selling their products, and therefore their financial information does not provide much information about how the venture is doing and will perform in the future. Due to this opacity, it is difficult to monitor the venture's progress and forecast its future cash flow. This difficulty requires a costly design of incentive mechanisms for the venture, and if this cost is too high, financing of such a venture is not viable—an underinvestment problem.[11]

Investors with technical expertise make the information problem less acute and may be willing to finance innovative ventures that investors without technical expertise are not willing to finance. Investors with technical expertise understand the technical milestones at various stages that new ventures have to hit in the course of commercialization. Therefore, investors with technical expertise can monitor new ventures better and can lessen the moral hazard problem (Michelacci and Suarez 2004). Investors with technical expertise are well aware of technical viabilities and financial prospects of the ventures. As a result, the asymmetric information problem also becomes less important (Chan 1983; Ueda 2004).

Second, innovative ideas often turn out to be unviable. If this happens, investors of the failed ventures are likely to be left with intellectual property of ventures, which are often the only assets in the venture. Selling such property at a reasonable price and maximizing the liquidation return require technical expertise such as familiarity with the venture's intellectual property and the industry landscape. Therefore, technical expertise is again important for financing innovations.

Evidence that typical VCs have technical expertise is mixed. Stuck and Weingarten (2005) report that less than 29 percent of typical VCs have advanced science degrees. Nevertheless, VCs may make up for their lack of science degrees by specialization and developing a network with scientific experts. Venture capitalists typically specialize in a small group of industries (Sahlman 1990b). This specialization presumably deepens technical knowledge about the industries in which a venture capitalist has been investing and therefore helps the venture capitalist to accurately evaluate business plans of firms in the same industries in the future.

Less Regulated Institutions

There are two reasons why less regulated financial institutions are more desirable for financing innovations. First, new innovative ventures experience a long time of no revenue and, due to their technical natures, have proprietary information. For this reason, they want to be as secretive as possible instead of being exposed to public scrutiny. Second, flexible contracting is particularly important for new innovative ventures that are expected to encounter a variety of unpredicted events (Amit, Brander, and Zott 1998). VC funds, at least in the United States, are less regulated than other financial institutions such as banks and hedge funds. There is little requirement for VCs to disclose their fund information and, therefore, VCs can also keep their portfolio firms from public scrutiny. Further, venture capitalists have more flexibility in the type of financial arrangements they can make with their portfolio firms than banks, who are not allowed to issue equity, except under special circumstances.

Summary

In view of the aforementioned theoretical linkages between venture capital and innovation, many scholars hypothesize that financial constraints are relaxed when supply of venture capital is plentiful, and, as a result, innovations by new firms flourish. Further, in such an environment, the number of new firms should rise as the presence of venture capital will improve expected returns to entry. Given that innovation tends to have spillover effects, a natural extension of this hypothesis is that an industry or a country becomes more innovative when the supply of venture capital is plentiful.

VENTURE CAPITAL AND INNOVATION: DATA

In this section, I am going to survey the empirical papers that study the relationship between venture capital and innovation at various levels.

Firm-Level Study

Consistent with the theory surveyed in the previous section, a variety of papers find that VC-backed firms are more innovative than non–VC-backed firms. Hellmann and Puri (2000) studied a survey of 149 recently formed firms in Silicon Valley and find that VC-backed firms tend to pursue an "innovator strategy," whereas non–VC-backed firms tend to pursue an "imitator strategy." Kortum and Lerner (2000) also find a similar positive association between VC backing and innovation. Studying 530 VC-backed and non–VC-backed firms in Middlesex County in Massachusetts, they find that the patents invented by venture-backed firms are more frequently cited than those invented by non–venture-backed firms. Studying a sample of VC-backed manufacturing firms that appears in the census data,

Chemmanur, Krishnan, and Nandy (2008) find that VC-backed firms experience a higher TFP growth than non–VC-backed firms after VC funding.

There are three caveats in interpreting this literature documenting that VC-backed firms are more innovative than non–VC-backed firms.

First, evidence suggests that VCs helps new firms to become more innovative at a later stage but not at an early stage. In particular, VCs may help commercialization of new ideas but not generation of new ideas. Hellmann and Puri (2000) find that VC-backed firms bring their products to market more quickly than their non–VC-backed counterparts. Nevertheless, studying the sample of German firms, Engel and Keilbach (2007) find that firms slow down their patenting after receiving VC investments. Caselli, Gatti, and Perrini (2009) find the same result as Engel and Keilbach for the sample of firms that went to public in the Italian Stock Exchange between 1995 and 2004.[12] Second, the innovativeness of VC-backed firms does not necessarily imply that VC helps new firms to innovate because innovative firms may attract VC. Indeed, Engel and Keilbach also find that VC-funded firms register more patents than the matched firms before receiving VC investments. A similar pattern is found in TFP. Chemmanur, Krishnan, and Nandy find that VC-backed firms already have higher TFP than non–VC-backed firms at the time of the initial VC funding. Peneder (2008) studies an unusually rich dataset of Austrian firms including both VC-backed and non–VC-backed firms. Employing innovative products' and/or services' share in the firm's sales revenues as the measure of innovation, Peneder finds that VC-backed firms tend to innovate more than their non–VC-backed counterparts. Nevertheless, controlling for the importance of formal protection of intellectual property rights (e.g., patents) to the firms, he finds that VC backing does not influence the firm's innovation.

Peneder also documents the reasons why Austrian VC-backed firms choose to finance through VC over other forms of financing. The majority of these firms report that bank loans, owners' funds, and public support are neither available nor sufficient and are often opposed to any types of strategic investors. Taken together, these results suggest that VC plays an important role in financing innovative firms with otherwise poor financial resources.

Finally, Dushnitsky and Lenox (2005) study the impact of VC investment on the VC's innovation rather than that of VC-backed companies. To be concrete, they focus on corporate VC programs and study the patent counts of investing firms instead of invested firms. They find that investing firms subsequently increased their patent counts relative to noninvesting firms, suggesting that corporate VC programs provide a valuable opportunity to scan new technology and enhance the investing firm's innovative ability.

Industry-, Regional-, and Country-Level Studies

Studies with units of observations bigger than the firm have been the mainstream in the study of innovation for a long time—for several reasons. First, innovation data such as R&D expenditures are available at the industry level but often not available or of bad quality at firm level. Second, due to nonexclusivity and spillover, innovative output is often shared by firms other than those who produced the innovation. Consequently, to measure these spillover effects, an analysis needs to go beyond innovation producers. Last, when studying the impact of subsidizing new or small firms, it is important to take into account general equilibrium effects. Subsidizing one type of firms may harm other types of firms. Therefore, from the public policy point of view, it is crucial to broaden the scope of data in order to understand the full effect of policies in question.

Whether higher supply of VC stimulates innovation is an important question. But it is difficult to test, because the supply of venture capital is often endogenous; more money is likely to flow in venture capital funds when new innovative firms are plentiful. Therefore, a positive correlation between VC funding and innovations does not necessarily imply the causality that increased VC funding stimulates innovation by new ventures. Increased innovations by new ventures can stimulate VC funding. To circumvent this causality problem, researchers typically use instrumental variables and/or long-lag specifications.

Kortum and Lerner (2000, 2001) examine the influence of VC investment on the patent count in the U.S. manufacturing sector from 1965 to 1992. To isolate the impact of VC on innovation from the opposite causality, they use the instrumental variables based on the 1979 clarification of the ERISA prudent man rule. This clarification is considered to have had a significant impact in motivating U.S. pension funds to invest in venture capital funds. By estimating a patent production function with VC investment, privately-funded R&D and federally-funded R&D as inputs, Kortum and Lerner find that VC investment not only positively affects patent count but also is substantially more efficient than privately-funded R&D in increasing patent count.[13] In particular, Kortum and Lerner (2000) write in page 674, "While the ratio of venture capital to R&D averaged less than 3% from 1980–1992, our estimates suggest that venture capital may have accounted for 8% of industrial innovations during that period." By dividing the sample used by Kortum and Lerner (2000, 2001), Gompers and Lerner (2003) find that the influence of VC on patent count is lower in the boom market, suggesting that the number of innovative firms is limited, and increased supply of VC during the boom market does not necessarily stimulate more innovation. Ueda and Hirukawa (2008) extend the sample period of the studies by Kortum and Lerner (2000, 2001) and Gompers and Lerner (2003) from 1992 to 2001 and examine the influence of VC investment on innovation during the 1990s when U.S. venture capital experienced an unprecedented boom. Unlike Gompers and Lerner, Ueda and Hirukawa do not find that the influence of VC on the patent count decreased during the 1990s boom market.

These industry-level results supporting the positive impact of VC on innovation may appear to be contradictory to the aforementioned firm-level patent results by Engel and Keilbach and by Caselli, Gatti, and Perrini that firms slow down their patenting once they receive VC funding. Nevertheless, this contradiction may arise from the long-run effect of increased VC supply. Expecting that VC money will continue to aid commercialization of patents by new firms, new firms may be more willing to innovate and patent. As a result, increased VC supply may stimulate innovations of new firms that may receive VC investment in the future.

A more substantial issue in the methodology of Kortum and Lerner is using patents as a measure of innovation, because increased VC supply may not only stimulate innovation but also make more innovations to be patented. As a result, the VC's impact on innovation may be overstated when patents are used as a measure of innovation. New firms are likely to use patents more often than established firms as a means to appropriate returns to innovation. Levin and colleagues (1987) find that large firms generally rate patents less effective mechanisms of appropriation than the other means such as secrecy, lead time, and sales or service efforts. Nevertheless, new firms, typically lacking their own manufacturing and marketing capacities, do not have any of these appropriation vehicles that established firms do.[14] Thus, new firms are more likely to depend on patents to protect their intellectual property rights, and their patent propensity is likely to be higher than established firms. (See Hall and Ziedonis [2001] for supporting evidence in the U.S. semiconductor industry.) Given that VC investment fuels these new firms, increased supply of VC should raise the patent propensity of industry.

Instead of patents, Ueda and Hirukawa (2008) employ TFP growth as a measure of innovation. Using the same regression specification as Kortum and Lerner, Ueda and Hirukawa do not find that VC investments have any significant impact on TFP growth in U.S. manufacturing industries. VC investment does, however, have a significant positive impact on labor productivity growth. Nevertheless, this impact comes from the technology substitution effect such that firms in VC-intensive industries shift their input from labor to either energy or nonenergy material.

In some other samples, VC investments have a positive impact on TFP growth. For instance, Tang and Chyi (2008) study the impact of VC investment on TFP growth of Taiwanese manufacturing industries. Using legal environments as instrumental variables for VC investment, they document the positive impact of VC investment on TFP growth. Romain and van Pottelsberghe (2004a) study a panel dataset of 16 OECD countries over the period from 1990 to 2001. They find that the elasticity of TFP with respect to VC stocks is higher than that to the stocks of business R&D and public R&D, suggesting that VC investment plays a more important role than business or public R&D in stimulating innovations. They also find that the intensity of VC funding has a positive effect on the elasticity of TFP with respect to the business R&D capital stock. From these results, the authors conclude that venture capital investments stimulate innovation not only directly but also indirectly through enhancing the absorptive capacity of the economy's knowledge stock. Nevertheless, Romain and van Pottelsberghe do not address the causality problem of VC investment, and therefore their results may be driven by exogenous innovations stimulating VC investment.

Lastly, the following two papers explore the VC's impact on other measures of innovation and find counterintuitive results. First, Zucker, Darby, and Brewer (1998) study causes of biotechnology start-up firms and find that controlling for the presence of local star scientists the size of historical VC market negatively affects the rate of biotechnology start-up. Second, Katila and Shane (2005) study the fate of licensed MIT patents and find that they are more likely to be commercialized if the licensee firms are in an industry with high VC investment. Nevertheless, puzzlingly, they find that this effect exists only if the licensee firms are established firms rather than new ones.

Reverse Causality

So far this chapter has surveyed studies that attempt to uncover VC's impact on innovations. Nevertheless, there also exist papers that study the impact of innovation on the size of VC markets. For instance, Romain and van Pottelsberghe

(2004b) study a panel dataset of 16 OECD countries from 1990 to 2000 and show that the stock of knowledge and the number of triadic patents (i.e., patents granted in EU, Japan, and the United States) affect positively and significantly the relative level of venture capital investment. Da Rin, Nicodano, and Sembenelli (2006) employ a panel of data for 14 European countries between 1988 and 2001 and study determinants of VC investment in high tech or early-stage firms. They find that these investments are positively related with R&D spending. Gompers and Lerner (1998) also find that R&D played an important role in the development of the U.S. VC market. Armour and Cumming (2006) study determinants of VC market size in 15 Western European and two North American countries for the period from 1990 to 2003. Interestingly, they find patenting activity in the previous year is negatively related with both fundraising and investing by venture capitalists.

Although these papers all indicate the presence of reverse causality, none of them address the potential endogeneity of innovation variables such as patent and R&D to VC investment. This does not come as a surprise, because it is difficult to identify a suitable instrument for innovations. Hirukawa and Ueda (2008) resort to study Granger causality between VC investment and innovation. They find that lagged TFP is often positively related with VC investment, suggesting the causality that innovations stimulate VC investment. Nevertheless, consistent with Engel and Keilbach, Caselli, Gatti, and Perrini, and Armour and Cumming, Hirukawa and Ueda find that lagging patent is often negatively related with VC investment.[15]

Summary

The firm-level evidence clearly supports that VC-backed firms are more innovative. However, interpretation of this relation requires caution. First, the selection effect that VC and innovative firms mutually select each other seems to be important. Second, venture capitalists may help their portfolio firms to commercialize their inventions but may not necessarily help them invent.

Evidence at more aggregate levels shows that VC investment stimulates patents. Nevertheless, evidence on VC's impact on TFP growth is mixed. Further, some studies suggest that the positive association of VC and innovation may be spurious. Finally, innovations are not only a consequence of VC investment but also likely to be a cause. Nevertheless, this reverse causality has been difficult to establish.

CONCLUSION

This essay surveys the literature on venture capital and innovation. It began with the definitions of venture capital and innovation, discussed the data on venture capital and innovation briefly, and then surveyed the theoretical and empirical literature. Given the importance of this topic, the literature in this area is continuously developing. Nevertheless, many questions still remain to be answered.

First, most existing literature studies VC alone and does not simultaneously consider business angels and/or strategic partners. These two categories of investors possess similar characteristics to venture capitalists (patient capital and technical and business expertise, etc.), and the amount of financing they provide to new ventures are estimated to be no smaller than VC investments. Comparative studies between venture capital and business angels or strategic partners would bring new perspectives with regard to the role of venture capitalists and their relationships with other types of investors that provide capital for financing innovations. Some interesting questions are, for instance, Is the impact on innovation different across these investors? Does VC's investment pattern indicate a presence of agency problems relative to the other financing sources, which are not intermediated? Does subsidizing venture capital reduce the investment from business angels or strategic partners? Is financing by strategic partners more often in the industry in which VC investment is large?

Second, although several papers study the impact of VC funding on the firms that receive it, little is known about the impact of VC funding on the competitors of VC-funded firms. Increased availability of VC funding makes the entry threat more credible and naturally affects the incumbent's strategy according to industrial organization studies. Existing industry-level studies partly address this industry-wide effect of VC investment. Nevertheless, few studies examine how the incumbent firms respond to VC investment in detail. Some interesting questions in this area are, for instance, how does the patenting strategy of incumbent firms respond to increased VC supply? Do incumbent firms patent more defensively to protect their competitive positions? Do they increase their R&D and try to be more innovative than VC-backed firms? Or do they cut down their R&D and buy innovations from VC-backed firms?

Third, existing studies have paid little attention to the role of different types of VC on innovation. Does investment by more reputable VCs have a bigger impact on innovation? How does this impact interact with legal environments of the countries in which VC-backed companies are located? Do corporate VC and government VC affect innovations of their portfolio firms differently from independent VC? All these questions are yet to be explored.

NOTES

1. For instance, Chan (1983) and Ueda (2004) contend that venture capitalists possess the ability to evaluate a new firm's potential profitability more accurately than other types of financiers. Nordeke and Schmidt (1998), Casamatta (2003), and Inderst and Mueller (2003) contend that venture capitalists provide their portfolio firms with valuable help and add value.

2. Sahlman (1990a) describes the process in which the founder of *Parenting Magazine* obtained start-up funding in 1989. It was difficult to find any venture capitalist willing to fund *Parenting Magazine* because publishing was not a typical area for venture capitalists. Time, Inc. was trying to develop a magazine similar to *Parenting* and understood well the need for such a magazine. As *Parenting* was farther along than its own venture, Time, Inc. decided to fund Parenting.

3. http://www.merriam-webster.com/dictionary/innovation.

4. Besides these three measures, industry-specific measures of innovations are available. For instance, for the drug and medical device industries, FDA approval is an important milestone to commercialization and can be used as a measure of innovation (see, e.g., Guedj and Scharfstein 2004).

5. Well-cited examples of recent questionable patents are "Method of Swinging on a Swing," U.S. Patent # 6,368,227, granted on Apr. 09, 2002 and "Thumb Sleeve for Thumb Wrestling Game," U.S. Patent # 6,704,937, granted on Mar. 16, 2004.

6. TFP growth is also called multifactor productivity growth.

7. In 1978, the U.S. Department of Labor clarified that investments in venture capital funds by pension funds do not violate the prudent man rule in Employment Retirement Income Security Acts (ERISA).

8. See Gompers and Lerner (1998) for details.

9. Enactment of the Bayh-Dole Act (P.L. 96-517), the Patent and Trademark Act Amendments of 1980, on December 12, 1980, created a uniform patent policy among the many federal agencies that fund research. Bayh-Dole enables small businesses and nonprofit organizations, including universities, to retain title materials and products they invent under federal funding. Amendments to the Act were also created to include licensing guidelines and expanded the law's purview to include all federally-funded contractors, (P.L. 98-620).

10. To avoid dilution of incentives, Casamatta (2003) shows that it is more efficient if a financier can provide advice than if an adviser is hired separately.

11. Jensen and Meckling (1976), Leland and Pyle (1977), and Myers and Majluf (1984) are classic articles that suggest the underinvestment problem caused by information frictions. Note that information frictions can also cause overinvestment. See deMeza (2002).

12. Stuck and Weingarten (2005) even contend that VC "thwarts innovation."

13. Examining German data, Tykvova (2000) also finds results similar to Kortum and Lerner (2000). Nevertheless, her results may be driven by the reverse causality.

14. Using the survey of U.S. manufacturing firms, Cohen, Nelson, and Walsh (2000) also find that propensity to patent process innovations is negatively related with the presence of complementary sales and service assets.

15. Hirukawa and Ueda (2008) also find that lagged VC investment is often negatively related with both TFP growth and patent count. This negative relation between lagged VC investment and TFP growth is consistent with the bubbles and crashes theory (e.g., Abreu and Brunnermeier 2003). This theory contends that economic booms will trigger subsequent crashes. As VC investments often increase during economic booms and TFP growth slows down during crashes due to low capacity utilization, the bubbles and crashes theory predicts that VC investment boom leads to slowdowns in TFP growth.

REFERENCES

Abreu, D., and M. K. Brunnermeier. 2003. Bubbles and crashes. *Econometrica* 71:173–204.

Acs, Z. J., and D. B. Audretsch. 1988. Innovation in large and small firms: An empirical analysis. *American Economic Review* 78:4:678–690.

Acharya, V. V., and K. Subramanian. 2007. Bankruptcy codes and innovation. CEPR Discussion Paper No. DP6307.

Amit, R., J. Brander, and C. Zott. 1998. "Why do venture capital firms exist? Theory and Canadian evidence." *Journal of Business Venturing* 13:441–466.

Armour, J., and D. Cumming. 2006. The legislative road to Silicon Valley. *Oxford Economic Papers* 58:596–635.

Black, B. S., and R. J. Gilson. 1998. Venture capital and the structure of capital markets: Banks versus stock markets. *Journal of Financial Economics* 47:243–277.

Caselli, S., S. Gatti, and F. Perrini. 2009. Are venture capitalists a catalyst for innovation? *European Financial Management* 15(1):92–111.

Casamatta, C. 2003. Financing and advising: Optimal financial contracts with venture capitalists. *Journal of Finance* 58:2059–2085.

Chan, Y. 1983. On the positive role of financial intermediation in allocations of venture capital in a market with imperfect information. *Journal of Finance* 38:1543–1568.

Chemmanur, T., K. Krishnan, and D. Nandy. 2008. How does venture capital financing improve efficiency in private firms? A look beneath the surface. Working paper, Boston College.

Cohen, W. M., R. R. Nelson, and J. Walsh. 2000. Protecting their intellectual assets: Appropriability conditions and why U.S. manufacturing firms patent (or not). NBER Working paper 7552.

Cumming, D., and J. G. Macintosh. 2006. Crowding out private equity: Canadian evidence. *Journal of Business Venturing* 21:569–609.

Da Rin, M., G. Nicodano, and A. Sembenelli. 2006. Public policy and the creation of active venture capital markets. *Journal of Public Economics* 90:1699–1723.

Dechenaux, E., et al. 2008. Appropriability and commercialization: Evidence from MIT inventions. *Management Science* 54(5):893–906.

deMeza, D. 2002. Overlending? *Economic Journal* 112:17–31.

Dushnitsky, G., and M. J. Lenox. 2005. Corporate venture capital and incumbent firm innovation rates. *Research Policy* 34(5):615–639.

Engel, D., and M. C. Keilbach. 2007. Firm level implications of early stage venture capital investment—An empirical investigation. *Journal of Empirical Finance* 14(2): 150–167.

European Commission. 1995. Green paper on innovation. Retrieved from http://europa .eu.int.

Freear, J., J. E. Sohl, and W. E. Wetzel Jr. 1995. Angels: personal investors in the venture capital market. *Entrepreneurship and Regional Development* 7:85–94.

Gilbert, R. J., and D. M. G. Newbery. 1982. Preemptive patenting and the persistence of monopoly. *American Economic Review* 72:514–526.

Goldsmith, R. W. 1969. *Financial structure and development.* New Haven: Yale University Press.

Gompers, P., and J. Lerner. 1998. What drives venture capital fundraising? *Brookings Papers on Economic Activity—Microeconomics* 149–192.

———. 2003. Short-term America revisited? Boom and bust in the venture capital industry and the impact on innovation. In *Innovation Policy and the Economy,* ed. Adam B. Jaffe, Josh Lerner, and Scott Stern (3). Cambridge: MIT Press, NBER Books.

Gorman, M., and W. A. Sahlman. 1989. What do Venture Capitalists do? *Journal of Business Venturing* 4(4):231–248.

Guedj, I., and D. S. Scharfstin. 2004. Organizational scope and investment: Evidence from the drug development strategies and performance of biopharmaceutical firms. http://ssrn.com/abstract=621322.

Hall, B. H. 2004. Exploring the Patent Explosion. *Journal of Technology Transfer* 30:35–48.

———. 2002. The financing of research and development. NBER Working paper 8773.

———, and Rosemarie Ham Ziedonis. 2001. The patent paradox revisited: An empirical study of patenting in the U.S. semiconductor industry, 1979–1995. *RAND Journal of Economics* 32(1):101–128.

Hellmann, T. F. 2002. A theory of strategic venture investing. *Journal of Financial Economics* 64(2):285–314.

———, L. Lindsey, and M. Puri. 2008. Building relationships early: Banks in venture capital. *Review of Financial Studies* 21(2):513–541.

_____, and M. Puri. 2000. The interaction between product market and financing strategy: The role of venture capital. *Review of Financial Studies* 13:959–984.

_____, and M. Puri. 2002. Venture capital and the professionalization of start-up firms: Empirical evidence. *Journal of Finance* 57(1):169–197.

Hirukawa, M., and M. Ueda. 2008. Venture capital and innovation: Which is first? CEPR Discussion Paper 7090.

Hyytinen, A., and O. Toivanen. 2005. Do financial constraints hold back innovation and growth? Evidence on the role of public policy. *Research Policy* 34(9):1385–1403.

Inderst, R., and H. M. Mueller. 2003. The effect of capital market characteristics on the value of start-up firms. *Journal of Financial Economics* 72(2):319–356.

Jaffe, A. B., and J. Lerner. 2004. *Innovation and its discontents: How our broken patent system is endangering innovation and progress, and what to do about it.* Princeton, NJ: Princeton University Press.

Jensen, M. J., and W. R. Meckling. 1976. Theory of the firm: Managerial behavior, agency cost, and ownership structure. *Journal of Financial Economics* 3:305–360.

Katila, R., and S. Shane. 2005. When does lack of resources make new firms innovative? *Academy of Management Journal* 48(5):814–829.

Kortum, S., and J. Lerner. 1998. Stronger protection or technological revolution: What is behind the recent surge in patenting? *Carnegie-Rochester Conference Series on Public Policy* 48 (June 1998):247–304.

_____. 2000. Assessing the contribution of venture capital to innovation. *Rand Journal of Economics* 31(4):674–692.

_____. 2001. Does venture capital spur innovation? In *Entrepreneurial Inputs and Outcomes*, vol. 13, ed. G. Libecap 1–44. Amsterdam: Elsevier.

Leland, H. E., and D. C. Pyle. 1977. Informational asymmetries, financial structure, and financial intermediation. *Journal of Finance* 32(2):371–387.

Lerner, J. (ed.). 1994. The syndication of venture capital investments (venture capital special issue). *Financial Management* 23(3):16–27.

_____. 2002. When bureaucrats meet entrepreneurs: The design of effective "public venture capital" programmes. *Economic Journal* 112:F73–F84.

Levin, R. C., A. K. Klevorick, Richard R. Nelson, and Sidney G. Winter. 1987. Appropriating the returns from industrial research and development. *Brookings Paper on Economic Activities* 3:783–820.

Levine, R., N. Loayza, and Thorsten Beck. 2000. Financial inter mediation and growth: causality and causes. *Journal of Monetary Economics* 46:31–77.

Melloan, J. 2005. Profiles of angel investors. *Groups. Inc* (June 16, 2005).

Michelacci, C., and J. Suarez. 2004. Business creation and the stock market. *Review of Economic Studies* 71(2):459-481.

Mowery, D. C., et al. 2001. The growth of patenting and licensing by U.S. universities: An assessment of the effects of the Bayh-Dole Act of 1980. *Research Policy* 30(1):99–119.

Myers, S., and N. Majluf. 1984. Corporate financing and investment decisions when firms have information that investors do not have. *Journal of Financial Economics* 13:187–221.

Noldeke, G., and K. M. Schmidt. 1998. Sequential investment and options to own. *RAND Journal of Economics* 29(4):633–653.

Peneder, M. R. 2008. The impact of venture capital on innovation behaviour and firm growth. Retrieved from http://papers.ssrn.com/sol3/papers.cfm?abstract_id=964954.

Puri, M., and R. Zarutskie. 2008. On the lifecycle dynamics of venture-capital- and non-venture-capital-financed firms. U.S. Census Bureau Center for Economic Studies. Paper No. CES-WP-08-13.

Reinganum, J. 1983. Uncertain innovation and the persistence of monopoly. *Bell Journal of Economics* 12:618–624.

Romain, A., and B. van Pottelsberghe. 2004a. The economic impact of venture capital. Discussion Paper Series 1: Studies of the Economic Research Centre, No. 18/2004. Deutsche Bundesbank.

_____. 2004b. The determinants of venture capital. Discussion Paper Series 1: Studies of the Economic Research Centre, No. 19/2004. Deutsche Bundesbank.

Sahlman, W. A. 1990a. *Parenting* magazine. Harvard Business School Case, #291015.

_____. 1990b. The structure and governance of venture-capital organizations. *Journal of Financial Economics* 27:473–521.

Sapienza, H. J., and A. K. Gupta. 1994. Impact of agency risks and task uncertainty on venture capitalists-CEO interaction. *Academy of Management Journal* 37(4):618–32.

Stuck, B., and M. Weingarten. 2005. How venture capital thwarts innovation. *IEEE Spectrum*, April 2005, 50–55.

Tang, M., and Y. Chyi. 2008. Legal environments, venture capital, and total factor productivity. *Contemporary Economic Policy* 26:468–481.

Tykvova, T. 2000. Venture capital in Germany and its impact on innovation. Retrieved from http://papers.ssrn.com/paper.taf?abstract_id=235512

Ueda, M. 2004. Banks versus venture capital: Project evaluation, screening, and expropriation. *Journal of Finance* 59, 601–621.

_____, and M. Hirukawa. 2008. Venture capital and industrial innovation. CEPR Discussion Paper 7089.

Zucker, L. G., M. R. Darby, and M. B. Brewer. 1998. Intellectual human capital and the birth of U.S. biotechnology enterprises. *American Economic Review* 88:290–306.

ABOUT THE AUTHOR

Masako Ueda received her Ph.D. in economics from the University of Tokyo. Dr. Ueda has held faculty positions in the United States, Spain, and Sweden. Her field of research is financing and strategy issues of new firms. She has published in academic journals including *Journal of Economic Theory*, *Journal of Finance*, *Journal of Political Economy*, and *Management Science*.

## CHAPTER 15

Reputation in Financial Intermediation

Evidence from Venture Capital

RAJARISHI NAHATA

Assistant Professor, Baruch College, CUNY

INTRODUCTION

Venture capital (VC) has emerged as one of the dominant forms of financing for technology-intensive industries. Many start-ups have flourished tremendously after receiving VC funding and have gone on to become industry leaders. Prominent examples include Apple, Cisco, Intel, Genentech, and most recently Google. VCs are important financial intermediaries channeling capital from investors to risky, unproven start-ups that otherwise would face a much more uphill task trying to raise capital. What also sets them apart from other traditional financial intermediaries—banks, other institutional investors, and so on—is their ability to provide expertise and other value-added services for start-ups' development.

In addition to providing expertise and value-added services that generate economic benefits, VC firms aspire to be active long-term players in the industry. These motivations critically influence and depend on VCs' reputational capital, a precious resource in the competitive VC industry beset by considerable information asymmetries between VCs and their investors, as well as between VC firms and start-ups. That a firm's reputation is a valuable asset that can generate future economic rents for the firm and provide its customers valuable information on products and services is well recognized (Shapiro 1983; Wilson 1985). This study surveys the literature on the important role of venture capitalists, particularly focusing on their reputation capital and its implications for companies.

More generally, financial intermediaries play an important role in financial markets by being conduits between providers and recipients of products and services. For example, corporations seeking money take help from banks and

Thanks to Douglas Cumming for the opportunity to write for *Venture Capital*. A survey by its very nature is limited in scope and focus, and many important papers are likely to have been left out from the discussion. I sincerely apologize to authors whose important work has been inadvertently omitted. I am responsible for all errors.

underwriters that channel the money from depositors and other investors to the companies themselves. A primary reason why companies raise money indirectly through a financial intermediary is because the investors may not know enough about the companies themselves to entrust them with their capital. By employing a financial intermediary, it is possible for one party to credibly signal its "better" quality to the other party to resolve the information asymmetry. "Signaling" can thus help mitigate the resulting adverse selection problem, which if not dealt with, can lead to market failure in its most extreme form (Akerlof 1970).[1]

A question arises: why can't the companies signal on their own instead of employing a financial intermediary to do their bidding? The reason is that it is often difficult for companies to credibly convey their private information and quality since they can signal falsely for short-term gains. In the absence of effective credible signals, investors are likely to be convinced that accurate information disclosure has occurred only if a third party, with reputation at stake, has asserted such on behalf of the company. Furthermore, the third party must be seen to be adversely and materially affected if its information production and certification turns out to be incorrect. As Booth and Smith (1986) and Megginson and Weiss (1991) note, for the third-party certification to be believable for investors, the certifying agent must have reputational capital at stake that would be forfeited by certifying falsely, and the value of the agent's reputational capital must be greater than the largest possible one-time wealth transfer or side payment that could be obtained by falsely certifying the transaction.

Thus, the greater the financial intermediary's reputation, the larger the short-term gain will have to be to induce the intermediary to certify falsely. This intuition has been formally captured in theoretical work in such diverse areas as auditing (Titman and Trueman 1986; Datar, Feltham, and Hughes 1991), securities underwriting (Chemmanur and Fulghieri 1994a), and loan monitoring (Chemmanur and Fulghieri 1994b).[2] In early work on the subject, Booth and Smith (1986) show that reputation can act as a credible bonding device. When at-stake reputation is large, it provides incentives to the intermediary to screen and monitor more intensely, which in turn leads to building up of even larger reputation capital. The reason why financial intermediaries invest in acquiring costly reputation is because they expect to earn economic benefits by providing valuable services.

Thus, reputation of financial services providers and the cost-benefit analyses of association with reputed actors are important considerations for companies interested in raising capital. External investors tend to rely on the reputation of the companies' associates in the absence of credible and adequate information about the companies themselves. For the private firms, this certification-based approach of relying on financial intermediaries' reputational capital assumes extreme importance because little is known about their operating history or track record. Furthermore, a segment of private firms that the venture capitalists largely focus on, deal with emerging technologies that are not only risky but whose outcome is also very uncertain. Thus, for such technology-intensive VC-backed private firms, the reputation of venture capitalists—their primary allies—is a key element in raising capital from both private and public sources.

While as a certification agent, VC reputation is important for the portfolio companies, the VCs themselves are also concerned about their reputation if they seek to be active long-term players in the financial markets. Given the highly networked nature of venture capital industry and the repeated need for funds, maintaining and enhancing reputation is critical for venture capitalists. A good reputation attracts potential investors and helps in developing useful working relationships with entrepreneurs, lawyers, investment bankers, auditors, and others who provide useful services to portfolio companies (Sahlman 1990). Reputable VCs can also benefit from less costly and larger fund-raising for future partnerships. In addition, reputation affects VC compensation, which in established funds is significantly more sensitive to performance, as shown by Gompers and Lerner (1999a). Finally, VCs earn most of their returns from IPOs and acquisitions of their portfolio companies and therefore have a strong incentive to establish a trustworthy reputation in order to retain access to the most profitable exit markets on favorable terms.

There exists some academic work studying the impact of financial intermediary reputation on performance of *private* firms with the VC literature providing most of the evidence in this area. While one strand of research has examined the impact of VC backing on firms contrasting VC-backed firms with those that are not, another branch has distinguished among VCs by their experience (or reputation) and analyzed its economic impact on VCs and their portfolio companies. In so doing, several intuitive measures of venture capital reputation have been suggested; examples include VC firm age, quantum of funds raised, cumulative aggregate investment, number of companies funded, number of investment rounds, capital under management, and number of companies taken public. Given the many disparate measures of VC reputation used in the literature, a few recent studies have focused on formulating a generally acceptable measure of VC reputation that is related to the performance of VC-backed companies in a consistent way.[3]

This survey on venture capital reputation is organized as follows. The next section offers an overview of the theoretical and empirical perspective on the importance of reputation capital for financial intermediaries, briefly surveying the underwriting, auditing, and commercial banking literatures. Then comes a discussion of the impact of reputation on venture capital firms as well as their portfolio companies. The following section summarizes the research focused on measuring VC reputation. Finally, the Conclusion sums up and discusses avenues for further research.

REPUTATION IN FINANCIAL INTERMEDIATION

There exists a large literature on the importance of financial intermediaries and their reputational capital. In particular, the theories of issuing equity have had a profound impact on the importance of financial intermediary reputation. Starting with Myers and Majluf (1984), the pecking order theory is based on the idea that insiders know more about their firms than outside investors and that firms maximize the wealth of current shareholders. Firms avoid issuing equity when they believe the stock is undervalued. Hence all firms with overvalued equity will issue stock, while only a fraction of firms with undervalued equity will, if say, they cannot afford to pass up their investment projects. Thus the average issuer in the market is likely to be overvalued. Rational investors anticipating this adverse selection problem will lower the offer price for the securities.

Thus the Myers and Majluf (1984) model predicts a negative stock price reaction to the announcement of equity issues because of potential adverse selection signaled by the decision to issue equity. Consistent with this prediction, empirical evidence suggests that firms perform poorly around seasoned equity offers, both in terms of poor stock returns (Asquith and Mullins 1986; Loughran and Ritter 1995; Spiess and Affleck-Graves 1995) and weak operating performance (Loughran and Ritter 1997; McLaughlin, Safieddine, and Vasudevan 1996, 1998).

A natural question that arises is whether the firms can decrease the negative impact on their stock returns around equity offerings or increase the likelihood of a successful equity offering.[4] A number of theoretical models imply that superior-quality issuing firms with significant information asymmetries can benefit substantially if specialized financial intermediaries can credibly certify firm values to less-informed investors. In other words, firms can signal favorable private information about their own values by choosing high-quality intermediaries (Booth and Smith 1986; Titman and Trueman 1986). In so doing, firms can avoid market failure by employing financial intermediaries to mitigate the adverse selection problem in equity offerings.

The role of underwriter reputation, for example, has been extensively studied in the context of both IPOs and SEOs. In a typical model, investment bankers produce and certify information about the companies that they have chosen to underwrite. The investment banks generally have an advantage over other investors in producing information at a relatively lower cost (Leland and Pyle 1977; Campbell and Kracaw 1980). Moreover, better-quality investment bankers can produce superior information about the companies they underwrite. For instance, Ljungqvist and Wilhelm (2003) find that price revisions increase with underwriting bank reputation suggesting that reputable banks extract more information from potential investors and incorporate it more aggressively in the issuers' offer prices. Similarly Corwin and Schultz (2005) find that the increased co-manager participation that accompanies reputable underwriters is related to more active offer price revisions, suggesting better information production for the issuers.

Furthermore, prestigious underwriters can have stricter standards for certification of issuing companies. For example, as Loughran and Ritter (2004) point out, reputable investment banks historically did not underwrite offerings by high-risk issuers. Thus, better reputable investment bankers are likely to back higher-quality companies, and the use of a better-quality investment banker is a positive signal about the issuing company's value. Moreover, a higher-quality company is willing to pay the additional fees associated with the use of a better-quality investment banker, because this can convey favorable information to outside investors who will then be willing to pay a higher price for the securities issued.

Despite the mostly clear empirical implications drawn from these models, empirical evidence on the topic is at best mixed. In early empirical research on investment banker reputation and IPOs, Tinic (1988); Beatty and Ritter (1986); Carter and Manaster (1990); Michaely and Shaw (1994); Carter, Dark, and Singh (1998); and Gompers and Lerner (1999b) find that investment banker reputation is associated with significantly lower underpricing. Carter and Manaster (1990) also show that low-dispersion or less risky issuers signal their quality by engaging reputed underwriters who in order to preserve their high reputation, market IPOs of less risky firms. Consistent with this argument, Michaely and Shaw (1994); Carter, Dark, and Singh (1998); and Gompers and Lerner (1999b) find that the long-run underperformance of IPOs managed by more prestigious underwriters is less severe. Other benefits that accrue to issuers backed by more reputable underwriters include an increased co-manager participation that in turn leads to an increased number of market makers and analysts covering the issuing firm (Corwin and Schultz 2005).

However, in more recent research, particularly on the data from the 1990s, IPOs are found to have *greater* underpricing when more reputable underwriters are involved (Beatty and Welch 1996; Loughran and Ritter 2004; Cliff and Denis 2004), which in part, is due to the research coverage provided by higher-ranked analysts affiliated with these underwriters. Also in contrast to the theoretical prediction, underwriters' gross spreads in IPOs have been found to be either generally close to 7 percent regardless of underwriter reputation (Chen and Ritter 2000), or lower for better reputed underwriters (James 1992; Corwin and Schultz 2005).

Although most models about the certifying ability of investment bankers, particularly the more reputable ones, are set in the context of IPOs, their implications are usually applicable to SEOs if the seasoned issuers are also subject to information asymmetries.[5] The Chemmanur and Fulghieri (1994a) model, for example, implies that the announcement period returns should be more positive for SEOs represented by more reputable investment bankers, and that better-quality investment bankers represent larger, less risky companies and bigger equity offerings.

Empirical evidence, however, again remains largely mixed. McLaughlin, Safieddine, and Vasudevan (2000) find a positive relation between investment banker reputation and announcement period returns when SEOs are announced, but no significant relation between investment banker reputation and long-run post-issue stock price performance. In recent work, Chuluun and Khorana (2007) report that the larger and more prestigious underwriting syndicates measured on the average reputation of all the underwriters in the syndicate are associated with lower SEO underpricing, which is consistent with the positive role of these specialized financial intermediaries. On the other hand, using a dataset of Canadian SEOs, Pandes (2008) shows that firms announcing equity offers experience more negative abnormal returns when underwriters to the offerings are more reputable. In a similar vein, Altinkilic and Hansen (2003) find that underwriter reputation is unrelated to the price discounts in primary seasoned equity offers (SEOs). In addition, the gross spreads in SEOs have been found to be either unrelated or inversely related to underwriter reputation (Butler, Grullon, and Weston 2005; Lee and Masulis 2008).

Although the evidence on fees is largely inconsistent with the theoretical prediction, some studies shed light on other potential ways by which reputable underwriters can benefit on account of their reputation. Analyzing the reasons for companies switching underwriters, Krigman, Shaw, and Womack (2001) show that issuing firms eventually gravitate toward more reputed underwriters. Corwin and Schultz (2005) find the number of underwriters and co-managers that participate in IPOs backed by reputable underwriters is significantly higher. This has important implications for underwriters in terms of risk diversification, independent expert appraisal, and certification provided by other underwriters, and formation of relationships that can result in future deal flow. Furthermore, persistence is observed in co-managers doing business with better reputed underwriters. These findings suggest that simply looking at spreads or fees may not be enough to capture the benefits accruing to the underwriters because of their better reputation.

A prominent issue is whether the performance of IPOs and SEOs is due to the reputation of underwriters or the quality of the issuing companies themselves. This reflects the well-known selection problem of more reputable underwriters choosing to associate with better-quality companies (Fernando, Gatchev, and Spindt 2005). If this endogenous nature of the company-intermediary matching is not taken into account, the inferences are likely to be misleading (Li and Prabhala 2005). In their analyses of IPO and post-IPO performance of equity-issuing companies, Chemmanur and Paeglis (2005) provide evidence on matching of better-quality companies with more reputable underwriters. However, even after controlling for management quality and underwriter reputation, the evidence on the certification role of underwriters is at best mixed. While companies represented by more reputable underwriters are able to attract a larger proportion of institutional investors as shareholders, they are also more underpriced.

In light of ambiguous evidence in the context of IPOs and SEOs, three recent studies, albeit in different settings, provide some evidence on the certification role of investment bankers. Raman (2007) explores the role of investment banks serving as placement agents in private placements of equity. Fang (2005) studies the role of investment bank reputation in a sample of public bond offers conducted during the 1990s. And Dai, Jo, and Schatzberg (2008) investigate the role of placement agents in the pricing of private investments in public equities (PIPEs). Most evidence from these studies is consistent with the theoretical prediction that investment bank reputation is informative of their clients' quality and that their underwriting decisions reflect their reputational concerns.

Most studies use the Carter and Manaster (1990) rankings to proxy for the underwriter reputation. The Carter-Manaster ranks, ranging from one to nine, are based on the relative placement of underwriter names in tombstone ads. These rankings have been found to be highly correlated with the underwriter market share, which has also been used in some studies to measure reputation.

From investment bankers and underwriters, we now turn to the certification role of auditors, which has been extensively analyzed as well. Early models by Titman and Trueman (1986) and Datar, Feltham, and Hughes (1991) imply that audit quality reduces IPO underpricing. The empirical evidence provided by Balvers, McDonald, and Miller (1988); Beatty (1989); and Michaely and Shaw (1995) is consistent with the predictions of these models. Specifically, companies that employed a Big Eight auditor were found to experience lower underpricing at their IPOs and better long-run stock return performance. The Big Eight auditors were found to be typically associated with much larger clients and thus had a larger market share based on their client revenues. Furthermore, Michaely and Shaw (1995) show that prestigious auditors are associated with less risky IPOs, which is consistent with matching of better-quality companies with more reputable auditors.

In the SEO context, Slovin, Sushka, and Hudson (1990) find that the stock price reaction to the announcement of seasoned equity offerings is a positive function of the quality of the auditing firm even after controlling for the reputation of the investment bank affiliated with the issuer and the quantity of bank debt in the issuer's capital structure.

An interesting study by Francis and Reynolds (2000) examines the auditors' trade-off between preserving reputation and the potential gains related to providing a low-quality product. They focus on large clients who can create an economic dependence that may cause auditors to compromise their independence and report more favorably to retain valuable clients. However, they find that such economic dependence (measured as a client's size relative to the size of the office that contracts for the audit and issues the audit report) does not prompt Big Five auditors to report more favorably on a client. This implies that auditors care about their reputation, which is consistent with the notion that financial intermediaries invest in acquiring costly reputation because they expect to earn economic benefits by providing valuable services.[6]

Some recent studies analyze the impact of an auditor's worsening reputation with the availability of an exogenous event, in the form of the indictment of Arthur Andersen (Andersen), by examining the reaction of companies to events that are damaging to an auditor's reputation. Chaney and Philipich (2002) investigate the impact of the Enron audit failure on auditor reputation and on the stock price of other Andersen clients. They show that other clients experienced significant negative stock returns upon Andersen's admission of fraud suggesting that investors downgraded the quality of the audits performed by Andersen. In Rauterkus and Song (2005), the authors find a 200 basis point more negative reaction to SEO announcements for companies audited by Andersen. The median firm in their sample loses $31.4 million more than a non-Andersen client.

Barton (2005) finds that 95 percent of Andersen's clients defected upon Andersen's formal indictment of criminal misconduct. Furthermore, Andersen clients defected sooner, mostly to another Big Five auditor, if they were more visible in the capital markets through more analyst and press coverage, had larger institutional ownership and share turnover, and raised more cash in recent security issues. This suggests that more visible companies try to build and preserve their reputation for credible financial reporting by engaging reputable auditors. In a related study, Asthana, Balsam, and Krishnan (2007) show that companies with relatively better corporate governance switched early upon Andersen's disclosure, and that companies switching from Andersen experienced positive excess returns during the three-day window around the announcement. Overall, these studies confirm that companies prefer reputed auditors for their certifying ability.

Regarding auditor compensation while several early studies (Beatty 1993; Craswell, Francis, and Taylor 1995) report that companies are willing to pay higher audit fees to receive audits from more reputable firms, recent research by Chaney, Jeter, and Shivakumar (2004) show that a reputable auditor premium, in terms of higher audit fees, disappears in a sample of privately-held companies once self-selection of auditors by these private companies is accounted for. This suggests that it is important to account for the endogenous nature of auditor-company matching (Menon and Williams 1991). Indeed, consistent with prior evidence Chaney, Jeter, and Shivakumar (2004) show that better-quality auditors are associated with an audit premium when selection bias is ignored.

Finally, any discussion on financial intermediation cannot ignore the large literature on commercial bank certification of their client companies, although an elaborate survey of this literature is beyond the scope of this study.[7] In contrast to the IPO/SEO and investment banking literature, however, much of the received wisdom from the commercial banking literature points toward bank certification being dominant even in settings where bank conflicts of interest are perceived to exist. For example, when banks underwrite securities of companies with whom they have lending relationships, they are potentially subject to conflicts of interest since the proceeds from securities' issues can be used to retire or refinance existing bank debt. While on one hand, the bank in its underwriting role can try to misrepresent the quality of the issuing company to potential investors, on the other the banks can credibly certify the quality of its borrowers to outside investors because it possesses private information about the borrowers (Puri 1999).

Banks are privy to much greater information about borrowers during the lending process (Fama 1985; Diamond 1991; Rajan 1992) as well as over the course of their relationship with the borrowers. Thus, if they emerge as certifiers of borrowers' quality outweighing potential conflicts of interest, it can have implications for borrowers in terms of lower yields on debt (Puri 1996; Gande, Puri, Saunders, and Walter 1997), reduced underpricing in equity issues (James and Weir 1990; Schenone 2004), higher wealth effects upon announcement of loans (Billett, Flannery, and Garfinkel 1995), and no significant underperformance after issues of debt (Ang and Richardson 1994; Kroszner and Rajan 1994; Puri 1994) or equity (Benzoni and Schenone 2008).

Credible certification also helps banks in building reputation that can be a valuable resource particularly for borrowers that lack a publicly known track record or are plagued by high information asymmetry. Indeed Hellmann, Lindsey, and Puri (2007) find that young borrowers prefer loans from banks that have an established reputation in the start-up market by virtue of a larger loan share.

On the relation between bank reputation and fees, most evidence is consistent with the findings in the IPO/SEO underwriting literature. For example, Yasuda (2005) finds that better reputable banks charge lower fees to their clients. Similarly Gande, Puri, and Saunders (1999) show that gross spreads in corporate debt underwriting are lower for banks that have larger market shares of corporate debt underwritings. There are at least two possible explanations for why the empirical evidence diverges from the theoretical prediction. First, there is endogenous matching of firms and banks with more reputable banks aligning with better-quality firms. Second, in return for future business opportunities, banks may be willing to pass on some of the benefits, say in terms of lower fees, to their clients. Consistent with this conjecture, Bharath, Dahiya, Saunders, and Srinivasan (2007) find that better reputable banks by their loan market share have a higher likelihood of receiving future lending business.

There are multiple ways by which bank certifying ability has been captured in the commercial banking literature. First, the presence of a bank having a lending relationship with the issuing firm has been shown to have a positive impact on the issuers of debt and equity (Puri 1996; Schenone 2004; Benzoni and Schenone 2009). Second, instead of a bank indicator, some studies include the size of bank stake to signify better incentives for bank certification that result from larger bank holdings (Gande, Puri, and Saunders 1999; Li and Masulis 2008). Third, a proxy for bank quality is explicitly designed as in Billett, Flannery, and Garfinkel (1995), who distinguish high-quality lenders from low-quality lenders by their credit ratings. Finally, many studies use the market share of loans (underwritten issues) to proxy for lending (underwriting) bank's reputation (Hellmann, Lindsey, and Puri 2007; Bharath et al. 2007, Gande, Puri, and Saunders 1999; Yasuda 2005).

In closing, we summarize the above evidence on reputational effects in financial intermediation as follows. First, better reputation of financial intermediaries is generally associated with their superior certification ability, and by and large the market reacts accordingly in a favorable manner. Even though the evidence from IPO/SEO underwriting literature is far from conclusive, the overwhelming evidence, at least in the banking and auditing literatures, is consistent with this conjecture. In analyzing commercial banks, much of the evidence points toward banks' certifying ability even when potential conflicts of interest exist.

Second, in return for creating and preserving reputation, the financial intermediaries expect to be compensated through higher fees and more business opportunities. These provide incentives to acquire costly reputation in the first place. However, most evidence points toward a better-reputation discount on fees. In other words, better reputable financial intermediaries are not found to charge higher compensation, but are frequently observed levying lower fees on their clients. There could be two primary reasons for this phenomenon. First, more reputable intermediaries are likely to select better-quality companies as their clients, and lower fees are simply a reflection of lessened adverse selection risk. Second, in return for future business opportunities, reputed intermediaries may be willing to pass on some of the benefits (in terms of lower fees or spreads) to their clients.

Third, maintaining and creating better reputation is one of the primary objectives of the financial intermediaries, and they are careful in selecting their clients. Matching of above-average companies with more reputable financial intermediaries is consistently observed in securities underwriting, auditing, and commercial banking literatures.

Fourth, deteriorating reputation of financial intermediaries has a negative impact on their clients. Furthermore, clients who switch intermediaries after worsening reputation of their affiliates witness the market rewarding them in terms of higher stock prices. Similarly, companies try to gravitate toward better reputable financial intermediaries in the long run.

Fifth, measures of intermediaries' reputation capital based on their market share have been used across these literatures, and by and large they perform well in most empirical studies, although other literature-specific measures of reputation exist as well. For example, although the well known Carter-Manaster rankings of underwriters are widely used in the investment banking literature, these are found to be highly correlated with the market share of the underwriting banks. Similarly, the auditing literature has typically used Big X ($X = 5$, 8, etc.) versus non–Big X classification to distinguish more reputable auditors from less reputed auditing firms, where Big X auditors are likely to have a larger market share of the audit market as well.

In the following sections, we discuss the role of venture capitalists and their reputation capital and tie in that evidence with the above synopsis, which is drawn from the overall empirical evidence found in the underwriting, auditing, and banking literatures.

VENTURE CAPITAL FIRMS AS FINANCIAL INTERMEDIARIES

As mentioned earlier, VC backing and their reputation are likely to be important factors in certification of private firms that lack a publicly-known track record.

In what follows we survey the evidence on implications of VC backing and reputation for both VC firms and their portfolio companies. We largely arrange the evidence as it has emerged in chronological order, although it becomes apparent from the discussion that VCs have influenced companies at various stages of their development as they develop from start-ups and in some cases go on to become successful public companies. Towards the end of this section, we discuss the impact of reputation on VC firms.

Some early papers in the VC literature emphasized the certification role of VCs by contrasting VC-backed and non–VC-backed IPOs, much akin to the securities underwriting literature. For example, in the context of IPO underpricing, Megginson and Weiss (1991) conclude that the presence of venture capitalists serves to lower the cost of going public. Matching VC-backed and non–VC-backed IPOs on industry and offer size, they show that VC backing reduces underpricing and gross spreads in a sample of firms that went public in the timeframe from 1983 to 1987. In a related study undertaken around the same period, although Barry, Muscarella, Peavy, and Vetsuypens (1990) do not find a significant impact of VC presence on IPO underpricing, they do show that experienced VCs underprice their IPOs less than their less-experienced counterparts. While the differences in the two studies on underpricing are attributable to how the samples are constructed, the Barry et al. (1990) study is notable in perhaps being the first in the literature to have analyzed the economic impact of VC experience.

Recent evidence, however, has somewhat overturned the conventional wisdom about the VCs' certification role in the context of IPO underpricing by showing that VC-backed IPOs are *more* underpriced than non–VC-backed IPOs (Lee and Wahal 2004). Using the propensity score technique to control for the endogeneity in VC funding of their portfolio companies (for example, reputable VCs are more likely to fund better-quality companies), they find that VC-backed IPOs experience larger first-day returns than comparable non–VC-backed IPOs, and that between the years 1980 and 2000, the average return difference has ranged from 5.01 percentage points to 10.32 percentage points. Although Lee and Wahal (2004) do not analyze the impact of high- or low-reputation VCs on underpricing, they shed some light on why VC firms underprice their companies at IPOs. In particular, they report that low-reputation firms—measured by VC age or number of previously backed IPOs—benefit more from underpricing as the subsequent inflow of funds into these VC firms is markedly higher. A higher IPO underpricing creates a market buzz that attracts a lot of attention from capital market investors, leading to this grandstanding behavior by less reputable VC firms.

In recent work, Li and Masulis (2008) analyze 1,479 VC-backed IPOs during the period from 1993 to 2000 and find that venture investments by multiple classes of financial intermediaries (investment banks, commercial banks, and insurance companies) have independent and incremental certification impact on the IPO process in terms of lower underpricing. The marginal effect of venture holdings by different classes of intermediaries is stronger when multiple classes of intermediaries are VC investors in the same issuer. Furthermore, the size of venture investments in issuer shares is associated with significantly less IPO underpricing, lower absolute price revisions, and higher IPO issuer return on assets (ROA) in the post-IPO period. The impact of venture investment positions is greater for IPO stocks with more information asymmetry, which is further support for the certification effect of intermediaries' venture investments. Likewise, the impact of intermediaries' venture investment positions is greater and more significant for IPO stocks backed by more reputable VCs, who are better able to reduce the asymmetric information problem facing outside investors.

In another study in the IPO setting, Lerner (1994a) sheds light on the VCs' market timing ability by showing that VCs, particularly more experienced VC firms by their age, are adept at bringing their companies public during better market conditions. Focusing on the biotechnology industry, the study evaluates the choices faced by VCs on whether to approach private investors or public capital markets for additional funding for their portfolio companies, and finds that VCs (and primarily more experienced VCs) are more likely to go public in better market conditions in the biotech industry.

Since IPOs, on average, are the most profitable of VC exits, Gompers (1996) utilizes this setting to analyze VC incentives to build reputation by analyzing a sample of 433 VC-backed IPOs in the timeframe from 1978 to 1987. Characterizing VC reputation by age, he finds that younger VC firms engage in grandstanding behavior by which they seek to establish a quick reputation in the venture capital industry by taking their portfolio companies public sooner than their more experienced counterparts.[8] However, this behavior has real adverse repercussions in that companies that go public earlier are more underpriced at their IPOs. Furthermore, younger grandstanding VCs are found to have spent less time with their portfolio companies, which can have implications for their development, since VCs provide expertise and other value-added services on a continuing basis.

In a related issue, Gompers et al. (2008a) analyze the timing of venture capital investment decisions, rather than timing of their exits. They study over 30,000 VC investments made during the period from 1975 to 1998 and evaluate the response of VC firms to shifts in public markets, particularly when valuations are high. They find that the greatest response to changes in the public markets is not by new or inexperienced VC firms, but by specialized organizations with considerable industry experience (measured by cumulative number of investments made by the VC firm). Although experienced VC firms increase their investments during market booms, there is no real degradation in their performance. These results suggest that experienced firms are better able to take advantage of shifts in public markets by increasing their investment outlays but without sacrificing their performance. In so doing, they further enhance their experience and reputation.

An important line of research, which shows the interaction between venture capital and corporate governance, asks whether VC firms inculcate good governance practices in the companies they back. Baker and Gompers (2003) examine board composition in a sample of more than 1,100 IPOs in the period from 1978 to 1987 and find that companies backed by VCs have fewer inside directors and more independent outsiders on their boards, and that the representation of independent outside directors increases with VC reputation (VC reputation is measured on both VC age and the average reputation of the underwriters the VC firm has associated with in its previous public offerings). They also show that the probability that a founder remains a CEO decreases with VC firm reputation. In related work based on a sample of nearly 17,000 VC investments made between 1990 and 2004, but using a different measure of VC reputation based on the number of prior investments a VC has made and the average size of VC syndicates in prior deals, Wongsunwai

(2008) reaches a similar conclusion that start-ups backed by higher-quality VCs have larger boards with more independent directors.

From a different corporate governance perspective, using a sample of nearly 1,800 companies that went public between 1983 and 1994, Hochberg (2008) shows that VC-backed companies have lower levels of earnings management than non–VC-backed companies at their IPOs and are also less likely to engage in aggressive accounting practices. Moreover, upon announcing the adoption of shareholder rights agreements, VC-backed companies experience significantly higher wealth effects than non–VC-backed companies. Distinguishing among VCs by their reputation, Wongsunwai (2008) shows that IPOs backed by higher-quality VCs have less aggressive financial reporting practices that manifest through lower abnormal accruals in the period after the IPOs and around their lockup expirations, and also have lower rates of subsequent financial restatements. Overall, the evidence is consistent with the notion that VC-backed companies have more shareholder-friendly corporate governance mechanisms, and reputable VCs inculcate significantly better corporate governance practices in their portfolio companies.

In a natural progression, some studies have examined the influence of VCs on post-IPO public companies. Brav and Gompers (1997) investigate the long-run performance of VC-backed and non–VC-backed IPOs brought to market from 1972 to 1992 to shed light on the primary source of IPO underperformance documented in several studies, including Ritter (1991) and Loughran and Ritter (1995). While they find VC-backed companies do not underperform, they also show that the documented IPO underperformance is not an IPO affect per se—the primary culprits are small, low book-to-market firms that do not receive VC backing.

IPOs and acquisitions are the two primary methods through which VCs profitably exit from their portfolio companies. It is well known that VC firms reap most of their profits from the subsample of their investments that exit either through IPOs or acquisitions (Cumming and MacIntosh 2003; Cochrane 2005). In many studies such as Gompers and Lerner (2000a); Brander, Amit, and Antweiler (2002); Hochberg, Ljungqvist, and Lu (2007); Sorensen (2008); and Zarutskie (2008), VC exits through IPOs and acquisitions denote successful outcome of VC investments. Hochberg, Ljungqvist, and Lu (2007) also show that this measure of VC success is a reasonable proxy for VC fund returns. Furthermore, companies going public are generally considered to be the most successful among all VC investments and also fetch the highest returns to VCs. Although the going public decision has been extensively studied, both theoretically and empirically, limited research exists on the acquisitions of private firms, particularly those that are VC-backed. A recent study by Poulsen and Stegemoller (2008) documents factors that determine the firm's choice of an IPO or an acquisition for a broad sample of privately held firms. In a logit framework estimating the likelihood of an IPO versus an acquisition on a sample of 1074 IPOs and 735 acquisitions from 1995 to 2004, VC backing is found to be an important positive predictor of companies going public. This evidence is again consistent with VC firms being an important source of information about the quality of the issuing companies.

Some recent studies that analyze the likelihood of successful VC exits include Hochberg, Ljungqvist, and Lu (2007); Sorensen (2007); Gompers, Kovner, Lerner, and Scharfstein (2008a); and Zarutskie (2008). The focus in Hochberg, Ljungqvist, and Lu (2007) is on analyzing whether VC network centrality affects

VC performance in terms of ability to profitably exit through IPOs and acquisitions. They construct five VC network centrality measures capturing the degree of VC connectedness with other VCs, based on the venture capital transactions syndicated in the recent past. The study based on a sample of VC investments made in 16,315 companies between 1980 and 1999 finds that VC network centrality is a significant predictor of VC performance supporting the conjecture that VCs that actively syndicate with other industry participants and are better connected have superior access to deal flow, investment opportunity sets, and information. Hochberg, Ljungqvist, and Lu (2007) use VC's aggregate investment in the venture capital industry as a measure of VC experience, but it does not emerge as a consistent predictor of portfolio companies' performance when VC network centrality is also accounted for. Even though the focus in Hochberg, Ljungqvist, and Lu (2007) is on showing the performance implications of networking in the venture capital industry, the network centrality measures are likely to be correlated with VC reputation.

In another interesting study, Sorensen (2007) separates the effects of VC sorting from value-addition to study their individual influences on the IPO rates. Using initial VC investments made in 1,666 companies between 1982 and 1995, he analyzes whether experienced VCs truly add incremental value to their portfolio companies, or do they simply have access to a more promising investment opportunity set? By employing a structural model based on a two-sided matching model, he is able to exploit the characteristics of the other agents in the market to separately identify and estimate the impact of VC influence and sorting on portfolio company performance. Sorensen (2007) proxies VC experience by the number of investment rounds made by a VC firm and shows that VC sorting is twice as important as VC influence in determining the portfolio company success.

While analyzing the performance implications of serial entrepreneurship, Gompers, Kovner, Lerner, and Scharfstein (2008b) highlight the role of more reputable VCs in selecting start-ups for funding. They find funding by more experienced venture capital firms enhances the chance of IPO success, but only for entrepreneurs without a successful track record. Moreover, experienced venture capitalists are able to identify and fund first-time entrepreneurs who are more likely to become serial entrepreneurs. Apart from emphasizing the impact of VC experience on IPO success, the results highlight the sorting skill of more reputable venture capitalists.

Finally, Zarutskie (2008) analyzes the background of human capital in VC firms by analyzing the biographical data for the 482 individual venture capitalists managing a sample of 222 first-time venture funds raised between 1980 and 1998. She finds that fund management teams with more task-specific human capital, measured by a greater number of managers having past experience as venture capitalists and by more managers having past experience as executives at start-up companies, manage funds with greater fractions of successful portfolio company exits. She also finds that fund management teams having more industry-specific human capital in strategy and management consulting and to a lesser extent, engineering and non-venture financing, manage funds with greater fractions of successful portfolio company exits.

From VC exits, we switch gears to analyze the value-added activities of VCs when they professionalize and monitor their portfolio companies. Hellmann and

Puri (2002) analyze the professionalization of start-up companies with the help of venture capitalists by primarily focusing on start-ups that have not yet approached public markets for funding. Using a combination of survey data, interview data, and publicly available data, they construct a dataset of over 170 young high tech firms based in the Silicon Valley to shed light on the nature of support that VCs provide in building up their portfolio companies. They find that VCs play an extensive role in professionalizing start-up firms through active intervention in designing human resource policies, executive compensation, and staffing of adequate personnel, particularly in sales and marketing. VC-backed companies are also twice as likely to replace the founders with outside CEOs faster. Furthermore, in another related study, using the same dataset, Hellmann and Puri (2000) show that venture capital is associated with a significant reduction in the time taken to bring a product to market, especially for start-ups that have innovative products. The evidence strongly supports the conventional view that VCs go beyond traditional financial intermediaries by playing an active role in managing and guiding their protégés toward eventual success.

Another strand of recent research, utilizing the U.S. Census Bureau data, focuses on analyzing the real impact of venture capital investments in terms of efficiency gains and productivity improvements generated in private companies. Focusing on companies in the manufacturing sector (SIC codes 2,000–3,999), and using a sample of 1,881 VC-funded and 185,882 non–VC-backed companies between 1972 and 2000, Chemmanur, Krishnan, and Nandy (2008) find that the overall efficiency measured by total factory productivity (TFP) is higher for VC-backed companies than for non–VC-backed companies, and this efficiency advantage of VC-backed companies arises from both screening and monitoring. In other words, not only is the efficiency of private companies prior to receiving VC financing higher than that of non-VC backed companies, but also the growth in efficiency subsequent to receiving VC financing is greater for such companies relative to non–VC-backed companies. Distinguishing VC firms by their reputation—based on cumulative fund raising by the VC firm—they find the increase in efficiency subsequent to VC financing is significantly higher for more reputable VC firms, and these efficiency gains arise from both an improvement in product market performance (sales) and from reductions in various input costs. In contrast, the efficiency gains generated by relatively less reputable VC firms arise primarily from improvements in product market performance. Finally, both the TFP level of VC-backed companies prior to receipt of VC funding and the growth in TFP subsequent to VC funding positively affect the probability of a successful exit via an IPO or an acquisition.

In a similar spirit, using data from the U.S. Census Bureau, Puri and Zarutskie (2008) look at the life-cycle dynamics of privately-held firms. As Puri and Zarutskie (2008) point out, much of our understanding of VC-backed companies is sourced from the analyses of companies that are successful, namely IPOs and acquisitions. We have little understanding of VC-backed companies that fail, or the privately-held firms that could use VC funding but did not. In tackling these questions, Puri and Zarutskie (2008) not only shed light on the life-cycle dynamics—growth, profitability, and failure—of private companies but also analyze which privately-held companies are likely to receive VC financing in the first place. Analyzing a matched sample of 7,632 VC-backed and 7,632 non–VC-backed companies, their findings

reveal that VCs typically invest in young firms, with potential for scalability being a particularly important criterion. Furthermore, relative to the non–VC-backed
companies, the VC-backed companies demonstrate larger scalability, both for successful and unsuccessful companies, at every point of their life cycle. However,
there is little difference in profitability measures between the two samples at the
time of VC exits. Finally, although VC-backed companies have lower failure rates
overall, the failure rates increase with the passage of time the VC has remained
invested in these companies.

Evidence at the aggregate level confirms VCs' impact on real economy as well.
Kortum and Lerner (2000) measure the influence of venture capital on technological
innovation in the United States from 1965 to 1992. Adopting an industry-level
analysis, they find that patenting patterns across manufacturing industries over
the three-decade period suggest that the impact of venture capital is positive and
significant, and their estimates suggest that venture capital accounted for about
8 percent of industrial innovations in the United States in the decade ending in
1992.

The evidence gleaned from this set of studies confirms that VCs are an important catalyst in the life cycle of privately-held companies emerging in new sectors
of economy, and play an important role beyond that of traditional financial intermediaries. Furthermore better reputable VCs are able to add more value to their
portfolio companies. We now focus on what VCs themselves gain from investing
in building and preserving their reputation.

While fund-raising is a challenging task for start-ups, it is not any easier for
VCs themselves. However, better reputation can certainly help in raising capital.
Analyzing the commitments to new VC funds from 1969 until 1994, Gompers and
Lerner (1998) report that better reputation, in the form of VC firm age and size,
positively affects the ability to raise new capital. Kaplan and Schoar (2005) in a study
of funds raised between 1980 and 2001 also show that more experienced firms—by
the number of funds raised—are more likely to raise capital, and raise larger follow-
on funds. Using a sample of about 250 private equity partnership agreements,
Lerner and Schoar (2004) show that the restrictions on limited partners' ability
to transfer funds are less common in later funds organized by the same private
equity group where information problems are presumably less severe because of
an established track record. This suggests that more reputable VC firms are less
worried about liquidity constraints because of an established reputation and that
when asymmetric information problems are more severe for future fund-raising
(for instance, for younger and less established VC firms) there is likely to be more
emphasis on selecting long-horizon investors.

On VC ability to raise funds for their portfolio companies, Bottazzi, Da Rin,
and Hellmann (2008) analyze data on 119 venture firms, 503 venture partners, and
1,652 portfolio companies that received VC investments between 1998 and 2001.
Using these data collected through a survey instrument sent to VC firms in 17
European countries, they find that reputable VCs (by firm age) are more effective
at fund-raising for their portfolio companies. In a slightly different vein, Lerner
(1994a) analyzes a sample of 651 investment rounds at 271 biotechnology firms
that received VC funding between 1978 and 1989. He confirms that prestigious
VC firms are more likely to syndicate with similar more reputable firms, which
not only decreases the capital requirements of a VC firm, but also facilitates in

diversifying risk, affords an independent appraisal of the project, and helps form relationships that are crucial for future deal flow.

On VC compensation, Gompers and Lerner (1999a) provide evidence from 419 U.S. venture partnerships formed between 1978 and 1992, which is generally consistent with the notion that reputation is an important determinant of compensation for venture capitalists. Using two proxies for reputation, the age and size of the venture organization, they find that the compensation of established funds is significantly more sensitive to performance and more variable than that of other funds. Older and larger firms have lower base compensation as well. In his early funds, the venture capitalist works harder even without explicit pay-for-performance incentives because, if he can establish a good reputation based on his portfolio companies' performance, he stands to gain additional compensation in later funds. Once a reputation has been established, explicit incentive compensation provides appropriate incentives to VCs.

Another way by which VCs can gain because of their better reputation is in their dealings with limited partners (LPs) and entrepreneurs. For example, reputational concerns can make opportunistic behavior less attractive for prestigious VC firms and reduce the need for covenants in their contracts with LPs. Gompers and Lerner (1996) examine covenants in 140 partnership agreements establishing VC funds and find evidence consistent with the notion that the likelihood of including covenants that restrict activities of the general partner is significantly reduced for reputable venture capital organizations. Alternately the evidence is also consistent with the notion that high-reputation VCs wield more bargaining power in their contract negotiations with LPs.

On VCs' interaction with their portfolio companies regarding contractual terms, Bengtsson (2008) finds that experienced VCs are more likely to receive board seats, and that they are more likely to invest in the earlier rounds of company's funding. In a similar spirit, based on their analysis of a European dataset comprising 223 entrepreneurial companies financed by 35 VC funds in 11 continental European countries, Cumming and Johan (2008) report that seasoned VCs are more likely to use convertible preferred equity and less likely to use common equity in their contracts with entrepreneurial firms.

In a more detailed analysis on contractual features, using cumulative number of investments made by the VC firm as a proxy for VC experience, Bengtsson and Sensoy (2008) show that more-experienced VCs use fewer contract terms that give the VCs downside protection. This evidence is consistent with the prediction that investors who are more able to mitigate agency and information problems through non-contractual means—such as monitoring or the threat of refusing follow-up financing—will use financial contracts with weaker downside protection. In their analysis based on a database of contractual provisions pertaining to investments by 646 private-partnership VCs in 1,266 start-up companies over 1,534 investment rounds, the authors construct a downside protection index (DPI) and relate it to VC experience. The DPI is an amalgam of six contractual features, namely cumulative dividend right, liquidation preference, redemption right, anti-dilution protection, participation right attached to the preferred stock, and pay-to-play feature for retaining rights in the event of future investments in the start-ups.

More evidence on the beneficial impact of VC reputation on contractual terms comes from Kaplan, Martel, and Stromberg (2007) who analyze VC investments in 23 non-U.S. countries and compare them to U.S. VC investments. They describe how the contracts allocate cash flow, board, liquidation, and other control rights. In univariate analyses, contracts differ across legal regimes. However, more experienced VCs implement U.S.-style contracts regardless of legal regime. VC firms that do not use U.S.-style contracts fail significantly more often, even after controlling for VC experience. The results are consistent with U.S.-style contracts being efficient across a wide range of legal regimes, and suggest that experienced VCs are able to negotiate for U.S.-style contracts with start-up companies regardless of the legal regime.

Along similar lines, but focusing on start-up valuations, Hsu (2004) shows that start-ups are often willing to turn down higher valuation offers in favor of more reputable VCs even if valuation offers are lower. His findings, based on a dataset of 149 start-up firms that received multiple offers from a total of 246 VC investors, imply that start-ups not only care about VC reputation but also willingly sacrifice higher valuation offers. Thus reputed VCs obtain higher compensation for their assistance, which is akin to a reputable underwriter or banker obtaining higher spread or fees for their services. The evidence in Hsu (2004) also implies that reputable VCs have a larger investment opportunity set, which can be thought of as an added incentive for VCs to acquire reputation.

On the impact of VC reputation on fellow VCs, Cumming and Dai (2008) present evidence consistent with VC reputation acting as a critical entry barrier for younger VCs. Based on a sample of U.S. VC investments made between 1980 and 2000, they find that more experienced and older VCs exhibit significantly stronger local bias in their investing. This behavior can be attributed to the unique two-sided matching in the VC market (Sorensen 2007). Unlike the investments in public equity, where fund managers have more control over which firms they invest in, in the VC industry VC investors are able to invest in entrepreneurial companies only when they are favored by the entrepreneurs. This significantly affects younger VCs' access to start-ups that are geographically located closer to more reputable VCs. It also increases the adverse selection risk for younger VCs since more reputable VCs prefer to align with better-quality companies.

Finally, a recent study sheds some light on the effects on VCs pursuant to a shock to their reputation. Atanasov, Ivanov, and Litvak (2008) study the repercussions of VC misbehavior and their worsening reputation by analyzing a sample of over 180 lawsuits involving venture capitalists. They analyze the relationship between lawsuits, VC fund-raising, and deal flow. Even though plaintiffs lose most VC-related lawsuits, litigation does not go unnoticed: in subsequent years, the involved VCs raise significantly less capital than their peers (matched on age, size, or performance) and invest in fewer and lower-quality deals. The biggest losers are VCs who are defendants in a lawsuit, who eventually lose the lawsuit, and who participate in multiple lawsuits.

In summary most evidence on the beneficial impact of VC backing and their reputation is consistent with theory. VCs (and particularly reputable VCs) add value to their portfolio companies and in so doing enhance their reputation. In return they are compensated through favorable start-up valuations, better contractual features in their agreements with limited partners and entrepreneurs, and increased fund-raising ability. However, in comparing and contrasting companies with and without VC-backing, or analyzing only the VC-backed companies, most studies use a measure of VC reputation about which little formal consensus exists in the literature. The next section discusses research that measures VC reputation and the emerging literature in this area.

MEASURING VC REPUTATION

As mentioned earlier, for the private VC-backed companies, the certification-based approach relying on financial intermediaries' reputation assumes extreme importance because little is known about their operating history or track record when they are trying to access public funding or explore potential acquirers. Even so, there is little consensus in the venture capital area on how to measure VC reputation, although some recent studies focus in that direction. This is surprising, considering both the importance of reputation in the VC industry and the preponderance of studies in other areas, notably the auditing and banking literatures that highlight the performance implications of reputation of financial intermediaries on public firms.

Some measures of VC reputation utilized in the literature include VC firm age, quantum of funds raised, cumulative aggregate investment, number of companies funded, number of investment rounds, capital under management, and number of companies taken public. Furthermore, the measures capturing VC network centrality in Hochberg, Ljungqvist, and Lu (2007) are also likely to be correlated with VC reputation. Most studies, however, do not focus on devising a consistent proxy for VC reputation or proposing a better measure (having more explanatory power) from the many measures hitherto utilized. Two recent studies that attempt to shed light on this issue are Ivanov et al. (2008) and Nahata (2008). While Ivanov et al. (2008) analyze the impact of VC reputation on long-run performance of IPOs, Nahata (2008) focuses on pre-exit portfolio companies to demonstrate a consistent measure of VC reputation that robustly predicts VC firm and portfolio company performance.

The empirical analysis in Nahata (2008) relates VC reputation to the performance of portfolio companies whose VC funding occurred between 1991 and 2001. The primary dataset consists of 33,539 identifiable VC investments in 12,124 portfolio companies. VC reputation is based on the cumulative market capitalization of IPOs backed by the VC firm in the IPO market. As Gompers and Lerner (2001) point out, IPOs are the most successful of all venture exits and fetch the highest returns to the venture investors. In guiding a portfolio company from a private start-up to an IPO, the VC firm adds to its reputation of being a successful venture investor. Furthermore, an IPO exit creates a buzz and enhances VC visibility in the industry. For each VC firm, the *dollar market value* of all companies taken public by the VC firm is cumulated until a given calendar year and normalized by the aggregate market value of all VC-backed companies that went public until the same calendar year. Kaplan and Schoar (2005) report a fair degree of return persistence in the private equity industry and Megginson and Weiss (1991) and Ivanov et al. (2008) argue that VCs enjoying continuing success create a greater visibility for themselves. The cumulative nature of the measure of VC reputation, referred hereafter as the *IPO capitalization share*, captures this effect.

On relating the aforementioned measure of VC reputation to VC firm and portfolio company performance, three major findings emerge in Nahata (2008). First, better reputable VC firms are more likely to lead their companies to successful exits—IPOs and acquisitions. This evidence holds upon analysis of both the performance of individual VC investments as well as the performance of the lead VC firm at the portfolio company level. Furthermore, these findings are robust when the probability of a successful exit is analyzed in the hazard framework. Thus reputable VCs are more likely to exit successfully with a lower expected duration.

Second, upon restricting the sample only to the successful exits, IPOs are found to be associated with more reputable VCs, even relative to acquisitions. Thus, a monotonic pattern emerges in which top brand VCs are more likely to be associated with IPOs, followed by medium brand VCs with acquisitions and the least reputable VCs with unsuccessful exits. Since IPOs on average, fetch the highest returns to the venture investors followed by acquisitions, this pattern is expected as the best VCs are expected to both select and nurture their portfolio companies toward the most successful exit.

Third, companies backed by more reputable VCs have higher asset productivity-ratio of revenues to total book assets at the time of their IPOs. Asset productivity is a means to determine the efficiency by which a company converts its investment in assets into sales. Reputable VCs are more likely to provide better value-added services that get translated into higher operating efficiency for their portfolio companies. The analyses control for other measures of VC experience or reputation used previously in the literature, for example, VC firm age, aggregate VC investment, VC connectedness, and cumulative investment rounds made by the VC firm. However, these do not emerge as consistent predictors of VC firm performance.

Since preserving and enhancing reputation is important for VC firms, reputable VC firms are more likely to invest in companies that have a greater potential to succeed. Companies too are willing to turn down higher valuation offers in favor of more reputable VCs even if valuation offers are lower (Hsu 2004). As mentioned earlier, Sorensen (2007) sheds light on this issue by distinguishing between *monitoring* by more experienced VCs from *sorting* in the VC market, which leads experienced VCs to invest in better companies. He finds both effects are significant, but sorting is almost twice as important as influence for the difference in IPO rates. In addition, the evidence in Nahata (2008) is consistent with Sorensen's findings when VC selection of investments is accounted for in the analyses.

One way to test whether VC reputation measured by IPO capitalization share effectively incorporates both VCs' selection as well as monitoring abilities, and predicts success of portfolio companies is by dividing the sample based on the developmental stage of portfolio companies when they were initially funded. Arguably, VCs are likely to expend more effort on monitoring, relative to screening, on early-stage portfolio companies. At the later stages of development, when companies are relatively closer to exit, the VC screening expertise assumes relatively more importance. On dividing the sample based on companies' being in seed/early or later/expansion stages at the time of their initial funding, and relating the likelihood of a successful VC exit to VC reputation, IPO capitalization share continues to predict the success of portfolio companies in both subsamples, suggesting that it effectively captures VCs' screening as well as monitoring expertise. This is important since a good proxy for reputation should ideally reflect both VC characteristics.[9]

In a complementary study, Ivanov et al. (2008) examine how VC reputation is associated with post-IPO long-term performance of portfolio companies. Using a primary dataset of 1,200 VC-backed and 1,302 non–VC-backed IPOs from 1993 to 2002, they measure issuer long-term performance on four standards: industry-adjusted operating performance (ROA), market-to-book ratio, long-run listing survival, and long-run abnormal stock returns. They also relate VC reputation to the probability of post-IPO acquisition, the takeover premium, and the expected growth rate of the issuing firm. These performance metrics are measured in the three-year post-IPO period.

Ivanov et al. (2008) create their reputation measure—IPO market share—based on VC's market share of completed venture-backed IPOs, which is very similar in spirit to IPO capitalization share, the measure proposed in Nahata (2008). One difference between the two measures is that while Nahata's (2008) measure is based on the market capitalization of companies going public, the proxy for VC reputation in Ivanov et al. (2008) is based on IPO gross proceeds. However, the two measures are likely to be highly correlated with each other. Notably, both are based on the VC firms' share of the VC-backed IPO market.

The IPO market share is found to have consistently significant positive associations with all the above long-term performance measures of the issuers. While VC backing improves a firm's post-IPO performance, they find VC reputation has even better explanatory power. Ivanov et al. (2008) also address the possibility of the results being an artifact of VC sorting rather than VC's ability to provide effective monitoring and other value-added services. Using an IV framework, they find evidence of both VC selection and nurturing in line with the evidence in Sorensen (2007).

Finally, Ivanov et al. (2008) explore some ways by which VCs nurture their portfolio companies by examining whether higher-reputation VCs are more actively involved post-IPO in their portfolio companies, and are associated with better-quality corporate governance. They find more reputable VCs are significantly more likely to continue to have large shareholdings and board positions one, two, and three years after an IPO, well beyond the standard lockup period. They also establish that better-quality VCs associate with portfolio companies exhibiting better corporate governance mechanisms, including fewer firms with either a CEO-Chair or founder-CEO duality. In summary, the superior post-IPO long-run performance of firms backed by more reputable VCs is consistent with their actively inculcating stronger corporate governance in their portfolio companies. Both studies show that the market share–based measure of VC reputation is effectively related to the performance of private firms both around VC exits and in the long run, which is consistent with the evidence on efficacy of market share–based reputation measures highlighted in other fields of financial intermediation.

CONCLUSION

Financial intermediation matters. Its importance is amply clear from the VC industry, which funds start-ups that otherwise would not receive funding directly from investors. Reputational capital is crucially important for VCs because it has significant implications for fund-raising, sorting, and harvesting. Research has consistently shown a positive impact of VC backing and particularly the importance of

Exhibit 15.1 Top 30 Venture Capital Firms

VC firm rankings are based on the dollar capitalization share of a VC firm in the IPO market, cumulated until the end of the year 2005. As a comparison, the 1998 rankings based on the dollar capitalization share of the VC firm in the IPO market until the end of that year are also presented. *indicates the VC firm was outside the top 100 bracket.

2005 Rank	Venture Capital Firm	IPO Capitalization Share (%)	1998 Rank
1	J.P. Morgan Chase Capital Partners	13.36	2
2	Kleiner Perkins Caufield & Byers	12.55	1
3	Integral Capital Partners	9.24	3
4	Goldman, Sachs & Co.	8.13	11
5	New Enterprise Associates	8.03	7
6	Sequoia Capital	7.98	5
7	Cisco Systems, Inc.	7.37	*
8	Intel Capital	6.99	*
9	Accel Partners	6.16	13
10	Amerindo Investment Advisors, Inc.	5.91	*
11	Worldview Technology Partners	5.55	*
12	Benchmark Capital	5.48	*
13	Vulcan Capital	5.42	*
14	Institutional Venture Partners	4.94	26
15	Bowman Capital	4.92	*
16	Crosspoint Venture Partners	4.80	60
17	Meritech Capital Partners	4.73	*
18	Matrix Partners	4.66	41
19	Technology Crossover Ventures	4.61	25
20	Oak Investment Partners	4.54	15
21	GE	4.47	*
22	Comdisco Ventures	4.45	*
23	Mayfield Fund	4.42	16
24	Microsoft Corporation	4.06	*
25	Sprout Group	4.01	24
26	Greylock	3.94	20
27	U.S. Venture Partners	3.72	10
28	Norwest Venture Partners	3.72	17
29	Kinetic Ventures LLC	3.64	72
30	Bessemer Venture Partners	3.54	19

reputation capital on nascent start-ups that transform into public companies and in some instances go on to dominate their industries. In real terms too, venture capital and particularly prestigious VCs have contributed by enhancing innovation and productivity in the economy.

While the VC literature has expanded exponentially in the previous two decades, some promising issues remain for future research. A persistently intriguing question is how is VC reputation formed? Some evidence on the formation of underwriter reputation is provided by Dunbar (2000), who analyzes the determinants of underwriters' IPO market share. Second, a wide majority of venture capital deals involve VC syndication. How does reputation of individual VC firms affect the formation of VC syndicates? Although some evidence on the topic is reported by Lerner (1994b), it may be worthwhile to analyze how different VC firms operating in their respective niches come together and provide complementary support to their portfolio companies. This may also shed some light on how different VCs (depending on their ability and operating niche) affect their portfolio companies in real terms (Hellmann and Puri 2000, 2002). Another promising avenue is to peek inside the black box and shed light on how reputation at the firm level interacts with the experience of personnel employed at the firm (Zarutskie 2008). These are issues worthy of further research.

NOTES

1. If investors know little about the companies, they are likely to view all companies—good or bad—uniformly and demand average prices for companies' securities, keeping some of the good companies from issuing them. This leads to bad companies being more likely to be selected by uninformed investors. Rational investors will continue to lower prices keeping out good companies from issuing securities, which can potentially lead to market failure.

2. A substantial body of research exists in the realms of auditing, commercial and investment banking, and public offerings literatures that examines the performance implications of reputation of financial services providers on public firms, both in the short term (for instance, underpricing in initial public offerings) and the long run. We briefly survey an extended body of research in these fields in the next section

3. In this study, I do not separate VC reputation from VC experience. Since reputation is diligently built upon experience, ability, and past performance, and is expected to broadly incorporate facets of each, I treat VC reputation as an inclusive measure of VC experience, ability, and past performance.

4. As mentioned earlier, if investors keep on lowering their offer prices for the companies' securities, it can keep some better-quality companies from issuing equity eventually leading to market failure.

5. However, because investors have relatively easier access to information on publicly-held companies and can also observe their market prices, the asymmetric information and adverse selection problems are likely to be less severe. Yet, investment banker certification will be important if the issuing company wants to signal its high quality to investors given that company insiders are usually much better informed than outside investors.

6. See also DeAngelo (1981), who argues that when incumbent auditors earn client-specific quasi-rents, larger auditing firms with a greater number of clients have more to lose by failing to report a discovered breach in a particular client's records. This collateral aspect increases the audit quality supplied by larger audit firms, who are likely to be more reputable as well.

7. For detailed survey evidence on bank certification in situations where banks use their private information from lending relationships to underwrite their borrowers' public securities, we direct interested readers to Drucker and Puri (2005) and the references therein. Banks have constant access to important information about borrowers during the course of their relationship with these companies, which can be beneficial to the borrowers in terms of reduction in information costs while accessing public markets. In addition to Drucker and Puri (2005), see the survey by James and Smith (2000) for evidence on banks' role as information producers and the resulting positive implications for borrowers.

8. In a similar spirit, analyzing all VC funded start-ups, Lindsey (2007) presents evidence that younger VCs, to build reputation, engage in an unusual amount of alliance activity on behalf of their portfolio companies.

9. The Appendix provides a ranking of the top 30 VC firms, by VC's dollar capitalization share in the IPO market (Source: Nahata, Rajarishi. 2008. Venture capital reputation and investment performance. *Journal of Financial Economics* 90:127–151).

REFERENCES

Akerlof, G. 1970. The market for "lemons": Quality uncertainty and the market mechanism. *Quarterly Journal of Economics* 84:488–500.

Altinkilic, O., and R. S. Hansen. 2003. The discounting and underpricing in seasoned equity offers. *Journal of Financial Economics* 69:285–323.

Ang, J., and T. Richardson. 1994. The underwriting experience of commercial bank affiliates prior to the Glass–Steagall Act: a re-examination of evidence for passage of the act. *Journal of Banking and Finance* 18:351–395.

Asquith, P., and D. W. Mullins. 1986. Equity issues and offering dilution. *Journal of Financial Economics* 15:61–89.

Asthana, S., S. Balsam, and J. Krishnan. 2007. Audit firm reputation, auditor switches, and client stock price reactions: The Anderson experience. Working paper. Temple University.

Atanasov, V., V. Ivanov, and K. Litvak. 2008. The effect of litigation on venture capitalist reputation. Working paper. University of Texas-Austin.

Baker, M., and P. Gompers. 2003. The determinants of board structure at the initial public offering. *Journal of Law and Economics* 46(2):569–598.

Balvers, R. J., W. McDonald, and R. E. Miller. 1988. Underpricing of new issues and the choice of auditor as a signal of investment banker reputation. *The Accounting Review* 63:605–622.

Barry, C., et al. 1990. The role of venture capital in the creation of public companies: Evidence from the going-public process. *Journal of Financial Economics* 27:447–472.

Barton, J. 2005. Who cares about auditor reputation? *Contemporary Accounting Research* 22:549–586.

Beatty, R. P. 1989. Auditor reputation and the pricing of initial public offerings. *Accounting Review* 64:693–709.

———. 1993. The economic determinants of auditor compensation in the initial public offerings market. *Journal of Accounting Research* 31:294–302.

———, and J. R. Ritter. 1986. Investment banking, reputation and the underpricing of initial public offerings. *Journal of Financial Economics* 15:213–232.

———, and I. Welch. 1996. Legal liability and issuer expenses in initial public offerings. *Journal of Law and Economics* 39(2):545–603.

Bengtsson, O. 2008. Relational VC financing of serial founders. Working paper. University of Illinois at Urbana-Champaign.

———, and B. Sensoy. 2008. Investor Abilities and Financial Contracting: Evidence from Venture Capital. Working paper. University of Illinois at Urbana-Champaign.

Benzoni, L., and C. Schenone. 2009. Conflict of interest and certification: long-term performance and valuation of U.S. IPOs underwritten by relationship banks. *Journal of Financial Intermediation*. In Press.

Bharath, S., et al. 2007. So what do I get: A bank's view of lending relationships? *Journal of Financial Economics* 85:368–419.

Billett, M., M. Flannery, and J. Garfinkel. 1995. The effect of lender identity on a borrowing firm's equity return. *Journal of Finance* 50:699–718.

Booth, J. R., and R. Smith II. 1986. Capital raising, underwriting and the certification hypothesis. *Journal of Financial Economics* 15:261–281.

Bottazzi, L., M. Da Rin, and T. Hellmann. 2008. Who are the active investors? Evidence from venture capital. *Journal of Financial Economics* 89:3:488–512.

Brander, J., R. Amit, and W. Antweiler. 2002. Venture capital syndication: Improved venture selection versus the value-added hypothesis. *Journal of Economics and Management Strategy* 11:423–452.

Brav, A., and P. Gompers. 1997. Myth or reality? The long-run underperformance of initial public offerings: Evidence from venture and non venture capital backed companies. *Journal of Finance* 52:1791–1821.

Butler, A., G. Grullon, and J. Weston. 2005. Stock Market Liquidity and the Cost of Issuing Equity. *Journal of Financial and Quantitative Analysis* 40:331–348.

Campbell, T. S., and W. Kracaw. 1980. Information production, market signaling, and the theory of financial intermediation. *Journal of Finance* 35:863–882.

Carter, R. B., F. H. Dark, and A. K. Singh. 1998. Underwriter reputation, initial returns, and the long run performance of IPO stocks. *Journal of Finance* 53:285–311.

Carter, R. B., and S. Manaster. 1990. Initial Public Offerings and Underwriter Reputation. *Journal of Finance*: 1045–1068.

Chaney, P., D. Jeter, and L. Shivakumar. 2004. Self selection of auditors and audit pricing in private firms. *Accounting Review* 79:51–72.

Chaney, P. K., and K. L. Philipich. 2002. Shredded reputation: The cost of audit failure. *Journal of Accounting Research* 40:1221–1245.

Chemmanur, T., and P. Fulghieri. 1994a. Investment bank reputation, information production, and financial intermediation. *Journal of Finance* 49(1):57–79.

_____. 1994b. Reputation, renegotiation, and the choice between bank loans and publicly traded debt. *Review of Financial Studies* 7:475–506.

Chemmanur, T., K. Krishnan, and D. Nandy. 2008. How does venture capital financing improve efficiency in private firms? A look beneath the surface. Working paper. Boston College.

Chemmanur, T., and I. Paeglis. 2005. Management quality, certification, and initial public offerings. *Journal of Financial Economics* 76:331–368.

Chen, H., and J. Ritter. 2000. The seven percent solution. *Journal of Finance* 55(3):1105–1131.

Chuluun, T., and A. Khorana. 2007. The structure and function of SEO underwriting syndicates. Working paper. George Institute of Technology.

Cliff, M., and D. Denis. 2004. Do IPO firms purchase analyst coverage with underpricing? *Journal of Finance* 59:2871–2902.

Cochrane, J. 2005. The risk and return of venture capital. *Journal of Financial Economics* 75:3–52.

Corwin, S., and P. Schultz. 2005. The role of IPO underwriting syndicates: Pricing, information production, and underwriter competition. *Journal of Finance* 60(1):443–486.

Craswell, A., J. R. Francis, and S. Taylor. 1995. Auditor brand name reputation and industry specializations. *Journal of Accounting & Economics* 20:297–322.

Cumming, D., and N. Dai. 2008. Local bias in venture capital investments. *Journal of Empirical Finance*, forthcoming.

Cumming, D., and S. Johan. 2008. Preplanned exit strategies in venture capital. *European Economic Review* 52:1209–1241.

Cumming, D., and J. G. MacIntosh. 2003. A cross-country comparison of full and partial venture capital exits. *Journal of Banking and Finance* 27:511–548.

Dai, N., H. Jo, and J. Schatzberg. 2008. The quality and price of investment banks' service: Evidence from the PIPE market. Working paper. SUNY-Albany.

Datar, S., G. A. Feltham, and J. S. Hughes. 1991. The role of audits and audit quality in valuing new issues. *Journal of Accounting and Economics* 14:3–49.

DeAngelo, L. 1981. Auditor size and audit quality. *Journal of Accounting and Economics* 3:183–199.

Diamond, D. 1991. Monitoring and reputation: The choice between bank loans and directly placed debt. *Journal of Political Economy* 99:689–721.

Drucker, S., and M. Puri. 2005. Banks in capital markets: A survey. In *Handbook in corporate finance: Empirical corporate finance*, ed. B. Espen Eckbo 189–232. North-Holland: Elsevier.

Dunbar, C. 2000. Factors Affecting Investment Bank Initial Public Offering Market Share. *Journal of Financial Economics* 55:3–41

Fama, E. 1985. What's different about banks? *Journal of Monetary Economics* 10:10–19.

Fang, L. 2005. Investment bank reputation and the price and quality of underwriting services. *Journal of Finance* 60:2729–2761.

Fernando, C., V. Gatchev, and P. Spindt. 2005. Wanna dance? How firms and underwriters choose each other? *Journal of Finance* 60:2437–2470.

Francis, J. R., and J. K. Reynolds. 2000. Does size matter? The influence of large clients on office-level auditor reporting decisions. *Journal of Accounting and Economics* 30:375–400.

Gande, A., M. Puri, and A. Saunders. 1999. Bank entry, competition, and the market for corporate securities underwriting. *Journal of Financial Economics* 54:165–195.

——, and I. Walter. 1997. Bank underwriting of debt securities: Modern evidence. *Review of Financial Studies* 10:1175–1202.

Gompers, P. 1996. Grandstanding in the venture capital industry. *Journal of Financial Economics* 43:133–156.

——, et al. 2008a. Venture capital investment cycles: The impact of public markets. *Journal of Financial Economics* 87:1–23.

——. 2008b. Performance Persistence in Entrepreneurship. Working paper. HBS.

Gompers, P., and J. Lerner. 1996. The use of covenants: an empirical analysis of venture partnership agreements. *Journal of Law and Economics* 39:463–498.

——. 1998. What drives venture capital fundraising? *Brookings Papers on Economic Activity. Microeconomics* 1998:149–204.

——. 1999a. An Analysis of compensation in the US venture capital partnerships. *Journal of Financial Economics* 51:3–44.

——. 1999b. Conflict of interest in the issuance of public securities: evidence from venture capital. *Journal of Law and Economics* 42:1–28.

——. 2000a. The determinants of corporate venture capital success: Organizational structure, incentives and complementarities. In *Concentrated ownership*, ed. Randall Morck (17–50). Chicago: University of Chicago Press.

——. 2001. *The venture capital cycle*. Cambridge: MIT Press.

Hellmann, T., L. Lindsey, and M. Puri. 2007. Building relationships early: Banks in venture capital. *Review of Financial Studies* 21(2):513–541.

Hellmann, T., and M. Puri. 2000. The interaction between product market and financing strategy: The role of venture capital. *Review of Financial Studies* 13:959–984.

——. 2002. Venture capital and the professionalization of start-up firms: Empirical evidence. *Journal of Finance* 57:169–197.

Hochberg, Y. 2008. Venture capital and corporate governance in the newly public firm. Working paper. Northwestern University.

Hochberg, Y., A. Ljungqvist, and Y. Lu. 2007. Venture capital networks and investment performance. *Journal of Finance* 62:251–301.

Hsu, D. 2004. What do entrepreneurs pay for venture capital affiliation? *Journal of Finance* 59:1805–1844.

Ivanov, V., et al. 2008. IPOs and venture capital reputation. Working paper. Case Western Reserve University.

James, C. 1992. Relationship-specific assets and the pricing of underwriter services. *Journal of Finance* 47:1865–1885.

_____, and D. Smith. 2000. Are banks still special? New evidence in the corporate capital-raising process. *Journal of Applied Corporate Finance* 12(4):8–19.

_____, and P. Weir. 1990. Borrowing relationships, intermediation, and the cost of issuing public securities. *Journal of Financial Economics* 28:149–171.

Kaplan, S., F. Martel, and P. Stromberg. 2007. How do legal differences and experience affect financial contracts? *Journal of Financial Intermediation* 16(3):273–311.

Kaplan, S. N., and A. Schoar. 2005. Private equity returns: Persistence and capital flows. *Journal of Finance* 60:1791–1823.

Kortum, S., and J. Lerner. 2000. Assessing the contribution of venture capital to innovation. *Rand Journal of Economics* 31:674–692.

Krigman, L., W. H. Shaw, and K. L. Womack. 2001. Why do firms switch underwriters? *Journal of Financial Economics* 60:245–284.

Kroszner, R., and R. Rajan. 1994. Is the Glass-Steagall act justified? A study of the U.S. experience with universal banking before 1933. *American Economic Review* 84:810–832.

Lee, G., and R. W. Masulis. 2008. Seasoned equity offerings: Quality of accounting information and expected flotation costs. *Journal of Financial Economics*.

Lee, P. M., and S. Wahal. 2004. Grandstanding, certification and the underpricing of venture backed IPOs. *Journal of Financial Economics* 73:375–407.

Leland, H., and D. Pyle. 1977. Informational asymmetries, financial structure, and financial intermediation. *Journal of Finance* 32:371–387.

Lerner, J. 1994a. Venture capitalists and the decision to go public. *Journal of Financial Economics* 35:293–316.

_____. 1994b. The Syndication of venture capital investments. *Financial Management* 23: 16–27.

_____, and A. Schoar. 2004. The illiquidity puzzle: Theory and evidence from private equity. *Journal of Financial Economics* 72:3–40.

Li, K., and N. Prabhala. 2005. Self-selection models in corporate finance. In *Handbook of corporate finance: Empirical corporate finance*, ed. B. Espen Eckbo 37–86. North-Holland: Elsevier.

Li, X., and R. W. Masulis. 2008. How do venture investments by different classes of financial institutions affect the equity underwriting process? Working paper. Vanderbilt University.

Lindsey, L. 2007. Blurring firm boundaries: The role of venture capital in strategic alliances. *Journal of Finance* 63(3):1137–1168.

Ljungqvist, A., and W. J. Wilhelm. 2003. IPO pricing in the dot-com bubble. *Journal of Finance* 58:723–752.

Loughran, T., and J. Ritter. 1995. The new issues puzzle. *Journal of Finance* 50:23–51.

_____. 1997. The operating performance of firms conducting seasoned equity offerings. *Journal of Finance* 52:1823–1850.

_____. 2004. Why has IPO underpricing changed over time? *Financial Management* 33:5–37.

McLaughlin, R., A. Safieddine, and G. Vasudevan. 1996. The operating performance of seasoned equity issuers: Free cash flow and post-issue performance. *Financial Management* 25(4):41–53.

_____. 1998. The information content of corporate offerings of seasoned securities: An empirical analysis. *Financial Management* 27(2):31–45.

_____. 2000. Investment banker reputation and the performance of seasoned equity issuers. *Financial Management* 29(1):96–110.

Megginson, W. L., and K. Weiss. 1991. Venture capitalist certification in initial public offerings. *Journal of Finance* 46:879–904.

Menon, K., and D. D. Williams. 1991. Auditor credibility and initial public offerings. *Accounting Review* 66:313–332.

Michaely, R., and W. H. Shaw. 1994. The pricing of initial public offerings: tests of adverse selection and signaling theories. *Review of Financial Studies* 7:279–319.

———. 1995. Does the choice of auditor convey quality in an initial public offering? *Financial Management* 24:15–30.

Myers, S., and N. Majluf. 1984. Corporate financing and investment decisions when firms have information that investors do not have. *Journal of Financial Economics* 13: 187–221.

Nahata, R. 2008. Venture capital reputation and investment performance. *Journal of Financial Economics* 90:127–151.

Pandes, A. 2008. Bought deals: The value of underwriter certification in seasoned equity offerings. Working paper. University of Calgary.

Poulsen, A., and M. Stegemoller. 2008. Moving from private to public ownership: Selling out to public firms vs. initial public offerings. *Financial Management* 37:81–101.

Puri, M. 1994. The long-term default performance of bank underwritten security issues. *Journal of Banking and Finance* 18:397–418.

———. 1996. Commercial banks in investment banking: conflict of interest or certification role? *Journal of Financial Economics* 40:373–401.

———. 1999. Commercial banks as underwriters: Implications for the going public process. *Journal of Financial Economics* 54:133–163.

———, and R. Zarutskie. 2008. On the lifecycle dynamics of venture capital and non venture capital financed firms. Working paper. Duke University.

Rajan, R. 1992. Insiders and outsiders: The choice between informed and arm's length debt. *Journal of Finance* 47:1367–1400.

Raman, K. 2007. Placement agents, reputation, and the cost of placing equity privately. Working paper. Bentley College.

Rauterkus, S., and K. Song. 2005. Auditor's reputation and equity offerings: The case of Arthur Andersen. *Financial Management* 34:121–135.

Ritter, J. 1991. The long-run performance of initial public offerings. *Journal of Finance* 46: 3–27.

Sahlman, W. A. 1990. The structure and governance of venture capital organizations. *Journal of Financial Economics* 27:473–521.

Schenone, C. 2004. The effect of banking relationships on the firm's IPO underpricing. *Journal of Finance* 59:2903–2958.

Shapiro, C. 1983. Premiums for high quality products as returns to reputations. *Quarterly Journal of Economics* 98(4):659–679.

Slovin, M., M. Sushka, and C. Hudson. 1990. External monitoring and its effect on seasoned common stock issues. *Journal of Accounting and Economics* 12:397–417.

Sorensen, M. 2007. How smart is smart money? A two-sided matching model of venture capital. *Journal of Finance* 62:2725–2762.

Sorensen, M. 2008. Learning by investing: Evidence from venture capital. Working paper. *Columbia University.*

Spiess, D. K., and J. Affleck-Graves. 1995. Underperformance in long-run stock returns following seasoned equity offerings. *Journal of Financial Economics* 38:243–267.

Tinic, S. 1988. Anatomy of public offering of common stock. *Journal of Finance* 43:789–822.

Titman, S., and B. Trueman. 1986. Information quality and the valuation of new issues. *Journal of Accounting & Economics* 8:159–172.

Wilson, R. 1985. Reputations in games and markets. In *Game-theoretic models of bargaining with incomplete information*, ed. A. Roth 27–62. Boston: Cambridge University Press.

Wongsunwai, W. 2008. Does venture capitalist quality affect corporate governance? Working paper. Northwestern University.

Yasuda, A. 2005. Do bank relationships affect the firm's underwriter choice in the corporate bond underwriting market? *Journal of Finance* 60:1259–1292.

Zarutskie, R. Forthcoming. Do venture capitalists affect investment performance? Evidence from first-time funds. *Journal of Business Venturing.*

ABOUT THE AUTHOR

Rajarishi Nahata obtained his Ph.D. in Management from Vanderbilt University. He specializes in empirical corporate finance with research interests in venture capital, private equity, entrepreneurial finance, corporate governance, mergers and acquisitions, and securities offerings. He has presented his research at prestigious academic conferences in the United States and abroad. His recent research has been published/accepted in the *Journal of Financial Economics, Journal of Financial and Quantitative Analysis*, and *Journal of Financial Intermediation*. Prior to his doctoral studies, he had been a corporate banker and software engineer.

CHAPTER 16

Investor Opportunism, and Governance in Venture Capital

BRIAN BROUGHMAN
Associate Professor, Indiana University Maurer School of Law

INTRODUCTION

There is a risk of ex post opportunism between entrepreneurs and investors in firms financed by venture capital (VC). The entrepreneur and VC investors have different interests with respect to numerous decisions, such as whether to replace a firm's CEO, whether to sell the firm, and whether to seek additional financing. These conflicts arise because the entrepreneur may receive nonpecuniary benefits (e.g., the joy of seeing her idea brought to market) that cannot be shared with the investors (Aghion and Bolton 1992), and because the parties may hold different financial claims (Kaplan and Strömberg 2003).

Such conflicts make the allocation of control particularly important. If either the entrepreneur or the VC investor has sufficient board seats and other governance rights to unilaterally control the firm, such party may behave opportunistically—causing the firm to take actions that benefit the controlling party at the expense of the firm as a whole. This problem exists because the ex ante financing contract is inherently incomplete and it cannot specify the firm's action for each contingency that may arise (Hart 1995). The financing contract can, however, allocate control, in effect determining *who* gets to decide contested issues.

VCs negotiate for decision-making (control) rights in their portfolio companies. This includes board seats, shareholder voting rights, and protective provisions (Kaplan and Strömberg 2003). VC control may improve firm performance by enabling VCs to monitor and replace the entrepreneur-manager if necessary (Lerner 1995; Gompers 1995; Hellmann 1998) and assists VCs in exiting their investment over the entrepreneur's objections (Klausner and Litvak 2001; Smith 2005).

Despite these benefits, VC control creates a risk of investor opportunism.[1] Academic commentators suggest three settings where VCs may behave opportunistically:[2]

1. *CEO replacement:* VCs in control of a start-up's board may opportunistically fire the founder-CEO in order to remove unvested stock options (Klausner and Litvak 2001) or to force her to sell back her vested equity at cost (Hellmann 1998).

2. *Later round financing:* Controlling VCs may cause a start-up to receive follow-on financing on terms that dilute entrepreneurs and other parties (Atanasov, Ivanov, and Litvak 2008; Gilson 2003).
3. *VC exit:* VCs may force the sale or IPO of the firm at a time or on terms that benefit the VCs at the expense of other parties (Fried and Ganor 2006; Broughman and Fried forthcoming; Cumming 2008; Gompers 1996).

The literature on venture capital contracting suggests potential solutions to the risk of opportunistic conduct, including renegotiation, state-contingent control, shared control, reputation/norms, and legal constraints. There is little data, however, on whether these constraints are effective at preventing opportunism, particularly by VC investors.

The remainder of this chapter is organized as follows. First, I address the source of conflict between entrepreneurs and VCs. I also explain how the allocation of control rights in the financing contract affects the risk of opportunism. Second, I outline several contractual and noncontractual solutions to the problem of ex post opportunism. Third, I summarize empirical studies of CEO replacement, follow-on financing, and VC exit.

VC FINANCING CONTRACT AND OPPORTUNISM

VC financing contracts are inherently incomplete (Aghion and Bolton 1992). The typical VC financing relationship lasts several years, during which numerous unforeseeable and nonverifiable contingencies may arise. The ex ante contract cannot fully align the parties' interests or specify the appropriate action for each contingency. Because of contractual incompleteness, the financing contract may be subject to underinvestment ex ante (Grossman and Hart 1986) and opportunistic behavior—the focus of this chapter—ex post (Aghion and Bolton 1992; Masten 1988; Williamson 1985).

The VC contracting literature recognizes two potential conflicts between entrepreneurs and investors. First, entrepreneurs receive nonpecuniary "private benefits" from the venture, while investors only receive financial returns (Aghion and Bolton 1992). For example, the entrepreneur may receive joy at seeing her idea brought to market, or she may receive various professional benefits from her employment with the start-up firm. The existence of such "private benefits" may cause the entrepreneur to prefer different strategies from the firm's VC investors. The entrepreneur's private benefits are generally assumed to be unverifiable and nontransferable, and as a consequence cannot be priced into the financing contract.

Second, the parties may hold different financial claims. VC-backed start-ups—at least in the United States[3] – typically issue two classes of stock: (1) common (held by entrepreneurs and employees) and (2) convertible preferred (held by VCs) (Kaplan and Strömberg 2003). Convertible preferred stock has two key features. First, it includes a liquidation preference. When the start-up is sold or dissolved, preferred stockholders are entitled to be paid the full amount of their liquidation preference before common shareholders receive anything (Barclay and Smith 1995). The liquidation preference usually equals the amount invested ("1x preferences") but can be a multiple of that amount (2x or 3x) and may include unpaid cumulative dividends and/or participation rights.[4] Second, the VCs' preferred stockholder includes a conversion right. A VC can choose to convert its shares into common stock at a prespecified ratio. Upon conversion, liquidation preferences and any other rights associated with the preferred stock are eliminated.[5]

Researchers suggest that convertible preferred stock creates efficiency gains and tax savings. Ex ante the entrepreneur may have better information than the VC regarding the feasibility of the project. Preferred stock reduces the risk of adverse selection, since the entrepreneur only profits if the firm is worth more than the VCs' liquidation preferences (Sahlman 1990). Also, preferred stock shifts additional risk to entrepreneurs and can provide stronger performance incentives to the entrepreneur than all common financing (Sahlman 1990). The dual class structure also creates tax benefit for U.S.-based start-ups. Issuing two classes of stock allows the firm to separately price the common stock issued to entrepreneurs and employees from the preferred stock issued to VC investors. As explained by Gilson and Schizer (2003), the start-up can shift some employee income from high ordinary tax rates to low capital gains tax rates by issuing preferred stock to the VC investors.

Regardless of whether preferred stock is used for efficiency reasons or for tax savings, it creates an additional conflict between a firm's entrepreneurs and VC investors. Because common shareholders and preferred shareholders have different cash flow rights, their interests in how the start-up is run can diverge (Fried and Ganor 2006). When a start-up is performing poorly, the VCs' liquidation preferences give them debt-like cash flow rights, while making common shareholders analogous to option holders.

Both conflicts—private benefits and divergent financial claims—impact a variety of important decisions frequently faced by VC-backed firms—whether to hire a new CEO, when to sell the firm, how much to invest in a new technology, and so forth. Neither party will always favor the strategy that maximizes the firm's aggregate welfare.

The existence of such conflicts makes the allocation of board control particularly important. The controlling party has the power to select the firm's choice of action. It may use this power opportunistically, causing the firm to pursue strategies that benefit the controlling party at the expense of the firm's aggregate welfare.

In start-up firms VC control of the board occurs approximately twice as often as entrepreneur control (Kaplan and Strömberg 2003).[6] Financing contracts are notably one-sided, protecting the VC investors but providing very few protections to the entrepreneur (Klausner and Litvak 2001; Atanasov, Ivanov, and Litvak 2008; Gilson 2003). The academic literature rationalizes the terms of the financing contract as responding to a standard agency conflict, with the VC viewed as the principal and the entrepreneur as the agent (Atanasov, Ivanov, and Litvak 2008; Klausner and Litvak 2001). Ex ante the VC may have little information regarding the feasibility of an entrepreneur's project. Consequently a one-sided contract may be necessary to protect the VC against adverse selection (Hellmann 1998) and to provide efficient incentives to the entrepreneur. Regardless of the reason, a typical VC financing contract addresses the risk of entrepreneur opportunism, but largely overlooks the risk of investor opportunism.[7] The next section considers alternative strategies that may reduce investor opportunism.

POTENTIAL SOLUTIONS

This section considers the following contractual and noncontractual mechanisms for preventing opportunistic conduct: (a) renegotiation, (b) state-contingent control, (c) shared control, (d) reputation/norms, and (e) corporate law. While none of these mechanisms can remove opportunism, collectively they reduce the risk.

Renegotiation

Renegotiation is emphasized by the incomplete contracting literature as a way to prevent ex post inefficiency (Hart 1995). Even though the parties cannot contract over the choice of action ex ante, they may be able to bargain over the action ex post when they have better information regarding their circumstances (Grossman and Hart 1986). Several financial contracting models, some specific to venture capital, allow for ex post renegotiation (Aghion and Bolton 1992; Hellmann 2006).

To illustrate how renegotiation could prevent opportunism in a VC-backed firm consider the following stylized example. Some time after receiving VC financing a start-up firm is considering whether to sell the business to an acquirer. Assume that the sale would be the efficient outcome; however, the entrepreneurs are opposed to the sale since they would lose their jobs and the sale would provide little payout to common stock. Furthermore, assume the entrepreneurs control the board and absent renegotiation they will block the sale. Renegotiation could solve this problem. The VCs, for example, could offer to give the entrepreneurs a side payment to obtain entrepreneur support for the sale. In fact, there is evidence that renegotiation of this sort sometimes occurs in start-up firms. In a study documenting the sale of VC-backed firms, Broughman and Fried (forthcoming) find that common stockholders at the target firm receive an additional "carveout" payment (i.e., a side payment) from the VCs in approximately one-quarter of the recorded transactions. The VCs were more likely to offer such carveout payments when the VCs did not control the board and needed the consent of common stockholders to sell the firm.

Provided there are no transaction costs or liquidity constraints, and the parties have symmetric beliefs, renegotiation of this sort will always lead to the ex post efficient outcome, regardless how control is allocated ex ante. This is a direct application of the Coase Theorem, with board control analogous to a property right. The ex ante allocation of board control will have a distributional consequence—it determines who has to bribe whom—but it will not affect the firm's choice of action (Coase 1960).

However, despite its potential advantages, there are several reasons to question how often the assumptions supporting Coasian renegotiation are satisfied. First, renegotiation may involve significant transaction costs. The cost of renegotiation may increase if there are several entrepreneurs or VC investors, as is often the case in start-up firms (Bartlett 2006), or if it is difficult to specify or enforce the new bargain. Second, if the parties have asymmetric beliefs, renegotiation may fail. It is often argued, for instance, that entrepreneurs are overly optimistic (Utset 2002). The entrepreneur may legitimately believe that the expected payoff from her preferred strategy is so high that there is no bargaining range to negotiate over. Third, liquidity constraints may limit the availability of renegotiation.

The entrepreneur, for example, may have limited wealth and thus be unable to pay the VC to take an alternative action (Aghion and Bolton 1992; Hellmann 2006; Broughman 2008a). Finally, even if renegotiation is available, it cannot generally solve ex ante underinvestment caused by the threat of ex post holdup (Hart 1995). So, while renegotiation could theoretically ensure an ex post efficient outcome, it may be limited in practice.

State-Contingent Control

The financial contracting literature models the allocation of control between an entrepreneur and an investor. Aghion and Bolton (1992) show that control should be awarded to the entrepreneur whenever possible to protect the entrepreneur's private benefits; however, investor control may often be necessary to ensure the investor's participation. The work of Aghion and Bolton (1992) is complimented by a number of recent articles, including Berglof (1994), Hellmann (1998, 2006), Dessein (2005), Kirilenko (2001), Black and Gilson (1998), Marx (1998), Schmidt (2003), Yerramilli (2006), and Gompers (1995), which focus on the allocation of control rights in VC-backed firms. Many of these studies recognize that the allocation of control need not be fixed at the time of the ex ante contract, but rather control can be contingent on future events.

For example, the financing contract could award the VC extra board seats if the firm fails to satisfy a verifiable performance target specified in the contract (Aghion and Bolton 1992). This arrangement may give the entrepreneur control in good states of nature and the VC control in bad states of nature ("State Contingent Control").[8] This form of state contingent control is desirable if the parties believe that the entrepreneur's incentives are better aligned with the firm's overall welfare when the firm is performing well, and VC's better aligned when the firm is performing poorly.

In their study of VC financing contracts, Kaplan and Strömberg (2003) find evidence that board seats and stockholder voting rights are sometimes contingent on future events. For example, in about 19 percent of the investment rounds in their sample the VCs gained the right to elect a majority of the firm's board if the company failed to redeem preferred stock on demand. This contingency, however, is less meaningful than it appears. VCs typically do not obtain the right to redeem their shares until five years after investment. Even after this period, redemption is rarely in the VCs' interest, since it would typically force a cash-strapped firm to liquidate itself at below market value. Kaplan and Strömberg (2003) find only one firm where the allocation of board seats is contingent on a contractual measure of financial performance. This suggests it is often difficult to find a verifiable measure of economic performance. Despite its advantages, state contingent control may be unavailable due to verifiability concerns.

Furthermore, state contingent control will not lead to the first best outcome except in situations where one of the party's incentives is perfectly aligned with the firm's overall welfare. It may often be the case—when there are several strategies to choose from—that neither the entrepreneur nor the VC has an incentive to pick the optimal strategy (Broughman 2008a). In such instances state contingent control by itself cannot lead to the efficient outcome. At best, it will lead to the lesser of two inefficiencies.

Shared Control

An alternative solution is to share board control with a third-party independent director holding the tie-breaking vote (Broughman 2008a, 2008b; Bratton 2003).

In practice this form of shared control is the most commonly used board arrangement. Kaplan and Strömberg (2003) classify each director into one of three categories: (1) VC, (2) entrepreneur, or (3) independent director.[9] They find that VC investors control the board 25 percent of the time and entrepreneurs 14 percent of the time. In the remaining firms (61 percent) control of the board is shared with third-party independent directors holding the tie-breaking vote(s). Broughman (2008a) refers to this arrangement as "ID-arbitration" to emphasize the independent director's tie-breaking position. The independent director can effectively "arbitrate" conflicts between the entrepreneur and VC.

Broughman (2008a) models the incentives created by ID-arbitration[10] and shows that ID-arbitration can reduce the risk of opportunism by moderating each party's ex post threat position. Under ID-arbitration neither the entrepreneur nor the investor can credibly threaten to pursue their preferred action. Instead, they must propose actions that would be endorsed by the independent director. Provided the independent director is relatively unbiased, this arrangement can lead to the efficient outcome in circumstances where alternative governance arrangements—entrepreneur control, investor control, or state-contingent control—are either unavailable or likely to lead to suboptimal results. The benefits of shared control, however, are limited if the independent director is biased or otherwise colludes with the entrepreneur or VC, or if the independent director has insufficient information about the firm's business to be an effective decision maker.

Reputational or Norm-based Constraints

Several writers argue that reputational considerations may help constrain opportunistic conduct in VC-backed firms (Black and Gilson 1998; Gilson 2003; Smith 1998; Klausner and Litvak 2001; Atanasov, Ivanov, and Litvak 2008). Even though the party with control of the board has the ability to act opportunistically, it may refrain from doing so if there is a sufficient reputational sanction attached to such conduct. Reputation is generally most effective in settings where both parties are in a long-term relationship or are repeat players. While the VC is generally a repeat player, the entrepreneur may not be. While some entrepreneurs ("serial entrepreneurs") form multiple start-up firms, most do not.

Even if the entrepreneur is not a repeat player, she may be able to communicate her experience with the VC to other entrepreneurs. Kreps (1990) demonstrates that this form of communication may be sufficient for reputation to develop in settings where one party is a repeat player and the other is not. Communication may be facilitated by web sites—such as www.thefunded.com—which encourage entrepreneurs to rate and describe their experiences working with different VC investors (Smith 1998). However, most postings on thefunded.com are anonymous, and it is difficult to verify whether an entrepreneur's complaints are due to VC opportunism or other factors.

The market for VC reputation requires "mechanisms transmitting [credible] information about VC behavior to future entrepreneurs and other contractual partners."[11] Litigation by entrepreneurs against VC investors may be one such mechanism. Even though VCs rarely lose at trial, Atanasov, Ivanov, and Litvak (2008) find that VCs involved in lawsuits raise significantly less capital in future years than their peers and invest in fewer and lower quality portfolio firms. This suggests that litigation may be a significant constraint on VC opportunism, not through the law itself but rather through an indirect reputational effect.

Finally, even though entrepreneurs may not be repeat players, they are typically represented by repeat player law firms that are actively engaged in VC. Such law firms may bolster the effectiveness of entrepreneurial business norms (Suchman and Cahill 1996). Reputation may be effective even if the entrepreneur will never directly work with VCs again.

A remaining problem is that reputation also points in other directions. The VC, for instance, also cares about its reputation among the limited partners (i.e., institutional investors) who invest in VC funds. Failing to act opportunistically in certain instances, will hurt the financial return received by the VC's limited partners. In this setting reputation could actually push the VC to act even more opportunistically than it would otherwise.[12]

Corporate Law

Fiduciary obligations under corporate law could, at least in theory, function as an alternative solution to the problem of VC opportunism. Preventing opportunistic behavior—particularly in cases where the parties are unable to adequately protect themselves through arms' length bargaining—is one of the conceptual justifications for imposing fiduciary obligations on the board (Hart 1993; Brudney 1997; Easterbrook and Fischel 1991).

Fiduciary obligations require each director to serve the best interests of the corporation, potentially reducing the scope for opportunistic behavior. To illustrate, a board under VC control may wish to sell the firm immediately to benefit preferred stock. Yet, this action may be deemed a violation of the board's fiduciary obligations, since it may reduce the expected value realized by common stockholders. In the extreme, all ex post inefficient outcomes could be deemed a violation of the board's fiduciary obligations. Under this (unrealistic) characterization, fiduciary obligations would accomplish what contract could not—effectively prohibiting opportunistic conduct that cannot be specified ex ante.

In practice, however, there are several reasons why fiduciary obligations are not an effective constraint on VC opportunism.

First, most of the disputes that may arise between entrepreneurs and VCs are protected from judicial review by the business judgment rule. The business judgment rule is a presumption in favor of a corporation's board of directors.[13] The business judgment rule effectively prevents courts from reviewing business decisions unless the board engaged in self-dealing. While it is technically possible for a plaintiff to overcome the business judgment rule, the standard of review makes it extremely difficult for plaintiffs to succeed.

Second, assuming plaintiffs can overcome (or avoid) the business judgment rule, it is unclear what type of obligation a board controlled by preferred stock owes to common stockholders. The conflict between the entrepreneur and the VC described above is essentially a conflict between common stock and preferred stock.

There are two basic scenarios where this conflict arises in VC-backed firms: (1) a board controlled by common stockholders takes actions which allegedly harm preferred stockholders, and (2) a board controlled by preferred stockholders takes actions that allegedly harm common stockholders. In both settings, Delaware law generally allows the controlling party to cause the firm to take actions that benefit it at the expense of noncontrolling classes of equity. Fried and Ganor (2006, 992) refer to this as a "control-contingent approach to fiduciary duties." According to Fried and Ganor (2006, 992), a preferred-controlled board does "not owe a fiduciary duty specifically to the common shareholders and it has wide discretion to benefit the preferred shareholders instead." This analysis makes it difficult for an injured entrepreneur, lacking board control, to claim fiduciary protection.

Third, fiduciary claims may need to be brought as derivative lawsuits as opposed to direct lawsuits.[14] Under derivative litigation any judgment would go to the entire firm. This can be a significant problem for entrepreneurs suing VC investors, since the entire judgment may go to the preferred shareholders when the firm is worth less than the liquidation preferences. Even though the entrepreneur may have been harmed by losing the option value of her common stock, the derivative form of fiduciary litigation will not recognize this damage.

DATA ON INVESTOR OPPORTUNISM

This section provides data on the allocation of board control and summarizes empirical studies of VC opportunism in three settings: (1) CEO replacement, (2) later-round financing, and (3) VC exits. Despite theoretical models built around opportunistic use of control, there is very little data measuring actual occurrences of ex post opportunism. Studies analyze the allocation of control rights in the ex ante contract (Kaplan and Stromberg 2003), but the effect that the allocation of control has on ex post behavior receives less attention in the financial contracting literature.

Observing ex post opportunism turns out to be extremely difficult. Many events that occur in the life of a start-up firm are open to multiple interpretations. For example, a firm under VC control may receive inside financing at a down valuation. Without knowing the firm's "true" valuation—an unobservable trait—it is hard to say whether a particular round of financing is dilutive or represents a real decline in the firm's valuation. A similar interpretive problem extends to CEO replacements and VC exits. The researcher needs to observe significant details about each firm to meaningfully interpret ex post behavior.[15]

Allocation of Control

VCs can only behave opportunistically to the extent that they have the power to control the relevant decision. Each of the three types of actions considered in this section requires board authorization. Consequently, the allocation of board seats may affect the risk of opportunism.

In a study documenting over 200 rounds of VC financing, Kaplan and Strömberg (2003) find that VC investors hold approximately 41 percent of the total board seats, entrepreneurs hold 35 percent, and independent directors (jointly appointed by a firm's VCs and entrepreneurs) hold the remaining 23 percent.

As noted above, board control is often shared with an independent director holding the tie-breaking vote. VCs only control the board in 25 percent of the financing observations.

These facts may understate the extent of VC control for a couple of reasons. First, VCs may have a significant influence over the selection of so-called independent directors. VCs have extensive professional networks, and significant ties to potential director candidates (Fried and Ganor 2006). To account for this concern, Broughman (2008b) creates a "de facto" classification, coding each "independent" director as a VC (entrepreneur) if the director was selected/nominated exclusively by the VCs (entrepreneurs), and did not have a relationship with the other party. On the other hand, if the entrepreneurs and VCs both participated in the director's selection then the director remains independent on a "de facto" basis. Broughman (2008b, 28) reports a "formal" and a "de facto" classification for each outside director in his sample.

Using Broughman's (2008b) database I describe the allocation of board seats from a sample of 47 start-ups located in Silicon Valley. Data are presented for each year of firm operation. Over all years the VCs hold approximately 44 percent of the board seats on a formal basis and 49 percent on a de facto basis. Because VCs are generally given additional board seats with each new round of financing, VC representation typically increases over time. After four years of operation, VCs control the board on a de facto basis in most of the sample firms. This suggests that the risk of VC misbehavior is greatest in the later years of a firm's life. Exhibit 16.1 illustrates the increase in VC board representation and control over time.

Second, VCs have a number of indirect control mechanisms that give them the power to influence corporate decision making even when the VCs do not control the board. For example, VCs can threaten to withhold later-round financing in order to gain leverage over various corporate decisions. Staged financing is an important source of implied authority (Aghion and Tirole 1997), particularly as the start-up runs low on cash (Gompers 1995). Furthermore, VCs may receive numerous contractual rights—drag-along rights, redemption/put rights, IPO registration rights, or a right of first refusal—that can be used to directly or indirectly influence various corporate decisions (Cumming 2008). While VCs may not have absolute control over their portfolio firms, they often have more influence over corporate actions than their board representation might suggest.

CEO Replacement

VCs frequently replace founder-CEOs (Gorman and Sahlman 1989; Broughman and Fried forthcoming). Hannan, Burton, and Baron (1996) find that the likelihood that the founder-CEO will be replaced is approximately 40 percent within the first 40 months, and over 80 percent after 80 months. Hellmann and Puri (2002) show that a VC-backed firm is twice as likely to replace its CEO with a non-founder as compared to a firm without VC financing. Some of this replacement appears to be driven by the required skill set of the CEO. For example, Wasserman (2003) finds that replacement often occurs either when product development is completed or when the firm raises additional financing, which often marks a change in the firm's stage of development (or the failure of the previous CEO to generate revenue).

(a)

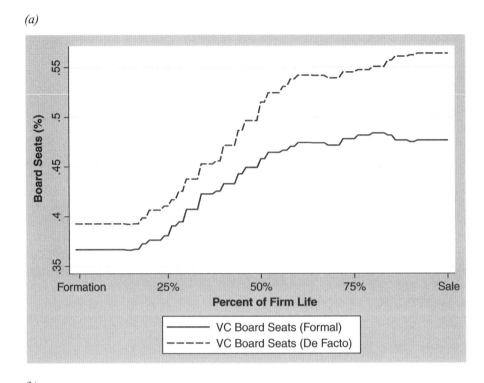

(b)

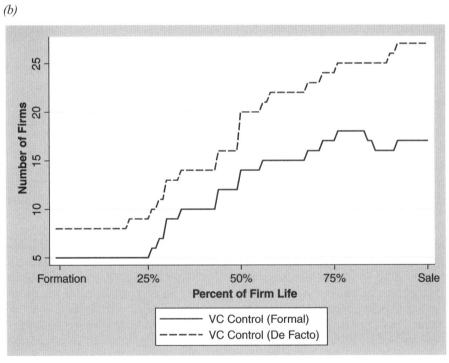

Exhibit 16.1   VC Control Timeline

On the other hand, VCs in control of a start-up's board may opportunistically fire founder-CEOs, either to strip founder-CEOs of their unvested equity and replace them with a cheaper manager (Klausner and Litvak 2001) or to force founder-CEOs to sell back their vested equity at cost, which may be well below its current value (Hellmann 1998). There is little to stop VCs in control of the board from opportunistically firing a founder-CEO. The entrepreneur's employment agreement generally does not provide significant severance protection, and she can generally be fired without cause (Hellman 1998).

Data from Broughman and Fried (2009a), however, finds no evidence of VC opportunism related to CEO replacement. Their study includes detailed data on the board structure of 47 VC-backed Silicon Valley firms. They find that the presence of VC board control has little effect on the likelihood of founder CEO replacement in a given year of operation. This conclusion is supported by entrepreneur interviews. The VCs did not force the replaced founder-CEOs to sell back vested equity at a low price. Most importantly, the entrepreneurs themselves did not generally perceive their replacement as opportunistic. This study is limited to a small sample from Silicon Valley and may not represent VC conduct in other settings. Nonetheless, it suggests that CEO replacement is rarely opportunistically motivated.

Later-Round Financing

When VCs control the board they may use their position to arrange follow-on financing rounds that dilute entrepreneurs and other common shareholders. Dilutive financings have been alleged in some of the lawsuits filed by entrepreneurs against VCs (Atanasov, Ivanov, and Litvak 2008).

In the initial round of financing there is no concern over dilution. The VCs have an incentive to seek a low valuation and high preferences. The entrepreneur, who initially controls the start-up, will seek a high valuation and lower preferences. The start-up's initial valuation and liquidation preferences emerge out of this arms-length bargaining process.

The situation is different in later rounds. In follow-on rounds of financing the existing VCs are effectively sitting on both sides of the bargaining table. If they control the board, the existing VCs may exploit their position to arrange a low valuation or high liquidation preferences so that, upon exit, they can capture a larger share of the proceeds. Such actions dilute the value of the entrepreneur's common stock.

The risk of dilutive financing is higher if the new financing is provided by existing investors (an "inside round"). By contrast if a new round of financing is provided largely by outside investors (an "outside round"), the current VC investors (like the entrepreneur in the initial financing round) have an incentive to negotiate for a high valuation (or lower preferences) to minimize the dilutive effect of the new financing on their interests in the firm.

Broughman and Fried (2009b) test for dilutive financing by comparing the valuation at the time a start-up is sold to the valuation assigned in the previous round of financing. They find little evidence of dilutive financing. In fact, firms that received inside financing under VC control tended to have higher valuations assigned in the new round of financing, suggesting that such rounds are not used by VCs to exploit entrepreneurs but rather to provide capital to failing firms that cannot obtain funds from outside investors.

These results do not find evidence of dilutive financing. One interpretation of this data is that existing VC investors are reluctant to syndicate their "lemons" with other VCs out of a concern over the reputational consequences they may suffer (Gompers and Lerner 1999).[16] Consequently, inside financing may be a signal that a firm is struggling rather than a signal of opportunism.

VC Exit

VC investments are of limited duration and are generally liquidated within the life of the VC fund. VCs exit either through an IPO or a sale of the firm (or if the firm is failing the VCs may simply write off their investment). VCs may use their position of control to manipulate the timing or form of exit, potentially redistributing value from the entrepreneurs to the VCs in the process.

A start-up firm may have to choose between an immediate sale versus re-maining independent. If the firm remains independent there is some chance that its future sale/IPO valuation will increase, but there is also a chance that it will decrease. Because of their liquidation preferences the VCs bear much of the downside risk if the firm remains independent, but are only entitled to a fraction of the upside benefit.[17] Fried and Ganor (2006) argue that preferred hold-ing VCs may force an immediate sale of the firm even if this is not the value maximizing strategy. Conversely, entrepreneurs may elect to keep a company independent even if a sale of the firm would be value maximizing (Hellmann 2006). Consistent with these predictions, Broughman and Fried (forthcoming) find that VCs sometimes award a carveout payment to a firm's entrepreneurs in order to obtain their support for a proposed sale of the firm. The likeli-hood and magnitude of such carveouts are higher when the VCs do not control the firm.

Gompers (1996) suggests another reason why VCs may rush to exit: they may need to signal their success to attract limited partner investments into their new fund. This motivation is particular relevant for younger VC firms, which do not have a long track record of success.

If a start-up is successful, the parties must choose whether to exit through an IPO or a sale of the firm. Entrepreneurs may prefer an IPO exit over a sale for two reasons. First, VCs' convertible preferred stock is subject to mandatory conversion in an IPO exit but not in a sale (Hellmann 2006). Second, the entrepreneur's private benefits are protected in an IPO, but likely to be lost if the firm is sold to an acquirer. Consistent with these observations, Cumming (2008) finds that VC control increases the likelihood that a start-up firm will exit by an acquisition as opposed to an IPO.

While these data emphasize trade-offs associated with VC control, we cannot conclude that VCs necessarily behaved opportunistically at the exit stage. Alter-natively, entrepreneurs may block efficient outcomes, and VC control may be nec-essary to avoid entrepreneur holdup. Additional research is needed to determine whether these trade-offs have efficiency consequences.

CONCLUSION

This chapter considers the issue of VC opportunism. VC investors receive extensive control rights in their portfolio firms. VCs may exercise their control opportunistically, benefiting themselves at the expense of the firm's entrepreneurs and other parties. This problem is magnified by the existence of significant conflicts of interest between entrepreneurs and VC investors. Financial contracting theory suggests several mechanisms—including renegotiation, state-contingent control, shared control, reputation/norms, and legal constraints—that may reduce the risk of opportunistic conduct. With few exceptions the literature has not tested the effect that these mechanisms have on ex post outcomes. Existing studies find little evidence of VC opportunism. Why this is the case, however, is unclear. Atanasov, Ivanov, and Litvak (2008) suggest that litigation may provide an indirect constraint on opportunism by damaging the reputation of VCs involved in litigation. Further research is needed to understand the consequences that alternative corporate governance arrangements and legal regimes have on ex post behavior.

NOTES

1. VCs are not the only residual claimant in a start-up firm, and consequently the VCs' interests may diverge from the firm's aggregate welfare.

2. There is also a risk of VC opportunism through "asset tunneling," described by Atanasov, Ivanov, and Litvak (2008, 7) as follows: "VCs often hold stakes in a number of firms in the same or related industries. . . . [VCs] could engage in transfer pricing, by arranging for one portfolio firm to purchase intellectual property, services, or other assets from another portfolio company at an inadequate or excessive price. . . . We call this 'asset tunneling.' If the VC holds different ownership stakes in different portfolio firms, it has an incentive to transfer assets from the firms with low ownership to the firms with high ownership." This chapter does not address asset tunneling. For more background on tunneling transactions see Atanasov, Black, and Ciccotello (2007).

3. Studies documenting VC investment in Canada (Cumming 2005a; 2005b), Europe (Schwienbacher 2005), and in developing countries (Lerner and Schoar 2005) show that convertible preferred is not the dominant form of investment outside the United States. One explanation for this pattern is that U.S. VCs are more sophisticated investors. An alternative explanation, however, is that U.S. tax law motivates the use of convertible preferred stock in the United States (Gilson and Schizer 2003).

4. VCs' convertible preferred stock sometimes includes participation rights (often referred to as "Participating Preferred"). Participating preferred entitles the holder not only to a liquidation preference but also to share with common shareholders, on a pro-rata basis, in any additional value available for distribution to shareholders, usually up to a specified amount.

5. A preferred stockholder will generally choose to convert into common stock only if the company is sold or liquidated for a sufficiently high price. However, if the firm is sold in an IPO meeting certain conditions, the financing agreement may require the VCs to convert to common (mandatory conversion) even if the preferred stock would offer a higher payout (Hellmann 2006).

6. However, neither the entrepreneur nor the VC typically controls the board. Board control is often shared with an independent director holding the tie-breaking vote (Broughman 2008a).

7. The VC is also protected by staged financing (Gompers 1995).

8. Aghion and Bolton's (1992) analysis of state contingent control is often used to explain the standard debt financing contract. In a typical debt financing the entrepreneur retains control of the firm as long as she does not default on the loan. However, if the entrepreneur defaults the creditor typically has the right to take control of the firm (through bankruptcy). In this example, control is contingent on the conditions of default defined in the debt contract.

9. The allocation of board seats is typically specified in the corporate charter and in voting agreements negotiated in connection with each round of financing. Class-specific board seats emphasize that the use of independent directors is not simply an accident of shareholder voting, but rather is explicitly contracted over by the parties.

10. Others have also noted the frequent use of independent directors in VC-backed start-ups (Bratton 2002; Smith 2005; Fried and Ganor 2006; Kaplan and Stromberg 2003).

11. See Atanasov, Ivanov, and Litvak (2008, 12).

12. To be sure, a fund's limited partners want the VC to attract quality entrepreneurs, which may limit their appetite for opportunistic conduct.

13. Smith v. Van Gorkom, 488 A.2d 858 (Del. 1985).

14. See Kennedy v. Venrock Assoc., 348 F.3d 548 (7th Cir. 2003) (illustrating the problem derivative litigation creates for plaintiffs).

15. One way to help interpret ex post behavior is with qualitative (i.e., subjective) data. With qualitative data the researcher can record the subject's interpretation of events. Qualitative analysis is limited, however, by the subject's interpretation, which may be subject to various cognitive biases. Furthermore, VC opportunism is most effective to the extent that it can be camouflaged or hidden from the entrepreneur, and consequently important data may be overlooked in studies relying primarily on qualitative data. Alternatively, the researcher could use litigation data as a proxy for opportunistic conduct (Atanasov, Ivanov, and Litvak 2008). Litigation is costly for the entrepreneur and is thus a credible signal of VC misconduct. Studies based on litigation, however, do not observe actual conduct by VCs. Litigation may be overinclusive to the extent that entrepreneurs file meritless strike suits, or underinclusive to the extent that the law fails to provide a cost-effective remedy for opportunism (Felstiner, Abel and Sarat 1980).

16. An alternative interpretation is that VCs may overvalue their portfolio firms—perhaps due to an endowment effect or other cognitive bias. An outside lead investor is not subject to such biases.

17. The VC's conversion right complicates the analysis. In circumstances implicating the VC's conversion right they may prefer greater risk. Put another way, the VC's equity claim is convex over certain range of outcomes and concave over another range.

REFERENCES

Aghion, P., and P. Bolton. 1992. An incomplete contracts approach to financial contracting. *Review of Economic Studies* 59:473–494.

Aghion, P., and J. Tirole. 1997. Formal and real authority in organizations. *Journal of Political Economy* 105:1–29.

Atanasov, V., B. Black, and C. Ciccotello. 2008. Unbundling and measuring tunneling. U of Texas Law, Law and Econ Research Paper No. 117; ECGI-Finance Working paper. Retrieved from SSRN: http://ssrn.com/abstract=1030529

Atanasov, V., V. Ivanov, and K. Litvak. 2008. The effect of litigation on venture capitalist reputation. Retrieved from SSRN: http://ssrn.com/abstract=1120994

Barclay, M., and C. Smith. 1995. The priority structure of corporate liabilities. *Journal of Finance* 50:899–917.

Bartlett, R. 2006. Venture capital, agency costs, and the false dichotomy of the corporation. *UCLA L. Rev.* 54:37–115.

Berglof, E. 1994. A control theory of venture capital finance. *Journal of Law, Economics, and Organization* 10:247–267.

Black, B., and R. Gilson. 1998. Venture capital and the structure of capital markets: Banks versus stock markets. *Journal of Financial Economics* 47:243–277.

Bratton, W. 2003. Venture capital on the downside: Preferred stock and corporate control. *Mich. L. Rev.* 100:891–945.

Broughman, B. 2008a. Independent directors and board control in venture finance. Working paper. Retrieved from SSRN: http://ssrn.com/abstract=1123840

_____. 2008b. The role of independent directors in VC-backed firms. Working paper. Retrieved from SSRN: http://ssrn.com/abstract=1162372.

_____, and J. Fried. Forthcoming. Renegotiation of cash flow rights in the sale of VC-backed firms. *Journal of Financial Economics*. U.C. Berkeley Public Law Research Paper No. 956243 Retrieved from SSRN: http://ssrn.com/abstract=956243

_____. 2009a. VC Replacement of founder-CEOs in Silicon Valley. Working paper. On file with the author, Indiana University Maurer School of Law.

_____. 2009b. Do VCs use inside financing to dilute founders? Retrieved from SSRN: http://ssrn.com/abstract=1442524

Brudney, V. 1997. Contract and fiduciary duty in corporate law. *B.C.L. Rev.* 38:595–665.

Coase, R. 1960. The problem of social cost. *Journal of Law and Economics* 3:1–44.

Cumming, D. 2005a. Capital structure in venture finance. *Journal of Corporate Finance* 11:550–585.

_____. 2005b. Agency costs, institutions, learning, and taxation in venture capital contracting. *Journal of Business Venturing* 20:573–622.

_____. 2008. Contracts and exits in venture capital finance. *Review of Financial Studies* 21:1947–1982.

_____, and J. MacIntosh. 2004. Boom, bust and litigation in venture capital finance. *Willamette Law Review* 40:867–906.

Dessein, W. 2005. Information and control in alliances and ventures. *Journal of Finance* 60:2513–2549.

Easterbrook, F., and D. Fischel. 1991. *The economic structure of corporate law*. Cambridge: Harvard University Press.

Felstiner, W., R. Abel, and A. Sarat. 1980. The emergence and transformation of disputes: naming, blaming, claiming. . . . *Law & Society Review* 15:631–654.

Fried, J., and M. Ganor. 2006. Agency costs of venture capitalist control in startups. *New York University Law Review* 81:967–1025.

Gilson, R. 2003. Engineering a venture capital market: Lessons from the American experience. *Stan. L. Rev.* 55:1067–1103.

_____, and D. Schizer. 2003. Understanding venture capital structure: A tax explanation for convertible preferred stock. *Harvard Law Review* 116:874–916.

Gompers, P. 1995. Optimal investment, monitoring, and the staging of venture capital. *Journal of Finance* 50:1461–1489.

_____. 1996. Grandstanding in the venture capital industry. *Journal of Financial Economics* 42:133–156.

_____ and J. Lerner. 1999. *The Venture Capital Cycle*. MIT Press, Boston, MA.

Gorman, M., and W. Sahlman. 1989. What do venture capitalists do? *Journal of Business Venturing* 4, 231–248.

Grossman, S., and O. Hart. 1986. The costs and benefits of ownership: A theory of vertical and lateral integration. *Journal of Political Economy* 94, 691–719.

Hannan, M., M. Diane Burton, and J. Baron. 1996. Inertia and change in the early years: employment relations in young, high technology firms. *Industrial and Corporate Change* 5, 503–536.

Hart, O. 1993. An economist's view of fiduciary duty. *University of Toronto Law Journal* 43:299.

_____. 1995. *Firms, contracts, and financial structure.* London:Oxford University Press.

_____. 1998. The allocation of control rights in venture capital contracts. *RAND Journal of Economics* 29 (1):57–76.

_____. 2006. IPOs, acquisitions and the use of convertible securities in venture capital. *Journal of Financial Economics* 81:649–679.

Hellmann, T., and M. Puri. 2002. Venture capital and the professionalization of start-up firms: Empirical evidence. *Journal of Finance* 57:169–197.

Kaplan, S., and P. Strömberg. 2003. Financial contracting theory meets the real world: An empirical analysis of venture capital contracts. *Review of Economic Studies* 70: 281–315.

Kirilenko, A. 2001. Valuation and control in venture finance. *Journal of Finance* 56: 565–587.

Klausner, M., and K. Litvak. 2001. What economists have taught us about venture capital contracting. In *Bridging the entrepreneurial financing gap: Linking governance with regulatory policy*, ed. M., Whincop (54–74) Aldershot, UK:Ashgate.

Kreps, D. 1990. Corporate culture and economic theory. In *Perspectives on positive political economy*, ed. J. E. Alt and K. A. Shepsle (90–143) Cambridge, UK: Cambridge University Press.

Lerner, J. 1995. Venture capitalists and the oversight of private firms. *Journal of Finance* 50:301–318.

_____, and A. Schoar. 2005. Does legal enforcement affect financial transactions? The contractual channel in private equity, *Quarterly Journal of Economics* 120:223–246.

Marx, L. 1998. Efficient venture capital financing combining debt and equity. *Review of Economic Design* 3:371–387.

Masten, S. 1988. Equity, opportunism and the design of contractual relations. *Journal of Institutional and Theoretical Economics* 144:180–195.

Sahlman, W. 1990. The structure and governance of venture capital organizations. *Journal of Financial Economics* 27:473–521.

Schmidt, K. 2003. Convertible securities and venture capital finance. *Journal of Finance* 58, 1139–1166.

Schwienbacher, A. 2005. An empirical analysis of venture capital exist in Europe and the United States. EFA 2002 Berlin Meetings Discussion Paper. Available at SSRN: http://ssrn.com/abstract=302001

Smith, D. Gordon. 1998. Venture capital contracting in the information age. *Journal of Small & Emerging Business Law* 2, 133.

_____. 2005. The exit structure of venture capital. *UCLA L. Rev.* 53, 315–356.

Suchman, M., and M. Cahill. 1996. The hired gun as facilitator: Lawyers and the suppression of business disputes in Silicon Valley. *Law & Social Inquiry* 21: 679–712.

Utset, M. 2002. Reciprocal fairness, strategic behavior & venture survival: A theory of venture capital-financed firms. *Wis. L. Rev.* 2002:45.

Wasserman, N. 2003. Founder-CEO succession and the paradox of entrepreneurial success. *Organization Science* 14:149–172.

Williamson, O. 1985. *The economic institutions of capitalism.* New York: Free Press.

Yerramilli, V. 2006. Joint control and redemption rights in venture capital contracts. Retrieved from SSRN: http://ssrn.com/abstract=967323

ABOUT THE AUTHOR

Brian Broughman is an Associate Professor at Indiana University Maurer School of Law. He received his Ph.D. from the University of California Berkeley, and a J.D. from the University of Michigan School of Law. His research interests include venture capital contracting, corporate finance, and corporate law. His dissertation examines the role of independent directors and the risk of opportunistic conduct in firms financed by venture capital. Dr. Broughman has presented his research at several academic conferences, including the conference on Empirical Legal Studies (CELS) and the American Law and Economics Association (ALEA) annual conference.

## CHAPTER 17

Conflicts of Interest and Litigation in the Venture Capital Industry

VLADIMIR ATANASOV
Assistant Professor, Mason School of Business, College of William and Mary

INTRODUCTION

Uncertainty and informational asymmetry in the venture capital (VC) industry generate various moral hazard and adverse selection problems and exacerbate any conflicts of interests between the parties involved. Complex contracts and reputational concerns prevent opportunistic behavior by most market participants. Still, a significant number of conflicts persist; some conflicts even lead to costly litigation. This chapter discusses the potential conflicts among VCs, investors in VC funds, entrepreneurs, and angels and other early-stage equity investors. It then examines VC contracts, reputation, and litigation as possible mechanisms to resolve conflicts of interest and reduce opportunistic behavior. While complex contracts largely resolve potential problems between VCs and their investors and protect the interests of VCs against entrepreneurial opportunism, reputation and litigation are the main mechanisms that prevent widespread VC opportunism against entrepreneurs.

Following the analysis of conflicts of interests in the VC industry and possible mechanisms to prevent them, the chapter discusses in more detail the existing law and finance literature on VC-related litigation with a focus on a recent study by Atanasov, Ivanov, and Litvak ("AIL") (2007), which has collected the most comprehensive VC lawsuits dataset available. The publicly available documents filed in connection with the AIL lawsuits reveal the most common types of conflicts that lead to contract failure and litigation. The direct outcomes of the lawsuits on average are minor and unlikely to deter opportunistic behavior ex ante. In contrast, the indirect impact of litigation on VC reputation leads to economically significant drops in fundraising and quantity and quality of deal flow. These reputational effects could serve as an important deterrent of VC opportunism, especially for older and more successful VCs.

The chapter presents a few policy recommendations. First, entrepreneurs should be aware of the possible conflicts of interests and opportunistic behavior by VCs. Second, to reduce the risk of dealing with opportunistic VCs, entrepreneurs need to perform rigorous due diligence of the reputation of the VCs and their past litigation record. Last, expert legal advice could be critical for improving the entrepreneur's expected return both at the stage of signing the investment agreement and accepting funds from a VC and in cases where opportunistic behavior leads to litigation.

CONFLICTS OF INTEREST

In their line of business VCs interact with many different parties. First, VCs raise capital from qualified investors like pension funds and university endowments. Second, VCs invest in start-up companies founded by entrepreneurs and often financed by angels in earlier rounds. In many cases VCs do not invest single-handedly but form syndicates and share control and monitoring of their ventures with other VCs. Third, VC-backed companies often seek debt financing from specialist banks like the Silicon Valley Bank. Last, VCs exit their investments by either bringing the start-up companies public via an IPO or selling them to other companies via an acquisition. In IPOs, VCs deal with public equity investors, investment banks and other gatekeepers like auditors, while in acquisitions VCs have to deal with the acquiring companies (and their advising investment banks). All of these complex interactions are associated with conflicts of interests that can motivate opportunistic behavior.

Little is known about the actual conflicts of interests between VCs and other parties involved in start-up companies. The deals are done in private, and researchers rarely have access to the terms of the deals or their outcomes. This section will conjecture what conflicts could arise in start-up financing involving VCs. The analysis of lawsuits in a subsequent section will shed some light on the frequency and nature of such conflicts, because the lawsuits generate publicly available documents that describe in detail the grievances of the plaintiffs and the alleged opportunistic behavior by the defendants.

Conflicts between VCs and Their Investors

U.S. venture capital funds usually operate as limited partnerships (Feng, Liang, and Prowse 1994). These partnerships are managed by VC companies who serve as a general partner and are capitalized by various investors serving as limited partners. Due to the illiquidity and long-term nature of VC investments, the limited partnerships have a 10-year life during which VCs are not required to disburse payments to limited partners. This 10-year period can be extended with limited partner approval for several more years.

The limited-partnership structure and significant informational asymmetries generate various channels for opportunistic behavior. First, when VCs solicit capital from investors they may misrepresent past performance. Many of the VCs' investments take a long period to exit, and while they are kept on the books of a VC fund, the VCs have discretion over the value at which they record such investments. One technique to misreport performance is suggested by Cumming and Walz (2007), who find evidence that many VCs around the world manipulate the value of unexited investments to boost the performance of their ongoing funds in order to attract funding for their new funds.

Second, once the limited partners have committed their funds, they have little say in the management of the partnership and its investment and disbursement policies. At this stage, the VCs can suspend any effort and can rely solely on income from annual asset management fees, or even misappropriate fund capital for perk consumption. VC partners can abandon the investments made in the fund and direct their efforts towards other funds. The investors have limited recourse against ongoing VC mismanagement as their money is held hostage for at least 10 years.

Limited partners can also act opportunistically against VCs. When limited partners commit to investing in a VC partnership, their capital does not flow to the fund immediately but is staged over the first several years of the partnership life (Litvak 2004). Large investors can hold up a VC by reneging on the agreement to deposit their capital on a timely basis and threaten to put the VC partnership in a liquidity crisis.

Conflicts between VCs and Entrepreneurs

As VCs can misrepresent the quality of their management team and the partnership performance and investment policy to their investors, entrepreneurs can mislead VCs about the quality of their start-up firms, their product potential, or technological advantages. Moreover, lower-quality start-ups have incentives to camouflage their performance more than higher-quality start-ups and create a classic lemon's problem *à la* Akerlof (1970). Many start-up companies do not have a long track record of generating sales or profits, their technology is in its infancy, and their founders are first-time entrepreneurs without proven management experience. Even if the fundamentals of the start-up at the time of fundraising are attractive, once the VC invests money in the firm, the entrepreneur can reduce her effort, start consuming excessive perks, and impact negatively the performance of the start-up. This is a manifestation of the classic Jensen and Meckling (1976) investor-manager agency problem.

Besides the investor-manager agency problem, the VC-backed start-up can potentially suffer from the reverse agency problem—opportunistic behavior by the VC to the detriment of the entrepreneur. In contrast to dispersed shareholders in public corporations, VCs have large ownership, several board seats, and strong contractual control rights. In many cases, VCs have the power to oust the entrepreneur and appropriate her ownership or utilize below–fair value issuance of new equity to dilute her stake. Such transactions, denoted by Atanasov, Black, and Ciccotello (2008) as equity tunneling, can transfer virtually all of the entrepreneur's ownership in the start-up to the VC.

Furthermore, VCs can transfer assets or future opportunities from the start-up to other companies they control in order to increase their value or the probability of a successful exit. Such asset tunneling techniques (Atanasov, Ivanov, and Litvak 2008) can be as effective as equity tunneling in transferring the entire start-up value to the VC. The concern that asset tunneling could be a significant problem in VC-backed start-ups has been raised by several theoretical studies: Ueda (2004); Dushnitsky and Shaver (2007); and Fluck, Garrison, and Myers (2006).

Last, the interest of the VC may not align with the interest of the entrepreneur when the VC is considering an exit from his investment. The VC and entrepreneur may disagree on the timing of the exit, the type of exit, or the terms of the exit. Oftentimes, the VC will have the upper hand and choose an early or inefficient exit that benefits the VC (perhaps because they need to demonstrate good performance, or the limited partnership is about to be liquidated) with negative effects for the entrepreneur (Fried and Ganor 2006). A recent paper by Masulis and Nahata (2008) demonstrates the VC conflicts of interests when a VC-backed company is acquired by a publicly traded corporation. The announcement effects for the acquirer are significantly larger when the VC sits on the acquirer's board or is in need of a quick exit (the life of their limited partnership is about to expire).

Conflicts between VCs and Other Start-Up Investors (Angels, Other VCs, Creditors)

Many of the conflicts of interest between VCs and entrepreneurs arise in the dealings between VCs and other VCs that have partnered with them in an investment syndicate or between VCs and angels and other early-stage investors in the start-up. A VC's later-round investments at oppressive terms may dilute early-stage investors, including other VCs.

Leavitt (2005) argues that the VCs have stronger incentives to implement equity tunneling techniques against early-stage investors like angels than against entrepreneurs, because (1) entrepreneurs may be necessary for the start-up success and the VCs could consider leaving them enough ownership to preserve their efforts, while the contribution of angels is fungible and could easily be replaced by the VCs; and (2) while entrepreneurs consume nonpecuniary benefits from being in control of their start-ups and will agree on dilutive investment terms proposed by the VCs to preserve the life of the start-up and their nonpecuniary benefits, angels and other early-stage investors value only monetary gains

VCs commonly invest in syndicates headed by one lead VC that has identified the deal and usually performs the bulk of due diligence and monitoring. In many cases the lead VC invests in the first round and then invites other VCs to participate in subsequent rounds. Once the lead VC has invested in the first round, it has incentives to misrepresent to outside VCs the future capital requirements of the start-up or its quality in order to achieve inflated pricing at the subsequent rounds (Admati and Pfleiderer, 1994; Cumming 2005).

When a VC initiates any asset tunneling technique, he will expropriate not only the founder-entrepreneur, but also the start-up itself and as a derivative all its other investors, including debt holders who will be left with no liquidation value if the company goes in default. Similarly, any exit strategy that is optimal for the VC but inefficient for the entrepreneur may harm other common stock holders as well.

Conflicts between VCs and Exit Counterparties

VCs aim to find a profitable exit from their investments. They can either bring the company public and after a period sell all their shares to public investors, sell the company to another corporation, or sell their stake back to the company or another investor. In the worse case, the company is liquidated and written-off as a failed investment. As with any IPO company, the insiders have incentives to inflate past performance in order to obtain better valuation from the underwriters. Similarly, in negotiations with a strategic buyer, VCs can misrepresent the value of the company or any potential synergies with the acquirer. These are adverse selection problems arising from the large informational asymmetries between VC and the buyers of the company stock (Cumming 2008).

CONTRACTUAL SOLUTIONS TO THE CONFLICTS OF INTEREST

The previous section presented a number of potential conflicts between VCs and other parties involved in early-stage companies. The industry seems full of possibilities for opportunistic behavior, which begs the question why this industry exists and has grown so successful in the last 25 years. One reason for this success is that most parties have developed complex contracts that reduce the occurrence of value-destructive opportunistic behavior (Lerner and Schoar 2005). The other reason is that most parties are repeat players with long horizons. These conditions create incentives to build reputation and avoid short-term opportunistic behavior. In this section, I will discuss the important contractual features designed to reduce some types of opportunistic behavior. The role of reputation in filling the contractual gaps is discussed in the next section.

Most contracts signed by VCs are not publicly available. There are a few limited cases when VCs have provided a small sample of contracts to researchers. In particular, for the analysis of VC-limited partner agreements I will rely on the findings of Litvak (2004); and for the analysis of VC-entrepreneur contracts on Kaplan and Stromberg (2003). A few other studies like Bienz and Hirsh (2006), Bienz and Walz (2006), Cumming (2008) or Lerner and Schoar (2005) document similar results.

VC Limited Partner Contracts

The typical VC partnership mandates that investors commit their capital for at least 10 years. The partnership is not required by law to publish any financial statements or provide other ongoing performance information, and is not protected by U.S. securities laws like the Investment Company Act of 1940. (This subsection will focus on VC contracts in the United States; for VC–limited partner contracts around the world see Cumming and Johan 2006.) These features combined with the risk of opportunistic behavior should make venture capital partnerships a rather unattractive asset class for all but the most risk-loving investors. Yet, starting from the late 1970s VCs have managed to attract billions of dollars of capital predominantly from sophisticated institutional investors. In order to attract such capital, VC partnerships have designed complex contracts and procedures that, while preserving VC flexibility and control, allow institutions to feel comfortable investing in this asset class.

The first important set of procedures designed to reduce adverse selection and moral hazard is the capital raising mechanism of VC funds. First-time VCs usually raise funds for a small fund and, if this fund does well, start raising capital for subsequent larger funds. Fund raising is done on average every three to five years, and VCs are continuously exposed to market pressure to perform well and build solid reputation with investors, even though the investors in each fund are committed for at least 10 years.

The payment structure of the VC management contracts is designed to align the interest of the VC with his limited partners. Typically, VCs receive a relatively small annual asset management fee (1 to 2 percent of partnership assets) and a percentage of the partnership profits (carry) which is much larger—20 to 25 percent. This fee structure combined with relatively small funds under management, assures that most VCs have interest to achieve large positive returns on the partnership capital. Still, if a partnership is large, the VCs can potentially run a lifestyle fund and live comfortably off asset management fees without returning any cash to investors. The 10-year life of the limited partnership resolves this concern, while also ensuring stable funding for illiquid and long-term investments.

In addition to the VCs pay-for-performance remuneration package, the contracts between VCs and limited partners often contain various covenants protecting the limited partners (Gompers and Lerner 1996). Covenants restrict the activities of the general partners, the types of investments that the fund can make and the fundraising of the venture capital company (see Metrick 2006, 38–40 for more detail). There are also detailed provisions stipulating the minimum number of hours that the VC partners should spend working on the fund investments (Cumming and Mackintosh 2004). The features are intended to further assure the VC's exclusive commitment to the management of the partnership and the fulfillment of her fiduciary duties towards the limited partners.

The last major feature of the limited partnership contract that protects investors' interest is the right to stage their capital inflows into the partnership. Typically, investors commit a certain overall sum, but they pay this amount in equal installments over the first three to five years of the partnership (Litvak 2004). Thus, they maintain flexibility and could forego paying the remaining installments if the VC violates his fiduciary duties. At the same time, giving investors the right to withdraw their capital commitments at any time can be detrimental to the VC and other limited partners. Therefore, the partnership agreement includes significant penalties for failed delivery of committed funds. Litvak (2004) studies the complicated nature of these penalty provisions and determines that they are an effective deterrent of limited partner opportunism.

VC—Entrepreneur Contracts

The relationship between a VC and limited partners is relatively straightforward to regulate with contracts. Contracts turn out to be not as successful in regulating the relationship between a VC and a start-up founder. Remember that the VC-founder relationship suffers from two potential agency problems: (1) entrepreneurs acting opportunistically to the detriment of the VCs and (2) the VCs acting opportunistically to the harm of entrepreneurs. In this subsection, I outline the main features of the typical VC-founder contract and discuss their role in solving each of the two agency problems. Due to the opposing nature of the two agency problems, in many cases a reduction in one leads automatically to an exacerbation of the other. Perhaps because VCs usually have larger bargaining power than entrepreneurs (or are better informed and use more sophisticated legal advice), I argue that the VC-entrepreneur contracts are on average biased in favor of the VCs.

Securities and Cash Flow Rights

Venture capital investments are predominantly structured as securities that both have liquidation priority over the founders and early equity investors' common stock on the downside and participation rights on the upside, usually implemented as convertibility into common stock. Kaplan and Stromberg (2003) find that more than 95 percent of their sample VC investments are structured as convertible preferred stock. In most cases the issue of convertible preferred stock is accompanied with liquidation preferences. Liquidation preferences explicitly specify a multiple of the VC's original investment that the start-up has to return to the VC before other investors can receive any payoffs.

The choice of convertible preferred equity or debt with liquidation preferences has been widely analyzed in the VC literature (see Casammatta's chapter of this book). The main rationale proposed by theoretical models for this security structure is that it ensures that entrepreneurs receive payoffs from the firm only when the VC's investment has been recovered.

These features make convertible preferred equity attractive for the VC, but they are not without cost for the entrepreneur and the start-up itself. Fried and Manor (2005) argue that the preferred equity position of the VC generates various conflicts of interest that are especially strong when the start-up has reached the exit stage. The VCs can opportunistically decide to sell the company prematurely and at a low price to ensure return of their capital via their liquidation preferences and leave little value for the entrepreneur and other common equity investors.

Antidilution and First Refusal Rights

Another set of terms present in the majority of VC-entrepreneur contracts are antidilution provisions and various rights granted to the VC to approve or veto future firm financing. The antidilution provisions serve the role of standard preemptive rights in protecting the VCs ownership stake from being diluted by the common stock holders in future rounds of financing. In addition to these reasonable protections granted in most private companies around the world, the antidilution provisions of the VC combined with their veto rights to approve future financing transfer most risk of future decline in firm value to the entrepreneur.

There are good arguments for the transfer of firm-specific risk to the party that is best informed about the firm and has the largest ability to improve firm performance. But, antidilution provisions transfer not only firm-specific risk but also industry or market risk to the entrepreneur. Moreover, these antidilution provisions, especially if implemented as "full ratchets" (see Kuemmerle [2004] for a definition of full versus weighted-average ratchets), enable an opportunistic VC to dilute the entrepreneur (and any other common stock investor). The VC only needs to initiate a new round of financing at a depressed price (a down-round), exclude the entrepreneur from participating, and transfer a large percentage of the entrepreneur's ownership stake in the company to himself.

The veto rights over future financing facilitate dilution even further by allowing the VC to shut down any alternative sources of capital and delay any financing until the start-up runs out of cash. Then, the VC can infuse capital at draconian terms and wipe out the common stockholders. The entrepreneur has no legal recourse, because if the VC did not infuse capital, the firm would have gone bankrupt and the common stock would have been worthless anyway (Bartlett and Garlitz 1995).

Corporate Governance and Control

The contracts between VCs and entrepreneurs include various corporate governance and control clauses. First, the contracts stipulate in detail the composition of the start-up's board of directors. A typical board consists of five members, two of which are appointed by the entrepreneur and two by the VC. The fifth member is an outsider approved by both parties. Kaplan and Stromberg (2003) document that with each subsequent investment round, the control rights and respectively the number of board members appointed by VCs increases. An increase in VC board representation can also occur under certain contingencies, the most common of which is the start-up's not meeting prespecified milestones.

Examples of milestones include a maximum time period during which the start-up has to achieve a certain sales number, have a completed product, or break even on a cash flow basis. Conditional on achieving such milestones, the entrepreneur maintains her ownership, board seats, and control. If milestones are not met, the VCs can increase their stake at the expense of the entrepreneur (by receiving free new shares, for example), receive more board seats and secure majority on the board.

The main value of milestones is that they remove any incentive for misrepresentation of future performance by the entrepreneur. If an entrepreneur exaggerates future performance projections, the VCs can set these projections as milestones in the contract, and when they are not met, the VC will take over, dilute, or even fire the entrepreneur. Thus, milestones punish overconfidence in entrepreneurs ex post, but allow them to keep their optimistic forecasts and beliefs ex ante. A fundamental flaw in milestones from an optimal contracting perspective is that they are usually absolute—not relative to industry or market performance. As a result, the founder bears not only firm-specific risk that she can modify and control through expending more effort, but also industry and market risk, which are exogenous to the entrepreneur.

Another common corporate governance contract clause is that VC capital will be transferred to the start-up not in one large sum but in several payments staged over a period of time. The transfer of future payments may be conditional on the start-up's meeting milestones or other conditions. Most importantly, the VCs usually retain complete control/approval rights over any future source of financing for the start-up. Arguably, staging creates value for all—the start-up saves on using expensive finance that it does not need immediately; the VC retains a real option to invest once some uncertainty has been reduced. In general, staging reduces the overall cost of capital for the start-up and maintains alignment of interests between VCs and entrepreneurs.

Nevertheless, staging can be costly for the entrepreneur. When a VC does not provide all necessary capital in one round, his control over future finance and antidilution rights makes founder dilution more effective. Imagine a scenario in which a start-up has received the first tranche of VC investment and is about to run out of cash to meet expenditures. The second tranche of VC money is due soon, but the VC delays it. As the start-up approaches insolvency, the entrepreneur is put in a difficult position. One possibility is that the start-up goes bankrupt and the VCs can take all useful assets in liquidation due to their preferred credit standing relative to the entrepreneur, or the VC can extend another infusion of equity capital, but this time at highly dilutive terms for the entrepreneur and other early equity investors.

Employment Terms

The last set of important contractual terms that are designed to control the entrepreneur's agency problem is the founder employment provisions. These terms are usually included in the term sheet and shareholder agreement. The most common employment term is vesting of founder shares. At the time of VC investment, the original founder receives a small percentage of his full promised ownership stake in the company. The remaining shares vest in regular increments over the next several years, conditional on the founder maintaining employment with the firm.

The founder employment agreement regulates the conditions under which the founder can be fired. In most cases, the entrepreneur can be fired by the board "at will," and usually no severance package is provided for in the contract (compare with the generous golden parachutes granted to CEOs in public corporations). Replacing the original entrepreneur by a professional CEO in VC-backed start-ups is common. In fact, it is the norm. Hannan, Burton, and Baron (1996) and Hellmann and Puri (2002) document that the majority of founders of VC-backed companies are replaced by professional CEOs within five to seven years of initial VC involvement.

The combination of vesting of entrepreneur's shares and "fire at will" board power provide, on one hand, incentives for the entrepreneur to work hard and generate value for both the VC and the start-up company (Hellman 1998), but on the other hand, grant ample opportunities for the VC to tunnel the entrepreneur's equity via a freezeout. The classic freezeout of minority shareholders in any corporation involves a forced purchase of minority shares by the controlling shareholder at a large discount to fair value. In VC-backed start-ups the freezeout transaction is usually implemented by first firing the founder from her CEO position and then invoking contractual terms that force the entrepreneur to forfeit any unvested shares. The freezeout is completed by contractual terms that often give the right to the VC to purchase all vested founder shares at cost (usually close to zero). This process results in the VC acquiring all founder common stock at a price well below fair value.

Contractual Protections for Entrepreneurs

The VC-entrepreneur contracts contain many clauses designed to protect VCs from opportunistic behavior by entrepreneurs. One would expect that these contracts will at the same time include a similar number of protections against VC opportunism. Surprisingly, only one such protection is included in most contracts—an automatic conversion of VC preferred stock into common stock when the company is going public at or above a prespecified minimum stock price. This protection has been analyzed theoretically by Hellmann (2006), who argues that it is designed to resolve a potential VC hold-problem. In the absence of automatic conversion provisions, a VC can extract a large side payment before he agrees to convert his preferred equity into common stock. This conversion is necessary because IPO investors are reluctant to invest in companies with complicated capital structure and multiple classes of shares.

The VC-entrepreneur contracts do not include any specific protections against situations when VCs force the start-up into an acquisition or other exit transaction at the expense of entrepreneurs and other investors. There are no explicit protections against asset transfers (tunneling), except for the occasional nondisclosure agreement during the due diligence stage.

In summary, VC-entrepreneur contracts are complex and apparently one-sided. Entrepreneurs have limited protections and bear a lot of risk, including industry and market risk, while VCs have tremendous contractual power, especially on the downside. All downward movements in performance lead to VCs' taking control of the board and diluting the existing founder stake via down rounds. The milestone provisions further dilute founder equity. Last, the fire-at-will and vesting provisions can wipe out the founder's stake completely. It is hard to believe that such contracts can exist in equilibrium if bargaining power is evenly split between VCs and entrepreneurs, entrepreneurs are sophisticated (or use sophisticated legal advice), or no other mechanisms exist to prevent VC opportunism. If any of these conditions are violated ex ante, it is likely that somewhere along the way, especially in a down market, some VCs will trigger their contractual powers, freezeout or dilute founders, transfer assets to other start-ups, or find other ways to behave opportunistically against the founders.

Although VC-entrepreneur contracts offer little protection against VC opportunism, other contracts could provide some protection for entrepreneurs as an unintended consequence. For example, Gilson (2003) argues that contracts between VCs and their investors help protect entrepreneurs against dilutive down-rounds, because when a VC depresses the price of an investment round, the VC has to use the same price to mark down his entire investment in the start-up. The mark-down will depress the reported value of the VC portfolio, and the VC will have to report poor annual performance to his investors. Gilson terms the unintended beneficial interactions between different contracts "contract braiding."

The interest of other parties involved in the start-up can also help protect entrepreneurs from certain VC opportunism. Fluck, Garrison, and Myers (2006) and Bachmann and Schindele (2006) argue that a VC syndicate will be less inclined to tunnel wealth than a single VC due to coordination and reputational costs. The existence of outside debt can help against asset tunneling, because if excessive asset tunneling brings the company into bankruptcy, the debt holders can allege fraudulent conveyance by the VC and claim these assets back. Such recourse, although not beneficial for entrepreneurs ex post (after all the company is already in bankruptcy and the entrepreneur equity is worthless), can still serve as a deterrent ex ante.

VC—Creditor Contracts

Traditionally, bank lending has not been viewed as a source of capital for start-up companies. Most banks have avoided the high-risk profile of start-ups. Nevertheless, a small number of specialized banks have committed a significant percentage of their capital to venture lending/leasing. The leader in this market segment is the Silicon Valley Bank (SVB). The lending contracts between SVB and start-ups are structured to align the incentives of VCs and entrepreneurs well with the interest of the lender. First, SVB invests only in start-ups backed by the most established and reputable VCs. Second, the debt financing is provided immediately after a large infusion of VC equity capital that provides a cash cushion for the debt holder. Third, in exchange for the debt financing, SVB receives warrants to purchase shares in the start-up at a fixed price. These warrants bring upside potential that augments the risk-return profile of the bank's investment.

Other contractual features are designed to limit downside risk—SVB's debt is secured with the start-up's equipment and other assets, SVB assumes control of the start-up if debt payments are not made. The central role of SVB in the venture capital community assures that nonpayment of its debt will result in large reputational costs for the delinquent VC. The venture lending contracts seem to prevent most adverse selection/moral hazard problems on the VC side, as long as the lender is an established bank with long-term interactions with the VC community like the SVB.

THE ROLE OF REPUTATION

VCs could behave opportunistically toward their limited partners, the start-up founders, or other participants in the VC industry. Yet if opportunistic behavior were too widespread, venture capital could not flourish as it has. So there must be some noncontractual constraints on VC behavior. One central mechanism that limits opportunistic behavior by VCs is reputation—with investors, other VCs, acquirers of VC-backed firms, investors in VC-backed IPOs, and current and potential entrepreneurs.

Reputation with Limited Partners in VC Funds

Because venture funds are organized as limited-term partnerships, VCs have to go back to investors to raise capital for new funds every few years. More reputable VCs are able to raise more capital, raise it faster, and negotiate better terms with their limited partners (for example, they may be able to charge higher management fees and/or take a bigger share of the profits of the fund). Reputational concerns in combination with the extensive contractual provisions in the partnership agreement contracts covered in the previous section should prevent most opportunistic behavior by VCs against their limited partners. Although, it is always possible for a few fraudulent VCs to secure funding from investors for a first fund, it is unlikely that such fraudulent behavior can persist in the long run. At the same time, investors that do not fulfill their capital obligations are also going to be first heavily penalized by contract and second ostracized by the VC community, leading to the disappearance of any investor opportunism in the industry.

Reputation with Entrepreneurs

A reputation for dealing fairly with entrepreneurs can generate future high-quality deal flow or better financing terms. For example, Black and Gilson (1998) argue that a central part of VC contracting with entrepreneurs is an implicit contract to return control to a successful entrepreneur by exiting through IPO, rather than through selling the company, if both options are available. Hsu (2004) shows that entrepreneurs are willing to accept lower valuations in order to secure financing from reputable VCs.

It is not possible to judge whether accepting lower valuations from more reputable VCs has increased entrepreneur wealth on average, but there is one setting when the wealth of the entrepreneur at exit is observable—when the start-up goes public in an IPO. The IPO prospectus includes data on the ownership stake of all major investors and managers and identifies the founders. Exhibit 17.1 reports an analysis of VC-backed IPOs between 1990 and 1999 and the expected wealth of founders who have received funding from above-median versus below-median reputation VCs. More reputable VCs leave larger ownership stake to founders and have slightly higher IPO valuations resulting in dramatic differences in founder wealth—a 50 percent increase in the medians.

Reputation with Other VCs, Acquirers, and IPO Investors

VCs often syndicate investments with other VCs. A VC with better reputation among other VCs will find it easier to syndicate its own investments and will

Exhibit 17.1 Mean and Median Founder Wealth at IPO by VC Reputation

The exhibit presents the mean and median ownership stake and dollar wealth of founders of 390 Venture-Backed firms that go public between 1992 and 1999. Founder ownership stake is the percentage of firm shares owned by founder listed in the IPO prospectus. Founder wealth computed at IPO offer price equals the ownership stake of the founder multiplied by the IPO offer price and the number of firm shares at IPO. Founder wealth computed at IPO closing price is computed using the first-day closing price of the IPO firm. We define Low-reputation VCs as VCs below median age, while High-reputation VCs are the VCs with above median age. The last column of the table reports the P-values of the t-test for means and Rank test for medians that the founder wealth measures are equal between the low- and high-reputation VC groups.

	Low-Reputation VCs	High-Reputation VC	P-value of Difference
Mean (median) founder ownership stake	0.138 (0.093)	0.167 (0.115)	**0.09** (0.14)
Mean (median) founder wealth computed at IPO offer price ($ Million)	33.854 (10.657)	44.085 (15.405)	0.20 (**0.06**)
Mean (median) founder wealth computed at IPO closing price ($ Million)	77.715 (13.076)	93.531 (17.987)	0.51 (**0.02**)

receive better syndication offers from other VCs. For example, Lerner (1994b) finds that reputable VCs tend to syndicate with other reputable VCs.

The need to preserve reputation with other VCs will constrain some VC activities that may harm entrepreneurs. Consider equity dilution. If all VCs from past rounds participate pro rata in an investment round, all can happily set a low price that dilutes common shareholders. However, if some VCs do not participate in the current round or participate less than pro rata, they will be diluted too if the current round price is too low. The interests of nonparticipating VCs will help to ensure the fairness of the investment price for common shareholders as well.

VCs exit from investments by selling them to acquiring companies or to public markets through an IPO. For both markets, a chief worry of buyers is the seller's superior information about the portfolio company's true value. There is ample empirical evidence on the importance of reputation during VC exits through IPO. Brav and Gompers (1997) show that VC-backed IPOs do not suffer the long-run underperformance that is found in other IPOs. Ivanov and colleagues (2008) find that IPOs backed by more reputable VCs enjoy better post-IPO long-run performance.

Measures of VC Reputation

The importance of VC reputation has warranted many approaches to measure it in the academic literature. Traditionally, VC reputation has been proxied by measures of VC experience—VC age (Lerner 1994a) and cumulative number of investment rounds that the VC has participated in (Sorensen 2007). More recently, Nahata (forthcoming) and Ivanov and colleagues (2008) have proposed measures of reputation based on the market share of a VC in past VC-backed IPOs. Nahata (2008) claims that his "IPO Capitalization Share" measure (the ratio of the sum of market capitalization of all past IPOs backed by a particular VC and the sum of the market capitalization of all VC-backed IPOs) most consistently predict future VC performance. Nahata (2008) proposes an alternative market share measure—"VC Investment Share"—defined as the sum of all portfolio investments by a VC scaled by all VC portfolio investments.

Other studies have argued that the performance of the VC is a good proxy for reputation and have used the proportion of successful exits. The reputation of VCs is also likely to be correlated with the reputation of their syndicate partners (Lerner 1994b) and the number of past syndicate partners (Hochberg, Ljungqvist, and Lu 2007). The latter study defines various measures of VC centrality based on the number of partners that a VC has invited to participate in past investment rounds led by the VC or the number of other VCs that have invited the VC to participate in their syndicated deals.

All of the academic measures discussed above require access to a large database of investment rounds of VC-backed start-ups. Such databases are provided by Thomson Financial–VentureXpert and Dow Jones–Venture One. The costs of subscription to such databases and the data manipulations required to calculate the VC reputation measures proposed by academics are usually beyond the means of entrepreneurs. To fill the need of entrepreneurs for access to VC reputation measures, a web site called theFunded.com provides a venue for entrepreneurs to discuss their interactions with VCs and evaluate them on a scale of 1 to 5 on five dimensions: track record, operating competence, pitching efficiency, favorable deal terms, and execution assistance. theFunded.com has been enormously successful and currently has evaluations for more than 4,500 VC companies by more than 10,000 entrepreneurs. An ongoing research project by faculty at Harvard Business School is studying the relation between the entrepreneur evaluations of VCs and the academic measures of VC reputation.

In summary, VC reputational concerns are an important, perhaps even the most effective, mechanism that prevents opportunistic behavior by VCs towards other participants in VC-backed start-ups. More reputable VCs are associated with better performing start-ups and higher wealth for entrepreneurs. Reputable VCs add more value to their investments, have access to higher-quality deal-flow, and consistently outperform their peers.

VC LITIGATION

After discussing possible conflicts of interest and opportunistic behavior in the VC industry and identifying contracts and reputational concerns as some of the solutions to reduce the occurrence of such behavior in the previous sections, this section sets to study acute conflicts that have resulted in litigation involving VCs.

The academic literature on litigation involving VCs is sparse. Cumming and MacIntosh (2004) offer a descriptive treatment and a few anecdotes. There are also several practitioner articles (Bartlett and Garlitz 1995; Christopher 2001; Fellers 2002; and Padilla 2001), offering advice to VCs about the litigation risks associated with "down rounds"—investment rounds at low prices, which result in significant dilution of entrepreneurs and other common stock investors. In many cases these down-rounds are a form of equity tunneling used by the VC to expropriate wealth from the common stockholders.

In comparison with the anecdotal treatment of VC litigation in the existing literature, the study by Atanasov, Ivanov, and Litvak (2007) has collected a comprehensive database of more than 200 lawsuits involving VCs. This database addresses various questions about the type of lawsuits involving VCs and sheds light on both the types of opportunistic behavior that occur in practice and the conditions under which reputation or contracts fail to prevent opportunism from occurring.

Two Case Studies

Before I turn to discussing the database used by Atanasov, Ivanov, and Litvak (2007), the following two case studies illustrate some of the conflicts of interests between VCs and entrepreneurs and provide examples of alleged opportunistic behavior by the VCs that has resulted in complete loss of ownership for the entrepreneur. The first case, Cooper v. Parsky, although decided in favor of the entrepreneur, did not provide any monetary reimbursement for the expropriation of the founder's 70 percent stake in a $100 million sales company. The second case, Kalashian v. Advent, resulted in a surprising $15 million settlement paid by the VCs to the two founders.

Cooper v. Parsky

Cooper v. Parsky, 140 F.3d 433, 2d Cir. (1998) combines almost all tunneling methods outlined above. The following narrative of the case is based on the plaintiff's complaint and the judge's opinion. The case was filed by Stanley Cooper—the founder, chairman, and CEO of U.S. Petroleum Corp (USP). Cooper incorporated USP in 1986 with the goal to build the first stand-alone petroleum wax refinery processing plant in the United States, as well as to acquire and develop other producing properties and refineries.

In 1987, USP received an investment from defendant Southwest Venture Partners II, a Texas VC. Southwest installed four directors to the board of USP. Southwest also obtained a voting agreement that gave the new USP board of directors a proxy to vote the Cooper's 71 percent majority interest in USP for 10 years, or until the occurrence of one of several specified triggering events. Cooper was assured by Southwest that the voting of his shares would be for administrative purposes and that under no circumstances was the Voting Trust to be used to dilute or eliminate the equity interest of the Coopers. Cooper also signed a five-year employment agreement with USP. That agreement provided that Cooper was to serve as a senior employee and to receive the same salary as the president of USP, and his employment was to be terminable only for cause. Five months after signing the employment agreement, Cooper was terminated and locked out of the USP premises.

In 1988, WSGP-International, Inc., a corporation 50 percent owned by the defendants Simon and Parsky, made an investment in USP via a limited partnership WSGP-USP LP. One of the other investors in WSGP-USP LP was Southwest—the original VC investor. Cooper was neither invited nor permitted to invest in this limited partnership. WSGP-USP LP then purchased majority control (50.1 percent) of USP for $7.2 million in a backdated agreement. The USP directors voted the Cooper stock in favor of this transaction, in which the Coopers were replaced as majority shareholders of USP. WSGP-USP LP became USP's new majority shareholder and lender.

On December 6, 1989, Petrowax PA Inc. was organized as a wholly owned subsidiary of USP to receive all productive assets of USP and acquire two wax refinery facilities. USP president and CEO Gene Blendermann's salary, upon which Cooper's salary was to be based under his employment agreement, was then split between USP and Petrowax. Gene Blendermann's salary from USP was reduced from $225,000 per year to $27,500.

In a series of equity tunneling transactions excluding Cooper, the USP's former 100 percent equity interest in Petrowax was reduced and diluted first to 44.96 percent and then to 15 percent. The transactions benefited WSGP, which acquired all of the remaining Petrowax common stock. In the end of 1991, USP's stake in its subsidiary Petrowax has been reduced to only 2.98 percent and USP transferred its remaining stake to Petrowax. This stock was the sole remaining asset of USP (all other assets were transferred previously to Petrowax).

In 1992, Petrowax filed under Chapter 11 in Delaware Bankruptcy Court. Petrowax was reorganized and had sales of about $100 million soon after the reorganization. In the same year, USP filed for bankruptcy under Chapter 7 in the Bankruptcy Court of the Southern District of New York.

Approximately seven months after being fired, Cooper initiated an arbitration proceeding seeking to enforce his Employment Agreement. The arbitrator found no "cause" basis for Cooper's termination and awarded Cooper salary, bonuses, incentive compensation, and health insurance for the period from November 22, 1988 through December 31. The arbitrator also found that USP could reinstate Cooper if it wished. Pursuant to this decision, USP reinstated Cooper, but calculated his compensation based on the $27,500 Blendermann was then receiving from USP. USP soon afterwards terminated Cooper again. On April 22, 1991, the New York Supreme Court ordered that Cooper recover from USP an amount equal to the salary and bonuses paid "directly or indirectly by USP or any related entity" to Blendermann from November 22, 1988, through the end of the original five-year term less one dollar per annum. The award amount was $676,000. To date, Cooper has obtained no payments from USP, because the company filed for bankruptcy and had no remaining assets. His claim against Petrowax was also expunged because USP was only a 2.98 percent shareholder of Petrowax at the time of Petrowax bankruptcy.

In addition to the employment arbitration, Cooper filed several lawsuits against Southwest, WSG, and Parsky seeking to recover their lost ownership stake in USP or USP's assets. All of these lawsuits were dismissed. The final result for Cooper was that after owning 70 percent of a 100 million dollar sales company, he eventually owned less than 50 percent of a bankrupt company with no assets.

Kalashian v. Advent (or the Alantec) Case

The following narrative is based on Padilla (2001): The Alantec Inc. dispute (Kalashian v. Advent VI L.P., No. CV739278 [Santa Clara Sup Ct. filed March 23,1994]) provides a good example of equity tunneling by VCs using down-round financing. Alantec was founded in 1987 by Michael Kalashian and Jagdish Vij. In 1988, the founders received a first round of venture capital money of $1.5 million. By the fall of 1990, venture capitalists had invested $16.5 million and acquired a 90 percent ownership and voting interest, as well as a majority of the directors on the board. The venture capital investors were dissatisfied with Alantec's management and Vij and Kalashian were ousted from the company by the end of 1990. The venture capitalists brought in John Wakerly to develop a new product and invested another $500,000 to support the development of this product.

At the time, Kalashian and Vij still owned all of the common stock, representing a combined 8 percent ownership interest in Alantec. The board decided to approve two new rounds of financing at highly dilutive terms to the two original founders. They did not inform the founders of the new rounds. To get around the majority vote of common stock needed to approve the financing, the board issued new common stock at $0.005 per share to the CEO and two other employees loyal to the investors, who then approved the new issues. By the end of the two rounds, the founders' ownership of the company went from 8 percent to 0.007 percent.

The new product proved a success and allowed Alantec to go public in 1994. In 1996, the company was purchased by Fore Systems for $770 million. The founders' final share was valued at about $600,000, while their predilution 8 percent interest would have been worth over $40 million.

Kalashian and Vij filed a lawsuit against the venture capitalists for the $40 million they allegedly lost because of the dilutive financings. After two weeks of trial testimony, the venture capitalists settled the suit for $15 million—a rather surprising outcome, which took the VC industry by surprise, resulted in significant media coverage, and perhaps motivated the slew of practitioner articles on down-rounds discussed above.

Analysis of the Lawsuits in the AIL Sample

The database of lawsuits involving VC collected by Atanasov, Ivanov, and Litvak (2007) includes more than 200 VCs and close to 300 lawsuits that have occurred in the period between 1975 and 2007. Atanasov, Ivanov, and Litvak (2007) find that VCs are listed as defendants in more than 70 percent of their lawsuits. The plaintiffs who bring suits against VCs include in order of frequency: start-up companies or their founders; other equity investors in start-ups; other VCs; nonfounder employees of start-ups; limited partners of venture funds (only two cases); and creditors of VC-backed start-ups (only 1 case).

About half of all VC-related lawsuits involve allegations of tunneling. Within the universe of tunneling cases brought against VCs, most popular allegations are wrongful transfers of assets; sales of companies on terms unfavorable to founders and other equity investors; expropriation of profitable opportunities; dilution and freezeouts. Plaintiffs in VC-related litigation usually fail, at least in cases that end up in court. Non-VCs win only 28 percent of resolved cases they bring. A large number of cases are dismissed for either procedural or substantive reasons.

Overall, the analysis of lawsuits in Atanasov, Ivanov, and Litvak (2007) is consistent with the discussion of contracts in this chapter. The most common conflicts resulting in lawsuits arise from the relationships between VCs and entrepreneurs and other common stock investors. The contracts that govern these relationships appear one-sided and afford the VCs plenty of channels for opportunistic behavior. In contrast, lawsuits arising from conflicts between VCs and their limited partners or their creditors are extremely rare, arguably because both the contracts that govern these relationships are balanced, and VCs' reputational concerns are stronger when repeatedly dealing with their capital providers.

Lawsuits and VC Reputation

Atanasov, Ivanov, and Litvak (2007) also analyze the determinants of the probability that a VC will be in litigation and the reputational costs associated with litigation. Their empirical analysis provides evidence of the importance of VC reputation in preventing opportunistic behavior. First, Atanasov, Ivanov, and Litvak (2007) find that on a per deal basis less reputable VCs are more likely to be litigated. Younger, smaller, and poorly performing VCs are more likely to be involved in litigation relative to the number of deals they have invested in. Another strong finding of Atanasov, Ivanov, and Litvak (2007) is that past litigation increases dramatically the probability of future litigation.

Second, a comparison of VCs that have been litigated with otherwise similar VCs that have not been subject to litigation reveals that following litigation, even though there are rarely monetary penalties awarded against defendant VCs, they experience significant decline in fund-raising relative to their peers. Litigated VCs also invest in fewer deals and the deals that they manage to invest in are lower-quality and less likely to result in successful exits. Last, litigated VCs are invited in fewer deals as a nonleading partner.

POLICY IMPLICATIONS

The venture capital industry in the United States is perhaps the most developed and best performing in the world. Previous studies posit that several reasons explain the success of VCs operating in the United States. Black and Gilson (1998) attribute this success to well-developed public markets and processes to bring start companies public via an IPO; Gilson (2003)—to contract braiding and reputation-building; Lerner and Schoar (2005)—to the complex VC-entrepreneur contracts; Armour and Cumming (2006)—to the U.S. legal system and especially the "temperate" bankruptcy laws.

The discussion of VC opportunism and the mechanisms to control it in the previous sections suggest that although the U.S. VC industry may be better than any other country, it can still suffer from costs associated with VC opportunism. In this section, I offer several policy implications that could help reduce these costs. First and foremost, entrepreneurs who consider raising capital from venture capitalists should be educated about the various possibilities for VC opportunistic behavior. Entrepreneurs need to be first aware of the problem before they can spend effort to alleviate it.

Second, due diligence on behalf of the entrepreneurs in their selection of VC investors is critical. I propose three main directions for due diligence: (1) read carefully the reviews and written comments about each potential VC investor on theFunded.com; (2) within reasonable resource boundaries collect data on academic measures of VC reputation; and (3) do a search of past litigation involving the prospective VCs. More intense due diligence by entrepreneurs will not only improve their choice of VCs, but also lead to better VC behavior overall, as VCs recognize that their opportunism can lead to reduced deal flow.

While entrepreneurs are the party most interested in effective VC investor selection, the thorough due diligence proposed in the previous paragraph will be likely more costly than what the average entrepreneur can afford. The market has already provided an important place for pooling entrepreneur experiences in selecting VCs—theFunded.com's web site. Still, government or nongovernment organizations aiming to stimulate entrepreneurship can help improve the process. These organizations can facilitate founder due diligence by granting entrepreneurs access to past litigation data and academic measures of VC reputation for a large number of VCs.

The analysis of lawsuits also suggests that in many cases entrepreneurs do not utilize the services of experienced lawyers. Forgoing expert legal help can be dangerous for the founders both at the stage of signing the shareholder agreement and unknowingly agreeing to erroneous contractual provisions granting excessive power to the VC without corresponding efficient gains (e.g., full ratchet provisions), and at the litigation stage when the entrepreneurs could kill a meritorious lawsuit by filing it in the wrong court, with the wrong claims, or the wrong evidence.

Again, careful choice of which lawyer to represent the founder in dealings with VCs can prove crucial for the founder's and the start-up's success.

CONCLUSION

The VC industry is plagued by various conflicts due to informational asymmetry. These conflicts are dealt with in complex contracts, but contracts are incomplete and often not sufficient in curbing opportunistic behavior. In fact, many of the terms included in VC-entrepreneur agreements while protecting the VC, at the same time invite opportunistic behavior by the VCs at the expense of the entrepreneur and other equity investors. This chapter argues that reputational concerns serve a major role in preventing most VC opportunism. Still, some conflicts lead to litigation that generates publicly available documents describing opportunistic behavior by VCs and other parties involved in start-up investments.

Atanasov, Ivanov, and Litvak (2007) have collected a large number of such lawsuits and documents, and this chapter discusses the lawsuits contained in their sample. Although litigation in most cases does not punish rogue VCs directly, they suffer losses to their reputation. These potential losses serve an important role in keeping the majority of VCs honest and prevent them from abusing their large contractual powers. Nevertheless, potential entrepreneurs need to be aware of possible VC opportunistic behavior and should protect themselves with thorough due diligence and expert legal advice.

REFERENCES

Admati, A., and P. Pfleiderer. 1994. Robust financial contracting and the role of venture capitalists. *Journal of Finance* 49:371–402.

Akerlov, G. 1970. The market for lemons: Quality uncertainty and the market mechanism. *Quarterly Journal of Economics* 89:488–500.

Armour, J., and D. Cumming. 2006. The legislative road to Silicon Valley. *Oxford Economic Papers* 58:596–635.

Atanasov, V., B. Black, and C. Ciccotello. 2008. Unbundling and measuring tunneling. Retrieved from SSRN: http://ssrn.com/abstract=1030529.

Atanasov, V., V. Ivanov, and K. Litvak. 2007. The effect of litigation on venture capitalist reputation. NBER Working Paper No. W13641. Retrieved from SSRN: http://ssrn.com/abstract=1037165.

Bachmann, R., and I. Schindele. 2006. Theft and syndication in venture capital finance. Working paper. BI Norwegian School of Management.

Bartlett, J. M., and K. R. Garlitz. 1995. Fiduciary duties in burnout/cramdown financings. *Journal of Corporation Law* 20:595–626.

Bartlett, R. P., III. 2006. Managing risk on a $25 million bet: Venture capital, agency costs, and the false dichotomy of the corporation. bepress Legal Series. Working Paper 1339. Retrieved from http://law.bepress.com/expresso/eps/1339.

Bengtsson, O. 2006. Repeated relationships between venture capitalists and entrepreneurs. Ph.D. Dissertation. University of Chicago.

Bienz, C., and J. Hirsch. 2006. The dynamics of venture capital contracts. CFS Working Paper No. 2006/11. Retrieved from SSRN: http://ssrn.com/abstract=929491

Bienz, C., and U. Walz. 2006. Evolution of decision and control rights in venture capital contracts: an empirical analysis. Retrieved from SSRN: http://ssrn.com/abstract=966155.

Black, B., and R. Gilson. 1998. Venture capital and the structure of capital markets: Banks versus stock markets. *Journal of Financial Economics* 47:243–277.

Christopher, A. 2001. VC and the law: Potential legal hurdles involved in funding the next big thing. *Venture Capital Journal*. February, 43-45.

Cumming, D. 2005. Agency costs, institutions, learning and taxation in venture capital contracting. *Journal of Business Venturing* 20:573–622.

_____. 2008. Contracts and exits in venture capital finance. *Review of Financial Studies* 21:1947–1982.

_____, and S. Johan. 2006. Is it the law or the lawyers? Investment covenants around the world. *European Financial Management* 12:553–574.

_____. 2008. Preplanned exit strategies in venture capital. *European Economic Review* 52:1209–1241.

Cumming, D., and J. Macintosh. 2004. Boom, bust and litigation in venture capital finance. *Willamette Law Review* 40:867–906.

Cumming, Douglas J., and U. Walz. 2007. Private equity returns and disclosure around the World. *Journal of International Business Studies*, forthcoming. Retrieved from SSRN: http://ssrn.com/abstract=514105.

Dushnitsky, G., and M. Shaver. 2007. Limitations to inter-organizational knowledge acquisition: The paradox of corporate venture capital. Working paper. Wharton School of Management, University of Pennsylvania.

Fenn, G., N. Liang, and S. Prowse. 1998. The private equity market: An overview. *Financial Markets, Institutions & Instruments* 6:4.

Fluck, Z., K. Garrison, and S. Myers. 2006. Venture capital contracting: Staged financing and syndication of later-stage investments. Working paper, Michigan State University.

Fried, J., and M. Ganor. 2006. Agency costs of venture capitalist control in startups. *New York University Law Review* 81:967–1025.

Gilson, R. 2003. Engineering a venture capital market: Lessons from the American experience. *Stanford Law Review* 55. Retrieved from SSRN: http://ssrn.com/abstract=353380.

Gompers, P., and J. Lerner. 1996. The use of covenants: An empirical analysis of venture partnership agreements. *Journal of Law and Economics* 39:463–498.

Gorman, M., and W. Sahlman. 1989. What do venture capitalist do? *Journal of Business Venturing* 4:231–248.

Hannan, M., D. Burton, and J. Baron. 1996. Inertia and change in the early years: Employment relations in young, high-technology firms. *Industrial and Corporate Change* 5:503–535.

Hellmann, T. 2006. IPOs, acquisitions and the use of convertible securities in venture capital. *Journal of Financial Economics* 81:649–679.

_____, and M. Puri. 2002. Venture capital and the professionalization of start-up firms: Empirical evidence. *Journal of Finance* 57:169–197.

Hochberg, Y., A. Ljungqvist, and Y. Lu. 2007. Venture capital networks and investment performance. *Journal of Finance* 62:251–301.

Hsu, D. 2004. What do entrepreneurs pay for venture capital affiliation. *Journal of Finance* 59:1805–1844.

Ivanov, V., C. N. V. Krishnan, R. Masulis, and A. K. Singh. 2008. Does venture capital reputation affect subsequent IPO performance? Working paper. Vanderbilt University.

Jensen, M., and W. Meckling. 1976. Theory of the firm: Managerial behavior, agency costs, and ownership structure. *Journal of Financial Economics* 3:305–360.

Kaplan, S., and P. Stromberg. 2003. Financial contracting meets the real world: An empirical analysis of venture capital contracts. *Review of Economic Studies* 70:281–316.

_____. 2004. Characteristics, contracts, and actions: Evidence from venture capitalist analyses. *Journal of Finance* 59:2177–2210.

Kuemmerle, W. 2004. Termsheet negotiations for Trendsetter, Inc. Harvard Business School Case and Teaching Note No. 5-802-226.

Leavitt, J. 2005. Burned angels: The coming wave of minority shareholder oppression claims in venture capital start-up companies. *North Carolina Journal of Law and Technology* 6:223–288.

Lerner, J. 1994a. Venture capitalists and the decision to go public. *Journal of Financial Economics* 35:293–316

———. 1994b. The syndication of venture capital investments. *Financial Management* 23:16–27.

———, and A. Schoar. 2005. Does legal enforcement affect financial transactions? The contractual channel in private equity? *Quarterly Journal of Economics* 120:223–246.

Litvak, K. 2004. Governance through exit: Default penalties and walkaway options in venture capital partnership agreements. Working paper, University of Texas Law.

Masulis, R., and R. Nahata. 2008. Venture capital conflicts of interest: Evidence from acquisitions of venture backed firms. *Journal of Financial and Quantitative Analysis*, forthcoming.

Metrick, A. 2006. *Venture capital and the finance of innovation.* Hoboken: John Wiley & Sons.

Nahata, R. Forthcoming. Venture capital reputation and investment performance. *Journal of Financial Economics.*

Padilla, J. 2001. What's wrong with a washout? Fiduciary duties of the venture capitalist investor in a washout financing. *Houston Business and Tax Law Journal* 1:269–306.

Sorensen, M. 2007. How smart is smart money? A two-sided matching model of venture capital. *Journal of Finance* 62:2725–2762.

Ueda, M. 2004. Banks versus venture capital: Project evaluation, screening, and expropriation. *Journal of Finance* 59:601–621.

ABOUT THE AUTHOR

Vladimir Atanasov received his Ph.D. in finance from the Pennsylvania State University and is currently an assistant professor at the College of William and Mary. Before coming to William and Mary, Vladimir Atanasov was an assistant professor at Babson College. His research is primarily focused on corporate governance and specifically on the effect of controlling block holders on firm value. He is also studying the effect of securities and corporate laws on the behavior of large investors and the relationship between certain legal statutes and capital market development. Other research projects that Professor Atanasov works on include the dilution of entrepreneurs in VC-backed firms and the effect of lawsuits on VC funding and deal flow. His research has been published in the *Journal of Financial Economics, Journal of Financial and Quantitative Analysis,* and *Journal of Corporation Law.* He has been funded by several grants from the U.S. Department of State, the Kauffman Foundation, and the Melbourne Center for Financial Studies.

## PART IV

Venture Capital Exits and Returns

CHAPTER 18

Venture Capital Exits

ARMIN SCHWIENBACHER
Associate Professor of Finance, Louvain School of Management, Université catholique de Louvain Research Fellow, University of Amsterdam Business School

INTRODUCTION

Venture capital has become an important source of funding in the economy, in particular because it finances new companies that may not get money otherwise. Although we lack strong empirical evidence on the overall impact of venture capital finance on economic growth and welfare,[1] a quick look at some successful companies that obtained venture capital in their early stage of development (such as Apple, Netscape, Microsoft, Intel, Cisco, FedEx, Sun Microsystems and Genentech), indicates that the impact is by far more important than the size of the venture capital market as compared to financial markets overall (see Black and Gilson [1998] for further evidence and comparisons with bank loans). Venture capitalists (VCs) have been successful in contributing to the development of innovation and converting innovation into profitable technologies. Many large corporations have recognized this and built their own venture capital units to foster growth opportunities and obtain access to innovative technologies before they reach the product market.

Venture capitalists invest important funds in start-up companies, for which typically they obtain an equity position in the company. These shares are usually highly illiquid in the initial phase so VCs tend to hold them for a few years before selling them. Moreover, since most ventures do not generate positive cash flows during their first years that would allow the payment of dividends to shareholders, the main way for VCs to earn money from their investments is to sell the shares they hold in their portfolio companies. This provides an additional source of investment uncertainty, since the visibility of exit options is rarely clear at the initial investment stage. The term "exit" therefore refers to the divestment of the company from the VC's portfolio—that is, the sale of the shares—and is the general topic of this chapter. The exit is the very last stage of involvement by the VC in the company and is crucial since exit conditions determine the potential gains that the VC can make. Therefore, the exit is as important as the entry decision itself. The analysis of possible exit options is a critical part of the due diligence process that VCs go through before deciding whether to invest.

The exit stage is also important for the venture capitalist as financier for many other reasons. First, VCs are not long-term investors. When investing, they want to see an exit option within the next few years. Since they are largely rewarded on the basis of the exit value, they also have incentives to divest at the most profitable opportunity without unnecessary delay. Second, the exit is also a way to evaluate the VC if investors do not know how good she really is. In this case, the exit outcome can be a signal of the VC's quality. Such a signal is a key element for successful follow-up fund-raising. And third, since venture-backed companies do not pay out dividends while the VC is involved, the exit is the only way to make a return on the investment.

Entrepreneurs also must be aware that venture capitalists will want to exit after a few years when the company stands on its own feet. This most often creates a difference in the time horizon between the VC and the entrepreneur, since the latter often wishes to remain in the firm beyond the venture capital investment period. Moreover, since the exit conditions determine the value of the venture, it may affect important decisions about business and R&D strategies, and the overall development of the firm. Therefore, an exit strategy must be developed and must include necessary measures to liquidate the investment at the highest possible return.

The aim of this chapter is to provide evidence on the importance of continuing research in the area of venture capital finance. Many important research questions remain unanswered. This chapter surveys a number of issues about the choice of exit route, and about the factors driving this choice. It presents an up-to-date overview of existing academic literature on venture capital exits, including theoretical and empirical literature. Since papers focused on exits directly are (still) rare, we take a broad view and interpret more general results in the literature within the scope of venture capital exits. We further provide the reader with some stylized facts reported in the empirical literature and highlight some open research questions.

The decision to exit has two main dimensions: type of exit route and timing of the exit. In this chapter, we argue that both dimensions can substantially affect the value of the investment and therefore the incentives of the venture capitalist and the entrepreneur in adding value.

This literature survey is structured as follows. First, we present the academic literature on financial contracting between venture capitalists and entrepreneurs related to exits. A strong emphasis is put on the contract-theoretical approach used in many other studies for the analysis of venture capital investments. We also detail some theoretical issues on the allocation of control rights and provide information on exit clauses often included in venture capital contracts in practice. Next, we describe the different exit routes used by VCs and provide some pertinent facts. We also discuss in greater detail empirical and theoretical findings on the two main exit routes, namely, the initial public offering (IPO) and the trade sale. Then, we discuss the time dimension of the exit. The follow-up section highlights some exit problems including potential agency problems that can make the optimal exit more difficult for the VC. The final section provides some open research questions.

FINANCIAL CONTRACTS AND CONTROL RIGHTS RELATED TO EXIT DECISIONS

From a financial perspective, the design of venture capital contracts—more commonly called share purchase agreements—typically responds to two major concerns of venture capitalists: on the one hand, the wish to protect themselves against downside risk in case things do not go well; and on the other hand, the wish to benefit from upside potential if the venture becomes very promising. This is well achieved through the use of convertible securities, among other ways.[2] The ultimate contracting outcome must further ensure appropriate incentives to the parties involved (Hellmann 1998). In some cases, VCs will even ask for "participating" preferred equity which, in addition to preferred dividends, provides them with a claim on common dividend payments.

But these are not the only concerns of the venture capitalist when negotiating with the entrepreneur. Given the importance for the VC to exit once the company can stand on its own feet, she typically retains important control rights with respect to exit decisions.[3]

In fact, a closer look at such contracts shows the concerns of the venture capitalist in her desire to retain options to exit in the future and thus make liquid the assets she holds in portfolio companies. Venture capital contracts are much richer and provide more flexibility in the design of claims and allocation of control rights than standard financial contracts, especially compared to public equity. These control rights are included in the contract in the form of specific clauses that provide the VC with intervention rights in order to secure her interests. Alternatively, they may be found in shareholder agreements.[4] These may affect both dimensions of exit—type and timing. The following clauses are typically included in contracts:[5]

Registration right (also called *demand right*) gives the right to force a listing of the company on a stock market.

Drag-along right is a call option given in a trade sale to the strategic buyer on a partner's shares (e.g., the entrepreneur's) when another partner (e.g., the venture capitalist) sells hers. For instance, if the VC decides to sell her stake, the strategic buyer has the right—but not the obligation—to buy the stakes of the entrepreneur and other investors under the same conditions.

Tag-along right (also called *go-along* or *piggy-back right*): in case one partner sells shares, this right gives a put option to the other partners to sell their shares under the same conditions. The strategic buyer is then forced to buy all the shares offered.

Call and put options: options given to one partner to buy and sell, respectively, some proportion of the shares of the other partner(s).

Other important clauses included in venture capital contracts, but not directly related to exit issues, are the following:

Right of first refusal (also called *right of first offer*) gives the right to inside investors at subsequent financing rounds to purchase shares before selling them to outside investors.

Preemptive rights: the right of a shareholder to retain some predetermined percentage of ownership in the firm when new shares are issued.

Buy-back provisions: the right (usually retained by founders) to buy back the shares at some future time (e.g., when investors wish to exit).

Vesting schedules: the timetable that specifies when options become exercisable and when the shares acquired through stock options can be sold. These schedules are generally imposed to founders and key employees, and are intended to avoid early departure with the full number of shares.

Noncompete clause: a clause included in employment agreements that is intended to prevent former employees from working for the employer's competitors for a specified period of time and, thus, to penalize employees who leave prematurely.

Next to board representation, these rights allow the venture capitalist to secure exit options and to avoid being locked-in with her shares; without the entrepreneur, often the venture is not worth much. In the case of the drag-along right, the intention is to make a trade sale possible. Since the VC typically is a minority shareholder and the strategic buyer only buys if he can acquire a majority in the company, the VC will typically exercise her right whenever she wishes to do a trade sale against the will of the entrepreneur. This allows the VC to increase her chances to make a deal with a potential buyer. Otherwise, if she only holds a small equity stake and the entrepreneur does not want to sell his, a trade sale may be difficult to do; in a trade sale, buyers usually want to acquire a bigger stake so that they can take control over the venture. A similar reasoning applies to other clauses; they are all intended to facilitate the VC's exit.

In other cases, the venture capitalist will also include very specific covenants and state-contingent intervention rights in the contract, such as "the right to sell the company if no IPO has occurred after five years" or "the right to sell if the company fails to redeem preferred stocks" (Kaplan and Strömberg 2003). In any case, it provides exit options to the VC if specific requirements are not met by the company.

Empirical studies have shown that venture capitalists guarantee themselves substantial rights in addition to cash flows, in particular at the beginning of their involvement and for seed financing, but less so for late-stage financing (Smith 2005). Empirical literature on contracting and exits is limited, largely due to the lack of available data. The few exceptions showing the relative importance of these clauses include Cumming (2008), Kaplan and Strömberg (2003), Cumming and Johan (2008), and Bienz and Walz (2008). The last two papers provide a dynamic analysis of how control rights evolve over time, in particular as parties reach the exit decision and depending on which exit route is more likely.

Next to covenants, venture capitalists typically require convertible securities instead of common shares for their investments (Kaplan and Strömberg 2003). Using a theoretical double moral hazard framework, Hellmann (2006) shows how convertibles may affect the outcome and thereby the likelihood of a venture to eventually go public as opposed to being acquired. Such securities enable the allocation of control rights based on the choice of exit route, whether it be an IPO or a trade sale. If both parties—entrepreneur and investor—need to provide costly value-adding effort, convertible securities become optimal when an IPO requires more time and with an uncertain outcome (in the model, a trade sale is less risky and allows earlier exit).

FIRST DIMENSION OF EXIT: TYPE OF EXIT ROUTE

In this section, we discuss the five main types of exit route used by venture capitalists to divest their portfolio companies. After an introductory presentation, we discuss in more detail the more important routes separately.

The five exit routes typically considered for venture capital are as follows:

1. Initial Public Offering (IPO): the company achieves a stock market listing so that the venture capitalist can also sell her shares to the public.

2. Trade sale (or acquisition): the sale of the portfolio company to an existing firm, possibly in the same industrial sector.
3. Management buyout (or repurchase): the venture capitalist sells her shares back to the entrepreneur.
4. Refinancing (or secondary sale): the venture capitalist's stocks are purchased by another institutional investor (e.g., another VC).
5. Liquidation (or write-off): the company files for bankruptcy.

Since the end of the 1990s, an important number of venture-backed companies were introduced on NASDAQ and on new European, high-growth stock markets, including the Alternative Investment Market (AIM), EuroNM (now closed), Nasdaq Europe (formerly Easdaq), and more recently Alternext and Marché Libre (part of Euronext).

These exit routes have different impacts on the market structure and incentives of the parties involved. This, in turn, substantially affects financing conditions and the allocation of control rights between venture capitalists and entrepreneurs. An important element that seems to affect the decision of the VC to exit and the value of the venture are the characteristics of the relevant product market (Schwienbacher 2008a). This can affect both dimensions of exit. Some interactions between the product market and the financing of ventures have been analyzed empirically by Hellmann and Puri (2000). They conclude that venture capital financing is related to time-to-market; that is, the time it takes to make the first commercial sale. Based on asymmetric information arguments, Cumming and MacIntosh (2001) further argue that causal links exist between investment duration (time until exit by the VC), the "quality" of the venture, the nature of the venture's assets (in particular, its degree of intangibility), and the exit strategy of the VC.

Exhibit 18.1 indicates how different exit routes evolved in Europe over time during the period from 1998 to 2005 as percentage of all divestments in each specific year. An important caveat is the fact that these data also include buyout transactions, since in Europe the distinction between venture capital and buyout is often not clearly made. To limit biases, we only provide these data and not ones weighted by deal size (where the bias is clearly larger, since buyout transactions are by far larger than venture capital transactions). First, the table shows that exit routes are mostly cyclical and thus may vary significantly from one year to another.[6] Second, it indicates that trade sales happen more often than IPOs. This is consistent with the general view expressed by many practitioners. And third, write-offs are an important exit route for private equity, indicating that these deals involve significant idiosyncratic risk. The particularly high fraction of write-offs in the years 2001 and 2002 are largely due to the burst of the Internet bubble that attracted huge interest of venture capitalists in the years from 1998 to 2000.

Regarding the United States, the relative importance of the IPO compared to the trade sale is similar and also varies significantly from year to year, although overall performance is known to be significantly higher for venture capital investments done in the United States than in Europe (Hege, Palomino, and Schwienbacher forthcoming). The ratio of trade sales to IPOs is 1.3 to 1.6 on average (depending on the stage of development of the venture at the time of the first investment round) when measured in number of exits (Giot and Schwienbacher 2007). Weighted on value, the ratio would presumably be somewhat lower.

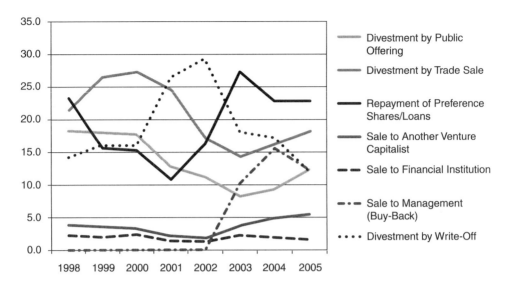

Exhibit 18.1   Relative Importance of Exit Routes
Exhibit 18.1 shows relative importance of exit routes, measured as a percentage of total amount of private equity (venture capital + buyout) divestments in Europe from 1998–2005.
Source: EVCA.

Initial Public Offering

When the firm is going public, the venture capitalist will also list her own shares and thus convert her private shares into public shares.[7] This allows her to subsequently sell them at the market price. Notice though that the IPO stage is not the exit per se but only a prestage since the VC is usually required to hold the shares after the IPO for a predetermined lock-up period. However, its length differs from one stock market to another and may also vary according to other contractual agreements among shareholders.

It is worth noting that most studies on the relationship of venture capital investments to IPOs do not focus directly on exit issues, but rather use the IPO event as a measure of performance of the venture capital investment or limit their observations on purpose to those venture capital investments that eventually become public because of increased data availability. In the latter case, these studies focus on a very specific subset of venture capital investments, usually the most profitable ones. In the former case, IPO exits are taken as the most successful venture capital investments, while other exit routes tend not.

Going public is the type of exit that has been most studied.[8] An IPO is generally viewed as the most profitable exit route for venture capitalists (see, for example, Sahlman 1990; Cumming and MacIntosh 2003a,b; Gompers 1995; and Black and Gilson 1998). Gompers (1995) reports the average annual rate of return for a venture capital in the United States is 60 percent when the exit occurs through an IPO and only 15 percent for a trade sale. Cumming and MacIntosh (2003a) further show that in Canada and the United States, ventures with highest market-to-book ratios more often go public.

Roëll (1996) provides a list of advantages for companies to go public. The main ones are access to new finance, enhanced company image, and publicity; motivating management and employees; and the possibility for cashing in. Disadvantages are all the possible costs and the danger of losing control over the company. For a general discussion on the decision to go public, see Jenkinson and Ljungqvist (2001).

From a more general perspective, some important differences have been observed between the IPO process of start-up companies and that of more established companies. First, for start-up companies, the decision whether to go public is closely related to the exit decision of the venture capitalist. For a non–venture-backed company with access to alternative financial resources, keeping the status quo (i.e., remaining private) is always an option; but for a venture-backed firm, the fact that the VC wants to exit rules out the option of a status quo. Also start-ups, as high-growth firms, do not simply time their IPO for hot issue markets as suggested in the paper by Myers and Majluf (1984); going public is vital for their survival, since they typically need substantial funds to stay in business. Thus, the decision to go public is not simply a way to adjust the firm's capital structure (i.e., debt/equity ratio), but is primarily driven by the need to raise more funds and to allow the VC to divest. Stock market conditions are therefore even more crucial for start-ups as their flexibility in timing their IPO is limited. Finally, a further distinction with conventional public companies is the absence of dividend payments for venture-backed companies that go public (Hege 2001). Once the venture-backed company is listed, potential gains for shareholders are limited to increases in the stock price.

Probably the most widely studied topic related to the IPO process is underpricing.[9] The price of shares needs to be discounted to guarantee that the less-informed investors purchase the issue in the presence of asymmetric information (Rock 1986). Otherwise, investors whose information is superior crowd out the others when good issues are offered—by overbidding the offer of less informed investors—and withdraw from the market when bad issues are offered, leading to the classical adverse selection problem. The offering firm must therefore price the shares at a discount in order to guarantee that uninformed investors purchase the issue. Taking the specific setting of venture capital finance into consideration, Neus and Walz (2005) show that the fact that venture capitalists are repeat players in the IPO market allows alleviation of some of the underpricing, since investors can punish a dishonest VC in the future.

Empirical studies on venture capital show that venture-backed IPOs are less underpriced than others. Barry and colleagues (1990) conclude that the quality of the VC's monitoring services appears to be recognized by capital markets through lower underpricing in an IPO. The main reasons put forward are the certification effect by the venture capitalist (Megginson and Weiss 1991) and the fact that VCs continue to hold significant equity stakes in the firms well after they have been taken public (Barry and colleagues 1990), which weakens the adverse selection problem through the signal they give to outside investors.

Trade Sale

There is very little empirical research on trade sales due to the particular difficulty in collecting data on this type of exit. In contrast to an IPO, a firm is not required to publicly disclose information under a trade sale. The literature that stands closest is that on mergers and acquisitions (M&A). From the point of view of the buyer, a trade sale is nothing more than a strategic acquisition of a venture for which the venture capitalist gets "immediate" cash in return. Therefore, it represents a change in ownership and a loss of control for the entrepreneur. The buyer typically aims at acquiring enough shares to achieve control over the acquired start-up company.

In some cases, the trade sale may take place through exchange of shares: a corporate buyer issues new shares in its own company to the venture capitalist in exchange for the shares in the start-up company. In this way, the VC gets shares of a less risky company in exchange for hers. These shares can then be distributed among the limited partners and/or sold later on the stock market.

Also, the strategic buyer can take an intermediate step by cofinancing (syndicating) the venture in later stages but before the venture capitalist exits, thus building a structure similar to that of a joint venture. In this way, it can reduce the potential problem of transfer of technology that is crucial in a trade sale.

Share Buyback and Secondary Sale

Other exit routes have attracted very little attention from academic researchers, although some have become more important in recent years (see Exhibit 18.1). Using Canadian data, Cumming and MacIntosh (2003b) provide empirical analysis of share buybacks and secondary sales as alternative exit routes in which venture capitalists sell their shares either back to management or to other institutional investors (with the entrepreneur in this case not selling his shares). In particular, they emphasize that fact that these routes involve only partial exits, in that not all shares are sold at once. Instead, VCs retain some equity stake in the investees as a way to signal quality when the degree of asymmetric information is severe. The reason for partial exits being more often observed in these two types of exit routes is explained by the fact that they typically involve ventures that fail to achieve their growth objectives, thus leading to relatively low returns. This in turn requires VCs to remain partially involved, or at least keep some form of financial commitment through an equity stake, to certify that these ventures are still worth keeping alive.

SECOND DIMENSION OF EXIT: TIMING OF EXIT

The second dimension of exit is timing. As already mentioned, venture capitalists aim at optimally timing their divestments, since their exit options are highly cyclical. In this section, we address some issues about the time dimension of VCs' divestment behavior.

Empirical evidence from the United States and Canada shows that venture capitalists on average stay four to six years with their portfolio companies before divesting them (Cumming and MacIntosh 2003a). A common way for VCs to time exits is by staging their financing in several rounds (Gompers 1995). In each round, the entrepreneur is given just enough financial resources to achieve the next intermediate development phase. This provides the VC with an option to exit at each financing round; she can either liquidate the venture if future prospects are bad, fully finance the next round, or reduce involvement through syndication (co-investment with other VCs). This is essential because entrepreneurs are unlikely to stop their own projects as long as others provide capital. Focusing on the biotechnology industry, Lerner (1994) examined the ability of VCs to time IPOs by going public when equity values are high and using private financing when values are low. Each financing round therefore involves an explicit decision to go public or postpone the exit. Furthermore, taking companies public when equity values are high minimizes the dilution of the entrepreneur's ownership stake.

Michelacci and Suarez (2004) point to the importance of exiting for the recycling of capital to redirect previously invested money into new, fresh start-ups and to raise capital for follow-up investments on the stock market through an IPO. This is especially important when there is limited supply of smart money, that is, money managed by skilled investors capable of assisting ventures in their start-up phase.

Notice that an exit strategy also needs to be considered in the event that the start-up company does not do well. Typically, entrepreneurs themselves do not voluntarily stop their own projects. Therefore, the decision whether to stop a project can hardly be delegated to the entrepreneur. The venture capitalist needs to be involved and make the decision based on her own information. Otherwise, this may lead to suboptimal continuation. Typically, it is best to stop when prospects of the venture fall too low to provide sufficient motivation for the entrepreneur to continue working hard. This may happen when most of the shares go to investors in follow-up rounds (Bergemann and Hege 1998; Bergemann, Hege, and Peng 2008).

A final possible reason for differences in timing among venture capitalists was proposed by Gompers (1996) and relates to reputation building (the so-called grandstanding effect). Exiting from a portfolio company by selling the shares is an effective way to signal the value of a company. In particular, if investors believe that going public is limited to high-quality firms, the VC can send a good signal to investors by listing the company. This provides an important reputational effect for an IPO. Gompers (1996) finds evidence that the building of reputation affects the timing of going public. Inexperienced VCs may not wait until the market is optimal to take firms public, because they need to signal their quality to potential investors in follow-on funds. Younger VCs would therefore tend to exit earlier from valuable companies to build a reputation; if VCs can demonstrate success to investors, this would improve their ability to raise new funds for future investments. Building on these findings, Lee and Wahal (2004) show that less-experienced venture capital firms take smaller and younger companies public. These results are consistent with the grandstanding hypothesis of Gompers (1996).

Several empirical studies have emphasized the strong importance of macroeconomic market conditions. A prominent study by Black and Gilson (1998) argues there is a strong link between a well-functioning venture capital market and an active stock market. The latter allows venture capitalists to exit from successful companies through an IPO. In the absence of a liquid stock market able to list young, high-growth companies, a VC would limit their investments due to the lack of viable exit options. This study, however, only examined one country, the United States, to draw such conclusions. Cumming, Fleming, and Schwienbacher (2006) show that in an international context (with focus on Asia-Pacific and the United States), this effect still persists; however, they also find that the quality of the country's legal environment is at least as important, if not more so, for facilitating venture capital exits than stock market development. In a related work, the same authors show that venture capital–backed companies may decide to relocate their facilities to a country with a better legal system (in the case of their study, mainly to the United States), as a way to provide better exit opportunities to investors (Cumming, Fleming, and Schwienbacher forthcoming). They show that these related companies benefit through higher returns at the exit phase.

The timing of the exit is further critically affected by the liquidity of exit markets. Cumming, Fleming, and Schwienbacher (2005) provide empirical evidence indicating that VCs adapt their exit and investment behavior according to the business cycle and the liquidity of exit markets. When markets are highly illiquid, VCs reduce their investments in anticipation of the lack of divestment opportunities ahead. Probably more interestingly, they show that, given the investments made, a large proportion of VCs invest in the early stage as a way to postpone exit needs. In contrast, VCs are more prone to invest in later-stage companies in hot issue markets in order to exit quickly.

Schwienbacher (2008b) provides pertinent facts on the European venture capital market. Although there are numerous similarities between the United States and Europe, there are also important differences, including the duration of the exit stage, which appears to be longer in Europe. The author argues that this difference is likely to be driven by the fact that markets that are relevant for venture capitalists are less liquid in Europe. This is true not only for the exit markets but also for the human resources that go into the ventures. This forces European VCs to shop around for longer periods when trying to sell their shares and makes replacement of key employees more difficult. Although, there exist important differences between the two venture capital markets and their related exit markets, there is no clear evidence showing that these differences persist in the long term. However, Hege, Palomino, and Schwienbacher (forthcoming) document that these disparities lead to significant performance differences, with U.S. investments generating higher returns than European ones.

The findings in Schwienbacher (2008b) support the idea that an IPO as an exit route may be limited to the most promising ventures while a trade sale seems to represent the more general exit route, that is, for both more and less promising ventures. With respect to exit choices, the likelihood for venture-backed companies to go public is affected by the number of financing rounds, the investment duration, and the reporting requirements of the investee to the venture capitalist.

One study that investigates both dimensions of exit (type and timing) simultaneously is that by Giot and Schwienbacher (2007). Using a detailed sample of more than 20,000 investment rounds, they analyzed the dynamics of exits for different exit routes using competing risk models, allowing for a joint analysis of exit type and exit timing, including their dynamic interplay. Most interestingly, they find evidence that the probability of going public follows a concave curve: it first increases after the entry of the venture capitalist until it reaches a plateau, followed by a decline. This pattern is consistent with the view that beyond a certain period of time a venture that "takes too much time" becomes less attractive for an IPO. This seems particularly true for ventures in the Internet industry. Interestingly, the steepness of the curve is most pronounced for later-stage than early-stage investments. This inverse U-shaped pattern for IPOs contrasts with the time-varying probability for trade sales, which vary very little over time. This confirms the view that the trade sale is a broad exit channel, not only limited to the most successful ventures.

AGENCY CONFLICTS AND EXIT PROBLEMS

In this section, we present some problems that may arise during the exit stage, some related to the strategic behavior of the entrepreneur (leading to so-called agency conflicts due to different objectives), and others stemming from external sources like liquidity of exit markets and information asymmetry with outside investors.

In the first subsection, we investigate some possible sources of conflict between the entrepreneur and venture capitalist regarding optimal exit route and timing. These often create additional exit barriers for the VC or distortions from the type of exit and/or optimal timing. Also, it is worth again stressing the fact that VCs are not long-term investors and thus usually have a different time horizon for their investments than entrepreneurs: VCs aim at exiting after a few years, while entrepreneurs are focused on a longer time horizon. This and other reasons are potential sources of conflict between the parties involved as their objectives differ. In the second subsection, we discuss different exit problems mentioned in the academic literature unrelated to internal agency problems.

Agency Conflicts

In this section, we discuss conflicts between entrepreneurs and investors (primarily venture capitalists) analyzed in academic literature.

Asymmetric information between venture capitalist and entrepreneur: Informational problems may either be present already before any contract is signed or may arise within the firm ex post, after the contract is signed. In the latter case, such asymmetry generally occurs in favor of the entrepreneur as he is more involved in the day-to-day process of the venture. He may then behave opportunistically (see, for instance, e.g., Trester 1998), which may negatively affect the return of the venture capitalist.

Termination: Bergemann and Hege (1998) show that a distortion from optimal timing may occur due to incentive problems, leading to earlier termination than the first best outcome. As mentioned earlier, the decision whether to stop the project cannot be optimally delegated to the entrepreneur, since he probably would not want to stop his own projects voluntarily.

Portfolio diversification of the venture capitalist: Sahlman (1990) points out that venture capitalists have incentives to create multiple funds over time and therefore have to allocate their limited time and capital optimally to their different projects. These incentives stem from economies of scale and scope, as well as learning effects over time. Each party's view about continuation may diverge, with the VC wanting to stop projects deemed profitable from the point of view of the entrepreneur, because the opportunity cost for the VC is too high given the effort she needs to exert. On a different perspective, Kanniainen and Keuschnigg (2003) present a theoretical framework in which VCs trade off portfolio size (number of companies in the portfolio) and the average value-adding services provided to each portfolio company. If risk aversion were introduced into the model, a similar relationship between risk level and number of investments would arise. Cumming (2006) provides empirical support for this trade-off.

Imperfect contractibility of innovation: Another important source of agency conflict is the noncontractibility of innovation. Aghion and Tirole (1994) stress the fact that "the exact nature of the innovation is ill-defined ex ante and that the two parties cannot contract for delivery of a specific innovation." The fact that an innovation is expected to be ill-defined ex ante generates a potential agency conflict between the venture capitalist and entrepreneur. It provides the entrepreneur with significant discretionary power over the choice of business and R&D strategies to adopt, which in turn potentially affects the riskiness of the project and exit outcomes of the VC.

Distorted innovation strategy: Schwienbacher (2008a) analyzes how the exit choice depends, among other things, not only on product market characteristics like innovation, but also on the type and extent of the venture capitalist's involvement. Based on explicit consideration of product market outcomes, the author shows that in various competition settings, an IPO can be more profitable than a trade sale when the new product is sufficiently innovative. This implies that highly innovative and profitable ventures are more likely to go public than ventures with more imitative products. Moreover, the decision of the venture capitalist concerning the exit route can induce an agency problem when the entrepreneur receives nontransferable private benefits from remaining independent in the firm after the exit of the VC. This agency problem stems from the implicit contracts inherent in the VC's option to list the company on a stock exchange. In this analysis, this factor induces the entrepreneur to attempt to differentiate his product from the competition more than would be optimal from a pure profit maximizing point of view. More generally, the analysis in Schwienbacher (2008a) supports the idea that important links exist between the product market and venture capital market, and derives several empirical predictions. The fact that the VC wants to sell her shares may generate a distortion in the R&D and business strategies of the company and thus also affects the optimal product market structure. Also, the choice of R&D and business strategy depends on the type of financial securities used, as it directly affects expected monetary gains of the entrepreneur.

Dilution: Finally, a crucial issue in venture capital financing is the incentives given to both parties to exert effort and thus to add value and avoid early termination (Bergemann and Hege 1998). Enough stocks must be allocated to both parties and dilution from subsequent financing rounds must be avoided. The ultimate dilution of the entrepreneur's stake will largely depend on the extent to which the company will be able to raise funds in subsequent rounds at sufficiently high prices. Also, stage financing may reduce dilution of the entrepreneur's stake, since investors do not need to inject the full amount upfront (Bartlett 1999). On the other hand, venture capitalists will typically retain some rights to avoid future loss of control from dilution—the so-called right of first refusal. In this way, they will require a right to participate in future financing rounds up to some level that avoids dilution.

Exit Problems

In this section, we discuss potential problems related to the exit process that are not directly generated by the strategic behavior of entrepreneurs.

Asymmetric information for outside investors: One problem when selling private equity is underpricing. This phenomenon, arising from informational problems, has been widely analyzed with respect to the IPO. However, underpricing can also appear for any other exit route. The venture capitalist will then be confronted with the dilemma of whether to sell her shares cheaper (underpriced) or remain involved in the venture until the problems creating the underpricing are resolved. The main reasons are hidden informational problems and hidden actions—that is, moral hazard. Different forms have been presented in the academic literature to explain IPO underpricing. Examples include (see Ibbotson and Ritter [1995] for a more complete list) costly information acquisition, winner's curse, signaling, ownership dispersion (leading to a lack of monitoring due to free-riding by all or most shareholders) and cascades (Welch 1992). Furthermore, if information collection is too costly for small investors, only a trade sale may be feasible (Chemmanur and Fulghieri 1999).

Liquidity risk: When investing in a project, the venture capitalist is faced with two asset-specific (idiosyncratic) risks. The first is the technological risk, that is, the risk that occurs when the entrepreneur is unsuccessful in his attempt to develop a profitable product or production process. The second is the liquidity risk, which "exists when the VC has difficulty exiting from an investment and receiving fair market value for the investment stake" (Norton and Tenenbaum 1993). Exit options for VCs are typically cyclical and therefore difficult to predict at the investment stage. This may force the VC to stay longer in the venture than expected. On the other hand, a more liquid market like a stock market, may make monitoring more effective because holding large stakes is less costly when the shares can easily be sold (see Maug [1998] and Aghion, Bolton, and Tirole [2000]). Cumming, Fleming, and Armin Schwienbacher (2005) provide an empirical investigation on the economic impact and the strategic investment behavior of venture capital funds in the context of uncertain exit options.

"Living dead": Another issue is asset specificity of innovation when there is a lack of market demand for a newly-introduced product. In this case, the greater the specificity of the assets, the lower the liquidation value of the venture (Shleifer and Vishny 1992). This can be particularly critical for venture-backed firms, since a major asset is the innovative idea, which is mainly intangible. And very often, if the entrepreneur and VC realize after some time that the idea will not yield a profitable product, it is not likely that other firms will believe the opposite to be true or that the highly asset-specific innovation can be used elsewhere. The liquidation value is therefore expected to be low in case of failure. Thus, it will affect the VC's follow-up investment decisions as in this case the liquidation value represents her outside option. This may affect the exit timing, since lower outside options (i.e., the value induced through liquidation) may provide incentives to remain involved for a longer period. This is also true for high bankruptcy costs, which may also lead to a longer (but possibly passive) involvement of the VC in the project.

SOME OPEN RESEARCH QUESTIONS

Many questions about venture capital exits remain unanswered. To complete this chapter, we suggest some areas for future research.

First, how can a venture capital market develop if the economy lacks exit routes such as a stock market allowing the listing of innovative companies? Vibrant stock markets have been identified as a key element for enabling a venture capital market to develop (Black and Gilson 1998; Da Rin, Nicodano, and Sembenelli 2006).

However, Black and Gilson (1998) have only tested this hypothesis on a single country, the United States. Cumming, Fleming, and Schwienbacher (forthcoming) extended this to several countries of the Asia-Pacific region and uncovered a more subtle picture of this relationship, with venture-backed companies relocating elsewhere as a way to facilitate exit of investors. At the same time, their work raises further questions as to the mechanics through which the legal environment may affect the degree of complementarity between the stock market and the venture capital market.

Second, how do prospects of available exit options affect the behavior of entrepreneur and investors? In particular, the threat by investors to leave a company is likely to affect entrepreneurial incentives to add value in the venture. Since the availability of exit options varies over time as the company matures, it inevitably affects the relative bargaining power of investors and the entrepreneur, as well as their respective incentives. This impacts conditions for timing the exit.

Other avenues for future research could be to examine how the availability of different exit options affects entrepreneurial behavior, for instance, in terms of innovation strategy to pursue; how to develop the company (e.g., a company that aims to go public must be a "complete" company, while one likely to be acquired may well only require a valuable technology); incentives to create value; choice of investors; and structure of financial contracts.

Many of these issues remaining to be investigated would provide valuable theoretical findings and empirical evidence to add to the literature on venture capital exits.

NOTES

1. A notable exception is Kortum and Lerner (2000) on the impact of venture capital financing on innovation (primarily measured by patent registrations). Further, from the macroeconomic perspective, Wasmer and Weil (2000) find significant positive impact of venture capital activities on short-term and long-term employment.

2. Similarly, venture capitalists in general want some seniority rights on future cash flows to protect themselves against downside risk. This is usually implemented through the use of preferred shares, which guarantees a predetermined dividend payment before any dividends are paid out on common shares, while the entrepreneur holds only common shares.

3. Control rights matter because they allow one party to make a decision in the event of conflicts. The literature on contract theory distinguishes between residual control rights and intervention rights (Grossman and Hart 1986). The venture capitalist typically retains the latter, while the entrepreneur reserves himself the former. Intervention rights are rights explicitly given to a party and written in the contract (sometimes rights are only given contingent on some state of nature), while residual control rights are retained by the party that manages the firm on a day-to-day basis and therefore often refer to rights on which it is not possible to contract on, as they relate to unmeasurable actions.

4. Chemla, Habib, and Ljungqvist (2007) offer a theoretical analysis of shareholder agreements, with specific focus on venture finance.

5. Bartlett (1999) offers a more complete presentation of rights/clauses that are typically included in the financial agreement between venture capitalist and entrepreneur. Chemla, Habib, and Ljungqvist (2007) provide a theoretical analysis of those rights/clauses used in venture capital contracts and, more generally, in shareholders agreements; they show

that puts/calls and clauses like drag-along and go-along rights may be useful for avoiding conflicts from ex post renegotiation or from unexpected exit by one party.

6. The fact that the available EVCA statistics indicate no buybacks before 2003 is most likely due to the fact that this type of exit route was included in the category "divestments by other means" until 2002 and only considered as a separate category later. Although this category is not explicitly reported in Exhibit 18.1, it is strictly positive throughout the time period considered. Moreover, the category "repayment of preference shares/loans" is largely attributable to buyout divestments and not venture capital divestments.

7. More general discussions on IPO activities are provided by Ritter and Welch (2002), Ibbotson and Ritter (1995), and Jenkinson and Ljungqvist (2001).

8. A recent paper by Ritter and Welch (2002) surveys the latest research developments on this topic in greater detail.

9. IPO underpricing is defined as the pricing of an IPO below its true market value. In empirical studies, it is measured as the difference between the offer price and the price at the end of the first trading day.

REFERENCES

Aghion, P., P. Bolton, and J. Tirole. 2004. Exit options in corporate finance: Liquidity versus incentives. Review of Finance 8(3):327–353.

Aghion, P., and J. Tirole. 1994. The management of innovation. *Quarterly Journal of Economics* 109:1185–209.

Barry, C., et al. 1990. The role of venture capital in the creation of public companies: Evidence from the going public process. *Journal of Financial Economics* 27:447–471.

Bartlett, J. 1999. *Fundamentals of venture capital*. Lanham, Madison Books.

Bergemann, D., and U. Hege. 1998. Venture Capital financing, moral hazard, and learning. *Journal of Banking & Finance* 22:703–735.

_____, and L. Peng. 2008. Venture Capital and sequential investments. Working paper. RICAFE Working paper # 68.

Bienz, C., and U. Walz. 2008. Venture capital exit rights. Working paper. Center for Financial Studies.

Black, B., and R. Gilson. 1998. Venture capital and the structure of capital markets: Banks versus stock markets. *Journal of Financial Economics* 47:243–277.

Chemla, G., M. Habib, and A. Ljungqvist. 2007. An analysis of shareholder agreements. *Journal of the European Economic Association* 5:93–121.

Chemmanur, T., and P. Fulghieri. 1999. A theory of the going-public decision. *Review of Financial Studies* 12(2):249–279.

Cumming, D. 2006. The determinants of venture capital portfolio size: Empirical evidence. *Journal of Business* 79:1083–1126.

_____. 2008. Contracts and exits in venture capital finance. *Review of Financial Studies* 21:1947–1982.

_____, G. Fleming, and A. Schwienbacher. 2005. Liquidity risk and venture capital finance. *Financial Management* 34:77–105.

_____. 2006. Legality and venture capital exits. *Journal of Corporate Finance* 12:214–245.

_____. 2009. Corporate relocation in venture capital finance. *Entrepreneurship Theory and Practice* 33 (5), pp. 1121–1155.

Cumming, D., and S. Johan. 2008. Preplanned exit strategies in venture Capital. *European Economic Review* 52:1209–1241.

Cumming, D., and J. MacIntosh. 2001. Venture capital investment duration in Canada and the United States. *Journal of Multinational Financial Management* 11:445–463.

_____. 2003a. Venture capital exits in Canada and the United States. *University of Toronto Law Journal* 53:101–200.

_____. 2003b. A cross-country comparison of full and partial venture capital exits. *Journal of Banking and Finance* 27(3):11–548.

Da Rin, M., G. Nicodano, and A. Sembenelli. 2006. Public policy and the creation of active venture capital markets. *Journal of Public Economics* 90:1699–1723.

Giot, P., and A. Schwienbacher. 2007. IPOs, trade sales and liquidations: Modeling venture capital exits using survival analysis. *Journal of Banking & Finance* 31(3):679–702.

Gompers, P. 1995. Optimal investment, monitoring, and the staging of venture capital. *Journal of Finance* 50:1461–1489.

_____. 1996. Grandstanding in the Venture Capital industry. *Journal of Financial Economics* 42:133–156.

Grossman, S., and O. Hart. 1986. The costs and benefits of ownership: A theory of vertical and lateral integration. *Journal of Political Economy* 94:691–719.

Hege, U. 2001. L'evaluation et le financement des start-up internet. *Revue Economique* 52:291–312.

_____, F. Palomino, and A. Schwienbacher. 2009. Venture capital performance: The disparity between Europe and the United States. *Revue Finance* 30(1), pp. 7–50.

Hellmann, T. 1998. The allocation of control rights in venture capital contracts. *Rand Journal of Economics* 29:1:57–76.

_____. 2006. IPOs, Acquisitions and the use of convertible securities in venture capital. *Journal of Financial Economics* 81(3):649–679.

_____, and M. Puri. 2000. The interaction between product market and financing strategy: the role of venture capital. *Review of Financial Studies* 13(4):959–984.

Ibbotson, R., and J. Ritter. 1995. Initial Public Offerings. In *Handbook of finance*, ed. R. Jarrow, V. Maksimovic, and W. Ziemba. Amsterdam: North-Holland, 993–1016.

Jenkinson, T., and A. Ljungqvist. 2001. *Going public: The theory and evidence on how companies raise equity finance*, 2nd ed. New York, Oxford University Press.

Kaplan, S., and P. Strömberg. 2003. Financial contracting theory meets the real world: An empirical analysis of venture capital contracts. *Review of Economic Studies* 70:281–315.

Kanniainen V., and C. Keuschnigg. 2003. The optimal portfolio of start-up firms in venture capital finance. *Journal of Corporate Finance* 9:521–534.

Kortum, S., and J. Lerner. 2000. Assessing the contribution of venture capital to innovation. *RAND Journal of Economics* 31(4):674–692.

Lee, P., and S. Wahal. 2004. Grandstanding, certification and the underpricing of venture capital backed IPOs. *Journal of Financial Economics* 73:375–407.

Lerner, J. 1994. Venture capitalists and the decision to go public. *Journal of Financial Economics* 35:293–316.

Maug, E. 1998. Large shareholders as monitors: Is there a trade-off between liquidity and control? *Journal of Finance* 53(1):65–98.

Megginson, W., and K. Weiss. 1991. Venture capital certification in initial public offerings. *Journal of Finance* 46:879–893.

Michelacci, C., and J. Suarez. 2004. Business creation and the stock market. *Review of Economic Studies* 71(2):459–481.

Myers, S., and N. Majluf. 1984. Corporate financing and investment decisions when firms have information investors do not have. *Journal of Financial Economics* 13:187–221.

Neus, W., and U. Walz. 2005. Exit timing of venture capitalists in the course of an initial public offering. *Journal of Financial Intermediation* 14:253–277.

Norton, E., and B. Tenenbaum. 1993. Specialization versus diversification as a venture capital investment strategy. *Journal of Business Venturing* 8(5):431–442.

Ritter, J., and I. Welch. 2002. A review of IPO activity, pricing, and allocations. *Journal of Finance* 57(4):1792–1828.

Rock, K. 1986. Why New Issues are underpriced. *Journal of Financial Economics* 15:187–212.

Roëll, A. 1996. The decision to go public: An overview. *European Economic Review* 40: 1071–1081.

Sahlman, W. 1990. The structure and governance of venture capital organizations. *Journal of Financial Economics* 27:473–521.

Schwienbacher, A. 2008a. Innovation and venture capital exits. *Economic Journal* 118(5):1888–1916.

———. 2008b. Venture capital investment practices in Europe and in the United States. *Financial Markets and Portfolio Management* 22: 3:195–217.

Shleifer, A., and R. Vishny. 1992. Liquidation values and debt capacity: A market equilibrium approach. *Journal of Finance* 47(4):1343–1366.

Smith, D. G. 2005. The exit structure of venture capital. *UCLA Law Review* 53:315.

Trester, J. 1998. Venture capital contracting under asymmetric information. *Journal of Banking & Finance* 22:675–699.

Wasmer, E., and P. Weil. 2000. The macroeconomics of labor and credit market imperfections. IZA Discussion Paper No. 179.

Welch, I. 1992. Sequential sales, learning, and cascades. *Journal of Finance* 47, 695–732.

ABOUT THE AUTHOR

Armin Schwienbacher is a tenured associate professor of finance at the Louvain School of Management, Université catholique de Louvain (Belgium), and a research fellow at the University of Amsterdam Business School (the Netherlands). He obtained his Ph.D. at the University of Namur (Belgium). His dissertation focused on exit strategies of venture capitalists. From 2001 to 2002, he was a visiting scholar at the Haas School of Business, U.C. Berkeley. He teaches courses in corporate finance and entrepreneurial finance at the master and MBA level. He has presented his research on venture capital and various other topics in corporate finance at numerous universities, financial institutions, and international conferences, and his work has been published in various international academic journals, including *Journal of Financial Intermediation, Economic Journal, Journal of Banking and Finance, Entrepreneurship Theory and Practice, Journal of Business Venturing* and *Financial Management*.

## CHAPTER 19

Returns to Venture Capital

MIKE WRIGHT
Professor of Financial Studies, Centre for Management Buy-Out Research,
Nottingham University Business School

RIYA CHOPRAA
Researcher, Centre for Management Buy-Out Research,
Nottingham University Business School

INTRODUCTION

The returns to private equity investment have become a vexed issue, attracting widespread debate in the media, government, and among researchers. Much of the attention has focused on later-stage buy-out investments, but there is a general move towards greater transparency and disclosure of the returns to both early and late-stage venture capital (VC) investments. Shortcomings in the information provided to investors may mean that limited partners are restricted in their ability to judge the investment record of the VC funds in which they seek to invest.

In this chapter, returns are examined at two levels. First, we examine returns at the level of VC funds. Second, returns at the investee firm level are discussed. The literature on returns to venture capital is, unsurprisingly, mainly concentrated in finance and economics journals, but a stream of studies has also appeared in entrepreneurship journals.

Reviews of the literature relating to the different stages of the venture capital investment process, from deal sourcing through to exit, are available in Wright and Robbie (1998) and Wright, Sapienza, and Busenitz (2003). In this review, we focus specifically on the earlier venture capital stage of the private equity market. Comparisons are made with the later management buy-out stage of this market where appropriate and where studies are available. Detailed surveys of the later buy-out stage of the private equity market are available in Wright (2007); Cumming, Siegel, and Wright (2007); and Bruining and Wright (2008). The main findings from the studies reviewed are summarized in Exhibit 19.1.

STRUCTURE OF VC FUND RETURNS

The venture capital fund manager receives a fee for the management of the funds and a share in the profits of the fund (Gilligan and Wright 2008). However, the fees received are typically an advance on carried interest, not in addition to the share

Exhibit 19.1 Summary of Studies of Returns to Venture Capital

Author	Sample Description	Data Source	Method of Analysis	Summary of Findings
Gompers and Lerner (1999)	419 U.S. venture capital partnership agreements and offering memoranda for funds formed between 1978 and 1992	Partnership agreements collected by three organisations: Aeneas Group, Kemper Financial Services, and Venture Economics	Multivariate regression analysis, including Ordinary Least Square (OLS) analysis	Compensation of established funds is significantly more sensitive to performance and more variable than that of other funds. Older and larger funds have lower base compensation, and performance and pay sensitivity do not appear to be related.
Dixon (1991)	30 London-based specialist UK venture capital companies, all listed on Stoy Hayward and represented approximately 20% of the total number of UK funds	Interviews with the executives constructed around a questionnaire	Mean scores, percentages of total sample mentioning it and standard deviations	The most important factor venture capitalists look for in a proposed investment is the experience of the management team, over the projected returns and turnover. The project's financing stage determines the risk premium, as the required rate of return is an arbitrary IRR to the proposal, not calculated through theoretical pricing models.
Wright and Robbie (1996)	74 UK venture capital institutions listed as full-time members of the British Venture Capital Association (BVCA)	Mail questionnaires to chief executives of the venture capital firms or senior colleagues	Mean scores, Standard Deviation, and Mann-Whitney U test of differences	Venture capitalists make greater use of discounted cash flow approaches and less use of asset-based methods, reflecting the use of IRRs as an important indicator of investment performance. They also use wide nonfinancial information to test the robustness of the accounting and financial projections.
Manigart et al. (1997)	136 venture capital firms from UK, France, Netherlands, and Belgium	Questionnaires filled by the senior managers of the venture capital firms	Correlation analysis	The most widely used valuation method in the UK is multiplication of past/future earnings with some price-earning ratio. In the Netherlands and Belgium it is the discounting of future cash flows, and in France it is the book value of net worth.

Manigart et al. (2002)	209 venture capital companies (66 from UK, 73 from U.S., 32 from France, 24 from Netherlands and 14 from Belgium)	Questionnaire survey	Chi-square analyses, limited dependent variable (LDV) technique, and ordinary least square (OLS) regressions	Stage diversification is associated with lower required returns for early-stage ventures. Being lead investor more often is associated with lower required returns for early-stage investments and fewer investments per VC manager associated with higher required returns. The required returns for independent VCCs are significantly higher than for captive and publicly supported firms for early-stage and expansion-stage investments.
Karsai et al. (1999)	18 venture capital firms (9 from Hungary, 6 from Poland, and 3 from Slovakia)	Questionnaire surveys and interviews administered to the managers in the VC firms	Mean scores on the basis of 1 = not important through to 5 = very important	Hungary and Poland have experienced marked growth in their venture capital markets, with the VC firms exhibiting greater involvement in the monitoring of their investees, while Slovakia remains underdeveloped, and VC firms in all three countries have less involvement in strategic decisions and more involvement in operational decisions, with major infrastructural impediments.
Robbie et al. (1997)	77 UK venture capital firms, which were full-time members of the British Venture Capital Association (BVCA) in 1996	A series of in-depth face-to-face interviews based on a structured questionnaire checklist, followed by a mailed questionnaire survey to the remaining UK venture capital firms (which were members of BVCA) not covered in the first stage	Chi-square test of independence to analyze the difference between independent and nonindependent venture capital firms	There exists a shift towards target IRRs set in relation to returns on other asset classes or returns for outperformers in the venture capital sector. An increased amount of performance targets are expressed in terms of target IRRs and cash amounts generated.

(Continued)

Exhibit 19.1 *(Continued)*

Author	Sample Description	Data Source	Method of Analysis	Summary of Findings
Lockett, Murray, and Wright (2002)	60 VC firms, which were full (investing) members of the British Venture Capital Association (BVCA) in 1999–2000	Telephone interviews conducted with the representatives of the venture capital firms	Z-tests of proportions, Mann-Whitney Z-test statistics and Wilcoxon signed ranks test Z statistics.	More generalist firms are now making more investments in technology-based companies. Target IRRs for technology-based investments are higher than the non–technology-based ones at the same stage.
Bygrave (1994)	All U.S. funds formed from 1969 through 1985	Venture Economics' Investment Benchmarks Report.	Weighted averages	The median IRR peaked in 1982 at 27%, with weighted average at 32%.
Kleiman and Shulman (1992)	14 Small Business Investment Companies (SBICs) and 12 Business Development Corporations (BDCs), that started after 1980 or dissolved before 1990	Venture Capital Journal, publicly available stock prices and NASDAQ monthly returns	Market model using Scholes and William (1977) technique and computing cumulative return of the funds	From 1980 to 1986, SBICs demonstrate significantly greater and unsystematic risk but significantly less systematic risk than BDCs. SBICs experience much higher returns, on a risk adjusted basis, than either the market proxy and BDCs.
Huntsman and Hoban (1980)	Returns generated by 110 private equity investments between 1960 and 1975, with investment size ranging from $1000 to $1.1 million	Three well-known venture capital firms (a publicly-held Small Business Investment Company, a partnership and a wholly-owned SBIC subsidiary of a large bank holding company), each representing a different type of institution	Algorithm developed by Lawrence Fisher	An attractive rate of return can be generated over time by well-diversified venture portfolios. Adequate diversification requires greater minimal capital levels than may be the case for portfolios containing securities of more mature enterprises with readily marketable securities.
Brophy and Guthner (1988)	12 publicly traded venture capital funds in existence during the time period from May 1981 to February 1985 and 12 open-ended mutual funds	Compuserve Executive Data Service and S&P Daily Price Index	Scholes and Williamson (1977) beta estimation technique	Superior results are realized on publicly traded venture capital funds when compared with portfolios of growth-oriented mutual funds and with the S&P 500 index.

410

Ljungqvist and Richardson (2003a)	73 mature private equity funds started between 1981 and 1993 with aggregate commitment of $36.7 billion and 8539 funds started between 1981 and 2001 with an aggregate commitment of $ 207 billion (in nominal terms)	Regression analysis, calculation of IRRs and their weighted averages thereof	Private equity generates excess returns on the order to 5% to 8% per annum relative to the aggregate public equity market. Source of outperformance of IRRs is not necessarily compensation for systematic risk, but it may be related to the type and the timing of the fund.
Ljungqvist and Richardson (2003b)	73 mature private equity funds started between 1981 and 1993 with aggregate commitment of $36.7 billion. These funds include both venture capital and buy-out funds.	Regression analysis	Existing funds accelerate their investment flows and earn higher returns when investment opportunities improve and the demand for capital increases. Increases in supply lead to tougher competition for deal flow and private equity fund managers respond by cutting their investment spending.
Cochrane (2005)	16,613 financing rounds with 7765 companies and a total of $112,613 million raised	VentureOne database, SDC Platinum Corporate New Issues and Mergers and Acquisition (M&A) databases, Market-Guide, and other online resources.	The smallest NASDAQ stocks have similar large means, volatilities, and arithmetic alphas, confirming that the remaining puzzles are not special to venture capital.
Phalippou (2007)	NA	Literature review of issues faced by private equity investors	The average investor has obtained poor returns from investments in private equity funds, potentially because of excessive fees. Investors need to gain familiarity with actual risk, past returns, and specific features of private equity funds.

(Continued)

411

Exhibit 19.1 *(Continued)*

Author	Sample Description	Data Source	Method of Analysis	Summary of Findings
Hwang et al. (2005)	5607 unique firms with financing data for a total of 12,553 rounds of funding, including 9706 rounds of private equity financing, plus 1307 IPOs, 896 acquisitions, and 644 shutdowns, covering the period from January 1, 1987 to March 31, 2000	Sand Hill Econometrics database	Repeat valuation model plus a correction for selection bias	The authors report a method for building an index for venture capital that can be used in much the same manner that the NASDAQ and S&P 500 are used as indices of prices of common stock.
Kaplan and Schoar (2005)	Two samples of funds covering the period from 1980 to 1997, excluding one with less than $5 million of committed capital. The first sample consists of 746 funds, officially liquidated or started before 1995. The second sample consists of 1090 funds, officially liquidated or started before 1997	Venture Economics	Regression analysis	Average fund returns (net of fees) approximately equal the S&P 500 although substantial heterogeneity across funds exists. Returns persist strongly across subsequent funds of a partnership. Better performing partnerships are more likely to raise follow-on funds and larger funds. This relationship is concave, so top performing partnerships grow proportionally less than average performers.

| Phalippou and Gottschalg (2009) | Base sample comprising 852 funds raised between 1980 and 1993, which are older than 10 years with size more than $5 million. The additional sample contains 476 different funds raised between 1980 and 1993 with more than 5 investments in the "investment dataset." Merged together, the base and the additional sample make what is called the "extended sample" in the study. | VentureXpert | Regression analysis | Average performance (net-of-fees) of funds is lower than that of S&P 500 by 3% per year, but gross-of-fees performance is above that of the S&P 500 by 3% per year. Newly raised funds have a performance similar to that of sample funds at the same age. It is also important to keep in mind that there is wide dispersion in performance and that performance is predictable to a certain extent only. |
| Metrick and Yasuda (2007) | 238 funds, of which 94 are venture capital funds and 144 are buy-out funds, raised between 1993 and 2006. These funds represent all prospective funds that the Investor considered investing in, not just the funds it ended up investing in. | Data from one of the largest private equity limited partners in the world, referred to as "the Investor" in the study. Other sources of data are Galante's Venture Capital and Private Equity Directory (Asset Alternatives, 2006), Private Equity. Performance Monitor 2006 (Private Equity. Intelligence, 2006), and Investment Benchmarks Report published by Venture Economics (2006a and 2006b). | Regression analysis | Buy-out (BO) fund managers build on their prior experience by increasing the size of their funds faster than venture capital (VC) managers do, leading to significantly higher revenue per partner and per professional in later BO funds. BO business is more scalable than the VC business, and past success has a differential impact on the terms of their future funds. |

(Continued)

413

Exhibit 19.1 (*Continued*)

Author	Sample Description	Data Source	Method of Analysis	Summary of Findings
Hellmann and Puri (2000)	149 start-up companies, with legal age no older than 10 years and with more than 10 employees, that are located in California's Silicon Valley	An assortments of surveys, publicly available information, and commercial databases (VentureOne and Venture Economics)	Cox proportional hazard regression model	Innovator firms are more likely to obtain venture capital than imitator firms. Venture capital is associated with a significant reduction in the time to bring a product to market, especially for innovators.
Engel and Keilbach (2007)	21375 non–venture-funded and 142 venture-funded firms, founded between 1995 and 1998, with at least one patent application and at least two entries with respect to their firm size to enable computation of a growth rate	Microlevel database on German firms developed and maintained by ZEW in Mannheim, Germany and DPA database (PATDPA)	Probit estimation of propensity scores	Firms with higher innovative output and with a highly educated management have a larger probability of getting venture capital. Venture-funded firms display significantly higher growth rates and larger numbers of patent applications, compared to their non–venture-funded counterparts.
Burgel et al. (2000)	362 and 232 firms from UK and Germany, respectively. These firms were formed between 1987 and 1996 and had at least 3 employees in 1997 and were primarily engaged in the production and development of new products, services, and processes.	Mail survey using a four-page identical questionnaire for both countries	OLS and probit regression models	Firms with international sales have higher sales growth than firms that sell domestically. Technological sophistication of products and the experience of entrepreneurs has a positive impact on growth.
Jain and Kini (1995)	136 VC-backed and 136 non-VC-backed IPOs	Going Public: The IPO Reporter and Investment Dealers Digest's Five-year Directory of Corporate Financing	Cross-sectional regression analysis	VC-backed IPOs exhibit relatively superior postissue operating performance compared to non-VC-backed IPO firms. Capital markets appear to recognise the value-added potential of VC monitoring, as reflectedd in the higher valuations at the time of IPOs.

Audretsch and Lehmann (2004)	341 firms that are/were listed on Neuer Markt in Germany between 1997 and 2002	Individual balance sheet data from IPO prospectuses, publicly available information from online data sources: German Patent Office and Deutsche Boerse	Probit approach and two-limit tobit model	Venture capital and debt provided by banks are not complements but substitutes. Banks play only a minor role in financing and controlling innovative firms.
Bottazzi and Da Rin (2002)	511 companies that went public on Euro.nm from their inception to December 2000	Listing prospectuses, annual reports of the companies and financing information from the venture capitalists	Probit regression analysis	Venture capital in Europe is not systematically associated with particularly dynamic companies, whether in terms of sales growth, new employment, or stock market performance.
Colombo and Grilli (2008)	439 Italian New Technology-Based Firms (NTBFs) operating in high tech sectors, established between 1/1/1980 and 1/1/2000	2004 release of Research Entrepreneurship in Advanced Technologies (RITA) database	Endogenous switching regression model	Founders' human capital has a direct positive effect on firm growth. VC investments are attracted by the perceived management competence of firms' founding team. The joint consideration of human capital variables and VC financing has the additional advantage of helping disentangle the relative importance of "scout" and "coach" functions performed by VC investors to the advantage of portfolio NTBFs.
Bertoni et al. (2008)	550 Italian New Technology Based Firms (NTBFs), observed over a 10-year period (1994–2003).	Hand collected longitudinal dataset drawn from the 2004 release of the RITA (Research on Entrepreneurship in Advanced Technologies)	Augmented Gibrat-law type panel data model with distributed lags and GMM-system estimation	VC financing has a positive effect on the subsequent growth of sales and employment of portfolio companies. The magnitude of this effect differs according to the type of investor, with the benefits of FVCs considerably exceeding those of CVCs.
Alemany and Marti (2005)	323 Spanish firms that are fully identified and for whom separate financial accounts exist	SABI database (Bureau Van Dirk)	chi-squared test of difference between proportions and nonparametric test of Kruskal-Wallis for different firm characteristics.	There exists a significant positive relation between the cumulative VC investment in a firm and the growth in employment, sales, gross margin, total assets, net intangible assets, and corporate taxes over time.

(Continued)

Exhibit 19.1 *(Continued)*

Author	Sample Description	Data Source	Method of Analysis	Summary of Findings
Davila et al. (2003)	494 start-up firms, of which 193 are venture-backed and 301 are non–venture-backed start-up firms	Several proprietary databases: Trivet (leading professional employer organisation), VentureOne (Reuters), and Venture Source (Venture Economics)	Auxiliary regression model	Companies that receive venture capital grow faster than the ones that did not have this type of financing.
Lee et al. (2001)	137 Korean technological start-up companies	Survey questionnaires, telephone interviews, and Korean Small and Medium Business Administration (KSMBA) web site.	Lagged dependent variable model, using identical fixed lag period	Technological capabilities and financial resources invested during the development period are positively associated with the start-up's performance. Entrepreneurial orientation has a positive and marginally statistically significant effect on performance.
Heirman and Clarysse (2005)	171 Resource Based Start-Ups (RBSUs) in Flanders (Belgium) founded between 1991 and 2000	Structured questionnaires	Uni (t-test, F-tests, Mann-Whitney U-tests) and multivariate (General Least Square) analysis	Raising large amounts of VC is a key driver for early employment and revenue growth. While most RBSUs are founded by pure technical founding teams, R&D experience has no effect on growth. Founding teams with commercial experience, on the other hand, grow significantly more in employees, revenues, and total assets. RBSUs, which are internationally oriented from the start, grow significantly faster in terms of revenues and total assets but not in employees. Firms that are closer to a market-ready product at founding do not grow significantly more in terms of revenues and employees, but firms that are earlier in the product development cycle grow more in total assets during the early growth path.

416

Study	Sample	Data source	Method	Findings
George et al. (2005)	889 Swedish SMEs, with data from 1997 to 2000	Statistics Sweden (the Bureau of Census)	Heckman correlation model, hierarchical OLS regression, and negative binomial regression models	Internal owners (CEOs and other senior executives) tend to be risk averse and have a lower proclivity to increase scale and scope of internationalization than external owners (venture capitalists and institutional investors).
Zahra et al. (2007)	384 SMEs representing 23 different industries, each with 500 or fewer full-time employees	Survey methodology, complemented with information gathered from secondary sources (SMEs' web sites, newsletters, and publications)	Moderated regression analysis	Top management team (TMT) ownership is strongly and positively associated with SMEs' investment in building the knowledge-based resources devoted to internationalization. A positive relationship exists between ownership by VCs and SMEs' investments in building two types of knowledge-based resources: human capital and proprietary. Outside directors serving on SMEs' boards fulfill a valuable enterprise role in the governance of these firms by offering new perspectives and ideas, and focusing managers' attention on the importance of building knowledge-based resources.
Lockett et al. (2008)	340 European VC-backed investments	Questionnaires targeted at senior management of the VC-backed firms, EVCA, Europe Unlimited and CMBOR databases, ONESOURCE, export-intensity online database EVCA directories	Heckman Selection estimates	External VC value-added resources have a greater impact on export intensity for early-stage ventures than late-stage ventures. External VC monitoring resources have a significant effect for late-stage MBO/I firms; however, no significant effect exists for early-stage firms.

(Continued)

Exhibit 19.1 (*Continued*)

Author	Sample Description	Data Source	Method of Analysis	Summary of Findings
Lerner et al. (2007)	838 funds raised between 1991 and 1998 with 4618 investments by 352 LPs in these funds	Asset Alternatives fund database (included as part of their Galante's Venture Capital and Private Equity Directory), supplemented from Venture Economics' online fund database, Private Equity Intelligence's 2004 Private Equity Monitor, Annual reports to written request forms mailed directly to the investors, confidential listing of investments by private investors, with whom the authors have personal relationships.	Pooled regression, Heckit sample selection regression and probit regression models	Endowments (and to a lesser extent, public pensions) are better than other investors at predicting whether follow-on funds will have high returns.
Jones and Rhodes-Kropf (2003)	1245 U.S. venture capital and private equity funds, formed between 1980 to 1999, with at least $5 million of committed capital. These funds exclude mezzanine and funds-of-funds.	Thomson Venture Economics	Time-series regression analysis	VC investments have positive alphas while investors in VC funds earn zero alpha. Even though fund investors expect zero alphas, funds that have more idiosyncratic risk ex post will earn higher returns.

Study	Data/Sample	Data source	Method	Findings
Gompers and Lerner (1999)	4069 professional U.S. venture financings of privately held firms taking place between January 1987 and December 1995, for which VentureOne was able to determine the valuation of the financing round	VentureOne	Hedonic regression approach, employing OLS specifications, log-log framework, Heckman sample selection regression analysis and instrumental variable regression analysis	The impact of venture capital inflows on prices is greatest in states with the most venture capital activity and segments with the greatest growth in venture inflows. Changes in valuation do not appear to be related to the ultimate success of the firms.
Gompers et al. (2005)	2179 venture capital firms investing in 16354 portfolio companies, resulting in 42559 unique observations of VC firms-portfolio company pairs. These investments were made between 1975 and 1998.	Thomson Venture Economics (Venture Economics)	Regression-based analysis	Venture capitalists with the most industry experience increase their investments the most when industry investment activity accelerates.
Cumming and Walz (2007)	221 PE funds managed by 72 PE managers, including 5038 observations of Portfolio firms (3824 are VC and 1214 late-stage mezzanine and buy-out) spanning a time period of 33 years (1971–2003) dispersed over 39 countries from North and South America to Europe and Asia. The observations represent 2419 fully realized investments, 1665 unrealized investments, and 954 partially realized investments.	Dataset collected by Center of Private Equity Research (CEPRES) in Frankfurt, Germany	Multivariate analysis of IRR performance based upon previous work (Cochrane 2005; Nikoskelainen and Wright 2007), multistep Heckman-like sample selection correction on realized/unrealized exits and full/partial exits	Less experienced PE managers as well as those involved in early-stage investments are more inclined to overvalue. Syndication proves to lower the incentives of PE funds to overstate the value of unrealized investments. Robustness and impact of accounting standards and legal framework are negatively related to the reporting behaviour of PE managers.

(Continued)

Exhibit 19.1 *(Continued)*

Author	Sample Description	Data Source	Method of Analysis	Summary of Findings
Zarutskie (2008)	318 first-time U.S. based VC funds, which are classified as "Private Equity Firms Investing Own Capital." These funds were raised between 1980 and 1998. These funds have nonmissing size information and have invested in five or more portfolio companies.	VentureXpert and hand-collected dataset describing the work/educational histories of the venture capitalists managing the VC firms selected from VentureXpert	Regression analysis	Fund management teams with more task-specific human capital manage funds with greater fractions of portfolio company exits. Fund management teams with more industry-specific human capital manage funds with greater fractions of portfolio company exits. Fund management teams that have more general human capital in business administration manage funds with lower fractions of portfolio company exits.
Dimov and Shepherd (2005)	112 independent venture capital firms in the U.S. that have made at least one investment in the wireless communication industry.	VentureXpert	Hierarchical regression analysis and canonical correlation analysis are used to analyse the data.	General human capital had a positive association with the proportion of portfolio companies that went public (IPO), whereas specific human capital did not. However, specific human capital was negatively associated with the proportion of portfolio companies that went bankrupt.
Bottazi; Da Rin, and Hellmann (2008)	119 venture capital firms from 17 countries, with 503 venture partners and 1652 portfolio companies. The venture firms are included were full-time members of European Venture Capital Association (EVCA) or of a national venture capital organisation in 2001, actively engaged in venture capital, and operational in 2002.	Survey conducted between February 2002 and November 2003, commercially available databases, Amadeus, Worldscope and VenturExpert, and trade publications like directories of venture capital associations and web sites of the respondents and their portfolio companies.	Univariate nonparametric tests and multivariate regression analysis including; probit models, conditional logit models, IV-Cum-Mills model, instrumental variable regression, Sorensen-Heckman model, and Ackenberg-Botticni model.	Prior business experience is an important predictor of investor activism. There exists a positive relationship between investor activism and the success of the portfolio companies, emphasizing the economic importance of human capital for financial intermediation.

Wright and Lockett (2003)	Sample 1 and Sample 2 consisted of 58 and 56 venture capital firms in the UK, respectively.	Mail questionnaires to the representatives of the venture capital firms listed in the BVCA directories of 1998–99 and 1999–2000 for Sample 1 and Sample 2, respectively	Mann-Whitney non-parametric tests statistics.	Reputation is highly important in encouraging other parties to continue to syndicate with a venture capital firm both for further investment rounds of a particular deal and for subsequent deals. The finance/risk-sharing motivation for syndication is stronger than the resource-based argument.
De Clerq and Dimov (2008)	200 randomly selected U.S.-based independent focal venture capital firms, with 14,129 initial investments of which 8,162 were first-round investments. These venture capital investments were made from 1962 to 2002.	VentureXpert	Ordered logit	Investing in industries in which the venture capital firm has more knowledge or investing with more or familiar partners enhances performance. Access to external knowledge is more effective when an incongruity exists between what the firm knows and what it intends to know.
Hochberg, Ljungqvist, and Yang (2007)	3,469 venture capital funds managed by 1974 venture capital firms that participated, in 47,705 investment rounds involving 16,315 portfolio companies. The sample considers all investments made by venture capital funds raised between 1980 and 1999, concentrating solely on investments by U.S.-based venture capital funds, excluding those made by angels and buy-out funds.	Thomson Financial's Venture Economics database	Graph theory and multivariate regression analysis	Better networked venture capital firms experience significantly better fund performance. Similarly, portfolio companies of better networked venture capital firms are significantly more likely to survive to subsequent financing and eventual exit.

(Continued)

Exhibit 19.1 *(Continued)*

Author	Sample Description	Data Source	Method of Analysis	Summary of Findings
Hege et al. (2004)	Sample 1 consisted of 171 VC firms, 67 from U.S. and 104 from 6 countries in Europe. Sample 2 comprises 274 observations from the EU—15 countries and 234 observations from the U.S. of portfolio companies that have at least one valuation observation in the VentureXpert and of which there is a financing round defined as "seed" or "early-stage" funding.	Questionnaire survey and data derived from the Thomson Financial's VentureXpert database	Tobit regression and OLS regression techniques	U.S. VC firms show a significantly higher performance on average than their European counterparts, both in terms of exit and rate of return. U.S. venture capitalists more often assert contingent control rights, indicated by convertible and decisions to replace entrepreneurs and have better capacity to screen projects and ensure their success in the early stages, than European venture capitalists.
Lerner and Schoar (2005)	210 transactions from 28 private equity groups occurring between 1987 and 2003, with the bulk of investments between 1996 and 2002. The transactions represent 30 distinct countries.	Survey in the private equity groups that invest in developing nations	Multivariate regression	Investments in nations with effective legal enforcement are more likely to employ preferred stock and to have more contractual protections for the private equity group, such as supermajority voting rights and antidilution provisions.
Kaplan and Stromberg (2009)	17,171 private-equity sponsored buyout transactions, which occurred between January 1, 1970, and June 30, 2007. The transactions that had been announced but not completed by November 30, 2007 are excluded.	CapitalIQ database	Trend analysis and regression analysis	On average, private equity creates economic value and therefore, has a substantial permanent component. Private equity activity is subject to boom and bust cycles, driven by recent returns as well as level of interest rates relative to earnings and stock market values, particularly for larger public-to-private transactions.

Study	Sample	Method	Findings
Wright et al. (2004)	357 venture capital firms from 9 countries in Europe, U.S. and Asia; covering a range of different legal systems	Multicountry data collected through mailing questionnaires and conducting face-to-face or telephone interviews	Kruskal-Wallis test and multivariate analysis using OLS regression	VC firms in Europe and Asia are significantly less likely than U.S. VC firms to use liquidation value methods but more likely to use PE comparators. European firms are significantly less likely to adopt DCF methods compared to U.S. VC firms. VC firms operating under German legal system are less likely to utilize information from financial press but significantly more likely to use interviews with entrepreneurs. VC firms operating under French legal system are more likely to utilise interviews with company personnel as well as sales and marketing information. VC firms in Europe and Asia are significantly more likely than U.S. VC firms to use financial press. VC firms in Asia are significantly less likely to make use of interviews with entrepreneurs or business plan data. VC firms in Europe are significantly more likely to utilize sales and marketing information.
Wright, Pruthi and Lockett (2005)	NA	NA	Literature review of international venture capital studies	Under-researched areas concern the influence of institutional context, especially the role of social networks and cultures. There exists major research gap in relation to work dealing with crossing of country borders by venture capital firms.

in capital growth. During the investment phase, the management fee will typically be 1.5 to 2.0 percent of the committed fund size.

The management fee was originally intended to pay for the operating costs of employing staff and other expenses associated with the fund manager's business, plus the reasonable salaries of the partners. Any excess over these costs is retained by the management company and may be paid to its partners/shareholders. Fund managers have to balance the use of fee income to reinvest in growing the personnel, infrastructure, and assets of the business with the requirement to recruit and retain their best partners by offering industry-competitive remuneration.

The share of capital profits ("carried interest" or "carry") is shared among the fund managers and their staff according to whatever arrangement they have agreed among themselves and their limited partners. The share is typically 20 percent once the investors have received an agreed minimum hurdle rate return (currently around 8 percent, but variable from fund to fund), less fees received. Gompers and Lerner (1999) find from a study of over 400 VC funds in the United States that the fixed element of compensation is higher for funds that are smaller, younger, and focused on early-stage and high tech deals. Over four-fifths of funds had a carry in the range 20 to 21 percent.

In addition to these fees and profit share that are common to most funds, other fees may be receivable by the fund managers. Monitoring and/or non-executive fees are widely payable by individual investee companies to defray some of the costs of employees and partners of PE managers monitoring the investment. These fees may be payable to the PE fund or to the manager, or split between them in a predetermined proportion. They are not usually material in a large fund.

Transaction costs incurred by the PE fund in making an investment are usually payable by the company being bought out and not by the PE fund. Abort costs of transactions that fail to complete may be borne by the fund or the manager or shared in a preagreed ratio.

PE fund managers may charge an arrangement fee to the investee company expressed as a proportion of the amount of money invested in a deal. These may be up to 3.0 percent of the equity invested (although less in larger deals). Usually these fees are credited to the fund but they may be split on a preagreed basis with the manager.

Typically the net of all these fees would be included in the calculation of the management fee and do not increase the overall rewards of the PE fund managers.

All of these individually negotiated arrangements within a fund manager's business impact the individual returns of investors over the long term.

TARGET RATES OF RETURN ON INVESTMENTS

UK studies of the target IRRs expected by UK VCs for portfolio firms for the 1980s (Dixon 1991) and early 1990s (Wright and Robbie 1996) show a benchmark of around 30 percent IRR. Target rates of return vary across countries. Manigart et al. (1997, 2002) find higher required rates of return by VCs located in the United States and UK compared with those located in France, Belgium, and the Netherlands. They infer that these differences are related to differences in institutional, legal, and cultural contexts. They suggest that the relative development of capital markets in a particular country is important, with the more developed U.S. and UK markets perhaps requiring more frequent valuation of companies.

Consistent with the resource-based view of the firm (RBV), Manigart and colleagues (2002) find that specialist early-stage VCs require a significantly higher return than other VCs when they invest in late-stage ventures. However, consistent with financial theory, they find that buy-out-stage specialists require a significantly lower rate of return than other VCs when investing in later-stage firms.

The target rate of return sought also appears to be related to the VCs' organizational form. Independent VCs tend to seek significantly higher rates of return than captive or public sector VCs (Manigart et al. 2002). In developed markets, target rates of return are generally based upon the characteristics of a specific investment. However, in transition economies, there is a lack of a clear relationship between return and investment stage (as a proxy for risk) (Karsai et al. 1999).

Funds providers (limited partners) have been found to adopt a variety of rate of return measures to judge the performance of VC funds. Robbie, Chiplin, and Wright (1997) find significant differences between the type of performance targets used by independent venture capital firms and other types of VC. While VCs tended to be set target IRRs expressed either as raw returns or percentage outperformance above other asset classes, captive VCs were also significantly more likely to be set an annual return on capital target. Robbie, Chiplin, and Wright (1997) also suggest an increase in performance target that is expressed in terms of target IRRs and cash amounts generated. Interestingly, this study found a generally low level of monitoring of VCs by the investors.

Lockett, Murray, and Wright (2002) also find a variety of valuation practices among UK VC firms investing in technology-based ventures. Mostly, different target IRRs were set for each investment stage separately within technology and nontechnology categories, but in other cases the approach adopted was to set higher target IRRs for technology proposals generally or to determine target IRRs on a deal-by-deal basis.

VC FUND RETURNS EVIDENCE

Venture capital associations worldwide have published analyses of the returns to venture capital funds for many years. Fund-level data published by national venture capital associations and the European Private Equity & Venture Capital Association (EVCA) consistently show that the internal rates of return (IRRs) on buy-out funds outperform any other form of private equity/venture capital investment. Exhibit 19.2, for example, shows the extent of returns for the upper quartile of funds. However, overall IRRs on early-stage investments for funds formed since 1980 were negative at the end of 2007 at a pooled IRR of –0.8 percent. VC industry comparisons with other benchmarks generally show that VC-stage investments underperform other indices such as the Morgan Stanley Euro Index and the HSBC Small Company Index but that buy-out–stage investments on average outperform these indices (EVCA 2008).

There is a long history of academic studies that have sought to provide deeper analysis of the rates of return to VC investments. These studies mostly relate to the United States and have attempted to estimate risk-adjusted rates of return and to identify whether venture capital deals generate better or worse returns than

Exhibit 19.2   Pan European IRRs (European Venture Capital Association) Data

Investment Stage	Upper Quartile Funds (Net Pooled IRR)							
	1999	2000	2001	2002*	2003	2004	2005	2006
Early	21.6	21.9	15.7	8.0	5.4	4.2	2.3	2.2
Development	13.7	13.8	13.4	10.0	8.5	7.4	9.0	8.9
Balanced	19.0	16.8	20.5	12.8	11.2	10.7	8.5	7.7
All Venture Capital	17.6	16.8	15.8	9.5	7.4	6.7	6.2	5.7
Buy-Out	23.9	21.0	19.8	17.8	17.0	16.5	17.8	16.7
Generalist	14.3	13.9	11.1	6.7	6.9	6.4	8.8	8.7
All Private Equity	19.4	18.3	17.2	12.2	10.9	10.6	10.6	10.4

Source: EVCA/Thomson Venture Economics.

investing in listed securities gross and net of fees. Various approaches have been used to adjusting for risk and survivor bias. There are differences between those studies that analyze early-stage venture capital as well as later-stage deals and those that only analyze the former or the latter. Some studies use data from single funds or single limited partners (LPs) while others involve large numbers of funds.

A review of nine early studies up to 1987 by Bygrave (1994) found that VC returns were substantially below the commonly held view of 30 to 50 percent IRRs. Rather, actual VC returns were generally in the tens with occasional periods in the 20 to 30 percent range and with rare highs above 30 percent. For funds raised in the period from 1969 to 1985, Bygrave (1994) finds that the median IRR reached a peak of 27 percent in 1982, with early-stage funds generating higher returns than later-stage funds.

An examination of the performance of publicly traded VC firms versus the performance of government-sponsored small business investment companies for the period from 1980 to 1986 by Kleiman and Shulman (1992) showed that the latter funds experienced greater returns on a risk-adjusted basis, but while having greater unsystematic risk had less systematic risk than publicly traded VC firms. These differences became insignificant in later years. Manigart and colleagues' (1994) analysis of 33 listed European VC firms for the period from 1977 to 1991 showed that only eight had returns higher than the market return, although systematic risk was lower than the market risk. They also noted that VC firms specializing in a particular investment stage had a higher return. Studies have noted that most, if not all, of the returns are earned by the top decile or quartile. Huntsman and Hoban (1980) show that by excluding the top decile the average return dropped from 18.9 to –0.28 percent.

Brophy and Guthner (1988), in the first study to look at the benefits from pursuing a fund of funds strategy for investors, distinguish between firm-specific and market-related risk in VC funds' returns. Their study examines weekly total returns over the five-year period from 1981 to 1985 for 12 listed VC funds compared with 12 randomly selected open mutual funds with the objective of maximizing capital gains. VC portfolios showed systematic risk below the S&P 500 and the sample of mutual funds and higher returns than both benchmarks. The study provides support for a fund of funds portfolio strategy by institutional investors as the correlation between VC fund returns is low, suggesting that firm-specific risk characteristics may be reduced by diversification.

Ljungqvist and Richardson (2003a, b) find that mature funds started in the period from 1981 to 1993 generate IRRs in excess of S&P 500 returns net of fees. These returns are robust to assumptions about timing of investment and portfolio company risk. They find that buy-out funds generally outperform venture funds; these differences partially reflect differences in leverage used in investments. However, the sample in this study was from one LP with a disproportionate share of (larger) buy-out funds.

Cochrane (2005) found that the gross returns of VC firms were high and that their log returns had negative alphas. Cochrane adjusted for the problem that missing financing rounds could bias returns upwards. Using the same dataset but with missing data issues addressed (Phalippou 2007), Hwang, Quigley, and Woodward (2005) find that gross of fees returns were lower.

Using data from funds raised during the period from 1980 to 1997, Kaplan and Schoar (2005) show average fund returns gross of fees outperform the S&P 500. However, net of fees returns are overall in line with returns on the S&P 500. Comparing VC funds and buy-out funds, they show that on a weighted capital basis only the former outperform the S&P 500. However, on an equal weighted basis, VC funds returns are lower than the S&P 500. Early and later-stage funds have higher returns than buy-out funds in funds raised during the period from 1991 to 1998 (Lerner, Schoar, and Wongsunwai 2007).

However, in an updated dataset covering U.S. funds raised from 1980 to 2003, Phalippou and Gottschalg (forthcoming) found that, after adjusting for sample bias and overstated accounting values for nonexited investments (many of which appeared to be living dead investments that had not been revalued), average fund performance changes from slight overperformance to underperformance of 3 percent per annum with respect to S&P 500. Venture funds underperform more than buy-out funds. They find that while there was a substantial gross of fees returns, this was not the case net of fees.

Metrick and Yasuda (2007) find that buy-out fund managers earn lower revenue per managed dollar than managers of VC funds. They also show that buy-out managers have substantially higher present values for revenue per partner and revenue per professional than VC managers. Buy-out managers build on prior experience by raising larger funds, which leads to significantly higher revenue per partner despite funds having lower revenue per dollar. Buy-out managers build on prior experience by raising larger funds, which leads to significantly higher revenue per partner despite funds have lower revenue per dollar.

A major reason that private equity firm managers are able to raise larger funds is their prior expertise (Metrick and Yasuda 2007) and the nature of management fees earned likely reflects the bargaining power arising from this experience. Metrick and Yasuda also find that there is variation between funds in the percentage management fee charged (over half of their sample had management fees of less than 2 percent, while 8 percent had fees above 2 percent) and that management fees decline significantly during the life of the fund. PE firms may also charge monitoring fees relating to the investments they make, which are substantially proportionately higher in smaller companies than in larger companies.

VENTURE CAPITAL AND INVESTEE PERFORMANCE

In addition to the literature on funds-level returns, a parallel literature has developed that examines firm level returns to venture capital investment.

Hellmann and Puri (2000) analyze whether the choice of investor impacts outcomes in the product market. The study is the first to examine the interrelationship between type of investor and aspects of market behavior of start-ups, specifically whether investee firms follow innovator or imitator strategies. They examine a stratified random sample of 149 VC and non–VC-backed firms in Silicon Valley during the period from 1994 to 1997. Using interviews and archival data they find that innovators are more likely to be financed by VCs than are imitators. Innovators were also faster in obtaining VC finance. VC-backed firms, especially innovators had a faster time to market. This study therefore highlights that VCs play different roles in different companies.

Other studies present mixed evidence regarding the relationship between VC backing and firm performance, particularly in terms of growth. Manigart and Van Hyfte (1999) find that VC-backed firms have higher asset growth than non–VC-backed firms in Belgium. Engel and Keilbach (2007) use propensity score matching to identify a control sample of non–VC-backed firms in Germany and find that VC-backed firms generate faster employment growth. In contrast, Burgel and colleagues (2000) find that VC backing has no impact on the growth of firms in Germany and the UK. Other studies of the growth of VC and non–VC-backed firms that went to IPO also show mixed results, with Jain and Kini (1995) and Audretsch and Lehmann (2004) finding positive effects of VC on growth, while Botazzi and Da Rin (2002) find no effect. Colombo and Grilli (2008) examine the influence of human capital and VC backing on the growth of VC-backed new technology based firms (NTBFs). Using a sample of 439 Italian NTBFs and after controlling for survivor bias and the endogeneity of VC funding, they find that once a NTBF receives VC backing the role of founders' skills becomes less important and the coaching skills of VCs become more important in contributing to firm growth. Important problems with these studies include their often cross-sectional nature and a typical failure to address the issue of endogeneity in VC backing. Bertoni, Colombo, and Grilli (2008) using a 10-year panel study of 550 Italian NTBFs show that VC backing, especially by financial VCs rather than corporate VCs, strongly spurs employment and sales revenue growth. A Spanish study of firms by Alemany and Marti (2005) using panel data analysis of VC-backed start-ups shows that both VC backing and its amount are associated with higher performance. Davila, Foster, and Gupta (2003) show that VC-backed firms have faster employment growth.

Lee, Lee, and Pennings (2001) found that the involvement of a VC in combination with the amount of financial resources invested in the first year after founding spurred the start-up's performance during the first two years. Heirman and Clarysse (2005) further refine this observation and add that VC involvement only makes sense if they invest significant amounts of money in the company at start-up, ranging from €1 to €5 million depending on the technology. They find that companies in which VCs only invested a small amount of money at start-up perform worse than those companies that start without any VC money at all. This suggests that venture capitalists in the first place invest money, and this might be the foremost important resource for start-ups.

Internationalization activities provide a further dimension of performance where the role of VCs may be important. George, Wiklund, and Zahra (2005) find that internal owners tend to be risk averse and have a lower tendency to increase scale and scope of internationalization than VC owners. Zahra, Neubaum, and Naldi (2007) find a positive relationship between the equity-holdings of VC firms and the development of knowledge-based resources for internationalization using a U.S. sample of firms.

Lockett and colleagues (2008) dig more deeply into what VC firms actually do to influence the performance of their investees. In contrast to Zahra, Neubaum, and Naldi (2007) they study VC investments in Europe that encompass both early-stage and late-stage management buy-out or buy-in (MBO/I) transactions. Their findings emphasize that the nature of the VC's involvement, monitoring versus added value, in influencing internationalization may vary between stages of investment. Employing a sample of 340 VC-backed firms, they show that monitoring resources are most effective in promoting export behavior for late-stage ventures and value-added resources in promoting export behavior in early-stage venture.

INFLUENCES ON RETURNS

Fund-level studies have suggested that the buildup of expertise through learning contributes to higher returns. Kaplan and Schoar (2005) find that experience matters: performance in one fund predicts performance in subsequent funds. In contrast, mutual funds do not show persistence. Phalippou and Gottschalg (forthcoming) also show that previous past performance was most important in explaining fund performance. However, Lerner, Schoar, and Wongsunwai (2007) find that there is considerable variation in returns by type of institution. The presence of unsophisticated performance-insensitive LPs allows poorly performing GPs to raise new funds.

A number of other influences on fund performance have been identified. Fund size, public market returns during a fund's life, fund sequence, having a VC objective, idiosyncratic risk, and level of investment opportunities appear to generate higher net of fee returns while competition for deal flow reduces returns (Kaplan and Schoar 2005; Jones and Rhodes-Kropf 2003; Ljungqvist and Richardson 2003a,b).

There is mixed evidence concerning the influence of the nature of competition in the market on fund returns. Ljungqvist and Richardson (2003a,b) find that competition for deal flow reduces VC fund performance. They also distinguish supply and demand conditions in the market and show that higher demand increases performance while higher supply decreases it. However, while the authors focus on demand side shock, supply may be driven by returns, not by demand for deals. Demand may not grow exogenously but be endogenously determined depending on the experience of GPs in being able to create quality deals or find diamonds in the rough. Moreover, apparent overpayment may differ between VCs depending on their level of experience. Deals that are riskier for young GPs may not be so risky for experienced GPs because they have the skills to select and add value. Hence experienced GPs may be able to pay more as they can find better deals and add more value.

Gompers and Lerner (2000) show that investments made during periods of high funds inflow do not generate greater success, while Cumming and Walz (2007) find a positive relationship between fund inflows and performance after correcting for sample selection bias. Gompers and colleagues (2005) using U.S. data show that prior experience helps VC firms to increase investments when deal opportunities improve and that this can lead to improved exit performance.

The literature on the effects of venture capital has developed from a simple examination of the presence or absence of venture capital investors to recognize their heterogeneity. A particularly important aspect of this heterogeneity concerns the role of the general and specific human capital of venture capital executives in generating returns as well as the role of social capital.

Fund-level analysis based on 318 U.S.-based VC funds raised between 1980 and 1998 shows that fund management teams with more task-specific human capital manage funds with proportions of portfolio company exits (Zarutskie forthcoming). Task-specific human capital was measured as having executives with past experience as VCs and as executives at start-ups. Fund management teams with more industry-specific human capital in strategy and management consulting manage funds with greater proportions of portfolio company exits. In contrast, fund management teams that have more general human capital in business administration have lower proportions of portfolio company exits.

Dimov and Shepherd (2005) provide an important contribution as they show that it is not simply the amount of human capital that is important but rather its nature. They use a human capital perspective to investigate the relationship between the general and specific human capital of executives in larger and more experienced VC firms and the performance of investee firms in the wireless communications industry. They find that although general human capital has a positive association with the proportion of portfolio firms that went public, specific human capital did not. However, specific human capital was associated with the proportion of investee firms that went bankrupt.

Richer insights are provided from a European study involving 119 VC firms and 1,652 portfolio companies, Bottazzi, Da Rin, and Hellman (forthcoming) explore the role of investor activism and its impact on portfolio firm performance. VC firms whose partners have prior business experience are significantly more active in investee firms. VC experience of the firm's partners is not significant, while the influence of a science background for executives is weak. Private independent VC firms are more involved in investees than other types of VC. The authors find that having more venture experience increases the likelihood that an executive will be put in charge of supervising portfolio firms. Examining whether investees made a successful exit or not, Bottazzi, Da Rin, and Hellman (forthcoming) find that, after using an instrumental variables approach to address endogeneity issues, there is a positive relationship between investor activism and exit performance that is both statistically and economically significant. This study is particularly interesting in terms of the nature and extent of the data collected. Data are based on a survey of VC firms in 17 countries augmented with data from VC firm web sites, commercially available databases, and VC directories. The study also distinguishes different investment stages. The authors collect data that comprises direct measures about the human capital of different partners and their roles inside VC firms.

VC firms engage in extensive syndication with other VCs for reasons of access to deal flow, access to greater expertise, and for risk spreading (Wright and Lockett 2003). These syndication networks both help identify better deals but also can provide access to resources that may help generate superior returns. De Clerq and Dimov (2008) examine the performance effects on 200 U.S. venture capital–backed firms of two knowledge-driven strategies, internal knowledge development, and external knowledge access through syndication. Performance is measured in terms of whether the investee firm went public, was sold, failed, and remained private. In an interesting longitudinal study they find that investing in industries in which a VC firm has more knowledge and investing with more or familiar syndicated partners increases the performance of investees. Access to external knowledge through syndication is most important when there is an incongruity between what the firm knows and what it intends to do.

Cumming and Walz (2007) find that syndication is positively related to gross of fees fund performance. Hochberg, Ljungqvist, and Lu (2007) also provide evidence of the linkage between the expertise that can be accessed through syndication and VC performance in their study of 16,315 companies that received their first VC funding in the period from 1980 to 1999. After controlling for other determinants of VC fund performance, such as fund size and the funding environment, they find that VCs that are better networked at the time a fund is raised subsequently report significantly better fund performance as measured by the rate of successful portfolio exits over a 10-year period. The most important influences on performance were found to be the size of the VC firm's networks, the tendency to be invited into other VCs' syndicates, and access to the best networked VCs. A one standard deviation increase in network centrality increased exit rates by approximately 2.5 percentage points from the 34.2 percent sample average. At the portfolio company level, a VC's network centrality had a significant positive effect on the probability that a portfolio firm survived to a subsequent funding round. Interestingly, Hochberg, Ljungqvist, and Lu (2007) find that when VC networks are controlled for, the beneficial effects of VC experience are reduced. Moreover, even when persistence in performance from one fund to the next is controlled for, network centrality continues to have a significant positive effect on performance.

Institutional context appears to play an important role in returns generation. Hege, Palomino, and Schwienbacher (2004) find that VC returns in Europe are below those for the United States. Cumming and Walz (2007) find, however, that less stringent accounting rules and weak legal systems are associated with overvaluation and misreporting of returns. Using a detailed dataset comprising individual investment details on over 5,000 portfolio firms and 221 PE funds spanning the period from 1971 to 2003 in 39 countries, they analyze potential reporting biases regarding current fund holdings using information from former fund holdings to construct benchmarks. They find systematic biases in the reporting of unrealized IRRs relative to forecast IRRs. Their research provides evidence that the reputational costs of misreporting are negatively related to the valuations of unrealized investments. Experienced PE managers tend to report significantly lower valuations than their younger counterparts. Specifically focusing on early-stage high tech unrealized investments, they find that these deals are on average of higher value than would be predicted based on realized early-stage high tech investments. Lerner and Schoar (2005) also find that both VC and buy-out funds in common law countries generate higher returns than these types of funds in other institutional environments.

SOME CAVEATS

Data availability has long created problems for the analysis of venture capital returns.

Accessing proprietary datasets may provide important access to otherwise difficult to obtain information but suffers from potential for selection bias since those selected may be better funds than those not included. Phalippou and Gottschalg (forthcoming), for example, attempt to address the potential selection bias in Kaplan and Schoar (2005) by using a fraction of a fund's successful exits as a proxy for performance as this is available for both selected funds and a subset of nonselected funds in the performance database used (Phalippou 2007). Kaplan and Stromberg (2009) comment, however, that the results obtained are qualitatively identical to those in Kaplan and Schoar (2005).

Proprietary datasets also typically relate to independent VC funds and thus accessing performance data on captive and public sector funds may be more problematical. These problems are also present in industry returns data. For example, Leleux (2007) notes that in compiling its European performance data the EVCA achieved only a 73 percent response rate to its request for performance information from all companies that participated in private equity activities in 2002. The extent to which this degree of nonresponse leads to bias in performance returns figures is, however, unknown.

In analyzing fund returns it is important to take account of whether returns are based on deals that have exited or on all investments in the fund. Focusing analysis on exited deals may inflate returns if the exited deals are the more successful ones. Alternatively, analyses based on all investments in a fund face the problem of valuing unexited deals. A potentially important problem however with non–legally binding guidelines is that underperforming VC funds may be reluctant to write down the value of unrealized investments, which may serve to hide their true performance (Phalippou and Gottschalg forthcoming). Moreover, heterogeneity in the nature of self-reported information may make comparisons of performance between VC funds difficult.

A further factor that needs to be taken into account is the difference between committed and drawn down funds. An investor making a $Xm commitment to a VC fund has very different risks and rewards than one investing $Xm in a unit trust (or similar fund) even if the underlying assets of the funds are the same. When comparing returns, a VC commitment should be viewed as providing a facility of up to $Xm not an investment (or stream of investments) of $Xm. The investors will have a return on the commitment in excess of the fees on committed investment if they receive interest in excess of the fee percentage. If the fee is 2 percent and the cash is deposited and undrawn at 3 percent, there is a positive 1 percent return even if the funds are not drawn down. This is clearly a negative NPV investment. The return on the commitment is therefore the sum of: Return on drawn down cash + Return on undrawn commitment. This contrasts with a direct investment in a quoted fund whereby the return = Return on drawn down funds + 0. Similarly, both the commitment and the fees of funds vary over the life of the fund. Typically there is an investment period and a "harvesting period" that may overlap in the middle of the fund's life. Fees decline after the investing period. This is an important distinction. Furthermore, there is no evidence in the academic body of work of the actual life of the funds and the variation over time.

Valuing early-stage firms poses major issues for VC firms and for assessing financial returns. Lack of objective information is particularly problematical. Various venture capital associations have attempted to promulgate recommendations for the valuation of investee companies. In Europe, guidelines produced by EVCA emphasize the reporting of Fair Values of investments (EVCA 2005), that is the amount for which an asset could be exchanged between knowledgeable, willing parties in an arms-length transaction. The guidelines recognize the subjectivity of the process but caution against VC firms being too cautious in their approaches to valuation.

A central issue concerns what methodology to use to arrive at a fair valuation given its subjective nature. The EVCA guidelines suggest that valuers should exercise judgement in the selection of the appropriate valuation method for a particular investment. Valuation methods adopted by VC firms vary between institutional environments. There is some tendency for more developed capital markets to use valuation methods that are more in line with standard corporate finance theory but even here, informational restrictions limited the extent to which the most sophisticated discounted cash flow (DCF) or options methods were used, with other methods such as P/E multiples and comparator transaction prices or industry benchmarks being used either alongside or instead of these methods (Wright and Robbie 1996; Manigart et al. 1997; 2002). A nine-country study covering the United States, Europe, and Asia by Wright and colleagues (2004) finds that the legal system and its implications for capital markets is especially important in explaining the information used in valuation methods. Cultural factors play an important role in the relative importance placed on information provided by entrepreneurs and in the business plan. This finding suggests that information sources are not easily transferred between different contexts. They also find that information sources may vary both between and within legal systems and geographic regions, emphasizing the heterogeneity of different environments and the need for fine-grained approaches.

CONCLUSION

In this review we have shown that an extensive and increasingly sophisticated literature has now developed to examine the returns to venture capital. Nevertheless, a number of areas for further research remain.

Further research continually needs to assess the returns to venture capital funds raised during different time periods. For example, if there is a learning effect in the VC industry over time, do returns increase over time, or are these competed away through increased competition for deals? Are the returns on funds raised in the boom period up to 2007 likely to be lower than in previous periods?

Further analysis may be required of the motives to invest in first-time funds if experienced funds generate greater returns. Naïve LPs may invest in first-time funds to gain experience, and a shortage of allocation from established funds may mean that new entrants cannot gain access to established funds. However, it is important to distinguish between first-time funds that are managed by inexperienced managers and those that are managed by experienced executives who have spun out of established funds. Further research may usefully examine this issue by obtaining data from web sites or fund documents on previous affiliations of executives, number of prior deals, successes versus failures, and so on.

Finally, further research may usefully be focused on the nature of the human and social capital resources VC firms bring to foreign markets that can enable them to enhance performance in those markets and overcome the liability of foreignness. There is some evidence that VCs adapt when they enter foreign markets in terms of their information, valuation, and monitoring behavior (Wright, Pruthi, and Lockett 2005), but there is an absence of evidence regarding the relative success of foreign VCs in aiding firms to internationalize.

REFERENCES

Alemany, L., and J. Marti. 2005. Unbiased estimation of economic impact of venture capital backed firms. Working Paper. ESADE Business School.

Audretsch, D., and E. Lehmann. 2004. Financing high tech growth: The role of banks and venture capitalists. *Schmalenbach Economic Review* 56:340–357.

Baden-Fuller, C., A. Dean, P. McNamara, and B. Hilliard. 2006. Raising the returns to venture finance. *Journal of Business Venturing*, 21:265–285.

Bertoni, F., M. Colombo, and L. Grilli. 2008. Venture capital financing and the growth of new technology based firms. WP Politechnico di Milano.

Botazzi, L., and M. Da Rin. 2002. Venture capital in Europe and the financing of innovative companies. *Economic Policy* 17:229–269.

Bottazzi, L., M. Da Rin, and T. Hellmann. Forthcoming. Who are the active investors? Evidence from venture capital. *Journal of Financial Economics*.

Brophy, D. J., and M. Guthner. 1988. Publicly traded venture capital funds: Implications for "funds of funds" investors. *Journal of Business Venturing* 3:187–206.

Bruining, H., and M. Wright. 2008. *Private equity and management buyouts*. Cheltenham, UK: Edward Elgar.

Burgel, O., et al. 2000. Internationalisation of high tech start-ups and fast growth: Evidence from Germany and UK. DP 00-35. Centre for European Economic Research, Mannheim.

BVCA. 2006. *The economic impact of private equity in the UK*. London: BVCA.

Bygrave, W. 1994. Rates of return from venture capital. In *Realizing Investment Value*, ed. W. Bygrave, M. Hay, and J. Peeters. London: Pitman.

Cochrane, J. H. 2005. The risk and return of venture capital. *Journal of Financial Economics* 75:9–11.

Colombo, M., and L. Grilli. 2008. On growth drivers of high tech start-ups: Exploring the role of founders' human capital and venture capital. WP Politechnico di Milano.

Cumming, D., and U. Walz. 2007. Private equity returns and disclosure around the world. Mimeo. Retrieved from SSRN: http://ssrn.com/abstract=514105

Davila, A., G. Foster, and M. Gupta. 2003. Venture capital financing and the growth of start-up firms. *Journal of Business Venturing* 18:689–708.

DeClerq, D., and D. Dimov. 2008. Internal knowledge development and external knowledge access in venture capital investment performance. *Journal of Management Studies* 45:585–612.

Dimov, D., and D. Shepherd. 2005. Human capital theory and venture capital firms: Exploring home runs and strike outs. *Journal of Business Venturing* 20:1–22.

Engel, D., and M. Keilbach. 2007. Firm level implications of early stage venture capital investment: An empirical investigation. *Journal of Empirical Finance* 14:150–167.

EVCA. 2005. *International private equity and venture capital valuation guidelines*. Brussels: EVCA.

George, G., J. Wiklund, and S. Zahra. 2005. Ownership and the internationalization of small firms. *Journal of Management* 31:210–233.

Gompers, P., and J. Lerner. 1999. An analysis of compensation in the U.S. venture capital partnership. *Journal of Financial Economics* 51:3–44.

———. 2000. Money chasing deals? The impact of fund inflows on private equity valuations. *Journal of Financial Economics* 55:281–325.

Gompers, P., et al. 2005. Venture capital investment cycles: The role of experience and specialization. *Journal of Financial Economics* 81:649–679.

Hege, U., F. Palomino, and A. Schwienbacher. 2004. Determinants of venture capital performance: Europe and the United States. WP HEC Paris and University of Amsterdam.

Heirman, A., and B. Clarysse. 2005. The imprinting effect of initial resources and market strategy on the early growth path of start-ups. Working Paper Series. Ghent University.

Hellmann, T., and M. Puri. 2000. The interaction between product market and financing strategy: The role of venture capital. *Review of Financial Studies* 13:959–984.

Hochberg, Y., A. Ljungqvist, and Y. Lu. 2007. Whom you know matters: Venture capital networks and investment performance. *Journal of Finance* 62:251–302.

Huntsman, B., and J. Hoban. 1980. Investment in new enterprise: Some empirical observations on risk, return and market structure. *Financial Management* (summer):44–51.

Hwang, M., J. Quigley, and S. Woodward. 2005. An index for venture capital, 1987–2003. *Contributions to Economic Analysis and Policy* 4:1–43.

Jain, B., and O. Kini. 1995. Venture capitalists' participation and the post-issue operating performance of IPO firms. *Managerial and Decision Economics*. 6:593–606.

Jones, C., and M. Rhodes-Kropf. 2003. The price of diversifiable risk in venture capital and private equity. Mimeo. Columbia Business School.

Kaplan, S., and A. Schoar. 2005. Private equity performance: Returns, persistence and capital flows. *Journal of Finance* 60 4:1791–1823.

Kaplan, S., and S., Per. 2009. Leveraged buyouts and private equity. *Journal of Economic Perspectives* 23:121–146.

Karsai, J., et al. 1999. Venture capital in transition economies—the cases of Hungary, Poland and Slovakia. In *Management buyouts and venture capital into the next millennium*, ed. M. Wright and K. Robbie. Cheltenham, UK: Edward Elgar.

Kleiman, R., and J. Shulman. 1992. The risk-return attributes of publicly traded venture capital: Implications for investors and public policy. *Journal of Business Venturing* 7: 195–208.

Knockaert, M., et al. 2006. Do human capital and fund characteristics drive follow-up behavior of early stage high-tech VCs? *International Journal of Technology Management* 34:7–27.

Lee, C., K. Lee, and J. Pennings. 2001. Internal capabilities, external networks, and performance: A study on technology-based ventures. *Strategic Management Journal*, 22:615–640.

Lerner, J., and A. Schoar. 2005. Does legal enforcement affect financial transactions? The contractual channel in private equity. *Quarterly Journal of Economics* 120:223–246.

Lerner, J., and W. Wan. 2007. Smart institutions, foolish choices: The limited partner performance puzzle. *Journal of Finance* 62(2):731–764.

Ljungqvist, A., and M. Richardson. 2003a. The cash flow, return and risk characteristics of private equity. NBER Working paper 9495.

———. 2003b. The investment behaviour of private equity fund managers. Working Paper. New York University.

Lockett, A., G. Murray, and M. Wright. 2002. Do UK venture capitalists *still* have a bias against investment in new technology firms? *Research Policy* 31:1009–1030.

Lockett, A., et al. 2008. The export intensity of venture capital backed companies. *Small Business Economics* 31:39–58.

Manigart, S., and W. Van Hyfte. 1999. Post investment evolution of VC backed companies. In *Frontiers of entrepreneurship research*, ed. P. Reynolds, W. Bygrave, S. Manigart, C. Mason, G. Meyer, H. Sapienza, K. Shaver. 419–432 Wellesley, MA: Babson College.

Manigart S., P. Joos, and D. De Vos. 1994. The performance of publicly traded European venture capital companies. *Journal of Small Business Finance* 3:111–125.

Manigart, S., et al. 1997. Venture capitalists' appraisal of investment projects: An empirical European study. *Entrepreneurship Theory and Practice* 21:29–44.

Manigart, S., et al. 2002. Determinants of required returns in venture capital investments: A five-country study. *Journal of Business Venturing*, 17:291–312.

Metrick, A., and A. Yasuda. 2007. The economics of private equity funds. Mimeo. Wharton School.

Phalippou, L. 2007. Investing in private equity funds: A Survey. Retrieved from http://ssrn.com/abstract=980243

Phalippou, L., and O. Gottschalg. Forthcoming. Performance of private equity funds: Another puzzle? *Review of Financial Studies*.

Robbie, K., B. Chiplin, and M. Wright. 1997. The monitoring of venture capital firms. *Entrepreneurship Theory and Practice*, 21:9–28.

Sorensen, M. 2007. How smart is smart money? A two-sided matching model of venture capital. *Journal of Finance* 62:2725–2762.

Wright, M. 2007. Private equity and management buy-outs. In *Handbook of research on venture capital*, ed. H. Landstrom. Cheltenham, UK: Edward Elgar.

_____, B. et al. 2006. University spin-out companies and venture capital. *Research Policy* 35(4):481–501.

_____, and A., Lockett 2003. The structure and management of alliances: Syndication in the venture capital industry. *Journal of Management Studies* 40:2073–2104.

_____, S. et al. 2004. Venture capital investors, institutional context, valuation and information: U.S., Europe and Asia. *Journal of International Entrepreneurship* 2:305–326.

Wright, M., S. Pruthi, and A. Lockett. 2005. International venture capital research: From cross-country comparisons to crossing borders. *International Journal of Management Reviews* 7(3):1–31.

Wright, M., and K. Robbie. 1996. Venture capitalists, unquoted investment appraisal and the role of accounting information. *Accounting and Business Research* 26:153–170.

_____. 1998. Venture capital and private equity: A review and synthesis. *Journal of Business Finance and Accounting* 25(5 & 6:521–570.

Wright, M., H. Sapienza, and L. Busenitz. 2003. *Venture capital*, vols. 1–3. Cheltenham, UK: Edward Elgar.

Zahra, S., D. Neubaum, and L. Naldi. 2007. The effects of ownership and governance on SMEs' international knowledge-based resources. *Small Business Economics* 29:309–327.

Zarutskie, R. Forthcoming. The role of top management team human capital in venture capital markets: Evidence from first-time funds. *Journal of Business Venturing*.

ABOUT THE AUTHORS

Mike Wright received his Ph.D. from the University of Nottingham. He is Director of the Centre for Management Buy-out Research (CMBOR), the first centre for the study of private equity and buy-outs, which he founded in 1986. He was Research Director of NUBS from 1991–2001. He has published widely on academic entrepreneurship, venture capital, private equity and related topics in journals such as *Academy of Management Review, Academy of Management Journal, Strategic Management Journal, Journal of Corporate Finance, Review of Economics and Statistics, Economic Journal, Journal of Management Studies,* and so on. He was an editor of

Journal of Management Studies from 2003 to 2008 and is currently an associate editor of *Strategic Entrepreneurship Journal*. He was ranked #1 worldwide for publications in academic entrepreneurship 1981–2005. His latest books include *Academic Entrepreneurship in Europe* (2007), *Private Equity and Management Buy-outs* (2008) and *Private Equity Demystified* (2008).

Riya Chopraa recently completed her M.Sc. in finance at Nottingham University Business School and is now a researcher at CMBOR.

## CHAPTER 20

Venture Capitalists' Control

Stimulating or Stunting?

APRIL KNILL
Assistant Professor, Florida State University, College of Business

INTRODUCTION

Some entrepreneurs prefer venture capital to alternative financing arrangements due to the active management role the venture capitalists (or "VCs") take (Hellmann 2000; Hellmann and Puri 2000, 2002). This managerial aspect provided by venture capitalists is desirable to entrepreneurs who excel in the service offered by their company (e.g., technology expertise for a high tech company entrepreneur), but lack the business savvy to succeed in the critical early years (Kaplan and Stromberg 2001). That said, many entrepreneurs start their own business because they don't want to have to answer to anyone. They want to be their own boss. Although entrepreneurs desire VCs to play an active management role, they still value autonomy.

Pursuant to the contract set up between the VC and the company in which it invests (the entrepreneurship, or equivalently, the "portfolio company" or "PC"), the VC has the freedom to be as attentive or as silent as he wishes. Surveys of VCs have shown different management styles (e.g., see Macmillan, Kulow and Khoylian 1988). On one end of the spectrum, the VC exudes a laissez-faire attitude or acts as a silent manager. Under this style, there is a lack of direct involvement in the operations of the portfolio companies in which it invests. One might say that this style is equivalent to the financing often achieved through angels.[1] This arguably lacks one of the main values touted by VCs—guidance (Renucci 2000; Sapienza, Manigart, and Vermeir 1996; Ehrlich and De Noble 1994; Sapienza 1992). At the other end of the spectrum, the VC exudes a very hands-on approach, or is a co-manager. One could argue that this style has the potential to be stifling and can translate into interference (Burkart, Gromb, and Panunzi 1997). At the very least it is the opposite of the autonomy many entrepreneurs seek out in starting a business. At most it could be stifling, squelching innovativeness, productivity, and more.

Given this spectrum of control, one could hypothesize that an optimal level of control exists wherein the firm may not only perform well but also flourish. To that end, this paper examines the control strategies of VCs to discern which levels result in optimal performance/outcome for the entrepreneurs. I find that the relationship between VC control and PC performance/outcome is in fact nonlinear. Analysis done at different levels of each proxy of VC control suggests that average VC control (versus either extreme) maximizes the positive impact on firm performance.

The rest of the paper is structured as follows. In the next section, I motivate the study. Following that, I provide the methodology of my examination. The data used is then described. Results are described and analyzed, and robustness tests are performed. Finally, the paper is concluded.

VC STYLES OF CONTROL

VCs do not have unlimited resources. They must divide their time among their existing investments (PCs) and their new investments (i.e., perform due diligence). If the control style of the VC is closer to a silent manager (co-manager), the time spent on new investments will be more (less). This amounts to a cost of involvement for the VC, which could ultimately impact the PC. If these costs become substantial, the performance and outcome of these fledgling firms could be negatively impacted, ultimately delaying the exit of these firms. Conversely, however, some entrepreneurs may find less VC involvement a positive factor.

Indeed, from the PC's perspective, VC control may be considered stifling. The self-selection process of entrepreneurs suggests that entrepreneurs seek out situations where they are not managed.[2] Such individuals often flourish when autonomous environments exist. Although too little control (i.e., management) is still a risk since some of these individuals lack important business savvy, excessive control can be just as damaging.

During the contract-writing phase of venture capital, certain control variables are established such as cash flow and voting rights. The essence of the control rights is formed at this stage of the VC/PC relationship (Kaplan and Strömberg 2003). It is this process that will set into motion the general level of involvement the VCs display (see Bergemann and Hege 1998 for a model of intertemporal risk sharing in the VC/PC relationship). As such, in order to maximize profit, VCs must know how much control they should exert on their portfolio companies before they set up the contract. Knowing the relationship between control and PC performance and outcome can help VCs make this important decision.

Vehicles of Control

The terms *control* and *ownership* in some senses may be interchangeably used. Kaplan and Stromberg (2003) and Cumming (2008) find that ownership may be an important factor in the performance of PCs. Specifically, they look at the provision of cash flow and control rights (e.g., through convertible securities) and how it affects PC performance. In this paper, I use ownership, a very important factor in the VC/PC relationship, as a proxy for control. I include a direct measure of ownership: the percent of the PC owned by the VC. To be thorough, I also define control in nonownership proxies thus defining control in the paper to imply a broader category than ownership.

Venture capitalists can maintain control over their investment by disbursing investment monies in smaller quantities across time (i.e., instead of in one lump sum).[3] As such, the average VC round investment may be an important means of controlling entrepreneurs.

The percentage of the VC's portfolio is a measure of how much the VC is relying on this PC to perform well. At the extreme—let's say 100 percent—the VC would likely be quite involved and would have the incentive to manage in a more co-managerial manner. At the other extreme, a small percentage, say under 5 percent, the VC would have an incentive to control the PC in a different manner. Given resource constraints and the more diversified approach of the VC in this scenario, a more laissez-faire managerial role would be taken. Given the differences in these logical approaches, this serves as an important proxy for control in the paper.

To address the fact that the level of management involvement may be affected by the VC's ability to travel to and from the PC, I include distance as a measure of control. The inclusion of this proxy follows the findings of Lerner (1995), who finds that the oversight of distant businesses is more costly than that of local firms.

Lastly, I include a proxy for the amount of time between rounds. Gompers and Lerner (1999b, 131) state, "Major reviews of progress and extensive due diligence are confined to the time of refinancing... [they] are designed to limit opportunistic behavior by entrepreneurs between evaluations." Extending this time between financings (and the reviews/due diligence between the rounds), in effect delaying (or even thwarting) the receipt of financing, could be perceived as a means of control. This is thus included as a proxy for control.

METHODOLOGY

To examine the impact of VC control, I identify ways in which the PC may benefit. Given data limitations (i.e., the scarcity) of performance data on PCs, I examine the impact of VC control on two proxies: their financial performance, where data is available, and their current status (i.e., outcome).

Entrepreneurial Performance

I test the hypothesis that there exists an optimal level of control a venture capitalist may exert over their portfolio companies that would enable that company to perform optimally using the following robust OLS regression.

$$Performance_{jt} = \alpha + \beta_0\,Control_{it} + \beta_1 PC_{jt} + \beta_2 VC_{it} + \beta_3 Y_t + \varepsilon \qquad (20.1)$$

where Performance is the financial performance level for PC_j at time t as measured by the level of sales, net income, and total assets (regressed separately). Standard errors are robust due to clustering around the PC. $Control_{it}$ is a proxy for the level of involvement VC_i exerts (over its PCs) at time t. Proxies include the average VC investment per round, the percentage of the VC portfolio comprised by the PC investment, the percentage of the PC the VC owns, geographic proximity, and the average amount of time between rounds. Proxies are regressed separately. PC_{jt} is a vector of PC investment characteristics such as IT Industry, an indicator variable that describes whether the PC is in the IT industry or not, Early Stage, an indicator variable that describes whether the PC is in the early stage or not, and Inv Term, which describes the number of years for which the PC has had funding. VC_{it} is a vector of VC characteristics such as Last Year Inv, which describes how much the VC invested in the PC last year, and Corporate VC, which is an indicator variable describing whether the VC is a corporate VC or not. Y_t is a vector of economic variables including S&P500 Return, GDP Growth, # Deals, and Bubble. S&P500 Return is the annual return on the S&P500 Index. GDP Growth is the percentage growth in gross domestic capital. # Deals is the number of VC investments at time t, and Bubble is a dummy variable included to control for the Internet Bubble era and its implications.

If there is a significant impact of VC control on PC performance, we would expect to see a statistically significant coefficient on control, β_0.

To discern whether there exists an optimal level of control for the VC with regard to the specific proxies for VC control, I add to equation (20.1) a squared term of the control proxy. This enables me to examine whether there is a possible maximum or minimum for each proxy. The regression is as follows:

$$Performance_{jt} = \alpha + \delta_0 \, Control_{it} + \delta_1 \, Control_{it}^2 + \delta_2 PC_{jt} + \delta_3 VC_{it} + \delta_4 Y_t + \varepsilon$$
(20.2)

All variables are as they were defined in equation (20.1). If there is indeed an optimal level, we would expect to see statistical significance in the coefficient on the squared control variable, δ_1, with a sign that is opposite to that of control, δ_0.

Entrepreneurial Outcome

To examine whether VC control has any impact on the current status of the PC (i.e., defunct, private, subsidiary, or public), I use a multinomial logit model to regress the following:

$$Pr(CurrentStatus_j) = \Psi(\alpha + \gamma_0 \, Control_{it} + \gamma_2 PC_{jt} + \gamma_3 VC_{it} + \gamma_4 Y_t)$$
(20.3)

where CurrentStatus is the current standing of the entrepreneurial (PC) company (i.e., defunct, private, subsidiary, or public).[4] Ψ is the cumulative logistic probability distribution function. All other variables are as they were previously defined. Once again a squared control term is added to check for the existence of an optimal level of control; this term is included in some but not all of the specifications.

DATA

Data is collected from SDC Platinum VentureXpert. The data is collected for all portfolio companies in the dataset. The timeframe included is from January 1, 1962 through July 31, 2008.[5]

Company-Specific Information

Portfolio company data included in my analysis includes Investment Term, IT Industry, and Early Stage. Investment Term is included to control for implications on performance and outcome. The longer a PC has been receiving investment from

VCs the more likely it is that it will be performing at a higher level and that it will exit via merger/acquisition ("M&A") or initial public offering ("IPO"). Company specifics such as their stage and industry reveal characteristics of the PCs, which in turn could offer insight into the level of control the VC should exert. Gompers (1995) finds that investment in early-stage firms is monitoring-intensive relative to other stages. Gompers and Lerner (1999a) and Norton and Tenenbaum (1993) explain that investment at certain stages entails more risk and, accordingly, more opportunity than others. Similarly, there are some industries that are riskier than others.

Venture Capitalist–Specific Data

VC characteristics that are included are Corporate VC and Last Year Inv. Corporate VC is included to control for the type of VC and Last Year Inv gives us a baseline for the amount that the VC invested in the PC last year.

Market Conditions

Macroeconomic variables such as Number of Deals, GDP growth, S&P 500 Return, and Bubble are included to control for the general state of the VC industry as well as the market in general. Number of Deals provides a proxy for the general fund-raising levels. GDP growth is included to control for business cycle effects. S&P 500 Return is included to control for public market conditions. This variable will likely pick up the counter-cyclical nature of the venture capital industry (Groshen and Potter 2003). Following studies such as Cumming (2006), I include an indicator variable Bubble to account for the increased probability of exit during the IT bubble period (from 1998 to 2000).

A list of summary statistics is found in Exhibit 20.1, Panel A.

Correlation

The vast majority of variables used within specifications do not exhibit any real conformance. The only real correlation within specifications is found in the macroeconomic variables. Correlation coefficients are displayed in Exhibit 20.1, Panel B.

RESULTS

Results for the impact of VC Control on PC financial performance and outcome are outlined below.

Firm Performance

Exhibit 20.2 displays the results from the base specification. Looking first to specifications (1) to (5) of Panel A, we see that all proxies of control significantly positively impact sales (at a 1 percent significance level). The marginal effect of the average VC round investment (specification [1]) represents an elasticity since both this variable and the dependent variable are transformed using the natural logarithm. The marginal effect is a 0.898 percent[6] increase in sales for a 1 percent increase in average round investment. The marginal effect of an increase in the percent of the VC's portfolio (specification [2]) is a 2.536 percent increase in sales. The marginal

Exhibit 20.1 Data Characteristics

Sales is the natural log of the level of sales for the PC. Net Income is the natural log of the level of net income for the PC. Total Assets is the natural log of the level of total assets for the PC. Avg VC Round Inv is the natural log of the average amount of VC investment per round. % VC Portfolio is the total amount the VC firm invested in the PC divided by the total amount the VC invested in all PCs. % PC Owned is total amount the VC invested in PC divided by total amount invested in PC. Distance is the natural log of the number of kilometers between the VC and the PC. Term Avg is the natural log of the average length of time between VC round investment dates. Inv Term is the difference between the year the PC received its first and last investments. Last Year Inv is the natural log of the amount ($Thous) the VC invested in the PC last year. IT Industry (Early Stage) is a dummy variable, which takes on a value of 1, if the PC is in the IT industry (Early Stage) and zero otherwise. S&P500 Return is the percentage return on the S&P500 at time t. GDP Growth is the percentage growth in gross domestic capital at time t. # Deals is the number of VC investments at time t. Bubble is a dummy variable that takes on a value of 1 if time t equals 1999 or 2000 and zero otherwise. Corporate VC is a dummy variable which takes on a value of one if the VC is a corporate VC and zero otherwise. Robust standard errors (clustered around PC) appear in brackets. *, **, *** indicate significance levels of 10, 5, and 1 percent, respectively.

Panel A. Summary Statistics

Variable	Observations	Mean	Standard Deviation	Min	Max
Sales	3,917	10.38	2.61	−2.04	18.06
Net Income	4,704	9.41	2.28	−4.61	17.91
Total Assets	5,423	11.67	2.35	0	18.32
% VC Portfolio	38,187	0.04	0.13	−0.06	1
Avg VC Round Inv	42,445	7.89	1.01	0.10	12.61
% PC Owned	38,179	0.36	2.24	0.00	275.36
Distance	19,238	1424.67	1577.09	0	12787.79
Term Avg	30,626	485.85	676.94	0	12964
Inv Term	42,445	2.67	3.64	0	40
Year Last Inv	42,445	2001.34	2.07	1998	2005
IT Industry	42,445	0.69	0.46	0	1
Early Stage	42,445	0.19	0.40	0	1
S&P500 Return	42,445	0.02	0.17	−0.22	0.28
GDP Growth	42,445	3.01	1.30	0.76	4.49
# Deals	42,445	8.42	0.39	7.99	9.00
Bubble	42,445	0.35	0.48	0	1
Corporate VC	42,445	0.11	0.31	0	1

Panel B. Correlation

	1	2	3	4	5	6	7	8	9	10	11	12	13	14	15	16
Sales (1)	1															
Net Income (2)	0.77	1														
Total Assets (3)	0.84	0.81	1													
VC % Port (4)	0.07	0.01	0.08	1												
Avg VC Round Inv (5)	0.33	0.27	0.32	-0.15	1											
% PC Owned (6)	0.18	-0.02	0.15	0.01	0.01	1										
Distance (7)	0.15	0.09	0.13	0.01	0.18	0.00	1									
Term Avg (8)	0.17	0.11	0.10	0.02	-0.01	0.00	0.02	1								
Inv Term (9)	0.01	0.07	-0.02	-0.01	-0.03	-0.06	0.06	0.58	1							
Year Last Inv (10)	0.01	0.06	0.05	0.03	0.00	0.00	-0.03	0.19	0.11	1						
IT Industry (11)	-0.23	-0.18	-0.22	-0.02	-0.03	-0.04	-0.05	-0.19	-0.08	-0.08	1					
Early Stage (12)	-0.12	-0.11	-0.12	0.03	-0.17	0.01	-0.07	-0.02	-0.01	0.04	0.07	1				
S&P500 Return (13)	0.00	0.00	-0.04	-0.01	-0.03	0.00	0.01	0.14	0.14	-0.02	-0.13	0.00	1			
GDP Growth (14)	-0.06	-0.06	-0.11	-0.02	-0.03	0.01	0.00	0.01	0.02	-0.18	-0.04	0.01	0.58	1		
# Deals (15)	-0.05	-0.06	-0.05	-0.02	0.01	0.01	0.01	-0.27	-0.22	-0.66	0.15	-0.01	-0.34	0.22	1	
Bubble (16)	-0.07	-0.08	-0.08	-0.02	0.02	0.01	0.01	-0.23	-0.19	-0.58	0.13	-0.01	-0.09	0.52	0.89	1
Corporate VC (17)	-0.05	-0.04	-0.06	0.07	0.05	-0.02	0.10	-0.04	-0.01	-0.02	0.09	0.00	-0.04	-0.01	0.04	0.04

Exhibit 20.2 Entrepreneurial Firm Performance

The following regression is utilized in Exhibit 20.2: $Performance_{jt} = \alpha + \beta_0\ Control_{it} + \beta_1 PC_{jt} + \beta_2 VC_{it} + \beta_3 Y_t + \varepsilon$. Performance is the level of performance for the PC and is proxied by sales in Panel A, net income in Panel B, and total assets in Panel C. Control is the level of control exerted by the VC over the PC and is proxied by one of the following: Avg VC Round Inv is the natural log of the average amount of VC investment per round. % VC Portfolio is the total amount the VC firm invested in the PC divided by the total amount the VC invested in all PCs. % PC Owned is total amount the VC invested in PC divided by total amount invested in PC. Distance is the natural log of the number of kilometers between the VC and the PC. Term Avg is the natural log of the average length of time between VC round investment dates. PC is a vector of variables that describes the PC investment and includes Inv Term, IT Industry, and Early Stage. Inv Term is the difference between the year the PC received its first and last investments. IT Industry (Early Stage) is a dummy variable, which takes on a value of 1 if the PC is in the IT industry (Early Stage) and zero otherwise. VC is a vector of variables that describes the VC and includes Last Year Inv and Corporate VC. Last Year Inv is the amount ($Thous) the VC invested in the PC last year. Corporate VC is a corporate VC. VC is a corporate VC and zero otherwise. Y is a vector of market condition variables that includes S&P500 Return, GDP Growth, # Deals, and Bubble. S&P500 Return is the percentage return on the S&P500 at time t. GDP Growth is the percentage growth in gross domestic capital at time t. # Deals is the number of VC investments at time t. Bubble is a dummy variable that takes on a value of 1 if time t equals 1999 or 2000 and zero otherwise. Specifications 6 through 10 include squared terms of the control proxies to test for optimality. Robust standard errors (clustered around PC) appear in brackets. *, **, *** indicate significance levels of 10, 5, and 1 percent, respectively.

Panel A. Sales

	1	2	3	4	5	6	7	8	9	10
Avg VC Round Inv.	0.641*** [0.036]					-1.207*** [0.311]				
(Avg VC Round Inv)^2						0.111*** [0.018]				
% VC Portfolio		1.263*** [0.407]					6.013*** [1.096]			
(% VC Portfolio)^2							-6.008*** [1.331]			
% PC Owned			1.174*** [0.126]					0.865 [0.554]		
(% PC Owned)^2								0.288 [0.504]		
Distance				0.173*** [0.030]					0.510*** [0.163]	

	(1)	(2)	(3)	(4)	(5)	(6)	(7)	(8)	(9)	(10)
(Distance)²						−0.031**				−2.521***
						[0.015]				[0.499]
Term Avg					0.450***					
					[0.077]					
(Term Avg)²										0.246***
										[0.040]
Inv Term	0.032***	0.009	0.054***	0.005	0.009	0.033***	0.011	0.054***	0.005	−0.017
	[0.011]	[0.012]	[0.013]	[0.014]	[0.016]	[0.011]	[0.012]	[0.013]	[0.014]	[0.016]
IT Industry	−0.941***	−1.087***	−0.904***	−1.245***	−0.875***	−0.892***	−1.054***	−0.900***	−1.237***	−0.813***
	[0.081]	[0.089]	[0.091]	[0.122]	[0.103]	[0.080]	[0.089]	[0.091]	[0.122]	[0.102]
Early Stage	−0.473***	−1.016***	−1.151***	−0.725***	−0.693***	−0.570***	−1.045***	−1.153***	−0.734***	−0.678***
	[0.154]	[0.164]	[0.166]	[0.245]	[0.195]	[0.155]	[0.164]	[0.167]	[0.246]	[0.194]
Last Year Inv	−0.068***	−0.068**	−0.062**	−0.086**	−0.063*	−0.069***	−0.070**	−0.062**	−0.086**	−0.056*
	[0.026]	[0.029]	[0.029]	[0.039]	[0.033]	[0.026]	[0.029]	[0.029]	[0.039]	[0.033]
Corporate VC	−0.206	−0.192	0.029	−0.288	−0.176	−0.144	−0.19	0.023	−0.272	−0.163
	[0.133]	[0.137]	[0.136]	[0.278]	[0.145]	[0.131]	[0.136]	[0.136]	[0.277]	[0.143]
S&P500 Return	0.497	0.521	0.614	−0.404	0.074	0.511	0.533	0.616	−0.385	0.093
	[0.374]	[0.434]	[0.432]	[0.597]	[0.484]	[0.373]	[0.431]	[0.432]	[0.595]	[0.481]
GDP Growth	−0.073	−0.154**	−0.152**	−0.007	−0.054	−0.090*	−0.148**	−0.151**	−0.007	−0.055
	[0.054]	[0.062]	[0.061]	[0.085]	[0.068]	[0.054]	[0.061]	[0.061]	[0.085]	[0.067]
# Deals	0.313	0.094	0.007	0.388	0.661*	0.214	0.1	0.009	0.379	0.581
	[0.311]	[0.347]	[0.347]	[0.473]	[0.397]	[0.311]	[0.346]	[0.347]	[0.475]	[0.396]
Bubble	−0.337	−0.149	−0.048	−0.725**	−0.492*	−0.275	−0.172	−0.05	−0.724**	−0.478
	[0.232]	[0.257]	[0.255]	[0.340]	[0.294]	[0.230]	[0.257]	[0.255]	[0.341]	[0.292]
Constant	139.768***	147.613**	135.170***	179.527***	128.311*	150.510***	151.439**	134.156**	177.828**	125.172*
	[53.528]	[59.371]	[58.869]	[80.718]	[67.274]	[53.128]	[59.174]	[58.874]	[80.723]	[66.976]
Observations	3,917	3,449	3,447	1,828	2,658	3,917	3,449	3,447	1,828	2,658
R-squared	0.15	0.07	0.09	0.10	0.07	0.16	0.08	0.09	0.10	0.09

(Continued)

Exhibit 20.2 (Continued)

Panel B. Net Income

	1	2	3	4	5	6	7	8	9	10
Avg VC Round Inv.	0.420*** [0.042]					−0.862** [0.396]				
(Avg VC Round Inv)^2						0.076*** [0.023]				
% VC Portfolio		−0.119 [0.453]					3.277*** [1.166]			
(% VC Portfolio)^2							−4.519*** [1.451]			
% PC Owned			−0.244 [0.152]					−1.113* [0.667]		
(% PC Owned)^2								0.787 [0.592]		
Distance				0.075* [0.040]					−0.077 [0.214]	
(Distance)^2									0.014 [0.019]	
Term Avg					0.102 [0.089]					−0.183 [0.520]
(Term Avg)^2										0.024 [0.043]

	(1)	(2)	(3)	(4)	(5)	(6)	(7)	(8)	(9)	(10)
Inv Term	0.059***	0.045***	0.036**	0.048***	0.040**	0.056***	0.047***	0.034**	0.048***	0.036*
	[0.013]	[0.014]	[0.015]	[0.016]	[0.019]	[0.013]	[0.014]	[0.015]	[0.016]	[0.020]
IT Industry	-0.554***	-0.734***	-0.786***	-0.642***	-0.647***	-0.504***	-0.708***	-0.780***	-0.646***	-0.636***
	[0.098]	[0.106]	[0.111]	[0.154]	[0.126]	[0.098]	[0.107]	[0.111]	[0.155]	[0.127]
Early Stage	-0.618***	-0.897***	-0.871***	-1.147***	-0.768***	-0.671***	-0.939***	-0.866***	-1.146***	-0.766***
	[0.185]	[0.208]	[0.209]	[0.336]	[0.251]	[0.185]	[0.208]	[0.209]	[0.336]	[0.251]
Last Year Inv	0.042	0.068*	0.067*	0.083*	0.079*	0.043	0.066*	0.068*	0.084*	0.080*
	[0.032]	[0.035]	[0.035]	[0.050]	[0.042]	[0.032]	[0.035]	[0.035]	[0.050]	[0.042]
Corporate VC	-0.114	-0.162	-0.209	-0.705	-0.175	-0.084	-0.149	-0.225	-0.712	-0.174
	[0.178]	[0.189]	[0.191]	[0.490]	[0.209]	[0.179]	[0.187]	[0.192]	[0.488]	[0.209]
S&P500 Return	0.752*	0.599	0.579	1.541**	0.722	0.731*	0.556	0.586	1.557**	0.722
	[0.420]	[0.455]	[0.456]	[0.692]	[0.540]	[0.419]	[0.454]	[0.455]	[0.693]	[0.540]
GDP Growth	-0.081	-0.125*	-0.122*	-0.154	-0.121	-0.092	-0.116*	-0.124*	-0.154	-0.122
	[0.064]	[0.070]	[0.071]	[0.099]	[0.084]	[0.063]	[0.070]	[0.071]	[0.099]	[0.084]
# Deals	0.860**	0.179	0.194	1.530***	0.952**	0.785**	0.161	0.187	1.554***	0.959***
	[0.371]	[0.403]	[0.402]	[0.589]	[0.484]	[0.375]	[0.402]	[0.402]	[0.588]	[0.483]
Bubble	-0.559*	-0.014	-0.027	-0.556	-0.177	-0.512*	-0.027	-0.014	-0.566	-0.187
	[0.299]	[0.326]	[0.325]	[0.446]	[0.414]	[0.299]	[0.325]	[0.326]	[0.445]	[0.413]
Constant	-85.499	-128.193*	-126.166*	-170.079*	-156.362*	-81.934	-124.462*	-126.733*	-170.969*	-157.279*
	[64.851]	[72.216]	[72.243]	[102.774]	[84.945]	[64.718]	[72.014]	[72.283]	[102.762]	[84.990]
Observations	1,972	1,694	1,693	805	1,172	1,972	1,694	1,693	805	1,172
R-squared	0.11	0.06	0.06	0.07	0.06	0.12	0.06	0.06	0.07	0.06

(Continued)

449

Exhibit 20.2 *(Continued)*

Panel C. Total Assets

	1	2	3	4	5	6	7	8	9	10
Avg VC Round Inv.	0.510*** [0.039]					-1.431*** [0.323]				
(Avg VC Round Inv)²						0.115*** [0.019]				
% VC Portfolio		0.956** [0.438]					4.882*** [1.244]			
(% VC Portfolio)²							-4.822*** [1.462]			
% PC Owned			0.632*** [0.133]					-0.848 [0.584]		
(% PC Owned)²								1.386** [0.541]		
Distance				0.127*** [0.031]					0.516*** [0.148]	
(Distance)²									-0.036*** [0.014]	
Term Avg					0.169** [0.080]					-2.013*** [0.514]
(Term Avg)²										0.182*** [0.041]

450

	(1)	(2)	(3)	(4)	(5)	(6)	(7)	(8)	(9)	(10)
Inv Term	0.013	−0.007	0.015	−0.013	0.001	0.009	−0.006	0.012	−0.014	−0.018
	[0.011]	[0.013]	[0.014]	[0.015]	[0.018]	[0.011]	[0.013]	[0.014]	[0.015]	[0.019]
IT Industry	−0.682***	−0.840***	−0.753***	−0.838***	−0.695***	−0.638***	−0.811***	−0.737***	−0.838***	−0.642***
	[0.084]	[0.092]	[0.095]	[0.124]	[0.108]	[0.084]	[0.092]	[0.095]	[0.124]	[0.107]
Early Stage	−0.516***	−0.831***	−0.884***	−0.833***	−0.661***	−0.568***	−0.845***	−0.881***	−0.840***	−0.649***
	[0.162]	[0.176]	[0.175]	[0.240]	[0.205]	[0.161]	[0.176]	[0.175]	[0.240]	[0.205]
Last Year Inv	0.02	0.026	0.034	0.037	0.043	0.019	0.024	0.037	0.037	0.048
	[0.027]	[0.030]	[0.030]	[0.041]	[0.034]	[0.027]	[0.030]	[0.030]	[0.041]	[0.034]
Corporate VC	−0.133	−0.159	−0.064	−0.326	−0.103	−0.069	−0.155	−0.084	−0.304	−0.08
	[0.129]	[0.131]	[0.132]	[0.272]	[0.140]	[0.127]	[0.130]	[0.133]	[0.271]	[0.140]
S&P500 Return	1.062***	1.078**	1.171***	0.909	1.056**	1.017***	1.065**	1.192***	0.932	1.026**
	[0.378]	[0.444]	[0.444]	[0.589]	[0.513]	[0.376]	[0.441]	[0.443]	[0.587]	[0.509]
GDP Growth	−0.181***	−0.220***	−0.222***	−0.13	−0.181**	−0.188***	−0.210***	−0.223***	−0.129	−0.178**
	[0.057]	[0.065]	[0.064]	[0.087]	[0.072]	[0.056]	[0.065]	[0.064]	[0.087]	[0.071]
# Deals	0.719**	0.59	0.527	1.384***	1.207***	0.643**	0.605*	0.546	1.369***	1.144***
	[0.326]	[0.361]	[0.362]	[0.495]	[0.424]	[0.325]	[0.361]	[0.363]	[0.496]	[0.423]
Bubble	−0.367	−0.246	−0.159	−0.894**	−0.543*	−0.324	−0.284	−0.173	−0.882**	−0.539*
	[0.245]	[0.268]	[0.267]	[0.349]	[0.306]	[0.241]	[0.266]	[0.267]	[0.348]	[0.304]
Constant	−38.096	−44.61	−60.875	−74.617	−85.194	−27.859	−39.87	−66.85	−75.484	−87.125
	[54.808]	[61.579]	[61.427]	[84.934]	[69.137]	[54.440]	[61.318]	[61.498]	[84.918]	[68.927]
Observations	2,469	2,186	2,184	1,222	1,657	2,469	2,186	2,184	1,222	1,657
R-squared	0.14	0.07	0.08	0.09	0.06	0.16	0.08	0.08	0.09	0.08

impact of the percentage of the PC owned (specification [3]) is a 2.235 percent increase in sales for a 1 percent increase in owned percent of the PC. The marginal impact of the distance between the VC and the PC (specification [4]) is a 0.189 percent for a 1 km increase in distance. The financing term average (specification [5]) is associated with a 0.568 percent in sales for a 1-day increase in the length of time between investment rounds. These results suggest that the percentage of the VC portfolio and the PC owned are the most influential proxies of control.

On further inspection, however, we see that this relationship is not linear. Adding a squared control term to the regressions shows that several of these control proxies have a nonlinear relationship with sales suggesting that there exists a maximum (i.e., where control>0 and control^2<0) or minimum (i.e., where control<0 and control^2>0) level of control. Indeed, specifications (6) to (10) suggest that Avg VC Round Inv and Term Avg have a convex relationship with sales and that % VC Portfolio and Distance have a concave relationship with sales. A convex relationship tells us that these proxies can either be small or large to maximize their impacts on sales levels. A concave relationship tells us that there exists a local optimal level for these proxies that maximizes.

Looking to Panel B, there is less evidence of the positive significant impact on net income. This is evidenced in fewer statistically significant marginal effects in specifications (1) to (5). In fact only Avg VC Round Inv continues to be statistically significant at 1 percent. Distance also retains significance, albeit at 10 percent. In looking at the nonlinear models we see that both the Avg VC Round Inv and % VC Portfolio proxies maintain their nonlinear convex and concave relationships, respectively. The economic impact of the marginal effects is also reduced in the net income regressions. Clearly, PC performance as measured by net income is not as heavily influenced by VC control as when measured by sales.

When measuring PC performance using total assets (Panel C), results are similar to those of sales in Panel A. Once again, the linear models in specifications (1) to —(5) show statistical significance of at least 5 percent for all VC control proxies. Results for the nonlinear models in specifications (5) to (10) show once again Avg VC Round Inv and Term Avg have a convex relationship and that % VC Portfolio and Distance have a concave relationship, this time with total assets.

VC Control Terciles

When looking at the results in Exhibit 20.2, it becomes evident that whether VC Control is beneficial for firm performance is dependent on the level of control. In order to take a closer look at the levels of VC Control for each proxy, the analysis shown in Exhibit 20.3 divides each control proxy into three distinct groups (i.e., terciles). The laissez-faire management group consists of those observations with a level of control for the individual proxies that belong in the bottom quartile (i.e., less than 25th percentile). The average management group consists of the middle two quartiles (i.e., greater than 25th percentile but less than 75th percentile). The co-management group consists of the top quartile (i.e., greater than 75th percentile).

The first observation from these results is that it is obvious that the impact on PC performance is not linear. If it were, we would see much more conformance across the levels of management. The second observation is that for every proxy save one (Term Avg), the optimal level of control is the average management. In other

Exhibit 20.3   Terciles of Control

The following regression is utilized Exhibit 20.3: $Performance_{it} = \alpha + \beta_0\,Control_{it} + \beta_1 PC_{it} + \beta_2 VC_{jt} + \beta_3 Y_t + \varepsilon$. Performance is the level of performance for the PC and is proxied by sales in Panel A, net income in Panel B, and total assets in Panel C. Control is the level of control exerted by the VC over the PC and is proxied by one of the following: Avg VC Round Inv is the natural log of the average amount of VC investment per round. % VC Portfolio is the total amount the VC firm invested in the PC divided by the total amount the VC invested in all PCs. % PC Owned is total amount the VC invested in PC divided by total amount invested in PC. Distance is the natural log of the number of kilometers between the VC and the PC. Term Avg is the natural log of the average length of time between VC round investment dates. PC, VC, and market condition controls are left out for brevity. Robust standard errors (clustered around PC) appear in brackets. *, **, *** indicate significance levels of 10, 5, and 1 percent, respectively.

	Relationship with Sales	Laissez Faire Management	Average Management	Co-Management
Avg VC Round Inv	Convex	−0.164	1.193***	0.799***
		[0.173]	[0.217]	[0.074]
Observations		704	1,603	1,610
R-squared		0.10	0.05	0.18
% VC Portfolio	Concave	0.214	1.125***	0.986***
		[0.386]	[0.160]	[0.280]
Observations		656	2,052	739
R-squared		0.03	0.09	0.13
% PC Owned	Insignif.	−0.177	1.233	1.023**
		[1.096]	[0.800]	[0.488]
Observations		694	1,339	1,414
R-squared		0.03	0.04	0.12
Distance	Concave	0.291**	0.405***	−3.021***
		[0.139]	[0.081]	[0.777]
Observations		364	996	468
R-squared		0.08	0.11	0.13
Term Avg	Convex	−0.450*	−0.358	0.911***
		[0.262]	[0.401]	[0.160]
Observations		662	1,085	911
R-squared		0.11	0.05	0.11

words, the marginal effect is most significantly positive in the middle management group. This suggests not only the nonlinear relationship of VC Control with PC performance, but also that extremes, whether they be too little or too much can be stifling to PC performance. Exhibit 20.4 demonstrates nicely the fitted values of PC sales performance with the nonlinear term included.

Entrepreneurial Firm Outcome

Results regarding the impact of VC control on PC outcome are slightly more mixed. In other words, the importance of VC control seems to depend more on the proxy, suggesting that the means of exerting control over the PC is important. Panel A of Exhibit 20.5 shows the base specification and Panel B, the specifications including the nonlinear (i.e., squared) term.

Avg VC Round Investment

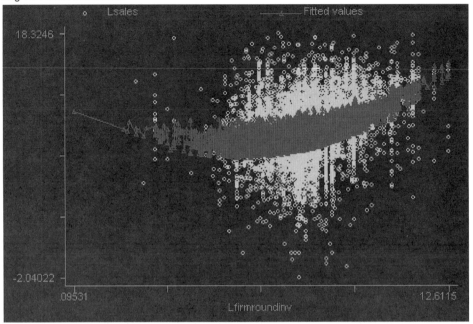

% VC Portfolio

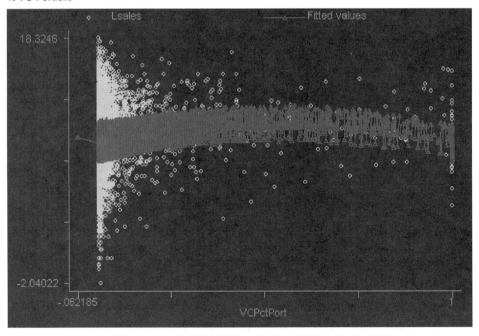

Exhibit 20.4   Nonlinear Relationships of Control with PC Performance

Distance

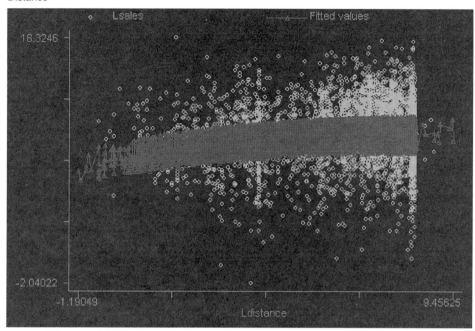

Investment Term

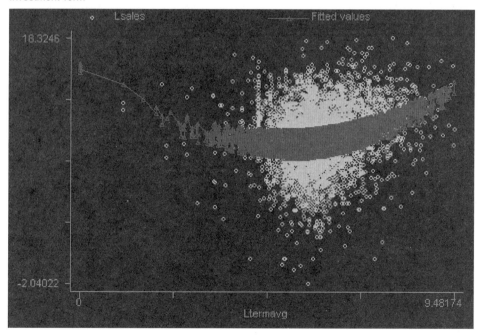

Exhibit 20.4 (*Continued*)

Exhibit 20.5　Entrepreneurial Firm Outcome

The following regression is utilized Exhibit 20.5: $Pr(CurrentStatus_j) = \Psi(\alpha + \gamma_0\, Control_{it} + \gamma_1 PC_{jt} + \gamma_2 VC_{it} + \gamma_3 Y_t + \varepsilon)$ where CurrentStatus is the current standing of the entrepreneurial (PC) company (i.e., defunct, private, public, or subsidiary). Ψ is the cumulative logistic probability distribution function. Control is the level of control exerted by the VC over the PC and is proxied by one of the following: Avg VC Round Inv is the natural log of the average amount of VC investment per round. % VC Portfolio is the total amount the VC firm invested in the PC divided by the total amount the VC invested in all PCs. % PC Owned is total amount the VC invested in PC divided by total amount invested in PC. Distance is the natural log of the number of kilometers between the VC and the PC. Term Avg is the natural log of the average length of time between VC round investment dates. PC is a vector of variables that describes the PC investment and includes Inv Term, IT Industry, and Early Stage. Inv Term is the difference between the year the PC received its first and last investments. IT Industry (Early Stage) is a dummy variable, which takes on a value of 1 if the PC is in the IT industry (Early Stage) and zero otherwise. VC is a vector of variables that describes the VC and includes Last Year Inv and Corporate VC. Last Year Inv is the amount ($Thous) the VC invested in the PC last year. Corporate VC is a dummy variable, which takes on a value of 1 if the VC is a corporate VC and zero otherwise. Y is a vector of market condition variables that includes S&P500 Return, GDP Growth, # Deals, and Bubble. S&P500 Return is the percentage return on the S&P500 at time t. GDP Growth is the percentage growth in gross domestic capital at time t. # Deals is the number of VC investments at time t. Bubble is a dummy variable that takes on a value of one if time t equals 1999 or 2000 and zero otherwise. Robust standard errors (clustered around PC) appear in brackets. *, **, *** indicate significance levels of 10, 5, and 1 percent, respectively.

Panel A. Base Specification

	Avg VC Round Investment	% PC Owned	% VC Portfolio	Distance	Term Avg
PC Current Status = Defunct					
Control	−0.001**	−0.040	−0.051***	−0.002	−0.045***
	[0.000]	[0.030]	[0.018]	[0.002]	[0.008]
PC Current Status = Private					
Control	−0.054***	0.016	0.043*	−0.005**	0.024***
	[0.003]	[0.014]	[0.023]	[0.002]	[0.009]
PC Current Status = Subsidiary					
Control	0.034***	0.018*	−0.045*	0.000	0.013
	[0.003]	[0.011]	[0.024]	[0.002]	[0.011]
PC Current Status = Public					
Control	0.020***	0.006	0.052***	0.007***	0.008
	[0.003]	[0.005]	[0.012]	[0.001]	[0.008]
Observations	42,445	38,179	38,187	18,388	39,840
Pseudo R^2	0.108	0.106	0.106	0.120	0.111

Panel B. With Squared Term

	Avg VC Round Investment	% PC Owned	% VC Portfolio	Distance	Term Avg
PC Current Status = Defunct					
Control	0.142***	−0.039	−0.105**	−0.011	0.042
	[0.030]	[0.025]	[0.050]	[0.008]	[0.042]
Control^2	−0.009***	0.000	0.069	0.001	−0.008**
	[0.002]	[0.000]	[0.055]	[0.001]	[0.004]

Exhibit 20.5 *(Continued)*

PC Current Status = Private					
Control	−0.173***	0.130***	0.001	−0.009	−0.136***
	[0.026]	[0.034]	[0.064]	[0.010]	[0.051]
Control²	0.008***	−0.001***	0.051	0.000	0.014***
	[0.002]	[0.000]	[0.074]	[0.001]	[0.004]
PC Current Status = Subsidiary					
Control	0.129***	−0.128***	−0.047	0.012	0.077
	[0.032]	[0.019]	[0.065]	[0.011]	[0.066]
Control²	−0.006***	0.001***	0.002	−0.001	−0.005
	[0.002]	[0.000]	[0.074]	[0.001]	[0.006]
PC Current Status = Public					
Control	−0.098***	0.038***	0.151***	0.009	0.017
	[0.014]	[0.006]	[0.033]	[0.007]	[0.054]
Control²	0.007***	−0.000***	−0.122***	0.000	−0.001
	[0.001]	[0.000]	[0.037]	[0.001]	[0.004]
Observations	42,445	38,179	38,187	18,388	39,840
Pseudo R²	0.110	0.110	0.106	0.120	0.111

Overall, the results suggest that all proxies of VC control thwart PC failure (i.e., PC Current Status = Defunct) as evidenced by the negative sign on all coefficients. That said, only three of the five show statistical significance. This would suggest that Avg VC Round Investment, % VC Portfolio, and Term Avg effectively reduce the probability that the PC will go defunct. Judging by the marginal impact, % VC Portfolio and Term Avg seem to be the most effective, a 1 percent increase in these proxies are associated with a 5.1 percent decrease and a 4.5 percent decrease in the probability of the PC going defunct, respectively.

Results for private firms are mixed. Both Avg VC Round Investment and Distance are associated with a reduction in the probability of the PC remaining private. % VC Portfolio and Term Avg, however, are associated with an increase in the probability of the PC remaining private. The former may be due to younger, less affiliated VCs that do not have the connections to quickly exit their investments. The latter may be better explained in the nonlinear model.

In general, results for PC exit (i.e., PC Current Status = Subsidiary or Public) suggest that VC Control increases the probability of exit at a statistically significant level. Only one exception to this applies—the impact of % VC Portfolio on PC exiting via M&A (i.e., Current Status = subsidiary). The impact here is a 4.5 percent reduction in the probability. That said, there is a corresponding increase in the probability of a PC exiting via IPO (i.e., PC Current Status = Public) of 5.2 percent for this VC control proxy.

The results from models with the squared control variable give us a closer look at the potentially nonlinear relationship between the VC Control proxies and PC Outcome. Results suggest that Avg VC Round Investment has a concave relationship with the probability that the PC will go defunct or with exit via M&A (PC Current Status = subsidiary) and a convex relationship with the probability that the PC will remain private or go public via IPO. This proxy remains pivotal to the PC as is evidenced by statistically significant marginal effects across the board. Although the existence of a concave relationship for both PC failure and exit via M&A may seem contradictory, resolution is found in examining the marginal effects themselves. Marginal effects on both the linear and the quadratic terms are different across the two allowing for local maximums, which can lead to a unique level/optimum. One can also surmise that VCs that invest more generally exit via M&A (versus IPO) and that the investment is either going to make it or fail.

% PC Owned also remains an important proxy. Only results for the PC going defunct lack significance. This is reassuring as it suggests that this form of VC Control does not substantially risk the viability of the PC. There exist concave relationships between the percent of the PC the VC owns and the PC remaining private and going public via IPO. A convex relationship exists between this proxy and the probability that a PC exits via M&A. Once again, differences in the marginal effects allow for local optimums.

The last three proxies, that is, % VC Portfolio, Distance, and Term Avg, matter less to PC outcome, as evidenced by a general lack in statistical significance in the coefficients. There are two exceptions. There exists a concave relationship between % VC Portfolio and the probability that PCs will go public via IPO. This can be seen as a good thing in that this proxy does not have an optimal level that impacts any of the other PC outcomes. Lastly, there exists a convex relationship between Term Avg and PCs remaining private. This suggests that VCs can minimize the probability that a PC remains private, which is actually beneficial since the payoff only occurs upon PC exit.

ROBUSTNESS

To ensure that results shown up to these point are not spurious, robustness tests are provided. These tests include alterations in test methodology (i.e., Heckman model) and the examination of differences across industries and VCs.

Nonrandomness of Exit

Since the choice of exit can cause a sample selectivity issue in the empirical analysis (see, e.g., Cumming 2006; Cochrane 2005), I use a two-step Heckman model (Heckman 1979) to ensure the integrity of the results. Specifically, I perform the following regression:

$$Pr(IPO_j | Exit) = \Psi(\lambda_0 \, Control_{it} + \lambda_2 PC_{jt} + \lambda_3 VC_{it} + \lambda_4 Y_t) \qquad (20.4)$$

Following the work of Cumming (2006) and Knill (2009), I include only Bubble year dummies in the first step of the regression (i.e., the choice of exiting versus not exiting) to avoid any multicollinearity in the specifications. Signs and significance are largely upheld once the nonrandomness of the decision to exit is considered, which serve to confirm those results found in Exhibit 20.5. Minor differences are found in the average round of investment where the level of significance drops from 1 percent to 5 percent and with % VC Port, where the magnitude of the marginal effect is cut in half.

Care must be taken, however, to realize that the interpretation here is slightly different. In Exhibit 20.5, the part of the exhibit displaying results for PC Current Status = Public (i.e., IPO) is referring to a limited dependent variable that indicates whether a PC has exited via IPO or not. A PC remaining private, failing, or a PC exiting via M&A are the same thing for this variable (dependent variable = 0). In the *Heckman Selection model*, however, the second-stage limited dependent variable describes whether the PC exits via IPO (dependent variable = 1) or M&A (dependent variable = 0). That said, the results imply that exerting control, specifically in the form of average VC round investment, % VC Portfolio, or Distance, is beneficial to the likelihood of the PC exiting via IPO. This is an important point given the literature's opinion that M&A is inferior to IPO as a form of exit (Schwienbacher 2002; Fleming 2004; Cumming and MacIntosh 2003a, 2003b). Results may be found in Exhibit 20.6.

Differences across Industries

To address the fact that results may be led by an investment in a particular industry, I reexamine the base analysis on different industries, namely three main industries important in venture capital: (1) information technology, (2) medical/health/life science, and (3) non–high technology. Results (found in Exhibit 20.7) reveal differences across industries when compared to the results found in Exhibit 20.2, Panel A. Results for information technology, a popular industry for venture capital investment during the term examined, are qualitatively identical. Signs and statistical significance are maintained. Even the magnitude of the marginal effects for the most part is maintained.

Differences in results for the medical/health/life sciences industry are mostly seen in a reduction in the statistical significance. Most of the drop in significance is seen once the nonlinear term is added. That said, the magnitude of the marginal effect in this industry in many cases exceeds those in the information technology subsample. Results for this industry may suggest that there does not always exist a clear optimum in the level of control in this industry, but when it does (i.e., with certain proxies) it is more meaningful.

Last, differences from previous results seen in the non–high technology subsample are seen throughout. There does not exist compelling evidence in this industry that an optimal level of control exists. A lack of statistical significance (save Avg VC Round Investment in the linear analysis and % VC Port in the nonlinear analysis) supports this contention.

Comprehensively, industry-specific analysis suggests that results are driven by the information technology industry (and to a lesser extent the medical/health/life science industry).

Differences across VCs

Venture capitalists differ on many dimensions beyond the management style that they practice. It is possible that results are driven by a certain type of VC or a

Exhibit 20.6 Nonrandomness of Decision to Exit

The Heckman Selection Model is used in Exhibit 20.5: $Pr(IPO_j|Exit) = \alpha + \beta_0 Control_{it} + \beta_1 PC_{jt} + \beta_2 VC_{it} + \beta_3 Y_t$, where the first stage regression is $Pr(Exit_j) = \delta_0 + \delta_1 T_j + \varepsilon$. Control is the level of control exerted by the VC over the PC and is proxied by one of the following: Avg VC Round Inv is the natural log of the average amount of VC investment per round. % VC Portfolio is the total amount the VC firm invested in the PC divided by the total amount the VC invested in all PCs. % PC Owned is total amount the VC invested in PC divided by total amount invested in PC. Distance is the natural log of the number of kilometers between the VC and the PC. Term Avg is the natural log of the average length of time between VC round investment dates. PC is a vector of variables that describes the PC investment and includes Inv Term, IT Industry, and Early Stage. Inv Term is the difference between the year the PC received its first and last investments. IT Industry (Early Stage) is a dummy variable, which takes on a value of 1 if the PC is in the IT industry (Early Stage) and zero otherwise. VC is a vector of variables that describes the VC and includes Last Year Inv and Corporate VC. Last Year Inv is the amount ($Thous) the VC invested in the PC last year. Corporate VC is a dummy variable, which takes on a value of 1 if the VC is a corporate VC and zero, otherwise. Y is a vector of market condition variables that includes S&P500 Return, GDP Growth, # Deals, and Bubble. S&P500 Return is the percentage return on the S&P500 at time t. GDP Growth is the percentage growth in gross domestic capital at time t. # Deals is the number of VC investments at time t. Bubble is a dummy variable that takes on a value of one if time t equals 1999 or 2000 and zero otherwise. Robust standard errors (clustered around PC) appear in brackets. *, **, *** indicate significance levels of 10, 5, and 1 percent, respectively.

Dependent Variable: Pr(Exit) in (2); Pr(IPO|Exit) in (1)

	Avg VC Round Investment		% VC Portfolio		% PC Owned		Distance		Term Avg	
	(1)	(2)	(1)	(2)	(1)	(2)	(1)	(2)	(1)	(2)
Inv Term	0.02***		0.02***		0.02***		0.03***		0.03***	
	[0.00]		[0.00]		[0.00]		[0.00]		[0.00]	
Year Last Inv	0.14***		0.12***		0.12***		0.14***		0.12***	
	[0.01]		[0.01]		[0.01]		[0.01]		[0.01]	
IT Industry	−0.31***		−0.32***		−0.32***		−0.28***		−0.24***	
	[0.03]		[0.03]		[0.03]		[0.03]		[0.03]	

Early Stage	-0.08*** [0.02]	-0.09*** [0.02]	-0.09*** [0.02]	-0.11*** [0.02]	-0.08*** [0.01]
S&P500 Return	0.00 [0.09]	-0.02 [0.09]	-0.02 [0.09]	-0.09 [0.10]	-0.03 [0.09]
GDP Growth	-0.09*** [0.01]	-0.10*** [0.02]	-0.10*** [0.02]	-0.14*** [0.02]	-0.08*** [0.02]
# Deals	-0.01 [0.09]	-0.04 [0.09]	-0.04 [0.09]	-0.09 [0.10]	0.09 [0.09]
Bubble	0.05 [0.09]	0.03 [0.08]	0.04 [0.09]	0.18* [0.09]	-0.02 [0.09]
Corporate VC	0.01 [0.02]	0.01 [0.02]	0.02 [0.02]	-0.04* [0.02]	0.01 [0.02]
Control	0.02* [0.01]	0.21*** [0.04]	0.00 [0.00]	0.01*** [0.00]	0.02 [0.02]
Invest in 1998	1.36*** [0.05]	1.32*** [0.05]	1.32*** [0.05]	1.48*** [0.05]	1.25*** [0.05]
Invest in 1999	1.22*** [0.04]	1.22*** [0.04]	1.22*** [0.04]	1.23*** [0.05]	1.13*** [0.05]
Invest in 2000	0.59*** [0.03]	0.62*** [0.03]	0.62*** [0.03]	0.59*** [0.03]	0.47*** [0.03]
	-0.83*** [0.01]	-0.88*** [0.01]	-0.88*** [0.01]	-1.27*** [0.02]	-0.77*** [0.02]
Constant	-270.48*** [18.82]	-246.01*** [18.96]	-245.41*** [19.27]	-284.14*** [21.52]	-230.42*** [20.55]
Model Chi^2	995.34***	917.80***	901.90***	888.30***	550.17***

Exhibit 20.7   Differences across Industries

The following regression is utilized in Exhibit 20.6: $Performance_{jt} = \alpha + \beta_0\,Control_{it} + \beta_1 PC_{jt} + \beta_2 VC_{it} + \beta_3 Y_t + \varepsilon$. Performance is the level of performance for the PC and is proxied by sales. Control is the level of control exerted by the VC over the PC and is proxied by one of the following: Avg VC Round Inv is the natural log of the average amount of VC investment per round. % VC Portfolio is the total amount the VC firm invested in the PC divided by the total amount the VC invested in all PCs. % PC Owned is total amount the VC invested in PC divided by total amount invested in PC. Distance is the natural log of the number of kilometers between the VC and the PC. Term Avg is the natural log of the average length of time between VC round investment dates. Industry subsamples include (1) information technology, (2) medical/health/life science, and (3) non–high technology. PC, VC, and market condition controls are left out for brevity. Robust standard errors (clustered around PC) appear in brackets. *, **, *** indicate significance levels of 10, 5, and 1 percent, respectively.

	Avg VC Round Investment	% VC Portfolio	% PC Owned	Distance	Term Avg	Avg VC Round Investment	% VC Portfolio	% PC Owned	Distance	Term Avg
Information Technology										
Control	0.617***	2.194***	0.997***	0.145***	0.472***	-1.163***	5.747***	-0.226	0.711***	-2.602***
	[0.054]	[0.751]	[0.175]	[0.039]	[0.109]	[0.429]	[1.725]	[0.721]	[0.227]	[0.833]
Control²						0.110***	-4.762**	1.175*	-0.052**	0.259***
						[0.026]	[2.285]	[0.677]	[0.021]	[0.068]
Medical/Health/Life Science										
Control	0.683***	1.632*	1.541***	0.181***	0.338*	-3.285***	6.870**	1.787	0.526*	-4.487***
	[0.100]	[0.897]	[0.333]	[0.062]	[0.175]	[0.977]	[2.939]	[1.297]	[0.317]	[1.332]
Control²						0.241***	-6.507*	-0.241	-0.033	0.375***
						[0.058]	[3.464]	[1.244]	[0.030]	[0.104]
Non–High Technology										
Control	0.513***	-0.186	0.056	0.096*	0.220*	-0.433	3.221**	0.438	0.072	-0.646
	[0.053]	[0.524]	[0.211]	[0.053]	[0.126]	[0.537]	[1.533]	[1.052]	[0.244]	[0.632]
Control²						0.055*	-4.159**	-0.336	0.002	0.073
						[0.030]	[1.791]	[0.916]	[0.023]	[0.053]

462

certain investment style of a VC. As such it is worth examining differences across VCs. To that end, I examine three factors of VCs dividing them into subsamples based on their annual median levels.

Based on the work of Knill (2009), the diversification of the VC can influence the performance of the PC. As such, it may be prudent to examine different levels of diversification taken by the VCs in the sample. Since diversification can be proxied on a number of different dimensions that would arguably complicate this robustness beyond the scope of the paper (i.e., domestic and international geography, industry, stage, and number of portfolio companies), I choose one of the most relevant from the aforementioned paper—stage diversification.

To control for the fact that not all of the venture capitalist in the sample are limited partnerships and that fund size may be fixed across the sample period, I examine base specifications across different sizes of the fund.[7]

Some VCs are just more knowledgeable than others due to experience and their gained skill set, leading to implications for PC performance.[8] To examine whether the level of expertise drives original results, I test the base specifications (with and without the nonlinear term) on two subsamples of VC expertise. The number of funds a VC has successfully raised derives this proxy. This proxy implicitly assumes retention of VC management. This assumption should not be problematic as long as venture capital firms are able to hire similarly talented executives to lead their firms.

The specifications in Exhibit 20.2, Panel A are performed once again on the subsamples described before. Exhibit 20.8 displays these results, Panel A without the nonlinear term and Panel B with the nonlinear term. The results in Panel A indicate no clear pattern in any of the VC characteristics. This implies that these VC characteristics do not alter systematically the impact of VC control on PC performance. Statistical significance in several of the marginal effects are diminished (especially in the case of VC fund size), but this is probably due to the loss of sample size based on the division of the sample and/or missing data.

The specifications with the nonlinear term (Panel B) overall confirm those in Panel A with one exception. When control is proxied by % VC Portfolio - VC Fund Size and VC Expertise seem to matter. The marginal effects of control and control^2 (−0.832 and 2.476, respectively) on performance are statistically insignificant for small funds. For large funds, however, these marginal effects are 5.309 and −5.645, both of them statistically significant (at 1 percent and 10 percent, respectively). The jump in both the economic and statistical significance from small to large funds is quite large. This suggests that for large funds, increasing the level of control, defined here by the % of the VC Portfolio comprised by the PC, is influential with regard to PC sales performance.

This is also the case, although only with regard to magnitude (i.e., economic significance) for VC expertise. The marginal effect of control and control^2 (as proxied by % of the VC Portfolio comprised by the PC) on PC sales performance more than doubles for more experienced VCs (from 5.230 to 11.594 for control and from −4.606 to −12.983 for control^2). This suggests that more experienced VCs can level more control more effectively. This may be due to the certification that they offer the PCs (Megginson and Weiss 1991; Hsu 2001) or their enhanced ability to successfully exit the PC.[9]

Exhibit 20.8   Differences across VCs

The following regression is utilized in Exhibit 20.8: $Performance_{jt} = \alpha + \beta_0\,Control_{it} + \beta_1 PC_{jt} + \beta_2 VC_{it} + \beta_3 Y_t + \varepsilon$. Performance is the level of performance for the PC and is proxied by sales. Control is the level of control exerted by the VC over the PC and is proxied by one of the following: Avg VC Round Inv is the natural log of the average amount of VC investment per round. % VC Portfolio is the total amount the VC firm invested in the PC divided by the total amount the VC invested in all PCs. % PC Owned is total amount the VC invested in PC divided by total amount invested in PC. Distance is the natural log of the number of kilometers between the VC and the PC. Term Avg is the natural log of the average length of time between VC round investment dates. VC difference sub samples include VC Diversification, which is based on the number of stages the VC invests in, VC fund size, and VC expertise, which is based on the number of funds the VC has successfully closed. PC, VC, and market condition controls are left out for brevity. Robust standard errors (clustered around PC) appear in brackets. *, **, *** indicate significance levels of 10, 5, and 1 percent, respectively.

Panel A. Base Specification

	Avg VC Round Investment	% VC Portfolio	% PC Owned	Distance	Term Avg	Avg VC Round Investment	% VC Portfolio	% PC Owned	Distance	Term Avg
			VC Diversification							
		Less Diversification						More Diversification		
Control	0.594*** [0.043]	0.687 [0.512]	0.898*** [0.169]	0.202*** [0.042]	0.490*** [0.102]	0.570*** [0.061]	1.398** [0.651]	1.196*** [0.184]	0.128*** [0.041]	0.356*** [0.112]
			VC Fund Size							
		Small						Large		
Control	0.327*** [0.095]	1.052 [0.830]	0.371 [0.351]	0.161** [0.077]	0.476** [0.187]	0.384*** [0.067]	1.389 [0.852]	0.049 [0.300]	0.119* [0.066]	0.476*** [0.152]
			VC Expertise							
		Less Experienced						More Experienced		
Control	0.596*** [0.054]	1.991*** [0.557]	1.097*** [0.187]	0.166*** [0.043]	0.480*** [0.109]	0.683*** [0.051]	1.944 [1.314]	1.144*** [0.193]	0.187*** [0.044]	0.413*** [0.114]

Panel B. With Squared Term

VC Diversification

	Avg VC Round Investment	% VC Portfolio	% PC Owned	Distance	Term Avg
	Less Diversification				
Control	-0.633* [0.351]	5.219*** [1.310]	1.19 [0.805]	0.521** [0.215]	-1.606*** [0.574]
Control²	0.072*** [0.020]	-5.870*** [1.603]	-0.27 [0.725]	-0.03 [0.020]	0.173*** [0.046]
	More Diversification				
Control	-1.621*** [0.538]	4.409** [1.891]	0.947 [0.748]	0.487** [0.233]	-3.319*** [0.822]
Control²	0.136*** [0.033]	-3.696 [2.259]	0.235 [0.694]	-0.033 [0.021]	0.306*** [0.067]

VC Fund Size

	Avg VC Round Investment	% VC Portfolio	% PC Owned	Distance	Term Avg
	Small				
Control	-1.284** [0.599]	-0.832 [2.294]	1.65 [1.631]	0.561 [0.409]	-0.672 [1.458]
Control²	0.107*** [0.038]	2.476 [2.720]	-1.146 [1.406]	-0.037 [0.039]	0.092 [0.112]
	Large				
Control	-1.295* [0.705]	5.309*** [1.865]	1.783 [1.548]	0.149 [0.362]	-1.695*** [0.636]
Control²	0.097** [0.040]	-5.645* [2.894]	-1.517 [1.313]	-0.003 [0.033]	0.191*** [0.054]

VC Expertise

	Avg VC Round Investment	% VC Portfolio	% PC Owned	Distance	Term Avg
	Less Experienced				
Control	-1.356*** [0.413]	5.230*** [1.462]	0.12 [0.789]	0.470** [0.233]	-2.191*** [0.531]
Control²	0.122*** [0.026]	-4.606** [1.963]	0.935 [0.738]	-0.028 [0.021]	0.222*** [0.043]
	More Experienced				
Control	-1.362*** [0.519]	11.594*** [2.107]	1.192 [0.858]	0.599** [0.238]	-4.506*** [0.858]
Control²	0.118*** [0.029]	-12.983*** [3.240]	-0.045 [0.772]	-0.038* [0.022]	0.405*** [0.070]

(Continued)

Exhibit 20.8 *(Continued)*

Variable	Definition	Source
	PC Performance Proxies	
Sales	The natural log of entrepreneurial company sales at time t.	SDC Platinum
Net Income	The natural log of entrepreneurial company net income at time t.	SDC Platinum
Total Assets	The natural log of entrepreneurial company total assets at time t.	SDC Platinum
	VC Control Proxies	
VC % Port	The total amount the VC firm invested in the PC divided by the total amount the VC invested in all PCs.	SDC Platinum
Avg VC Round Inv	The natural log of the average amount of VC investment per round.	SDC Platinum
% PC Owned	The total amount the VC invested in PC divided by total amount invested in PC.	SDC Platinum
Distance	The natural log of the number of kilometers between the VC and the PC.	SDC Platinum
Term Avg	The natural log of the average length of time between VC round investment dates.	SDC Platinum
	PC Investment Specifics	
Invest Term	The year VC last invested in PC minus year VC first invested in PC.	SDC Platinum
IT Industry	A dummy variable that takes on a value of one if the PC is in the IT industry and zero otherwise.	SDC Platinum
Early Stage	A dummy variable that takes on a value of one if the PC is in the Early stage and zero otherwise.	SDC Platinum
	VC Characteristics	
Corporate VC	A dummy variable that takes on a value of one where VC is a corporate venture capitalist and zero otherwise.	SDC Platinum
Last Year Inv	The amount VC invested in PC last year.	SDC Platinum
	Market Conditions	
Number Deals	The natural log of the number of VC deals (investments) at time t.	VentureXpert
GDP Growth	The percentage growth rate in the gross domestic product	World Development Indicators
S&P500 Return	The return on the S&P 500 index.	Standard & Poor's
Bubble	A dummy variable that takes on a value of one if time t is during the market bubble (t=1998, 1999, 2000).	SDC Platinum

466

ALTERNATIVE EXPLANATIONS AND FUTURE RESEARCH

It is possible that my proxies for control are proxying for something else, namely, ownership. Although I define control more broadly than ownership in this paper, as Kaplan and Stromberg (2003) and Cumming (2008) suggest, it may be ownership that is compelling and not the actual control the VC exerts over the PC. To the extent that data is available, it would be interesting to do a similar analysis using contract specifics and/or security type (in the same vein as the papers mentioned above). I leave this endeavor to future research.

CONCLUSION

Studies have found that there is value in the hand holding provided by VCs. VC control over the PC can actually benefit the PC with regard to performance or outcome (i.e., whether or not a firm exits via M&A or IPO, remains private, or even fails). One could imagine, however, that too much (little) involvement could be stifling (less than stimulating) to the PC.

This paper finds that the relationship between VC control and PC performance and outcome is nonlinear. In many cases there exists a local maximum (optimum) level of management. I find that extremes in VC control, as proxied by average VC round investment, the percent of the PC the VC owns, the percent of the VC's portfolio comprised by the PC, and the average number of days between investment rounds, provides less than optimal impacts on firm performance. These results suggest that there is a happy medium when it comes to VC control. Average levels of control maximize the positive impact offered by VCs.

NOTES

1. Some angel investors do provide managerial support. An "angel" is an alternative source of capital for portfolio companies. These wealthy individuals provide their own capital (versus funds raised from others) and do so in smaller amounts. According to www.angelcapitaleducation.org, this amount is generally $5,000 to $100,000.

2. Entrepreneurs of PCs are not always able to shop around for VC funding. See Gompers and Lerner (1998) for a study of the determinants of supply of VC funding.

3. Ownership can change across these financing rounds, so this proxy of control is not independent from ownership.

4. PC outcome = private is the base outcome.

5. In looking at the breakdown of fund investment type, approximately 7,000 are private equity investments. Since this represents such a small percentage of observations (4 percent of the sample) and excluding these observations leads to qualitatively identical results, the paper is written from the perspective of the venture capitalist (VC).

6. This number is calculated as exp(coefficient on % VC Portfolio)—1.

7. Cumming (2006), for example, demonstrates that "returns to scale are in fact diminishing ... for the number of investee firms in a VC fund portfolio." (p. 1117) suggesting that there could be a point at which VCs would optimally want to limit growth.

8. Expertise also serves to control for VC grandstanding, which was brought to light by Gompers (1996).

9. See also Lerner (1994) for an examination of the ability of more experienced VCs to take PCs public, particularly at market peaks.

REFERENCES

Bergemann, D., and U. Hege. 1998. Venture capital financing, moral hazard, and learning. *Journal of Banking and Finance* 22:703–735.

Burkart, M., D. Gromb, and F. Panunzi. 1997. Large shareholders, monitoring, and the value of the firm. *Quarterly Journal of Economics* 112:693–728.

Cumming, D. 2006. The determinants of venture capital portfolio size: Empirical evidence. *Journal of Business* 79:1083–1126.

_____. 2008. Contracts and exits in venture capital finance. *Review of Financial Studies* 21:1947–1982.

_____, and J. MacIntosh. 2003a. Venture capital exits in Canada and the United States. *University of Toronto Law Journal* 55:101–200.

_____. 2003b. A cross-country comparison of full and partial venture capital exits. *Journal of Banking and Finance* 27:511–548.

Ehrlich, S., et al. 1994. After the cash arrives: A comparative study of venture capital and private investor involvement in entrepreneurial firms. *Journal of Business Venturing* 9: 67–82.

Fleming, G., 2004. Venture capital returns in Australia. *Venture Capital: An International Journal of Entrepreneurial Finance* 6:23–45.

Gompers, P. 1995. Optimal investment, monitoring, and the staging of venture capital. *Journal of Finance* 50:1461–1489.

_____. 1996. Grandstanding in the venture capital industry. *Journal of Financial Economics* 43:133 156.

_____, and J. Lerner. 1998. What drives venture capital fundraising? *Brookings Papers on Economic Activity: Microeconomics*, 49–192.

_____. 1999a. An analysis of compensation in the U.S. venture capital partnership. *Journal of Financial Economics* 51:3–44.

_____. 1999b. *The venture capital cycle*, 1st ed. Cambridge: MIT Press.

Groshen, E., and S. Potter. 2003. Current issues in economics and finance. *Federal Reserve Bank of New York* 9:1–7.

Hellmann, T. 2000. Venture capitalists: The coaches of Silicon Valley. In *Silicon Valley edge: A habitat for innovation and entrepreneurship*, ed. W. Miller, C. M. Lee, M. Hanock, and H. Rowen. Stanford, CA: Stanford University Press.

_____, and M. Puri. 2000. The interaction between product market and financing strategy: The role of venture capital. *Review of Financial Studies* 13:995–984.

_____. 2002. Venture capital and the professionalization of start-up firms: Empirical evidence. *Journal of Finance* 57:169–198.

Hsu, D. 2001. What do entrepreneurs pay for venture capital affiliation? *Journal of Finance* 59:1805–1844.

Lerner, J. 1994. Venture capitalists and the decision to go public. *Journal of Financial Economics* 35:293–316.

_____. 1995. Venture capitalists and the oversight of private firms. *Journal of Finance* 50:301–318.

Kaplan, S., and P. Stromberg. 2001. Venture capitalists as principals: Contracting, screening, and monitoring. *American Economic Review* 91:426–430.

_____. 2003. Financial contracting theory meets the real world: An empirical analysis of venture capital contracts. *Review of Economic Studies* 70:281–315.

Knill, A. 2009. Should venture capitalists put all their eggs in one basket? Diversification versus pure play strategies in venture capital. *Financial Management* 38:441–486.

Macmillan, I., D. Kulow, and R. Khoylian. 1988. Venture capitalists; involvement in their investments: Extent and performance. *Journal of Business Venturing* 4:27–47.

Megginson, W., and K. Weiss. 1991. Venture capitalist certification in initial public offerings. *Journal of Finance* 46:879–903.

Norton, E., and B. Tenenbaum. 1993. Specialization versus diversification as a venture capital investment strategy. *Journal of Business Venturing* 8:431–442.

Renucci, A. 2000. Optimal claims and tightness of relationships with a value-enhancing investor. GREMAQ, Université de Toulouse.

Sapienza, H. 1992. When do venture capitalists add value? *Journal of Business Venturing* 7: 9–27.

_____, S. Manigart, and W. Vermeir. 1996. Venture capitalist governance and value added in four countries. *Journal of Business Venturing* 11:439–469.

Schwienbacher, A. 2002. An empirical analysis of venture capital exits in Europe and the United States. Working paper. University of Amsterdam.

ABOUT THE AUTHOR

April Knill received her Ph.D. from the University of Maryland at College Park in August of 2005. While pursuing her doctoral degree she worked at The World Bank as a consultant. Upon graduation, she went to work at Florida State University. Her research interests are venture capital/private equity and international finance. She has published in academic journals such as *Journal of Business* and *Financial Management*.

## PART V

International Venture Capital and Public Policy

## CHAPTER 21

Cross-Border Venture Capital and Private Equity

MARKKU V. J. MAULA
Professor of Venture Capital, Institute of Strategy, Department of Industrial
Engineering and Management, Helsinki University of Technology

INTRODUCTION

Historically, venture capital has been considered by many to be a regional cottage industry (Gompers 1994) with investments being made primarily within short driving distance from the offices of venture capital and private equity firms (Griffith, Yam and Subramaniam 2007). That picture has changed dramatically during the past 10 years or so (Baygan and Freudenberg 2000; Bottazzi, Da Rin, and Hellmann 2004; Maula and Mäkelä 2003). Currently, most venture capital firms operate internationally or are considering doing so in the near future (Deloitte 2007). The rapid internationalization of the venture capital and private equity industry has had major implications on how venture capital and private equity firms operate. The globalization of the VC industry has also had major implications to related policy making with increasing attention being paid to removing obstacles for cross-border venture capital and private equity (see European Commission 2007). The rapid globalization of venture capital and private equity has even forced major changes in how private equity data and statistics have to be collected to get a correct picture of the activity. In Europe, the traditionally nationally organized data collection was centralized in 2007 to gather more accurate data on cross-border activity.

At the same time, the research on venture capital and private equity has started to examine various new questions arising from the increasingly international activities of venture capital and private equity firms. That development started from the comparison of domestic investment activities in different countries and has more recently expanded to the internationalization of investments (Wright, Pruthi, and Lockett 2005). During the past decade, cross-border venture capital has emerged

I would like to acknowledge funding from Tekes, the Finnish Funding Agency for Technology and Innovation for the project "Venture Capital and Private Equity in a Global Economy." I would also like to thank Mirela Ene, Jennifer Vandermosten, Grégoire Samain, and PEREP_Analytics and the European Venture Capital and Private Equity Association (EVCA) for statistics, Risto Tukkinen for comments and some analyses, and Tomi Alén for superb research assistance.

as a new rapidly growing stream in venture capital and private equity research (Maula and Mäkelä 2003).

In this chapter, I take stock of the current body of literature on cross-border venture capital and private equity. The rest of the chapter is structured as follows. First, the body of literature on cross-border venture capital and private equity is reviewed, summarized, and evaluated. Then, underlying theoretical and method-ological approaches are discussed. Thereafter, implications for various stakehold-ers are discussed. Finally, avenues for future research are suggested.

THE INTERNATIONALIZATION OF VENTURE CAPITAL AND PRIVATE EQUITY

The venture capital and private equity market has internationalized rapidly since the late 1990s (Baygan and Freudenberg 2000; Bottazzi, Da Rin, and Hellmann. 2004; Maula and Mäkelä 2003; Wright, Pruthi, and Lockett 2005). For instance, Exhibit 21.1 shows how venture capital and private equity fundraising has become more international, with more than half of the funds being raised from foreign limited partners since the beginning of the millennium.

In parallel with the internationalization of fund-raising, investment scopes of general partners have also internationalized rapidly (Bottazzi, da Rin, and Hellmann 2004). Currently, according to a recent survey, most venture capital firms operate internationally or are considering doing so in the near future (Deloitte 2007). Exhibit 21.2 shows that in European venture capital and private equity the

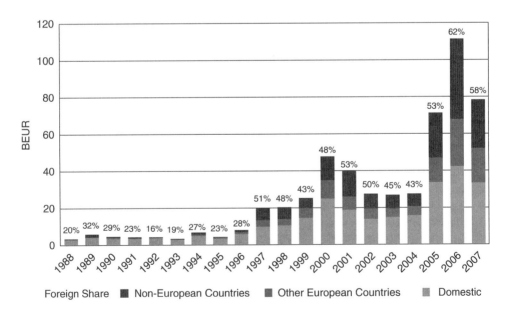

Exhibit 21.1   Cross-Border Fundraising in Europe, 1988 to 2007

Note: Exhibit 21.1 presents European cross-border venture capital and private equity fund-raising volumes from 1988 to 2007. Percentages over columns refer to share of foreign commitments in new funds. Analysis is based on data from EVCA and PEREP Analytics.

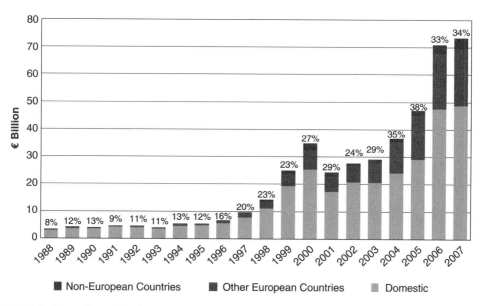

Exhibit 21.2   Cross-Border Investing in Europe, 1988–2007

Note: Exhibit 21.2 presents European cross-border venture capital and private equity investment volumes from 1988 to 2007. Percentages over columns refer to share of foreign investments. Analysis is based on data from EVCA and PEREP Analytics.

share of foreign investments of all investments has grown rapidly since the late 1990s to about one-third of all investments 2004. Exhibit 21.3, based on 2007 data, shows that the share of foreign investments varies strongly between countries.

Although cross-border venture capital has been prevalent in Europe, recently Asia has received significant amounts of cross-border investments. Nevertheless, the relative winner in the competition for foreign venture capital investments appears to be Israel, with Israeli companies raising $1.6 billion venture capital investments in 2007 of which two-thirds were from foreign VCs.

Although there has been a general growing trend in cross-border investment flows, there is also some cyclical fluctuation around that trend. It appears that whereas bull markets lead to increasing the role for cross-border investments, the relative share decreases in bear markets. During bad times, investors tend to focus on their home base. Although the recent market downturn may slow down the internationalization trend for a while, there are clear drivers for the globalization trend of the venture capital and private equity market to continue. In the following section, I review the existing studies on cross-border venture capital and private equity.

RESEARCH ON CROSS BORDER VENTURE CAPITAL AND PRIVATE EQUITY

In classifying and reviewing literature on cross-border venture capital and private equity, I follow the stages of the venture capital cycle (Gompers and Lerner 1999)

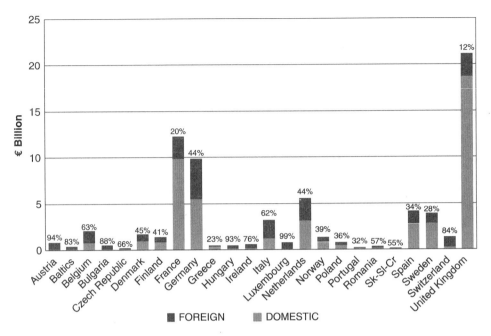

Exhibit 21.3   Cross-Border Investing in Europe by Country in 2007

Note: Exhibit 21.3 presents European cross-border venture capital and private equity investment volumes using the market approach by investor office location in 2007. Percentages
over columns refer to share of foreign investments. Analysis is based on data from EVCA
and PEREP Analytics.

starting with the raising of a VC fund, proceeding through the investing in, monitoring of, and adding value to portfolio firms, continuing as the VCs exit their
investments and return capital to investors, and finally renewing through raising
the next fund. Selected studies on cross-border venture capital and private equity
are summarized in Exhibit 21.4 below and reviewed in the following sections.

Cross-Border Fundraising

The literature suggests that cross-border fund-raising is largely driven by the need
for the limited partners to diversify their investments internationally and the attractiveness of various regions as targets for investment.

On the macro level, the existing research has shown that the maturity and
transparency of the VC market and the perceived potential of target companies in
the foreign markets improve the attractiveness and fund inflows in those markets.
However, problems in tax and legal environment can reduce the attractiveness of
countries as investment targets for institutional investors (Cumming and Johan
2007; Heikkilä 2004). In an analysis of the determinants of cross-border fund-
raising in Europe between 1991 and 2003, Heikkilä (2004) demonstrated the effects
of market attractiveness and tax issues on cross-border fund-raising. Similarly,
in a recent global survey of potential limited partners by Groh, Liechtenstein,

Exhibit 21.4 Summary of Selected Studies on Cross-Border Capital and Private Equity

Exhibit 21.4 summarizes selected studies that have directly examined cross-border venture capital and private equity

Reference	Key Concepts	Key Variables	Key Predictions and Findings	Key Contribution	Method and Sample
Cross-border Fund-raising					
Heikkilä (2004)	Cross-border fund-raising, market attractiveness, tax environment	Cross-border fund-raising	Cross-border fund-raising is positively related to a liquid exit-market and a well performing and mature VC fund manager base and negatively to fund managers investing a large share of funds in foreign companies and by tax problems (permanent establishment problem)	Demonstrates the effects of market attractiveness and tax issues on cross-border fund-raising	Country-year level panel data analysis of cross-border fund-raising in Europe between 1991 and 2003
Cumming & Johan (2007)	Fund investments, regulatory harmonization	Private equity allocations (dv), regulatory harmonization	Regulatory harmonization is related to the level of investment, geographic concentration, and vehicle for investment	Demonstrates that regulatory harmonization facilitates investment in private equity, as well as international investment in private equity	Institutional investor level analysis of domestic and cross-border private equity fund investments by 100 Dutch institutional investors in 2005
Groh et al. (2008)	Cross-border fund investments	Cross-border fund investments	From limited partner perspective, key factors influencing foreign fund investments include property rights and the need to find local quality General Partners, the quality of management and skills of local entrepreneurs, and the expected deal flow. Bribery and corruption is a major negative factor. Public funding and subsidies are not, significant, and the IPO activity and the size of local public equity markets have only a minor role	Identifies factors influencing cross-border fund investments from institutional investor perspective	Survey of 75 limited partners worldwide

(Continued)

477

Exhibit 21.4 (*Continued*)

Reference	Key Concepts	Key Variables	Key Predictions and Findings	Key Contribution	Method and Sample
Groh et al. (2008)	Country attractiveness for limited partners	Fund-raising inflows, tens of variables describing entrepreneurial opportunities, economic activity, capital market, taxation, corporate governance and investor protection, and human and social environment	Attractiveness of countries for limited partners to allocate capital can be measured using a broad index covering entrepreneurial opportunities, economic activity, capital market, taxation, corporate governance and investor protection, and human and social environment	Develops a validated index on country attractiveness for limited partners	Analysis of 42 country-level data series from various databases for European countries to develop an index

Cross-border investing

Reference	Key Concepts	Key Variables	Key Predictions and Findings	Key Contribution	Method and Sample
Meyer & Shao (1995)	VC internationalization, portfolio diversification, agency costs	VC firm's international diversification, domestic and foreign risk and return parameters	VCs can reduce risks by diversifying internationally	Demonstrates the potential benefits and trade-offs in international diversification of VCs	Theoretical
Wright et al. (2002)	International investment behavior of VCs	Risk assessment, sources of information	Foreign VCs (in India) overemphasize product market factors and accountants' reports and underemphasize management in risk assessment and overemphasize independent information sources in comparison to domestic investors.	Demonstrates that VCs adapt to foreign markets rather that apply recipe from domestic markets	VC firm-level statistical analysis of 31 Indian and 73 U.S. VC firms between 1996 and 2000

Hall & Tu (2003)	International expansion	VC firm's willingness to invest abroad (dv), VC firm's size (iv)	VC firm's willingness to invest overseas positively related to its size	Identifies the role of size as a determinant of foreign expansion of VC firms	VC firm level logistic regression analysis of 128 British VC firms in 2000
Maula & Mäkelä (2003)	Value-added of cross-border VCs	Foreign revenues of portfolio companies, foreign VCs	The existence of foreign external investors is positively related to the expected revenues from foreign software product business.	Demonstrates the value adding role of foreign VCs in internationalization of portfolio companies	Portfolio company-level regression analysis of 228 Finnish software product companies
Mäkelä & Maula (2005)	New venture internationalization, isomorphism, legitimacy, liability of foreignness	VC internationalization support (dv), existence of cross-border-VC (iv), target market fit, pressure to conform	Foreign VCs located in a venture's target market of internationalization can be valuable for the venture by legitimizing the unknown new venture in that market. The benefits may turn into disadvantages if the target market differs from the home markets of the foreign VC	Demonstrates the role of foreign VCs in internationalization of new ventures	Portfolio-company-level inductive case analysis of cross-border VC financing of nine Finnish ventures between 1997 and 2002
Mäkelä & Maula (2006)	Interorganizational commitment	Interorganizational commitment, investors' expectations, distance, embeddedness, and financial importance	Changes in a venture's prospects influence investors' commitment levels. This is amplified by the remoteness of the investor and mitigated by the investor's embeddedness in local syndication networks and the relative investment size.	Demonstrates the specific challenges of managing cross-border VC relationships	Investment level inductive case analysis of 29 investment relationships in 8 cross-border VC syndicates in Finnish ventures between 1997 and 2002

(Continued)

Exhibit 21.4 (*Continued*)

Reference	Key Concepts	Key Variables	Key Predictions and Findings	Key Contribution	Method and Sample
Tykvová & Schertler (2006)	Internationalization of VCs, maturity of VC industry, syndication	Number of bilateral cross-border VC investments (dv), syndication, maturity of VC industry, market growth differentials (iv)	Cross-border VC investments are primarily targeted in markets with established local VCs suggesting complementarity rather than rivalry. VCs also respond more strongly to growth differentials between foreign and domestic markets if investments can be syndicated with an experienced local investor.	Demonstrates the importance of established local VC industry for attracting foreign VC investment flows	Country-pair-year level panel regression analysis of cross-border investments between 23 countries from 2000 to 2004. Also deal level analysis
Bottazzi et al. (2007)	Role of trust for VC cross-border investments	Investments (dv), trust, control variables	Trust influences investments	Demonstrates that the Eurobarometer measure of trust among nations significantly affects investment decisions.	Survey and investment data on European venture capital firms and their investments
Kaplan et al. (2007)	Cross-border contracting	Contracts in foreign VC investments	More experienced VCs are able to implement U.S.-style contracts regardless of legal regime. VC experience and trust are more influential in explaining the use of U.S.-style terms than legal regime or other legal, and institutional variables. VCs who use U.S.-style contracts are substantially and significantly less likely to fail. The VCs who switched styles all moved from non-U.S. to U.S.-style contracts. VCs do not appear to use U.S.-style contracts to trade off downside protection for upside	Demonstrates that more experienced VCs implement U.S.-style contracts regardless of legal regime	Deal-level analysis of 145 investments in 107 companies in 23 countries by 70 different lead VCs

Guler & Guillén (2007a)	Internationalization of VCs, home country networks	Propensity to internationalize, status (Bonacich centrality), network brokerage	Social status of VCs in syndication networks and brokerage and the presence of partners on firms' foreign market entry	Demonstrates that home-country syndication network position influences foreign expansion of VCs	VC-country-year-level analysis of the propensity of 1,010 U.S. VCs to internationalize in 40 foreign countries between 1990–2002
Guler & Guillén (2007b)	Internationalization of VCs, transnational connections, attention-based view of the firm, neo-institutional theory, the world-society approach to globalization	Propensity to internationalize (dv), trade, transnational communities, previous collaboration	Trade, migration, and the presence of syndication partners increase the rate of entry and mitigate the adverse effects of uncertainty	Demonstrates that transnational connections from trade, migration, and previous interorganizational collaboration influence foreign market entry	VC-country-year-level analysis of the propensity of 1,010 U.S. VCs to internationalize in 95 foreign from 1990 to 2002
Guler & McGahan (2007b)	Cross-border VC syndication	Syndicate size (dv), venture location, venture industry	VCs do not syndicate more broadly internationally than in the United States	Demonstrates that VCs do not appear to adapt their syndication practices in cross-border investments	Portfolio company level analysis of 13,415 (8,672 U.S and 4,743 non-U.S). VC-backed ventures founded between 1989 and 2001
Guler & McGahan (2007a)	Cross-border VC syndication	Syndicate size (dv), level of intellectual property protection, legal system, development local VC industry, and VC reputation	Legal environment (both intellectual-property protection and the strength of ownership rights based on common law) influences the breadth of syndication	Demonstrates the role of legal institutions in determining the use of syndication	Portfolio company-level analysis of 12,640 (8,672 U.S. and 4,265 non-U.S). VC-backed ventures founded between 1989 and 2001

(Continued)

Exhibit 21.4 (*Continued*)

Reference	Key Concepts	Key Variables	Key Predictions and Findings	Key Contribution	Method and Sample
Manigart et al. (2007)	VC internationaliza-tion, human resources	VC internationalization (dv), VC human resources incl. their number, education, and experience (iv)	The number and international experience of VC executives increase the likelihood of internationalization of the VC firm	Demonstrates the role of VC human resources in explaining VC internationalization	VC firm level regression analysis of 195 VCs in five European countries between 2002 and 2004
Meuleman & Wright (2007)	Cross-border VC syndication, inter-nationalization process, institutional theory, learning theory	Cross-border syndication (dv), cultural distance, legal context, organizational learning	Cultural and legal differences and organizational learning influence the use of syndication in cross-border investments	Demonstrates that staged expansion theory and organizational learning theory can explain cross-border syndication.	Investment-level logistic regression analysis of 754 cross-border investments of UK PE investors in Europe between 1990 and 2005
Aizenman & Kendall (2008)	Cross-border VC flows	Cross-border VC flows (dv), distance, common language, colonial ties	Distance, common language, and colonial ties positively related to flows. Also the presence of high-end human capital, a better business environment, high levels of military expenditure, and deeper financial markets are important local factors that attract international venture capital. Also evidence of path dependency and persistence in VC and PE flows, indicating network effects and fixed costs of entry may be at work	Demonstrates on macro level the effects of distance, common language, and colonial ties on cross-border VC flows	Country-level analysis of cross-border investment VC flows between more than 100 countries between 1992 and 2007

Study	Key concepts	Variables	Findings	Contribution	Sample/Method
Alhorr et al. (2008)	Cross-border VC flows, economic integration	Cross-border VC outflows (dv), adoption of common market (iv), adoption of common currency (iv)	Country will have higher cross-border VC outflows after adopting common market and common currency	Demonstrates on macro level the impact of economic integration on cross-border VC flows	Country-level analysis of cross-border VC investment flows in 24 European countries between 1985 and 2002
Bottazzi et al. (2008)	Impact of legal systems for domestic and foreign VCs	Investor behavior (dv) investor and portfolio company legal system characteristics, control variables	Develops a model to examine how optimal contracts and investor actions depend on the quality of the legal system	Demonstrates that investor's legal system is more important than that of the portfolio company in determining investor behavior	Conceptual analysis and analysis of 1,431 venture deals from 124 venture capital firms in 17 European countries
Fernhaber & McDougall (2008)	New venture internationalization	Portfolio company international sales intensity (dv), VC investment, VC reputation, and VC international knowledge (previous cross-border investments) and their interactions	VC investment, reputation, and international knowledge are positively related to portfolio company international sales intensity and have a positive interaction effect	Demonstrate that VCs act as catalysts for internationalization	Portfolio company level tobit regression analysis of the international sales intensity of 161 U.S. VC-backed high tech new ventures that underwent an IPO between 1996 and 2000
Mäkelä & Maula (2008)	Cross-border investment readiness, international social capital	Likelihood of receiving cross-border VC, cross-border investment readiness, experience, market focus, local VC role	Local VCs play an important role in facilitating cross-border investment readiness and likelihood of receiving foreign VC investments. This is moderated by venture management experience, and market focus	Demonstrates the role of local VC in attracting foreign VCs in cross-border syndicates	Portfolio-company level inductive case analysis of cross-border VC financing of nine Finnish ventures between 1997 and 2002

(Continued)

Exhibit 21.4 (Continued)

Reference	Key Concepts	Key Variables	Key Predictions and Findings	Key Contribution	Method and Sample
Schertler & Tykvová (2008)	Cross-border private equity flows, fiscal environment	Number and volume of bilateral cross-border VC investments (dv), differences between countries in private equity intermediaries fiscal environment (iv)	Countries with a favorable legal environment have a higher level of domestic investment and also attract a higher amount of private equity from abroad	Demonstrates that an improvement in the intermediaries' fiscal environment will cause a shift in the supply curve, which will increase domestic investments, generate a positive return differential between foreign and domestic investments, and thus encourage private equity investors from going abroad. Investors systematically exploit cross-country differences in fiscal environments.	Country-pair-year level panel regression analysis of cross-border investments between 15 countries in 2000–2006
Tykvová & Schertler (2008)	Cross-border syndication, distance, transaction costs	Number and volume of bilateral cross-border VC investments (dv), distance and syndication (iv)	Distance decreases bilateral cross-border investments with small investments affected more than large ones. Syndication with VCs in recipient countries reduces the effect of distance	Demonstrates how cross-border syndication mitigates the transaction costs in cross-border investments	Country-pair-year level panel regression analysis of cross-border investments between 30 countries in 2000–2006. Also deal level analysis

Author	Key concepts	Variables	Findings	Data/Method
Khavul et al. (2009)	Cross-border VC syndication, complementary assets	VC syndication tie (dv), geographic distance and industry experience difference between potential syndication partners	Demonstrates search for complementary knowledge drives the choice of new syndication partners	Syndicate level analysis of 5376 syndicated VC investments by domestic and foreign institutional investors in the emerging Israeli high technology venture market between 1992–2002
		Geographic distance and similarity of industry expertise between VCs have an interacting effect on syndicate partners choices		
Cumming et al. (2009)	Corporate relocation of VC-backed companies	Corporate relocation and financial returns (dv), market characteristics, investor characteristics, target characteristics	VC-backed companies (a) located in countries with less-developed law and financial systems are more likely to relocate to countries with more-developed law and financial systems in order to improve governance, mitigate information asymmetries, and improve the expected rate of return of the investment, and (b) companies located in countries with weaker economic conditions and lower populations are more likely to relocate to countries with stronger economic conditions and greater populations in order to be closer to potential customers at the time of exiting the investment and improve the expected rate of return of the investment	Econometric analysis of data from 53 venture capital funds involving 468 investee companies and 12 countries in the Asia-Pacific
			Demonstrates that relocations to the U.S. yield much greater returns to Asia-Pacific VCs than investing in companies already based in the United States at the time of VC investment. Further, more experienced Asia-Pacific VCs have greater success with their investee relocations to the United States, and these relocations yield higher returns relative to staying in their country of origin.	

(*Continued*)

485

Exhibit 21.4 (*Continued*)

Reference	Key Concepts	Key Variables	Key Predictions and Findings	Key Contribution	Method and Sample
Cross-border exits					
Cumming et al. (2006)	Foreign exits, legality	Exit outcome (dv), legality index	Increase in the Legality index increases the probability of an IPO exit	Demonstrates a relationship between legality and VC exit outcomes	Investment level analysis of 468 VC investments in Asia-Pacific
Hursti and Maula (2007)	Foreign IPOs	Foreign vs. domestic IPO (dv), foreign pre-IPO ownership, international operations, international experience, size, high-technology focus	Foreign VCs and corporate investors as well as international experience are positively related to foreign IPOs	Demonstrates the effects of foreign pre-IPO ownership and experience on the likelihood of foreign IPOs	Portfolio company level rare events logistic analysis of foreign vs. domestic IPOs of European companies between 1991–2001

Jääskeläinen & Maula (2008)	Foreign IPOs and trade sales exits, local bias, direct and indirect network ties	Propensity of cross-border exit and exit to specific markets (dv), direct and indirect foreign VC ties	Direct and indirect foreign VC ties influence the exit market choice, but differ in their effects: indirect ties with broad reach facilitate foreign trade sales exits, but direct ties with stronger certification effects are important in foreign IPOs	Venture-exit market pair-level longitudinal analysis of 4,436 European VC backed ventures between 1990 and 2008
Wang (2008)	Foreign exits		Argues that VCs have to adapt their strategies when investing in transitional economies because of limited exit opportunities	Literature review, theoretical
Reviews				
Wright et al. (2005)	Internationalization of VC (all phases)	—	The literature on internationalization of VC has recently evolved from country comparisons to cross-border VC.	A comprehensive literature review	Literature review

and Canela (2008), institutional investors raised the protection of property and investors' rights as the most important factor influencing the attractiveness of countries as targets for private equity allocation followed by the availability of high quality local general partners, expected entrepreneurial management quality and skills, expected deal flow, and transparency of the market (lack of bribing and corruption). Availability of public funding and support for companies was not seen as important by potential limited partners. In a subsequent analysis, Groh, Liechtenstein, and Lieser (2008) developed country attractiveness indices and found that while corporate governance and the investor protection regime and the size and the liquidity of capital market were important, the attractiveness of countries reflected many other factors. However, in general, the attractiveness scale correlated strongly with observed fund-raising inflows. In line with these surveys, an in-depth analysis by Cumming and Johan (2007) shows that perceived regulatory harmonization increases fund inflows from institutional investors.

On the micro level, there is little research examining the cross-border fund-raising processes and determinants. However, based on private equity firm-level and fund-level studies, the track record and contacts of general partners influence their ability to attract foreign investments in addition to the market specific factors.

Cross-Border Investing and Value Adding

Concerning cross-border investments, the current body of literature already provides a quite developed picture of the determinants of investment activities both on the macro and the micro level.

On the macro level, recent research has shown that investment flows between countries can be largely explained by the balance between the demand and the supply of capital and the frictions influencing how easily the supply can meet the demand (Aizenman and Kendall 2008). The demand for cross-border venture capital is largely related to the existence of a strong pool of attractive investment opportunities indicated, for instance, by high quality human capital (Aizenman and Kendall 2008; Tykvová and Schertler 2008), patents (Guler and Guillén 2007), world class science emanating from universities (Wright et al. 2007), higher GDP growth rate (Tykvová and Schertler 2008), and supportive exit markets including mergers and acquisitions ("M&A") and IPO opportunities (Cumming, Fleming, and Schwienbacher 2005; Da Rin, Nicodano, and Sembenelli 2006; Jeng and Wells 2000). The supply of venture capital is positively related to a functioning tax and legal framework for raising venture capital funds (Schertler and Tykvová 2008). The frictions reducing the cross-border flows include, for instance, distance (Aizenman and Kendall 2008; Bottazzi, da Rin, and Hellmann 2007; Tykvová and Schertler 2008), foreign language (Aizenman and Kendall 2008), different currencies (Alhorr, Moore, and Payne 2008), not belonging to a common market (Alhorr, Moore, and Payne 2008), trade relations (Bottazzi, da Rin, and Hellmann 2007; Guler and Guillén 2007), lack of availability of experienced co-investors (Guler and Guillén 2007; Meuleman and Wright 2007; Mäkelä and Maula 2008; Tykvová and Schertler 2008), lack of information and trust (Bottazzi, da Rin, and Hellmann 2007; Jääskeläinen and Maula 2008), and lack of regulatory environment that investors know and trust. Countries that have investment opportunities, developed financial institutions, migration, and potential syndication partners are more likely to attract cross-border investments (Guler and Guillén forthcoming, 2007).

When reviewing central studies in this stream, the studies by Bottazzi, da Rin, and Hellmann (2007), Alhorr, Moore, and Payne (2008), Aizenman and Kendall (2008), Schertler and Tykvová (2008), and Tykvová and Schertler (2006; 2008) merit further attention. In a sophisticated analysis on European cross-border investments, Bottazzi, da Rin, and Hellmann (2007) found that trust facilitates investments and investor behavior. Their findings suggest that countries can expect foreign investments to come mostly from countries with well established trust for the recipient country. Demonstrating on the macro level the impact of economic integration on cross-border VC flows, Alhorr, Moore, and Payne (2008) found in their country-level analysis of cross-border investment flows in 24 European countries between 1985 and 2002 that a country will have higher cross-border VC outflows after adopting common market and common currency. Similarly, demonstrating the macro-level effects of distance, common language, and colonial ties on cross-border VC flows, Aizenman and Kendall (2008) conduct a country-level analysis of cross-border investment VC flows between more than 100 countries between 1992 and 2007. They find that distance, common language, and colonial ties positively related to flows. Also the presence of high-end human capital, a better business environment, high levels of military expenditure, and deeper financial markets are important local factors that attract international venture capital. Also evidence of path dependency and persistence in VC and PE flows, indicating network effects and fixed costs of entry may be at work.

Among other important studies in this stream, Tykvová and Schertler have conducted a string of studies on the macro-level analysis of cross-border investment flows. In the first study in this series, Tykvová and Schertler (2006) examine the importance of an established local VC industry for attracting foreign VC investment flows. In a country-pair-year level panel regression analysis of cross-border investments between 23 countries from 2000 to 2004, they find that cross-border VC investments are primarily targeted in markets with established local VCs, suggesting complementarity rather than rivalry. VCs also respond more strongly to growth differentials between foreign and domestic markets if investments can be syndicated with an experienced local investor. In another study, Tykvová and Schertler (2008) find that distance decreases bilateral cross-border investments with small investments affected more than large ones. Syndication with VCs in recipient countries reduces the effect of distance. This country-pair-year level panel regression analysis of cross-border investments between 30 countries from 2000 to 2006 demonstrates how cross-border syndication mitigates the transaction costs in cross-border investments. Finally, Schertler and Tykvová (2008) find that countries with a favorable legal environment have a higher level of domestic investment and also attract a higher amount of private equity from abroad. They conclude that an improvement in the intermediaries' fiscal environment will cause a shift in the supply curve, which will increase domestic investments, generate a positive return differential between foreign and domestic investments, and thus encourage private equity investors to go abroad. They find that investors systematically exploit cross-country differences in fiscal environments.

On the micro level, the body of literature is even finer grained. Several papers have examined the use of information in deal screening (Wright, Lockett, and Pruthi

2002), determinants of foreign investments (Guler and Guillén forthcoming, 2007), syndication of cross-border investments (Khavul et al. 2009; Mäkelä and Maula 2006, 2008), and the value adding roles (Fernhaber and McDougall 2009; Maula and Mäkelä 2003; Mäkelä and Maula 2005).

Concerning the VC decision to invest abroad, Meyer and Shao (1995) first argued that VCs can reduce risks by diversifying internationally. Their findings demonstrated the potential benefits and trade-offs in international diversification of VCs. Thereafter, Hall and Tu (2003) found in their analysis of 128 British VC firms in 2000 that size was positively related to internationalization. Later, more detailed studies have tested various theoretical explanations for internationalization of VCs. For instance, Guler and Guillén (forthcoming) studied the effects of social networks in their analysis of the propensity of 1010 U.S. VCs to internationalize in 40 foreign countries between 1990 and 2002. They found that home-country syndication network position influences foreign expansion of VCs. In another study, using a related sample, Guler and Guillén (2007) found that transnational connections from trade, migration, and previous interorganizational collaboration influence foreign market entry.

Manigart and colleagues (2007) took another perspective and examined the role of human resources in internationalization. In their analysis of internationalization of 195 VCs in five European countries between 2002 and 2004, they found that the number and international experience of VC executives increased the likelihood of internationalization of the VC firm. The study clearly demonstrated the role of VC human resources in explaining VC internationalization.

In a stream of research examining the role of syndication in cross-border venture capital, Maula and Mäkelä (2003) and Mäkelä and Maula (2008), based on an inductive case analysis of cross-border VC financing of nine Finnish ventures between 1997 and 2002, demonstrated the important role of local VC in attracting foreign VCs in cross-border syndicates. In another study on cross-border syndication, Khavul and colleagues (2009) conducted a syndicate-level analysis of 5,376 syndicated VC investments by domestic and foreign institutional investors in the emerging Israeli high technology venture market between 1992 and 2002. They found that search for complementary knowledge drives the choice of new syndication partners.

In another study on cross-border syndication, Guler and McGahan (2007a) conducted a portfolio company level analysis of 12,640 (8,672 U.S. and 4,265 non-U.S.) VC-backed ventures founded between 1989 and 2001. They found that legal environment (both intellectual-property protection and the strength of ownership rights based on common law) influences the breadth of syndication. Using a related sample Guler and McGahan (2007b) demonstrated that VCs do not appear to adapt their syndication practices in cross-border investments. Finally, Meuleman and Wright (2007) examined how cultural and legal differences and organizational learning influence the use of syndication in cross-border investments. Their investment-level logistic regression analysis of 754 cross-border investments of UK PE investors in Europe between 1990 and 2005 demonstrated that staged expansion theory and organizational learning theory can explain cross-border syndication.

In research examining contracting, monitoring and value-adding in cross-border venture capital, Wright, Lockett, and Pruthi (2002) first showed, by analyzing the investment behavior of 31 Indian and 73 U.S. VC firms between 1996 and 2000, that VCs adapt to foreign markets rather than apply recipes from domestic markets. For instance, foreign VCs in India overemphasized product market factors and accountants' reports and underemphasized management in risk assessment and overemphasized independent information sources in comparison to domestic investors. With regard to differences in contracting, Kaplan, Martel, and Strömberg (2007) conducted a deal-level analysis of 145 investments in 107 companies in 23 countries by 70 different lead VCs and found that more experienced VCs were able to implement U.S.-style contracts regardless of the local legal regime. VC experience and trust were found to be more influential in explaining the use of U.S.-style terms than the local legal regime or other legal and institutional variables. VCs who used U.S.-style contracts were found to have a lower risk to fail. When VCs changed their contracting, they always moved from non-U.S. to U.S.-style contracts. Regarding value adding Bottazzi, da Rin, and Hellmann (2008) found in their modeling and analysis of 1,431 venture deals from 124 venture capital firms in 17 European countries that the investor's legal system is more important than that of the portfolio company in determining investor behavior. Foreign investors coming from better legal environment provide more value added for portfolio companies than local investors.

Among studies examining the effects of cross-border investments on portfolio company internationalization, Maula and Mäkelä (2003) analyzed 228 Finnish software companies and found that foreign external investors were positively related to the expected revenues from foreign software product business. In more detailed case studies on internationalization support of foreign VCs, Mäkelä and Maula (2005) conducted inductive case analysis of cross-border VC financing of nine Finnish ventures between 1997 and 2002 and found that foreign VCs that were located in a venture's target market of internationalization were valuable for the venture by legitimizing the unknown new venture in that market. However, they also found that the benefits from foreign VCs could turn into disadvantages if the target market differed from the home markets of the foreign VC. In general, the study demonstrated the potentially important role of foreign VCs in internationalization of new ventures. In line with this case analysis, Fernhaber and McDougall (2009) analyzed the effects of cross-border venture capital on the international sales intensity of 161 U.S. VC–backed high tech new ventures that became public between 1996 and 2000. They found that VC investment, reputation, and international knowledge were positively related to portfolio company international sales intensity and had a positive interaction effect. The results supported the view that VCs act as catalysts for internationalization. Finally with regard to internationalization-related aspects, Cumming, Fleming, and Schwienbacher (2009) found in their analysis of 468 investee companies of 53 venture capital firms in 12 countries in the Asia-Pacific how VC induced international relocations of their portfolio companies are motivated by economic conditions and better legal environment. These relocations produce improved financial returns for investors.

However, concerning the downside of cross-border investors, Mäkelä and Maula (2006) examined the commitment of cross-border investors using inductive case analysis of 29 investment relationships in 8 cross-border VC syndicates in Finnish ventures between 1997 and 2002. They found that changes in a venture's prospects influenced investors' commitment levels. This was amplified by the remoteness of the investor and mitigated by the investor's embeddedness in local syndication networks and the relative investment size. The study pointed some specific challenges of managing cross-border VC relationships, especially in a context of declining market conditions.

Cross-Border Exits

Concerning cross-border exits, the current literature suggests that cross-border exits are largely driven by the lack of domestic exit opportunities (Wang 2008) as well as the credibility and connections of the portfolio company and their investors in the foreign target markets (Hursti and Maula 2007; Jääskeläinen and Maula 2008).

On the macro level, there are no studies examining the flows between countries. However, some micro-level studies such as Jääskeläinen and Maula (2008) highlight the importance of similar factors for cross-border investing such as distance and common language. Furthermore, Cumming, Fleming, and Schwienbacher (2006) examine the effects of legal environment on cross-border exits using a sample of 468 VC investments in Asia-Pacific and find that an increase in the legality index increases the probability of an IPO exit.

On the micro level, several studies have examined the determinants of cross-border exits (e.g., Hursti and Maula 2007; Jääskeläinen and Maula 2008). In a study concerning the determinants of foreign IPOs by European companies between 1991 and 2001, Hursti and Maula (2007) found that international experience of the management team and pre-IPO ownership by foreign investors are positively related to foreign initial public offerings. In another study examining the roles of direct and indirect network ties of financial intermediaries as mechanisms for mitigating information problems in cross-border exits, Jääskeläinen and Maula (2008) found that direct and indirect ties through VC investors to foreign markets influenced the probability of trade sales and IPO exits to those markets.

THEORETICAL AND METHODOLOGICAL UNDERPINNINGS

Despite the relatively early phase of development of the research on cross-border VC, the phenomenon has already attracted a very multidisciplinary group of scholars to examine various aspects of the internationalization of venture capital and private equity. While much of the initial work has been done by scholars from financial economics and entrepreneurship fields, the breadth of scholarship has grown rapidly and covers a large variety of theoretical backgrounds and research designs.

Among theoretical lenses adopted in the analysis of different stages of cross-border VC, researchers have adopted for instance institutional theory (Guler and Guillén 2007; Mäkelä and Maula 2005), agency theory (Meyer and Shao 1995), diversification literature (Meyer and Shao 1995), commitment theory (Mäkelä and Maula 2006), social capital (Mäkelä and Maula 2008), learning theory (Meuleman and Wright 2007), and attention-based view (Guler and Guillén 2007).

Among research designs used, several early studies in the analysis of the phenomenon adopted inductive case analysis (Mäkelä and Maula 2005, 2006, 2008). Different types of regression analyses have been very common (Hursti and Maula

2007). In the later studies, various types of longitudinal research designs including panel data analysis and survival analysis have become increasingly common (Jääskeläinen and Maula 2008). Also, network analysis has been a popular choice as a part of many studies (Guler and Guillén forthcoming; Jääskeläinen and Maula 2008). In recent works increasing attention has also been paid to the challenges from potential endogeneity in variables explaining different aspects of cross-border VC (Cumming Fleming, and Schwienbacher 2006; Jääskeläinen and Maula 2008). In general, the evolution of research methodology in research on cross-border venture capital and private equity has reflected the evolution and maturity of this research stream and the underlying disciplines (see, e.g., Aguinis et al. 2009).

IMPLICATIONS FOR STAKEHOLDERS

The internationalization of the venture capital and private equity market has various implications for stakeholders. In the following sections, we review these implications from the perspectives of entrepreneurs, general partners, limited partners, and policy makers.

Implications to Entrepreneurs

For entrepreneurs, the increasing globalization of venture capital and private equity has many benefits but also some challenges. First, increasing cross-border activity improves the choice of investors. Entrepreneurs are no longer completely dependent on domestic availability of venture capital. Cross-border venture capital and private equity mean that there are more potential investors that can invest in a venture located in a given country. This also increases competition between investors since VCs can no longer maintain regional strongholds in which they do not have to compete for deals. This improves the negotiation power of entrepreneurs that are in a position to attract foreign investors.

Cross-border VC and the larger set of investors in a given geographical area also influence the value added received by entrepreneurs. Broader geographical scopes and increasing competition in geographical areas often leads to more focus in terms of industry specialization. Subsequently, entrepreneurs have better opportunities to attract an investor that is specialized in their industry and operates in the internationalization target market and can therefore support their international growth (Mäkelä and Maula 2005).

However, there are also some challenges for entrepreneurs stemming from the increasingly international market for entrepreneurial finance. Entrepreneurs have to be able to attract and collaborate with international investors. Investment readiness in an international context is clearly more demanding than in a domestic context. The international operation of many funds also tends to increase costs and thereby the lower limit of deals that can be justified. This may cause problems in the availability of smaller investments.

Implications to General Partners

For general partners, the cross-border activity gives broader deal flow but often necessitates more focused industry specialization. Organizationally, general partners will have to develop new solutions to cover broader geographical areas. Many general partners have established offices in several countries and operate as virtual teams. However, given the generally thin organizations, such international operation may be very different compared to traditional venture capital.

The expanded geographical scope also often means the need to profile in some dimension and develop a focus, for instance, in a certain industry sector to differentiate from competition. Partnering with other VCs established in other locations has become increasingly important. As shown in several studies (Mäkelä and Maula 2008), a trusted partner in the local market is important for syndication.

Finally, although internationalization is an interesting strategy to expand deal flow, identify attractive business opportunities, and diversify internationally, it is not an easy one. For instance, managing a portfolio consisting of portfolio companies located in different countries will require a lot of traveling. It also takes a lot of time and effort to develop contacts and reputation in foreign markets to be able to attract the best deals. The paradox is that many international operations of GPs have been too short-lived to make it possible to succeed (e.g., the wave of cross-border VC at the turn of the millennium).

Implications to Limited Partners

For limited partners, geographical diversification is obviously beneficial from a risk management perspective just as in other asset classes. Venture capital and private equity markets differ in their maturity and development, and diversification reduces the risks related to any single market. From a practical perspective, geographical diversification poses challenges for limited partners. Although strong market insight is very important in all asset classes, investments in venture capital and private equity funds have some differences compared to public equity. Compared to public equity where investments can be made online, private equity requires due diligence and negotiations that cannot be done remotely. Therefore, geographical diversification leads to more traveling for institutional investors. However, the increasing internationalization of many general partners somewhat reduces the need for geographical diversification on the fund level since internationalized GPs can cover broader geographical markets. Also funds of funds can support institutional investors in remote geographical markets.

Implications to Policy Makers

From a policy perspective, it is well established that venture capital plays an important role in facilitating the growth and development of many of the most successful young innovative growth companies and in contributing positively to innovation and economic and employment growth (Achleitner and Klöckner 2005; Alemany and Martí 2005; Belke, Fehn, and Foster 2003; Bertoni, Colombo, and Grilli 2008; Engel and Keilbach 2007; Kortum and Lerner 2000; Meyer 2006; Romain and Van Pottelsberghe 2004). Given the primary interest in facilitating growth companies rather than investors, the availability of venture capital and private equity for companies established in the focal country is an important policy issue in many countries in the world.

One way to improve the conditions for stronger entrepreneurial ventures and to improve the availability of entrepreneurial finance is to reduce the fragmentation of the venture capital marketplace. The reduction of fragmentation essentially means making it easier for venture capital investors to cover larger geographical areas than just individual countries. In practice this means increased harmonization of the regulations that investors have to deal with when investing in foreign countries and reduction of the various kinds of tax and legal environment–related barriers to cross-border investments that still exist in many countries.

Although many of the factors influencing cross-border venture capital flows are such that they are difficult to change, especially in the short term, there are some that are easier to address. The most central and easy approaches are the removal of legal uncertainty and the improvement of the informational basis for investment decisions.

DIRECTIONS FOR FUTURE RESEARCH

Although research on cross-border VC has evolved very rapidly during the past few years, the number of published articles is still quite modest, and most of them have opened more new questions rather than exhausted opportunities for contribution. Regarding directions for future research, a few ideas are presented here.

What is apparent from the review of existing studies on cross-border VC is that it is a complex, multifaceted phenomenon requiring multiple lenses and research designs to be properly understood. Examined from the perspective of the venture capital cycle, it appears that most of the current research has focused on explaining investments, that is, why do VCs invest abroad and, if so, which countries would they invest in and why. Furthermore, many studies have examined how foreign investments differ from domestic ones and why. However, there is still relatively little research on cross-border fund-raising or exits. Given that fund-raising influences investments, and exits influence fund-raising, it can be expected that more contributions are needed in fund-raising and exit stages of the VC cycle. Furthermore, there is also relatively little research examining and explaining the performance of cross-border VC. Also the roles and interplay of different types of investors and intermediaries (e.g., corporate VCs, public VCs, and business angels) in the cross-border context offers opportunities for contributions.

Regarding research design aspects, the existing research quite clearly shows that determinants of cross-border VC are often a combination of market attractiveness aspects and connections between individual actors that explain whether investments are being made. Such interaction between different levels of determinants calls for increased adoption of methods suitable for multilevel analysis (Hitt et al. 2007). Another important issue to consider more seriously in future research on cross-border VC is the potential endogeneity of explanatory variables. Quite often, it can be argued that choices concerning different aspects of cross-border VC are strategic and dependent on the expected profitability of those choices under given circumstances (Hamilton and Nickerson 2003; Li and Prabhala 2006). In general, increased attention is needed to ascertain the causality in the examined relationships.

CONCLUSION

In parallel with the globalization of the venture capital and private equity market, a new stream of literature examining cross-border venture capital and private equity investments has emerged. Starting from more descriptive studies and questions concerning the motivations and determinants of VC internationalization, research has expanded to cover all phases of the VC cycle and has already adopted various theoretical perspectives and research designs. Despite this, the stream is still in its infancy with a lot of potential for new contributions.

REFERENCES

Achleitner, A., and O. Klöckner. 2005. Employment Contribution of private equity and venture capital in Europe. Munich, Germany: Center for Entrepreneurial and Financial Studies, Technische Universität München.

Aguinis, H., et al. 2009. First Decade of organizational research methods: Trends in Design, measurement, and data-analysis topics. *Organizational Research Methods* 12(1):69.

Aizenman, J., and J. Kendall. 2008. The internationalization of venture capital and private equity: NBER Working Paper No. 14344. http://www.nber.org/papers/w14344.

Alemany, L., and J. Martí. 2005. Unbiased estimation of economic impact of venture capital backed firms. EFA 2005 Moscow Meetings Papers.

Alhorr, H. S., C. B. Moore, and G. T. Payne. 2008. The impact of economic integration on cross-border venture capital investments: Evidence from the European Union. *Entrepreneurship: Theory & Practice* 32(5):897–917.

Baygan, G., and M. Freudenberg. 2000. The internationalization of venture capital activity in OECD countries: Implications for measurement and policy. Paris: Organization for Economic Co-operation and Development. STI Working Papers-2000/7.

Belke, A. H., R. Fehn, and N. Foster. 2003. Does venture capital investment spur employment growth? CESIFO Working Paper No. 930.

Bertoni, F., M. G. Colombo, and L. Grilli. 2008. Venture capital financing and the growth of new technology-based firms. SSRN working paper. http://ssrn.com/abstract=1102233.

Bottazzi, L., M. Da Rin, and T. Hellmann. 2004. The changing face of the European venture capital industry: Facts and analysis. *Journal of Private Equity* 7(2):26–53.

_____. 2007. The importance of trust for investment: Evidence from Venture Capital. ECGI-Finance Working Paper No. 187/2007.

_____. forthcoming. What is the role of legal systems in financial intermediation? Theory and evidence. *Journal of Financial Intermediation*.

Cumming, D. J., G. A. Fleming, and A. Schwienbacher. 2005. Liquidity risk and venture capital finance. *Financial Management* 34(4):77–105.

_____. 2006. Legality and venture capital exits. *Journal of Corporate Finance* 12(2):214–245.

_____. Corporate relocation in venture capital finance. *Entrepreneurship Theory and Practice* 33 (5): 1121–1155.

Cumming, D. J., and S. A. Johan. 2007. Regulatory harmonization and the development of private equity markets. *Journal of Banking & Finance* 31(1):3218–3250.

Da Rin, M., G. Nicodano, and A. Sembenelli. 2006. Public policy and the creation of active venture capital markets. *Journal of Public Economics* 90(8):1699–1723.

Deloitte. 2007. Global trends in venture capital 2007 survey. Deloitte Touche Tohmatsu.

Engel, D. and M. Keilbach. 2007. Firm-level implications of early stage venture capital investment—An empirical investigation. *Journal of Empirical Finance* 14(2):150–167.

European Commission. 2007. Removing obstacles to cross-border investments by venture capital funds. (COM(2007) 853 final). Brussels, Belgium: Commission of the European Communities.

Fernhaber, S. A., and P. P. McDougall. 2009. Venture Capitalists as catalysts to new venture internationalization: The impact of their investments, reputation and knowledge resources. *Entrepreneurship Theory and Practice* 33(1):277–295.

Gompers, P. 1994. The Rise and Fall of Venture Capital. *Business and economic history* 23(2):1–26.

———, and J. Lerner. 1999. *The venture capital cycle*. Cambridge: MIT Press.

Griffith, T. L., P. J. Yam, and S. Subramaniam. 2007. Silicon Valley's "one-hour" distance rule and managing return on location. *Venture Capital: An International Journal of Entrepreneurial Finance* 9(2):85–106.

Groh, A. P., H. Liechtenstein, and M. A. Canela. 2008. International allocation determinants of institutional investments in venture capital and private equity limited partnerships. IESE Working Paper WP-726.

Groh, A. P., H. Liechtenstein, and K. Lieser. 2008. The European Venture Capital and Private Equity Country Attractiveness Index(es). IESE Working Paper WP-773.

Guler, I., and M. F. Guillén. forthcoming. Knowledge, Institutions and Organizational Growth: The Internationalization of U.S. Venture Capital Firms. *Journal of International Business Studies*.

———. forthcoming. Home-country networks and foreign expansion. Academy of Management Journal.

———. 2007. Transnational connections and strategic choice: Venture capital firms' entry into foreign markets. Working paper. Boston University.

Guler, I., and A. M. McGahan. 2007a. The more the merrier? Institutions and syndication size in international venture capital investments. Working paper. Boston University.

———. 2007b. Syndication in international venture investing. Working paper. Boston University.

Hall, G., and C. Tu. 2003. Venture capitalists and the decision to invest overseas. *Venture Capital: An International Journal of Entrepreneurial Finance* 5(2):181–190.

Hamilton, B. H., and J. A. Nickerson. 2003. Correcting for endogeneity in strategic management research. *Strategic Organization* 1:51–78.

Heikkilä, T. 2004. European single market and the globalisation of private equity fundraising: barriers and determinants of foreign commitments in private equity funds. Master's thesis. Espoo, Finland: Helsinki University of Technology.

Hitt, M. A., et al. 2007. Building theoretical and empirical bridges across levels: Multilevel research in management. *Academy of Management Journal* 50(6):1385–1399.

Hursti, J., and M. V. J. Maula. 2007. Acquiring financial resources from foreign equity capital markets: An examination of factors influencing foreign initial public offerings. *Journal of Business Venturing* 22(6):833–851.

Jääskeläinen, M., and M. V. J. Maula. 2008. Do networks of financial intermediaries help reduce local bias? Evidence from cross-border venture capital. Working paper. Helsinki University of Technology.

Jeng, L. A., and P. C. Wells. 2000. The determinants of venture capital funding: Evidence across countries. *Journal of Corporate Finance* 6:241–289.

Kaplan, S. N., F. Martel, and P. Strömberg. 2007. How do legal differences and experience affect financial contracts? *Journal of Financial Intermediation* 16(3): 273–311.

Khavul, S., et al. 2009. Who hooks up with whom? Initial selection of international partners in an emerging market. Working paper. University of Texas at Arlington.

Kortum, S., and J. Lerner. 2000. Assessing the contribution of venture capital to innovation. *Rand Journal of Economics* 31(4):674–692.

Li, K., and N. R. Prabhala. 2006. Self-selection models in corporate finance. In *Handbook of corporate finance: Empirical corporate finance*, vol. A, ed. B. E. Eckbo. Amsterdam: Elsevier/North-Holland.

Mäkelä, M. M., and M. V. J. Maula. 2005. Cross-border venture capital and new venture internationalization: An isomorphism perspective. *Venture Capital: An International Journal of Entrepreneurial Finance* 7(3):227–257.

———. 2006. Interorganizational commitment in syndicated cross-border venture capital investments. *Entrepreneurship Theory and Practice* 30(2):273–298.

———. 2008. Attracting foreign venture capital: The role of a local investor. *Entrepreneurship and Regional Development* 20:237–257.

Manigart, S., et al. 2007. Human capital and the internationalisation of venture capital firms. *International Entrepreneurship and Management Journal* 3(1):109–125.

Maula, M. V. J., and M. M. Mäkelä. 2003. Cross-border venture capital. In *Financial systems and firm performance: Theoretical and empirical perspectives*, ed. A. Hyytinen and M. Pajarinen (269–291). Helsinki: Taloustieto Ltd.

Meuleman, M., and M. Wright. 2007. Cross-border private equity syndication: Cultural barriers, legal context and learning. Nottingham, UK: Centre for Management Buyout Research. CMBOR Occasion Paper.

Meyer, J. E., and J. J. Shao. 1995. International venture capital portfolio diversification & agency costs. *Multinational Business Review* 3(1):53–58.

Meyer, T. 2006. Private equity, spice for European economies. *Journal of Financial Transformation* 19:61–69.

Romain, A., and B. Van Pottelsberghe. 2004. The economic impact of venture capital. Discussion Paper Series 1: Studies of the Economic Research Center, N 18/2004: Deutsche Bundesbank.

Schertler, A., and T. Tykvová. 2008. Stay at home or go abroad? The impact of fiscal and legal environments on the geography of private equity flows. Working paper. Kiel University.

Tykvová, T., and A. Schertler. 2006. Rivals or partners? Evidence from Europe's international private equity deals. ZEW Discussion Paper No. 06-091.

———. 2008. Syndication to overcome transaction costs of cross-border investments? Evidence from a worldwide private equity deals' dataset. Working paper. ZEW Mannheim.

Wang, X. 2008. Exit and foreign venture capital firms' behavior in transitional economies Presented at the Academy of Management Meetings 2008, Anaheim, CA.

Wright, M., B. C., P. Mustar, and A. Lockett. 2007. *Academic Entrepreneurship in Europe*. Cheltenham, UK: Edward Elgar.

Wright, M., A. Lockett, and S. Pruthi. 2002. Internationalization of western venture capitalists into emerging markets: Risk assessment and information in India. *Small Business Economics* 19(1):13–29.

Wright, M., S. Pruthi, and A. Lockett. 2005. International venture capital research: From cross-country comparisons to crossing borders. *International Journal of Management Reviews* 7(3):135–165.

ABOUT THE AUTHOR

Markku V. J. Maula is Professor of Venture Capital at Helsinki University of Technology TKK, Institute of Strategy, Finland. His research interests focus on issues related to value creation in business strategy and corporate finance with a particular focus on venture capital and private equity, technology-based new firms, corporate venturing, and innovation policy. His research has received international awards and been published in leading scholarly journals including *Strategic Management Journal, Journal of Business Venturing, Entrepreneurship Theory & Practice,* and *Research Policy*. In addition to his research and teaching roles, he has acted as an advisor to firms and government agencies in issues related to venture capital, corporate venturing, and innovation policy.

## CHAPTER 22

The Canadian Public Venture Capital Market

CÉCILE CARPENTIER
Professor, Laval University, School of Accountancy

JEAN-MARC SURET
Professor, Laval University, School of Accountancy

INTRODUCTION

Venture capital (VC) is typically associated with the private placement of equity or quasi-equity by specialized institutional investors. For Gompers and Lerner (2001, 155), "specialized financial intermediaries, such as venture capital organizations, can alleviate the information gaps, which allows firms to receive the financing that they cannot raise from other sources." VC investors have developed methods, expertise, and tools to screen, fund, advise, and monitor the most promising ventures. Even if some of them act as business angels, individual investors are generally not associated with VC activities. This is probably because, as Fenn, Liang, and Prowse (1996, 1) note, "few investors had the skills necessary to invest directly in this asset class, and those that did found it difficult to use their skills efficiently." Accordingly, a public VC market, where individual investors finance emerging companies, should not succeed or even survive. In Europe, several countries have implemented new (or junior) stock markets, devoted to the financing of growing companies. They apply more lenient listing rules and often do not require profitability. To be listed, companies must meet the minimal listing requirements that exclude nascent companies. These junior markets are commonly used as an exit vehicle by private VC providers and are generally considered as failures (Bottazzi and Da Rin 2002). This verdict is consistent with the proposition that public markets are not well suited for financing growing companies, even if these companies are no longer in the early stage of development. In this context, the creation of a public VC market devoted mainly to early-stage companies can be considered an unrealistic objective.

Nonetheless, this type of market has long been active in Canada. To our knowledge, the TSX Venture Exchange (TSXV) is the only public VC market in the world. Although one might argue that the London Alternative Investment Market (AIM) and First North in the Nordic countries could claim this status because they apply principle-based listing standards instead of quantified minimum listing requirements, firms listed on the AIM are very similar to those listed on the main Canadian stock market, the Toronto Stock Exchange (TSX). On First North, the mean market capitalization and initial public offering (IPO) gross proceeds represent respectively 4 and 10 times those observed on the TSXV.

The Canadian situation provides a unique opportunity to analyze the extent to which a public VC market can stimulate the success of emerging businesses while mitigating the multiple consequences of the large asymmetry of information prevailing in this type of financing. This situation also allows us to compare the outcome of two approaches to growing business finance. The TSXV is totally free of public policy grants and advantages, while the VC market is heavily distorted by generous public policies, in particular the Labour-sponsored VC fund program, which represented approximately half of the Canadian VC activity during the period examined (Cumming and MacIntosh 2007).

This chapter describes and analyzes how a stock exchange can be used to finance emerging companies and to assume the role usually played by private VCs. We find that this public VC market has a success rate that is approximately four times the corresponding rate for private VC. The public VC market provides approximately seven times as many new listings to the main market as private VCs (Carpentier, L'Her, and Suret forthcoming). For a five-year horizon, the delisting rate of newly listed companies is much lower than the failure rate observed for the private VC sector in Canada. Finally, the comparison of the returns shows that the public VC market outperforms the private one. We conclude that a public VC market is indeed able to compete with a private one, even if it does not have the tools, skills, and value added capabilities usually attributed to private VCs.

The rest of the chapter is organized as follows. In the following section, we analyze the public VC market from a conceptual perspective and evidence the large differences between the public and the private approach to VC. The various mechanisms new firms use to enter the TSXV and to raise successive financings are described in the following section. We also summarize, in this section, the main characteristics of the newly listed companies. After that, we study the results of this experimentation, both in terms of failures and successes (graduation to the main exchange). The next section compares the rate of return of the public and the private VC markets in Canada. The last section is devoted to discussion of the lessons of the Canadian experimentation in terms of regulation, public policy, and financing strategy for growing firms.

DESCRIPTION AND CONCEPTUAL ANALYSIS OF THE SITUATION

The Canadian Stock Market and Venture Capital Market

In Canada, nascent companies wishing to obtain equity finance after the seed money–stage of development can choose between two paths, as illustrated in Exhibit 22.1. The first option is to turn to the Canadian classic VC market, which is generally considered the third-largest in the world in terms of available funds. The second path is the TSXV, the public VC market. At the entrance, subsequent rounds of financing, and exit stages, both markets present similarities. Newly created companies with no history or sales are allowed to list on the TSXV because of very

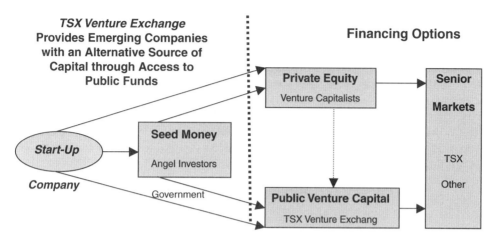

Exhibit 22.1 The Canadian Market for Growing Business Financing, as Depicted by a Professional in the Field

Source: Public Venture Capital. Kevin Strong, Manager, Winnipeg Office. TSX Venture Exchange. May 10, 2006. www.sata.ca.docs.2006%2005%2010%20SATA.ppt.

lenient listing requirements. They can enter the market using a reverse merger (RM) on a public shell, an IPO, or a capital pool company (CPC). The CPC program has been implemented in Canada as a clone of the U.S. blind pool program, to help emerging companies access the stock market. Similar to the classic VC market, the TSXV offers several equity financing avenues. In both markets, investors can provide subsequent rounds of financing. Private placements are also commonly used by the TSXV-listed companies. Lastly, just as the most profitable exit for classic VCs is an IPO, the objective of the TSXV is to graduate its best performers to the TSX.

In addition to the TSX and the TSXV, there are two secondary and more recently created markets: the NEX and the Canadian National Stock Exchange (CNSX).[1] There were 1,578 issuers listed on the TSX and 2,261 issuers listed on the TSXV as of November 30, 2008. The main market itself is equivalent to the London AIM in terms of characteristics of listed companies, and can be considered a market devoted to growing companies (Rousseau 2006). All but the largest 245 companies on the TSX are small or micro-capitalization companies according to Nicholls (2006, 160). A leading law firm in the country considers that the AIM and the TSX offer "a real exit for mature companies not ready for the pros."[2] The TSXV aims to feed this market. This creates an original situation where a junior market is fed by a public VC market whereas in most countries, the conventional VC market is the natural feeder of the junior exchange.

The TSXV[3] calls itself a "public venture market." Kevin Strong, the manager of the Winnipeg Office of the TSXV, describes this market as a "national market for publicly traded venture companies offering venture companies and their investors a quality, liquid and efficient environment for capital raising and investing," and "a fully-regulated national stock exchange that exists to improve access to capital and provide public company experience and mentorship to emerging companies prior to graduation to a senior stock exchange."[4] Notably, the TSXV aims to provide the management of newly public companies with mentoring and stream-lined graduation to the TSX.[5] This exchange has very low initial and ongoing listing requirements. New companies can list with no revenues. Their stock price should be higher than CAN$0.15, and their minimum net tangible assets, includ-ing the IPO proceeds, have been set at CAN$500,000 or CAN$750,000 depending on the period.[6] If we apply the definitions of small and micro caps stated by the Advisory Committee on Smaller Companies (SEC 2006), about 98 percent of the TSXV companies could be considered micro capitalization companies (Nicholls 2006). The TSXV lists a large number of resources companies, a sector in which VC involvement is traditionally low. It is generally assumed that over 50 percent of the world's traded mining companies are listed on one of the two main Canadian Exchanges, and resources companies represent approximately 50 percent of the new listings on the TSXV. In this sector, the listing requirements are minimal. For a Tier 2 listing, an Exploration Company should have spent at least CAN$100,000 in the past three years, must have geologic merit, and a planned work program valued at CAN$200,000 or more. At the time of listing, the company must have sufficient funds to carry out the planned work program plus meet all required property or option payments and general and administrative costs for 12 months. No requirements apply to net tangible assets.

The consequences of these very low listing requirements are illustrated in Exhibit 22.2, where we report the distribution of stock prices and market capital-ization at the end of 2006. Accordingly, this table illustrates that than 82.07 percent (97.79 percent) of TSXV-listed stocks trade at prices lower than one (five) Canadian dollars, and 80.53 percent of TSXV firms have a market capitalization lower than CAN$30 million.

The large relative weight of resources companies is probably a partial explana-tion for the growth of this public VC market in Canada. Classic VCs generally do not invest in natural resources, and the public market could be required to obviate the lack of equity financing for this sector. However, the Canadian situation can also be attributed to the inefficiency of the conventional VC market, largely influenced by public policies promoting poorly designed Labour-Sponsored VC funds (Cum-ming and MacIntosh 2006; Cumming and MacIntosh 2007). In consequence, the stock market has been largely used as a substitute for the VC market. As Cumming (2006, 221) notes, "the comparatively lower quality of Canada's VC market gives rise to a need for Canadian companies to access public capital markets earlier than their counterparts in the U.S." In Canada, new business financing provided by the public VC market has largely exceeded that provided by the private market since 2002, as illustrated in Exhibit 22.3.

Most of the theoretical research devoted to venture capitalists (VCs) concludes that a public VC market could not succeed in the long run. The next section explains why.

Why a Public VC Market Should Not Succeed

Several theoretical arguments assert that the development of new ventures through a stock market is not feasible, consistent with the evidence provided by experi-mentation with new markets in Europe. A stock market and individual investors have neither the tools nor the capacity to resolve the agency and asymmetric

Exhibit 22.2 Main Characteristics of TSVX-Listed Companies at End of 2006, According to *TSVX Review*

Stocks not traded during the year are set to 0. Panel A reports the stock price distribution in Canadian dollars. Panel B reports the market capitalization in CAN$ million.

	Frequency	Relative Frequency %	Cumulative Frequency %
Panel A: Stock Prices, in Canadian dollars ($)			
$0	51	2.39	2.39
$0.05	92	4.32	6.71
$0.1	165	7.74	14.45
$0.2	418	19.62	34.07
$0.3	274	12.86	46.93
$0.4	201	9.43	56.36
$0.5	152	7.13	63.49
$0.75	247	11.59	75.08
$1	149	6.99	82.07
$1.5	139	6.52	88.60
$5	196	9.20	97.79
$10	32	1.50	99.30
More than $10	15	0.70	100.00
Total	2,131	100.00	
Panel B: Market Capitalizations, in CAN$ million ($M)			
$0 M	51	2.39	2.39
$1 M	152	7.13	9.53
$2 M	182	8.54	18.07
$5 M	362	16.99	35.05
$10 M	368	17.27	52.32
$15 M	230	10.79	63.12
$20 M	169	7.93	71.05
$30 M	202	9.48	80.53
$50 M	159	7.46	87.99
$100 M	146	6.85	94.84
$500 M	100	4.69	99.53
More than $500 M	10	0.47	100.00
Total	2,131	100.00	200.00

information problems associated with new and growing businesses. As Amit, Brander, and Zott (1998) posit, information asymmetries are the key to understanding the VC industry. To circumvent these asymmetries, VCs have developed particular tools and methods, which are briefly presented in Exhibit 22.4 along with the equivalent (if any) in the public VC market.

The first, and perhaps most significant, difference between the private and the public market lies in the screening of venture projects. A stock market with listing requirements based on minimal quantitative benchmarks cannot perform a due diligence review of listing candidates. All firms fulfilling the minimal listing requirements can list on the TSXV, while the VCs generally finance a very low proportion of the projects they analyze. VCs choose a project following a thorough

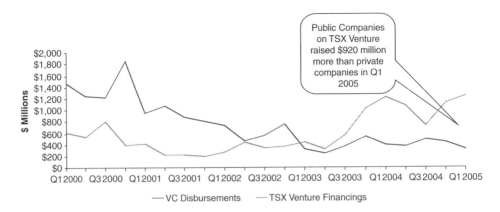

TSX Venture figures include Resources (Mining and Oil and Gas)
and Real Estate sectors financing statistics.

Exhibit 22.3 Financing on TSVX Compared with VC Disbursements, 2000 to 2005
Source: Public Venture Capital. Kevin Strong, Manager, Winnipeg Office. TSX Venture Exchange. SAT,
May 10, 2006. www.sata.ca.docs.2006%2005%2010%20SATA.ppt. The data originate from TSX Group
and Macdonald and Associates as of March 2005.

due diligence process concerning the various dimensions of the venture, including
its management and the market for the product or service. A second important
difference between the public and the private market is the use, by the latter, of
incentive contracts and specially designed securities. These tools serve to control
agency problems and associated risks. The public venture market has only conventional stocks and warrants at its disposal. Private VCs are presumed to provide
value-added services in several areas of firms' activities. The public market cannot
provide these services, and the sponsor's role is limited to ascertaining that the firm
is suitable for the market. Moreover, in several cases, the sponsor is not involved
in the listing process. The stock exchange exempts an issuer from the sponsorship
requirements when it raises an IPO, and the prospectus is executed by at least one
member of the exchange, and, since the 2002 revision of the TSXV policy, a CPC
is no longer required to retain a sponsor for an IPO, provided that it has an agent
sign the CPC prospectus as an underwriter.[7]

One can argue that firms that opt for the public venture market cannot benefit
from value-added activities usually provided by VC. Further, firms financed by
the public VC market are likely to reach the main market under less favorable
conditions than companies backed by VCs. These VCs spend considerable time
monitoring firm management before the IPO (Gompers 1995) because they have
incentives to set strong governance structures in their portfolio firms (Hochberg
2006); this is known as the "monitoring effect." Moreover, as underlined by Lerner
(1995) and by Barry and colleagues (1990), VCs frequently retain a seat on the
newly listed firm's board even after cashing out. Lerner argues that it may be
expected that these firms will experience fewer agency problems because VCs
are specialized providers of oversight. VCs have strong incentives to set optimal
governance systems before their portfolio firm goes public, because their returns
depend on the share price when the lockup rules permit them to sell their stake. This
is called the "oversight effect." Finally, Chemmanur and Loutskina (2006) evidence

Exhibit 22.4   Comparison of Tools and Skills Available to Conventional and Public Venture Capital (VC) Markets

Tools, Methods, and Skills	Conventional VC Market	Public VC Market
Selection of more promising deals	Specific analysis tools, knowledge of the sectors. VCs have a direct and strong incentive to select the best projects.	No selection. New companies must fulfill minimal listing requirements. No incentive to select the best projects.
Information collection	VCs use due diligence process and their knowledge of the technologies and market to determine the value of the projects.	Prospectus if the listing is done via an IPO; notice and minimal information when the listing is done by RM in several provinces.
Management valuation and knowledge	Management experience is assessed.	Officers, directors, and holders of more than 10% of a company's voting securities complete information forms, allowing the TSXV to conduct background checks before approving a listing.
Incentive contracts	Generally used. Shareholders agreements adapted to the specific context.	Not available.
Monitoring and value added service	Value-added services in several areas of management, including strategy, marketing, and finance.	A participating organization can provide a sponsorship letter. Sponsors confirm whether the issuer satisfies the initial listing requirements and comment on the ability of the firm to meet its obligations as a public company.
Networking capacity	Significant, mainly for sector specialized VCs.	None.
Exit mechanism	VCs possess market power and knowledge of the IPO process. VCs remain involved in the newly listed firm, because the value they get from the IPO is determined by the stock price at the end of the lock-up period.	Graduation toward a more senior exchange. The exchange provides technical help for graduation, but it has neither the motivation nor the resources to provide the graduating companies with the services usually provided by VC at the IPO exit time.

a "market power effect." VCs develop long-term relationships with participants in the IPO market, such as underwriters, institutional investors, and analysts. These relationships increase the participation by these market players in the IPOs.

The comparison between the tools, resources, and skills of a private and a public market for VC illustrates that only the former can resolve the asymmetry, risk, and agency problems that prevail in the financing of new ventures. As Korcsmaros (2002, 4) maintains, "the jury is still out on the accomplishments attained by stock exchanges dedicated to serving SMEs and the extent to which they have been successful in bringing SMEs to the capital market." There is support for the notion that, especially for emerging economies, stock exchanges are particularly relevant to help medium-sized indigenous firms gain access to finance and promote local market development. However, there are specific doubts regarding the suitability of financing emerging ventures through an exchange. Consequently, the analysis of the Canadian public venture market is of great interest.

ENTRANCE MECHANISMS
The Penny Stock IPO Process

In the United States, several regulatory changes strongly restrict the issuing of penny stock IPOs. The Penny Stock Reform Act of 1990 (PSRA) was mainly an attempt to curb fraudulent security issues by placing severe restrictions on IPOs priced below $5. As evidenced by Bradley and colleagues (2006), penny stock IPOs are rare in the United States. From 1990 to 1998, these authors mention 251 penny stock IPOs and 2,707 ordinary IPOs. However, the gross proceeds of the penny stocks of their sample ($5.7 million) are approximately four times those reported in Canada during the same period. This illustrates the distinctive situation of the stock market in Canada. This situation prevails because the Canadian and U.S. stock exchanges and regulators have followed opposite paths. In Canada, there are no requirements for minimum stock price, and companies are allowed to list at a prerevenue stage, with minimal shareholders' equity and prices generally lower than one Canadian dollar.

The initial listing requirements have changed several times over the years and vary by sector. As a result, characterization of the newly listed companies illustrates the requirements more clearly than the list of criteria would. For the last 20 years, the median issue price, preissue shareholders' equity, and gross proceeds were CAN$0.75, CAN$180,000 and CAN$550,000 respectively. Almost 59 percent of issuers report no revenues, and 84 percent report negative earnings. The majority of Canadian IPOs can be considered penny stock IPOs, while in most countries, minimal listing requirements exclude microcapitalization and start-up companies from the market. However, consistent with the arguments of several practitioners and academics that the listing rules are too restrictive, alternative listing modes have been developed and actively promoted by the exchanges. They include the RM listing method and the use of the CPC Program.

Reverse Mergers

An RM listing is a merger between a public shell company, generally inactive, and the target, a privately held company. The shell generally has a very low market value. For the illustration presented in Exhibit 22.5, we use a value of CAN$1

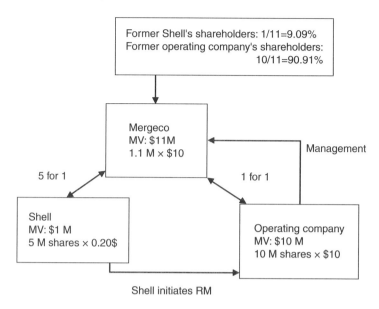

Exhibit 22.5 Illustration of the Reverse Merger Listing Method Used on the TSVX Market

million, comprised of 5 million shares priced at CAN$0.20. Operating closed firms that seek listing generally have a much higher value: for illustration purposes, we attribute to such a firm a value of 1 million shares priced at CAN$10. The resulting company, which we name Mergeco, results from the merger of the two former firms. The merger entails an exchange of shares, and a private placement is often raised. Because of the difference in value between the shell and the operating company, the shareholders of the operating company acquire the majority of the shares of the resulting entity. These shareholders ultimately control the public shell company, which is why this transaction is called a *reverse* merger. RMs take place in the exempt market: this means that newly listed companies are exempt from filing a prospectus and need not comply with the registration requirements prevailing for IPOs.[8] Moreover, during an RM, the company cannot issue equity publicly, because these transactions are not considered public offerings and are not associated with the approval of a prospectus by the authorities. As a result, the private company becomes public by buying the shell and does not need to issue a prospectus, sell new shares to the public, or meet the minimum listing requirements.

The frequency of RM is constrained by the availability of shells. "Classic" shells are once-active companies that failed to develop and ceased or strongly reduced their activities. They are mostly NEX listed companies that could not meet the ongoing listing requirements of the other exchanges. "Manufactured" shells are created specifically from zero, using the CPC program.

The CPC Program

The first Junior Capital Pool program was launched in Alberta at the end of 1986. This program was an adaptation of the U.S. Blind Pool (Blank Check Company, BCC) program. In 1997, a similar program was adopted in British Columbia. The CPC program replaced the two previous programs following the merger of the

Vancouver and Alberta Stock Exchanges in November 1999. In Ontario and Quebec, the program has been in force on the TSXV since 2002. The CPC program is a two-stage process. The first stage involves the completion of the IPO and the listing of the CPC on the exchange. The CPC is a listed corporation with no assets or business plan, no operating history, and no assets except cash. Its sole goal is to find and acquire assets or companies as takeover targets. The second stage involves an agreement in principle relative to a qualifying transaction. Once this transaction is completed, the new entity must satisfy the exchange's minimum listing requirements for the particular industrial sector. The resulting issuer (RI) may be listed for regular trading either in Tier 1 or Tier 2. In the United States, BCCs commonly used in the 1980s as shells have been severely restricted by the Securities and Exchange Commission (SEC), which enacted Rule 419 in 1992, designed to protect investors against fraud in RM transactions (Feldman 2006, chap. 4). However, creative lawyers developed the special purpose acquisition company ("SPAC")[9] to work around the new regulations without defeating the regulations' purpose of investor protection (Heyman 2007).

A Picture of the New Listings

In Exhibit 22.6, we report the main characteristics of the firms that have accessed the TSXV during the last two decades, by subperiod and by type of listing method. These firms are microcapitalization corporations: their premoney shareholders' equity is approximately CAN$300,000. The listing does not coincide with collection of significant amounts of cash. If we consider the private placements occurring during RM as the equivalent of the IPO's gross proceeds, we get a median (mean)

Exhibit 22.6 Main Characteristics of 3,857 New Listings on the TSVX from 1986 to 2006, by Listing Method

CPC means Capital Pool Companies. Mean and median gross proceeds, assets and shareholders' equity are in CAN$ million ($M). % means percentage. EPS means earnings per share.

Type of listing	Initial Public Offering	Reverse Merger	Resulting Issuer from CPC	All New Listings
Number	1,982	825	1,050	3,857
Mean Gross Proceeds, in $M	1.61	2.94	2.36	2.08
Median Gross Proceeds, in $M	0.55	0.66	1.14	0.65
Assets, in $M	0.54	1.60	0.80	0.71
Shareholders' Equity, in $M	0.18	0.71	0.32	0.26
% of High Tech Issuers	16.04	14.67	29.12	19.29
% of Natural Resources Issuers	55.55	41.58	39.27	48.14
% of Issuers without Revenues at the Issue	58.68	41.00	29.96	49.26
% of Issuers with Negative EPS at the Issue	83.57	77.84	72.33	80.14

Source: Carpentier, L'Her, and Suret (forthcoming).

gross proceeds of CAN$650,000 (CAN$2 million) for all new listings. Moreover, 80.14 percent of newly listed firms report negative earnings at the listing time, and close to 50 percent of companies access the market at a prerevenue stage. These issuers have median assets of CAN$0.71 million. There are only slight differences between the companies, depending on the listing mode. The median shareholders' equity is larger for RMs (CAN$710,000) than for IPOs (CAN$180,000) and RIs of CPCs (CAN$320,000). The proportion of companies reporting no revenues (earnings) at the listing time ranges from 30 percent (72 percent) for RIs of CPCs to 59 percent (84 percent) for IPOs. Overall, the operational characteristics of firms financed through the TSXV resemble those of firms that can be financed by early-stage private VCs.

A very large proportion (more than 48 percent) of newly listed companies specialize in natural resources, including energy and mining. The proportion of technological firms (19.29 percent) appears low compared with the proportion of such investment by VCs in the United States, which is generally between 80 percent and 90 percent.[10] However, Brander, Egan, and Hellmann (2008) report that 33 percent of private VC investees are in technology sectors in Canada. The focus of VC thus differs sharply between the two countries.

According to Baygan (2003), in 2001, deals valued at CAN$5 million and above represented about 80 percent of all Canadian VC transactions, and the average deal size reached CAN$4.5 million at the beginning of the 2000s. Similar figures are provided by Industry Canada: the average deal size in VC reached CAN$3.0 million in 2002, after peaking at CAN$4.3 million in 2000—a 72 percent increase from the CAN$1.8 million average in 1996 (Industry Canada 2002). Accordingly, the median proceeds raised by newly listed Canadian companies (CAN$0.65 million) are significantly lower than the average deal in the Canadian VC market. The TSXV indeed competes with the early-stage component of the VC market, but the TSXV new listings are even smaller than the firms financed by private VCs. By summing the gross proceeds and the premoney shareholders' equity, we estimate the median postmoney shareholders' equity at CAN$1 million.

Subsequent Financing Rounds

In the conventional VC market, staging is a current practice, and the financed companies are provided with successive financing rounds. The situation is similar in the public VC market, where the listed companies issue a large number of private placements and subsequent public offerings. Most of these financing rounds occur when the companies do not report positive earnings or even sales. Exhibit 22.7 summarizes the financing activity of firms that listed on the TSXV between 1993 and 2006. A surprising result is that a large proportion of the firms analyzed had no financing activity following the listing. 39.38 percent of the IPOs issue neither private nor public equity. The same situation prevails for RMs (44.26 percent) and RIs of CPCs (46.10 percent). The reasons such companies list are unclear, but growth financing does not seem to be among them. The most plausible explanation is that a large proportion of newly listed companies do not fulfill the minimal conditions required to secure private or public outside equity.

Based on an extensive analysis of 3,720 private VC investments from 1996 to 2004, Brander, Egan, and Hellmann (2008, 12) report that "as of five years after first

Exhibit 22.7 Distribution of Subsequent Financing Activity between 1993 and 2006, of Companies Newly Listed on the TSVX

Total gross proceeds (GP) are in CAN$ million. Mean and median time until the first subsequent financing is in months. IPO means initial public offering. RM means reverse merger. CPC means capital pool company.

	# of firms	%	Private Placements				Seasoned Offerings			
			#	mean time	median time	total GP	#	mean time	median time	total GP
Panel A: IPO										
no financing	484	39.38	—	—	—	—	—	—	—	—
1 financing	379	30.84	197	28.65	16.39	2351.88	182	20.49	13.68	6363.46
2 financings	168	13.67	98	26.21	13.83	2461.55	70	20.15	13.22	3723.65
3 financings	85	6.92	46	23.64	17.18	1542.91	39	18.67	14.19	7005.91
>=4 financings	113	9.19	62	18.88	9.30	3154.69	51	13.72	11.27	16410.04
Total	1229	100.00	403	25.98	14.32	9511.03	342	19.20	12.57	33503.05
Panel B: RM										
no financing	274	44.26	—	—	—	—	—	—	—	—
1 financing	186	30.05	91	28.06	13.86	868.54	95	19.95	7.82	1098.37
2 financings	74	11.95	53	18.17	10.51	779.16	21	10.85	2.40	1061.27
3 financings	40	6.46	27	14.14	5.75	525.12	13	15.16	8.48	1110.18
>=4 financings	45	7.27	32	17.15	6.97	1339.24	13	7.49	3.32	680.43
Total	619	100.00	203	21.91	9.40	3512.05	142	17.02	6.80	3950.25
Panel C: Resulting Issuers from CPC										
no financing	378	46.10	—	—	—	—	—	—	—	—
1 financing	278	33.90	132	28.48	15.72	707.68	146	15.04	6.19	656.18
2 financings	78	9.51	47	22.97	6.90	557.60	31	12.75	4.60	603.69
3 financings	44	5.37	36	14.58	7.74	607.15	8	15.26	7.79	399.79
>=4 financings	42	5.12	33	26.68	18.04	907.99	9	19.03	14.06	493.26
Total	820	100.00	248	25.18	12.32	2780.42	194	14.87	6.11	2152.92

investment, about 10 percent of venture-supported enterprises have an IPO, about 25 percent are acquired by a third party, about 45 percent go out of business, and the remainder either experience another type of venture capital exit or simply continue as a venture-supported privately held enterprise." The proportion of TSXV newly listed companies that do not get subsequent rounds of financing is in the same range as the failure rate observed in the private VC market.

Following listing, a large proportion of firms (16 percent) issue private placements exclusively. Our analysis of these private placements indicates that they are essentially provided by individual investors. This is a puzzling result, especially for the backdoor new listings. Indeed, if these firms do not raise public offerings, they will never create a public market for their shares, and their stock liquidity will be low. One of the main advantages of a public listing is the decrease in the cost of equity through the creation of a liquid market for shares. Our analysis shows that the firms listed on the TSXV are not actively seeking this advantage.

The total financing obtained by the 854 firms involved in private placements is low: CAN$15.8 billion or CAN$18.5 million per firm over an average timeframe of 10 years. Only 25.41 percent of the newly listed firms get financing through a subsequent public offering. The mean time to raise this financing is approximately 17 months after the listing date. The median time ranges from 6 months for RIs of CPCs to 13 months for IPOs. Overall, a small subsample of firms (7.50 percent) obtained 4 financings or more, but they raise 41.48 percent of the total gross proceeds. From the financing strategy standpoint, firms that choose the public market exhibit a pattern of staged finance similar to the one observed in the private market.

PERFORMANCE OF THE PUBLIC VENTURE MARKET IN DEVELOPING NEW VENTURES

The performance of a venture market can be measured in several ways. We focus on the following dimensions.[11] First, we analyze the failure—or delisting—rate of new listings. Second, we study the success rate of the same listings. For VCs, the most successful exit is the IPO. In Canada, Brander, Egan, and Hellmann (2008, 18) consider that the IPO market is divided into two segments: "the senior exchanges (TSX), which signal that an enterprise has achieved a certain maturity and viability, and the junior exchanges, which do not guarantee either maturity or viability of the enterprise." We then compare the rate of VC-backed IPOs on the TSX with the rate of graduation from the TSXV to the same main market. A third pertinent dimension is the rate of return investors earn.

Definition and Measures

Delisting

In Canada, the delisting rules have allowed securities to stay listed for a very long period, even if they are traded at a very low price or not at all. For example, in December 2001, 313 stocks listed on the TSXV had prices equal to 3 cents or less. Several of these stocks have been used as shell companies during an RM listing. Before the creation of the NEX in 2003, companies falling below TSXV's ongoing listing standards were designated inactive and given 18 months to meet the standards or be delisted. However, the delisting is not systematic; the stock exchange uses flexibility and discretion in applying the rules.[12] The ongoing listing standards to Tier 2 of the junior market refer to a minimal market capitalization of CAN$100,000 (in 2007), minimal working capital of CAN$50,000, and significant operating revenues in the previous 12 months; or at least CAN$100,000 in expenditures directly related to the development of assets in the previous 12 months. No conditions apply to the stock price. By comparison, similar limits for the NASDAQ are $5 million for market capitalization and $1 for the stock price, under standard 1.[13]

To be able to estimate a failure rate, we applied a rule that mimics the NASDAQ delisting practice as well as the decision criteria used by Demers and Joos (2007), among others. We consider as "dead" any stock that maintains a price lower than CAN$0.10 for seven consecutive months. We use the 10-cent limit given that Canadian IPO prices are on average one-tenth of prices in United States.[14] This rule affects approximately 10 percent of newly listed companies, yet in many cases, the application of the rule has the sole effect of producing a delisting rule that is earlier than the date reported by the exchanges. We also consider as nonsurviving a stock that is used as a shell for an RM, all companies whose stocks were delisted by the exchange, or subject to an issuer cease trade order at the time of the analysis, failed companies that are not yet delisted, and those whose stocks are only traded OTC or NEX.

Mergers and Acquisitions
In the case of mergers, we assume that the resulting company is a continuation of the issuer. The issuer status is then one of a merged company. In the case of acquisitions, we collected the acquisition price per share (including the value of share exchanges) and qualified as failures the cases where the acquisition price is lower than CAN$0.10.

Success
The TSXV considers that a company succeeds if it graduates to the main Canadian market. To graduate, TSXV-listed companies have to comply with the TSX minimal listing requirements. Even if these requirements are higher than those prevailing on the TSXV, they appear to be very low relative to international standards. In 1998, the TSX introduced the "technology company standards," which required that companies have a minimum of CAN$10 million in treasury, adequate funds to cover all planned research and development (R&D) expenditures, general and administrative expenses and capital expenditures for a period of at least two years, and a minimum two-year operating history that included R&D activities. Accordingly, these listing standards allow developing companies to access the market easily while reporting negative earnings, even at a prerevenue stage of development.[15] For mineral exploration and development-stage companies, the only quantified requirements are working capital of at least CAN$2 million and net tangible assets of CAN$3 million. For industrial companies "forecasting profitability," the TSX requires net tangible assets of CAN$7.5 million and evidence (satisfactory to the TSX) of earnings from ongoing operations for the current or next fiscal year of at least CAN$200,000.

As its web site states, the TSXV promotes the migration of growing companies, which it strives to help graduate from the TSXV to the TSX "in a more efficient and economical manner than ever before.... Once a company has gained the skills necessary to operate successfully as a public venture and built a solid financial foundation, it's possible to graduate to a senior exchange such as TSX." The TSXV proposes the following benefits for graduation:[16] TSX listing application fee will be waived for eligible TSXV issuers; certain issuer information on file with TSXV can be accessed by the TSX; sponsorship requirements may be waived for qualified TSXV issuers; and a business development service helps the company in the graduation process. Graduations are proudly highlighted on the web site. The opportunity to graduate is a central argument in the promotion of actions organized by the exchange to attract new listings.[17]

The Results of the Public VC Market

An extensive data collection process enabled us to establish the status of 3,430 of the 3,857 newly listed firms included in the initial sample (88.93 percent). The missing observations mostly concern firms that list at the beginning of our period of analysis for which no data are subsequently available. A status of failure is probably the best guess for these firms. Exhibit 22.8 presents the distribution of the status by cohort and by listing method. We group RMs and RIs of CPCs (backdoor listings) because we do not observe material differences between these two categories in terms of evolution and status.

Overall, Panel A shows that, at the end of the study period, nonsurviving issuers represent 51.98 percent of the sample. The success rate (graduation or cross-listing) is 7.67 percent for the whole period. A proportion of 40.34 percent of issuers remains listed, but they do not graduate to a higher exchange. Therefore, in the long run, approximately 5 out of 10 new issuers in Canada fail, 1 succeeds, and 4 survive but do not progress. The failure rate of IPOs is slightly higher than the rate observed for the firms that use a backdoor listing method (56.91 percent versus 46.77 percent), and the success rate is also lower for the first group (6.76 percent versus 8.64 percent). This can indicate that IPO firms are, on average, of lower quality than the firms that use the backdoor listing method. However, no definitive conclusion can be reached without carefully controlling for sector and size of newly listed companies.

Panel C of Exhibit 22.8 allows a comparison with the results of previous studies, where failure and survival rates are generally estimated after three, four, and five years. The proportion of nonsurviving firms thus falls to 23.12 percent. Three U.S. studies deal specifically with penny stocks, comparable to, albeit larger than Canadian IPOs. Weber and Willenborg (2003) report a delisting rate of 25.3 percent after four years, Bradley and colleagues (2006) a rate of 31.5 percent after three years, and Dalbor and Sullivan (2005) estimate the failure rate at 44 percent. In a recent paper, Espenlaub, Khurshed, and Mohamed (2008) estimate the delisting rate at 21.68 percent after only two years for newly listed companies on the AIM. Despite listing requirements that are significantly more permissive than in the United States and even the fact that a large proportion of new issuers report no sales, the survival rate of new issuers in Canada after about five years seems to be lower or in the same range as the rate observed in other countries. This situation can probably be explained by the capacity of developing listed firms to issue private or public equity, even with negative earnings or no revenues, which would allow

Exhibit 22.8 Distribution of IPOs, Backdoor Listings (BLs), and All New Listings (All) between 1986 and 2006 by status at the end of the study period (June 2007, Panel A), ten years after listing (Panel B), and five years after listing (panel C).

Classifications by status at the end of the study period (June 2007, Panel A), 10 years after listing (Panel B), and 5 years after listing (Panel C). BL means backdoor listings.

	Total	Nonsurviving		Surviving, No Success		Success (Graduation)	
		Nb	%	Nb	%	Nb	%
Panel A: Status at the end of the study period, 1986–2006							
IPOs	1982	1128	56.91	720	36.33	134	6.76
Backdoor listings (BL)	1875	877	46.77	836	44.59	162	8.64
All new listings	3857	2005	51.98	1556	40.34	296	7.67
Panel B: Status 10 years after listing							
IPO 1986–1990	1126	391	34.72	693	61.55	42	3.73
IPO 1991–1995	266	106	39.85	145	54.51	15	5.64
IPO 1996–1997	137	63	45.99	60	43.80	14	10.22
IPO 1986–1997	1529	560	36.63	898	58.73	71	4.64
BL 1986–1990	158	98	62.03	53	33.54	7	4.43
BL 1991–1995	368	194	52.72	143	38.86	31	8.42
BL 1996–1997	160	75	46.88	65	40.63	20	12.50
BL 1986–1997	686	367	53.50	261	38.05	58	8.45
All 1986–1990	1284	489	38.08	746	58.10	49	3.82
All 1991–1995	634	300	47.32	288	45.43	46	7.26
All 1996–1997	297	138	46.46	125	42.09	34	11.45
All 1986–1997	2215	927	41.85	1159	52.33	129	5.82
Panel C: Status 5 years after listing							
IPO 1986–1990	1126	178	15.81	938	83.30	10	0.89
IPO 1991–1995	266	28	10.53	228	85.71	10	3.76
IPO 1996–1997	379	93	24.54	269	70.98	17	4.49
IPO 1998–2002	37	11	29.73	23	62.16	3	8.11
IPO 1986–2002	1808	310	17.15	1458	80.64	40	2.21
BL 1986–1990	158	60	37.97	93	58.86	5	3.16
BL 1991–1995	368	72	19.57	276	75.00	20	5.43
BL 1996–1997	685	224	32.70	420	61.31	41	5.99
BL 1998–2002	151	67	44.37	74	49.01	10	6.62
BL 1986–2002	1362	423	31.06	863	63.36	76	5.58
All 1986–1990	1284	238	18.54	1031	80.30	15	1.17
All 1991–1995	634	100	15.77	504	79.50	30	4.73
All 1996–1997	1064	317	29.79	689	64.76	58	5.45
All 1998–2002	188	78	41.49	97	51.60	13	6.91
All 1986–2002	3170	733	23.12	2321	73.22	116	3.66

emerging firms to finance their growth. Moreover, the failure rate observed on a 5-year horizon is lower than the rate reported by Brander, Egan, and Hellman (2008, 12) for the Canadian private equity market; they estimate that, at five years after first investment, about 45 percent of venture-supported enterprises go out of business. According to this statistic, the rate of mortality of newly financed firms is lower for the TSXV than for the private VC market.

Panel B of Exhibit 22.8 allows a comparison with the few studies that report failure rates over a long horizon (e.g., Fama and French 2004). The table shows that 41.85 percent of the new listings did not survive after 10 years. This rate is lower than the rate reported by Henser, Rutherford, and Springer (1997) for the same time horizon (55.1 percent). It is also consistent with the one reported by Fama and French (2004) for their IPO issuers whose assets are below those of the median NYSE firm, but the size of these NASDAQ-listed companies is much larger than that of firms observed on the TSXV. Albeit much smaller and less mature than their U.S. equivalents, Canadian newly listed companies exhibit a similar or higher survival rate.

We report, in Exhibit 22.8, the failure rates by cohort of newly listed companies, for each listing mode. This value indicates the extent to which the failure rate is increasing, as asserted in the United States by Fama and French (2004). After five years (Panel C), the rate of failure increases sharply for IPOs, from 15.81 percent to 29.73 percent for the cohort from 1998 to 2002. This failure rate also increases for backdoor listings and, overall, the proportion of failure at five years has doubled from the end of the 1980s to the beginning of the 2000s. The examination of the failure rate after ten years does not evidence a similar pattern (Panel B). For all the new listings, the rate increases from 38.08 percent to 46.46 percent. This rate of failure increases for IPOs and decreases for backdoor listings. The large increase in failure that we observe for the five-year horizon is partially attributable to listing of emerging firms in the sector of Internet and technologies. However, this phenomenon is not a fully satisfactory explanation, given that the failure rate increases for firms listed during the previous subperiod.

We report, in the rightmost column of Exhibit 22.8, the number of newly listed companies that graduate to the TSX by entry mode. For IPOs, the average graduation rate is 6.76 percent (Panel A): only 134 of the 1,982 IPOs of the period graduate. The proportion is 8.64 percent for backdoor listings (162 graduations per 1,875 listings). Overall, the success rate of the TSXV is 7.67 percent. Comparable statistics are provided by Brander, Egan, and Hellmann (2008) for the conventional VC market, after an extensive survey of all the VC investments in Canada over the period from 1996 to 2004. They examine 3,720 VC-backed firms, and show that 115 of these firms subsequently raise an IPO, 68 of which are followed by listing on a main exchange and 47 on the TSXV. The success rate reported by Brander, Egan, and Hellmann for the conventional VC market is thus a meager 3.1 percent for the population. The rate decreases to 1.8 percent if we consider IPOs on the TSX only. By comparison, the rate we estimate for the VC stock market is 7.67 percent. Although we cannot test the significance of this difference using the available data, the public venture market in Canada seems to provide a graduation rate for TSXV-listed companies that is approximately four times the exit rate by IPOs on the main market estimated for VCs.

Exhibit 22.9   Comparison of Canadian Raw Returns

The internal rate of return of the conventional venture capital (VC) comes from the Canadian VC Association. Portfolios are value-weighted. NA means not available.

	Annual Return	Standard Deviation
1,626 newly listed firms on the TSXV, 1986–2006	15.69%	35.40%
TSX S&P Index, 1986–2006	10.70%	14.34%
TSXV S&P Index, 01/2001 to 12/2006	23.57%	23.07%
TSX S&P Index, 01/2001 to 12/2006	13.08%	11.19%
1,144 newly listed firms on the TSXV, 06/1995 to 06/2005	11.96%	34.78%
Internal rate of return of conventional VC, 06/1995 to 06/2005	−3.00%	NA

Source: Carpentier, L'Her, and Suret (forthcoming).

THE PERFORMANCE OF THE PUBLIC VENTURE MARKET: THE INVESTOR'S PERSPECTIVE

Comparing the returns of a VC and a public market is a challenging task. VC returns are internal rates of return. The comparison with the classic rates of return of indexes cannot be based on statistical tests. Moreover, in Canada, indexes are available only from 1995 to 2005. The estimation of returns for the TSXV is also problematic, because this market results from the merger of several markets. The S&P TSXV index was created in 2002. Previously, a CDNX index was available since 1999. Before that time, the venture market was composed of several entities, each with its own index. As a result, we cannot use the official indexes for a long-term analysis. Moreover, the S&P TSXV index does not include newly listed companies. For these reasons, our analysis cannot provide a definitive conclusion on the relative performance of both markets. Nonetheless, the results are striking. Exhibit 22.9 reports the value-weighted returns of an index of new listings on the public VC market. We use all the stocks that list on the TSXV or its predecessors, from their listing date. The new listings include IPOs, RMs, and RIs of CPCs. The weights are based on the market capitalization at the beginning of each month.[18] For comparison purposes, we report (1) statistics on the return distribution of the TSX for the same period, (2) the official index returns for both markets, from 2001 to 2006, and (3) the new listings' return for the period from 1995 to 2005, for a comparison with the conventional VC market's return.

Our first observation is that the TSXV outperforms the main market. The newly listed firm index posts an average rate of return of 15.69 percent, while the return of the main market was 10.70 percent. Nonetheless, the standard deviation is 35.40 percent for the former market vs. 14.34 percent for the latter one. We get similar results when the official indexes are used. Note that this market is highly volatile and illiquid, and is dominated by small and growth stocks. The TSXV probably does not compensate investors adequately for the various forms of risk associated with the ownership of small and growth stocks.

The second observation is that the public VC market outperforms the private one considerably. From June 1995 to June 2005, the private VC industry reports a meager net annual internal rate of return of −3 percent.[19] The net annual rates of return are in the same range for early-stage VC (−3.4 percent), balanced VC (−2.8 percent), and later-stage VC (−3.3 percent). During the same period of time, the new listings index posts an 11.96 percent annual rate of return. The VC market's performance is abnormally low in Canada relative to the United States, which reports an annual return of 27.6 percent for the same period, according to the Canadian Venture Capital Association (CVCA). The difference between the returns of the public and private venture markets is economically very large, but we cannot assess its statistical significance because the two returns are not estimated the same way.

This unexpected result contradicts the proposition that conventional VCs benefit from significant advantages in financing new ventures. In Canada, the public VC market outperformed the private one. One explanation for this is that the reported VC return is abnormally low, because it includes the very poor return of Labour-Sponsored VC Funds, which receive large tax subsidies but suffer from poor governance (Cumming and MacIntosh 2006). According to this explanation, during the studied period the larger players in the VC market have not demonstrated the capacity and skill usually attributed to private VCs. A second explanation could be that the TSXV is heavily exposed to the natural resources sector, while the VC is not. Nonetheless, excluding this sector does not change the conclusion, since the difference between the public and the private market return is still higher than 1000 basis points per year (Carpentier, L'Her, and Suret forthcoming). A third explanation for the observed difference could be a competition effect. With quicker and lighter procedures (mainly in the case of RMs) the TSXV may have captured a significant market share of promising companies usually oriented toward traditional VC. We have left the test of these propositions for further research.

CONCLUSION

This paper describes and analyzes how a stock exchange can be used to finance emerging companies and to assume the role usually played by private VCs. Our analysis of the population of new listings in the Canadian venture stock market—the TSXV—during the period from 1986 to 2006 illustrates the openness of this market to early-stage companies. The size and the gross proceeds of newly listed companies are generally lower than those reported for VC investments, and far less than those observed in the junior markets in Europe. The TSXV is indeed a public market for VC, which provides equity to early-stage companies well before they reach the profitability stage, and even before they report revenues.

Canada has developed a specific path to finance emerging firms, probably because of the poor performance of a VC market hampered by questionable public policies and minimally interested in small deals, combined with the steady rate of business creation in the natural resources sector, where VC involvement is typically low. The Canadian experience thus illustrates that a mode other than classic VC can provide businesses in the preprofitability stage with equity. The question is whether such a tool can be economically viable. Several dimensions of this experimentation deserve attention.

We measured the success rate of new entrants and estimated the rate of failure/ success. We then compared these data with data reported for traditional VCs, which usually consider an IPO to be a success. We find that the success rate of the public venture market is approximately four times the corresponding rate for traditional VC. This surprising result is not consistent with the lack of screening and monitoring by the venture stock exchange. However, the public venture market admits more new firms than the VC market usually does, and seems to accept companies at an earlier development stage. The bottom line is that during the period under analysis, the ratio of graduations to the total sample of VC-backed IPOs is approximately seven to one (Carpentier, L'Her, and Suret forthcoming).

For a horizon of five years, the delisting rate of newly listed companies is lower than the one reported in the United States and much lower than the failure rate observed for the private VC sector in Canada. This result is surprising because of the apparently poor quality of the new issuers on the public market and the lack of value-added activity usually associated with conventional VC providers. In particular, the delisting rate is much lower than the failure rate of 45 percent reported from 1996 to 2004 by Brander, Egan, and Hellmann (2008) for private VCs. This situation is probably attributable to two factors. First, a Canadian company can easily issue private or public equity, even if it has not reached the profitability or even the sales stage. In this sense, the Canadian seasoned equity market contrasts sharply with the U.S. market. The second explanation is the tolerance of the exchange for delisting of nonoperating companies. The exchange is probably less prone to delist than VCs are to write off. Nevertheless, the observation that a public market devoted to early-stage companies exhibits a lower failure rate than the private VC market is not in line with the theoretical literature, which gives private VC a strong advantage in financing new ventures. In the same vein, the observation that the rate of return of a public VC market can surpass that of a private VC market, in the same country, is another unexpected result. Further research is needed to determine if the poor performance of the Canadian VC market is linked to the existence of the public VC market, and to what extent these markets are competing with each other. In any case, this evidence clearly argues in favor of a reexamination of public policy devoted to VC in Canada.

NOTES

1. CNSX, formerly known as the Canadian Trading and Quotation System inc. (CNQ), listed 100 securities in November 2008 (see www.cnsx.ca). NEX is a separate trading board of TSXV where firms that do not fulfill the ongoing listing requirements are moved. According to NEX's web site: "NEX issuers have the opportunity to refinance, reactivate or reinvent themselves in order to re-apply to TSX Venture Exchange provided they can evidence their compliance with TSX Venture Listing Requirements."

2. See Eric M Levy, Heenan Blaikie LLP, Alternative capital markets for U.S. issuers: TSX and AIM, at http://www.abanet.org/buslaw/committees/CL650000pub/materials/goingpublic.pdf.

3. We use the term "TSXV" to refer to this exchange and its predecessors. In 2001 the TSX Group acquired and renamed the Canadian Venture Exchange (CDNX), previously created by the merger, in 1999, of the Alberta and Vancouver Exchanges. In 2001, the Montreal Exchange opted to specialize in derivatives, and transferred its small capitalization securities to the CDNX.

4. See Kevin Strong, Manager, Winnipeg Office, TSX Venture, Public Venture Capital. Exchange, May 10, 2006, slide 9 at www.sata.ca.docs.2006%2005%2010%20SATA.ppt.

5. See http://www.tsx.com/en/pdf/TSXVentureSuccessStories.pdf.

6. To list on NASDAQ from June 1999 to June 2001, a company had to post a stock price higher than US$4, shareholders' equity of US$4 million, and market capitalization of US$5 million at least.

7. http://www.tsx.com/en/pdf/ManualUpdateAug-2002.pdf.

8. The disclosure requirements for these transactions vary over time and between provinces. In 2005, the exchange modified the policy to require prospectus-like disclosure.

9. An SPAC is a company that has no specific business plan or purpose or has indicated that its business plan is to engage in a merger or acquisition with an unidentified company or companies, other entity, or person within a specified time period, typically within a span of 18 months, according to the SEC. These companies are "development-stage companies." There are considerable differences between BBC and SPACs in terms of regulation, size, and the number of shareholders. The average proceeds of the 62 IPOs of SPACs analyzed by Jog and Sun (2007) from 2003 to 2006 are US$65 million, an amount that is unrelated to those found in the CPC program.

10. From PWC data at http://www.pwcmoneytree.com/moneytree/nav.jsp?page=notice& iden=B.

11. This section and the next section of the chapter draw upon the papers by Carpentier and Suret (forthcoming) and Carpentier, L'Her, and Suret (forthcoming).

12. According to the TSX Manual (2007, policy 2.5, 3) "If an Issuer has a viable business although it does not meet certain elements of the Tier 2 TMR, the Exchange may determine that it is not appropriate to transfer the Issuer to NEX. The Exchange will consider the seasonal or other cycles which affect an Issuer's business. If an Issuer's Working Capital is low because of seasonal or other temporary conditions, the Exchange may delay enforcement of this Policy but will continue to monitor the Issuer."

13. According to the Listing Standard and Fees document, available on the NASDAQ site (last visited January 15, 2009), at http://www.nasdaq.com/about/nasdaq_listing_req_fees.pdf.

14. Demers and Joos (2007) report a mean and median issue price in the vicinity of US$15 to US$16. The corresponding value is US$2 (CAN$3).

15. See Harris (2006) for an analysis of this change in the listing requirements, and more generally of the listing standards in Canada.

16. See http://www.tsx.com/en/listings/venture_issuer_resources/graduation_to_tsx/index.html.

17. The TSXV organizes "Accessing Public Venture Capital Workshops" that "go beyond the basics of public venture capital and delivers compelling, first person perspectives on public financing, building your business and sustaining growth. And it provides access to leading public venture capital experts—investment bankers, lawyers, auditors and TSX Venture professionals." The cases of graduating companies are presented as success stories (http://www.tsx.com/en/pdf/TSXVentureSuccessStories.pdf).

18. To limit the influence of the outliers, we set the maximum monthly return to 1000 percent (roughly 0.03 percent of the distribution). The equally weighted index is largely influenced by the spectacular returns of several very small stocks, which soar from 1 to 10 cents. Consequently, we report and discuss the value-weighted returns exclusively.

19. See Canadian VC & Private Equity Industry Performance data, online on the site of Reseau Capital (the Quebec VC and Private Equity Association), last visited January 15, 2009, at http://www.reseaucapital.com/Statistiques/Stat2005/Performance%20Study%20June%202005.pdf. The performance of the U.S. VC industry is also available (last visited January 15, 2009) at http://www.reseaucapital.com/Statistiques/Stat2006/2006_Q4_ForumCanada-France.pdf.

REFERENCES

Amit, R., J. Brander, and C. Zott. 1998. Why do venture capital firms exist? Theory and Canadian evidence. *Journal of Business Venturing* 13(6):441–466.

Barry, C. B., et al. 1990. The role of venture capital in the creation of public companies: Evidence from the going-public process. *Journal of Financial Economics* 27:447–471.

Baygan, G. 2003. Venture capital policies in Canada. OECD Science, Technology and Industry Working papers, 2003/4. OECD Publishing.

Bottazzi, L., and M. Da Rin. 2002. Venture capital in Europe and the financing of innovative companies. *Economic Policy():European Forum* 17:34, 231–269.

Bradley, Daniel J., et al. 2006. Penny stock IPOs. *Financial Management* 35:1:5–29.

Brander, J. A., E. J. Egan, and T. F. Hellmann. 2008. Government sponsored venture capital in Canada: Effects on value creation, competition and innovation. NBER conference on international differences in entrepreneurship. Retrieved from http://www.nber.org/~confer/2008/IDE/hellmann.pdf.

Carpentier, C., J. L'Her, and J. Suret. Forthcoming. Stock exchange markets for new ventures. *Journal of Business Venturing.* Retrieved from http://ssrn.com/abstract=1132285.

Carpentier, C., and J. Suret. 2008. The survival and success of penny stock IPOs: An analysis of the consequences of low listing requirements. Retrieved from SSRN: http://ssrn.com/abstract=1070855.

Chemmanur, T. J., and E. Loutskina. 2006. The role of venture capital backing in initial public offerings: Certification, screening, or market power? Retrieved from SSRN: http://ssrn.com/paper=604882.

Cumming, D. 2006. Do companies go public too early in Canada? Research Study Commissioned by the Task Force to Modernize Securities Legislation in Canada.

_____, and J. MacIntosh. 2006. Crowding out private equity: Canadian evidence. *Journal of Business Venturing* 21:5:569–609.

_____. 2007. Mutual funds that invest in private equity? An analysis of Labour sponsored investment funds. *Cambridge Journal of Economics* 31:3:445–487.

Dalbor, M. C., and M. J. Sullivan. 2005. The initial public offerings of restaurant firms: The case of industry-specific micromarket capitalization offerings. *Journal of Small Business Management* 43:3:226–242.

Demers, E. A., and P. Joos. 2007. IPO failure risk. *Journal of Accounting Research* 45(2):333–371.

Espenlaub, S., A. Khurshed, and A. Mohamed. 2008. Is AIM a casino? A study of the survival of new listings on the UK Alternative Investment Market (AIM). European Financial Management IPO Symposium 2008, Oxford. Retrieved from http://efmaefm.org/0EFMSYMPOSIUM/oxford-2008/Susanne.pdf.

Fama, E. F., and K. R. French. 2004. Newly listed firms: Fundamentals, survival rates, and returns. *Journal of Financial Economics* 73(2):229–169.

Feldman, D. N. 2006. *Reverse mergers: Taking a company public without an IPO.* New York: Bloomberg Press.

Fenn, G. W., N. Liang, and S. Prowse. 1996. The economics of the private equity market. *Federal Reserve Bulletin* (January):1–69. http://www.federalreserve.gov/pubs/staffstudies/1990-99/ss168.pdf.

Gompers, P. A. 1995. Optimal investment, monitoring, and the staging of venture capital. *Journal of Finance* 50(5):1461–1489.

_____, and J. Lerner. 2001. The venture capital revolution. *Journal of Economic Perspectives* 15(2):145–168.

Harris, A. D. 2006. The impact of hot issue markets and noise traders on stock exchange listing standards. *University of Toronto Law Review* 56 (Summer):223–280.

Hensler, D. A., R. C. Rutherford, and T. M. Springer. 1997. The Survival of Initial Public Offerings in the Aftermarket. *Journal of Financial Research* 20:1, 93–110.

H., D. K. 2007. From blank check to SPAC: The regulator's response to the market, and the market's response to the regulation. *Entrepreneurial Business Law Journal* 2(1):531–552.

Hochberg, Y. 2006. Venture capital and corporate governance in the newly public firm. Working paper, Kellogg School of Management, Northwestern University. Retrieved from http://www.kellogg.northwestern.edu/faculty/hochberg/htm/VCCG.pdf.

Industry Canada. 2002. Canadian venture capital activity: An analysis of trends and gaps 1996–2002. Ottawa: Industry Canada.

Jog, V., and C. Sun. 2007. Blank check IPOs: A home run for management. Retrieved from SSRN: http://ssrn.com/abstract=1018242.

Korcsmaros, K. 2002. Can capital markets meet the financing needs of SMEs. *Infrastructure and Financial Markets Review* 8(4):4–6.

Lerner, J. 1995. Venture capitalists and the oversight of private firms. *Journal of Finance* 50(1):301–318.

Nicholls, C. 2006. The characteristics of Canada's capital markets and the illustrative case of Canada's legislative regulatory response to Sarbanes-Oxley. Research Study Commissioned by the Task Force to Modernize Securities Legislation in Canada.

Rousseau, S. 2006. The competitiveness of Canadian stock exchanges: What can we learn from the experience of the alternative investment market? Research Study Commissioned by the Task Force to Modernize Securities Legislation in Canada.

SEC. 2006. Final report of the advisory committee on smaller public companies to the U.S. Securities and Exchange Commission. Washington, DC: SEC.

Weber, J., and M. Willenborg. 2003. Do expert informational intermediaries add value? Evidence from auditors in microcap initial public offerings. *Journal of Accounting Research* 41(4):681–720.

ABOUT THE AUTHORS

Cécile Carpentier received a Ph.D. in finance from the Lille II University (France). She is a Chartered Accountant (France) and a Chartered Financial Analyst (CFA). She specializes in corporate finance and small business finance. She has published in several academic journals such as the *Journal of Business Venturing, Small Business Economics, Venture Capital, Canadian Tax Journal* and *Canadian Public Policy.* She is a CIRANO Fellow.

Jean-Marc Suret received a Ph.D. in finance from Laval University (Canada). He is a Canadian Business Valuator (CBV). He specializes in corporate finance, public policy, and financial accounting. He has published many articles in academic journals such as the *Journal of Business Venturing, Contemporary Accounting Research, Small Business Economics, Journal of International Business Study* and the *Financial Review.* He served as Director of the School of Accountancy of Laval University from 1999 to 2006. He is a CIRANO Fellow.

## CHAPTER 23

Public Policy, Venture Capital, and Entrepreneurial Finance

CHRISTIAN KEUSCHNIGG
Professor, University of St. Gallen, Institute of Public Finance and Fiscal Law

INTRODUCTION

Venture capital (VC) has become an important source of finance but also a source of professional support for new firms in high-technology industries. A firm's transition from birth of the idea to a marketable product involves more than just technological experiments and development of prototypes. Developing marketing strategies, attracting key clients and reliable suppliers, hiring new personnel, and raising further financing requires managerial skills. Start-up entrepreneurs typically lack the necessary capital and often would benefit from professional assistance. Venture capitalists (VCs) can fill these gaps. They have access to capital and are endowed with managerial and industry know-how. They dispose of a well connected network of suppliers, customers, and key personnel. Indeed, the defining characteristic of VC is the combination of financing and commercial assistance. The main functions of VC financing consist of screening, contracting, and advising (see Kaplan and Stromberg [2001] for a concise statement of the stylized facts). Gompers and Lerner (1999) and Kaplan and Stromberg (2003, 2004) provide detailed empirical evidence. In contrast to more passive bank financing, VCs arrange for entrepreneurs to receive support by creating links to suppliers and possible customers, attracting key personnel, providing strategic and marketing advice, and helping the professionalization of the firm.

Venture capital started out in the United States half a century ago and has grown impressively since then. Almost half of new firms in the United States that are sold off at IPOs (Initial Public Offerings) have been backed by VC (see Gompers and Lerner [2001]). In Europe, VC emerged significantly later. Only in the most recent years have VC firms become prominent financiers of young technology firms there. Statistics published by EVCA (European Private Equity and Venture Capital Association) report a total investment of €71 billion in 2006, up from 10 billion in 1997 and 24 billion in 2001.[1] As in previous years, seed and start-up investment constituted only a minor part (8.3 percent in 2006) while expansion and replacement investments absorbed 21 percent. The major part was in financing buy-outs (70.7 percent). In 2005, 5.2 percent of total investments was allocated to seed and start-up, 26.6 percent to expansion and replacement investments, and 68.2 percent to financing buy-outs. The EVCA statistics further reveal marked differences across countries. Sweden, the UK, and the Netherlands had the largest private equity/VC markets in Europe (1.44, 1.26, and 1.05 percent of GDP in 2006, respectively), while France's share was slightly above the European average of 0.57 percent. Germany and Switzerland recorded only around 0.2 percent of GDP.

Innovation generates large social returns. Jones and Williams (1998) suggest that the social rate of return on R&D is about 30 percent while private returns are much lower, between 7 to 14 percent. These authors argue that, from a social perspective, R&D investments should be two to four times higher than what is actually observed! While VC accounts for a rather small part of total investment, it is concentrated in the most innovative sectors. Kortum and Lerner (2000) found that VC is responsible for a disproportionately large share of overall industrial innovation in the United States. A dollar of VC appears to be about three times more potent in stimulating patents than a dollar of traditional corporate R&D. According to their estimates, VC accounted only for about 3 percent of corporate R&D from 1983 to 1992 but was responsible for about 8 percent of industrial innovation in this decade. Given an unchanged potency of venture funding, VC investments should have accounted for about 14 percent of U.S. innovative activity in 1998. Policy makers and the business community have thus taken a strong interest in improving the conditions for financing new firms, and in the development of an active VC industry in particular. Young VC-backed firms are considered an important source of innovation and growth. Several questions arise when developing a policy perspective. Is there enough risk capital available? Do administrative procedures and requirements hinder entrepreneurship in the first place? Are government grants and subsidies to new firms appropriate? Do taxes block the creation and development of start-ups? Do taxes deter the support and advisory effort of VCs to their portfolio companies?

The VC industry regularly evaluates public policy with respect to whether it is suitable to promote the development of private equity and VC markets and to encourage entrepreneurship. For instance, EVCA in 2003 and again in 2004 published a benchmarking report on the tax and legal environment in its member countries (see EVCA 2004). The assessment evaluates 13 indicators relating to both the supply-side (i.e., investors in private equity and VC funds and fund managers investing directly in companies) and the demand side of private equity and VC (i.e., creation of entrepreneurial firms). Among the tax indicators covered are (1) company tax rates, with special attention to those applicable to small and medium-sized companies; (2) capital gains tax rates for individuals; (3) income tax rates for private individuals; (4) tax incentives for individual investors investing in private equity; (5) the entrepreneurial environment; and (6) fiscal incentives to enhance research and development.

The benchmarking report reflects a firm belief that taxes matter for entrepreneurship. Empirical research in public finance indeed testifies to the importance of taxes for entrepreneurship. For example, Rosen (2005) in summarizing his research with a series of co-authors produces ample evidence that once started, the decisions in new firms regarding employment, capital investment, and production are markedly influenced by taxes. Gentry and Hubbard's (2000) empirical analysis demonstrates that the progressivity of the tax schedule is important for entrepreneurship. They argue that the progressivity of the income tax acts like a success tax that taxes successful ventures generating high incomes at particularly high rates and thereby significantly reduces the probability of entrepreneurial entry. Gordon (1998) and Cullen and Gordon (2007), on the other hand, argue that high personal tax rates could actually encourage entrepreneurial activity when individuals are able to exploit the option to incorporate. The argument is that entrepreneurs would choose to be noncorporate in the early stage when the business makes losses. They would then save taxes by offsetting these losses against other personal income. Once the business starts to record profits, an entrepreneur prefers to incorporate in order to exploit low corporate taxes. According to this view, high personal income tax rates can encourage entrepreneurship because they imply high tax savings from offsetting losses in the early phase. Boadway and Tremblay (2005) offer a broad overview of the theoretical public finance literature on entrepreneurship and examine various rationales for policy intervention with respect to start-up entrepreneurship.

Apart from this public finance literature on entrepreneurship, there is little theoretical or empirical work on the effects of public policies on VC-financed entrepreneurship. Exceptions are a few contributions by Poterba (1989a,b) and Gompers and Lerner (1998). These authors find some evidence of a moderately negative effect of the capital gains tax on VC investments and fund-raising. Capital gains taxation tends to depress demand for VC by discouraging entrepreneurial entry. Since the entrepreneur's income from starting a firm mainly consists of capital gains earned in the start-up period, the capital gains tax makes VC-backed entrepreneurship less attractive relative to dependent employment. The capital gains tax can also importantly affect contracts. Cumming (2005) found for Canada that a lower capital gains tax can significantly increase the use of convertible preferred equity. The capital gains tax can also hamper fund-raising since investors' returns mainly consist of capital gains as well. In addition, Gompers and Lerner (1998) found that liberalization of pension fund investment regulations is an important source of new capital and can thereby stimulate the expansion of the industry. Da Rin, Nicodano, and Sembenelli (2006) have found that the corporate capital gains tax hurts VC investments in Europe, in particular for early stage investments.

None of this empirical literature has actually been able to identify how taxes may change the relative performance of VC-backed compared to other firms by affecting the incentives of VCs to provide support and add value to their portfolio companies. Our own previous theoretical work has aimed to shed light on how exactly taxes as well as subsidies can affect the number of VC-backed firms and the incentives of entrepreneurs and VCs to exploit the full potential of these firms (see Keuschnigg 2003, 2004a-b, and Keuschnigg and Nielsen 2003a-b, 2004a-b).

The effectiveness of subsidies to capital and research investments of young firms has been investigated empirically by Lerner (1999) and Wallsten (2000), among others. These authors conclude that programs such as the Small Business Innovation Research (SBIR) program in the United States can significantly raise the growth of awardee firms compared to other matched firms. This superior performance was confined to awardees in areas with substantial new firm creation. Wallsten found significant crowding-out effects although he too argued that the program could help firms to attract additional private funding. The program may thus have a certification role in the sense that participation in the program makes firms more likely to attract additional venture financing.

This paper discusses the effects of taxes and subsidies levied at different stages of a firm's life cycle. We explore how they impact on VC and bank-financed investment and entrepreneurship. In particular, we examine subsidies representing the various investment grants, interest subsidies, and subsidies to capital expenditure in research and development that are prevalent in many countries. We explore the taxation of capital gains in new firms when sold off to new investors, the taxation of wages in an alternative occupation, and corporate income taxation. Our analysis indeed shows that a limited focus on the taxation of early stage firms cuts too short. The taxation of mature companies is as important for start-ups as the direct taxation of infant companies. Corporate and dividend taxes reduce entrepreneurship even though these taxes are typically paid only by mature companies rather than young ones. Indeed, Djankov and colleagues (2008) estimate that the impact of the corporate tax on aggregate investment occurs to a large extent on the entry (entrepreneurship) margin. The basic insight is that taxes that reduce the value of mature firms thereby diminish the gains from setting up new companies as well.

To organize the review of the literature, this chapter develops a small model of heterogeneous firms. The most profitable firms receive active VC financing on top of passive bank loans while the less profitable ones exclusively rely on bank financing. Investment levels are determined by the firms' financing capacity, that is, their ability to raise external funds. The main results concern the effects of tax and subsidy policies. We show how they influence investment levels of different types of firms, how firms self-select into bank and VC financing, and how they affect start-up incentives and entry. For example, investment subsidies boost investment, firm values, and entry. They also benefit to a larger extent the more profitable firms and, therefore, induce a larger share of start-ups to go for VC financing. Success taxes such as corporate tax or dividend and capital gains taxes reduce the cash flow and, thus, financing capacity and investment levels per firm. They also reduce firm value and entry, and they harm the more profitable VC-backed firms relatively more, so that a smaller fraction of start-ups ends up with VC support. The analysis also reveals that the type of investment incentives and the timing of tax liabilities over a firm's life cycle are important. For example, subsidies given in a fixed amount are more attractive to companies with low investment returns while subsidies proportional to the investment scale favor the more profitable companies that invest at a larger scale.

Finally, alternative capital income tax systems have different implications for more and less profitable firms and, in turn, on the choice between VC and bank financing. The tax reform literature postulates two types of so-called investment neutral corporate tax systems: a cash flow tax allows for immediate expensing of investment but denies deduction of costs of finance such as interest expenses or imputed cost of equity. Such a system implies a high tax liability at the cash flow stage when the return to investment accrues, and a low tax burden at the investment stage. In contrast, an ACE (allowance for corporate equity) allows for full deduction of the costs of finance but denies immediate investment expensing. Compared to a cash flow tax, the tax burden is shifted from the late cash flow to the early investment stage. First of all, we show that these investment neutral tax systems are not neutral when the firms' ability to invest is restricted by their limited financing capacity. We then show that an ACE system favors highly profitable relative to less profitable firms. In consequence, this system induces a larger fraction of firms to go for VC financing, raises expected firm value at the start-up stage and encourages entrepreneurship relative to a cash flow tax.

The following section presents a small model of VC and bank financing of heterogeneous firms. After that comes a review of the empirical evidence on VC value added and illustrations of the consequences for investment and entrepreneurship when the VC sector becomes more efficient. The following section turns to tax policy and compares the results of the present model to the insights of the existing literature. After that comes a discussion of adverse selection and then consideration of other important areas of public policy.

A MODEL OF VENTURE CAPITAL AND BANK FINANCING

What are the effects of taxation when the market for start-up financing is shared among banks and VC firms? There is some research to explain what determines entrepreneurs' choice between bank and VC financing, such as Ueda (2004) or Winton and Yerramilli (2006). Landier (2003) and Inderst and Mueller (2006) similarly discuss the special role of VC firms as compared to banks. None of these papers investigates how taxes may differentially affect bank and VC-financed firms, market splitting among banks and VC funds, entrepreneurship, and aggregate income. A first attempt is Keuschnigg and Nielsen (2005), who suggest a search model where VC-backed firms earn excess returns over bank-financed firms due to active VC support. Among all entrants, a segment of firms is matched (rationed) with a limited number of VC firms and earns excess returns. The remaining part is left with passive bank financing. Ex post, VC, and bank-financed firms are different, but all firms within each class are identical. In this chapter, we introduce a novel model of heterogeneous firms with variable investment where the more profitable firms go for more expensive VC financing while the less promising but still viable ones remain with bank financing. The model is a generalization of Tirole (2001, 2006) and Holmstrom and Tirole (1997) and merges this with a model of heterogeneous firms as pioneered in Melitz (2003). It offers a formal framework to discuss potential policy effects and to compare with the existing literature.

External Financing: Risk-neutral entrepreneurs are endowed with a single project, which they can run at a variable scale. The sequence of events is this: (1) entrepreneurs' entry decision; (2) investment return v becomes known and firm chooses VC or bank financing; (3) firm obtains external funds and invests; (4) entrepreneur and VC choose effort; (5) firm succeeds or fails. Given limited own assets A, entrepreneurs raise external funds from VCs or banks to leverage investment I. After start-up, the return to investment $v \in [v_0, v_1]$ differs across firms, leading them to choose different financing modes. If successful, the venture yields an end-of-period return (cash flow) vI that increases linearly with investment. In case of failure, there is no return at all, and investment must be completely written off. If the expected surplus per unit of investment is positive, firms wish to invest as much as possible until they exhaust their financing capacity. The firm's success probability depends on the entrepreneur's effort, yielding $p > p_L$ if effort is high. The VC's active role in the company can raise the success chances by q, reflecting the value added of VC financing and giving a total success probability of $p + q$. With bank financing, success depends only on the entrepreneur's effort.

The government subsidizes investment costs and claims part of the company's profit in case of success. The net present value of taxes paid over subsidies received is

$$\tau = [(p + q)t - s]I - z \tag{23.1}$$

where z is a fixed and s a proportional investment subsidy and tI refers to profit taxes paid when the company reports a positive cash flow. This tax is meant to include all success taxes such as corporate, dividend, and capital gains taxes. When the company fails, the return is zero, and no tax is paid.

When the company is able to obtain VC financing, it also takes additional bank loans to further leverage own capital. Returns per unit of investment are shared among stakeholders where a part v^m or v^b is reserved to repay VCs (index m for monitoring investor) and banks and a part t is claimed by government as a success tax. The entrepreneur collects the residual share v^e. The private surplus net of τ is divided according to $\pi = \pi^e + \pi^m + \pi^b$, or

$$
\begin{aligned}
\pi^e &= (p+q)v^e I - A, \quad v^e = v - v^m - v^b - t \\
\pi^m &= (p+q)v^m I - cI - \kappa - I^m \\
\pi^b &= (p+q)v^b I - [(1-s)I - z - I^m - A] \\
\pi &= \rho I - \kappa + z, \quad \rho \equiv (p+q)(v-t) - c - 1 + s
\end{aligned}
\tag{23.2}
$$

Except for I, I^m, and v, all parameters are constants. VCs not only contribute money in the amount of I^m, but also business advice and monitoring services, which raise the success probability by q. The monitoring and advising cost, $cI + \kappa$, consists of a fixed cost plus a term linearly rising with the investment scale. The fixed cost is incurred before investment and reflects the VC's initial cost of learning the details of the project.[2]

We assume perfect competition among financial intermediaries and a perfectly elastic supply of funds where the deposit rate is normalized to zero. There is no shortage of financial funds. The entrepreneur extracts the entire joint surplus π when intermediary profits are zero, $\pi^m = \pi^b = 0$. However, the financing constraints below limit the amount of external funds. When the VC gives a loan I^m, the firm requires an additional bank loan equal to the square bracket in (23.2), or $I - I^m - A$ in the absence of tax. If the investment return is large enough to yield a positive margin ρ, the entrepreneur obtains a surplus $\pi = \rho I - \kappa + z$ which increases linearly with investment. Hence, the firm raises external funds and expands investment until financing capacity is exhausted.

The firm's financing capacity reflects the pledgeable income available for repayment, which depends on effort towards a high success probability. Once investment is sunk, the entrepreneur may prefer to consume private benefits bI

and accept a low success probability p_L, instead of focusing on the core business. Similarly, the VC firm may prefer to avoid the variable monitoring cost cI (after the initial cost κ is sunk) and get not sufficiently involved in the firm so that the success probability declines by q. In this situation of double moral hazard, both the entrepreneur and VC must have sufficient incentives to provide the required effort for a high success probability $p + q$. At this stage, investments I and κ are already sunk and profit shares are fixed. The incentive constraints for full effort are $pv^e \geq p_L v^e + b$ and $q \cdot v^m \geq c$ or

$$IC^e : v^e \geq \beta \equiv b/(p - p_L), \quad IC^m : v^m \geq \gamma \equiv c/q \qquad (23.3)$$

The minimum shares necessary to guarantee the entrepreneur's and VC's contribution for a high success probability are, thus, $v^e = \beta$ and $v^m = \gamma$, respectively.[3]

Since monitoring services make VC more expensive than bank loans, bank credit is preferred. Hence, the firm cedes a minimum share $v^m = \gamma \equiv c/q$ to assure managerial advice and monitoring services. Given competition in investment financing, the VC is also asked for a loan and breaks even if

$$I^m = (p + q)v^m I - cI - \kappa = p\gamma \cdot I - \kappa \qquad (23.4)$$

To maximize own surplus, the firm attracts additional bank loans to expand investment. Given the VC's contribution, the entrepreneur accepts the minimum incentive compatible share β to maximize pledgeable income and, thereby, the firm's debt capacity. The bank lends as long as $(p + q)(v - t - \gamma - \beta)I \geq (1 - s - p\gamma)I + \kappa - z - A$, that is, as long as pledgeable income is large enough to guarantee repayment. The right-hand side is the required bank loan when the VC finances a part I^m. Assuming that pledgeable income grows slower than the need for bank loans, investment expansion will ultimately be bounded by the financing constraint, leading to an investment level of (use $q\gamma = c$)

$$I = \frac{1}{\theta} \cdot (A - \kappa + z), \quad 0 < \theta \equiv (p + q)\beta - [(p + q)(v - t) - c - 1 + s] < 1$$
$$(23.5)$$

Suitable parameter restrictions are discussed in a separate technical Appendix. They imply $0 < \theta < 1$ so that own equity is leveraged with external financing to expand investment, $I > A - \kappa + z$.

Banks Versus Venture Capital: Some firms may not benefit from VC since the extra advising and monitoring services must be separately compensated, making VC more expensive. The alternative is to rely exclusively on a standard bank loan. In this case, the firm does not benefit from managerial support ($q = 0$) but also avoids the compensation of consulting costs ($c = \kappa = 0$). The firm claims a minimum share β to maximize pledgeable income and boost its financing capacity. A lower index is introduced to refer to the source of finance. Without benefits and costs of managerial advice, the leverage factor and profit margin under pure bank financing are

surplus $\qquad \pi_b^e = \dfrac{\rho_b}{\theta_b}(A + z) + z, \quad \pi_m^e = \dfrac{\rho_m}{\theta_m}(A - \kappa + z) - \kappa + z$

profit margin $\quad \rho_b = p(v - t) - 1 + s, \quad \rho_m = (p + q)(v - t) - c - 1 + s$ $\qquad$ (23.6)

leverage factor $\quad \theta_b = p\beta - \rho_b, \quad \theta_m = (p + q)\beta - \rho_m$

Firms are heterogeneous with respect to investment returns. After start-up, returns are drawn from an interval $v \in [v_0, v_1]$. Knowing v, the firm chooses the financing mode. We generally assume taxes and subsidies to be small, that is, close to zero. The following parameter restrictions, discussed in a separate Appendix, imply that (1) profit margins ρ_j are strictly positive; (2) leverage factors $1/\theta_j$ are finite and larger than unity in the entire interval; and (3) low return projects prefer pure bank financing while firms with very profitable investment opportunities opt for VC financing:

$$v > \beta, \quad q > pc, \quad \frac{p + q}{q} > \frac{A}{\kappa} \qquad (23.7)$$

After learning its investment productivity v, a firm opts for the financing mode that yields the larger surplus, $\pi_m^e \lessgtr \pi_b^e$. At low realizations, bank financing is preferred; high-return projects go for VC financing with additional bank credit. Over the entire range, the net present value always increases with project returns. There must thus be a single crossing of the profit lines, and, at the point of indifference v_* when the two curves cross, the value under VC financing rises faster than under bank financing. Exhibit 23.1 illustrates.

The indifference condition $\pi_b^e(v_*) = \pi_m^e(v_*)$ yields $[(1 - s)q - cp](A + z) = (p + q)\theta_b\kappa$ which is further manipulated to obtain a closed form solution for the

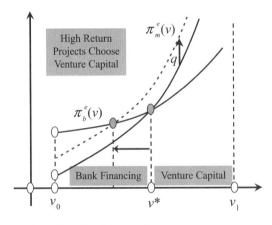

Exhibit 23.1 Venture Capital vs. Bank Financing

cut-off value

$$v_* = \beta + t + \frac{1-s}{p} - \frac{(1-s)\,q - cp}{(p+q)\,p} \frac{A+z}{\kappa} \qquad (23.8)$$

where v_* is, of course, in the admissible interval $[v_0, v_1]$. We limit attention only to small taxes and subsidies close to zero.

Entry: A priori, project returns are distributed with density $g(v)$ and an associated cumulative distribution function $G(v)$. To start a firm, an entrepreneur must irrevocably give up alternative income w. She is willing to do so if the expected net present value is large enough. Upon start-up, the company must anticipate the financing choice once it learns the project return. Expected net present value is, thus,

$$\bar{\pi}^e = \int_{v_0}^{v_*} \pi_b^e(v) \cdot dG(v) + \int_{v_*}^{v_1} \pi_m^e(v) \cdot dG(v) \geq w \qquad (23.9)$$

Obviously, everything that strengthens expected profit by allowing for a higher incentive compatible investment leverage encourages entry.

THE VALUE ADDED OF VENTURE CAPITAL

A firm's success rests on the entrepreneur's effort and due diligence (see the empirical results reviewed in Rosen [2005]). In addition, VCs add value by establishing contacts, giving strategic business advice, and generally helping in the professionalization of young firms. There is substantial empirical evidence on the value-added role of VCs. Hellmann and Puri (2002) show that VC-backed start-ups in Silicon Valley are much faster in introducing stock option plans for highly skilled personnel and in hiring a professional sales manager. Also, the presence of a VC makes it more likely that the entrepreneur will be replaced by a professional CEO from outside if her lack of managerial abilities turns out to be an impediment to the firm's rapid growth. The VC's influence is particularly strong in the early phase of business development when the informational problems are the largest, but becomes insignificant later on when the firm has successfully matured. Hellmann and Puri (2000) show that VC-backed firms introduce more radical innovations and pursue more aggressive market strategies compared with other start-ups. For example, once a VC joins the firm and provides finance, the probability of introducing the new product on the market jumps up by a factor of more than three!

Part of this superior performance of VC-backed firms may result from VCs being able to locate the more profitable firms than banks. In line with the theory of the preceding section, the empirical work of Sorensen (2007) implies that selection and value-added effects are simultaneously important. He finds important sorting effects in the sense that the most experienced investors get the best deals. The probability of success of a firm financed by the most experienced investor in his sample is 39 percent, which compares with only 15 percent of firms financed by the least-experienced investors. These findings are in line with Bottazzi, Da Rin, and Hellmann (forthcoming) or Gompers, Kovner, Lerner, and Scharfstein (2006), who emphasize human capital of VCs, showing that more experienced

VCs are significantly more involved with their portfolio companies and are able to generate larger returns on exit. The results hold when controlling for sorting effects. Sorensen (2007) calculates that sorting (the best investors getting the best deals) explains 58 percent of this increase in success probability while the investor's influence explains 42 percent.

Apart from investor experience, the productive contribution of VCs to business growth also rests on the existence of appropriate incentives on the part of the financier. Indeed, the empirical evidence on the impact and value added of VC is less clear-cut in Europe than in the United States (see Bottazzi and Da Rin [2002] for a skeptical view while Audretsch and Lehmann [2004], arrive at a more positive picture). Finance theory has addressed VC incentives in terms of a double-sided moral hazard problem, where both the entrepreneur and VC must exert effort in the company (see Holmstrom [1982]; Aghion and Tirole [1994]; Casamatta [2003]; Inderst and Mueller [2004]; Repullo and Suarez [2004]; Schmidt [2003]; and our own previous work mentioned above).

To illustrate the importance of the value-added function, we investigate in our model the consequences of VCs getting more experienced and efficient. With the same monitoring cost, advice increases the success probability to a larger extent, by $dq > 0$. The Appendix of this chapter linearizes the model and derives comparative static results.[4] A more active style of VC financing raises the firm's success probability and, in turn, pledgeable income and debt capacity. Firms are thus able to expand investment by leveraging own equity to a larger extent (see A23.5). VC-backed firms become larger than those relying on exclusive bank financing. The value added of VC financing boosts performance of VC-backed relative to bank-financed firms. These firms would be larger anyway because they are the more profitable ones, but they grow even larger on account of VC support. Much of the extra investment financing comes from additional bank lending rather than borrowing from VCs. To see this, we compute the change in $I^m = (pc/q)I - \kappa$ in (4) and get $dI^m = -\frac{pc}{q}I \cdot \hat{q} + \frac{pc}{q} \cdot dI$ which is, in fact, ambiguous. Given an unchanged monitoring cost, it becomes cheaper to incentivize VCs when they are more productive. They get a smaller share $\gamma = c/q$ per unit of investment, which also restricts their financial contribution. On the other hand, when the firm's total investment is larger, VCs also lend a larger amount. However, this does not cover the total need for increased external funding, so that bank lending $dI - dI_m = \frac{pc}{q}I \cdot \hat{q} + \frac{q-pc}{q} \cdot dI$ clearly increases since $q > pc$. This relates to the certification role of VCs, that is, the presence of a VC raises the firms' pledgeable income and allows them to borrow more from banks. When VCs become more productive, this certification role is emphasized.

When VC value added as reflected in q gets larger, the expected surplus of a VC-backed firm rises since both the profit margin as well as the leverage factor increase in q. As a result, the cut-off return v_* declines, see (A23.8). Since a more active style in VC financing (higher q) benefits only VC-backed firms, it shifts up the π_m^e-line in Exhibit 23.1, leading to a lower cut-off return. A larger share of start-ups prefers VC financing. At start-up stage, when the subsequent financing choice is anticipated, the expected value of a new firm in (23.9) also rises, which strengthens incentives for entry. Note that a small variation of the cut-off value has no impact on expected value since the discrete financing choice implies $d\bar{\pi}^e/dv_* = [\pi_b^e(v_*) - \pi_m^e(v_*)]g(v_*) = 0$. Only the direct effect of more valuable VC support is important, which is relevant only for VC-backed firms. Expected profit ex ante, before the investment return is realized, changes by

$$d\bar{\pi}^e = \int_{v_*}^{v_1} \frac{\partial \pi_m^e(v)}{\partial q} dG(v) \cdot dq$$

Prior to learning the project return, a firm always has some chance that its innovation will turn out to be very profitable and suitable for VC financing. Using the elasticity in (A23.7) and dividing by $w(= \bar{\pi}^e$ if free entry with zero profits, thus $\hat{\bar{\pi}}^e \equiv d\bar{\pi}^e/w)$ yields

$$\hat{\bar{\pi}}^e = \int_{v_*}^{v_1} \left[\frac{1}{\rho_m} + \frac{v - \beta}{v\theta_m} \right] vq \frac{\rho_m I_m}{w} dG(v) \cdot \hat{q} \qquad (23.10)$$

Via ρ_m, I_m and θ_m, the integrand depends on the return v. A more productive VC industry not only leads to a larger share of start-up firms to opt for VC financing (selection effect, v_* falls), but also encourages entry in general (level effect, $\bar{\pi}^e$ rises which attracts new entrants). The performance of VC-backed relative to bank-financed firms rises.

TAX POLICY AND THE VENTURE CAPITAL SECTOR

The life cycle of a young firm involves a typical sequence of events. The government defines a policy environment. From the perspective of the entrepreneur, starting a firm is an occupational choice problem. Entrepreneurship is worthwhile only if it promises a higher expected present value of income than an employed career. Starting a company typically requires some early seed investment to turn the idea into a project and develop a business plan which can be presented to a financier. Often, this limited seed investment is financed from own resources, family, business angels, and so on.[5] When the project is innovative and the firm's investment promises high returns, own equity is typically far from sufficient to finance expansion investment and fully exploit the growth potential. The firm must thus approach an external investor. However, the entrepreneur typically needs more than just money. Experience at this stage is often mainly with technical product development rather than the management of a growing company. The firm thus needs both money and managerial advice and will ideally be able to enlist VC financing. Experienced VCs can help with industry experience, managerial know-how, a network of contacts, and can give strategic business advice. On the other hand, VC is more expensive than standard bank financing since the monitoring and advising services must be compensated and is thus suitable only for the most profitable projects. When expansion investment is successful, and the firm's product is successfully launched, the returns to investment materialize and give rise to profits. The firm enters this more mature stage with access to standard market finance. At this point, it can be sold to new investors, possibly in an IPO on a stock market for young technology companies. The VC firm typically divests, and entrepreneurs often realize part of their stake.

Public policy influences private decisions at different stages of the firm's life cycle. The relative tax burden on labor compared to cumulative capital income tax, consisting of the present value of corporation, dividend and capital gains taxes, affects incentives for entrepreneurship and determines the rate of business creation. The amount of external finance needed is reduced by investment subsidies. Such subsidies are offered by numerous government programs, such as direct investment tax credits paying for part of the investment cost, subsidized interest for small businesses, credit guarantees, and so on. Public credit guarantees, at a cost to the government in case of failure, allow banks and investors to charge lower interest than would otherwise be possible.

When firms successfully mature to the production stage, they start to earn positive profits that are subject to corporation tax and, when distributed to private investors, dividend and capital gains tax. The corporate tax together with depreciation rules and other provisions in the tax base such as interest deductibility, immediate write-offs, tax treatment of research expenditures, and so on influence the further growth of mature firms. The capital gains tax kicks in and cuts into the privately earned gains during the start-up period when the entrepreneur sells part of her stake. These taxes subtract from cash flow and pledgeable income and thereby reduce firms' investment scale by reducing their ability to raise external funds. Success taxes all reduce the private value of companies, independent of their implications for the scale of investment. Although not paid during the start-up period but only much later, they have an important negative impact on start-up activity and incentives in the early stage of business development. All these taxes reduce the company value that can be expected when starting a business and putting in effort to enhance survival chances. It's not only the capital gains tax that is relevant for venture capital backed entrepreneurship. We now discuss the principal policy impact in the context of our theoretical model, discussed earlier, and relate the results to the existing literature.

Wage Tax

The rate of business creation depends on the expected capital income by starting one's own firm relative to the entrepreneurs' alternative career prospects. For this reason, wage taxation is quite relevant for start-up activity as the empirical literature mentioned in the Introduction emphasizes. The wage tax exclusively influences the occupational choice decision. In reducing the opportunity cost of entrepreneurship w in (23.9), it stimulates entry and business creation. If a high tax load on labor relative to capital income, as in countries with a dual income tax such as the Nordic countries, strongly boosts entrepreneurship, new firms may possibly start to compete down prices in their specialized market segments so that the return to investment v declines. The tax may thus discourage investment and the net present value of young firms. If firms are finance-constrained, this reduction in investment scale is welfare reducing because, being constrained, investment is too low in private equilibrium. Simply pushing agents into entrepreneurship may not be a good policy because it would only lead to more start-up firms but a smaller scale of them. If this happened, more entrepreneurship would reduce efficiency and welfare, because investment tends to be too low already in the untaxed market equilibrium.[6]

The mirror image of this result is that low capital income taxes increase entrepreneurship. However, part of it may only be motivated to convert highly taxed labor income into lightly taxed capital income (Gordon 1998, Crawford and Freedman 2007, and Egger, Keuschnigg, and Winner 2008). This income shifting has lead to substantial losses in tax revenue in some Nordic countries with a dual income tax regime (Soerensen 2005). However, tax shifting may be less of a problem with innovative, VC-backed firms in search of large growth opportunities.

Success Taxes

Profit or success taxes include corporate taxes, dividend and capital gains taxes. They all have in common that they reduce the cash flow or income that is created by successful investment. In a purely neoclassical model of the firm, taxes impair investment because they reduce the return to investment. In the model of the second section of this chapter, this channel is, in fact, excluded because the return to investment v results upon drawing from a return distribution and is exogenously given thereafter. In line with substantial empirical evidence, tax effects operate entirely by their impact on financing constraints. The level of investment per firm depends on two measures, the amount of equity or own assets A, and the amount of pledgeable income available for incentive-compatible repayment of external funds. The novel channel for tax effects in the present model is that success taxes reduce pledgeable income. They thereby reduce the financing capacity and the firm's ability to expand investment by raising more external funds. We thus find in (A23.2) and (A23.5) that the tax reduces the investment scale of VC and bank-financed firms by $\hat{I}_m = -((p+q)/\theta_m) \cdot \hat{t}$ and $\hat{I}_b = -(p/\theta_b) \cdot \hat{t}$, respectively. An increase in the tax t per unit of capital, where tI_j is the total tax paid by a firm of type j, depresses VC-backed investment more severely than bank-financed investment since the success probability $p+q$ and the leverage factor $1/\theta_m$ are higher with VC financing. Similarly, within each group, the tax is relatively more harmful to more profitable firms which are those with a larger leverage.

Clearly, success taxes reduce firm values under either financing mode, see (A23.4) and (A23.7) or $\hat{\pi}_b^e = -(1/\rho_b + 1/\theta_b)(\rho_b I_b/\pi_b^e)p\hat{t}$ and $\hat{\pi}_m^e = -(1/\rho_m + 1/\theta_m)(\rho_m I_m/\pi_m^e)(p+q)\hat{t}$, respectively. The explicit solution in (A23.8) implies that the value line for VC financing is shifted down in Exhibit 23.1 to a larger extent compared to pure bank financing. Consequently, the pivotal investment return rises. Success taxes thus discriminate against VC financing so that, in the end, fewer firms demand VC. Finally, since the tax reduces the value of all types of firms, it clearly diminishes expected value π^e of a start-up company upon entry before the profitability of investment is revealed. Extracting a larger net present value of taxes from firms relative to the tax load on alternative activities clearly reduces incentives to start new firms. Success taxes discourage business creation and entrepreneurial entry.

Success taxes are particularly damaging and have first-order negative welfare effects even with small tax rates. To see this, note that the social surplus of bank and VC-financed firms is equal to $\pi_b = (pv - 1)I_b$ and $\pi_m = ((p+q)v - c - 1)I_m - \kappa$, respectively. Given positive profit margins (see the discussion of 23.7), a larger investment scale would yield a strictly positive social surplus at the margin but is not possible in private equilibrium due to finance constraints. Hence, if policy tightens finance constraints and thereby reduces the investment scale, welfare must fall since investment is already too low in private equilibrium. In making finance constraints more tight and thereby reducing investment, success taxes impose first-order welfare losses.

This welfare result is in parallel to the results in our previous own research (see the review in Keuschnigg and Nielsen [2006] and the specific results in Keuschnigg and Nielsen [2003a-b and 2004a-b]). In line with a large part of the theoretical VC literature, we have included variable effort by the entrepreneur and VC but a fixed investment size. In this work, underinvestment is reflected in too little entrepreneurial effort and VC advice and, therefore, overly high rates of business failure. By way of contrast, the present model treats effort as a discrete all or nothing decision so that it is not variable at the margin. Underinvestment is thus not reflected in effort but rather in the scale of investment as determined by the financing constraint. While there is not much empirical evidence on differences in effort and success rates across VC-backed and comparable other firms, the empirical literature clearly suggests that VC-backed firms are able to raise more capital, which points to the certification role of VC as in this paper. The policy conclusions are, however, broadly consistent and qualitatively the same in both frameworks.

Corporate Tax: Particularly important among success taxes is the corporate tax. All in all, the tax may reduce economic efficiency on three fronts. First, by discouraging mature firm investment after the exit of a VC,[7] the tax reduces private firm value by more than it adds to the present value of tax revenue. The corporate tax thus involves an excess burden or deadweight loss like any other tax that discourages private activity. The impact of the tax on size and value of mature firms depends importantly on depreciation allowances and other deductions as well. Second, the tax burden gets capitalized in the firm value. In reducing mature firm value, the corporate tax is likely to magnify financing frictions during the start-up and expansion phase considered here. By reducing the financing capacity and early expansion investment, the corporate tax leads to a first-order welfare loss since investment scale is already too low in the market equilibrium. This first-order welfare loss is much more severe than the tax distortion of mature firm investment, which results only in a second-order welfare loss and would thus disappear for small taxes. Third, given the above-average innovation potential of young VC-backed firms, the loss in aggregate innovation will not be made up by increased innovation of established firms. By its negative effect on firm creation, the corporate tax is likely to reduce the rate of innovation and economic growth. In view of the knowledge spillovers created by new firms, entry of young innovative firms may be too low even in the absence of taxes. If there are important external effects from private innovation activity, the tax again reinforces a preexisting market distortion and is therefore particularly harmful. There are thus two additional reasons that raise the cost of the corporate tax beyond the usual deadweight loss that is associated with other taxes as well. In consequence, the effects of the corporate tax on VC-backed innovative entrepreneurship are particularly harmful.

Dividend and Capital Gains Taxes: At the investor level, corporate income can accrue either as dividends or capital gains and is subject to personal taxes. A young growth company, be it VC-financed or not, will typically not pay dividends during the start-up phase, since cash flow, if there is one at all, will be needed to finance further investment before acquiring additional external financing. Once firms have survived to a mature production stage and have accumulated a large enough capital stock, they will start paying dividends. Dividend payments are typically observed only at a more mature stage when the VC firm has already exited by means of an IPO, management buyback, or sale to another firm. The fact that start-up firms are usually not paying dividends does not mean, however, that dividend taxation wouldn't be relevant for their performance. Quite the contrary. Capitalization of dividend taxes paid during the mature stage reduces firm values, irrespective of whether there is any impact of dividend taxes on mature firm investment or not.[8] Lower firm value reflects a reduced cash flow, which can be distributed to the stakeholders of the company, thereby reducing pledgeable income, debt capacity, and investment at earlier stages, and eventually reduces entrepreneurship. Except for the potentially different impact on value and size of mature firms, the effects on business creation and investment in the start-up phase are qualitatively similar to the corporate tax.

The capital gains tax is generally believed to be the most relevant tax impediment to VC-financed investments, the reason being that the return to investment both to entrepreneurs and VC firms mostly accrues in form of capital gains during the start-up period. It would be seriously incomplete, though, to limit attention only to the capital gains tax. The size of the capital gains is determined by the value that is realized when the VC firm divests, by IPO, acquisition, buyback, or write-off. The value of the firm at this stage depends on future profits net of taxes if the company hadn't failed already before the transition to the mature state. Since corporate and dividend taxes are capitalized into firm value, they reduce the capital gains that can possibly be created during the start-up phase. The focus in the VC literature on the capital gains tax is too narrow.

So far, we have assumed full loss offset in capital income taxation. The consequences of incomplete loss-offset are analyzed by Keuschnigg and Nielsen (2003b) in a model of fixed investment and variable effort. In the present context, one can anticipate two consequences. First, a restriction in loss offset raises the effective tax burden and should thus reduce entry. And second, loss offset limitations make failure more costly and could strengthen incentives, making it cheaper to incentivize the entrepreneur and thereby strengthening pledgeable income and financing capacity.

A lower capital gains tax may stimulate fund inflows by individual investors but less by tax-exempt institutions such as pension funds. The empirical literature (Poterba 1989a, b and Gompers and Lerner 1998) finds that the capital gains tax mainly affects entrepreneurial entry rather than fund inflows. Our theoretical framework thus starts from the presumption that fund-raising is not a limiting factor. In fact, there may be too much money chasing too few attractive investments (Gompers and Lerner 2000). If at all, VC financing is probably constrained by the possible shortage of management skills and entrepreneurial know-how required in VC investing (Bottazzi, Da Rin, and Hellmann forthcoming; Gompers et al. 2006), rather than a shortage of financial funds.

Subsidies to the Cost of Capital

Many policies to encourage business creation include direct subsidies to investment spending. In the United States, empirical research on the Small Business Innovation Research (SBIR) has shown that grants significantly raise the growth of awardee firms compared to others (see Lerner [1999, 2002]). Wallsten (2000) found significant crowding out effects although he too argued that the program could help firms to attract additional private funding. Our theoretical model shows indeed that investment subsidies raise investment by helping firms to raise more external funds from outside investors and also points to the fact that the impact may systematically differ across different types of firms. Investment subsidies are either given in a fixed absolute amount z or as a fraction s of the chosen investment level. Both types of subsidies boost investment of all firms, although with different impact. A flat subsidy z acts like an increase in own equity but has no impact on investment multipliers $1/\theta_j$. By (A23.2) and (A23.5), it triggers a proportional increase in investment, $\hat{I}_m = \hat{z}/(A - \kappa) > \hat{I}_b = \hat{z}/A$. The fixed cost associated with VC financing uses up part of own assets and thereby reduces the amount of external borrowing by VC-backed firms. Hence, the percent increase in investment is larger for VC-backed compared to bank-financed firms. Further, the absolute increase in investment, $dI_b/dz = I_b(v)/A = 1/\theta_b(v)$, is larger for more profitable firms, which are leveraged to a larger extent. The same holds for VC-backed firms, which are similarly heterogeneous in their investment returns.

A proportional investment subsidy magnifies the leverage factor by $\hat{\theta}_j = -\hat{s}/\theta_j(v)$, and thereby investment by $\hat{I}_j = -\hat{\theta}_j$, where $j \in \{b, m\}$. A higher return reduces the factor θ at rate $p + q$ for VC-backed companies, compared to p for bank-financed firms. Hence, a proportional investment subsidy not only has a relatively larger impact on VC-backed relative to bank-financed firms. Different from a flat subsidy, it boosts investment of more profitable firms to a larger extent also within each class. Hence, in general, a proportional subsidy favors investment of more profitable companies relatively more. Intuitively, since the best companies invest at a much larger scale, a proportional subsidy also subsidizes them to a larger extent compared to smaller, less profitable firms.

VC-backed firms benefit more. The subsidies thus reduce the cut-off value v_* and induce more firms to demand VC support. Independent of this selection effect, the subsidies raise the net present value of both types of firms. From (A.4) and (A.7),

$$\hat{\pi}_j^e = \left(\frac{1}{\rho_j} + \frac{1}{\theta_j}\right) \frac{\rho_j I_j}{\pi_j^e} \left[\hat{s} + \frac{1}{I_j} \cdot \hat{z}\right] \tag{23.11}$$

where $\pi_b^e = \rho_b I_b$ and $\pi_m^e = \rho_m I_m - \kappa$ in an initial untaxed equilibrium. Within each class, the investment scale I_j increases with a firm's profitability. The square bracket thus shows that the value of a flat subsidy becomes relatively less important for more profitable firms, while an ad valorem subsidy is given in proportion to the investment level and, thereby, favors the highly profitable firms to a larger extent. Since a subsidy boosts profits of all types of firms, it also raises the expected value $\bar{\pi}^e$ prior to the productivity draw as given in (23.9) and thereby clearly encourages firm entry and business formation.

Revenue-Neutral Policies

All of the isolated policies considered up to now either increase or decrease the present value of net tax revenue per firm. We have also emphasized the fact that one and the same policy change can have rather different effects on different types of firms as distinguished by their investment productivity. In the following, we discuss two policy strategies that keep the net present value of tax revenue constant and yet favor the most productive VC-backed companies at the expense of less profitable bank-financed firms.

Flat versus Proportional Subsidies: In reality, investment subsidies differ in non-trivial form. Some subsidies are limited to a maximum amount per firm and are independent of investment scale; others are strictly proportional. Suppose now that the government replaces flat by proportional investment subsidies in a way that keeps tax revenue constant. The net present value of a specific firm's tax liability is given in (23.1) and yields an aggregate value of net tax payments equal to $T = \int_{v_0}^{v_*} \tau_b(v) dG(v) + \int_{v_*}^{v_1} \tau_m(v) dG(v)$. The policy raises s and reduces z, starting from values of zero, in a way that keeps tax revenue unchanged, $\hat{T} = dT = 0$, or

$$\hat{T} = -\bar{I} \cdot \hat{s} - \hat{z} = 0, \quad \bar{I} \equiv \int_{v_0}^{v_*} I_b(v) dG(v) + \int_{v_*}^{v_1} I_m(v) dG(v) \qquad (23.12)$$

Denote the average investment level per firm by $\bar{I}$. Shifting investment incentives from flat to proportional subsidies thus requires $\hat{z} = -\bar{I} \cdot \hat{s}$. Using this in (A23.2) and (A23.5) and noting $I_b = A/\theta_b$ and $I_m = (A - \kappa)/\theta_m$ yields

$$\hat{I}_b = (I_b - \bar{I}) \frac{1}{A} \cdot \hat{s}, \quad \hat{I}_m = (I_m - \bar{I}) \frac{1}{A - \kappa} \cdot \hat{s} \qquad (23.13)$$

Clearly, the suggested policy affects firms rather differently. In particular, note that the leverage factor for VC-backed firms rises rapidly for the best projects with a return near the upper bound. These firms clearly invest more than average, $I_m > \bar{I}$, and will correspondingly benefit from the policy. One can show that at the cut-off value v_*, investment levels are $I_b(v_*) > I_m(v_*)$ since the fixed cost of VC investing reduces the investment scale. We can thus not prove whether marginal firms near the cut-off return are above or below average. Since the least profitable firms clearly choose bank financing, one can safely assume that firms with a return near the lower bound invest below average, $I_b(v) < \bar{I}$, and therefore lose from the policy. To sum up, shifting investment incentives from flat to proportional subsidies favors the largest, most profitable, VC-financed firms and discriminates against the smallest bank-financed companies.

Similar conclusions are obtained when inspecting the impact on firm values. Substituting the policy into (A23.4) and (A23.7) yields

$$\hat{\pi}_b^e = (I_b - \bar{I}) \left(\frac{1}{\rho_b} + \frac{1}{\theta_b} \right) \frac{1}{I_b} \hat{s}, \quad \hat{\pi}_m^e = (I_m - \bar{I}) \left(\frac{1}{\rho_m} + \frac{1}{\theta_m} \right) \frac{\rho_m I_m}{\pi_m^e} \frac{1}{I_m} \hat{s} \qquad (23.14)$$

As before, the policy favors the most profitable, VC-backed firms with the highest investment scale and harms firms with very low returns, which are most likely bank-financed. For the same reason as before, we cannot show how profits of pivotal firms in either financing mode are affected. It is thus not possible to determine whether the policy induces more firms to opt for VC financing or not. Given that firm values increase for both types of firms, expected value $\bar{\pi}^e$ ex ante also rises, which makes start-up entrepreneurship more attractive.

Fundamental Tax Reform: The general tax reform literature recommends two rivaling concepts of "investment neutral" tax systems: cash flow taxes as proposed in the Meade Report (1978), Hall and Rabushka (1985), or the U.S. President's Panel (2005), among others. The rival concept is the allowance for corporate equity (ACE), pioneered by Boadway and Bruce (1984) and introduced into the tax reform debate by the IFS Capital Taxes Group (1991). The choice between cash flow versus allowance for equity is again on the agenda of the current Mirrlees review for tax reform.[9] These alternative proposals for investment neutrality are generally thought to be equivalent and to give rise to the same present value of tax burden and tax revenues; see, e.g., Bond and Devereux (2003). It is also acknowledged that the two concepts, while equal in present value terms, differ in terms of the timing of tax payments. The cash flow tax gives immediate tax relief to current investment but denies any deduction of the costs of financing (no deductions of interest on debt or of imputed cost of equity). Hence, tax liability is low at the early investment stage and high when the firm earns the cash flow from successful investment. The cash flow tax is back loaded and shifts the tax burden into the future. In contrast, the ACE tax with an allowance for the cost of financing at the cash flow stage (deduction of interest on debt and of imputed cost of equity) but no deductions at the investment stage shifts the tax burden to the present and is front loaded. In a purely neoclassical investment model with perfect information, the timing of tax burden is irrelevant. We now show that the timing of tax liability becomes very important in a world with financing constraints. In particular, moving from a cash flow to an ACE system strengthens the financing capacity of the most profitable firms and favors VC financing.

Consider now a marginal, revenue neutral move from an ACE to a cash flow tax system, which shifts a firm's tax liability from the early investment stage (reduce s) to the late cash flow stage (raise t). To implement this policy package, we first define the average success probability over all bank and VC-financed firms,

$$\bar{p} \equiv \left[p \int_{v_0}^{v_*} I_b(v)dG(v) + (p+q) \int_{v_*}^{v_1} I_m(v)dG(v) \right]/\bar{I}, \quad p < \bar{p} < p+q \qquad (23.15)$$

where I is defined in (23.12). Clearly, this average success probability is an endogenous concept, depending on firms' selection into bank and VC financing and on investment scales of different types of firms. In computing the change in aggregate tax revenue as before, we again start from an untaxed position (reducing tax base effects) and find, after substituting from (A23.1),

$$\hat{T} = \bar{I} \cdot (\bar{p} \cdot \hat{t} - \hat{s}) = 0 \Leftrightarrow \hat{s} = \bar{p} \cdot \hat{t} \qquad (23.16)$$

To mimic the move from an ACE to a cash flow tax in a revenue neutral way, we raise the success tax by $\hat{t}$ (denying a deduction for costs of finance raises the tax liability in the cash flow stage), and allow for a proportional investment subsidy in the amount of $\hat{s} = \bar{p} \cdot \hat{t}$ (moving to a cash flow tax with immediate expensing reduces the tax liability at the investment stage). Although the government abstains from taxing more or less in the aggregate, this self-financed policy change has nontrivial consequences. Consider the investment responses in (A23.2) and (A23.5), leading to $\hat{I}_b = [\hat{s} - p \cdot \hat{t}]/\theta_b$ or

$$\hat{I}_b = \frac{\bar{p} - p}{\theta_b} \cdot \hat{t} > 0, \quad \hat{I}_m = -\frac{p + q - \bar{p}}{\theta_m} \cdot \hat{t} < 0 \tag{23.17}$$

Clearly, replacing an ACE tax with a cash flow tax shifts the tax burden from the investment to the cash flow stage and thereby discriminates against investment of the most profitable firms, which tend to be VC-financed, in favor of the least profitable firms, which are bank-financed. The discrimination against the more profitable VC-backed firms is also reflected in the relative changes in firm values in (A.4) and (A.7), giving $\hat{\pi}_b^e > 0 > \hat{\pi}_m^e$,

$$\hat{\pi}_b^e = (\bar{p} - p)\left(\frac{1}{\rho_b} + \frac{1}{\theta_b}\right) \cdot \hat{t}, \quad \hat{\pi}_m^e = -(p + q - \bar{p})\left(\frac{1}{\rho_m} + \frac{1}{\theta_m}\right)\frac{\rho_m I_m}{\pi_m^e} \cdot \hat{t} \tag{23.18}$$

Obviously, this also holds for the pivotal firm with return v_*. By shifting up in Exhibit 23.1 the value line for bank-financed projects and shifting down the line for VC-backed firms, the policy raises the pivotal investment return and, thereby, discourages firms to demand VC. Evaluating (A23.8) yields

$$\hat{v}_* = \left[p - \bar{p} + \frac{A}{\kappa}\frac{q}{p+q}\bar{p} \right]\frac{1}{pv_*} \cdot \hat{t} > 0 \tag{23.19}$$

Since $p < \bar{p} < p + q$, the sign is guaranteed to be positive. The square bracket is $(A - \kappa)q/\kappa$ and, thus, positive when $\bar{p} = p + q$, and it is $\frac{A}{\kappa}\frac{q}{p+q}p$ when $\bar{p} = p$. Hence, moving from a cash flow to an ACE system (reduce t and raise s) makes the tax system more front loaded by shifting the tax burden from the late cash flow to the early investment stage. This policy favors investment and firm values of the more profitable VC-backed companies at the expense of less profitable ones and, thereby, leads more firms to demand VC financing. An ACE system should thus be more conducive to the expansion of the VC industry. Since the expected values of bank and VC-financed firms are affected in opposing ways, it remains unclear whether the policy boosts entry.

A revenue neutral policy that cuts success taxes and finances the revenue losses with a reduction in upfront investment subsidies then favors VC-backed companies but harms bank-financed firms. In earlier work (see Keuschnigg and Nielsen [2003a-b], for example), we have assumed a fixed investment scale of firms but allowed entrepreneurial and VC efforts to vary continuously, leading to an endogenous success probability p. The impact of VC support was not on external funding and investment leverage but rather on the success probability of firms. In that framework, both efforts were found to be too low, and failure rates too high, since both the VC and entrepreneur had to bear the full cost of managerial and advising effort but were entitled to only part of the returns. In the present model, investment is too low due to finance constraints. Both formulations have in common that a reduction in success taxes financed by a reduction in upfront subsidies favors VC-backed companies even if the net present value of tax revenues remains unchanged.[10] A low tax burden late in the firm's life cycle either increases the reward to effort and, thus, raises firms' survival chances, or it raises the financing capacity and boosts investment scale. The reform could thus contribute to a more active or a larger VC industry without throwing more money at it. The key rationale for this policy is not to stimulate entry but to sharpen incentives and raise pledgeable income. Keuschnigg (2004) showed how the policy could give rise to knowledge spillovers and boost innovation-based growth.

SELECTION VERSUS VALUE ADDED

The suggested front-loading should favor VC-backed over bank-financed firms. Note that $p < \bar{p} < p + q$ in our model. Comparing (23.16) and (A23.1) shows that the present value of tax payments falls for VC-backed and rises for bank-financed firms. Since it remains unchanged on average, the policy has not a clear-cut effect on entry. However, more start-up activity is probably not desired. For entirely different reasons, the literature based on De Meza and Webb (1987), see De Meza (2002), for a more recent statement, and the evidence discussed and presented in Cressy (1996, 2002) and Parker (2003), argue that entry should actually be actively discouraged since entrepreneurship may be too high when there is cross-subsidization from good to bad firms in bank financing. Firms are probably very heterogeneous with respect to their success probability and/or value created (De Meza and Webb 1999).

Cross-subsidization occurs when banks cannot easily distinguish between high and low quality firms. While entrepreneurs may be fully aware of the quality and success chances, a bank may have difficulties to judge from outside what the potential of a new firm without a past track record really is. Banks thus tend to offer uniform financing conditions to heterogeneous firms and may be unable to prevent cross-subsidization in their credit portfolio. Lending conditions are then too unattractive to the very best firms, but too favorable for low quality firms. As a result, credit conditions allow entry of less able entrepreneurs who would not get financed if banks had a chance to correctly assess individual risk. If a correct risk assessment of young firms without track record is not possible from outside, the bank makes a loss while the marginal entrepreneur just breaks even. In consequence, the net present value of the venture is negative from a social perspective. Policy should be concerned to reduce entry rather than encourage it. From a normative perspective, the literature has argued for interest taxes and other measures to increase the cost of capital, rather than start-up subsidies. Interpreted in the light of the framework of the preceding section, the net present value of taxes on the company and investor level should be positive and exceed the wage tax burden to discourage entry.

The recent synthesis and generalization of the literature based on Stiglitz and Weiss (1981) and De Meza and Webb (1987) by Boadway and Keen (2005)—see also the discussion of Boadway and Tremblay (2005)—makes the point that firms differ not only in one but possibly in several dimensions with no clear correlation pattern of success probabilities and returns of different types. In not being able to distinguish different firm types, banks will again offer uniform credit conditions. However, with heterogeneity in several dimensions such as survival probabilities or market potential, uniform bank lending does not give rise to a clear-cut pattern of cross-subsidization, or only in rather special cases (one being the DeMeza-Webb framework). To cut a long discussion short, the implication is that bank financing leads to excess lending and overinvestment of some types of firms while lending would be too restrictive and entrepreneurial investment too low in other types of new ventures. Clear-cut policy recommendations are no longer possible. If banks are unable to distinguish heterogeneous firms, government is expected to be even less able to differentiate. As a default rule, tax policy should arguably remain neutral towards the entry margin. Other reasons such as knowledge spillovers might still call for a policy to encourage entry of more innovative firms.

Keuschnigg and Nielsen (2008) have analyzed issues of adverse selection in a model of VC financing. Apart from the potential cross-subsidization in VC portfolios, the paper also shows how convertible securities are useful to induce desired self-selection of entrepreneurs, see Cumming (2006a) for empirical results in this direction. Compared to banks, VC firms use more flexible contractual forms such as convertible securities and stage financing to tailor financing needs to the specific character of firms (Kaplan and Strömberg 2003, 2004, document the rich nature of actual VC contracts).

OTHER AREAS OF PUBLIC POLICY

Taxes and subsidies are by far not the only important area of public policy towards innovative entrepreneurship and VC financing. There might be policy complementarities leading to mutually reinforcing effects (e.g., Cumming 2007). One omission of the present review is the tax treatment of stock options for employees (Gilson and Schizer 2003). Substantial tax savings may be possible due to tax deferral when stock options are taxed only at the date when the option is exercised and income actually is realized, rather than at the date of issue.[11] A favorable tax treatment of employee stock options could help young technology firms to attract key personnel at a lower wage cost at a time when cash flow is low or nonexistent.

One important precondition for an active VC industry is access of young technology companies to liquid stock markets. Liquid stock markets allow VCs to exit from their portfolio companies faster and more profitably. This exit possibility also helps the entrepreneur to regain control over the company when the concentrated stake of the VC firm is broadly dispersed over smaller market investors at an IPO. Since entrepreneurial independence is a main motivation for entrepreneurship in the first place, the presence of specialized stock markets makes potential entrepreneurs more willing to start a firm (Black and Gilson 1998). It also makes the value added of VC financing more attractive to entrepreneurs since the intense control of VCs is expected to last only for a limited time period. According to Micchelacci and Suarez (2004), the presence of liquid stock markets allows VCs to exit faster and to reshuffle their activities to new early-stage companies where VC support is needed the most. In equilibrium, liquid stock markets boost innovation and growth because the faster turnover of VC allows for a larger rate of VC-backed entrepreneurship. The empirical analysis of Da Rin, Nicodano, and Sembenelli

(2006) indeed finds that the presence of stock markets significantly stimulates VC activity.

There are other important areas of public policy, unrelated to taxes and subsidies. Among them are entry regulations and administrative barriers to start firms (Fonseca, Lopez-Garcia, and Pissarides 2001); patent protection to allow young firms to safely appropriate their innovation rents, and investor protection and reporting rules (e.g., Armour and Cumming 2006); bankruptcy laws that do not permanently stigmatize failed entrepreneurs (diminished job prospects in case of failure make innovators less willing to start a firm in the first place; see Gromb and Scharfstein [2003]; Landier 2003); or liberal pension fund regulations to allow pension funds to diversify by allocating funds to VC firms, which facilitates fund-raising (Gompers and Lerner 1998).

CONCLUSION

The creation of young firms is a significant factor in promoting employment and innovation. VC has become an increasingly important source of funding for start-up firms. In combining financing with active advice and monitoring, VC can help the professionalization of portfolio companies and add value. Therefore, VC-backed firms appear to outperform similar firms without access to VC, making them a particularly important source of job growth and innovation. Policy makers are thus much concerned about creating the right policy environment for a dynamic VC industry.

Our policy analysis implies that success taxes such as the capital gains tax may be quite harmful to VC-financed entrepreneurship. The corporate tax is harmful to investment and valuation of mature firms and is most likely to be even more harmful to finance constrained start-up firms. In reducing the returns to effort, the corporate tax impairs the incentives for effort and advice at the firm's start-up stage and may, thus, contribute to an overly high failure rate and harm the quality of VC investments. Alternatively, as in the framework of this chapter, the tax reduces pledgeable income and the financing capacity of young firms and thereby restricts investment. The analysis lends some support to the advocates of cutting the capital gains tax or giving corporate tax relief to small innovative firms. However, such tax relief should be confined to VC-backed firms only. In terms of practical tax policy, two issues should be noted. First, the burden of the capital gains tax may already be quite low compared to other capital income taxes. The deferral of capital gains until realization implies interest gains that significantly reduce the actual tax burden. Second, there may be some practical difficulties in selectively applying a tax break to VC-backed firms only.

Many programs to stimulate business creation involve investment subsidies. In reducing the present value of net tax liability, they favor entry. The analysis has also shown that the specific form of the subsidies is important. Compared to flat subsidies given in a fixed absolute amount, proportional subsidies are more favorable to the more profitable firms, which are more likely to receive VC support. The analysis has also shown that subsidies are relatively less effective in boosting investment by VC-backed firms, compared to a cut in success taxes. For the same reason, a profit tax with an allowance for financing costs also favors the more innovative and, thus, more profitable VC-backed firms, compared to a cash flow tax, which gives tax relief up front. Shifting the tax burden from the late cash flow stage when the returns to effort and investment accrue, to the early investment stage sharpens incentives for effort and strengthens the financing capacity of the most profitable firms even if the net present value of tax liabilities remains unchanged. Hence, the structure of investment subsidies and the details of capital income taxes regarding the definition of the tax base, have non-trivial consequences for investment and growth of bank versus VC-financed firms.

APPENDIX: COMPARATIVE STATICS

The hat notation denotes logarithmic derivatives such as $\hat{q} \equiv dq/q$. For small policy changes starting from an untaxed position of $t = s = z = 0$, define $\hat{\tau} = d\tau$, $\hat{s} = ds$ and $\hat{z} = dz$. The net present value of tax payments in (23.1) depends on the firm's profitability v. Compared to a VC-backed company, a bank-financed firm owes $\tau(v) = (pt - s)I(v) - z$. Starting from an untaxed position, one can ignore tax base effects via changes in I. The tax liability of a type j firm with investment $I_j(v)$ thus changes by

$$\hat{\tau}_b = I_b \cdot (p \cdot \hat{t} - \hat{s}) - \hat{z}, \quad \hat{\tau}_m = I_m \cdot [(p + q) \cdot \hat{t} - \hat{s}] - \hat{z} \quad (A23.1)$$

Bank-financed Firms: Investment in (23.5–23.6) changes by

$$\hat{\theta}_b = -\frac{1}{\theta_b}[pv \cdot \hat{v} - p \cdot \hat{t} + \hat{s}], \quad \hat{I}_b = -\hat{\theta}_b + \frac{1}{A} \cdot \hat{z} \quad (A23.2)$$

Profits are $\pi_b^e = \rho_b I_b + z$ and change by $\hat{\pi}_b^e = \hat{\rho}_b + \hat{I}_b + (1/\pi_b^e)\hat{z}$, where the effect on the profit margin is

$$\hat{\rho}_b = \frac{1}{\rho_b}[pv \cdot \hat{v} - p \cdot \hat{t} + \hat{s}] \quad (A23.3)$$

Combining with the preceding results and collecting terms gives

$$\hat{\pi}_b^e = \left(\frac{1}{\rho_b} + \frac{1}{\theta_b}\right)\left[pv \cdot \hat{v} - p \cdot \hat{t} + \hat{s} + \frac{1}{I_b} \cdot \hat{z}\right], \quad \frac{1}{\rho_b} + \frac{1}{\theta_b} = \frac{p\beta}{\theta_b \rho_b} \quad (A23.4)$$

VC-backed Firms: Investment in (23.5–23.6) changes by

$$\hat{\theta}_m = -\frac{1}{\theta_m}[(v - \beta)q \cdot \hat{q} + (p + q)(v \cdot \hat{v} - \hat{t}) + \hat{s}], \quad \hat{I}_m = -\hat{\theta}_m + \frac{1}{A - \kappa} \cdot \hat{z} \quad (A23.5)$$

where $v > \beta$ since profit margins are assumed to be positive over the entire range as was discussed in the context of (23.7). Values $\pi_m^e = \rho_m I_m - \kappa + z$ under VC financing change by $\hat{\pi}_m^e = \frac{\rho_m I_m}{\pi_m^e}(\hat{\rho}_m + \hat{I}_m) + \frac{1}{\pi_m^e}\hat{z}$, where the effects on the profit margin are

$$\hat{\rho}_m = \frac{1}{\rho_m}[(p+q)(v \cdot \hat{v} - \hat{t}) + \hat{s} + qv \cdot \hat{q}] \qquad (A23.6)$$

Combining and collecting terms gives

$$\hat{\pi}_m^e = \left(\frac{1}{\rho_m} + \frac{1}{\theta_m}\right)\left[\frac{\rho_m I_m}{\pi_m^e}\left[(p+q)(v \cdot \hat{v} - \hat{t}) + \hat{s}\right] + \frac{\rho_m}{\pi_m^e} \cdot \hat{z}\right]$$
$$+ \left(\frac{1}{\rho_m} + \frac{v - \beta}{v\theta_m}\right)\frac{\rho_m I_m}{\pi_m^e}qv \cdot \hat{q} \qquad (A23.7)$$

Equilibrium: The pivotal return v_* equates firm values in the two financing modes. The direct derivative of (8), evaluated at the untaxed position, yields

$$\hat{v}_* = \frac{1}{v_*}\hat{t} - \frac{q - cp}{(p+q)\,pv_*\kappa}\hat{z} - \left[\frac{p+q}{q} - \frac{A}{\kappa}\right]\frac{q}{(p+q)\,pv_*}\hat{s} - \frac{(1+c)q}{(p+q)^2 v_*}\frac{A}{\kappa}\hat{q} \qquad (A23.8)$$

Clearly, the cut-off increases with success taxes, implying that they discriminate against choosing VC, while both types of investment subsidies favor VC financing by reducing the cut-off value.

NOTES

1. See EVCA Barometer June 2005 on http://www.evca.com.
2. Since advising and coaching is time intensive, the portfolio of VC firms compared to banks tends to be much smaller and more focused. Kanniainen and Keuschnigg (2004) have developed a theory of VC portfolio size where the quality of advice and VC support is traded off against the number of portfolio firms. Cumming (2006b) provides empirical evidence in support, and Keuschnigg (2004a) explores the tax consequences. These issues are beyond the scope of the present analysis.
3. We assume that the project is not viable and is not financed if incentive constraints were violated. This would always be the case if $p_L = 0$. Hence, we assume p_L to be low enough.
4. The hat notation, e.g., $\hat{q} \equiv dq/q$, indicates percentage changes relative to values in the initial equilibrium. As an exception, we use absolute changes, e.g., $\hat{t} \equiv dt$, $\hat{s} \equiv ds$ and $\hat{z} \equiv dz$, for small policy variables which are initially zero.
5. In the model of the second section of this chapter, the VC's fixed cost of investigating the project could equivalently be interpreted as an early seed investment of the entrepreneur. After self-financing of seed investment, the firm is left with own assets to finance expansion investment.
6. The welfare implications are discussed more extensively in the next subsection.
7. The investment return may itself depend on what happens after successful completion of the start-up phase and exit of a VC.
8. There is an unresolved debate about whether mature firms, in response to dividend taxes, reduce investment or not (new versus old view of dividend taxation). A general consensus seems to be that dividend taxes do not distort investment of large, mature

firms that can finance their investments fully with retained earnings, but they reduce investment by young and growing firms. This is precisely what our framework implies for VC-financed growth companies.

9. Ongoing research under the Mirrlees Review commissioned by the editorial team can be accessed under www.ifs.org.uk/mirrleesreview/index.php.

10. In earlier work, we have exclusively concentrated on VC financing and have not discussed any selection effects between bank and VC-financed firms.

11. The problem is similar to the tax advantage of applying the realization principle in capital gains taxation, rather than taxation upon accrual.

REFERENCES

Aghion, P., and J. Tirole. 1994. The management of innovation. *Quarterly Journal of Economics* 109:1185–1209.

Armour, J., and D. Cumming. 2006. The legislative road to Silicon Valley. *Oxford Economic Papers* 58:596–635.

Audretsch, D., and E. Lehmann. 2004. Debt or equity? The role of venture capital in financing high-tech firms in Germany. *Schmalenbach Business Review* 56:314–357.

Black, B. S., and R. J. Gilson. 1998. Venture capital and the structure of capital markets: Banks versus stock markets. *Journal of Financial Economics* 47:243–277.

Boadway, R. W., and N. Bruce. 1984. A general proposition on the design of a neutral business tax. *Journal of Public Economics* 24:231–239.

Boadway, R. W., and M. Keen. 2005. Financing and taxing new firms under asymmetric information. Discussion paper, Queen's University and IMF.

Boadway, R. W., and J. Tremblay. 2005. Public economics and start-up entrepreneurship. In *Venture capital, entrepreneurship and public policy*, ed. V. Kanniainen and C. Keuschnigg. CESifo Seminar Series, Cambridge: MIT Press, 198–219.

Bond, S. R., and M. P. Devereux. 2003. Generalized R-based and S-based taxes under uncertainty. *Journal of Public Economics* 87:1291–1311.

Bottazzi, L., and M. Da Rin. 2002. Venture capital in Europe and the financing of innovative companies. *Economic Policy* 34:231–269.

_____, and T. Hellmann. Forthcoming. Who are the active investors? Evidence from venture capital. *Journal of Financial Economics*.

Casamatta, C. 2003. Financing and advising: Optimal financial contracts with venture capitalists. *Journal of Finance* 58:2058–2085.

Crawford, C., and J. Freedman. 2007. Small business taxation. A Special Study in selected issues undertaken for the *Mirrlees Review*, Working paper.

Cressy, R. 1996. Are business start-ups debt rationed? *Economic Journal* 106:1253–1270.

_____. 2002. Introduction: Funding gaps. *Economic Journal* 112:F1–F16.

Cullen, J. B., and R. H. Gordon. 2007. Taxes and entrepreneurial activity: Theory and evidence for the U.S. *Journal of Public Economics* 91:1479–1505.

Cumming, D. J. 2005. Agency costs: Institutions, learning, and taxation in venture capital contracting. *Journal of Business Venturing* 20:573–622.

_____. 2006a. Adverse selection and capital structure. *Entrepreneurship Theory and Practice* 155–183.

_____. 2006b. The determinants of venture capital portfolio size: Empirical evidence. *Journal of Business* 79:1083–1126.

_____. 2007. Financing entrepreneurs. Better Canadian Policy for venture capital. C.D. Howe Institute Commentary No. 247.

Da Rin, M., G. Nicodano, and A. Sembenelli. 2006. Public policy and the creation of active venture capital markets. *Journal of Public Economics* 90:1699–1723.

David De Meza. 2002. Overlending? *Economic Journal* 112:F17–F31.

_____, and D. C. Webb. 1987. Too much investment: A problem of asymmetric information. *Quarterly Journal of Economics* 102:281–292.

_____. 1999. Wealth, enterprise, and credit. *Economic Journal* 109, 153–163.

Djankov, S., et al. 2008. The effect of corporate taxes on investment and entrepreneurship. NBER WP 13756.

Egger, P., C. Keuschnigg, and H. Winner. 2008. Incorporation and taxation: Theory and firm-level evidence. University of St. Gallen, WP Series in Finance No. 93.

EVCA (European Private Equity and Venture Capital Association). 2004. Benchmarking European tax & legal environments. May 2004.

Fonseca, R., P. Lopez-Garcia, and C. A. Pissarides. 2001. Entrepreneurship, start-up costs, and employment. *European Economic Review* 45:692–705.

Gentry, W. M., and R. G. Hubbard. 2000. Tax policy and entry into entrepreneurship. *American Economic Review* 90:283–287.

Gilson, R., and D. M. Schizer. 2003. Understanding venture capital structure: A tax explanation for convertible preferred stock. *Harvard Law Review* 116:875–916.

Gompers, P. A., et al. 2006. Skill vs. luck in entrepreneurship and venture capital: evidence from serial entrepreneurs. Discussion paper, Harvard University.

Gompers, P. A., and J. P. Lerner. 1996. The use of covenants: An empirical analysis of venture partnership agreements. *Journal of Law and Economics* 39:463–498.

_____. 1998. What drives venture capital fundraising? *Brookings Papers on Economic Activity—Microeconomics*: 149–192.

_____. 1999. *The venture capital cycle.* Cambridge: MIT Press.

_____. 2000. Money chasing deals? The impact of fund inflows on private equity valuations. *Journal of Financial Economics* 55:281–325.

_____. 2001. The venture capital revolution. *Journal of Economic Perspectives* 15:145–168.

Gordon, R. 1998. Can high personal tax rates encourage entrepreneurial activity? *IMF Staff Papers* 45:49–80.

Gromb, D., and D. Scharfstein. 2003. Entrepreneurship in equilibrium. Discussion paper, London Business School and Harvard Business School.

Hall, R. E., and A. Rabushka. 1985. *The flat tax.* Stanford: Hoover Institution Press.

Hellmann, T., and M. Puri. 2000. The interaction between product market and financing strategy: The role of venture capital. *Review of Financial Studies* 13:995–984.

_____. 2002. Venture capital and the professionalization of start-up firms. *Journal of Finance* 57:169–197.

Holmstrom, B. 1982. Moral hazard in teams. *Bell Journal of Economics* 13:324–340.

_____, and J. Tirole. 1997. Financial intermediation, loanable funds, and the real sector. *Quarterly Journal of Economics* 112, 663–691.

IFS Capital Taxes Group. 1991. Equity for companies: A corporate tax for the 1990s. Commentary No. 26, London: Institute for Fiscal Studies.

Inderst, R., and H. M. Mueller. 2004. The effect of capital market characteristics on the value of start-up firms. *Journal of Financial Economics* 72:319–356.

_____. 2006. Early-stage financing and firm growth in new industries. Discussion paper, London School of Economics and New York University.

Jones, C. I., and J. C. Williams. 1998. Measuring the social return to R&D. *Quarterly Journal of Economics* 113:1119–1135.

Kanniainen, V., and C. Keuschnigg. 2004. Start-up investment with scarce venture capital support. *Journal of Banking and Finance* 28:1935–1959.

Kaplan, S. N., and P. Stromberg. 2001. Venture capitalists as principals: Contracting, screening, and monitoring. *American Economic Review* 91, 426–430.

_____. 2003. Financial contracting meets the real world: An empirical analysis of venture capital contracts. *Review of Economic Studies* 70:281–315.

———. 2004. Characteristics, contracts, and actions: Evidence from venture capital analysis. *Journal of Finance* 59:2173–2206.

Keuschnigg, C. 2003. Optimal public policy for venture capital backed innovation. CEPR DP 3850.

———. 2004a. Taxation of a venture capitalist with a portfolio of firms. *Oxford Economic Papers* 56:1–22.

———. 2004b. Venture capital backed growth. *Journal of Economic Growth* 9:239–261.

———, and S. B. Nielsen. 2003a. Tax policy, venture capital, and entrepreneurship. *Journal of Public Economics* 87, 175–203.

———. 2003b. Taxes and venture capital support. *European Finance Review* 7:515–539.

———. 2004a. Start-ups, venture capitalists, and the capital gains tax. *Journal of Public Economics* 88, 1011–1042.

———. 2004b. Taxation and venture capital backed entrepreneurship. *International Tax and Public Finance* 11:369–390.

———. 2005. Public policy for start-up entrepreneurship with venture capital and bank finance. In *Venture capital, entrepreneurship and public policy*, ed. V. Kanniainen and C. Keuschnigg (221–250). Cambridge: MIT Press, CESifo Seminar Series.

———. 2006, Public policy, start-up entrepreneurship and the market for venture capital. In *The life-cycle of entrepreneurial ventures, International Handbook Series on Entrepreneurship*, vol. 3, ed. Simon Parker (227–257). New York: Springer.

———. 2008. Self-selection and advice in venture capital finance. University of St. Gallen, WP Series in Finance No. 17.

Kortum, S., and J. Lerner. 2000. Assessing the contribution of venture capital to innovation. *RAND Journal of Economics* 31:674–692.

Landier, A. 2003. Start-up financing: From banks to venture capital. Working paper, Graduate School of Business, University of Chicago.

———. 2006. Entrepreneurship and the stigma of failure. Working paper, Stern School of Business, New York University.

Lerner, J. 1999. The government as venture capitalist: The long-run impact of the SBIR program. *Journal of Business* 72:285–318.

———. 2002. When bureaucrats meet entrepreneurs: The design of effective "public venture capital" programmes. *Economic Journal* 112:F73–F84.

Meade, J. E. 1978. The structure and reform of direct taxation (Meade Report). Boston: Allen and Unwin.

Melitz, M. J. 2003. The impact of trade on intra-industry reallocations and aggregate industry productivity. *Econometrica* 71:1695–1725.

Micchelacci, C., and J. Suarez. 2004. Business creation and the stock market. *Review of Economic Studies* 71:459–481.

Parker, S. C. 2003. Asymmetric information, occupational choice and government policy. *Economic Journal* 113, 861–882.

Poterba, J. M. 1989a. Capital gains tax policy toward entrepreneurship. *National Tax Journal* 42:375–389.

———. 1989b. Venture capital and capital gains taxation. In *Tax policy and the economy*, vol. 3, ed. L. H. Summers (47–67). Cambridge: MIT Press.

Repullo, R., and J. Suarez. 2004. Venture capital finance: A security design approach. *Review of Finance* 8:75–108.

Rosen, H. S. 2005. Entrepreneurship and taxation: Empirical evidence. In *Venture capital, entrepreneurship and public policy*, ed. V. Kanniainen and C. Keuschnigg (251–279), Cambridge: MIT Press. CESifo Seminar Series.

Schmidt, K. M. 2003. Convertible securities and venture capital finance. *Journal of Finance* 43:1139–1166.

Soerensen, P. B. 2005. Neutral taxation of shareholder income. *International Tax and Public Finance* 12:777–801.

Sorensen, M. 2007. How smart is smart money? A two-sided matching model of venture capital. *Journal of Finance* 62:2725–2762.

Stiglitz, J. E., and A. Weiss. 1981. Credit rationing in markets with imperfect information. *American Economic Review* 71:393–410.

Tirole, J. 2001. Corporate governance. *Econometrica* 69:1–35.

———. 2006. *The theory of corporate finance.* Princeton, NJ: Princeton University Press.

Ueda, M. 2004. Bank versus venture capital. Project evaluation, screening, and expropriation. *Journal of Finance* 59, 601–621.

U.S. President's Advisory Panel on Federal Tax Reform. 2005. Simple, fair, and pro-growth. proposals to fix America's tax system. Retrieved from www.taxreformpanel.gov.

Wallsten, S. J. 2000. The effects of government-industry R&D programs on private R&D: The case of the Small Business Innovation Research Program. *RAND Journal of Economics* 31:82–100.

Winton, A., and V. Yerramilli. Forthcoming. Entrepreneurial finance: Banks versus venture capital. *Journal of Financial Economics.*

ABOUT THE AUTHOR

Christian Keuschnigg received a Ph.D. from the University of Innsbruck and the Habilitation from the University of Vienna, and is Professor of Public Economics at the University of St. Gallen. He specializes in public economics with a focus on business taxation. Professor Keuschnigg has published many articles in academic journals such as *Journal of Public Economics, Journal of Economic Growth, European Finance Review, Journal of Banking and Finance* as well as several books including *The Economics of Taxation* (Mohr Siebeck 2005) and *Venture Capital, Entrepreneurship and Public Policy* (MIT Press 2005, co-editor).

## CHAPTER 24

Twelve Meditations on Venture Capital

Some Heretical Observations on the Dissonance Between Theory and Practice When Applied to Public/Private Collaborations on Entrepreneurial Finance Policy

GORDON MURRAY
Chair in Management (Entrepreneurship), University of Exeter Business School

DAVID LINGELBACH
Assistant Professor of Business, School of Business and Leadership, Stevenson University, and Professorial Lecturer, Johns Hopkins School of Advanced International Studies

Meditation (definition)

>   a. *The action or practice of profound spiritual or religious reflection or mental contemplation.*
>   b. *Continuous thought on one subject; (a period of) serious and sustained reflection or mental contemplation.*
>
> Shorter Oxford English Dictionary, 2

INTRODUCTION

For practicing Buddhists, meditation is an important aid to self-knowledge and enlightenment. In the context of this policy-oriented paper, we use this concept in order to raise an important set of questions. Can organizations also become enlightened? Is it possible for a governmental or state agency to undertake "serious and sustained" reflection? Put another way, can a public agency create, and subsequently employ effectively, a collective memory of past actions and consequences? We would suggest and will argue in this paper that, from the empirical evidence available, government organizations are often rather poor at learning from their own past experiences or borrowing from the relevant experiences of equivalent agencies in other countries.

There are many reasons that may account for this partial and imperfect learning. Civil servants are specialists in the multifaceted and often highly politicized processes of government but not generally in the mastery of specific content. Thus, able public servants in administrations in most advanced polities regularly move across the government machine, taking disparate roles in several departments in their progress to senior office. Reflection also takes time and space in the agenda, two commodities very scarce in contemporary governments, constrained by shrinking budgets and growing demands in an age of state decline (van Creveld 1999). And, invariably, rational and depersonalized Weberian bureaucratic actions will always be overlaid, second-guessed, or trumped by the contemporary political imperative.

It is in this policy context that we would argue that the professional academic "outsider" may have a role. By definition, a scholarly analysis demands reflection, a theoretical compass, and a menu of appropriate methodologies. These are applied to situations that are often viewed over time and across different conceptual geographies in order to reach robust generalizable conclusions. The academic process is both comparative and evaluative. On occasions it may also be prescriptive. It is in offering this differently rigorous and more longitudinal perspective that the academic may complement the shorter-run agendas of the policy practitioners. Indeed, in some circumstances, the specialist academic outsider may have a *greater* knowledge and understanding of historic policy actions and their consequences than the current cohort of responsible policy makers.

We make the strong assumption of a different type of academic knowledge. In consequence, our objective in this paper is perhaps ambitious ... even heroic. Namely, we wish to inform government policy makers of the consequences of their actions and to stress how well-grounded theory from economics, management, and entrepreneurship disciplines may usefully inform their policy choices. Specifically, and academics by definition should always be specific, we wish to illustrate our premise with reference to the financial services industry. We will argue how the applications of early-stage, venture capital (VC) financing policy by several governments—undertaken with little reference to this wider body of research—have often resulted in adverse consequences far removed from their original aspirations. We seek to give explanations as to why these divergences occur by reference to both observed practice and established theory. Our focus and illustrations are exclusively focused on "early stage" VC activity where government and private interests have come together to jointly finance "hybrid" investment funds (OECD 2004, 2008). Our deliberations are informed by over 20 person-years involvement in academic research and policy advice/evaluation across a number of developed and developing economies. It is precisely because we are not practitioners that our analysis may have merit.

Importantly, the purpose of the paper is neither to criticize nor to indict the actions of policy makers or, indirectly, practitioners. Rather, the authors' ambition is to raise a hand of caution and gently to request that aspiring policy makers reflect, however briefly, on the historical record of public/private interventions in order that new initiatives may at least be measured against, and more importantly informed by, the template of past experience and its formal analytical interpretation. To borrow from a Buddhist *koan* (riddle), we urge our policy maker readers to "listen to the sound of one hand clapping."

Our observations reflect on public/private co-investment arrangements in a specialist area of financial services involving the financial support of young, innovative, and entrepreneurial firms. After the unprecedented chaos of global financial services starting in the fall of 2008, which has lead to publicly funded rescues (i.e., equity purchases) of many of the Western worlds' major banks, we now find that the management of public/private partnerships in financial services has become a current and multitrillion dollar issue. The state has once again become a major player, perhaps the most important player, in global capital markets. The policy dimension of public and private concerted actions has become an issue of the utmost economic importance. Also we have heard several commentators mirroring public bafflement ask, "Why was it not possible to learn more from previous experience of financial and market failures?!"

ACADEMIC ENGAGEMENT—OR WHY DON'T THEY EVER LISTEN TO US?

The degree to which management scholars should or should not actively engage in advising or influencing policy or practitioner constituencies remains a permanent element of academic introspection and debate (Van de Ven 2007). For many scholars, too close an association with the commercial or public activities of professional managers and their organizations is seen as engendering a risk of compromised intellectual freedom, objectivity and integrity. Jermier (1998) notes that applied managerial research is too often designed and focused on issues determined at the behest of the established, élite cohorts of top management and/or majority stock holders. By implication, the research goals may often be counter to the interests of labor, consumers, or the average citizen (a large and passive group increasingly termed "Main Street"). The direction of much of applied management research is seen as possibly laden with value assumptions inimical to the liberality of many social scientists. Management research may actually be *damaging* to workers' interests. (It is therefore not surprising that John Doe rarely demands an academic opinion.) On occasion, academic advice may not be good for anyone. Ghoshal (2005), citing the disastrous governance failures of Enron, Tyco, and Global Crossing, argued that some theoretical underpinnings of management thinking may actively condone bad management practice (pathologies). He specifically examples the important, financial economics concept of "Principal-Agency theory" with its explicit assumption of self-interested and adversarial action as the norm of management behavior. Here, the need to incentivize management agents beyond other interest groups can be interpreted as an intellectual legitimization of the self-serving and destructive rapacity of top management teams. Merchant bankers please note![1]

For others, an academic career is more properly conducted in a reflective and disinterested environment removed from the "noise" of the factory floor or executive suite. Here, the quality and relevance of academic endeavor is more properly determined by fellow academicians who judge output largely within the narrow and self-referencing criteria of peer-reviewed journal articles, research council grants, conference appearances, and other indications of exclusively scholarly esteem and recognition. In each case, the contribution to and influencing of current behavior in the commercial or policy arenas is of subordinate interest and importance. Prescription is seen as the domain of the consultant. Despite consultancy being one of the largest employers of business and management school graduates, the term has a pejorative connotation to many academics. Consultancy advice is often excoriated by scholars as atheoretic, nonrigorous, and fashion driven, although there exists some recent evidence of a change in heart as so-called researcher/user "engagement" assumes a greater academic salience (Van de Ven 2007).

If scholars' ability and desire to influence commercial organizations is seen as limited, the impact of social sciences research on policy formation and execution is perhaps even more parlous. Rynes and Shapiro (2005) lament that the accumulated knowledge of management and organizational behavior professors appears to have had negligible influence on the U.S. government in its addressing of the major organizational and political challenges of the day. This belief of the general failure of theoretical and empirical scholarship to influence government's perspective or actions is lamented by several other authors (Abrahamson and Eisenmann 2001; Bazerman 2005; Pfeffer 1998). Perhaps, the most obvious exception to this "iron rule of irrelevance" can be seen in the influential role that economists have played and continue to play in both commercial and public policy debates. This is despite the assertion by many critics of economics' policy hegemony that economic theory has consistently proven to be "systematically wrong" (Bazerman 2005, 25). Where economists have appeared to be more consistently successful than other social scientists is in their engagement with both public and private practitioner constituencies, and in their ability to communicate using an institutionally accepted (if not widely understood) language and vocabulary (Ferraro, Pfeffer, and Sutton 2005). More critically, according to Bazerman (2005), the influence of economists is founded on their ability and willingness to offer *prescriptive* advice and detailed analytical recommendation to practitioners. In so doing, economists have arguably communicated and worked with the subjects and users of their research in a more widely and deeply integrated manner than perhaps any other discipline in the social sciences.

In the increasingly global, inter-related (and thus volatile) policy and commercial environments of the New Millennia, Abrahamson and Eisenman (2001) suggest that academics have to redefine themselves as "knowledge entrepreneurs" if they do not wish to see themselves as marginalized in what these authors believe is an increasingly commoditized knowledge market. This extreme interpretation would ironically seem to place academic researchers firmly in the domain of consultants, similarly obliged to hustle in order to find research opportunities in a world of competing experts. We find this projection implausible if for no other reason than that much top quality academic research is not a commodity (unlike much consultancy) but is highly branded and personalized in both its form and delivery.[2] However, the question of a sensible balance between the creation of intellectual value and its practical application remains. The policy actions of government are hugely material both in their direct and indirect impact on all citizens as well as in the considerable resources they consume. Academic researchers largely funded by public taxes cannot easily ignore either their actual cost or their potential contribution to society. Greater engagement with the policy process may well provide value to research producers and consumers alike. It is on this optimistic premise that this paper has been written.

THE TWELVE MEDITATIONS

The following twelve meditations are a personal reflection. They are both a summary and a critique of popular government actions in the field of entrepreneurial finance. In the area of early-stage entrepreneurial finance, government activity is increasingly becoming the main driver of new forms of financial provision to start-up and young firms (Jääskeläinen, Maula, and Murray 2007; Pierrakis and Mason 2008). Here an important clarification is necessary. In our examples and references, we are not describing a form of finance available and relevant to the great majority of small and medium-sized enterprises (SMEs) that have few ambitions for growth. Rather, we are talking about forms of equity finance (i.e., risk capital) that are appropriate to that exceptional and small minority of new and young businesses, often termed "Gazelles," that are very strongly growth focused (Acs, Parsons, and Tracy 2008; Autio 2008).

Each of the twelve meditations seeks to illuminate a particular area of public/private activity and its related policy actions and consequences. They are presented as a set of statements that are testable, and thus potentially of academic credibility:

Government innovation & finance policy makers fit into two camps. They either believe in Charles Darwin or the Book of Genesis. In reality, most prefer the creation story.

The State as "Creationist"

In 1996, a report commissioned by the Industry R&D Board of the Australian Commonwealth government suggested that Australia should consider an "equity enhancement' program (similar to that employed in the Small Business Investment Companies Act in the United States) in order to stimulate an increased investment of early-stage, risk capital into technology-based young firms. The report's author suggested that Australia had an "hour glass problem" (Murray 1996a), that is, a systemic constraint in the sources of start-up and early-stage growth finance available to high-potential young firms. Within 18 months, the Australian Commonwealth government had created the Innovation Investment Fund (IIF) with an initial A\$100 million budget. The IIF was designed specifically to address capital rationing in young firms by crafting a supply-side policy instrument that provided private VC funds with public leverage of up to 2:1 (Cumming 2007). Australian policy makers and legislators acted with impressive speed to address a major concern of economic policy. The logic underpinning the creation of the IIF program was to remove a constriction in the capital market and thus assist the rapid development of an emerging, Australian venture capital industry (Wan 1989).

This enthusiasm to kick start an Australian venture capital industry, while understandable, took little cognizance of the protracted period and the necessary environmental and institutional preconditions required to form a viable and profitable a venture capital industry. American family trusts were doing *proto*-venture capital, equity financings in the 1930s (Gompers 1994). The first "classic" VC firm, American Research and Development, incorporating a limited liability

Exhibit 24.1 Examples of Profit Distribution Structure in Government Supported VC Funds

Feature	Description	Profit Distribution Effects	Examples (present and past)	Category Based on Effects on Profit Distribution
Public investor co-investing with private investors	Government matching the investments by private investors	Helps in setting up a fund. Also helps to build a sufficiently big fund to benefit from economics of scale. Investing in *pari passu* with private investors does not have profit distribution effects	Public participation: <50% of the fund: Europe/EIF Finland/FII Israel/Yozma; >50% of the fund: Australia/IIF and Pre-seed Fund USA/SBIC and SSBIC UK/regional venture capital funds	*Pari Passu*
Timing of cash flows	Ordering of the cash flows so that public investor puts the money in first and gets the money out last	The IRR of the private investor can be enhanced through timing of cash flows improving the attractiveness of the fund	UK/regional venture capital funds	Differential timing of the investor of public and private investors
Public participation as a loan	Government provides its share of capital as a loan with interest	The loan with interest creates a leverage effect on the return of private investor when the returns from the fund exceed the interest rate. Correspondingly, losses are increased with low performance	USA/SBIC/UK/ECF	Leveraging the return to private investors with a loan
Capped return for public investors	After the all time investors including the public invested have recieved certain IRR, the rest of the cash-flows are distributed to private investors only	Capped return for the government increases the expected IRR for private investors. This distribution increases the compensation for good performance. This in turn creates a strong incentive for the private investors to incentivize the general partners to make successful investments and add value to portfolio companies	UK/regional venture capital fund: Australia pre-seed fund Chile/CORFU	Limiting the profits entitlement of the public investor

Buy-put option for private investors	Private investors are given the option to buy the share of the government at (or until) a specific point of time at a predetermined price (typically nominal price + interest)	The effects on the IRR of private L.P. are similar to the "capped return" structure. However, there are two additional benefits: (1) the buy-out option gives both the public and the private L.P. an opportunity to demonstrate success earlier and more visibly than in the capped return alternative; (2) in the case of success, government gets a quick exit from the fund and can reinvest the money instead of waiting for the returns on fund termination	Israel/Yozma New Zealand/New Zealand venture investment fund
Downside protection	Downside protection means the government underwriting losses from the portfolio	Downside protection helps support the IRR, when partial loss of invested capital is probable	Germany/WFG Germany & KfW France/SOFARIS Denmark/the equity guarantee program	Guarantee of compensation to the private investor for loss of invested capital
Fund operating costs	Government subsidizes the management company to cover same of the costs from running the fund	Subsidies create an effect similar to the structure with asymmetric timing of cash flows. Magnitude of the effect depends on the size of subsidy	Europe/European seed capital scheme	Not examined

Source: Jääskeläinen, Maula, and Murray 2007.

partnership legal structure was formed in the United States in 1946 by Professor Doriot (Hsu and Kenney 2005) aided by significant support from Harvard University. Yet, the U.S. VC industry could only credibly be seen as an autonomous, and mature, asset class by the early 1980s—some *40* years later (Avnimelech and Teubel 2004). Similarly, the UK government employing the offices of the Bank of England created the Industrial and Commercial Finance Corporation (ICFC) and the Finance Corporation Industry (FCI) in 1945 as part of Britain's post–World War II reconstruction. These two organizations became the forerunner of 3i plc.[3] The ICFC and the FCI were a policy response to the "equity gap" first identified in Britain by the Macmillan Committee during the Great Depression and then reaffirmed by periodic official government reviews of the financial circumstances of small and medium-sized enterprise finance (Macmillan 1931; Bolton 1971; Wilson 1979). Yet, the UK as the second-largest VC industry in the world by the year 2000 was only a significant recipient and user of investment funds for early-stage risk capital investments from the mid-1990s onwards. While there is some evidence that the more recently established national VC industries have taken less time to become operational and professionalized—see, for example, the Finnish VC industry (Maula and Murray 2003; Jääskeläinen, Maula and Murray 2007)—the reality remains that the creation of a VC industry in even the most conducive legal, economic, and technological environments is the product of decades of incremental and evolutionary change compatible with the wider commercial and political environments.

Management scholars have long recognized the necessary precursors to effective strategic action at the level of the firm, industry, or economy. Diffusion models, industry life cycles, and stage theories of development, while often challenged (see, for example, Rogers [2003]; Klepper [1997]), do acknowledge the time and cultural dimensions required for material change (Tushman and Anderson 1986; McDougall et al. 1994). Similarly, advocates of "resource based theories of the firm" indirectly recognize that knowledge resources and particularly tacit competencies are not easily or speedily acquired (Kay 1993). Above all, economic historians have counseled us as to the slow pace and long gestation of *real* industrial change (North 2005; Clark 2007).

Yet, political imperatives demand rapid action with the creation of immediate (and preferably novel) policies and programs. Civil servants are often obliged to be complicit in such haste. Policy horizons do not easily extend beyond the interstices between elections in a democratic state, which has now become the dominant form of political organization. Thus, publicly financed incentives are set up to encourage initiative and to remove the inertia of limited activity by the targeted constituencies. The result is often the emergence of national VC industries and related programs that have solely domestic relevance, attract little institutional finance from foreign investors, and are heavily dependent on public support for both investment funds and operational costs. This reality is currently being ignored in a host of emerging countries across the world as they seek to emulate advanced Western economies by the promotion of de novo venture capital industries.

Market failure is what happens when you don't give me money; and a rational, objective, and rigorous economic analysis is what has happened when I don't give you money.

The State as "Apologist"

Technically, a "market failure" exists when the price established in the market does not equal the marginal social benefit of a good and thereby results in an undersupply from producers. Market failures occur for four main reasons: the abuse of market power resulting in imperfect competition; markets ignoring the impact of economic activity on those outside the market; when markets attempt to provide many types of public goods; and the presence of asymmetric information or uncertainty confounding optimal decisions. Early-stage equity finance in unproven young firms seeking to commercialize novel technologies in nascent or immature markets potentially can give rise to several types of market failure. For example, when the market does not provide sufficient finance to meet the demands of young firms regardless of their willingness to pay the price required (interest payment, collateral guarantee, and so on). Asymmetric information increases the uncertainty and risks for providers of capital, many of which would rather leave the market than provide finance under these unknown (and unknowable) conditions. The absence of finance means that existing companies fail through lack of access to necessary resources or growth is restricted and new companies are not formed.[4] Each of these outcomes may represent a significant social and economic cost to society.

It can be taken as a sine qua non that governments in free market economies would prefer not to intervene in financial markets unless there is clear evidence of a market failure leading to a serious misallocation of resources. Further, governments have to be convinced that their actions will effectively address the identified problem at an acceptable level of public costs. Thus, governments (and the appropriate competition authorities) need to be convinced both that a market failure exists and that it should be addressed. The fact that many financial institutions are loath to finance young firms is not per se evidence of a market failure. Indeed, if the young firms are highly risky and the expected return of any external investment does not provide an acceptable risk-adjusted return to investors, then the decision to deny finance is unquestionably rational. Those arguing the case for intervention have to demonstrate that there are specific and resolvable circumstances that prevent capital markets from acting efficiently and finding an equilibrium price at which the market clears. In short, given the robustness with which many markets work despite willful public attempts at intervention, the onus of proof should be on those critics that argue that the market is not working.[5]

Absence of information leading to the decision not to offer finance at any price would constitute a market failure, which could justify some form of government intervention. Perverse incentives that bias the normal matching of supply and demand would also constitute a market failure. For example, loan guarantees may, on occasion, have this effect on the actions of both capital providers and users (Riding and Haines 2001). There is a substantial literature on the interests and actions of the key actors in the venture capital process and the effect of their behavior on the optimal allocation of finance to potentially attractive young businesses.[6] This literature centers on a treatment of the genesis, effect, and management of agency costs as faced by the providers of capital (limited partners), the users of capital (portfolio firms), and the allocating intermediary agents (the venture capitalists or general partners). The effect of moral hazard issues on the behavior of actors in this market is central to these arguments (Burgemann and Hege 1998). That an agent can act in a manner that adversely affects the supply or demand of capital, is in part based on the absence of full and equal information available to all the parties to the transaction, that is, the information asymmetry problem. Thus, the actions of government, in addition to providing more capital from public resources, also focus on correcting the causes of market failure in order that public interventions in private markets remain effective and temporary. For example, the popular promotion and subsidization of business angel networks is one means by which several governments seek to address a continuing information gap in the immature, informal investor markets (Mason and Harrison 1997).

Thus, the case for public intervention is largely predicated on the belief that some correctable inefficiencies exist in the market's allocation of finance to SMEs. These are seen as particularly harmful to national economic interests (welfare) in the case of high potential / high impact, young, growth-oriented firms. Knowledge-based young firms whose assets are largely tacit in nature, such as intellectual property rights, are seen as especially vulnerable to constraints in the supply of finance given their modest internal resources and a general inability to attract debt finance at formation and early stages of growth because of their irregular and immature cash flows (Storey and Tether 1998). In short, their future value is not fully reflected in a present level of collaterizable assets that are sufficiently attractive to lenders.

That financial markets can discriminate against SMEs is not a new concept. The Macmillan Report (1931) argued that small British firms seeking sums under £250,000 (approximately £7 million at current prices) were discriminated against. Seventy-two years later, HM Treasury (2003) in the United Kingdom has argued that a market failure continues to exist at between £250,000 and £1 million, with sums under £2 million being still very difficult to access. The assumption that capital market failures exist for young firms is virtually taken as a given in government policy documents at both national and international levels including the European Commission, the OECD, and the World Bank.

Yet, contemporary national studies of SMEs' business environments find it is only in exceptional cases that small and medium-sized firms are repeatedly denied access to finance. In the UK Small Business Survey conducted by academic researchers on behalf of the UK government's Department of Business, Enterprise and Regulatory Reform (BERR), only 17 percent of firms interviewed between 2004 and 2007 reported any constraint on access to finance with 12 percent receiving an outright refusal. Being a "growth oriented firms" was not seen as a significant variable in any refusal to access finance (Cosh et al. 2008). Similarly, Maula and Murray (2003) using Finnish data also noted that only 6 to 7 percent of fast-growth SMEs were observed to have any problem with access to finance. These figures would suggest that it would be more sensible to have the statement "no evidence of market failure exists" as the Null Hypothesis, at least in countries with well-developed financial markets. Yet, the actual policy reality is that the existence of a market failure is commonly taken as a given "fact" in several advanced industrialized economies. All too often government policy documents repeat the term "market failure" with little acknowledgement to the paucity of research evidence supporting such a strong assertion. In reality, the research evidence is that many studies purporting to investigate this phenomenon are skeptical as to the generic existence or material effect of a SME "financing gap" although disentangling supply and demand factors in determining whether such a gap exists can be technically challenging (Berger and Udell 2006).

This is not to suggest that market failure does not or cannot exist. Indeed, there are structural circumstances that suggest it is uneconomic for VC firms to provide small tranches of money to young firms (Murray and Marriott 1998; European Commission 2005). Many VC firms in the membership of the powerful trade association, British Venture Capital Association (BVCA), no longer wish to offer applicant investee firms sums of money under a minimum of £5 million.[7] However, this debate on the minimum scale of VC investment masks the fact that many firms seeking finance *are not attractive enough* to professional investors in an asset class where the risk reward ratio has persistently acted against the interests of investors. The concept of "market readiness" is only just coming into policy fashion. This approach reappraises the market for SME finance from a demand-side perspective. It seeks to answer the conundrum that many SMEs argue—that access to finance is extraordinarily difficult—while at the same time venture capitalists state with equal conviction that they have more money than opportunities in which to invest (Queen 2002).

The rest of the world is not America. We can borrow but ultimately we have to find our own solutions.

The State as Groupie

The United States with the largest and most established VC industry[8] in the world is the single benchmark against which all other VC industries are compared (European Commission and U.S. Department of Commerce 2005). This is sensibly so, as the United States has consistently been one of the most profitable VC markets (Rosa and Raade 2006) in addition to having identified and financed some of the world's most outstanding new companies (Gompers and Lerner 1999). The returns to the U.S. top quartile VC firms have been attractive (and for some investments quite spectacular) and have greatly advantaged both the general partnership's managers and their limited partner investors. This U.S. success is in marked contrast to the disappointing returns that early-stage, classic VC has recorded in the UK, continental Europe, and beyond. It appears that the U.S. industry remains exceptional in its greater ability to recognize, nurture, and benefit from the investment in early-stage companies across a series of new and disruptive technologies and markets (Murray and Lott 1992; Dimov and Murray 2007).

It is thus not remarkable that government A or B may state that official government policy is to emulate as closely as possible the successes of an American exemplar. Yet, this goal is often little more than an aspirational slogan. For example, in the UK, public ambitions have covered creating a Silicon Fen (Cambridge), a Silicon Valley (South Wales), and a Silicon Glen (the Edinburgh-Glasgow corridor in Scotland). Further, we have Ireland, Finland, Belgium, New Zealand, and a host of other smaller countries each assuming policy targets for VC financing that are based on emulating the actions and history of the (presently) largest economy in the world, with the most successful technology-based corporations and, similarly, the most advanced educational infrastructure in science and technology research.

Regardless of the implausibility of such goals (Leslie and Kargon 1996), they are an abnegation of the peculiar and unique processes by which individual national economies develop. If we ascribe to the logic of "path dependency," a UK, Brazil, India, or China cannot replicate the U.S. experience (Teece, Pisano, and Shuen 1997; Kenney and von Burg 1999). At best, national policy makers may be able to draw out a number of generalizable lessons from the U.S. experience. For example, much of the present success of Silicon Valley is based on the foundation of several large companies intimately connected to the defense industry from the 1930s onwards (Saxenian 1994; Leslie and Kargon 1996; Page, West, and Bamford 2005). The idea that creating a military industrial complex comparable to the one in the United States (and possibly Israel) may be a precondition of a successful VC industry only emphasizes the need to think in terms of peculiar national histories rather than electing to follow blind emulation.[9]

What nations may be able to do is to understand the reasons and precursors for the formation of U.S. systems for the financing of young and novel industries in order to make their own adaptations. Israel has colonized an early-stage VC space very successful as an *off-shoring* of U.S. technology particularly (but not exclusively) in its civil application of originally military products and services, such as encryption and other security software. Similarly, Ireland has historically been highly successful as a low tax European entrepôt and destination for foreign corporations wishing to have a trading base within the European Union. Its early-stage VC activity has been strongly oriented around servicing the large community of foreign owned, technology-based corporations resident in Ireland. For Finland, its decision to become an innovation-based, knowledge economy was hugely influenced by the collapse of its Soviet export market in the early 1990s (Sabel and Saxenian 2008). The need to finance speculative innovative ideas outside traditional financing channels led to Finnish government support for the emergence of a VC industry in the mid-1990s (Maula and Murray 2003). In the developing world, India created a vibrant VC industry in response to the emergence of the outsourced software services industry (Dossani and Kenney 2002), while South Africa has struggled to develop VC despite a promising enabling environment (Lingelbach, Murray, and Gilbert 2008). What unites each of these illustrations is the *uniqueness* of each country's history and the specific circumstances leading to the formation of a national VC industry.

In fact, we would argue that it remains an open question as to whether or not VC is mainly an American innovation that has been diffused and adapted for various other national environments. A credible argument can be made that risk capital is a global phenomenon of several distinct variants and with historical antecedents predating American VC activity. Thus, it may well be that the potential for significant venture or risk capital activity is endemic to several or a majority of societies but that weak institutional environments have inhibited their development when compared to a number of advanced Western economies (La Porta, Lopez-de-Silanes, and Shleifer 1998, 2000).

The question is not whether the United States is an exemplar in VC activities. In reality, the United States is not an exemplar. Rather, a small number of American locations or clusters have sufficient size and centrality to enjoy world-scale impact in knowledge-based investment. These include Northern California, Greater Boston, and arguably North Carolina, Dallas, and Seattle. Outside these centers, the United

States has little obvious advantage over Europe or other regions. Policy makers should sensibly be asking themselves what are the preconditions for successfully creating an industry based on entrepreneurial risk—and do such preconditions exist in their own economy? Only after meeting these requirements is it credible to start looking at the technical questions of knowledge asset production and scale and scope economies in technology or other product markets in order to ascertain the probabilities of economic survival and success.

If you believe that all men are born equal, don't become a venture capitalist. Socialists make lousy venture capitalists.

The State as Wimp

One of the biggest challenges for policy makers in seeking to implement a U.S. model of VC activity is to attempt to introduce a new model of behavior without also importing or recognizing the social and cultural underpinnings of the American model. This model of economic activity relies on market forces as the pre-eminent allocation and signaling mechanisms. Like Darwin's evolutionary theory of natural selection, entrepreneurial markets allow relatively few winners but demand many losers. To operate in this market takes a form of physical and mental toughness that is unusually pre-eminent in the Anglo-Saxon competitive and individualistic culture. Max Weber in 1904 termed this set of enabling characteristics, the Protestant Ethic. It contrasts strongly with more paternal European social models in which the state is both protector and allocator of publicly owned resources.[10] The U.S. model is meritocratic and elitist. Its citizens have a passion for winning and broadcasting the benefits of success. Of equal importance, Americans appear noteworthy in their more tolerant acceptance of failure as a concomitant and necessary requirement to the celebration of success. This muscular American economic individualism can be compared with, in Hoffstede's (2001) terms, the "lower masculinity" of, for example, Nordic economies with their preferred emphasis on a societal as opposed to a predominantly individual perspective.

Given that democratic governments usually reflect broadly the cultural norms of their electorates, while similarly many economists theorize in terms of the behavior of the *owners* of assets rather than concentrating on the entrepreneurial *arrangers* of assets (Cantillon 1755; Say 1815), it is very easy to misunderstand the environmental preconditions for entrepreneurial behavior. Accordingly, one of many persistent weaknesses in developed, democratic Western governments is their attempts to introduce fairness, equity, and balance into the entrepreneurship policy equation. Entrepreneurial action is exceptional in all communities. Entrepreneurs are a small minority in the adult population generally. Even in the United States, only 12 percent of adults are actively involved in the entrepreneurial process of starting new firms (Bosma et al. 2008). For a majority of European countries, "Total Entrepreneurial Activity"[11] within the national adult population is consistently recorded at less than half of the United States value. Such estimates are stable over several annual surveys. Government incentives that do not discriminate in favor of its more entrepreneurial citizens—who may often be the more educated, the richer, or the more foreign—unwittingly trade economic advantage for apparent social equity. An entrepreneurial policy that does not actively discriminate in favor of growing businesses and their owners commanding more and/or better quality assets, including human capital, is at best ineffective and at worst hypocritical.

Governments have as much chance of becoming effective venture capitalists as tax collectors have of being loved.

The State as Loser

If government policy makers on the evidence available believe that the capital markets are imperfect in the supply of finance to SMEs, they have a number of choices. The provision of direct grants is one means by which the state can circumvent the market allocation process by transferring public finance directly to targeted firms on the basis of a set of selection criteria that policy makers believe are appropriate. Criteria employed may include firm size, firm sector, firm location, priority industry sector, R&D intensity, limited collateral, and so on. Conversely, they can themselves replicate the services supplied by private market principals. In this case, the government itself becomes a venture capital provider and addresses the missing or insufficient supply of services and actions of the private sector funders. A number of countries have set up such commercially focused funds, effectively recruiting investment managers to become public employees. For example, the Finnish Industry Investments, the China Hi-Tech Venture Capital Corporation, and Bahana Artha Ventura in Indonesia are all publicly owned investment funds with significant VC activity. Such activities are direct replications of private VC funds but are normally constrained in their investment focus—at least in developed countries—to that area of the market that is seen as problematic, such as seed capital and start-up finance particularly to high tech ventures.[12] Given that the state is providing a service that private, profit-motivated agents have eschewed, usually for reasons of poor fund performance, it is not surprising that such initiatives have often been characterized by high costs and poor returns (Murray 1998). Public venture capital firms are disadvantaged in competing in an area where professional investment competences are scarce and accordingly highly rewarded in professional labor markets.[13] There is a further agency problem in that while public investment executives may wish to be remunerated in a comparable manner to their private peers, they are not personally at risk from the negative outcome of their poor investment decisions.[14] Thus, public funds are commonly hampered by limited experience and low competence levels as well as by less well aligned managerial incentives.

It is these structural limitations of publicly owned VC funds that have occasioned greater contemporary interest in what are termed "hybrid" VC funds (OECD 2004).The genesis of this model is the seminal experiment in the United States of creating "Small Business Investment Companies" under the auspices of the Small Business Administration. While certainly not free of problems in its execution (Kleiman and Shulman 1992), the generic characteristics of the SBIC "equity enhancement" model have now been adopted in a range of modified forms by several other countries (including Australia, Finland, New Zealand, and the UK). The central logic of the use of public funds to leverage private investor returns is that it is efficient for the state to use public finance in order to engineer a range of incentives that encourage private VC firms to work in partnership with the state in promoting greater investment activities in areas of interest to public policy. In order to attract private interest, the state has to create incentives that address the key structural factors that make early-stage investing unattractive to the commercial investor. In essence, inducements have to be engineered that materially rebalance the risk/reward ratio of speculative risk capital investment in start-up and early-stage companies. There are several variants to the hybrid model, but essentially the public treasury becomes directly or indirectly a limited partner in the hybrid fund and provides a substantial proportion of the finance available to the fund and to investments made to the target group of companies. (In the specific case of the SBIC, the government becomes a guarantor or underwriter to the private investors thereby increasing the amount of funding that can be raised from commercial sources at an attractive rate of interest.) Frequently, the state will provide funding on a 2 to 1 basis as a "special" investor in the fund as, for example, in the UK's Enterprise Capital Fund scheme or Australia's Industry Investment Fund. In additional, the state will often require only a nominal return in the event of a successful investment. If the investment fails, the state will be a subordinated investor preferentially writing off its own proportion of the monies committed to the portfolio firm or to the aggregate fund.[15]

Recognizing the sensitivity of VC fund returns to "the time cost of capital," some schemes allow the public LP to invest before private fund money is committed. The state will only seek a repatriation of its own finance when all other private LPs in the fund have first received an agreed share of capital gain contingent on a successful investment. Thus, the private fund gains the benefit of substantial public investment at a lower cost of capital and with the public LP bearing a greater risk of loss in the event of a partial or complete investment failure. This public leverage effect can have a material effect on the performance of the fund. Jääskeläinen Maula, and Murray (2007) estimate that these asymmetric public/private risks and rewards can increase the terminal, net "cash to cash" returns (i.e., internal rate of return) to private LPs by up to 8 percent. However, these authors caution that such engineering of incentives can only work to increase the returns of a hybrid fund that has generated some positive capital gain via its investment decisions.

Downside guarantee funds do just that—they guarantee that there will be a downside.

The State as Sucker

The most attractive incentive to a private investor occurs if the state is prepared to guarantee the level of risk of the investor (LP) by underwriting part or all of the contingent loss of individual portfolio investments made or the aggregate losses of the fund. Guaranteed underwriting of the investments of private agents in order to encourage them to undertake actions desired by the state has a considerable history that long predates its involvement with VC (Irwin 2007; European Commission 2001, 2005). However, guarantees become especially useful in circumstances where there is a high level of unquantifiable uncertainty. For example, the large and subordinated position of the state as a "special" limited partner in the UK's Regional Venture Capital Funds was necessary before private investors (including the publicly owned international financing agency, the European Investment Fund) were prepared to co-invest in the new program. The terms accepted by the state as a "special" limited partner included being "the first investor in and the last out"; a cap on its returns; and, above all, the recipient of first losses. These conditions meant that in effect the state guaranteed the downside of the fund up to the level of its total public investment. Likewise in the United States, the SBA's underwriting of loans taken out by SBICs has the same guarantee effect. Such schemes have also been in evidence in continental Europe with France, Denmark, and Germany specifically providing guarantees to private sector risk capital investors (see, for example, WFG, tbg & KfW in Germany, SOFARIS in France, and the Equity Guarantee Program in Denmark). In the United States, a number of states have also provided guarantees to support local VC funds, including Oklahoma, Arkansas, Iowa, Ohio, Utah, and Michigan (NASVF 2006).

The central issue with a guarantee scheme centers on exactly the nature of the incentive to the private investor and the conditions under which it will be triggered. Equity leverage using subordinated state finance has a multiplier effect on the investor's return, amplifying both the rewards and costs of good and bad investments, respectively.[16] In contrast, a guarantee gives no incentive for the general partner to make good investments but reduces the cost to the limited partners of making a poor or ill-judged investment. Accordingly, the guarantee blunts the salience of negative market signals by reducing the impact of their consequences (Gilson 2003). The guarantee can thus allow the creation of a "moral hazard" whereby the investor does not bear the full commercial consequences of his actions. Accordingly, an injudicious but rational investor has an incentive to make riskier investments than would be the case if no underwriting was available given the asymmetric responsibilities.[17] In the authors' opinion, any public scheme that serves to lessen the costs of poor decisions while being neutral to good decisions is problematic. This is especially so when (as noted) public funds or private funds working at the most challenging early stages of the investment market are likely to have greater problems in attracting the involvement of the most experienced and successful investment managers.

Venture capitalists believe that seed capital is very important—so long as they don't have to provide it.

The State as Pocket Money

In a British Venture Capital Association sponsored survey in 1990, the top 20 venture capitalists in the UK were asked their opinion as to the greatest shortcoming of the industry in its first decade of significant operation (Murray 1992).[18] The respondents, who included representatives from both "classic" VC and Private Equity (Management Buy Out) fund managers, were unanimous in their opinions. They cited the inability of the UK to find a means of financing start-up and early-stage, high potential enterprises as successfully as the VC industry in the United States. The dearth of seed funding was particularly noted. This situation remains similar, and arguably worse, nearly 20 years later. Seed and other early-stage capital has remained a chronically unsuccessful investment focus outside the possible exceptions of East and West Coast America. Targeted primarily at technology-based new enterprises with products yet to be commercialized, seed capital investment combines multiple uncertainties from technology, market, and managerial sources. In addition, seed investing is particularly unattractive for VC investors, in that it demands very considerable managerial input from the general partnership of the VC firm into the fledgling enterprises while at the same time employing very little capital from the funds under management.

Accordingly, the European VC model with its concentration of small, *specialist* early-stage funds has been characterized by very low returns and several failed funds. This has resulted in an exit of commercial-focused VC firms from this market. Consequently, seed, start-up, and early-stage financing is now an area of the risk capital market where public funded VC firms predominate (Small Business Service 2006b; Pierrakis and Mason 2008). An earlier evaluation of the European Commission's European Seed Capital Pilot Program showed that one-quarter of the 21 country funds surveyed would have become insolvent within three years—even without making an investment—given the very high start-up and transactions costs in relation to the funds under management (Murray 1998). Classic VC funds in the UK have addressed this challenging asymmetry between the (high) management costs incurred and the (low) returns generated from exits and fee income from the modest funds managed by either abandoning seed activity or by increasing funds under management and refocusing activities on later-stage growth and development capital investments. A number of general partnerships have reallocated their efforts entirely from venture capital to private equity deals. Nor is this situation unique to the UK. The FII program in Finland was sanctioned for being set up to undertake early-stage investments while in practice concentrating its resources in private equity deals (Maula and Murray 2003). Similarly, South African private equity funds that have established VC funds in the past are now scaling back or abandoning those efforts for much the same reasons.

The U.S. model of seed investing implicitly recognizes that seed capital is, in isolation, not a viable commercial product, at least not when delivered by a VC fund. Rather, it is the first, "intelligence seeking" stage of a holistic investment process that will normally provide multiple rounds of follow-on finance to successful firms up to an exit event via either an IPO or a trade sale. Accordingly, U.S. VC firms undertaking seed capital are multistage investors and are commonly managing funds of over $1 billion. By such means, the strategically important but extraordinarily high risk/return ratio of seed capital deals are attenuated in being amortized across the total range of activities of the fund (Dimov and Murray 2007).

> *The archetype venture capitalist has razor-sharp teeth, can smell blood at three kilometers, has a paranoid/psychotic need to achieve lucrative deals, reveres capital gain above all things—and likes flower arranging.*

The State as Innocent Abroad

In order for the state to work effectively with venture capitalists, policy makers need to understand the modus operandi of the private sector organizations and commercial managements with which they wish to collaborate. Without such an understanding of the instrumentality and aggressively meritocratic and professional culture of the risk capital sector, there is a high probability that they will not be able to engineer sufficiently attractive incentives to ensure investment professionals' collaboration. Perhaps even more likely, less-experienced public departments will devise incentives that are inappropriately generous, thereby diminishing the potential public welfare by the degree of overpayment to their private agents.

Venture capitalists have very demanding interests as investors. Ideally, they wish for a very high return with negligible risk. They do not court risk but rather manage it professionally—for a price broadly measured in their significant ownership of the portfolio company's stock. Governments' interest in encouraging VC firms to invest in early-stage activities requires the incentivization of general partners who would otherwise seek to moderate risk by abandoning start-ups and moving toward later-stage and more certain investments. Thus, it becomes important to understand the motivations of the private collaborators in order to design incentives that encourage them to meet government's desired outcomes.

In reality, the government will not attract the best venture capitalists to engage in hybrid activities, at least in countries with already-established private equity and venture capital industries. The investment record of such general partnerships ensures that they are well known to institutional investors. Indeed, established VC firms with an upper quartile performance have a waiting list of institutions wishing to be allowed to participate in their next fund-raising. Thus, the partnerships available to the state are either VC firms with less enviable track records or, frequently, commercial but untested investment managers anxious to enter the VC/PE market and seeing a government leveraged fund as one means of entry. For such managers, the hybrid fund becomes a "loose brick" in the wall surrounding the VC/PE community (Prahalad and Hamel 1990). If such an investment team can be accepted and can subsequently demonstrate a clear competence as professional equity investors, they have the opportunity to raise substantial follow-on funds on the back of their own performance. Thus, publicly supported hybrid funds have become one of the few channels by which new entrants can enter a rapidly maturing VC and PE market.

Governments have belatedly recognized their negotiating power. Recent calls for the design and management of new hybrid funds in the UK's Enterprise Capital Fund scheme (Small Business Service 2006) were put out to public bidding. The state by employing its own professional advisers was able to undertake due diligence on the investment teams that sought to be part of the scheme. Somewhat ironically, the VC firm applicants were subjected to the same type of scrutiny that they commonly impose on potential investee firms. The UK government, through its involvement in a series of new VC fund programs since 1997, has been able to accumulate its own professional competence in both designing and staffing public/private investment funds. With greater enterprise policy networking, venture-focused skills sets are now being disseminated between policy makers from several countries. As the playing field has leveled, venture capitalists now need to understand the nature of the (public) beast as much as the policy makers need to understand their private sector agents.

Kleiner Perkins, Atlas Venture, Apax and Technologie Holdings require their investors to wait 10 years for full returns—the Government would prefer to give you one year.

The State as Importunate

As noted above, in order to engage successfully with the VC industry and meet its own objectives, the state has had to learn the paradigms and heuristics by which this specialist form of entrepreneurial finance is conducted. These industry practices and routines often evolve for highly pragmatic reasons. Equity funding in a classic VC scenario will follow the well known "J Curve" (Meyer and Mathonet 2005) with the cumulative value of the fund being less than the money committed for the first years of the fund's operations. Bürgel (2000) in one of the first forensic studies of VC performance analyzed detailed investment cash flows on a sample of some 80 UK-based funds. He demonstrated that funds typically did not start to show a positive net gain in value until around the fifth year of operation. It is because of the long gestation of many young enterprises before demonstrating any significant commercial value (Miller and Friesen 1984; Agarwal and Audretsch 2001) that the GPs have to require of limited partners that their investment is locked in for an industry standard (in the United States and Europe) of a minimum 10-year period.

Yet, the time needed to demonstrate a clear investment performance and the time given to publicly supported funds to provide evidence of such an effect is often out of kilter. The provision of public financing to a private fund raises considerable governance issues. The state rightly wishes to see the positive consequences of its risk-bearing actions. Yet, the demands made on such funds for evidence of success or, more vaguely, public value-added are often importunate and made unreasonably early into the investment cycle. Auditing the present value of a highly immature portfolio firm is illusory, and the industry recommended practice of carrying investments at cost until an independent evaluation event is appropriate given the high uncertainty. It is a source of added pressure on less informed investors that failed investments are much more likely to be realized before investment successes. In the argot of the industry, "lemons ripen before plums."

All industries have their peculiar and specific practices and conditions. Again, public investors who are unaware of the heuristics of the industry are unlikely to do other than increase the destructive pressures on early-stage, hybrid fund arrangements.

> *Specialist users of advanced technological products and services rarely insist that the technology they purchase was conceived, designed and manufactured in a nomadic community of 200 souls on the north side of a fjord some 500 miles from the nearest Starbucks.*

The State as Romantic or Holy Fool

The state has a constitutional responsibility to protect and nurture all of the diverse communities and groups within its borders. This is in part articulated in a redistributive function that transfers resources from the nation's centers of highest economic activity to regions or communities more remote or otherwise disadvantaged. A significant proportion of total public activity is allocated to these tasks and involves education, training, employment, and capital investment activities across a range of public administration offices. At the same time as having a range of social policy actions, the state is also interested in stimulating future economic activity by investing in new, innovative, and productive capacity both at the research and commercial stages (Small Business Service 2004). Resources to create new high tech industries are attractive to all regions in an economy and no more so than for economically depressed regions that have often declined from an illustrious industrial past. Yet, the reality of scale and scope advantages, particularly within networked economies that demonstrate exponential benefits of proximity and growth, is that new investment in technology and other new knowledge assets is likely to be much more fruitful if added incrementally alongside other existing assets in so-called clusters (Porter 1998).

Thus, policy makers face a conflict between their heads and their hearts. The more effective allocative decision would be to invest in existing areas of research excellence and hope that trickle down development theories actually work. At best, most countries outside the largest 10 world economies will only have a very small number, if any, of centers of genuinely world-class technology-based activity. In reality, few policy makers will be left to make such important decisions without political sanction. The political process rightly must assume responsibility for redistributive actions, regardless of technical optimization. In an ideal world, the stage is set for an informed debate over priorities, means, and ends. The reality is often quite different.

Much of regional policy is more accurately understood as a social transfer masquerading as an investment in innovative capacity. This is beautifully articulated by one policy maker who said to one of the authors: "I know that the fund has been created for early-stage technology investments but with a little money and patience this could once again be a first class television factory." The statement has the charm of truth. Essentially public money allocated for equity investments in new technology applications was to be diverted in order to sustain the operations of an uncompetitive factory producing a commodity product in a remote region of a highly developed Western economy. The region was also the home territory of a powerful, ruling party politician anxious not to see a major increase in local unemployment if the factory closed down. Here, an innovation policy program provided a convenient pork barrel.

Publicly supported venture capital funds have been particularly vulnerable to being hijacked by social and regional interests. Venture capital is politically sexy and smacks of modernity, highly educated and well paid work forces, clean industries, and warm images of California. As a result, the less economically developed regions of most advanced Western economies (and some developing countries) are littered with small early-stage VC funds with weak managements, weaker balance sheets, and negligible deal flow. They commonly do not survive beyond the exhaustion of the public subsidy. (Such funds for obvious reasons are rarely in receipt of genuine "matched" private financing.) They are the outward manifestation of policies that have uncritically seen the link between venture capital and innovation as causal and sufficient. The overlaying of a European economic development, investment infrastructure through the European Commission can add another layer of opportunity and sometimes policy confusion for European states. Indeed, the rules of much European development funds activity proscribes placing finance into areas which are not officially classified as economically disadvantaged. The term "disadvantaged" can often be translated as meaning regions that have neither the supply nor the quality of universities, research laboratories, large and small technology businesses, knowledge workers, or managerial manpower. Yet each of these resources is required for the construction and execution of an innovation policy that is able to be assisted by venture capital activity. Thus, the very places that can use this funding least efficiently are often the places most likely to be in receipt of this form of financing. Hans Christian Anderson was prescient. It is not just kings that do not have new clothes. Regions can be equally naked.

In explaining the misallocation of innovation funding and entrepreneurial finance activities into social programs, we are *not* suggesting that poor or less advantaged regions be left in a virtual *laager* of poverty and deprivation. In a decent and democratic society such discrimination should be unacceptable. What we are suggesting is that to suborn a specific set of (innovation) policy instruments in order to engage in separate (social) policy actions is likely to be suboptimal for both innovation and social policy, irrespective of the criteria employed. Frequently, the objective of local public servants is to maximize inward transfers of public monies regardless of the opportunity cost of their allocation. Thus, in the case of a VC initiative, antecedent questions determining the quality and volume of technological opportunities sufficient to sustain a fund structure with a reasonable probability of attractive returns are rarely asked. The criteria and operational conditions of public schemes can work to frustrate the goals they seek to achieve. A worst case scenario in such policy making may occur if a primary reason for the local establishment of such a fund is national/regional pride, that is, *region X has one and they are certainly no better than us!* In these rather common circumstances, public attempts to subsidize the emergence of a local VC industry via the financing of a number of small stand-alone funds can result in little more than the temporary creation of a status symbol or policy fashion accessory.

The good thing about evaluating seed and incubator funds on the cost of capital (IRR) to the government is that it is relatively unambiguous, clear, and simple. The bad thing is that such a method of evaluation is completely inappropriate.

The State as Irrational Rationalist

Venture capital has become in the last 20 years a new asset class primarily available for institutional investors that wish to introduce a further level of diversity and variance into their core portfolios of equities, bonds, and other alternative investments (see the industry promotional literature of the NVCA, BVCA, EVCA). Early investors into upper quartile VC and private equity funds have seen highly attractive long-term returns (Rosa and Raade 2006). A core requirement of an asset class is sufficiently long-term and credible quantitative metrics in order that professional investors and actuaries may be able to construct mixed instrument portfolios of desired risk/return trade-offs. The very nature of a typically 10-year, fixed-term VC fund is such that performance metrics are not instantly available compared to a traded public stock. However, over the investment cycle investors can gain an increasingly accurate representation of terminal fund performance from year five and beyond (Bürgel 2000). Internal rate of return (IRR) and capital gain multiples are the two most common measurements of VC fund performance (Fenn, Liang, and Prowse 1995; Gompers and Lerner 1999). Such measures, which reflect the opportunity costs of investment allocations, are entirely appropriate for commercial investors in their assessment of the effectiveness of the general partners of their funds. Over time, standardized investment guidelines imposed by VC and PE national associations on their members have reduced the idiosyncrasies and occasional misinformation of GPs' performance reporting to institutional investors (LPs).

It is entirely reasonable that early-stage funds conform to industry practice in their reporting procedures. However, when such funds are public/private hybrids, the information provided only allows for a strictly economic or commercial evaluation. While this is of pre-eminent importance to the private partners in such a relationship, it is only of partial value to the public investor. It needs to be remembered that most public limited partners agree to subordinated returns in order to ensure the necessary leverage incentives to their private co-investors in the fund. For the public investor, often requiring a base return determined by the cost of the state's capital, a commercially attractive return is important only in ensuring the continued participation of the private partners. The objective of their public support of the hybrid fund is in the long-run, public welfare returns contingent on the new investment activity. Thus, the state is primarily interested in creating an infrastructure and competencies conducive to the accelerated production of new knowledge assets and, critically, their effective commercial exploitation.

The celebrated Israeli Yozma Program started in 1993 as a public initiative from the Office of the Chief Scientist before being privatized in 1997. It signaled these wider interests by offering, at its formation, to sell the public involvement in the 10 new VC funds created by the program back to the participating private investors within the first 5 years.[19] In essence, the Israeli state acted as a catalyst in promoting the emergence of a VC industry. It then withdrew from a direct commercial involvement when the investment results clearly indicated the commercial viability of investment activities fueled by Israeli intellectual property and publicly-supported, advanced research capabilities (Avnimelech, Kenney, and Teubal 2004). In the United States, the Small Business Administration's SBIC program is arguably the best known, and most emulated, of such state-assisted schemes. However, the running of two quite separate SBIC schemes has added some confusion to outsiders. The *debenture* SBIC program, which was created in 1958 and uses the state to facilitate loans to licensed SBICs in order to leverage private capital, has been judged a success (U.S. Small Business Administration 2003). A second program, the *participating securities* SBICs, started as an experiment in 1994 and was designed to encourage early-stage investments by the SBA, investing additional equity directly in the SBICs via a public investment. This latter scheme was terminated in 2004 after the sharp market turndown in technology stocks in the year 2000 left the SBA with a total investment exposure of over $11 billion. A strictly commercial appraisal would be positive to both the Israeli Yozma program and the UK's 3i initiative, which was also successfully privatized in 1994. The SBA's debenture SBICs would be seen as commercially positive, and the participating securities variant would be judged a commercial failure. Yet, such a partial conclusion would greatly underestimate the SBICs' impact on the three of the largest and most successful VC industries in the world. The U.S. and UK programs were materially responsible for training the first national cohort of professional venture capitalists in the postwar period up until the early-to-mid 1980s. Similarly, the Yozma program replicated an advanced risk capital investment infrastructure in Israel in by the late the 1990s. Their impact has been very considerably larger than an exclusive analysis of fund performance would suggest.

However, all too often, the state's efforts are measured against the benchmark of private investor interests. Wider cost-benefit analyses should incorporate mechanisms that price the externalities and spillovers of the fund's activities: for example, the training of investment managers; the orientation of university research departments to commercial spin-out activities; the construction of a professional SME support network of accountants, lawyers, patent attorneys, and so on; the dissemination of innovative practices throughout the wider business community are usually remarkable as evaluation criteria because of their general absence outside academic studies. This is not to argue that the performance of the fund is of secondary relevance to the state. A failed fund is likely to produce little of the desired externalities and spillovers noted. However, the investment activity's financial performance is a necessary but insufficient benchmark. Public program evaluations have to address both the advantages and limitations of using market measures in a policy context if they are not to draw erroneous policy conclusions.

It is evident that the institutions of state can change and adapt to meet new ideas and opportunities. After all, the Dark Ages in Europe only lasted five hundred years.

The State as Architect, Not Mechanic

One can kick start a motorbike but not a VC industry. It is all too infrequently noted that the evolution of a credible VC industry is measured in decades rather than in single years (see issues of path dependency in the second Meditation). It is also tempting for policy makers to concentrate on the "tactics" of setting up a new fund without a wider understanding of the necessary "strategies" that need to be put into place to create an environment compatible with risk capital activity. As noted, a frequent question posed by policy makers is how one can emulate the successes of a U.S. or UK industry. In seeking to answer this question the new institutional economics of North (1990 and 2005) and others is of considerable utility. Institutional writers have recognized, in seeking to define conducive entrepreneurial and investment environments, the critical importance of "context" and, perhaps above all, of "the rule of law" (La Porta, Lopez-de-Silanes, and Shleifer 1998; La Porta, Lopez-de-Silanes, Shleifer, and Vishny 2000). A growing awareness of the importance of context is also similarly being seen in the field of entrepreneurship research and policy formation (Phan 2004; Audretsch, Grilo, and Thurik 2007). To date, entrepreneurship as a subject area has largely been dominated by individual-level and dispositional approaches (Shane 2004; Shane and Venkataraman 2000; Sorensen 2007).[20] Accordingly, the three conditions that Gilson (2003) argues must exist simultaneously if a VC industry is to emerge—that is, entrepreneurs, funds for investment, and an investment vehicle that creates the right incentives—are quite correct. However, they are "necessary but not sufficient" conditions. Their creation and employment is only possible if institutional precursors allow an environment in which such resources can be mobilized.

That the importance of a transparent, open, and honest trading environment to entrepreneurial activity might come as a revelation to academics would surprise most high technology entrepreneurs. An abiding concern as to the piracy of their intellectual property by dishonest firms both at home and abroad is one of the single most defining characteristics of the young innovative firm. The need to protect their intellectual assets and the associated economic rents strongly influences how, when, and where they announce innovations, set up their businesses, protect their IP, sell their products, and services and with whom they will trade and collaborate (Coeurderoy and Murray 2008). The security provided by the institutional and legal environments to vulnerable young firms has a profound effect on their actions. Without the entrepreneur's confidence in the protection of the firm's valuable and innovative assets via recourse to national institutions that defend individual property rights regardless of the status of the owner (foreigner/citizen, large firm/start-up firm, etc.), the economy's credibility is severely undermined.

Pettigrew recently observed that government agencies must focus on both policy and process.[21] The process by which a viable VC industry emerges still remains poorly understood, although recent research has begun to focus on the various motors involved (political, economic, and commercial) and their interrelationships (Lingelbach, Gilbert, and Murray 2008). Market-oriented programs to stimulate VC tend to focus both on enabling contexts and incentives that will attract private-sector involvement and co-investment.[22] Yet, the relatively small number of sustainable, national VC industries to date and the failure of several efforts to create more examples belie such confidence. Neither governments nor researchers appear to understand adequately the VC emergence process.

CONCLUSION

Since starting to write this paper we have witnessed the onset of chaos in the global financial markets. In the face of the cataclysmic events starting in the fall of 2008, which can for once accurately be described as "without parallel," it could be argued that the relevance of this paper disappears. The authors also at first entertained a similarly gloomy prognosis. However, on greater reflection, we would argue that our paper is exceptionally timely. We have seen in the unprecedented two weeks of late September/early October 2008, several of the central banks of the world's largest economies purchasing large or controlling shares in several of their major private banks. At virtually a stroke, the growing international market liberalism of the Reagan-Thatcher years, which had continued from the early 1980s to the present day, seems to have stalled and started to reverse. The focus of our paper has been on how the state and the private sector may both learn to live with and gain benefit from each other's participation in the relatively arcane world of early-stage venture capital. A parallel model of public/private co-investment is now being played out in the worlds' major financial centers and is underpinning the survival of many banks. Our observations and thoughts—albeit addressing a problem of a more modest scale—can be seen as both timely and relevant.

This paper is not intended to be an antigovernment polemic. We do not take an ideological or a political stance. Our interest is purely instrumental. We are interested in the efficacy of government intervention as measured by the promotion of "desirable" outcomes including, for example, the genesis and growth of new enterprises or the conversion of intellectual property from university laboratory or other sources of innovation into new or better goods and services via the medium of new market entrants. We have no interest in criticizing government efforts to promote early-stage venture capital activity. Rather, we write as interested academic observers committed to fostering a debate on the nature of productive public engagement in entrepreneurship policy. We clearly see a role for venture capital in the innovative process—be it from formal or informal sources. At the earliest stages of investment, we also see a role for the state to be both a supporter of, and an investor in, privately managed risk capital activity.

By design or not, government has become a major player in shaping and stimulating the environment in to which the "classic" venture capital industry has emerged. We recognize that, in the United States, government policy has gone well beyond simply creating a conducive environment for the creation and financing of new enterprise. Indeed, U.S. public policy on enterprise and innovation has been highly interventionist both at the federal and state levels (Lazonick 2008). Similarly, UK investors and entrepreneurs in the second-largest VC industry in the world have benefited directly from purposeful and sustained intervention by the British government (Murray 2007). The public administrations of both countries have seen the provision of risk capital for innovative young firms via the agency of profits-seeking, private organizations as being important and, on occasions, too important to leave to the vagaries of the capital market.

Advocates of state intervention can and do argue the need for public support in order to catalyze the emergence of a new industry. The citing of market failures as a justification for the state's active intervention is often, but not always, credible. Yet, the harsh reality remains that the emergence of an active and viable early-stage "classic" VC industry seems to be the exception rather than the rule among the developed economies of the world. This emergence process is not trivial, nor has it been found to be easily emulated. Even a nascent industry has lots of moving parts, and it is embedded in complex market and social processes including simultaneity requirements (Gilson 2003), diffusion of the VC model (Rogers 2003), cyclicality (Gompers and Lerner 2005), and the need for co-production between government investors and fund managers (Lingelbach, Gilbert, and Murray 2008).

We also share Pettigrew's (2008) concern that government often focuses too much on policy goals and too little on the process by which policy outcomes are realized. Government support for VC is an example of a process of change. Yet, both government and academia have, until recently, given too little thought to what kind of process VC emergence might be and what are the implications for better policy. Instead, reflecting the dominance of economics in VC research, bureaucrats and academics alike have focused their attention on getting the market to work efficiently. While this focus may be necessary, it does not seem to be sufficient, especially given the slow pace at which VC as an asset class has grown and internationalized in comparison to other financial innovations of a similar vintage.

A process-oriented research agenda in VC might seek to answer the following general questions:

> What type of process is VC emergence?
> What are the constituent processes of VC emergence?
> How has the process of VC emergence varied by country and over time?
> What are the policy implications of the different ways in which VC has
>   emerged?
> In what ways can government policy accelerate or retard emergence?

Thus, there are several preconditions that appear to have to be met before the state can hope to intervene positively in a nascent or immature market. It must have the resources (including capital, information, and technical knowledge) that make it able to analyze and negotiate a resolution of present weaknesses in supply and demand. Its intervention must also demonstrably support private market interests in order to realize the necessary actions to improve the effectiveness of the market.

Above all, the state must communicate, and be prepared to justify publicly, the logic of its actions to its commercial partners. It is in its inability to formulate a consistent, evidence-based policy—including the consequent choices for prescriptive action—that the state is frequently most culpable. As we have tried to demonstrate with our "12 meditations," an efficient market is a hard and implacable taskmaster. For a government to become involved as a co-producer with private agents in the provision of risk capital services, it must be as informed and as professional as any other party. Such skills are delegated to others by public servants at their peril. The state's social goals can only be reached by first achieving its partners' commercial objectives.

Early-stage venture capital activity remains one of the most intellectually and practicably demanding areas of investment finance. Most governments are novitiates in these activities and at present remain bereft of enlightenment. The Buddhist master will remind his students regularly that at the center of the eight-spoked "wheel of life" or Dharmachakra, lie three symbolic creatures. These are the pig, the snake, and the cockerel. This latter symbol exists to impress Buddha's followers of the evil to mankind of ignorance. We would issue a similar reminder to policy makers.

NOTES

1. The draft was written before the announcement in December 2008 of the Bernard Madoff pyramid selling scandal at an alleged cost of $50 billion losses to investors in his funds.

2. Clearly, many large consultancies would also see themselves as branded providers of expert advice. However, the primary focus on the named individual producer and the subordination of the profit motive in mainstream academe to the public enhancement of knowledge makes the two activities profoundly different in practice.

3. The name 3i—an acronym for Investors in Industry—was given to the merged organization formed from ICFC and FCI in 1983.

4. This situation is currently occurring in several market economies as of spring 2009 as banks reduce lending in preference for building up their severely depleted balance sheets.

5. Readers may smile at these comments in the light of the unprecedented chaos in financial markets since the fall 2008. However, we do not believe that this maelstrom should be taken as the norm and thus seen as the context in which most financial transactions will occur over time.

6. For a review of this literature, see Gompers and Lerner (2005).

7. For example, 3i plc, an extremely successful venture capital firm that was originally formed by the UK government in 1945 specifically to address the problems facing small businesses identified in the Macmillan Report, no longer invests in the start-up and

early-stage markets. Similarly, Apax Partners, an important early VC funder of start-up firms, in 2003 formally announced that requests for risk capital finance of under £10 million would no longer be considered.

8. Here we define "classic" venture capital in accord with common practice and exclude private equity investments in mature and established companies, particularly management buy-outs.

9. To date, only Israel has also been able to harvest a comparable (albeit much smaller) civilian innovation premium from its high defense spending unlike Russia or South Africa.

10. This question of different styles of capitalism with different roles for the state has assumed enormous importance in the chaotic capital markets of the fall 2008. See the *Economist* October 4, 2008:4546.

11. See the Global Entrepreneurship Monitor (GEM) project at http://www.gemcon sortium.org.

12. When public-financed VC funds compete in a product area where there are already private providers, the government is vulnerable to charges of crowding out private investors.

13. Corporate venture units have similar problems to public VC funds in attracting professional investment managers to work in environments where their actions are constrained by noncommercial objectives and their remuneration is influenced by factors outside of their investment record (Hill et al. Forthcoming).

14. General partners in a private VC or PE fund are required to also invest a part of their wealth personally in to their fund. GPs' share of the capital gain of the fund is also commonly conditioned on reaching a "hurdle" of minimum performance return linked to the cost of capital of the investors in the fund.

15. Later public VC schemes in the UK have seen the state negotiate a position as preferred creditor (e.g., Enterprise Capital Fund Scheme) rather than as subordinate investor (e.g., Regional VC Fund Scheme).

16. In the event of a failed investment, the state may still seek a minimum return on its cost of capital. The later ECF funds have this preferential requirement for the state's interests imposed on recipient funds.

17. Exactly the same criticism is being used to discuss the system of giving bank employees large performance bonuses. Market traders were incentivized to take considerable risks given that they did not bear the full costs of any negative outcomes.

18. The author arranged for the forthcoming survey to be announced in the *Financial Times*. The article stated that the researcher would meet the UK industry's top VC investors as identified by the British Venture Capital Association. Accordingly, some 40 plus chairman and CEOs of venture capital companies contacted the author requesting that he meet them urgently!

19. While the Israeli government required a predetermined exit premium, private partners in 8 of the 10 supported funds bought out the public interest to become exclusively private VC funds.

20. I am grateful to Erkko Autio for guidance in discussions on the role of context to entrepreneurial research.

21. Seminar address at the Academy of Management's Annual Conference, Anaheim, California, August 2008.

22. The UK government and the Small Business Service post 1997 would be an exemplar of market-oriented policies with a strong co-investment focus. The Regional VC Funds, the

Enterprise Capital Funds, the High-Tech Fund, and the more socially focused Bridges Fund were each launched with public money for a policy purpose yet managed by a strongly incentivized private sector.

REFERENCES

Abrahamson, E., and M. Eisenman. 2001. Why management scholars must intervene strategically in the management knowledge market. *Human Relations* 54(1):67–75.

Acs, Z., W. Parsons, and S. Tracy. 2008. *High-impact firms: Gazelles revisited.* Report to the SBA. Washington, DC 20037: Corporate Research Board, LLC.

Agarwal, R., and D. B. Audretsch. 2001. Does entry size matter? The impact of the life cycle and technology on firm survival. *Journal of Industrial Economics* 49(1): 21–43.

Audretsch, D. B., I. Grilo, and A. R. Thurik. 2007. Explaining entrepreneurship and the role of policy: A framework. In *Handbook of Research on Entrepreneurship Policy*, ed. David B. Audretsch, I. Grilo, and A. Roy Thurik (1–7). Cheltenham, UK: Edward Elgar.

Autio, E. 2008. *Gazelles innovation panel: Summary and conclusions from panel discussions.* Brussels: European Commission, Europe INNOVA.

Avnimelech, G., M. Kenney, and M. Teubal. 2004. Building venture capital industries: Understanding the U.S. and Israeli experiences. *Berkeley Roundtable on the International Economy.* Working paper 160.

Bazerman, M. H. 2005. Conducting influential research: The need for prescriptive implications. *Academy of Management Review* 30(1):25–31.

Bergemann, D., and U. Hege. 1998. Venture capital financing, moral hazard and learning. *Journal of Banking & Finance* 22(6–8):703–735.

Berger, A. N., and G. F. Udell. 2006. A more complete conceptual framework for SME finance. *Journal of Banking & Finance* 30(1):2945–2966.

Bolton, J. E. 1971. *Small firms: Report of the committee on inquiry on small firms.* London: Her Majesty's Stationery Office.

Bosma, N., et al. 2008. *Global entrepreneurship monitor: 2007 executive report.* Babson Park, MA, and London: Babson College and London Business School.

Bürgel, O. 2000. *UK venture capital and private equity as an asset class for institutional investors.* London: British Venture Capital Association.

Cantillon, R. 1755/1931/1959. *Essai sur la Nature du Commerce en Général*, trans. and ed. H. Higgs. London: Frank Cass.

Clark, G. 2007. *A farewell to alms.* Princeton, NJ: Princeton University Press.

Coeurderoy, R., and G. Murray. 2008. regulatory environments and the location decision: Evidence from the early foreign market entries of new-technology-based firms. *Journal of International Business Studies* 39: 670–687.

Cosh, A., et al. 2008. *Financing UK small and medium-sized enterprises. The 2007 survey.* Cambridge: Centre for Business Research, University of Cambridge.

Cumming, D. 2007. Government policy towards entrepreneurial finance: Innovation investment funds. *Journal of Business Venturing* 22(2):199–235.

Dimov, D., and G. Murray. 2007. An examination of the determinants of the incidence and scale of seed capital investments by venture capital firms. *Small Business Economics* 30(2):127–152.

Dossani, R., and M. Kenney. 2002. Creating an environment for venture capital in India. *World Development* 30(2):227–253.

Economist, The. 2008a. Lessons from a crisis. October 4, 2008.

Economist, The. 2008b. Market failure. December 5, 2008. Retrieved from www.economist .com

European Commission. 2001. *Final report: Innovative instruments for raising equity for SMEs in Europe*. Brussels: European Commission.

European Commission. 2005. *Best practices of public support for early-stage equity finance: Final report of the expert group*. Brussels: European Commission.

European Commission and U.S. Department of Commerce. 2005. *Working group on venture capital: Final report*. Brussels: European Commission.

Fenn, G. W., N. Liang, and S. Prowse. 1995. *The economics of the private equity market*. Washington: Board of Governors of the Federal Reserve System.

Ferraro, F., J. Pfeffer, and R. I. Sutton. 2005. Economic language and assumptions: How theories can become self–fulfilling. *Academy of Management Review* 30(1): 8–24.

Ghoshal, S. 2005. Bad management theories are destroying good management practices. *Academy of Management Learning & Education* 4(1):75–91.

Gilson, R. J. 2003. Engineering a venture capital market: Lessons from the American experience. *Stanford Law Review* 55:1067–1103.

Gompers, P. 1994. The rise and fall of venture capital. *Business and Economic History* 23(2):1–26.

———, and J. Lerner. 2005. Equity financing. In *Handbook of Entrepreneurship Research*, ed. Zoltan A. and David B. Audretsch (267–298). New York: Springer.

Gompers, P., and J. Lerner. 1999. *The venture capital cycle*. Cambridge: MIT Press.

HM Treasury. 2003. *Bridging the finance gap: A consultation on improving access to growth capital for small business*. London: Her Majesty's Stationery Office.

Hill, S., et al. Forthcoming. Transferability of the venture capital model to the corporate context: Implications for the performance of corporate venture units. *Strategic Entrepreneurship Journal*.

Hofstede, G. 2001. *Culture's consequences: Comparing values, behaviors, institutions, and organizations across nations*. Thousand Oaks, CA: Sage.

Hsu, D. H., and M. Kenney. 2005. Organizing venture capital: The rise and demise of American research and development corporation 1945–1973. *Industrial and Corporate Change* 14(4):579–616.

Irwin, T. C. 2007. *Government guarantees: Allocating and valuing risk in privately financed infrastructure projects*. Washington: World Bank.

Jääskeläinen, M., M. Maula, and G. Murray. 2007. Performance of incentive structures in publicly and privately funded "hybrid" venture capital funds. *Research Policy* 36(7):913–929.

Jermier, J. M. 1998. Introduction: Critical perspectives on organizational control. *Administrative Science Quarterly* 43: 235–256.

Kay, J. 1993. *Foundations of corporate success*. Oxford: Oxford University Press.

Kenney, M., and U. von Burg. 1999. Technology, entrepreneurship, and path dependence: Industrial clustering in Silicon Valley and Route 128. *Industrial and Corporate Change* 8(1):67–103.

Kleiman, R. T., and J. M. Shulman. 1992. The risk-return attributes of publicly traded venture capital: Implications for investors and public policy. *Journal of Business Venturing* 7(3):195–208.

Klepper, S. 1997. Industry life cycles. *Industrial and Corporate Change* 6(1):145–182.

La Porta, R., F. Lopez-de-Silanes, and A. Shleifer. 1998. Law and finance. *Journal of Political Economy* 106(6):1113–1155.

———, and R. Vishny. 2000. Investor protection and corporate governance. *Journal of Financial Economics* 58:3–27.

Lazonick, W. 2008. Entrepreneurial ventures and the developmental state: Lessons from the advanced economies. Helsinki: United Nations University—World Institute for Development Economics Research. Discussion Paper 2008/01.

Leslie, S. W., and R. H. Kargon. 1996. Selling Silicon Valley: Frederick Terman's model for regional advantage. *Business History Review* 70(4):435–472.

Lingelbach, D., G. Murray, and E. Gilbert. 2008. The rise and fall of South African venture capital. Halifax, Canada: Presentation at 2008 International Council for Small Business World Conference.

Macmillan, H. 1931. *Report of the committee on finance and industry*. CMND 3897. London: His Majesty's Stationery Office.

Mason, C. M., and R. T. Harrison. 1997. Business angel networks and the development of the informal venture capital market in the U.K.: Is there still a role for the public sector? *Small Business Economics* 9(2):111–123.

Maula, M., and G. Murray. 2003. *Finnish industry investment ltd.: An international evaluation*. Report to Finnish Ministry of Trade and Industry. Helsinki: MTI.

McDougall, P. P., S. Shane, and B. M. Oviatt. 1994. Explaining the formation of international new ventures: The limits of theories from international business research. *Journal of Business Venturing* 9(6):469–487.

Meyer, T., and P. Mathonet. 2005. *Beyond the J-curve: Managing a portfolio of venture capital and private equity funds*. New York: John Wiley & Sons.

Miller, D., and P. H. Friesen. 1984. A longitudinal study of the corporate life cycle. *Management Science* 30(1):1161–1183.

Murray, G. 1992. A challenging market place for venture capital. *Long Range Planning* 25(6):79–86.

———. 1996a. *The relevance of "new technology based firms" and related support mechanisms to the commercialisation of Australia's federal research & development activities*. A Summary Report Prepared for the Industrial Research and Development Board. Canberra: IRDB.

———. 1996b. A synthesis of six exploratory European case studies of successfully exited, venture capital-financed, new technology-based firms. *Entrepreneurship Theory and Practice* 20: 41–60.

———. 1998. A policy response to regional disparities in the supply of risk capital to new technology-based firms in the European Union: The European seed capital fund scheme. *Regional Studies* 32: 5:405–419.

———. 2007. Venture capital and government policy. In *Handbook of research on venture capital*, ed. H. Landström (113–151.) Cheltenham: UK: Edward Elgar.

———, and J. Lott. 1995. Have venture capital firms a bias against investment in high technology companies? *Research Policy* 24: 283–299.

———, and R. Marriott. 1998. Why has the investment performance of technology-specialist, European venture capital funds been so poor? *Research Policy* 27: 947–976.

National Association of Seed and V. Funds. 2006. *Seed and venture capital: State experiences and options*. Chicago: National Association of Seed and Venture Funds.

North, D. C. 1990. *Institutions, institutional change, and economic performance*. Cambridge: Cambridge University Press.

———. 2005. *Understanding the process of economic change*. Princeton, NJ: Princeton University, Press.

OECD (Organization for Economic Cooperation and Development). 2004. *Venture capital: Trends and policy recommendations*. Paris: OECD.

———. 2008. *OECD framework for the evaluation of SME and entrepreneurship policies and programmes*. Paris: OECD.

Pfeffer, J. 1998. *The human equation: Building profits by putting people first*. Boston: Harvard Business School Press.

Phan, P. H. 2004. Entrepreneurship theory: Possibilities and future directions. *Journal of Business Venturing* 19(5):617–620.

Pierrakis, Y., and C. Mason. 2008. *Shifting sands: The changing nature of the early stage venture capital market in the UK*. London: National Endowment for Science, Technology and the Arts.

Porter, M. E. 1998. Clusters and the new economics of competition. *Harvard Business Review* 76(6):77–90.

Prahalad, C. K., and G. Hamel. 1990. The core competence of the corporation. *Harvard Business Review* 68(3):79–91.

Queen, M. 2002. Government policy to stimulate equity finance and investor readiness. *Venture Capital* 4(1):1–5.

Riding, A. L., and G. Haines Jr. 2001. Loan guarantees: Costs of default and benefits to small firms. *Journal of Business Venturing* 16(6):595–612.

Rogers, E. M. 2003. *Diffusion of innovations*. New York: Free Press.

Rosa, C., D. Machado, and K. Raade. 2006. Profitability of venture capital investment in Europe and the United States. Brussels: European Commission. Economics Paper No. 245.

Rynes, S. L., and D. L. Shapiro. 2005. Public policy and the public interest: What if we mattered more? *Academy of Management Journal* 48(6):925–927.

Sabel, C., and A. Saxenian. 2008. *A fugitive success: Finland's economic future*. Helsinki: Sitra. Sitra Reports, no. 80.

Saxenian, A. 1994. *Regional advantage*. Cambridge: Harvard University Press.

Say, J. 1815/1821. *Catéchisme d'économie politique*, trans. John Richter.

Shane, S. 2004. An evolving field: Guest editor's introduction to the special issue on evolutionary approaches to entrepreneurship in honor of Howard Aldrich. *Journal of Business Venturing* 19(3):309–312.

———, and S. Venkataraman. 2000. The promise of entrepreneurship as a field of research. *Academy of Management Review* 25(1):217–226.

Sørensen, J. B. 2007. Bureaucracy and entrepreneurship: Workplace effects on entrepreneurial entry. *Administrative Sciences Quarterly* 52(3):387–412.

Storey, D. J., and Bruce S. Tether. 1998. Public policy measures to support new technology-based firms in the European Union. *Research Policy* 26: 9, 1037–1057.

Teece, D. J., G. Pisano, and A. Shuen. 1997. Dynamic capabilities and strategic management. *Strategic Management Journal* 18(7):509–533.

Tushman, M. L., and P. Anderson. 1986. Technological discontinuities and organizational environments. *Administrative Science Quarterly* 31(3):439–465.

UK Department of Business, Enterprise, and R. Reform. 2007. *Annual survey of small businesses' opinions 2006/07*. London: UK Department of Business, Enterprise, and Regulatory Reform.

UK Department of Business, Enterprise, and Regulatory Reform and Cambridge Centre of Business Research. 2008.

UK Small Business Service. 2004. *Annual survey of small businesses: UK, 2003*. Brighton: Institute for Employment Studies.

UK Small Business Service. 2006a. Annual *survey of small businesses: UK, 2005*. Brighton: Institute for Employment Studies.

U. Small B. Service. 2006b. Annual *survey of small businesses: UK, 2004/05*. London: UK Small Business Service.

U.S. Small Business Administration. 2003. *Small business investment company report fiscal year 2002 special report*. Washington: U.S. Small Business Administration.

Van Creveld, M. 1999. *The rise and decline of the state*. Cambridge: Cambridge University Press.

Van de Ven, A. H. 2007. *Engaged scholarship: A guide for organizational and social research*. New York: Oxford University Press.

Wan, V. 1989. The Australian venture capital market. *Journal of Small Business Management* 27(3):75–78.

Weber, M. 1992. *The Protestant ethic and the spirit of capitalism* London: Harper Collins.

West III, G. P., and C. E. Bamford. 2005. Creating a technology-based entrepreneurial economy: A resource based theory perspective. *Journal of Technology Transfer* 30(4): 433–451.

WilsonCommittee. 1979. *The financing of small firms: Interim report of the committee to review the functioning of the financial institutions.* London: Her Majesty's Stationery Office. CMND 7503.

ABOUT THE AUTHORS

Gordon Murray received his Ph.D. from the University of East Anglia. His research interests are focused on the genesis and growth of new knowledge-based firms, early-stage venture finance, and international comparison of government policies towards enterprise. Dr. Murray has conducted policy-focused research for the UK, German, Finnish, Irish, and other European governments, the Australian Commonwealth and the European Commission in addition to undertaking consulting commissions for several financial service providers and the British and European Venture Capital Associations.

David Lingelbach completed his Ph.D. at the University of Exeter and holds undergraduate and graduate degrees from MIT. His research interests are focused on entrepreneurship in developing countries, with a special interest in entrepreneurial finance. Following a career as a banker, venture capitalist, and fund manager, he has served as a policy advisor on venture capital and entrepreneurship to development finance institutions and national governments in the Middle East, Asia, Africa, and Latin America.

Index